OF KENNEDYS AND KINGS

Books by Harris Wofford

OF KENNEDYS AND KINGS

EMBERS OF THE WORLD: CONVERSATIONS WITH
SCOTT BUCHANAN (*editor*)

INDIA AFIRE (*with Clare Wofford*)

IT'S UP TO US

OF KENNEDYS AND KINGS

Making Sense of the Sixties

HARRIS WOFFORD

FARRAR · STRAUS · GIROUX   New York

Library of Congress Cataloging in Publication Data
Wofford, Harris. Of Kennedys and Kings.
Includes index.
    1. United States—Politics, government, and civil rights
—1960–1969. 2. Kennedy, John Fitzgerald, Pres.
U. S., 1917–1963. 3. Kennedy, Robert F., 1925–
1968. 4. King, Martin Luther, Jr., 1929–1968.
5. King, Coretta Scott. 6. The Peace Corps. I. Title.
E841.W56   1980   973.922′092′2   80–12558

For my father

CONTENTS

OF KENNEDYS AND KINGS

PROLOGUE · Nevertheless

In The African Queen, *after the boat by that name has sunk,*
Katharine Hepburn is fished out of the lake by German officers, who
ask how she and Humphrey Bogart got there.
   "We came down the Ulanga River," says Katharine.
   One interrogator, knowing the enemy forts along the way, the
crocodiles, and the unnavigable rapids, declares: "That's impossible."
   "Never-the-less," she replies firmly, "we came down it."

It was a long river, with many rapids, and the passage was too fast, yet
for all the wrong turns and terrible mistakes, the sixties were an extraordinary time of social invention and constructive politics. An era of unprecedented convergence of popular initiative and public power, the early
1960s saw a surge in the spirit of national service, with people in surprising numbers really interested in what they could do for their country.
Talent and intelligence were widely enlisted to work on the nation's
problems. A Peace Corps was formed and went into action in fifty countries. Through a combination of nonviolent action and government
response, civil rights were established in law and made a reality in important parts of American public life. A battle against poverty was begun.
   In the world at large, the coming of John Kennedy coincided with
the remarkable period when John XXIII was updating the Catholic
Church and Khrushchev was trying to de-Stalinize the Soviet Union. It
was a time of peaceful competition and cooperation in the exploration of
space, when man first set forth toward the moon and nuclear tests in the
atmosphere were finally banned.
   Yet it was also a time when the Central Intelligence Agency of the
United States, with or without presidential approval, sought to assassinate foreign leaders, and even conspired with organized crime to kill
Castro; when the United States Air Force dropped more bombs on one
small country in Asia than were used in all of World War II; when the
Federal Bureau of Investigation used its power to disrupt the movement
for civil rights and defame its most prophetic leader; when a President of
the United States, a candidate for President, and the chief spokesman
for black rights and nonviolence were murdered.
   To those who find it impossible to believe that so much good and so

3

much bad could have happened in one intense time, the recollections and reflections in this book add up to the shorthand reply: *Nevertheless.*

Making sense of the sixties is important unfinished business because the widespread misreading of that curious and critical decade is one of the reasons it is so hard for anyone, including Jimmy Carter, to succeed as President. The inflation of John Kennedy's short-lived Presidency into the nonsense of Camelot needed to be punctured, but revisionist historians and ideologues have deflated and distorted that period in American politics almost beyond recognition. In doing so, they contributed to the cynicism about all government that has paralyzed our politics.

One of the legacies of the 1960s is that people learned, perhaps too well, how to say no—and apparently lost the capacity to say yes. Negative insights are important, and the ability to block policies and oppose Presidents is part of self-government. But nothing would have more disappointed John Kennedy, Robert Kennedy, and Martin Luther King, the three chief subjects of this book, than having merely a negative message drawn from their interlocking lives and deaths.

In foreign policy in the sixties, however, there *was* a negative message: the brightest were not the best. Clearly IQs do not make the difference between no vision or bad vision and the vision without which people perish. We will never know whether John or Robert Kennedy would have found the wisdom needed. Nevertheless, their search for it, like Martin Luther King's, went further than the present generation seems to understand. Lyndon Johnson's role was also more complex than is usually recognized; he wanted above all to wage and to win a war against poverty, but for reasons that still need to be plumbed, he became obsessed with another kind of war—in Indochina.

The peculiar route by which I came to work with these men and be a witness to these events led to disagreements, in matters of civil rights and foreign policy, that may be important to tell. I was deeply critical of the decision to go ahead with the CIA plan for an invasion of Cuba, and of the military machismo and cold-war view of the world that led to the Bay of Pigs and its aftermath. As I learned details of the bizarre efforts to overthrow or eliminate Castro, a secret program known as Operation Mongoose, I was appalled; and the related displacement (as Undersecretary of State) of Chester Bowles, one of the few official opponents of all this, only made it worse.

When Johnson sent U.S. troops into the Dominican Republic while Peace Corps Volunteers continued to serve and sympathize with the rebellious populace, some of us talked of "the Peace Corps *versus* the War Corps." But most of the time in American policy-making during those years, from the Bay of Pigs to Vietnam, no one was a match for the military. Nevertheless, it is wrong to look on John and Robert Kennedy simply as cold warriors. In the peaceful resolution of the Cuban missile crisis, they showed that another course was possible and preferable. They took the time to assemble and analyze all the available facts, and consider the most disastrous hypotheses. Then, going contrary to most of their military and geopolitical strategists' advice, they prevailed by focusing on the most hopeful, instead of the most threatening, elements in Khrushchev's messages. We need to come to terms with the sixties—with all their conflicting messages—in some such way.

Since politics as drama seems to offer a more illuminating perspective than ideology, I have tried to present issues in dramatic form. Readers can thus participate and draw their own conclusions. At center stage are the two Kennedy brothers, each of whom contained contradictions in his character and gave conflicting messages. Reviewing and reconsidering the events of that decade, I found, to my surprise, that the characters of John and Robert Kennedy, and the character of their family and its role in American life, seem as significant as the political causes they championed. Above all, in writing this book I came to see more sharply the growth and change in Robert Kennedy, from the narrow-minded moralist of the 1950s who would use almost any means to get his ends, to the broad-visioned and strangely transfigured candidate for President in 1968.

In this skeptical age, it is hard to acknowledge heroes, and Americans cannot regain their lost innocence. In classic drama, however, the hero is not one without great flaws; indeed, he is usually brought down by some combination of those flaws and fate, but out of the fall comes new understanding. In comedy, as pride and presumptions are punctured, the audience laughs and learns. In tragedy, the hero and all who identify with him should attain more profound enlightenment through suffering. The sixties saw both kinds of drama in full measure.

The ingredients for comedy were there in abundance: the unprecedented nepotism enjoyed by the young brothers from Boston; the unceasing pressures brought on sons by two stubborn and devoted fathers, Joseph Kennedy and Daddy King; the altruistic presumption of the President and the Congress in sending very young and sometimes very old Peace Corps Volunteers to do good on three continents; the strange sight of civil rights crusaders marching, singing, sitting down, and going to jail "with love in their hearts" for George Wallace, "Bull" Connor, and a variety of adversaries; and the odd paradox of a President who won in part through black votes being unable for a long time to execute the stroke of a pen he had promised, while his successor, declaring "We shall overcome" in a Texas accent, was able to push through Congress the most sweeping civil rights legislation in American history. There were even allegations of extraordinary sexual adventures (the seedbed of classic comedy), leading to unpredictable predicaments and exacting a high posthumous price in public opinion.

John and Robert Kennedy and Martin Luther King were comic heroes in the best and most American sense: young, romantic, and over-reaching. But above and beyond them, there was the larger drama of America and its relationship with the world during that era of great expectations. Once again, in the early sixties, a youthful and optimistic America caught the imagination of people on all continents. Recalling and recapturing some of that "public happiness" (as John Adams put it) may be part of the cure for the anti-politics now afflicting America.

But what started out so hopefully turned into tragedy before our eyes. Such was the case of Martin Luther King. Overcoming his own fears and those of his wife and father, and wrestling with messianism, King put the educational and redemptive power of suffering at the center of his theory of nonviolent action, and for thirteen years practiced what he preached. In doing so, he developed as a political leader and broadened his view of the reforms needed in America's domestic and foreign policies; he grew and deepened but he did not fundamentally change.

Robert Kennedy, however, came to tragedy by a quite different path. He might have lived a long life of effective political action but for his brother's assassination. Keeping from the public facts about the CIA, the FBI, and the Mafia crucial to the investigations of his brother's and King's murders must have caused him special suffering. His desire for the unvarnished truth, his sympathy for the weak and the poor, and his restless ambition drew him finally into the campaign that ended in Los Angeles. Yet there was something in his basic character, temperament, and religious convictions that led naturally toward tragedy. In his poem *For Robert Kennedy 1925–68*, Robert Lowell wrote: "Doom was woven in your nerves."

John Kennedy would have guffawed if anyone tried to make him a tragic hero. He enjoyed irony, and was armed with a comic spirit. When asked how he became a war hero, he said, "It was involuntary—they sank my boat." Irrepressibly self-confident, he had what his wife (in a 1953 poem about, and for, her husband) called a "too proud heart," and he, too, was destined for a tragic fate.

"Understanding, which is an art and a science, is also a passion," says Octavio Paz, poet and diplomat of Mexico. Without sympathy or sometimes antipathy, "the encounter from which the spark of under-standing springs does not take place." In the encounters described in this book there was certainly sympathy and sometimes antipathy. I write with the special vantage point of one who was both committed and critical. Neutrality is not one of the vices on display.

In 1950, my wife Clare and I wrote a book, *India Afire*, reporting our studies on that subcontinent and proposing, among other things, the adoption of a Gandhian strategy by the American civil rights movement. This led to an early association with Martin King, who once joked that I was the only lawyer he knew who understood why he wanted—on occasion in peaceful protest—to go to jail, and who was willing to help him get there. Our book also led to collaboration with Chester Bowles, after he returned from being Ambassador to India, in efforts to reshape Democratic Party foreign policy. I was first drawn to John Kennedy in 1957 (and assisted him from time to time as a speechwriter) because of his call for a new foreign policy that would take us beyond the cold war and establish a strong relationship with Asia, Africa, and Latin America.

During this period I became counsel to Father Theodore Hesburgh on the U.S. Commission on Civil Rights and an editor of the commission's first report to the President and Congress in 1959. While teaching at Notre Dame Law School the winter of 1959–60, at John Kennedy's request I edited a book of his speeches on foreign policy, *The Strategy of Peace*. In 1960, he and Robert Kennedy asked me to organize and co-ordinate the Civil Rights Section of the presidential campaign, during which I brought King and Kennedy together, with unforeseen results. After the election I worked with Sargent Shriver in the talent search for top presidential appointments. In 1961 and 1962 I served on the White House staff as Special Assistant to the President for Civil Rights, and helped with the organization of the Peace Corps. Then, for two years, we lived in Addis Ababa, where I was the Peace Corps' Special Representative for Africa and director of its Ethiopia program, after which I returned to Washington as Associate Director of the Peace Corps.

It was in Addis Ababa on November 22, 1963, that I was awakened with the news of President Kennedy's assassination. A few weeks later, at Kenya's independence celebration—Uhuru—I first heard Harry Belafonte sing, "Have you seen my friend Abraham? And where is my friend John?" The next time I heard him sing it, in 1968, the refrain ended, "Abraham, Martin, Bobby, and John." It was a decade later, back in Africa on a trip for Bryn Mawr College, from the distance of a dozen years as a college president, that I decided to write this book.

At first I wondered whether the title, *Of Kennedys and Kings*, is too confusing; these accounts of the Kennedys and the Martin Luther Kings, and their interaction at the heart of American politics, have nothing to do with foreign monarchs, the jet set, or the "beautiful" people who act like royalty. But the confusion may be appropriate for a phenomenon that fascinates and repels so many onlookers: three generations out of Ireland, the Kennedys not only act like an American royal family, they have almost been accepted as such by millions of Americans. Almost, but not quite, for the electoral process and opinion polls are as fickle as the media, which together crown our unordained kings and queens.

The Kennedys are not the first American family to become a political dynasty. There were the Adamses, the Roosevelts, the Tafts, and, more recently, the Rockefellers. But in our time the sons of Rose and Joseph Kennedy have occupied a unique position, arousing more loyalty and love—and more fear and hatred—than any other public figures. Their lives and deaths, and what Edward Kennedy after Chappaquiddick called the "curse" on the Kennedys, constitute an American epic. On a different scale the same can be said of Martin Luther King and his family.

Epics as verifiable history, as Robert Lowell has warned, have many pitfalls. "But the great epics," he added, "must mean something, not by didactic pedagogy, propaganda, or edification—but by their action, a murky metaphysical historical significance, a sober intuition into the character of a nation. . . ." Whether or not the sagas of the Kennedys or the Kings amount to such an epic, they deal with central figures of our time.

Shortly before Robert Kennedy was killed, I was telling some of these stories to Scott Buchanan, the philosopher who planned the great books program at St. John's College in Annapolis. He noted that I went back and forth between matters of state and the inner struggles within the minds of John and Robert Kennedy and Martin King, and he pointed to ancient authority for such alternation. In *The Republic*, when Socrates was in trouble defining justice for the state, he turned to look at justice in the individual soul—and vice versa. Buchanan told me of the time his colleague Stringfellow Barr, the president of St. John's, had complained, "Dialectic is too abstract for me—I'm not up to Socratic dialogue." "Yes, you are," Buchanan reassured him, "but you're a Southerner, and you do it through stories." In 1968 when I said to Buchanan that I wished I could convey both the comedy and the tragedy of the sixties, but didn't think I was up to it, he replied, "Just tell your stories straight—it will all be there."

Ten years later that is what I set out to do.

8

I

The Making of a President: Another View

Sometimes you look for one thing and you find another.
—Sancho Panza

1 · Calling Mrs. Martin Luther King

It was a gray day in March 1965, and we were about six miles outside Selma on Highway 80. Coretta Scott King was walking with her chin high and looking straight ahead as she had learned to do during a long decade of civil rights marches. I had not seen her since John Kennedy was killed. At the front, leading the march to Montgomery, Andy Young signaled that we could rest on the roadside. Coretta saw me a few ranks behind and in her slow, measured way welcomed me back to Alabama—"There is plenty to be done here." Then with her usual steady calm, she turned to the subject we had never discussed after the 1960 election: "They say that his call to me made the difference, that it elected him President. I like to think so. He was beginning to do so much, he and his brother."

Much has been made of Kennedy's action and Nixon's inaction while Martin King was in a Georgia jail in October 1960. The impact on black voters and on electoral votes has been analyzed and reported. But the full story of the reactions of John and Robert Kennedy and of Coretta, Martin, and Daddy King has not been told. The complexity and spontaneity and the irony of accident that surrounded and caused the call have nowhere been accurately conveyed.

The facts have sometimes been turned upside down. In his *Report of the County Chairman*, James Michener wrote that "when John Kennedy leaves the White House in 1968 he ought to erect a statue to the man who suggested that he make his urgent phone call . . ." but Michener had the call being made to Martin instead of Coretta King, which misses the point. In a television dramatization of King's life on NBC in 1978, Kennedy's motivation was assumed to have been cynical and merely political. In other versions the episode is treated as an example of an all-efficient, ever-calculating, well-coordinated Kennedy machine. The reverse is closer to the truth. Motivation was mixed, but at the time no one could predict whether the political consequences for Kennedy would be good or bad.

Kennedy's call was, in fact, precipitated by Coretta's call to me the day her husband was sentenced by a Georgia judge to four months of hard labor for driving with an out-of-state license. "They are going to kill him, I know they are going to kill him," she told me. The thought of the Georgia chain gang stirred old memories and fears. She wanted to do something and was turning anywhere for help. Having heard that Senator John Kennedy was concerned, she called me, an old friend, now the Senator's civil rights coordinator.

It was the second time I had heard her predict her husband's death. Late one evening in 1957, I was driving Martin and Coretta King from a meeting in Baltimore to their Washington hotel, and suddenly in the back seat she started telling my wife about a terrible, recurring dream in which Martin was killed. As a girl growing up in Marion, Alabama, near Selma, she had come to fear the violence of white people; her home had burned down under suspicious circumstances, and then her father's sawmill was burned by a white logger. "They will do anything," she said.

In October 1960, King had hoped there would be no new racial controversy during the presidential election. As the head of the nonpartisan Southern Christian Leadership Conference, he did not intend to endorse Kennedy, but he was "neutral against Nixon." He was impressed and encouraged by the far-reaching Democratic civil rights platform, and preferred to use the campaign period to negotiate civil rights commitments from both candidates, but particularly from Kennedy. When the Student Nonviolent Coordinating Committee, including Julian Bond and Marion Barry, proposed a sit-in against segregation in restaurants and lunch counters in downtown Atlanta stores, King urged a delay until after the election. When the young militants decided to go ahead anyway, King tried to arrange to be out of town on the day scheduled. He confided this to me when I had to cancel a meeting he had set with Kennedy for that day in Miami; with his one good reason for not being in Atlanta gone, he did not think he could avoid participating in the sit-in.

Negotiations for the meeting with Kennedy had been going on for weeks, with one complication after another. King had a larger personal following than any other Negro leader and could reach the mass of Negro voters as no one else then could. ("Black" was not yet the acceptable term.) We in the Civil Rights Section of the campaign wanted somehow to demonstrate Kennedy's support for King and King's respect for Kennedy, and thought a well-publicized meeting of the two would help. They had met privately earlier in the summer, after the Democratic convention, and King had urged Kennedy to "do something dramatic" to assure Negroes of his commitment to civil rights. In later discussions I had with King, he suggested a meeting in the South as one way to do this. That would symbolize Kennedy's concern and courage. Afterwards King would be willing to tell a news conference that he appreciated the Democratic Party's strong platform on civil rights and had confidence in the Senator's determination and ability to carry it out as President. Not quite an endorsement, but a near equivalent. We thought it would add important momentum to the campaign, and help counteract the anti-Catholic mood of many deeply Protestant Negro clergymen. King's own father, a

12

Baptist minister, had signed a newspaper advertisement for Nixon, solely on religious grounds.

The difficulty was Martin's condition that the meeting take place in the South. Kennedy suggested Nashville, but King didn't think that was Southern enough to make the point. Deeper South, he urged. Kennedy would not agree to Atlanta because his chief supporters there—Griffin Bell, Governor Ernest Vandiver, Robert Troutman (an old friend from Choate)—thought it would lose a state he otherwise had a good chance to win. Finally Miami was agreed to, although it was not what King had meant by the Deep South.

Perhaps because of that venue and because both Kennedy and Nixon were to be in Miami to address the American Legion convention, King told us he would have to offer to meet Nixon, too. Since Nixon was more and more following a Southern strategy, he probably would have refused such a meeting, but Kennedy did not want to fall into a trap: Nixon might meet King and thus convey a sense of King's neutrality, diluting any pro-Kennedy effect among Negroes, while the Kennedy meeting, with its emphasis on the Democratic civil rights platform, would intensify the Southern white resentment. Reluctantly, I had to call off the Miami meeting. King stayed in Atlanta, joined the sit-in, and went to jail.

On Wednesday, October 19, 1960, cheered on by hundreds of supporters and jeered at by surprised white customers, some seventy-five Negroes sought luncheon service at ten downtown Atlanta stores. It was a dramatic break with tradition and prevailing law. "There was hardly a place outside our own neighborhoods," Coretta King wrote of the event, "where a Negro could even get a soda except by going to the side door of a drugstore and having it handed out." Martin King was in the forefront of those asking to be served in the Magnolia Room restaurant in Rich's, one of the largest department stores in the South. He and fifty-one others were arrested and charged with violating the anti-trespass law. Refusing to put up bail, King said, "I'll stay in jail a year, or ten years, if it takes that long to desegregate Rich's."

Thursday, several hundred Negroes sat in at or picketed some fifteen establishments, forcing the closing of many eating places; twenty-five protesters were arrested. Friday, few stores attempted to offer food service; one that did, Woolworth's, was closed when Negroes sat in and whites gathered threateningly. Two Negroes were arrested.

Saturday morning, October 22, I was home in Alexandria, Virginia, playing with our children and enjoying a brief break from night-and-day campaigning. The radio reported that the Ku Klux Klan was parading on downtown Atlanta streets. King's Southern Christian Leadership Conference had telegraphed both presidential candidates asking for help. At Kennedy headquarters we were daily becoming more concerned that even without the Republicans pressing the point, a Negro backlash against all Democrats might result from Atlanta's reminder of the segregation-forever stand of white Southern Democrats. But what brought me to telephone Atlanta was a simpler thought: King had been in jail four days and I, a friend and Kennedy's civil rights man, had done nothing.

In Atlanta, Morris Abram, a leading lawyer and civil libertarian, listened while I joshed him, seriously: "Atlanta's supposed to be the enlightened leader of a New South, Hartsfield's the best mayor in the country, and you're a lawyer who can do anything. So why is Martin still in jail?" Morris said that it was fortuitous I had called; he was leaving for a meeting at City Hall with Mayor Hartsfield and a group of Negro leaders. He would tell Hartsfield of my call and they would see what they could do. Senator Kennedy did not know of my call, I emphasized, but I knew he would appreciate a satisfactory resolution, with King's release from jail as soon as possible.

Two or three hours later the phone rang. "Sit down and hold on to your seat," Morris began. "The mayor has just told press and television people outside City Hall that in response to Senator Kennedy's personal intervention he has reached an agreement with Negro leaders for the release of King and the other sit-in prisoners."

"But Kennedy knows nothing about my call—I told you I was acting on my own," I said, holding on to my seat.

"The mayor knows that, but it is a good agreement and he wants to talk to you."

"This is Bill Hartsfield," a familiar voice said. "Now I know that I ran with the ball farther than you expected, Harris, my boy, but I needed a peg to swing on and you gave it to me, and I've swung on it. You tell your Senator that he and I are out on the limb together, so don't saw it off. I'm giving him the election on a silver platter, so don't pull the rug out from under me."

While Hartsfield was talking, in his warm Southern drawl, I began to think how I would explain the situation to Kennedy. Hartsfield *was* one of the best mayors, a Southern Fiorello La Guardia, and the agreement he had reached with Negro leaders for a thirty-day halt in demonstrations while he worked with business and civic leaders to desegregate downtown Atlanta exemplified why Atlanta was the most progressive city in the South: when the Civil Rights Commission held hearings on housing in Chicago, New York, and Atlanta in 1958 and 1959, Hartsfield was one of the star witnesses in the sessions I had organized in Atlanta; and his story was more promising than anything we heard in the Northern cities. But Kennedy's Georgia and Southern campaign managers were not going to be persuaded; they would consider the unauthorized intervention intolerable. Later Bobby Troutman told me that he was taking his kids to a ball game when he heard the mayor's announcement on the radio; he stopped the car and hurried into a phone booth to call Bob Kennedy and be assured that nothing like that had happened.

Racing against time to prevent the kind of denial that would damage both Kennedy and Hartsfield, I finally got through by radiophone to Kennedy's car in a motorcade in Kansas City. Pierre Salinger or Kenneth O'Donnell took the call. "Hartsfield said *what*? You did *what*?" I don't recall who spoke or the exact curses that came next. After a short argument and consultation with Kennedy, it was agreed, grumpily, that Salinger would issue a low-key explanation that did not saw the limb from under all of us. When I read it on the wire service, I did not like its inaccuracy but it did not pull the rug out from under the mayor or the sixty Negro leaders who had joined in the agreement:

> As a result of having many calls from all over the country regarding the incident in Atlanta, Senator Kennedy directed that an inquiry be made to give him all the facts on that situation and a report on what properly should be done. The Senator is hopeful that a satisfactory outcome can be worked out.

Georgia campaign chief Griffin Bell, then a leading Atlanta attorney, did not sound so hopeful. On behalf of Governor Vandiver, Congressman George Smith III, his campaign co-chairman, and himself, he declared, "We know that Senator Kennedy would never interfere in the affairs of a sovereign state." Bell added that "Martin Luther King has violated a state law. He is charged with trespassing on private premises, has been offered bail, and refused it because he wants to be a martyr. He must stand trial and he will get equal treatment just as any other common law violator."

While consternation spread among white Southern Democratic leaders, Negroes were momentarily jubilant. Coretta King went to the victory celebration to greet the prisoners released from jail; to her dismay, Martin was not there. The previous spring he had been charged with driving without a Georgia license (he had his Alabama license). He had been stopped by a policeman who saw him driving with a white woman—the novelist Lillian Smith—whom he and Coretta were taking to a hospital in De Kalb County, a stronghold of the Ku Klux Klan. He had been fined twenty-five dollars and placed on twelve months' probation. Just as Mayor Hartsfield was arranging the release of prisoners, a De Kalb County judge declared that King's arrest for the sit-in violated his probation and reinstated the earlier conviction.

King was taken to the county jail outside Atlanta and ordered to serve six months in a state prison at hard labor. On the traffic charge—which did not involve a law that King considered unconstitutional, as he did segregation laws—he was ready to post bail and appeal while on bail, but the judge refused to let him out.

At the sentencing, Coretta King cried in public, "for the first time," she said later, "since the Movement began in 1955." She feared that "such a long sentence meant that our baby would arrive while he was in jail." She was five months pregnant and the judge had announced a six-month sentence (later reduced to four). Daddy King scolded her for crying, but was shocked and upset himself. When they saw him in his cell, Martin said, "We must prepare ourselves for the fact that I am going to have to serve this time."

What should Kennedy do now? The incredible sentence to hard labor was causing worldwide comment and was a red-hot issue among millions of American Negroes. Mayor Hartsfield announced: "We wish the world to know that the City of Atlanta had no part in the trial and sentencing of Dr. King for a minor traffic offense." But the state of Georgia and its Democratic governor were parties to King's imprisonment, and Kennedy's earlier expression of concern seemed to have been ineffective. I argued that at least we should issue a strong public statement. That would increase the pressure for King's release and improve Kennedy's standing among Negro voters. I prepared a draft to which he at first agreed, but the telephone lines between Washington and Georgia were soon buzzing with protests from Governor Vandiver, Griffin Bell, and others around the South. Kennedy was told he would lose Georgia and several other states if he issued such a statement. Bell, however, was a fair man and was shocked by the four-month sentence; he thought King should be freed on bail and prepared a more moderate draft to that effect. Finally, the governor was said to have promised to get "the son of a bitch" released if Kennedy would refrain from any further public statement. "I agreed," Kennedy told me. "What we want most is to get King out, isn't it?"

It was certainly what we wanted. Yet three days after all the other prisoners had been released, King was still in the county jail. The judge was delaying a hearing on bail. It was at this point that I received the phone call from Coretta King, her voice breaking. Frustrated because I could not tell her about the governor's promise and Kennedy could not make any public comment on the case, I could only say we were doing everything possible. This was not very reassuring to a wife who felt her husband's life was in danger every minute he remained in jail.

Stirred by the desperation in her voice, I asked Louis Martin to commiserate with me over some beer. Aside from Sargent Shriver, who had overall responsibility for our Civil Rights Section, Louis was my closest colleague in the campaign.

"Who cares about public statements?" I said to Louis. "What Kennedy ought to do is something direct and personal, like picking up the telephone and calling Coretta. Just giving his sympathy, but doing it himself."

"That's it, that's it!" said Louis. "That would be perfect."

We pondered the proposal for a while and then decided to try to get it to Kennedy right away. This time, however, I could not get through to him or to any of his key associates, and Shriver's number didn't answer. The Kennedy aides didn't return my phone calls, probably fearing more pressure for public action.

Concerned about Coretta, I thought it would be good to have someone she respected reach her to express support that night, so I called Chester Bowles.* When I explained the situation, he said he would dial her immediately and tell her that every effort was being made to assure Martin's safety and achieve his early release. Moreover, he said, Adlai Stevenson was there for dinner, and he would get him to talk to her, too.

The next morning she called me to say that she had tremendously appreciated the warm talk with Chester Bowles; she didn't mention Stevenson. Later Bowles explained that he had tried to persuade Stevenson to come on the telephone but Adlai said he couldn't do it because he had never been introduced to her. Whether he really held back out of such scruples or because the call had an emotional quality he found distasteful, or because he didn't want to offend white Southern leaders who might support him for Secretary of State, or for some other reason, Stevenson's response reflected the reticence that appealed to some as a guarantee against demagoguery but so often frustrated those who sought decisive action.

Most urgently on Coretta's mind, however, was a fear that her

---

* As Ambassador to India from 1950 to 1952 and in his *Ambassador's Report* and other writings, Bowles had championed the idea of Gandhian action. The Kings particularly liked his article, "What Negroes Can Learn from Gandhi," in *The Saturday Evening Post* (August 20, 1957), on which I had collaborated.

nightmare was coming true. In the middle of the night Martin had been awakened roughly in his cell, put in handcuffs and leg chains, hurried out into a car, and driven two hundred miles into rural Georgia. He wondered whether he was being taken out to be lynched. When dawn came the car finally deposited him at the Reidsville state prison and he was able to telephone his wife. For Coretta, Martin's transfer that far out into "cracker country" was a terrible turn for the worse.

In fact, Morris Abram assured me a few minutes later, the move itself was a wise one, though the way it had been done was inexcusable. King indeed had been in great danger in a small county jail; he was much safer in a state prison where a reasonable warden was in charge. The last thing the governor of Georgia or the Georgia white establishment wanted was King's blood on their hands. Encouraged, but still concerned about both Martin and Coretta and about Kennedy's role, I talked with Sargent Shriver in Chicago and brought him up to date. He had been given the civil rights assignment in the campaign because of his long-standing involvement as head of the Catholic Interracial Council of Chicago. During the Montgomery bus boycott he had introduced Martin King to his first public audience in Chicago; I knew he would be responsive.

"The trouble with your beautiful, passionate Kennedys is that they never show their passion," I said. "They don't understand symbolic action. Last night Louis and I suddenly knew what Kennedy should do, but we couldn't get through to him and you weren't home, so Chester Bowles did it." I had hardly stated the idea when he said, "It's not too late, Jack doesn't leave O'Hare for another forty minutes, I'm going to get it to him. Give me her number and get me out of jail if I'm arrested for speeding."

When Shriver reached Kennedy's room at the O'Hare International Inn, he saw the usual set of top associates and knew that if he broached it in their presence, someone would shoot the idea down. He waited until Ted Sorensen had gone off to finish a speech, Salinger left to see the press, and O'Donnell went to the bathroom. Then he mentioned King's middle-of-the-night ride to the state prison and said, "Why don't you telephone Mrs. King and give her your sympathy?" Shriver recalls giving him a simple case for the call: "Negroes don't expect everything will change tomorrow, no matter who's elected. But they do want to know whether you care. If you telephone Mrs. King, they will know you understand and will help. You will reach their hearts and give support to a pregnant woman who is afraid her husband will be killed."

Kennedy listened intently and, after a thoughtful pause, said, "That's a good idea. Why not? Do you have her number? Get her on the phone." In another minute, while everyone else was out of the room, he was talking with her warmly, seriously, reassuringly.

Even before any word from Shriver, I heard from Mrs. King. She was very moved, and grateful. I asked her what Kennedy had said, and she quoted him as saying: "I want to express to you my concern about your husband. I know this must be very hard for you. I understand you are expecting a baby, and I just wanted you to know that I was thinking about you and Dr. King. If there is anything I can do to help, please feel free to call on me."

Soon afterwards Morris Abram called. "It's happened!" he said. "Kennedy's done it, he's touched the heartstrings." Martin's father and Coretta had just come to his law office and told him about the Kennedy call. "Daddy King says if Kennedy has the courage to wipe the tears from Coretta's eyes, he will vote for him whatever his religion." We agreed that Morris would urge the senior Dr. King to make his conversion public.

About this time, Anthony Lewis of *The New York Times* called to query me, and perhaps to goad me, about the King affair and Kennedy's apparent silence and inaction. I said that if there was any action it wouldn't be in Washington but in Atlanta, and that he should keep in touch with Mrs. King, not me. He called back shortly to say the *Times* correspondent in Atlanta reported the odd response that Mrs. King would not talk to him unless Harris Wofford approved. I called her and asked if Senator Kennedy had requested her not to make any comment. When she said he had made no such request, I said I was sure Kennedy wouldn't be issuing any statement but she should feel free to say anything she considered appropriate. Louis Martin and I sat back and waited.

We didn't have to wait long. John Seigenthaler, Bob Kennedy's close aide, called with a summons: "Bob wants to see you bomb throwers right away." A fine and compassionate Pulitzer Prize-winning newspaperman from Nashville, John sounded worried.

In his Washington headquarters, Bob was pacing back and forth, angrily. On the plane to Detroit the candidate had rather nonchalantly told Salinger, "And by the way, I telephoned Mrs. Martin Luther King this morning." Salinger, sensing danger, had radioed the word to Bob, who had exploded. With fists tight, his blue eyes cold, he turned on us. "Do you know that three Southern governors told us that if Jack supported Jimmy Hoffa, Nikita Khrushchev, or Martin Luther King, they would throw their states to Nixon? Do you know that this election may be razor close and you have probably lost it for us?"

He gave us no chance to state our case. When he ordered that there be no publicity, I said that nothing could keep the story from spreading in Atlanta and was about to tell him that the *Times* was already on the track. Louis also knew that the New York *Post* was pursuing the story. But Bob declared that the Civil Rights Section was not to do anything more that was controversial—no new press release, no new editorializing literature, no nothing—and dismissed us.

Now it was our morale that was low. Late that night when the Senator landed in New York, a newsman asked him if it was true he had called Mrs. King. He is said to have muttered something under his breath about a traitor in his camp, but publicly he confirmed the call. "She is a friend of mine and I was concerned about the situation." The next morning the *Times* attached a very small item about the call at the end of a long story on King's transfer to the Reidsville prison. (Anthony Lewis says the Washington bureau had submitted a substantial article on the call, but the editors did not see the event's significance.) The *Times* quoted Mrs. King briefly and then noted that some Republicans had urged a statement on the King case from Nixon but that "an aide said the Vice President would have no comment."

In the Atlanta press Coretta King was quoted at greater length:

> It certainly made me feel good that he called me personally and let me know how he felt. I had the feeling that if he was that much concerned he would do what he could that Dr. King was let out of jail. I have heard nothing from the Vice President or anyone on his staff. Mr. Nixon has been very quiet.

Unknown to any of us at the time, Nixon and Eisenhower were in fact considering issuing a statement. In his book *Six Crises*, Nixon says that upon learning of the King case he immediately talked with Attorney General William Rogers, who recommended strong White House action. The Department of Justice prepared a draft for President Eisenhower to read on television:

> It seems to me fundamentally unjust that a man who has peacefully attempted to establish his right to equal treatment, free from racial discrimination, should be imprisoned on an unrelated charge, in itself insignificant. Accordingly, I have asked the Attorney General to take all proper steps to join with Dr. Martin Luther King in an appropriate application for his release.

Who decided against it, and why, we do not know. It would have matched the Kennedy initiative, with less risk to Nixon since the action would have been Eisenhower's, still a magic name, North and South.

From my experience with Eisenhower's White House in the late 1950s (when I was with the Commission on Civil Rights), I suspect that the President merely maintained his consistent resistance to any action in the area of civil rights. This was one of the many times when Eisenhower could have given Nixon crucial assistance and didn't. But in this case Nixon himself also had the option to do or say something, and didn't.

Also unknown to me, sometime during this period Lyndon Johnson is said to have told Senator Kennedy, "Well, we'll sweat it out—but you'll have the privilege of knowing that you did the right thing."

While we were sweating it out late in the afternoon of October 27, the day after the call, David Brinkley of NBC called to say that a bulletin had just come over the wires reporting that a brother of Senator Kennedy had called the De Kalb County judge to ask for King's release. "Did someone really call the judge?" he asked. Knowing how Bob felt and certain that Ted, in California, would not have intervened, I assured him no brother could have done it, and no brother-in-law either, I felt sure. Brinkley said he wouldn't use the story on the evening news.

Not long afterwards, John Seigenthaler got me on the phone. Bob was on the line from New York, asking us to draft a statement explaining why he called the county judge. John had already denied the story and could not believe Bob had done it; nor did he think it a good move, politically or legally.

"Can't you just say I was inquiring about Dr. King's constitutional right to bail?" Bob asked, sounding uncharacteristically sheepish.

"What did you say to him? Why did you call him?" we asked.

"I said that if he was a decent American, he would let King out of jail by sundown. I called him because it made me so damned angry to think of that bastard sentencing a citizen to four months of hard labor for a minor traffic offense and screwing up my brother's campaign and making our country look ridiculous before the world."

That is how I remember it, although his language was no doubt more colorful. But oral history is inexact, and John Seigenthaler recalls that Bob said, "It just burned me all the way up here on the plane. It grilled me. The more I thought about the injustice of it, the more I thought what a son of a bitch that judge was. I made it clear to him that it was not a political call; that I am a lawyer, one who believes in the right of all defendants to make bond. . . . I felt it was disgraceful." The conversation, Kennedy said, had been restrained, and the judge had not sounded hostile.* Bob had not told his brother about it.

---

* In his 1964 oral history interview with Anthony Lewis, Robert Kennedy recalled that the suggestion to call the judge came from Governor Vandiver himself,

Very late that night—he thinks around 3 a.m.—Louis Martin was awakened by the telephone. "This is Bob Kennedy," the caller said. "Louis, I wanted you especially to know that I called that judge in Georgia today, to try to get Dr. King out." Louis shook himself awake, not believing his ears, and made Kennedy repeat himself; there seemed to be quiet pride in Bob's voice as he recounted his action.

"*You* are now an honorary Brother!" Louis Martin said. Ever afterwards, Bob claimed that title in dealing with Martin ("Tell him his honorary Brother needs his help," he would say to Martin's secretary), and in turn Martin would always be able to get through directly to Kennedy with those magic words.

On balance I, too, was as pleased by Bob's passion as I was surprised by his procedure. The impropriety of the call was obvious. The Canons of Professional Ethics of the American Bar Association provide that "a lawyer should not communicate or argue privately with the Judge as to the merits of a pending cause, and he deserves rebuke and denunciation for any device or attempt to gain from a Judge special personal consideration or favor." Yet that canon notwithstanding, if the call in fact influenced the judge to let King free on bail, Kennedy's political instincts—if not his legal tactics—were right. If King had remained in jail, the Senator's call to Mrs. King might have seemed a symbol without substance—the worst fate for any symbolic act. Not long after Bob's call, the judge, noting pressure "from both sides," released King on $2,000 bond.

Outside the prison, King said, "I am deeply indebted to Senator Kennedy, who served as a great force in making my release possible. For him to be that courageous shows that he is really acting upon principle and not expediency." He added, "There are moments when the politically expedient can be morally wise." To a reporter he said, "I hold Senator Kennedy in very high esteem. I am convinced he will seek to exercise the power of his office to fully implement the civil rights plank of his party's platform." He noted he had not heard from Nixon and did not know of any effort in his behalf by anyone in the GOP.

That Friday evening, October 28, some eight hundred people filled the Ebenezer Baptist Church in Atlanta to welcome Martin home. "We must master the art of creative suffering," he said. "We must continue to

---

probably via Griffin Bell. Kennedy said he called the judge from a pay booth and told him that King's release would be very helpful. According to Kennedy, the judge had responded, "Bob, it's nice to talk to you." After the election Kennedy said that the judge called on him at the Department of Justice and they had a friendly visit.

have the courage to challenge the system of segregation whether it is in schools, public parks, Christian churches, lunch counters or public libraries. We must be prepared to suffer, sacrifice and even die." While he did not endorse Kennedy outright, the Atlanta *Journal* reported that "he did just about everything short of it." To the congregation he said, "I never intend to be a religious bigot. I never intend to reject a man running for President of the United States just because he is a Catholic. Religious bigotry is as immoral, undemocratic, un-American and un-Christian as racial bigotry."

Dr. King, Sr., chose that evening to make his public announcement:

> I had expected to vote against Senator Kennedy because of his religion. But now he can be my President, Catholic or whatever he is. It took courage to call my daughter-in-law at a time like this. He has the moral courage to stand up for what he knows is right. I've got all my votes and I've got a suitcase and I'm going to take them up there and dump them in his lap.

There were just ten days left before the election. The press had carried the Kennedy-King story far and wide, but most of its readership was white. White bigots, North and South, were likely to know what one or both of the Kennedy brothers had done. At Democratic headquarters dire predictions were being made about how many votes—and states— the King affair had cost. Louis Martin and I wanted to do everything in our power to see that the prophesied losses were made up by a surge of black votes.

Negro-owned newspapers, mostly weekly publications with modest circulation, could not reach the mass of black voters in time. Yet we knew that the story, if well told, would convince many to switch from Nixon, and even more importantly, would inspire many registered but apathetic Democrats to vote who might otherwise stay at home. We thought we could arrange mass distribution of a good pamphlet, but with Bob Kennedy having directed us to publish no new statements or editorializing literature, we were stymied.

Putting the problem to Shriver, still in Illinois, we asked him to help persuade Bob to let us print and distribute a little pamphlet on the King case. "What do you want to put in it?" he asked. We said that all we wanted to do was reproduce the statements made by leading Negroes in the public press. "So you don't need to editorialize or make any new statement?" he said. "Then you don't need to ask Bobby's permission. He might say no, but what you're planning is not within his ban. Let's do it. If it works, he'll like it. If we don't do it, and we don't get enough Negro votes, he and Jack wouldn't like that, and we would all be kicking ourselves for a long time."

In six hours we went to press with *The Case of Martin Luther King*. To avoid embarrassing the Democratic National Committee we arranged for it to be published and sponsored by "The Freedom Crusade Committee" headed by two Philadelphia ministers (one of them the father of Congressman-to-be William Gray, Jr.). We stretched the non-editorializing rule to—or beyond—the limit with one bold caption: "*No Comment*" *Nixon versus a Candidate with a Heart, Senator Kennedy*. Otherwise, it simply contained, in very readable type, the statements by Coretta, Martin, and Dr. King, Sr., along with the following comments by Ralph Abernathy of the Southern Christian Leadership Conference, Gardner Taylor, president of the Protestant Council of New York, and the New York *Post*.

"I earnestly and sincerely feel that it is time for all of us to take off our Nixon buttons," Abernathy was quoted as saying. "Senator Kennedy did something great and wonderful when he personally called Mrs. Coretta King and helped free Dr. Martin Luther King. This was the kind of act I was waiting for. It was not just Dr. King on trial—America was on trial. . . . I learned a long time ago that one kindness deserves another. Since Mr. Nixon has been silent through all this, I am going to return his silence when I go into the voting booth."

The Reverend Gardner Taylor said, "This is the kind of moral leadership and direct personal concern which this problem has lacked in these last critical years." The New York *Post* editorial said that Senator Kennedy responded "with full awareness that his words and deeds would inflame the Southern racists and multiply his difficulties in Dixie. . . . In this dramatic human episode Senator Kennedy has looked a lot larger and warmer—and bolder—than his opponent."

During the weekend of October 29–30, the first 50,000 copies of the pamphlet, printed on light blue paper and dubbed "the blue bomb," rolled off a Washington press and were mailed in bundles all over the country. By Tuesday, November 1, Shriver had called and said they were reprinting 250,000 (later 500,000) copies in Illinois for distribution before every Negro church in Chicago and other cities in Illinois and Wisconsin on the following Sunday, two days before the election. As orders for hundreds of thousands of new copies came from Civil Rights Section campaign workers in many states, we telephoned around the country to organize a massive Sunday distribution at Negro churches. In a number of cities, extra copies were printed on local presses. Near dawn on Sunday, November 6, we loaded the last large shipments on

Greyhound buses headed for Virginia and North and South Carolina. They were met at the terminals and the pamphlets taken straight to the churches. In all, nearly two million copies were distributed.

The printed word and churches were not our only recourse. Streetwise Louis Martin called Harlem leader Raymond Jones and other Northern Negro Democrats, suggesting they send runners into the bars with the word that Kennedy called Coretta and got Martin out of jail. When "Ray the Fox" reported back that the bars of Harlem were all going our way, and when we got widespread reports of whole congregations of Negro Baptists and Methodists standing up and pledging to vote for Kennedy, we sensed that a tide was running for the Senator in practically every Negro community, North and South.

When the votes were counted that Tuesday, it became clear that more than two-thirds of the Negroes voting were for Kennedy. (Gallup and Harris polls found 68 to 78 percent for the Senator.) Moreover, a higher proportion had voted—and had voted Democratic—than in 1956. In Illinois alone, which Kennedy carried by 9,000 votes, some 250,000 Negroes are estimated to have voted for him. Theodore White, in *The Making of the President 1960*, concluded that "it is difficult to see how Illinois, New Jersey, Michigan, South Carolina or Delaware (with 74 electoral votes) could have been won had the Republican-Democratic split of the Negro wards and precincts remained as it was, unchanged from the Eisenhower charm of 1956." If two or three of those states had gone Republican, Kennedy would have lost. He won by 84 electoral votes, with a popular margin of only 120,000 votes.

Afterwards, President Eisenhower in irritation blamed "a couple of phone calls"—by John and Robert Kennedy—for the decisive shift of Negro votes. Nixon, in turn, wrote in *Six Crises* that had the White House issued the statement that the Justice Department had recommended, "the whole incident might have resulted in a plus rather than a minus." Instead, Nixon wrote, despite what he considered a strong personal record in support of civil rights legislation, and earlier friendly association with Martin King himself (when they met in Ghana), "this one unfortunate incident in the heat of the campaign served to dissipate much of the support I had among Negro voters." He added that if he had "called the judge or done something similarly 'grandstand,'" it might have been a sure road to victory—one of sixteen such possible roads he listed.

Curiously, Nixon blamed it all on Bob Kennedy and made no reference to the Senator's call to Mrs. King. He explained the "no comment" attributed to him as a reaction to Bob's call to the judge. He said that on learning of Bob's call he told his press secretary, Herb Klein, "I think Dr.

King is getting a bum rap. But despite my strong feelings in this respect, it would be completely improper for me or any other lawyer to call the judge. And Robert Kennedy should have known better than to do so." Klein, according to Nixon, concluded it would be better simply to say "no comment." Whatever he may have said later to Klein about Bob Kennedy, the "no comment" to *The New York Times* was given after the Senator's call to Mrs. King—the day before Bob's call to the judge.

Two days after the election, Nixon's chauffeur said, "Mr. Vice-President, I can't tell you how sick I am about the way my people voted in the election. You know I had been talking to all my friends. They were all for you. But when Mr. Robert Kennedy called the judge to get Dr. King out of jail—well, they just all turned to him." Nixon replied, "If there was any fault involved it was not with your people: it was mine, in failing to get my point of view across to them."

In such a narrow victory, credit goes to every successful part of the campaign, back to the very beginning, and to all the actions and inactions of the candidate (and in this case, the candidate's brothers, sisters, brothers-in-law, wife, mother, and father). Accidental and elusive factors play their part, too. Bernard Segal of Philadelphia, former president of the American Bar Association, tells how his and Bob Kennedy's mutual love of chocolate led by a circuitous route to Bob's close association with Congressman William Green, Sr., James P. Clark, and other key Philadelphia Democratic leaders, without whose support the crucial Pennsylvania delegation might not have cast their decisive convention votes to nominate John Kennedy. But if the election had been lost no one would have known about Bernard Segal's chocolates; the call to Mrs. King could easily have been singled out for a large share of the blame.

In his *Report of the County Chairman*, James Michener calls the King affair "the single event which came closest to being the one vital accident of the campaign." When King was jailed, Michener assumed it "was a situation that must work to the Democrats' disadvantage, for if Senator Kennedy did nothing, he would lose Negro support in the vital northern cities, and if he did something, he would alienate the South, where he had to pick up electoral votes." Michener concluded:

> What happened is history. . . . John Kennedy took the risk and did the gallant thing. . . . In doing this he did not lose Georgia or South Carolina or Texas. Instead he won the Negro vote in New York and Chicago and Philadelphia, and thus the Presidency.

In the original draft of *The Making of the President*, White had it that a single "command decision" was made for the candidate to call

Mrs. King and for brother Bob to call the judge. After I gave him a very different version, he modified the account of the Senator's call but still wrote that "Bobby Kennedy, informed in the course of the day of the command decision . . . the next morning telephoned . . . the Georgian judge." And again, on the plan for the pamphlet, he wrote that since the "command decision had been made, the Kennedy organization could by now follow through." His view of a centralized super-efficient Kennedy operation would not let him write otherwise, but that is not how it happened.*

Bob Kennedy never discussed the calls to Mrs. King or the judge with me, except for that morning when he gave Louis Martin and me hell for suggesting his brother's action and the night he confessed to calling the judge. The New York *Post* writer Murray Kempton reported that he had asked Bob, after the election, whether he was glad he had called the judge. "Sure I'm glad," Kennedy said, "but I would hope I'm not glad for the reason you think I'm glad."

John Kennedy never, to my knowledge, made any public comment on his call to Mrs. King, except the brief confirmation that he had done it, but in a conversation about it with John Kenneth Galbraith he said, "The finest strategies are usually the result of accidents."

On Sunday, October 30, while the blue pamphlets were being printed, I went to meet Senator Kennedy at Washington National Airport. It was the last time I was to call him "Senator" or "Jack," for he was about to fly off for his final campaign in Pennsylvania, New York, and California (where he would propose the Peace Corps). Our Civil Rights Section had one piece of unfinished business: the release of the report of the Conference on Constitutional Rights that Kennedy had convened in New York in mid-October. It was a document that had been cleared and then, for one reason or another, delayed. Kennedy had agreed to sign the covering letter at the airport.

He read it carefully, no doubt noting the far-reaching specific recommendations covering practically every area of civil rights. Then in his quizzical, sympathetic but humorous way, he looked me in the eye and

---

* Attributing more generous motives to Kennedy, White retold the story of the call to Mrs. King in his 1978 book, *In Search of History*. But the call was not an entirely humanitarian act either. Nor was the account in Sorensen's *Kennedy* correct. Kennedy phoned, according to Sorensen, against the advice of "almost all his advisers" who "initially opposed [it] as a futile 'grandstand' gesture which would cost more votes among Southerners than it would gain among Negroes." There was prior advice against issuing a public statement about King, but no advice about the call, except Shriver's, since none of the other "advisers" knew of it in advance.

asked, "Tell me honestly whether you think I need to sign and release this today in order to get elected a week from Tuesday. Or do you mainly want me to do it to go on record?" I had to agree that the release would have little effect on voters; it involved commitments for his presidency. By now he had shot his bolt for civil rights in the campaign and done it well.

"Then we can wait, and release it when I'm elected," he said. "You can consider me on record—with you."

I walked with him out on the runway to his plane, the *Caroline*. He was carrying his three-year-old daughter on his back, and my five-year-old son, Daniel, was on mine. The sun was shining and his gaiety that day had the air of victory about it.

Then, in the only reference I ever heard him make to the King affair, he asked, "Did you see what Martin's father said? He was going to vote against me because I was a Catholic, but since I called his daughter-in-law, he will vote for me. That was a hell of a bigoted statement, wasn't it? Imagine Martin Luther King having a bigot for a father!"

He said it lightly, and as we parted, he grinned and added, "Well, we all have fathers, don't we?"

2 · On the Campaign of 1960

In many ways *The Making of the President* 1960 captured the character of Kennedy's presidential campaign, but on one important issue I thought White was wrong. The picture White portrayed of a smooth, tightly run, hierarchical Kennedy political organization contrasted sharply with the spontaneity, creative chaos, and unbureaucratic response to conflicting pressures that I experienced.

That I should be claiming any expertise about Kennedy—even that I should have been in his campaign at all—is surprising. When I first encountered Jack Kennedy at Clare Boothe Luce's home in Greenwich, Connecticut, in 1946, when he was running for Congress (and I was about to enter college), I never would have guessed that I might someday support him for President. Clare Luce whispered to me that "if old Joe has his way, Jack will be President of the United States." With several young women in tow, Kennedy demolished the food and headed for the tennis court. After several efforts to engage him in conversation, during which he made it clear that tennis and the girls were his priority on such a sunny day, I concluded that the certain-to-be-elected congressman was a lightweight. He no doubt considered me oddly overcommitted to political ideas at age twenty, while I found him at age twenty-nine disappointingly undercommitted to anything except perhaps his political career.*

During the McCarthy period, he joined in the attack on Owen Lattimore and talked loosely about our "losing China," as if we ever had it. But I was struck favorably by his refusal to go along with most other New England politicians in asking Truman to pardon the convicted but still very popular Mayor Curley of Boston, and he once attacked the

---

* Clare Luce had expected us to find much in common. As veterans, we had each attended and written articles about the 1945 San Francisco Conference at which the United Nations was founded. At twenty-three, in 1940, Kennedy had published his expanded senior thesis at Harvard, *Why England Slept*; at twenty, in 1946, I had just finished *It's Up to Us*, a book about the national Student Federalist organization I started in high school. Although one of Kennedy's first talks in 1946 was on the theme of world interdependence, his approach was more pragmatic. At San Francisco, after hearing another young veteran, Cord Meyer, who was about to lead United World Federalists (and later to become a mastermind of CIA covert action), Kennedy had written in his notebook: "Admittedly world organization with common obedience to law would be the solution. Not that easy. If there is not the feeling that war is the ultimate evil, a feeling strong enough to drive them together, then you can't work out this internationalist plan. Mustn't expect too much. . . . There is no cure-all."

selfishness and shortsightedness of the American Legion. Then in 1951 he visited Asia and "saw firsthand that in Indochina we had allied ourselves with a colonial regime that had no real support from the people." My wife Clare and I had just published our book on India, and we agreed with Kennedy's warning to Congress that to try to check Communism in Vietnam primarily by force of arms "apart from and in defiance of innately nationalist aims spells foredoomed failure."

Aside from that brief foray into foreign policy, Kennedy's record in the House did not warrant much enthusiasm when he was elected to the Senate in 1952. One wondered how far charm, money, and a determined, famous father would take him. At the Democratic convention in 1956 Stevenson selected Kennedy to make the nominating speech for him—a major opportunity for a nationwide audience—but finally decided to throw the vice-presidential nomination to an open convention. Kennedy, Humphrey, and Kefauver were the leading contenders, and supporters of each had about twelve hours before the balloting. I stayed up all night working against Kennedy's nomination.

Most liberals were for Humphrey. Hubert Horatio Humphrey had caught their imagination at the 1948 convention when he stirred the delegates to adopt a civil rights plank that would take the party "out of the shadow of States Rights into the sunshine of Human Rights." I had cheered him from the galleries on that occasion. Later my wife, a Minnesotan, and I had come to know, like, and respect him, as he successfully reformed a corrupt city government and built a new Democratic-Farmer-Labor Party that was to make Minnesota a center of progressive politics for years to come—something John Kennedy could never claim about Massachusetts. When we were writing our book on India in 1950, he gave us its title—*India Afire*. Pacing up and down, after quickly picking up some of our main points, he kept repeating, "Those people constitute one-fifth of the human race, and India's afire." India wasn't, just then, but Hubert Humphrey always was. As a senator, Humphrey had begun to prove his legislative effectiveness and national leadership. Yet much as I admired him, his image as a loud and militant liberal was not, in that era of stolid moderation, what I thought Stevenson needed to have a chance against Eisenhower.

On the other hand, Kennedy seemed the wrong candidate, backed by the wrong forces. He had written *Profiles in Courage*, but on the most controversial issue in American politics in those years—the excesses of Senator Joseph McCarthy—John Kennedy had been largely distinguished by his silence. His brother Robert had even worked for a time on McCarthy's staff, and their father was known as one of McCarthy's friends and supporters. There was more to the matter than this, I learned later, but in 1956 I agreed with Eleanor Roosevelt's chastisement in front of a number of people when Kennedy sought her convention support. She described him as "someone who understands what courage is and admires it, but has not quite the independence to have it."

Some were opposed to Kennedy because of his father or his religion. No one doubted the senior Kennedy's independence and courage; whether standing up to Franklin Roosevelt and Winston Churchill or opposing American intervention in World War II and in the cold war that followed, he had often been in the thick of controversy and had earned a host of enemies. Although he belonged to a Jewish golf club in Palm Beach, his own salty tongue had given rise to rumors of anti-Semitism. For their part, liberals tended toward anti-Catholicism. When Kennedy supporters circulated a memorandum written by Theodore Sorensen, indicating that a Democratic ticket could win if it was able to recapture those Catholics who had switched to Eisenhower, many liberals took offense.

My own opposition to Kennedy was on different ground. The big-city machines and Southern conservatives rallying to Kennedy appeared to be an unholy alliance to defeat Estes Kefauver. In chairing the first major congressional investigation of organized crime, the Tennessee senator had uncovered a vast network of corruption embarrassing to his party. In Illinois this contributed to the defeat of a fellow senator, Scott Lucas. The Democratic establishment was dead set against Kefauver and was not ready to swallow Humphrey.

Not all of the old leaders were for the thirty-nine-year-old Kennedy. Many of his fellow Catholics feared an anti-Catholic backlash. Mayor David Lawrence of Pittsburgh warned that the nomination of a Catholic would assure defeat. "America is not ready for a Catholic," Jim Farley told Stevenson. My own, non-Catholic concern was about a different kind of backlash. Estes Kefauver, in 1956 as in 1952, had gone to the people and scored extraordinary primary victories. Stevenson had finally prevailed, but if the vice-presidential nomination was now denied Kefauver, millions of people would be angered; justice and good politics alike seemed to call for Kefauver's nomination.

In the balloting, Kennedy showed unexpected appeal across conventional lines of region and ideology, even discounting the anti-Kefauver vote. When Lyndon Johnson cast all 56 votes of Texas "for that fighting senator who wears the scars of battle . . . John Kennedy," the young man from Massachusetts nearly attained a majority. Ironically, it was the crucial votes thrown to Kefauver by Catholic "bosses"—Lawrence of Pennsylvania and Mike DiSalle of Ohio—that stopped the Kennedy tide from going over the top. In the future, Kennedy would thank all those who blocked him in 1956, on the ground that if he had won and gone down to disastrous defeat with Stevenson, his Catholicism would have shared the blame and his chance for the presidency might never have come.

Meeting Robert Kennedy in early 1957 did nothing to make me want his brother to become President. Bob had recently accompanied Justice Douglas on a trip to the Soviet Union and I was helping Chester Bowles plan a visit to some of the same cities in Soviet Asia. Friends suggested that Bobby—as everyone then called him—could give us some helpful advice and interesting contacts in Tashkent and Samarkand.

Already Bobby's reputation was that of an arrogant, narrow, rude young man, but I told myself that Justice Douglas, whom I had known and admired since our days in India, would not have taken him along on a difficult journey if he did not see something better in him. Bobby's clash and near fistfight with Roy Cohn during the McCarthy hearings had demonstrated his spunk; as chief counsel for the new Senate Select Committee on Improper Activities in the Labor or Management Field, he was now fighting on the new frontier of labor racketeering. We were the same age, in the same profession and city, and active in the same party; I looked forward to meeting him.

He sat at one end of a long cavernous office in the basement of the Old Senate Office Building. I was shown to a seat at the other end, while a Negro attendant brought him a luncheon tray. He ate his lunch, talked on the telephone, worked on his papers, while I waited; my own lunch hour was almost gone and I had no time to spare from a case I was working on. Finally, he signaled me to come up to his desk. He gave a short glum account of his Russian trip, warned that they spied on you night and day, in hotels and even in hospital rooms, and said he had nothing special to suggest. Then he went into a diatribe against the Soviet regime, which he explained was a great evil and an ever-present threat, and bid me goodbye.

Having come to anti-Communism early, I did not appreciate his moralizing. Khrushchev's 20th Party Congress denunciation of Stalin had just occurred, and it was a time of ferment in the Soviet empire. Bobby had given no insights or clues about the new developments and showed little interest.

Later, Justice Douglas's wife, Mercedes, explained to me that Joe Kennedy had insisted that his old friend take his son along and Douglas had complied, grudgingly, because he felt he owed his Supreme Court seat to Kennedy's intervention with President Roosevelt. On the trip Bobby had seemed almost paranoid about the Russians, refusing most of the food and at first refusing to have "a Communist doctor" when he was taken seriously ill with a high fever. In exasperation, Douglas one night urged Bobby to stop trying to convert Communists; after that, Kennedy seemed to listen more. Douglas was impressed by the young man's pluck and persistence, particularly on hard mountain treks. "Bobby was an all-out," he said. "If he was climbing a peak or hiking a trail there was nothing else in the world to do but that." Douglas added that Bobby "worked hard on that trip and came back with some considerable insight" and concluded that it was for the young Kennedy "the final undoing of McCarthyism." Before the trip he saw Russians as soulless fanatics; afterwards, according to Douglas, he saw them as "people with problems." In his ardent and comprehensive biography, *Robert Kennedy and His Times*, Arthur Schlesinger stresses the importance of this Russian experience but adds that it "took time to penetrate."

When I saw Bobby there was no sign of penetration. He no doubt regarded Bowles as an arch-liberal and a possible rival of his brother's, with whom he had no desire to cooperate. Anyway, by then he was "all-out" on the trail of Jimmy Hoffa, and probably nothing else in the world mattered. Excuses aside, my first impressions of Bobby further colored my thinking about Jack Kennedy; if the senator was not guilty by association with his father, there was this insufferable brother.

Returning to Washington after a ten-week tour in the U.S.S.R., Poland, Yugoslavia, Afghanistan, Pakistan, and India, I felt that our country and its leaders were out of touch with the changes and revolutionary pressures in the developing nations and the Communist world. In newspapers, magazines, and books, Bowles resumed the public debate against America's cold war policies that he had been carrying on since his replacement as Ambassador to India in 1953. Although he had the assistance of a number of young lawyers such as Abram Chayes and myself, he was relatively lonely on the public stage. Justice Douglas, with whom he saw eye to eye, was limited by his duties on the highest bench; Humphrey, who shared their point of view, was busy speaking out on dozens of domestic issues; and Stevenson, who had aroused so many Americans to a new interest in politics, remained relatively indifferent to the developing nations.

On July 2, 1957, John Kennedy rose in the Senate to give the first of two major foreign policy addresses. They were a direct challenge to the Eisenhower and Dulles policies by a popular new member of the Senate Committee on Foreign Relations.

The single most powerful force in the world is man's desire to be free, said Kennedy, and the single most important task of American foreign policy was to meet the challenge of both Western and Soviet imperialism. He took as critical test cases the situations in Algeria and Poland. He called upon France to negotiate with the Algerian rebels for a peace that assured self-determination, and he called for America to cease supporting the French effort at a military solution. "Instead of abandoning African nationalism to the anti-Western agitators and Soviet agents who hope to capture its leadership," he said, "the United States, a product of political revolution, must redouble its efforts to earn the respect and friendship of nationalist leaders."

Six weeks later, in a long, detailed analysis of the crisis of Russian imperialism in Eastern Europe, he castigated the failure of the American policy that had encouraged—and then let down—the armed uprising in Hungary. He called for America to stop seeing Communism as a monolith, in black-and-white terms—to begin to differentiate between the shades of gray—and specifically to promote diversity within the Soviet bloc by offering trade and aid to Poland. He contrasted "the total repression which gripped that country" when he visited it in 1955 with "the gradual increases in freedom we have witnessed since last October," and urged America to support the Polish evolution. In a bold step, the anti-Stalinist new Polish government had asked for $300 million of American aid; after months of haggling and indecision, the United States had offered a loan for less than one-third of the request. "Our action was too little and too late," said Kennedy. He called for "an increase of people-to-people contacts, of cultural, scientific, and educational exchanges" to "break through the long isolation from the Western world." In short, he suggested that the necessary condition for the freedom of Eastern Europe was peace.

Kennedy's proposals on Poland did not receive much attention, but a storm of criticism about the Algerian talk swirled around the Senator. Although French opponents of the war in Algeria were encouraged and the full text was carried in *L'Express*, the French government was furious. So was the U.S. State Department. *The New York Times*, which in 1954 had written that "in Dienbienphu the French are fighting heroically the battle of the free," now defended the French position against the upstart Senator. Most leading Democrats, except Chester Bowles and Hubert Humphrey, were silent or opposed. (On the Senate floor, Humphrey had called Kennedy's address "a service to the cause of American foreign policy.") Stevenson, whom Arthur Schlesinger saw in Paris a few days after the talk, "was appalled: Kennedy was criticizing an ally . . ." Dean Acheson publicly denounced the Senator's talk as a juvenile's "impatient snapping of the fingers."

Six days after the talk, Kennedy went back to the Senate floor and held his ground:

Mr. President, the reaction to my remarks both at home and abroad has further strengthened my conviction that the situation in Algeria is drifting dangerously. . . . No amount of hopeful assertions that France will handle the problem alone, no amount of cautious warnings that these are matters best left unmentioned in public, and no amount of charges against the motives or methods of those of us seeking a peaceful solution can obscure the fact that the Algerians will someday be free. Then, to whom will they turn—to the West, which has seemingly ignored their plea for independence; to the Americans, whom they may feel have rejected the issue as none of our affair while at the same time furnishing arms that help crush them; or to Moscow, to Cairo, to Peking, the pretended champions of nationalism and independence?

Not long afterwards Kennedy became chairman of the African Subcommittee of the Senate Foreign Relations Committee and continued his involvement with the decolonization of that continent. One day about that time I wrote Kennedy a letter saying that his two talks seemed to me the most thoughtful, responsible, and important statements so far made in the Senate during the 1950s. I was then an associate in the law firm of Covington and Burling, of which Dean Acheson was a senior partner. After the former Secretary of State's attack, Kennedy was amused to find support from someone at the bottom of the Covington letterhead.

Ted Sorensen, who had helped draft those talks, began to give me other speeches and writings of the Senator—and to make the case for his presidential candidacy. Sorensen was persistent and persuasive; at thirty, he was also arrogant, brash, analytical, and totally dedicated to John Kennedy, for whom he had been working for five years. His cool front covered a warm and strong commitment to a new role for America in a revolutionary world. From a populist Nebraska background, he came naturally to a concern for human rights at home and abroad. For me, it was a good sign that Kennedy was drawn to, and more and more drawing upon, Sorensen. Their collaboration on talks and writings had become a crucible in which the Senator's ideas and policies were shaped and tested.

Before long, Sorensen asked me to draft a foreign policy speech for the Senator, which I did, and then another. When he asked if I would consider working full-time, I said I still had to be convinced Kennedy was the best candidate. With detail and earnestness, Sorensen proceeded to deal with my chief doubts.

On Joe McCarthy, he gave a cogent account of the Senator's carefully prepared speech in favor of censure that he was prevented from making because of his back operation; then of Kennedy's subsequent duel with death and the ordeal of a long-drawn-out recovery, and of his several controversial actions, before and after the censure vote, that showed his revulsion and resistance to all forms of McCarthyism. If Sorensen had been completely candid he would have conceded that Kennedy was also held back by his father's and brother's relations with McCarthy, and by his own political instincts. "Hell, half my voters in Massachusetts look on McCarthy as a hero," the Senator had said to Arthur Schlesinger. Only a few senators did stand up early against McCarthy's Communist witch-hunt—notably Herbert Lehman, Estes Kefauver, William Benton, and Millard Tydings, and the latter two were beaten as a result. Still, Mrs. Roosevelt was right that a Catholic war hero might have given a stronger profile in courage.

Beyond details on voting record and public stands, what impressed me most was Sorensen's case for Kennedy's capacity for growth. I had not realized how much physical pain the Senator endured during most of his adult years—"at least one-half of the days he spent on this earth," according to his brother Bob—and how close to tragedy he had lived, in war, in his own recurring illnesses, and in the death of his elder brother and sister and the mental retardation of another sister. In much the words he later used in his book *Kennedy*, Sorensen stated his theory that the Senator's experience with tragedy had produced in him both a desire to enjoy the world and a desire to improve it. These desires, Sorensen conceded, had sometimes been in conflict, particularly before 1953 (the year he began as a senator, married Jacqueline, and employed Sorensen). Agreeing that Kennedy had "fiddled around as a congressman," Sorensen felt when he met the new senator "that an inner struggle was being waged for the spirit of John Kennedy—a struggle between the political dilettante and the statesman, between the lure of luxury and lawmaking." According to Sorensen the statesman had won out.

In the spring of 1959, as counsel to Father Theodore Hesburgh on the Commission on Civil Rights, I was working on the commission's first report to the President and Congress when Senator Kennedy's office called to ask me to come up to Capitol Hill. No doubt well briefed for our private talk by Sorensen, Kennedy went straight to the point most likely to win me. In rapid-fire blunt fashion, the Senator said (in approximately these words):

> The key thing for the country is a new foreign policy that will break out of the confines of the cold war. Then we can build a decent relationship with developing nations and begin to respond to their needs. We can stop the vicious circle of the arms race and promote diversity and peaceful change within the Soviet bloc. We can get this country moving again on its domestic problems.
>
> Stevenson may see this, but he's a two-time loser and has no real

chance; nor has Bowles or Humphrey, with whom I agree even more. The most likely alternatives are Johnson or Symington, but if either of them is nominated we might as well elect Dulles or Acheson; it would be the same cold-war foreign policy all over again.

I have a good shot at the nomination and election, and am the only electable candidate who will bring about the change we need. Will you help me do it?

His arguments were obviously honed to my interests; nevertheless, by the time we finished I was impressed by his apparent candor, conviction, and determination, and agreed to think about his offer to join his campaign staff full-time. If his record in civil rights was undistinguished, his interest in foreign affairs went back over years and now seemed genuine and more deeply rooted than I expected. I found his directness and combination of seriousness and humor appealing; out of his inner struggle, tempered by gaiety, it seemed to me that Kennedy's personal charm was being transformed into effective political charisma.

After a few days I told the Senator that he had my full support for 1960, though not my full time in 1959 because of a commitment to teach at Notre Dame Law School. Sorensen did not give up. Even the night before the moving van came to take our things to South Bend he came to our house to keep me from making a major mistake. He badly needed relief from constant speechwriting and said they were able to use my drafts without many changes, which was not then true of anyone else available. If I joined the staff now, at the beginning of the campaign, I would be on the inside, Sorensen said; if I didn't, I would have missed an opportunity that might never come again.

No doubt he was right. To understand why the commitment to Notre Dame took precedence, one would need to know Father Hesburgh. He saw the establishment of a civil rights center at Notre Dame as an essential continuation of the work we had started at the Commission on Civil Rights. His skepticism about the Senator, magnified by his reaction to the highhandedness he had experienced from the Senator's father, left him in no mood to release me from my obligation. Knowing how he felt and wanting to carry out his plans, I did not ask him to do so.

Soon after we were settled in South Bend, in September 1959, Father John Cavanaugh, former president of Notre Dame, invited me to dinner on what he said was a very confidential and very embarrassing mission. "Joe wants me to get you back to Washington," he finally explained. A friend and confidant of Joe Kennedy, Cavanaugh was not unused to such pressure but worried how I would react. Mr. Kennedy had called him and said his son wanted a fellow to work for him who felt he had a prior moral obligation to Notre Dame. If his son needed some-one for his campaign, then Cavanaugh should tell Hesburgh to forget the moral obligation and get that fellow on the first plane to Washington. It had been put in more vivid language than Cavanaugh wished to repeat.

We agreed not to tell Hesburgh; it would have been the last straw in his relations with Joe Kennedy, and we still hoped to win his vote. Hesburgh's negative attitude, to my surprise, was shared by most of my colleagues at Notre Dame in the fall of 1959. Dire predictions that Kennedy would be snowed under by an avalanche of Protestant votes in Wisconsin and West Virginia were widespread on campus. I found only one Catholic member of the faculty who was openly and actively for the Senator; the priests were particularly dubious. A statement by Kennedy in *Look* magazine had been offensive to many serious Catholics, who found one passage unduly secular and a denial of the higher moral claim of natural law. "Whatever one's religion in his private life may be," Kennedy had said, "for the officeholder nothing takes precedence over his oath to uphold the Constitution and all its parts."

Later that fall when I told Sargent Shriver about Joseph Kennedy's call to Father Cavanaugh, he said, "Don't ever underestimate Mr. Kennedy." This was the only time I personally saw the long hand of Joe Kennedy, but if he would intervene so vigorously on such a small matter, I could imagine what he was like when he dealt with Mayor Daley for delegates. "And that is exactly who did deal with Daley most of the time," said Shriver. John Kennedy would go in to see Daley when he visited Chicago, but it would be a ceremonial visit, lasting five or ten minutes. The long, tough talks were between the mayor and Joe Kennedy. Shriver said this was true of the negotiations with the Philadelphia leader, Congressman William Green, and with other Irish-Americans of the old school who were in key positions in a number of city and state Democratic organizations, including California and New York.

"You should have seen Mr. Kennedy in the 1952 Senate campaign," Shriver said. Stevenson had turned down Shriver's offer to campaign full-time for him, free, saying he did not know how he would use the young man's talents. Mr. Kennedy then "persuaded" Shriver to come to Massa-chusetts and campaign for Jack. Shriver had been an early Stevenson supporter, and his heart was in the national effort, but Mr. Kennedy said, "If Adlai is that stupid, then he'll never win, so get on the plane to Boston and help Jack." Shriver arrived in time for Jack's first paid-for television broadcast. Mr. Kennedy had assembled at Hyannis Port the top executives of the advertising agency hired to plan Jack's media cam-paign. They sat glued to the television set, with Mr. Kennedy following his son's every word and move. "What did you think?" he asked when

Jack finished. One by one the admen said that Jack had looked fine, done fine. Hating sycophants, Mr. Kennedy exploded with anger Shriver witnessed only two or three times, and said, "The hell he did! He was lousy, the show was lousy, and you know it." Jack had been stiff and somewhat pompous in his earnestness. Mr. Kennedy fired the man responsible for the approach and kept working with the others until a very different style and format were developed. He insisted that his son should be informal and direct, as if he were talking personally to the audience in their living rooms. That approach was given much credit in Kennedy's victory over the well-established Henry Cabot Lodge. Another successful proposal by Joe Kennedy was the mobilization of the whole family for tea parties in friendly homes all over the state.

The money provided by Joe Kennedy was only one-tenth of his contribution, said Shriver. The father's critical, driving determination, his telephonic arm-twisting of key contacts all over the country, and his constant moral support of his sons played a far-reaching and fundamental role in the making of America's thirty-fifth President. "You do what you think is right," Joe Kennedy told his son after he was elected to the Senate, "and we'll take care of the politicians." When the Senator was under heavy fire for his Algerian talk, Joe Kennedy (who in fact thought it was bad politics) cheered his son: "You lucky mush. You don't know it and neither does anyone else, but within a few months everyone is going to know just how right you were on Algeria." Jack Kennedy once commented, "My father would be for me if I were running as head of the Communist Party."

Joseph Kennedy's long-standing anti-colonialism and his criticism of U.S. cold war policies had probably contributed to his son's controversial stand. In *Robert Kennedy and His Times*, Arthur Schlesinger recounts Joseph Kennedy's opposition to the Truman–Acheson "program of minding other people's business on a global scale," which he considered "warbreeding." "The basic world policy for the U.S.," he wrote in 1946 in *Life*, "should be to prevent World War III." The "real dangers at home" —budget deficits, inflation, depression—seemed to him "far more real" than the Soviet threat. In 1950, after MacArthur's forces had invaded North Korea, Mr. Kennedy (at a University of Virginia Law School students' forum arranged by Robert) asked: "What business is it of ours to support French colonial policy in Indochina or to achieve Mr. Syngman Rhee's concepts of democracy in Korea?" The containment policy had "solidified Communism, where otherwise Communism might have bred within itself internal dissensions." With peace, he predicted, differences in European Communism "will destroy the singleness that today characterizes Russian Communism," and "Mao in China is not likely to take his orders too long from Stalin. . . ." In 1956, Mr. Kennedy warned against "an imperialism of the mind, the attempt to make every state into a copy of America." He wrote that if Communism was expanding, it was "because of the vacuum of the spirit created by our own preoccupation with economic and military problems alone."

While I did not desert Notre Dame at Joseph Kennedy's imperial command, I agreed to work for his son in my spare time. Goaded by the continuing opposition to the Senator among academics and liberals generally, and especially by those who discounted his ability in world affairs but had never read one of his speeches, I suggested that his foreign policy talks should be collected, edited, and published as a book. Sorensen replied that the Senator thought this a good idea; would I do it? Soon cartons of speeches arrived for Clare and me to sort, read, select, and edit. Where gaps occurred, we proposed new talks and sometimes I supplied drafts; I prepared short introductory essays for the Senator to publish with each section.

In the spring of 1960 Harper & Row brought out *The Strategy of Peace*. Sorensen says the mass mailing of the book was the "largest single effort to woo the intellectuals." In his book *Kennedy*, he reports how editors, scientists, columnists, educators, reporters, authors, publishers, labor leaders, clergymen, public opinion leaders, and liberal politicians in great number received copies of the book "personally" from the Senator. One previously pro-Humphrey professor replied: "*The Strategy of Peace* is incontestably the best campaign document I can imagine, for it communicates what various other books and most news reports inadequately convey. . . . You emerge from the book as the kind of reflective and purposeful candidate that many of us seek."

Thomas Hughes, an old friend who had left Senator Humphrey to become the chief assistant to newly elected Congressman Chester Bowles, was not so readily swept into Kennedy's camp. On reading the book, he was struck by the consistent Kennedy-Bowles-Humphrey (and, to a lesser extent, Stevenson) view of the world that emerged, and wondered whether this truly reflected the candidate or was the result of natural selection by the editor. Having worked with me as a draftsman and editor of Bowles's earlier books, *Ambassador's Report* and *The New Dimensions of Peace*, he detected a familiar hand.

The resemblance to Bowles, however, was not limited to the new material prepared for the book. No one comparing Bowles's writings with this collection of Kennedy's speeches over six years could fail to note the congruence of viewpoints throughout. This is not to suggest that Bowles was a predominant influence. Yet he was a significant figure in the national foreign policy debate, with whom Kennedy generally agreed.

In early 1960 Kennedy appointed Bowles his "chief foreign policy adviser." This was in part a political move designed to encourage the liberal wing of the party at a time when most Democrats of that persuasion were holding out for Humphrey or Stevenson. Nevertheless, Kennedy was not stretching the truth when he wrote Bowles, "I have long been impressed with your own insights and your ability to articulate the fundamental foreign policy issues facing the American people."

With the support of his father and a Louis Harris poll, but over the opposition of his brother and staff, Kennedy had finally decided to enter the Wisconsin primary. It became his first crucial test. In the snows of New Hampshire he had campaigned well, but his predictable victory started no snowball. Wisconsin was different and difficult: more than two-thirds of the voters were Protestant, the Midwest never takes easily to New England and Harvard, and Humphrey was all but a favorite son. To win in Wisconsin, Kennedy had to prove that he could bring back into the Democratic fold the Catholic Democrats who had deserted to Eisenhower, but equally important, he had to draw a substantial part of the Protestants—which meant, among other things, appealing to Wisconsin liberals, one of whose heroes was Hubert Humphrey.

The state was inundated with Kennedy family and friends, including all the Senator's brothers, sisters, and brothers-in-law. Humphrey complained that he was "a corner grocer running against a chain store," but for all the family glamour there was no one from outside the clan speaking effectively to the many Wisconsin voters loyal to the Progressive tradition of Robert La Follette. By 1960 few Wisconsin Democrats were willing to admit they had ever supported Joe McCarthy, who had beaten their own younger La Follette; Kennedy was being seriously hurt by charges that he had not adequately opposed McCarthyism and that too many of those within his clan had actually been sympathetic to McCarthy.

"You must help get Chester Bowles to campaign in Wisconsin," Sargent Shriver said to me in an urgent call that I returned after a Notre Dame law class in February 1960. During the primary, Shriver was in charge of the campaign in the First and Second Wisconsin congressional districts, including Madison, a liberal stronghold.

With students and faculty at the University of Wisconsin and with the editors of *The Progressive* (founded by La Follette), as with many Democrats throughout the state, Bowles would carry considerable weight. Moreover, there was no liberal Democrat then publicly in support of Kennedy who was as well known and respected as Bowles. Having just been appointed Kennedy's foreign policy adviser, he was the obvious choice; it would cause negative comment if he didn't go.

But Bowles had privately told Kennedy and Sorensen that there was one condition for his support: that he would not campaign directly against two long-time friends, Stevenson and Humphrey. Kennedy and Sorensen said they understood, but their understanding included the suspicion that Bowles did not want to burn his bridges in case Kennedy lost in Wisconsin. They knew Bowles wanted to be Secretary of State, no matter who became the next Democratic President, and they doubted that his earlier presidential ambitions were burned out.

Dealing deftly with a still possible rival, Kennedy in late 1959 had told Bowles that if it became clear that he himself could not get the nomination, "I want you to know that my support will go to those who were the first to support me." Bowles says he "recognized this as a bit of political seduction, not as a serious statement of intent." Nonetheless, he found such seduction stimulating. An incipient "draft Bowles" movement was springing up around the country, not instigated by him, but not displeasing to him either. Those behind it were ardent believers in Bowles and not then inclined at all toward Kennedy; they and many Humphrey and Stevenson supporters would have been angry if Bowles had gone to Wisconsin.

Key people around Kennedy put heavy pressure on Bowles to go, and I added my case. The logic of becoming Kennedy's foreign policy adviser required that he go all the way, I thought. In almost the terms Sorensen had used with me, I argued that if he went, he would be inside the Kennedy camp in a way he might never be if he refused at a time of need. If he didn't go, he should not expect to have much chance of being Kennedy's Secretary of State. But Bowles would not budge.

At this point, Shriver asked me to come as a substitute and speak to a large rally at the university. To our dismay, about twenty people were scattered about the good-sized law school lecture hall when I arrived. My main theme was that Kennedy "has approximately the same view of the world as Humphrey, Stevenson, and Bowles" and that no one but Kennedy had the ability to carry the majority of the people along with him in that viewpoint. I said I would love to see Humphrey President, but in a race with Nixon I felt sure he would lose. Although neither Humphrey nor Kennedy had a record on McCarthy to be proud of, I contended that "the worst response in the whole period was Humphrey's amendment to outlaw the Communist Party, adopted in the Communist Control Act of 1954." That act "out-McCarthyed McCarthy." Once it was proposed "practically everyone went along with it, but it hurt to have a Democrat and liberal taking the initiative."

To reach the audience that didn't come, Shriver printed the talk and sent thousands of copies around Wisconsin. He badly wanted Kennedy's nomination to come through liberal support (along with the more natural Irish and Catholic constituency), not through an alliance with Southern conservatives. Kennedy was saying that himself during this period—at least to liberals. Shriver well knew that there was a tug-of-war within Kennedy and within the family not just between the lure of luxury and lawmaking but between the liberal and conservative poles. Kennedy spoke disparagingly of those "doctrinaire 'liberals' . . . who are so opposed to me" but said that if "professional liberals made him uncomfortable" he "knew too many conservatives in politics with whom I have nothing in common" to identify with their camp. When asked whether he would be a liberal or conservative President, he had replied, "I hope to be responsible." Shriver hoped Kennedy would find himself responding to a convention and campaign in which the liberal wing gave him decisive support.

Kennedy's victory in Wisconsin was impressive but too narrow to be decisive. Although he demonstrated his appeal to rank-and-file Catholics, he did not do well enough with Protestants and Humphrey held most of the liberal vote. Humphrey was determined to go on for another battle in West Virginia (where there would be very few Catholics). Reading a copy of my Madison talk, Humphrey wrote me a bitter note, the thrust of which was *Et tu Brute*. Although we later worked together warmly on several occasions, in connection with civil rights and the Peace Corps, our relationship was never fully restored; I was sorry to have hurt him and also to discover that he was not always the Happy Warrior. It made me more understanding of Bowles's reluctance to bring pain to someone to whom he had long been close.

About this time a member of the Parliament of India, a follower of Gandhi and a friend whose insights I respected, met with all the major presidential prospects in both parties, and was most impressed with Humphrey and Kennedy. "But Humphrey's spring has sprung—he is uncoiled," Asoka Mehta concluded. "Kennedy's spring has not sprung."

When Kennedy came to Notre Dame in April 1960, right after Wisconsin, he moved his audience to a standing ovation. His co-religionists were losing their caution and the Irish were claiming their own. Even Father Hesburgh was impressed in their talk together; "I guess I will opt for vigor and youth," he said afterwards. Kennedy renewed his request to me to join his staff full-time, and I agreed to go to Washington as soon as classes ended, the first of May. He talked soberly of the long road ahead.

Ted Sorensen took me to lunch on my first day in Washington. First, in his usual blunt fashion, he said that his prediction had been borne out;

a year before, I was the one speechwriter he could use and needed most, but now, in May 1960, there was Richard Goodwin, who was their key man. Second, he had noted that I had worked with Shriver in Wisconsin, and he advised that being close to him would not be useful to me for the future. He was viewed by the family as "the house Communist"— too liberal, unduly idealistic, a Boy Scout. This was a jocular use of "Communist" but also an indication of how little it took to be on the left in the Kennedy family in those years. Third, he appreciated my association with Chester Bowles and knew that Bowles and I had strong views about what was right and wrong in the world, with most of which the Senator probably agreed, but he wanted to make sure I knew the Kennedy staff's definition of good and bad: whatever helps assure the nomination and election of John Kennedy is good; whatever hinders it is bad.

A warm reception! Sorensen was trying to be helpful, sensing a romantic strain that needed to be subdued, but his bucket of cool realism merely left me with a definition of good and bad that I wished I had not heard. In the fever of a campaign, anything that brings victory nearer seems good, and I was ready to go all-out for Kennedy, but I didn't want to win with that definition ringing in my ears. Ironically, in my experience Sorensen was one of those close to Kennedy most able to maintain a commitment to a larger view of the common good. Until he wrote his book *Kennedy*, he kept his own romantic side concealed, but even under great pressures he often demonstrated that you can be critical and committed at the same time.

Shriver's role within the family and the campaign was more complicated than Sorensen suggested. If John Kennedy had not been running for President, Shriver might well have been the Democratic candidate for governor of Illinois, with support from both liberal reformers and the city Democratic organization—and the assistance of Joseph Kennedy. The elder Kennedy had picked the attractive and energetic young lawyer-journalist to edit the papers left by his eldest son, Joe, and then sent him to Chicago to help run one of his main properties, the vast Merchandise Mart, which Shriver did with great success. Shriver and the oldest Kennedy daughter, Eunice, had married in 1953; they had many things in common, including a serious interest in the Church—each had once considered belonging to special Church orders. She devoted great time and organizing effort to the Special Olympics for handicapped and retarded children; he became president of the Chicago Board of Education. Together and separately they made a strong impression.

In the winter of 1959–60 I had attended a large dinner of Chicago school officials; almost everyone at my table predicted that Shriver would someday be governor. Several who had worked with him closely said he was the most imaginative, effective, and humane executive they had ever known. "To tell you the truth," one of them added, "he's my real choice for President."

When I first met Shriver in the fall of 1959 I did not know of his Kennedy connection. In a talk at the Chicago City Club on the work of the Civil Rights Commission, I had referred to the power of Gandhian symbolic action. A man in the audience asked, "As someone who has studied Gandhi, what would you suggest that the school board of the city of Chicago do—what symbolic action could it take—to help break the vicious circle of race and poverty in our school system?" Not getting much of an answer, he came up afterwards and said he was president of the school board and was very serious about the question. Would I please take the time to think about it and write him? The name on his card was Sargent Shriver. About a week later I got a note from him saying that because of de facto segregation in housing, the school system was in real racial trouble and if I had any ideas, send them. Then, a few weeks later, the phone rang and it was Shriver in town for a Notre Dame football game, asking me to join him at the stadium. Off and on for two hours he laid out the Chicago problem and pressed me for suggestions—all the time following the game. By the fourth quarter he had enlisted me to spend some time at the school board in Chicago, reviewing the facts and brainstorming about solutions.

Before anything substantial—or symbolic—had come of this, Shriver was swept full-time into the Kennedy campaign and had to resign from the school board and put aside his gubernatorial ambition. One Catholic, at the top of the ticket, would be all that prairie, Protestant downstate Illinois could take. In Shriver, Kennedy gained his most effective family emissary to liberals, and one of his most successful campaigners.

Robert Kennedy and some others in the family no doubt considered Shriver too liberal. He had helped found the national Catholic interracial movement, and headed its Chicago branch. With his friend William McCormick Blair, one of Stevenson's law partners, he had been among the first to work to draft Adlai in 1952. From Joe McCarthy's first wild charges he had been opposed to the Wisconsin demagogue, and found himself on the other side of the fence from Bob and others in the family. He had a sharp political argument with Eunice when she took a table at the Irish Fellowship Society dinner to hear McCarthy; Shriver and Bill Tuohy, a leading city Democrat, went off to dinner by themselves, remarking that they were the only Democrats with Irish blood in Chicago who were not honoring McCarthy that night.

Joseph Kennedy seldom let ideology determine his judgment of a man; he appreciated Shriver's energy, imagination, and skills. If Mr. Kennedy's emphasis was on success in this world, his wife, Rose, particularly admired her son-in-law's continuing religious search. Nevertheless, even with Shriver's resilient combination of idealism and pragmatism, it was not an easy family to enter by marriage. He was no doubt bolstered by his own family pride. When I first met his mother, she made it clear to me that the Shrivers belonged to the old Maryland Catholic aristocracy, unlike the Kennedys. Shriver had grown up in a home where Cardinal Gibbons was a familiar visitor and where former President Taft had once spent an afternoon. Showing her own competitiveness, Mrs. Shriver said to me, "We go back three hundred years in Maryland, when they were still in Ireland."

There was to be little time for competition with Dick Goodwin as a speechwriter. A few days after I joined the staff, Senator Kennedy called me in to ask if I thought he was in trouble with Negroes, and if so, what he should do. Although I had not focused on the question, I knew that the few Negro advisers he had enlisted were not in the mainstream of civil rights leadership and that his reputation was not strong among Negro leaders I knew best, including Martin Luther King. He said that his chief interest had been foreign affairs, and that he had never been in a position to know many Negroes. Whom should he see?

King and Roy Wilkins, head of the National Association for the Advancement of Colored People, were among the first I arranged for him to meet, separately. In each case, there was a candid exchange and the talk went well, although King commented that Kennedy did not have a "depthed understanding" of civil rights.

When I had gone to see Wilkins, he agreed that Kennedy's record was not bad; the Senator had voted for every major civil rights measure. However, in 1957 he had supported the so-called jury trial amendment, which provided that before someone could be sentenced to more than forty-five days in jail for contempt of court in a civil rights case, a jury trial would be required. The NAACP had attacked this provision as a concession to the South, but many supporters of the 1957 act, including me, had favored it. Kennedy's position, however, was being effectively used against him; it reminded people of the remarkable Southern support he had received at the 1956 convention.

Wilkins told me that his wife, a Catholic, was ardently for Kennedy, but he was still dubious. Then he said, "If you ask me who, of all the men in political life, I would trust to do the most about civil rights as President, it would be Lyndon Johnson." After dealing with him for many years, the NAACP chief felt Johnson had a deep, inner determination about this that stemmed from his intimate knowledge of the damage racial discrimination was doing not only to the South but to the whole country. Wilkins admitted that it would be impolitic within the Negro and liberal community to confess such heresy publicly, but if the convention should turn to Johnson he could support him with enthusiasm.

Soon after this, in early May, Bob Kennedy called me down to campaign headquarters at the foot of Capitol Hill. "We're in trouble with Negroes," he said, measuring me with his intense blue eyes. "We really don't know much about this whole thing. We've been dealing outside the field of the main Negro leadership and have to start from scratch." He said that he and the Senator wanted me to work full-time on the problem; they were asking a man in the family, Sargent Shriver, who had long been interested in civil rights, to supervise the work—"he knows all these things." "We want you to head up a Civil Rights Section and work through Sarge and do everything you need to do to deliver every Negro delegate going to the convention. We'll call you the coordinator. It's up to you. Tell us where we are in all this and go to it."

So we went to it. Almost immediately a key test arose: Kennedy had a good chance to win over the important Michigan delegation, but Michigan Negroes were particularly cool to him; Governor Mennen Williams considered their support crucial. Williams and Democratic committeewoman Mildred Jeffrey of the United Automobile Workers union suggested that there ought to be an occasion when Kennedy talked and answered questions in a no-holds-barred session with Michigan civil rights and Negro leadership. Fearing that Kennedy would be put on an embarrassing spot, some Kennedy staff men were opposed, but we persuaded him to take the gamble. He invited the governor to fly the state's top civil rights leadership to Washington, for a breakfast and an all-morning discussion at his home in Georgetown.

Jacqueline Kennedy looked askance at the relatively militant group that trooped through her house to the elegant breakfast she had arranged in the courtyard. Most of them looked and sounded skeptical, and a few were hostile.

It was a beautiful sunny morning and Kennedy was at his best; Chester Bowles was at his side as he listened seriously, answered questions candidly, and went further in committing himself to a strong civil rights platform at the convention and program as President than I had ever heard him go. Quickly measuring the mood, he knew he had to respond in a clear, affirmative way. He "stated categorically" (as the notes recorded by the Michigan group reported) that the civil rights issue was "of overwhelming moral significance to him and if elected President he would use the full prestige and weight of his office to completely eliminate second-class citizenship in America." His on-the-spot judgment was right; almost every guest left wearing a Kennedy PT-boat pin, with an unexpected enthusiasm about their new candidate.

The close association between the Kennedy brothers and the Reuther brothers during the investigation of labor racketeering had laid the foundation for support by the UAW, but Kennedy's position on civil rights and the reaction of Negro leadership were important to the Reuthers. The morning's success gave further momentum to the move to Kennedy by a union that was often decisive in Michigan politics. It was evident that many of Governor Williams' own doubts had been resolved. Unknown to me at the time, Kennedy had in his briefing papers on Mennen Williams, or "Soapy" as the governor liked to be called, a staff memorandum advising him that:

> Williams is a man of strong convictions. He takes himself very seriously and believes that he is an instrument of God's will in furthering liberal, humanitarian causes. He is a devout Episcopalian . . . [who] sees himself as having been tapped to put the Sermon on the Mount into governmental practice. This is not a pose but reflects a sincere, if unusual, conviction.

Kennedy was warned that "any approach to him which overlooks this strong religious drive . . . will miss the mark." Kennedy did not miss the mark.

From the warmth generated among the visitors that morning, favorable word spread throughout the civil rights leadership around the country. We also saw that the way to help Kennedy feel at home and assert leadership in civil rights was to put him in just such direct encounters. From then until the convention, we tried to capture as much of his time as possible for one-to-one or small discussions with key Negro Democrats. There were times when we had Negro leaders in different rooms of his Georgetown house at the same time, waiting to see the Senator, and being ushered to him separately so they would not run into each other.

In West Virginia, where Negroes (and Catholics) were less than 5 percent of the population, Kennedy had another kind of encounter. Fresh from a few days in the sun of Montego Bay, Kennedy was appalled by the high proportion of people out of work, living on federal food packages of surplus lard and corn meal. "Imagine, just imagine kids who never drank milk," he said one night.

If poverty had been the central issue, Humphrey probably would have carried West Virginia; instead, the primary turned on the question of religious tolerance. Over and over again, Kennedy said that in taking the oath of office he would be swearing on the Bible to respect the separation of church and state, and in the end the Protestants of West Virginia believed him. Proving that they could rise above prejudice may have been a significant part of their motivation. After Wisconsin many of us had worked hard to persuade friends around Humphrey to get their candidate to withdraw so that the religious showdown in West Virginia could be avoided. Yet it was Kennedy's ordeal and triumph there, on that issue, that overcame the chief obstacle to his nomination. If Kennedy had not had Humphrey to fight and beat (by 61 to 31 percent) in West Virginia, he might well have been stopped at the convention.

As we flew to Los Angeles for the opening of the convention, July 11, arithmetic told us a first-ballot majority was within reach. But in the weeks before, an American U-2 high-altitude plane was shot down over the Soviet Union on the eve of a summit conference in Paris; the United States spokesman denied the mission until the captured pilot, Gary Powers, confessed that he was an aerial-photographic spy; and the summit collapsed under Khrushchev's charges against Eisenhower. Adding to world tensions, the newly independent Congo broke into civil war, the Korean government of Syngman Rhee fell as a result of student demonstrations, and Castro defiantly seized United States property in Cuba. The first political effect of these international crises was to threaten Kennedy.

The forty-three-year-old Senator had criticized the timing of the U-2 flight and the official falsehoods, and said the United States should have expressed "regret" and given assurances it would not happen again. Lyndon Johnson charged Kennedy with appeasement and vowed he would never "apologize" to Russia; he said it showed that Kennedy was too young for the White House—the country required someone "with a touch of gray in his hair." Next Harry Truman joined the effort to stop the young Senator. On July 2, the former President went on televison to denounce Kennedy and propose instead Stuart Symington, Lyndon Johnson, Chester Bowles, Governor Robert Meyner of New Jersey, and several others, saying that in a world crisis we needed "a man with the greatest possible maturity and experience."

Truman's direct appeal to Kennedy to "be patient" invited a direct response. On the Fourth of July, Kennedy replied that Truman's age test "would have kept Jefferson from writing the Declaration of Independence, Washington from commanding the Continental Army, Madison from fathering the Constitution . . . and Christopher Columbus from even discovering America." (Sorensen's inclusion of Jesus of Nazareth on the list was mercifully omitted.) If "fourteen years in major elective office is insufficient experience," the Senator said, "that rules out all but three of the ten names put forward by Truman, all but a handful of American Presidents, and every President of the twentieth century—including Wilson, Roosevelt, and Truman." Other nations were choosing younger leaders "who can cast off the old slogans and delusions and suspicions," he said. To Truman's question, "Senator, are you certain that you are ready?" Kennedy gave Lincoln's reply, on the eve of his presidency: "I see the storm coming and I know His hand is in it. If He has a place and work for me, I believe that I am ready."

The first storm coming was the belated but unpredictably powerful movement to draft Stevenson. A Stevenson-Kennedy ticket suddenly was being advanced on many sides as the answer to a world in ferment. The public banner was carried boldly by Eleanor Roosevelt, who visited delegations and went on television, calling on Kennedy to take the vice-presidency, in which he could "grow and learn." Behind the scenes, Senator Mike Monroney of Oklahoma and skilled veterans of Stevenson's two previous campaigns mobilized old loyalties, the latent anti-Kennedy feeling in the camps of defeated candidates, and the new or renewed enthusiasm of volunteers around the country. In corridors of convention headquarters in the Biltmore Hotel and out on the streets I met and had heated arguments with many friends who had put vacations and jobs aside to go to California to draft Adlai. It was still my conviction that he could not carry a national majority, even with Kennedy as a running mate, but there was a spirit in the air that could not be easily denied.

When my wife and I arrived at the Sports Arena for the convention opening, we found thousands of Stevenson supporters marching and chanting, "We want Stevenson." Inside other thousands in the galleries were continuing the cry at each opportunity. The next afternoon, when Stevenson himself entered to sit in the Illinois delegation, he received a huge ovation and was almost carried to the platform in a sea of enthusiasm. It was not enough to remark, as Kennedy's aide Kenneth O'Donnell did, "I never said he couldn't be elected mayor of Los Angeles," for the pressure was coming from many parts of the country and within many delegations; indeed, the memory was stirred of every Democrat who had given his heart to Adlai in 1952 or 1956.

The fever mounted when pro-Stevenson rebellions broke out in the California, Minnesota, and New York delegations, among others. Kennedy's hold on a number of states could be lost by a switch of one or a very few delegates. There is a mysterious momentum in a convention that can overturn all calculations, and a new wind was blowing. Sometime after midnight, Tuesday, Adlai Stevenson emerged from seclusion to meet a large group of delegates and others. I squeezed into the overflow-

ing hall to hear him indicate his readiness to run and—at this last minute
—to fight for the nomination. There was a surge of excitement at the end
as he quoted Robert Frost's lines:

> *"The woods are lovely, dark and deep,*
> *But I have promises to keep,*
> *And miles to go before I sleep,*
> *And miles to go before I sleep."*

None of us slept very much any night that week. Early each morning, for a couple of hours, our civil rights contingent operated a hospitality suite in the Biltmore. By now this group included Kennedy's early
black supporters and civil rights activists in a dozen delegations. Delegates came to talk, to question Kennedy's record, and to ask what they
could do to help.

When we arrived two days in advance, we knew that more than a
majority of the estimated 250 or so black delegates and alternates (out of
a total of about 4,500) were with Kennedy. The day before the convention, the Senator had spoken effectively at a large NAACP rally. Adam
Clayton Powell had come out for Johnson, but practically every other
leading black Democrat was by then for Kennedy, and almost none for
Stevenson. One could hear repeated stories of disappointment with Adlai;
they paralleled my own experience. In 1959 Stevenson had invited me to
spend an afternoon talking with him about the report of the Civil Rights
Commission; I left depressed by his ambivalence, discomfort, and weari-
ness about racial issues. The noticeable lack of black support for Stevenson was a significant depressant to the Stevenson movement at Los
Angeles. We were quick to call delegates' attention to the fact that there
were almost no blacks in the Stevenson demonstrations.

The strongest new momentum for Kennedy among black delegates
and civil rights advocates came from an uncoordinated combination of
Chester Bowles and Bob Kennedy on the platform. In the spring, Bowles
had been appointed chairman of the Democratic Platform Committee,
and he had made it a more active enterprise than ever before in the
party's history, holding regional hearings in different parts of the country.
In mid-May, Bowles showed Senator Kennedy an early draft of the platform, including a strong civil rights plank, but the candidate gave it only
a cursory glance. On the plane to Los Angeles, Bowles showed it to
Sargent Shriver, who liked it. At breakfast the day before the platform's
presentation Bowles insisted that Bob Kennedy read the final draft; the
campaign manager did so and made no comment.

What Bowles may not have made clear to any of them was that the draft on civil rights was a maximal position he had asked me to prepare with his Platform Committee aides, Tom Hughes and Abram Chayes. We also proposed a minimal position, on which there should be no compromise. But none of us expected the adoption of the original plank.

"We've got Southerners on the committee, and we don't have a flaming civil rights majority," Bowles had said. "But we'd better begin with a maximum plank. We'll draft the plank that says everything we can think of that we ought to do, and we'll negotiate as much of it as we can." We had included practically all of the Civil Rights Commission recommendations, and more.

Bob Kennedy had talked with me in general about the platform and concluded that our delegates should be asked to support a strong civil rights plank, but he had not taken the time to listen to details and I had not expected him to go very far in his support. Instead of checking further, Bob stood on a chair in Suite 8315 on the morning the Platform Committee was to decide, and as part of his daily briefing told the large assembly of Kennedy workers to support the full Bowles draft. Loud applause encouraged him to repeat, "Remember, all the way with the Bowles platform."

Soon afterward, to Bowles's amazement, some of the committee members he had expected to find pressing for compromise were silent or even speaking up for the very strong version; the Southerners saw how outnumbered they were and, with only minor modifications, the whole maximal plank was adopted. Later, in a conversation with me about the far-reaching platform, John Kennedy seemed to take it in his stride and be amused at the mix-up. In his book, Sorensen says that "in Kennedy's private view" the platform promised "too many antagonistic specifics that could not be fulfilled, raising too many unwarranted hopes and unnecessary fears." Here again, Theodore White's description of Kennedy's organization was wide of the mark. "Control as exercised from 8315," he wrote of the convention operation, "was precise, taut, disciplined. . . ." Not quite.

On the afternoon of the nomination, the ring of chanting Stevenson supporters outside the Sports Arena was larger than ever. Inside, the galleries went wild when Senator Eugene McCarthy placed Stevenson's name before the convention. But barring some emotional tide sweeping the floor, the battle by then was over. Shriver was working closely with the Illinois delegation and knew that Daley was holding firm for Kennedy. Stevenson that afternoon had finally reached the mayor to make a personal appeal. He reminded Daley that he was the first Illinoisan to run for President since Abraham Lincoln—but to no avail. When the roll call came to Illinois, there were only 2 votes for Stevenson, 61½ for Kennedy.

"You know where Daley probably was when Adlai was trying to get him?" Shriver said. "At Joe Kennedy's." While he never came to the convention hall, Mr. Kennedy had encamped at Marion Davies' villa in Santa Monica. Throughout the week, many of the old-time leaders of the party, like Daley, Congressman Green of Philadelphia, and others from New York and California, were to be found at the villa, around the swimming pool with Mr. and Mrs. Kennedy. It was to his parents and their pool that John Kennedy had gone that afternoon, eluding the newsmen at the front door of his apartment by climbing down a back fire escape and over a fence.

On the convention floor we had the pleasure of knowing that almost every black delegate had voted for Kennedy; the few exceptions were mainly in the home states of other candidates. Soon afterwards, with the nomination won, in the midst of exultation and mutual embraces, I found myself just outside the little house on the edge of the arena which had been the Kennedy communications center. Leaders of the party arrived and crowded in to greet the nominee before he was introduced to the convention. Daley, Bailey, DiSalle, Lawrence, Prendergast, Green, Harriman, McCormack, Ribicoff—they were all there, with only Mennen Williams from our operation, except for Shriver, who was talking with Bob Kennedy. As John Kennedy finally arrived in a brightly lit police motorcade, received the proffered congratulations, and moved through a pressing crowd to the convention rostrum, it came over me what a small part anyone plays in the large process of such a campaign. In the almost empty headquarters of Johnson, Symington, and Stevenson, with discarded placards and unused pamphlets, other men and women were at the same time wrestling silently with other thoughts.

That night at around 2:30 a.m. Shriver was awakened by a phone call. "Lyndon will? All right, I'll get the word to Jack first thing in the morning," he said. Drowsily from the next bed I asked what the call was about; we had both stayed in the Biltmore to be ready for any contingency. "Johnson will accept the vice-presidential nomination if Jack offers it to him—that caller has firsthand information and wants to make sure Jack knows it and makes no mistake. We've got to wake up early so I can warn him before any move is made."

Unknown to us, at about the same hour John Kennedy was himself calling Johnson's suite, but a sleepy aide said that Johnson could not be disturbed. In the book *Johnny, We Hardly Knew Ye*, Kennedy's close friend David Powers recalls that after the Senator's secretary, Evelyn Lincoln, had played "When Irish Eyes Are Smiling" on the piano and the several guests had left the hideaway, Kennedy read again a line from Johnson's cordial telegram of congratulations: "LBJ now means Let's Back Jack." Unable to reach the Majority Leader, Kennedy left a message for Mrs. Lincoln to arrange a meeting with Johnson at 10 a.m. Getting into his bed, Powers said to himself, "My God, he's going to offer it to Lyndon Johnson."

Around seven-thirty Shriver and I went to Kennedy's suite and were there when the nominee arrived around eight. Shriver talked with him quietly and soon afterwards Mrs. Lincoln arranged for Kennedy to go down to Johnson's suite at ten. Then Robert Kennedy came in and seemed to be upset. He and his brother went into the bedroom and closed the door. When they came out, David Powers recalls, Bob said, "If you're sure it's what you want to do, go ahead and see him."

Bob went to take a bath and while soaking in the tub asked Pierre Salinger to add up the electoral votes in the states we were sure of, and to add Texas. Hearing this, Ken O'Donnell said, "Don't tell me it's Johnson." Bob replied, "I guess it is. He's seeing him now." O'Donnell later described his reaction: "I was so furious that I could hardly talk. I thought of the promises we had made . . . that Johnson would not be on the ticket if Kennedy won the nomination. I felt that we had been double-crossed."

Meanwhile in the Kennedy suite, Shriver told me that Jack wanted to consult with party leaders and that while he was calling the ones Kennedy had listed, I should call others, like Governor Williams, Bowles, the Reuthers, and some key Negro colleagues in our civil rights contingent. "There's still a chance to stop this if there's enough opposition," he said.

By the time Kennedy returned from Johnson's suite, Bailey, Daley, Lawrence, DiSalle, and Ribicoff were there, congratulating him on the offer. When Bob Kennedy came back, John took him aside and, according to Bob's 1965 account to Arthur Schlesinger, said, "You just won't believe it. . . . He wants it." To which Bob says he replied, "Oh, my God!"

Bob claimed that his brother offered the nomination to Johnson "entirely *pro forma*" and "never dreamt that there was a chance in the world that he would accept it." Sorensen wrote, "Neither Kennedy nor anyone else could have expected that Johnson would accept." But this view that Johnson's nomination was by accident does not square with the facts. Having had indications from Shriver and others that Johnson would accept, the nominee should have been ready to believe it when Johnson said yes.

The evidence suggests that Johnson had been in Kennedy's mind as a real possibility for some time, but that he kept his cards close to his chest.

Chester Bowles recalls that earlier in the convention Kennedy had told him he thought Johnson would be the wisest choice. When Bowles protested that talent in legislative manipulation did not mean ability in world affairs, Kennedy had smiled and said, "But he'll never accept." Yet the day before the convention, Philip Graham, publisher of the Washington *Post* and a close friend of Johnson, urged the choice of Johnson and was strongly backed by Joseph Alsop. Kennedy had seemed sufficiently affirmative for Graham to encourage the *Post* to report that Johnson would probably get the nomination.

When the *Post* article appeared, the whole Michigan delegation and many others close to our civil rights effort were upset. Shriver and I were commissioned to assure them there was no such plan. Kenneth O'Donnell said he gave "the same assurance, with Kennedy's knowledge," to wavering liberal and labor delegates. Before his own nomination, Kennedy clearly sensed that he could not afford to be seen leaning toward Johnson (except perhaps with a few chosen Johnson friends). Simultaneously, to Symington's friend Clark Clifford, Kennedy had intimated Symington was his choice. Meanwhile, Robert Kennedy was saying to Edwin Guthman, then of the Seattle *Times*, that Henry Jackson was his choice and "Jack likes him."

Just what went on in John Kennedy's mind will never be known. It is possible that after his conversations with Bob and Shriver, he spoke to Johnson in a tentative fashion, hoping for a refusal, and that Johnson seized the suggestion and held him to it. Whatever happened between them that morning, it is clear that the opposition he encountered that day shook him and may have made him wish that Johnson would withdraw. Robert Kennedy told Schlesinger, "We both promised each other that we'd never tell what happened—but we spent the rest of the day alternating between thinking it was good and thinking that it wasn't good . . . and how could he get out of it."

There in the suite, I saw—and to some extent helped bring on—the hell that broke loose around the Kennedy brothers as key members of their staff and liberal, labor, and civil rights supporters besieged and beseeched them. Sensing that O'Donnell was about to explode, the nominee took him into the bathroom, where, Ken recalls, he told Kennedy, "This is the worst mistake you ever made. You came here . . . like a knight on a white charger . . . promising to get rid of the old hack machine politicians. And now, in your first move after you get the nomination, you go against all the people who supported you." Kennedy listened, pale and livid with anger, and then, according to O'Donnell, said:

I'm forty-three years old, and I'm . . . not going to die in office. So the vice-presidency doesn't mean anything. I'm thinking of something else, the leadership in the Senate. If we win, it will be by a small margin and I won't be able to live with Lyndon Johnson as the leader of a small majority in the Senate. Did it occur to you that if Lyndon becomes the Vice-President, I'll have Mike Mansfield as the leader in the Senate, somebody I can trust and depend on?

It is easy to say that a presidential candidate should think of nothing but which vice-presidential candidate would be best qualified to be President, yet in the turmoil before and after a nomination it is hard to think at all. Bob Kennedy said, "My God, this wouldn't have happened except that we were all too tired last night."

Bob looked embarrassed every time we passed each other in the suite that day. Reuther and Meany had come in, talked to Kennedy, conveyed their total opposition, and left in anger. Late in the morning, Kennedy was meeting in the bedroom with a group of Southern governors, who were pleased with the choice, when Mennen Williams walked in. The Michigan governor listened for a while and then announced loudly—some say, shouted—that he would lead a fight against the nomination on the convention floor. O'Donnell says that one of the Southerners jumped up to take a punch at Williams, but Ribicoff intervened.

During a lull around midday, Shriver took me over to the window and asked, "What do you really think? Is it as bad an idea as we're saying it is?" I said I had been arguing back and forth with myself and about an hour ago had decided I was for it. Not only might it mean carrying Texas, it might break the Southern monolith against civil rights and bring the South back into the mainstream of politics. I recalled Roy Wilkins' prediction that Johnson would do more for civil rights than any other politician. And if Symington and Jackson were the alternatives, they were no better—probably worse on foreign policy.

"You bastard!" Shriver said. "That's about the way I come out, but I was keeping it to myself, doing my duty by all our friends and breaking my back to get them all in to see Kennedy and stop it." We laughed, in mutual relief, and agreed that anyway Kennedy needed to hear and deal directly with that opposition.

There are differing accounts of what happened next. Everyone agrees that in the early afternoon Bob Kennedy went down to Johnson's suite, reported that there might be a floor fight against him, and asked him if he would consider becoming the chairman of the Democratic National Committee instead. (To that suggestion, Sam Rayburn is said to have told Bob, "Shit!") In Johnson's suite a different argument had apparently been raging, with some of the Southerners present insisting that "for Johnson to run on such a ticket of civil rights and Catholicism would be treason to the Old South."

Philip Graham and others close to Johnson believed that Bob Kennedy went there on his own, not at his brother's behest. Graham called John Kennedy to protest Bobby's intervention. In a subsequent memorandum, Graham wrote that the nominee disavowed his brother and said, "Bobby's been out of touch, and doesn't know what's happening." Five years later, talking about it to Schlesinger, Robert said he was "flabbergasted" by the charge that he was on a lark of his own—"my brother's asleep, so I'll go see if I can get rid of his Vice-President." He said that his brother and he "decided by about two o'clock that we'd try to get him out of there and not have him," and that he was sent down to Johnson to "get him to withdraw and still be happy." Robert said that as he gave his message, Johnson "shook and tears came into his eyes, and he said, 'I want to be Vice-President, and, if the President will have me, I'll join with him in making a fight of it.'"

The differing recollections in this *Rashomon* tale of how a fateful political decision was made suggest that Robert and John were not entirely of the same mind, or fully coordinated in their actions. They changed their minds eight times (according to Robert in 1964). In any case, at about three o'clock John Kennedy talked to Johnson and confirmed the offer; they agreed that it would be announced at a four-thirty press conference.

Kennedy cleared everyone out of the bedroom, but the rest of us stayed in the suite, not knowing what had been decided. Delegations were still coming in to get their points across to the candidate, who was no longer available. Three Minnesota leaders cornered me to make a case for their governor, Orville Freeman. As they did so, at length and with enthusiasm, I noticed on the television screen behind them that something was happening; Kennedy was shown leaving his room and moving down the corridor. I tried to stop the Minnesotans to say that it looked as if Kennedy was about to go on television, but they were undaunted. Finally they turned around to see Kennedy come on the screen and announce that he had selected Lyndon Johnson.

Before long, from the floor of the Sports Arena the cameras showed Joe Rauh, Americans for Democratic Action leader and civil rights attorney in the Washington, D.C., delegation, appealing ardently, "Don't do it, Jack!" and threatening a floor fight against Johnson. Many Northern delegates were in consternation, the TV reporter said, and a rank-and-file revolt might yet take place. Though Shriver and I had planned to watch that session on television, after hearing Joe Rauh, Shriver said,

"Let's show the flag." Soon we were on the floor, hearing the charges of betrayal and making the best case we could for the unity ticket of Boston and Austin.

Though many Michigan delegates were bitter, Reuther or some other UAW emissary had secured written assurance from Johnson that he would support the civil rights platform. Governor Williams remained opposed, but after a caucus Michigan did not nominate anyone else. Other labor resistance had been moderated by the word from David Dubinsky that picking Johnson was a political masterstroke.

With his parents at Marion Davies' house that evening, according to Charles Bartlett, the candidate and his father talked about the decision. "Don't worry, Jack," Mr. Kennedy said. "Within two weeks they'll be saying it's the smartest thing you ever did." Mr. Kennedy had been urging Johnson's selection and hoping that he would accept.

The next evening I was among the 80,000 who heard Kennedy and Johnson accept their nomination in the Los Angeles Coliseum. Kennedy called on people to choose "between the public interest and private comfort" and confront the "uncharted areas of science and space, unsolved problems of peace and war, unconquered pockets of ignorance and prejudice, unanswered questions of poverty and surplus." Saying that "we stand today on the edge of a New Frontier," he pointed specifically to "a peaceful revolution for human rights—demanding an end to racial discrimination in all parts of our community life," and said "the times demand invention, innovation, imagination, decision."

In August 1960, driving to his Senate office, John Kennedy saw me waiting for a taxi near his Georgetown house. "Jump in," he said. Then, his left hand tapping the window of his red convertible, he said, "Now in five minutes tick off the ten things a President ought to do to clean up this goddamn civil rights mess."

With one stroke of the pen he should sign an Executive Order against discrimination in federally assisted housing, I said. For more than a year since Father Hesburgh and I had drafted that proposal and the Civil Rights Commission had unanimously recommended it, Eisenhower had failed to act. The other actions I listed in the few minutes it took to reach Capitol Hill came straight from the recommendations of the commission or the Democratic platform, but the main theme was the great unused potential for executive action. Frustrated by the impasse in the special session of Congress, Kennedy grabbed at anything that would bypass the legislative branch. His whole campaign at that moment seemed bogged down in a morass of congressional debate, which daily dramatized the divisions within the Democratic Party.

Republicans had introduced as bills the most controversial items in the Democratic civil rights platform, and Senator Hugh Scott and others were taunting Kennedy to press for legislative action. If he did, there was certain to be a Southern filibuster that would stretch into the fall and block the passage of any bill. Yet if Kennedy and the majority of Democrats voted to table the civil rights bills, it would look as if they were disowning the platform. Kennedy would be made to look either ineffective or hypocritical. The best response, he thought, was for a majority of Senate Democrats to condemn the tricky Republican maneuver and vote to table, while firmly pledging to enact and carry out the full civil rights platform promptly in a new Democratic administration.

Kennedy asked me to prepare a statement for him to take to his Senate colleagues. He went over the draft with Johnson and others, and then they and a number of us took it to every possible Democratic signer. Just as we finished getting the signatures of a solid majority, Kennedy called to say he had agreed with Senator Richard Russell of Georgia to modify the statement. We then took the new version to the potential signers and again secured a majority. The press release was prepared and about to be issued when Kennedy called again with new reasons for delay. Then Senator Joseph Clark of Pennsylvania and others committed to civil rights demanded that a line be strengthened. This went on, back and forth, perhaps a half dozen times over ten days. Finally time ran out and just before the showdown on the bills we released a statement signed by Kennedy and most Northern and Western Democratic senators.

Despite the modifications, it was a strong pledge, and it needed to be; the choice of Johnson had set back the momentum toward Kennedy among blacks and liberals. On the other hand, Kennedy also had to be concerned about the even higher level of potential rebellion among Southern Democrats. It was during this period, after a session with Kennedy on our draft statement, that Senator Russell reported unhappily to Senator Harry Byrd of Virginia "that Kennedy will implement the Democratic platform and advocate civil rights legislation beyond what is contained in the platform."

Missing from the list of signers was the name of one liberal Northern senator, Eugene McCarthy. Though Kennedy had remarked that McCarthy's speech nominating Stevenson was the best at the convention, the junior senator from Minnesota had no compliments for Kennedy when I went to ask him to sign the statement. "What have the Kennedys ever done for me?" he asked sourly. "Why should I lift a finger for them?" I don't remember many other details of his sardonic thrusts, but it was an unpleasant encounter. The interests of civil rights, as well as of the campaign against Nixon, both causes McCarthy purported to champion, called

59

for the maximum number of Democratic signers; McCarthy's refusal seemed to me inexcusably petty.

By this time the Civil Rights Section was part of a larger issues division of the campaign, under Shriver's overall direction. Shriver had enlisted Adam Yarmolinsky to organize an Urban Affairs Section, and others to help him build organizations of Farmers and Business and Professional People for Kennedy. In addition to guiding these ventures, Shriver had important regular campaign responsibilities in Illinois and several other Midwestern states.

The Civil Rights Section was given increased support because of the initial adverse effect of the Johnson nomination. Frank Reeves, who had NAACP contacts all over the country, was selected to travel with the candidate. Marjorie Lawson, an attorney with special ties to professional, religious, and women's groups, was designated director and concentrated on the state and local organization of black Democrats. Congressman William Dawson of Chicago, senior Negro member of Congress and long-time head of the Minorities Division of the Democratic National Committee, was titular chairman. Bob Kennedy made it clear that the operating responsibility remained with me as the coordinator, reporting to Shriver.

The most important addition, after the convention, was Louis Martin, a salty Negro publisher who had just spent a year in Nigeria establishing a radio and newspaper network there. At Los Angeles, Martin had declined to commit himself before the nomination, saying, "I'm just back from Africa and I don't know anything." He knew a lot in many corners of American politics. The management of all Kennedy advertising in Negro newspapers and magazines, his first assignment, was only one of many contributions. He soon became our chief counselor, colleague, and co-conspirator. "Let's get all the horses on the track!" was his constant refrain, a motto very much in line with the general Kennedy strategy. Before fully throwing in his lot with us, he insisted that the Democratic National Committee pay Negro publishers thousands of dollars of bills from previous campaigns.

One of the untamed steeds, with wide popular appeal among blacks, was Congressman Adam Clayton Powell of Harlem. Though he had backed Johnson, Powell was finally enlisted by Louis Martin, with the help of a sizable financial inducement approved by Kennedy's brother-in-law, Stephen Smith. When Powell spoke around the country, he took along a huge blown-up facsimile of a restrictive covenant Nixon had signed on purchasing his house. The deed's prohibition of the sale or lease of the property to Negroes, Jews, etc., was circled in red, with the word "Shame!" added as commentary.

Another man difficult to keep on the track was Congressman Dawson. This elderly stalwart of the regular Democratic organization in Chicago had warm ties to old-line Southern leaders in Congress, and disliked the new approach of a Civil Rights Section, beginning with its name. "Let's not use words that offend our good Southern friends, like 'civil rights,' " he advised at our first meeting. He was wary of the civil rights leaders we were bringing into the campaign. Dawson preferred the all-Negro enclave of the Minorities Division of previous campaigns, without interlopers like me, or the candidate's brother-in-law, or other white colleagues in the Civil Rights Section.

Since the Civil Rights Section was a *fait accompli*, the immediate issue with Dawson was his office. Shriver had taken a whole floor of a building on K Street, near Bob Kennedy's headquarters, and insisted on keeping it an open space, a practice that had proven itself in the Merchandise Mart. We all had desks and our own phones, and the floor was a whirl of activity. Congressman Dawson came in to visit his "office," looked around, shook his head, and said it was totally impossible for him to operate out in the open that way. Shriver finally yielded and ordered the construction of one enclosed office, right in the middle of all the open space. Some of the caustic young blacks called it "Uncle Tom's Cabin."

The registration of black voters was one of our priorities. Since a much lower proportion of blacks were registered than whites, even where there was no racial obstruction, and a much higher proportion of blacks tended to vote Democratic, we knew that a massive registration drive among Negroes would help Kennedy. We concluded that it would be better not to have such a drive sponsored by the Democratic Party; if conducted under the auspices of Negro churches, a nonpartisan registration effort could be financed by tax-exempt contributions rather than difficult-to-secure political dollars. We arranged for former NAACP attorney Franklin Williams to take leave from his post as California's assistant attorney general and spearhead the program. One of those asked to make a major donation to the drive still fondly recalls making out his check to the Friendship Baptist Church and wondering whether it really existed. It did, and the drive resulted in thousands of extra voters.

Another aspect of the civil rights campaign, with wider ramifications, concerned Africa. Kennedy's chairmanship of the African Subcommittee of the Senate Foreign Relations Committee became a political asset. Although Negro leadership had largely spurned connections with Africa a decade before, by 1960 the sense of identity was at a high point, as, one by one, African states were becoming independent. To Nigeria's independence celebration in August 1960, Kennedy sent as his personal representative Theodore Berry, a Negro leader and later mayor of Cin-

cinnati; we made much of the fact that Eisenhower sent no Negro on the official American delegation. Kennedy repeatedly talked about America's concern for African freedom and development. He pointed out that this continent, so long "behind God's back" and ignored by American policy, would soon poll one-fourth of all the votes in the United Nations General Assembly. Of the 6,000 members of the whole Foreign Service, he noted, only 23 were of African descent.

When the State Department, after dragging its feet for a long time, refused to support a large airlift of students from Kenya to the United States, which Tom Mboya had arranged as a way to speed up the preparation of Kenyans to run their own society, Shriver persuaded the Kennedy Foundation to grant the necessary funds. Nixon hurried to reverse the State Department decision, but by then the Kenya leader said he preferred the Kennedy Foundation support which had been offered when he needed it. The transaction was celebrated at a well-publicized meeting between Mboya and Kennedy at Hyannis Port. Seeing the easy rapport of these two young men, each heading for the top leadership of his nation, I had a sense that day of the far-reaching changes to come in the relationship between America and Africa.

Throughout the campaign we were busy supplying material for the candidate to use on the campaign circuit and in statements sent to various groups. One controversial issue was the wave of student sit-ins to integrate public facilities that, in February 1960, had begun in Greensboro, North Carolina, and was spreading through the South. In a message to the youth of the country, Kennedy said that the peaceful civil rights demonstrations were not "something to be lamented, but a great sign of responsibility, of the American spirit. It is the American tradition to stand up for one's rights—even if the new way to stand up for one's rights is to sit down."

For the first debate with Nixon on September 26, I took out to Chicago the kind of facts Kennedy liked to absorb. While Nixon dodged the whole subject of civil rights, Kennedy gave a vivid description of racial injustice:

> The Negro baby born in America today . . . has about one-half as much chance of completing high school as a white baby born in the same place on the same day, one-third as much chance of completing college, one-third as much chance of becoming a professional man, twice as much chance of becoming unemployed, about one-seventh as much chance of earning $10,000 a year, a life expectancy which is seven years shorter, and the prospects of earning only half as much.

In the second debate, on October 7, Kennedy told the listening nation what he often said in talks to Negro groups: that by one stroke of the pen Eisenhower should sign the proposed executive order against discrimination in housing, and that he, Kennedy, would do so as soon as he took office.

Recurring opposition to our Civil Rights Section came from those in the party who contended that Negro voters were primarily interested in economic issues. Byron ("Whizzer") White, a Colorado attorney who headed the national Citizens for Kennedy organization, argued strongly that the emphasis on civil rights was inflammatory and unnecessary. A former football star, Rhodes Scholar, and war veteran, he was a formidable critic; both John and Robert Kennedy liked him and listened to him. Despite his grumbling objection and that of others on the staff, we had persuaded Kennedy to let us convene, in his name, a national advisory conference on civil rights. In deference to Johnson, who advised that "constitutional rights" would be more acceptable in the South, we used that term; in fact, it was no doubt more acceptable generally, North and South.

The conference was a considerable gamble. We invited all the major leaders in the field, whether they were Democrats or for Kennedy or not; they were to divide into workshops, hear witnesses give evidence, and make recommendations to which Kennedy would respond. Some feared the conference would be a "runaway grand jury," making impossible demands and putting the candidate in an untenable position. It was to conclude in a major public rally in Harlem, which could be a fiasco if the conference did not go well.

More than four hundred participants had come from forty-two states when Hubert Humphrey opened Kennedy's two-day National Conference on Constitutional Rights in New York on October 11. They separated into workshops on legislation and on executive action in education, voting, the administration of justice, employment, housing, and public facilities. Then, overruling those who wanted him merely to send a message, Kennedy came and listened to reports of the findings and recommendations. In response, Kennedy said he agreed with Eleanor Roosevelt's comment that this was the kind of conference that could have been usefully called by the President in 1954 and 1955 before the crisis of desegregation had overtaken the country. The conference, he said, "establishes an important principle of consultation between those who bear responsibility in the government and those who live as citizens and work in the field." He promised not only support for civil rights legislation but executive action "on a bold and large scale." He continued: "The presidency is, as Franklin Roosevelt said, above all a place for moral leadership. As this is a moral question, the central responsibility will bear upon the President." Mrs. Roosevelt said, "It took courage to call this conference," and announced she was now convinced that "Senator Kennedy will fight to get prompt action on civil rights."

At the Harlem rally of many thousands in front of the Theresa Hotel, Kennedy was flanked by a score of the nation's civil rights leaders. This was the hotel where Castro had recently stayed and where Khrushchev had embraced Castro. Behind that drama, Kennedy said:

> There is another great traveler in the world, and this is the travel of a world revolution in a world of turmoil. . . . We should not fear the 20th Century, for this world-wide revolution which we see all around us is part of the original American revolution. When the Indonesians revolted after the end of World War II, they scrawled on the walls, "Give me liberty, or give me death" and "All men are created equal." Not Russian slogans, but American slogans. When they had a meeting for independence in Northern Rhodesia, they quoted Jackson, they quoted Franklin Roosevelt. They don't quote any American statesman today. . . .

In the high spirits of that day, before an enthusiastic crowd, he was carried away, saying that in Africa "there are children called George Washington. There are children called Thomas Jefferson. There may be a couple called Adam Powell. . . ." To laughter, Congressman Powell said, "Careful, Jack!"

Two shadows soon fell over the campaign. Martin Luther King was arrested in Atlanta, and, the day after King's arrest, Kennedy seemed to commit himself to support the armed overthrow of Castro.

Kennedy's thrusts on Cuba and allegations of a missile gap with the Russians finally did irritate Eisenhower enough to campaign for Nixon. If Kennedy had pressed on these lines sooner, Eisenhower might well have begun campaigning vigorously in time to make the difference. Major and sustained intervention on Nixon's behalf by Eisenhower could have swung the election to the Vice-President, and that could have come in connection with either King or Cuba. Mort Sahl noted that Ike at last was "now in the campaign, although he has not committed himself on civil rights." The comic critic added: "I really—after his great record of eight years—hate to see him get involved in politics." Kennedy was sorry, too.

On October 21, I found myself in the anomalous and uncomfortable position of agreeing with Nixon in the fourth TV debate when he chastised Kennedy for suggesting an illegal intervention in Cuba. Kennedy's repeated references to the Communist threat in Cuba, Ghana, and Guinea disappointed me. But with the climax of the Martin Luther King case at just this point, there was little time to dwell on disagreement with what I hoped was just campaign oratory. Moreover, during these last days, in proposing the Peace Corps, Kennedy lifted the level of the campaign. It was the one new idea advanced by either side.

On election day, the wily, street-wise Harlem Democratic leader, Ray ("the Fox") Jones, called me to say that the Constitutional Rights Conference and then the King call had been one-two knockout blows, that there was a massive turnout of Negroes for Kennedy throughout New York, and that he wanted to take his hat off to the Civil Rights Section about which he had first been skeptical. "It was like a symphony," he said, "working up to a great last movement."

Symphony was hardly the way it had felt or sounded to most of us. A jazz band was more like it; from time to time John or Robert had let the trumpet blast, or it took off by itself—sheer improvisation.

A veteran of Adlai Stevenson's two campaigns made a comparison that was also pleasing: for all of Adlai's love of ideas and Kennedy's more pragmatic bent, he said there had been a greater concentration of energy on ideas and issues in the Kennedy campaign than with Stevenson in either 1952 or 1956. Shriver and the sections he led were responsible for much of that. Working separately in Cambridge was the academic group around Archibald Cox. But at the center, aided directly by Sorensen, Feldman, and Goodwin, was Kennedy himself, a lean and learning man always on the move, who picked things up quickly and responded well.

Late on election night, with Nixon still not conceding and the returns from Illinois, California, Michigan, and Minnesota uncertain, John Kennedy walked across Bob Kennedy's lawn at Hyannis Port toward his own home and bed. In the dark his companion thought he said, "I'm angry." In the original manuscript he showed me, Theodore White pegged *The Making of the President 1960* on that incident. What finally broke the calm of this cool, contained Kennedy and caused him to display such heat? To answer this, White (in his first draft) flashed back over all the miles traveled, talks given, hands shaken, and deals made, beginning long before the primaries and culminating in that outburst in the early hours of Wednesday, November 9, 1960.

"Even if Kennedy said that, don't build your book on it," I advised White. Irony, gaiety, grace, restless curiosity, antipathy to ideology, concern for the common good, a thirst for power, and a respect for reason were his dominant qualities, I contended. No doubt, on occasion, anger too, but if he was angry you would feel it; he wouldn't declare it solemnly. While Nixon was almost always solemn, Kennedy was almost never.

While I was making the case against marring an excellent book with such an uncharacteristic anecdote, White stopped me. "Don't worry," he said. "When Kennedy read the manuscript that was the only thing he said I had to change."

"That's not what I said," the President-elect told White. "What I said was 'I'm hungry.'"

3 · Search for the Brightest and the Best

In his first press statement as President-elect, Kennedy announced that Allen Dulles would stay on as head of the CIA and J. Edgar Hoover would continue for the thirty-seventh year as Director of the FBI. A few days later, a postcard came from Thomas Hughes, then the chief congressional aide to Chester Bowles, reminding me of the Wisconsin campaign talk in which I had spoken, with some hyperbole, of a "Kennedy-Bowles-Stevenson-Humphrey world view" and had said Kennedy was the one most able to bring into office an administration that would represent that view "from top to bottom." Hughes's card read: "I want you to know that I voted for your Kennedy–Bowles–Stevenson–Humphrey–Lyndon Johnson–Allen Dulles–J. Edgar Hoover view of the world."

Kennedy's public reason for reappointing Dulles and Hoover was to establish their posts as nonpolitical. Within the campaign staff we were told that the narrow margin of victory made it unwise to affront either the millions of Americans who revered Hoover or the scores of legislators and leaders of the foreign policy establishment who respected Dulles. Not until dawn of the morning after the election, when Illinois and Michigan finally fell into the Kennedy column, was a majority in the Electoral College assured. With 49.7 percent of the voters for Kennedy and 49.6 percent for Nixon, neither had a popular majority.

Both appointments seemed ominous to me. In the Civil Rights Commission we had repeatedly run up against the indifference or resistance of the FBI, whose agents in the South, all white, had been of almost no help to us. Kennedy had acted before Martin Luther King or other civil rights leaders could warn and press him not to keep Hoover, whose antipathy to Negroes and the cause of equal rights was well known. Perhaps Kennedy moved fast in order to forestall just such pressure.

When the President-elect decided on Allen Dulles, he did not know that the CIA was planning the invasion of Cuba or that Dulles had approved plans for the assassination of Lumumba and Castro. He reappointed this symbol of the cold war before he had chosen his own top advisers on world affairs in the State Department and the White House. They had no chance to urge an immediate change in the CIA command.

My Wisconsin formula for Kennedy's world view was, of course, an oversimplification. The President-elect was a complex political leader in a complex situation. He was not anyone's man—not Stevenson's or Bowles's, and not Mayor Daley's or John Bailey's; not the Civil Rights Section's, and not the Southern senators'; not his father's, and not

Bobby's. He had one foot in the cold war and one foot in a new world he saw coming; one hand in the old politics he had begun to master, one in the new politics that his campaign (and Stevenson's before him) had invoked. Kennedy would have considered even those polarities misleading, and would have insisted that the contradictions and tensions in his politics reflected the realities of America in 1960. Whatever the precise description, Kennedy's inner struggle would now be reflected in an extended political one, within his administration, over the course for the nation to take in domestic and world affairs.

Between the election and the inauguration, John Kennedy had seventy-two days to pick a Cabinet, make hundreds of key appointments, review the federal budget waiting for submission to Congress, prepare an inaugural address setting the nation's new direction, and complete myriad other tasks. Watching him on television as he was driven to the Hyannis armory for his first press conference, I enjoyed his exuberance and recognized the sign of impatience as the camera alternated between his smiling face and his fingers constantly tapping the automobile window.

Two days after the election, I received a phone call from Shriver. "If you thought you were going on vacation, enjoy it quickly—between now and Sunday," he said. "Monday morning we go to work." He had just finished a long planning session with Kennedy and his key associates in Hyannis Port. "Jack has asked me to organize a talent search for the top jobs—the Cabinet, regulatory agencies, ambassadors, everything. We're going to comb the universities and professions, the civil rights movement, business, labor, foundations, and everywhere, to find the brightest and the best people possible." Shriver recalls that Kennedy used that phrase, "the brightest and best." It was much later that we discovered the 1811 hymn by Bishop Heber—"Brightest and best of the sons of the morning, / Dawn on our darkness, and lend us thine aid"— and later still that Lyndon Johnson used that phrase in a far less happy context.

To my protest that two of the most important jobs had been filled without any search, one with crucial impact on civil rights and the other on foreign policy, Shriver said the fight was just beginning. With this new assignment we would have the first responsibility and opportunity to recommend names for the most critical departments—State, Defense, Treasury, and Justice and for all the other Cabinet and sub-Cabinet posts. Shriver wanted Louis Martin, Adam Yarmolinsky (coordinator of the campaign's Urban Affairs Section), and me to meet him at the Mayflower Hotel first thing Monday. Before then we were to find out everything we could about previous presidential transitions and see what had already been prepared for this one.

No Democrat had taken over from a Republican since 1932. In the transition from Hoover to Roosevelt, there had been a breakdown in national policy-making at a critical point in the Depression. In the 1952 change from Truman to Eisenhower, despite innovations in joint planning, particularly in handling the budget and foreign affairs, the cooperation was far from satisfactory. Even in the best of transitions, the engine of the United States government would slow down long before the election and not operate with full power for some months after the inauguration. With a nuclear arms race underway and crises in the Congo, Korea, and Cuba, even more was at stake in 1960 than in 1952.

Fortunately, the Brookings Institution had undertaken comprehensive studies to assist the new administration (whoever won in 1960) in understanding the inexorable demands of the calendar, the problems likely to arise, and the available sources of help. One Brookings study noted that during World War II German submarines achieved striking successes against Allied convoys by attacking just after the changing of the watch—during the some twenty minutes it took for fresh eyes to adjust to the night. In a changing of the presidential watch, the country could not afford any period of bad vision on crucial matters of national security.

Kennedy had often used the term "Commander in Chief" to add weight to his concept of an active, powerful presidency, but it was necessarily still something of an abstraction to him. In a sobering interview for Brookings, James Killian, Eisenhower's adviser on science and technology, described how modern weaponry had transformed the role of the Commander in Chief. From the moment Kennedy took the oath he would be responsible for America's nuclear bombers hovering in the air around the world, ready to destroy the cities of Russia in the event of a Soviet surprise attack. Would the new President be factually and psychologically prepared, Killian wondered, to decide, on word of an apparent Soviet attack, whether or not to order the Strategic Air Command to proceed to targets?

Another point in a number of interviews was Eisenhower's surprising hostility toward Truman. Eisenhower, who seemed so congenial in public, apparently would not forgive Truman for some of his sharp criticism, particularly the charge that Eisenhower had not had the courage to defend George Marshall against attacks by Senator Joe McCarthy. Truman was not to revisit the White House until Eisenhower departed. Truman's Republican Undersecretary of State, Robert Lovett, emphasized that an incoming executive can get a lot of help from his predecessors and from the continuing civil servants if he is not a stuffed shirt who thinks he knows it all. Ike's thinking that it was "consorting with the enemy" to have close relations with the outgoing administration was one of the ways Lovett thought the incoming Republicans in 1952 had been "damn stupid."

Stupidity was not one of Kennedy's faults. In their post-election messages and when they met, mutual respect and graciousness prevailed between the outgoing and incoming Presidents. Eisenhower was said to be much impressed with the young man. A spirit of cooperation spread downward, smoothing the way for the newcomers to take over.

By the time Shriver met with Martin, Yarmolinsky, and me at the Mayflower on Monday, November 14, he was pursuing some promising leads, including Robert Lovett and McGeorge Bundy, dean of Harvard's faculty of Arts and Sciences, whom he had seen en route to Washington. Before getting offices or discussing criteria for the search, we were off and running to provide urgent information to the President-elect. Shriver knew the kind of man Kennedy wanted. More accurately, since Kennedy worked well with and respected a wide range of types, Shriver knew the kind *not* wanted: the too ideological, too earnest, too emotional, and too talkative—and the dull.

One of the first leads led, a month later, to a Secretary of Defense. The day after the election Robert McNamara had been chosen as president of the Ford Motor Company. Reading that news, Shriver remembered hearing enthusiastic accounts of McNamara in the mid-1950s. One of the wartime "whiz kids" brought into the Pentagon as a team of management experts, McNamara was a man whose career Shriver had followed with admiration. At Hyannis Port after the election, he had mentioned McNamara and the President-elect said to look into him. Next Shriver found that Lovett, as Assistant Secretary of War during World War II, had been responsible for assembling the whiz-kid team and considered McNamara the best of them—and an excellent prospect for Secretary of the Treasury or of Defense.

Adam Yarmolinsky, who had met and liked McNamara, told us how the Ford executive had broken tradition and refused to settle in the usual company suburb, choosing instead to commute from Ann Arbor in order to keep close ties with the university community there. As a lover of great books seminars, I was happy to discover that McNamara belonged to one. Learning that McNamara was reading *The Phenomenon of Man*, Shriver commented, "How many other automobile executives or Cabinet members read Teilhard de Chardin?" McNamara was a Republican who had supported Kennedy (and in 1940 had been one of two out of 198 members of the Harvard Business School faculty to support Roosevelt). He contributed to the NAACP and the American Civil

Liberties Union. With each call made about McNamara, we heard further commendation of his judgment, analytic ability, and administrative efficiency. He emerged as a man who could effectively help a President cope with the military-industrial complex which Eisenhower had warned was so difficult and dangerous.

While the press was predicting that Stuart Symington or Henry Jackson would become Secretary of Defense, Shriver proposed that Kennedy make an all-out effort to persuade McNamara to leave his new Ford presidency, for either the Defense or the Treasury post. McNamara's acceptance would symbolize the new administration's power to draw top talent, even from the ranks of business. In early December, Kennedy reviewed Shriver's file of recommendations on McNamara, and then said, "Let's do it." He authorized Shriver to fly secretly to Detroit and tell McNamara the President-elect wanted him to be either Secretary of Defense or Secretary of the Treasury.

It was a bold gamble, but the boldness of the offer was one reason McNamara gambled on Kennedy. He ruled out the Treasury right away, but agreed, despite great reluctance to leave a job he had just started, to fly to Washington to meet Kennedy. They took to each other; after thinking it over for some days, in mid-December McNamara decided to forgo his business career and its large income for the public challenge as Secretary of Defense.

At the last minute, just as everything seemed set, an urgent question came to us from Kennedy: Was McNamara a Catholic? *Who's Who* didn't say. There mustn't be too many in the Cabinet, the first Catholic President said. Within a few minutes we were able to send the word back: No, he was not a Catholic.

In terms of the new President's capacity to take command of the whole government, and first of all its budget for the coming year, the most pressing need was for a Director of the Bureau of the Budget. When Shriver had called John Kenneth Galbraith, he talked about another Harvard faculty member, David Bell, who had worked in the Budget Bureau and the White House during the Truman administration and then for some years had served as an economic adviser in Pakistan. Galbraith thought Bell was probably too young to be the director, but said he would be an outstanding associate director. While Yarmolinsky and I were calling people for opinions about Bell, Shriver flew to Boston one night to see him. After a few hours, Shriver was sure this was the man for Kennedy.

"He was low-key, well informed, experienced, unideological, sensitive, quick, somewhat ironic, and good-humored—just the sort Kennedy responds to best," Shriver explained to us later. To Kennedy, he had added, "He's like Chuck Spalding"—an old, close friend of Kennedy's who possessed some or all of those characteristics. Bell went to talk with Kennedy, and the selection of a Director of the Budget was soon announced. The forty-three-year-old President-elect did not consider the forty-year-old Bell too young.

"Good work," Kennedy said to Shriver. "But next time you bring me an academic who doesn't have a Ph.D., make sure I have the facts straight so I don't sound stupid." The President-elect had called Bell "Doctor" and been corrected. One of my first lessons in the talent search was to overcome a prejudice against holders of Ph.D.s who call themselves "Doctor." Shriver admonished me: "That's an Eastern, Ivy League bias. West of the Mississippi, almost every academic with a Ph.D. is called 'Doctor' and is proud of it." When Governor Orville Freeman of Minnesota was named Secretary of Agriculture, he joked that he was chosen only because Harvard had no school of agriculture. Actually his chief competitor, with the biggest farm-belt backing, bored Kennedy to the point that he had fallen asleep listening to him.

Looking back, I suspect that our biggest bias was an inclination toward lawyers—not a new phenomenon in Washington. Shriver, Yarmolinsky, and I had all gone to Yale Law School, and we soon enlisted regular help from Washington attorneys Paul Warnke and Thomas Farmer. Shriver did work hard to develop a network of informants in every region. Nevertheless, I remember how often one of us would call Eugene Rostow, then dean of Yale Law School, who had kept track of generations of lawyers, or would check with someone in the Cambridge academic group.

Louis Martin made sure that the breadth of the hunt included blacks, whom Kennedy had promised to appoint in unprecedented numbers. When Shriver called Martin after the election to ask him to join the hunting team, one of Louis's friends said, "Well, you've been telling all those lies in the campaign. You'd better go on down there and help make them come true." Before the search was over, Martin had compiled a list of 750 Negro prospects. "I had a candidate for almost every job," he recalled afterwards. "I don't give a damn what the job was, I came up with a Negro. It got to be a joke."

Our talent search operated from a suite in the headquarters of the Democratic National Committee. On the other side of the entry hall were the offices where Larry O'Brien, Ralph Dungan, and Richard Donohue were in touch with party workers, seeking to find appropriate positions for the most deserving. Shriver and all of us in his search were naturally interested in the politics of each appointment and in the fate of the political people we cared about. Yet O'Brien, Dungan, and Donohue were primarily seeking the right positions for particular political supporters, while we were seeking the right people, regardless of politics, for particular positions. The difference in the two approaches seemed greater than the distance separating the two sides of the building, and seldom the twain did meet. We called it a state of friendly competition.

In the reception room and halls, there would usually be a throng of people seeking jobs or trying to push someone for a job. As the word spread about the talent search, we were flooded with letters and callers, most of them concerned about jobs at levels lower than we were likely to reach. No matter how clearly, sympathetically, and firmly we explained that we were not dealing with the positions they were interested in, many of them persisted. Most of them did not know or care to know about the distinctions between our talent search and O'Brien's political placement operation; they just wanted to be seen or heard by somebody, if not everybody.

Fortunately, Shriver gave up the idea of an all-open office; unlike the Civil Rights Section, we had doors behind which we could escape. From morning to night the halls were filled with supplicants who felt sure their future depended on seeing Shriver, O'Brien, or one of us. One day when we were under intense pressure to get answers to Kennedy about someone he was considering for the Cabinet, my secretary was pressed by a man I had known slightly who insisted that he had to have an appointment; when she explained I couldn't see him that day, he announced he was going to sit outside my office all day and night until I saw him. He was sitting there at 8 p.m. when I finished the memorandum for Kennedy. Having to deal decently with so many anxious job seekers was one of the most painful experiences in my life. It reminded me of Carl Sandburg's account of Lincoln trying to escape from petitioners crowded into the White House halls.

Mitigating this was the intoxication of being involved in decisions that would affect the country. Others enjoyed it, too. Once I telephoned Courtney Brown, then dean of the Columbia School of Business, to get his opinion of several possibilities for Secretary of the Treasury. When asked what he thought about Averell Harriman, Robert Roosa, Eugene Black, and Douglas Dillon, he chuckled. "Well, Averell's sitting right here in my office now," he said. "Averell—this is the Kennedy people down in Washington. They're calling to find out what kind of a Secretary of the Treasury you'd be." My father, a colleague of Brown's, who happened to be in the meeting, said that Harriman replied jovially, "Tell them I'm available."

Once while we were riding high, Kennedy himself was unamused.

There had been a number of leaks to the press about prospective Cabinet appointments—none, I think, from any of us, but everyone was under suspicion. One night, while we were at supper, a call came for Shriver or one of us. When a secretary said we were all out, the caller asked in irritation, "Well, who are you?" The young woman replied emphatically, "*I am Mr. Adam Yarmolinsky's* secretary!" To which the caller, in an unmistakable accent, said, "And I am John Kennedy and I want you to tell me who is leaking these Cabinet names." He told her to tell Mr. Yarmolinsky and Mr. Shriver and Mr. Wofford and anyone else up there that if they were doing it, they better damn well stop. Later we learned that most of the leaks had in fact come from the President-elect, who liked to try out ideas on friends in the news media, expecting them to keep it secret.

Kennedy relished flexible lines of authority and multiple sources of information. When Richard Neustadt, then a professor at Columbia, who had worked in Truman's White House and just written a provocative book, *Presidential Power*, was enlisted to assist in the transition, he asked how he should relate to Clark Clifford, another adviser on how to staff the administration. Kennedy said, "I don't want you to relate to Clark Clifford. I can't afford to confine myself to one set of advisers. If I did that, *I* would be on *their* leading strings."

Throughout these weeks the pressure was intense. From Palm Beach, where Kennedy spent much of the time, Shriver was under a constant barrage. As he gave his brother-in-law names and information on possible appointments, he would get in return more names suggested by Kennedy's expanding network of advisers, including, from the beginning, his ever active and influential brother Bob. The same names, of course, appeared on many lists; Kennedy complained about "old faces." New or old, the suggestions had to be researched and information double-checked if possible so that no blunder would be made.

Faced with impossible deadlines, we did preposterous things. Once Kennedy had decided upon an appointment, it was not supposed to be announced until the FBI had reported on the man's loyalty, character, and background. Even on a crash basis, a full field investigation would take weeks, during which the appointee could not take office. Before the era of Alger Hiss and Joe McCarthy, such investigations of top-level people were minimal; in the Truman-Eisenhower transition they had been a problem, but now they threatened to be a major log jam. Yet they could not be waived without great political risk, and in some cases risk to the country's security. Therefore, even though Shriver held no government post, he sent the FBI lists of prospects to be investigated *before* the

74

President-elect had acted on an appointment, and during this brief inter-lude of cooperation with the incoming administration, J. Edgar Hoover complied.

Our lists included many who had no idea they were being con-sidered and some whom Kennedy never did consider seriously. Some were flattered and intrigued when their associates reported that FBI agents had come to see them about their colleague's fitness for a high but unspecified government position—and some of these were let down when nothing was subsequently offered. Others, who had no intention of ac-cepting any role in the administration, were furious about being investi-gated. One of these was Dean Acheson, back in his law firm and not then inclined at all toward John Kennedy, whom he considered an "unformed young man." His partners thought it funny and a little late for the FBI to be checking into the loyalty of the former Secretary of State. "I've told Jack Kennedy I'm not going to take any job, but you know the Ken-nedys!" a livid Acheson told his friends.

Compounding the situation was our working hypothesis that those who came seeking jobs were probably not the ones who should get them. This proposition that those best fit to fill the leading positions in the state would not desire to take them, and would have to be persuaded, is as old as Plato's *Republic* and makes some sense. But it contrasts sharply with the way John Kennedy and almost every other President had been chosen. To respect everyone's pride, including the job seekers', we spoke of "pros-pects," not "candidates" for a job.

Actually, as our files for each of the several hundred major presi-dential posts began to fill, the lines between "prospects" and "candidates" became blurred. In many cases, our search would lead to an interesting possibility who, as he learned of our interest, became interested himself and with different degrees of subtlety then participated in a campaign for the position. In other cases, the prospect was a candidate for that or another high post from the beginning.

One of those who in no way sought a job was Paul Freund, a respected professor of law at Harvard whom many leading lawyers (and the *New York Times* writer on law, Anthony Lewis) hoped to see on the Supreme Court. Freund seemed to be an outstanding choice for Solicitor General. He demurred, but we still pressed the recommendation, and Kennedy himself tried to convince him. Freund was advised that if he agreed he would be in line for an appointment to the Supreme Court. After he finally refused, he wrote me a note saying, "I hope you will understand that they also serve who only stay and teach."

Freund, Robert Lovett (who at sixty-five and in poor health firmly said no to any post), and a few others notwithstanding, it became clear that Kennedy's call to the Washington Frontier was hard for most people to resist. Not since the early New Deal had so many citizens, young and old, felt the attraction to public service. Once again the federal government was a powerful magnet for the idealistic and the ambitious. The interested and even excited way many people responded to our telephone calls indicated how strongly Kennedy had caught their imagination. Sometimes, when the person we called realized we were asking advice about someone else, we could detect the disappointment.

Ours was largely a search by telephone, although Adam Yarmolinsky designed a handy form for written information, including space for comments as to the prospect's *judgment, integrity, ability to work with others, industry, devotion to Kennedy's programs,* and *toughness.* There was public teasing about the last category, but for better and worse it was certainly a criterion the President used, beginning with his key White House staff. Kenneth O'Donnell, for example, resembled a cobra, sensing every danger, ready to strike—he had the kind of toughness Kennedy wanted next to him in an appointments secretary.

"Devotion to Kennedy's programs"—or his "principles," as one version of our form sheet had it—was a difficult category because the programs and principles were not always so clear. In checking on prospects for the Secretary of the Treasury we knew that Kennedy wanted someone who would be reassuring to Wall Street and to a conservative Congress, yet at the same time be a fresh face and a person with innovative ideas. But what kind of innovative ideas?

When Galbraith and Arthur Schlesinger came down from Cambridge to go over their slate of recommendations with Shriver, they were disturbed to find serious consideration being given to Douglas Dillon (and several bank presidents) for Treasury. An investment banker, son of one of the founders of Dillon, Read and Company, Undersecretary of State in the outgoing administration, a Republican who had contributed thousands of dollars to Nixon's campaign, Dillon was presumed to champion conservative fiscal policies. Favoring a Treasury Secretary committed to the use of monetary policy to stimulate economic growth, the Cambridge group pressed for Harriman, or a legislator like Senator Albert Gore, Congressman Henry Reuss, or Congressman Richard Bolling.

When Schlesinger took their case against Dillon to Kennedy, he replied, "Oh, I don't care about those things. All I want to know is: is he able? and will he go along with the program?" Since at that point there was no set program, how was one to know whether Dillon would go along?

76

The dynamics of the appointments process were fascinating to watch. After he had appointed Dillon to the key Treasury post, and had thus aroused liberal opposition, Kennedy involved himself actively in selecting other top officials in Dillon's department and in the other agency focused on economic policy, the Council of Economic Advisers. For chairman of the Council, he chose Walter Heller, a Hubert Humphrey Democrat at the University of Minnesota, and in the Treasury Department itself Dillon soon found himself surrounded by avowed Democrats.

From the beginning Dillon worked well with the relatively liberal economic team Kennedy assembled. With important leadership and help from Budget Director Bell, a Kennedy economic program was put together that Dillon championed. Not only did Dillon go along with all this; before long he became the Cabinet member who was probably closest to the President and his family. Bob Kennedy as well as his father had at first opposed giving such a key post to an active Republican, fearing that Dillon would resign and embarrass the President. By 1967, however, Bob named his son Douglas Harriman Kennedy in honor of two men, Douglas Dillon and Averell Harriman, about both of whom he had been dubious in 1960.

The Cabinet appointee who made the most use of the talent search staff was Robert McNamara. Adam Yarmolinsky and Paul Warnke had been primarily responsible for Defense Department recommendations and had an impressive file, but when we met McNamara for a long, early breakfast in the Ford Company suite at the Shoreham Hotel, he already had cards with as many names as we had. When we didn't have information on his names, he would say, "Will you check him out today?" By the time we finished, each of us, including Shriver, had specific assignments, and we agreed to meet again the next morning at dawn. This went on for three or four days, when we realized that we had all been co-opted for McNamara's own talent hunt. Soon we were spending most of our time on the Defense Department and falling behind everywhere else. Shriver finally said, "It's your shop now, Mr. Secretary. Nobody else is doing the job you are in finding people. We're needed in other places."

McNamara's drive, precision, and ability to draw people into his orbit and get the best from them were extraordinary. Although open to new suggestions, he was firm in rejecting a presidential proposal he disagreed with. He resisted considerable pressure to pick Kennedy's friend and active supporter, Franklin Roosevelt, Jr., as Secretary of the Navy, and selected instead John Connally of Texas. He soon asked Yarmolinsky to become his special assistant and continue the talent search for other key posts in the department. Of all the "finds" in his talent search, Shriver took most pride in McNamara.

Kennedy was most concerned and most uncertain about the selection of a Secretary of State. It was inevitably what interested me most: if anything like a "Kennedy-Bowles-Stevenson-Humphrey view of the world" was to prevail in the new administration's foreign policy, it would need to be represented at the top. The lower ranks of the State Department and Foreign Service were trained in the old diplomacy and imbued with the spirit of the cold war.

Press speculation centered on Stevenson, Bowles, David Bruce, Ralph Bunche, McGeorge Bundy, Senator William Fulbright, Robert Lovett, John McCloy, and, toward the end, Dean Rusk. In fact, Lovett and McCloy (then chairman of the Chase Manhattan Bank) had withdrawn. The appointment of Bunche, a black Nobel Peace Prize winner, then the Undersecretary-General of the United Nations, would have been a dramatic move, but we had no indication that he was ever under active consideration. Knowing the opposition to Bowles among conservative Republicans and in the foreign policy establishment, and the difference in style between Bowles and Kennedy, I knew his appointment was unlikely unless a process of elimination left Kennedy with no other good choice.

We did not then know the force with which one long-time foe sought to eliminate Bowles. A few days after the election, Kennedy arranged to visit Nixon at Key Biscayne. In the campaign, one of Nixon's favorite themes in the South was to say that "the party of Schlesinger, Stevenson, and Bowles" was "a far cry from the party of Jefferson, Jackson, and Wilson." Now, while playing golf along with their mutual friend Senator George Smathers, Nixon told Kennedy that he understood political debts, and if the President-elect owed Stevenson the office of Secretary of State, he, Nixon, could accept it. But there was one man, he warned, whose appointment he would oppose with all his strength. If Kennedy made Bowles Secretary of State, he would interrupt his vacation and campaign to block Bowles's confirmation in the Congress.

The Nixon-Bowles antagonism went back to the days when Nixon was a young lawyer in the Office of Price Administration under OPA Director Bowles, but his current complaint was that Bowles was soft on Red China. Nixon was particularly worried because immediately after the election Kennedy had designated Bowles as his representative in Washington to meet with foreign diplomats who wanted to see Kennedy during the pre-inaugural period.

Kennedy had been playing a cat-and-mouse game with both Bowles and Stevenson for many months. In early 1960 his designation of Bowles as his chief foreign policy adviser served as leverage on Stevenson, who also wanted to be Secretary of State (if not President). When the nomination was most in doubt, Kennedy might have reluctantly agreed to give Stevenson the job if Adlai had offered his support then and thus assured a first-ballot victory at Los Angeles. Instead, Stevenson wavered and belatedly succumbed to an effort to stop Kennedy, thereby reinforcing the impression of unreliability and vacillation Kennedy had taken from his earlier experiences with Adlai.

After the nomination, when Bowles had to decide whether to run for re-election to Congress or withdraw in order to work full-time in the presidential campaign, Kennedy urged him to run for Congress. He argued that Bowles could win by campaigning in Connecticut for two or three weeks while giving most of his time to the national campaign; then, if Kennedy had won, Bowles could resign and take a high post in the administration. Kennedy feared that if Bowles withdrew, Stevenson and some of his supporters might assume Bowles had been assured the job of Secretary of State and diminish their support.

When Bowles nevertheless withdrew from the congressional race in order to serve Kennedy, Stevenson had to be reassured that no commitment had been made to Bowles. Kennedy asked Stevenson to prepare a basic position paper on foreign policy for use after the election. Matters were further confused when a few weeks later Kennedy announced a committee on national security policy, headed by Paul Nitze, and including David Bruce and Roswell Gilpatric. The overlapping assignments bothered Stevenson, but some of his friends say that until late November he fully expected to be Secretary of State. Backing him strongly, as ever, was Eleanor Roosevelt. After the election, when Kennedy asked her what he could do to overcome her lingering skepticism about him and win her full blessing, she said, "Make Adlai Secretary of State."

In mid-November, a long Stevenson foreign policy paper covering a wide range of issues and making proposals for the organization of the State Department was taken to Palm Beach by a Stevenson colleague, John Sharon; it had been largely prepared by another close Stevenson associate, George Ball. Impressed, Kennedy asked Sharon to organize further task forces on Africa, the Foreign Service and State Department personnel, foreign economic policy, the U.S. overseas information program, and arms control. He suggested that Bowles head one or two of the task forces. The Stevenson camp was encouraged by Sharon's broad—and Bowles's limited—assignment.

During this period I happened to be traveling with Stevenson and the trustees of the Field Foundation on a trip to Atlanta and outlying Georgia towns. We sat next to each other on a long bus ride and talked about the Kennedys and about his report, which I had just read. It was clear how much he hoped to become Secretary of State. Southern economic development and race relations were the subjects of the tour, but at each stop a crowd had gathered to greet Adlai Stevenson. The warmth and enthusiasm, in rural Georgia, must have heartened him. We were all reminded of the large constituency Stevenson still represented.

By late November I could sense from the questions coming from Palm Beach and from what Shriver said—and didn't say—that Stevenson was out of the running. Lovett was reported to have asked Kennedy, "Tell me honestly, are you looking for a Secretary of State or are you looking for an Undersecretary?" Kennedy was said to have replied wryly, "I guess I am looking for an Undersecretary." Stevenson was too independent and too large and international a figure to be an Undersecretary. Moreover, there was strong opposition to Stevenson from Kennedy's father, his brother Robert (who had voted for Eisenhower in 1956), and some of his closest political supporters and staff.*

In fact, the President's own deep negative reaction to Stevenson had probably ruled him out all along. Arthur Schlesinger reports that in meetings with Kennedy, Stevenson "tended to freeze a little . . . and, instead of the pungent, astute and beguiling man he characteristically was, he would seem stiff, even at times solemn and pedantic." Among other negative points about Adlai in his oral history interviews, Robert Kennedy said his brother simply "didn't want to spend any time with him."

One day Shriver returned from the small family christening of John Kennedy, Jr., amused by the priest's problem in quieting the argument over who should be Secretary of State long enough to perform the ceremony. As soon as the rite was over, the argument broke out again, between John and Robert Kennedy and the others assembled, including artist William Walton and columnists Charles Bartlett and Joseph Alsop.

Walton was one of the humane and open-minded influences close to Kennedy; he was urging some important role in world affairs for Averell Harriman, then sixty-nine and somewhat deaf but still eager for a new assignment. (Robert Kennedy later wondered why they had never seriously considered Harriman for Secretary of State. Instead they had joked about his having to get a hearing aid before he would be any use.) Bartlett, another good friend, supported Senator Fulbright for the post.

---

* William Green, Sr., the political leader of Philadelphia, for example, in delivering Pennsylvania convention delegates to Kennedy in 1960, had asked that Stevenson get no Cabinet post. During the 1956 Stevenson campaign, Green had visited the Democratic candidate in a hotel suite. Green was told that after he left the room Stevenson said, "Open the window and let some fresh air in—and get the odor of corruption out."

As to Alsop, I knew without anyone telling me which men the hard-line columnist would be most against. During the campaign, after the first television debate in Chicago, Bob Kennedy invited me to join him and Alsop in a crowded booth at the hotel bar. With his unusual combination of colorful macho language and effete manner, Alsop had assaulted Kennedy's association with Bowles and Stevenson and urged Bob to press for a tougher stand against Cuba and Russia. Alsop's presence in the inner family circle was no source of reassurance.

My reaction to Alsop was not just based on reading and disagreeing with him for years; in 1957, at a Moscow dinner with Ambassador Charles Bohlen, I had seen the mutual antipathy between Alsop and Bowles. They had clashed on almost every point of foreign policy. Yet much as I disliked Alsop's way of dominating the argument by talking tougher than anyone else, he could be very persuasive. Already he had used his powers of persuasion ardently and effectively on behalf of Johnson for Vice-President and Dillon for Secretary of the Treasury. Later Robert Kennedy was to note that Alsop was a tremendous booster of Dillon and "in view of all the favors that Alsop had done I don't think there's any question that this was a factor." Alsop was backing David Bruce for Secretary of State.

So Kennedy wanted all the information we could get on Bruce. Though he had been considered a good Ambassador to France and Germany and a competent Undersecretary of State, he seemed to be very much of the old school, with Europe the touchstone of his thinking. He had given no sign of sharing the foreign policy views espoused by Kennedy in *The Strategy of Peace*. One colleague of the sixty-two-year-old Bruce described him as "dead from the neck up." Whatever criteria Kennedy had in mind, we knew he wanted someone who was very much alive. Shriver argued within the family against Bruce's appointment. Lovett also was reported to be negative. In retrospect I came to realize that our report on Bruce was wrong. As Kennedy's Ambassador to Britain, he wrote perceptive, lively, and wise analyses of events and, as secret documents on the CIA later revealed, he had given one of the first warnings against that agency's abuses.*

We were also (I came to think) wrong about Fulbright. By December 1960 it had become evident to many of us, and to some of the President-elect's friends in the press, that Kennedy's own preference was the chairman of the Senate Foreign Relations Committee. After first having considered Fulbright rather pompous and opinionated, Kennedy had learned to respect the insight and wit of this former Rhodes Scholar

---

* See page 456.

and university president from Arkansas. Yet Fulbright's appealing laconic manner was coupled with a lackadaisical approach to work and a disconcerting quality of resignation in the face of obstacles. Though he had sponsored the legislation that led to the Fulbright international scholarship program, he had become skeptical of foreign aid. In the fall of 1960 I, like most of the supporters of Bowles or Stevenson, saw him as a threat.

"At this point," reports Arthur Schlesinger, "some of Bowles's backers, acting without his knowledge, began stirring up Negro and Jewish organizations against Fulbright. . . . Kennedy had almost decided on Fulbright; but finally, after rather heated arguments, the President-elect yielded and struck Fulbright's name from the list." Civil rights forces, including Negro leaders, were indeed against Fulbright, because he had signed the Southern Manifesto and filed a court brief against school desegregation; influential Jewish organizations considered him pro-Arab. Some of us who were Bowles or Stevenson backers may have fanned the anti-Fulbright flames, but the protests to Kennedy were ignited by the public press reports.

Robert Kennedy himself pressed the case against Fulbright on racial grounds. "I was extremely strong against it and ultimately prevailed," Robert wrote in a confidential memorandum for the record in February 1961. What finally dissuaded the President, his brother thought, was the fear that in a United Nations in which the majority of nations were colored, the United States would be vulnerable with a Secretary of State known for his stand against Negro rights. In retrospect, Bob Kennedy —and many of us—regretted that we worked to block Fulbright, because for all his shortcomings he was one of the wisest men in Washington. As Secretary of State his counsel might have kept America out of the Vietnam War.

Fulbright must have regrets of his own. It is clear, I think, that if he had been courageous on civil rights in the late 1950s, he would have been Kennedy's Secretary of State. But, as he said in his ill-fated *amicus* brief in *Aaron v. Cooper*:

> The people of Arkansas endure against a background not without certain pathological aspects. They are marked in some ways by a strange disproportion inherited from the age of Negro slavery. The whites and Negroes of Arkansas are equally prisoners of their environment. No one knows what either of them might have been under other circumstances.

At the end of November, Kennedy asked Stevenson to be the Ambassador to the United Nations, with Cabinet status; he explained that with the slim Democratic majority in Congress, he needed a Secretary of

State who was not so controversial. Stevenson would not accept without knowing who would be the Secretary of State. He was alarmed by word from Walter Lippmann that Kennedy was thinking of McGeorge Bundy, who had voted against Stevenson in 1952 and 1956. Adlai's strong opposition probably played a part in eliminating Bundy in the final sweepstakes. Stevenson's refusal to accept the UN Ambassadorship on the spot so irritated Kennedy, according to Robert Kennedy's later account, that the President-elect "was about to tell him that he couldn't have even that."

With Stevenson out of the running for the Secretaryship, and the prospects for Bruce, Bundy, and Fulbright dim, there seemed perhaps a chance for Bowles. The Bowles-Kennedy relationship also suffered from mutual stiffness; Kennedy never saw Bowles at his best, though each time the two met, Bowles came away convinced that they were in full agreement on the issues discussed. After his unsettling session with Adlai, Kennedy invited Bowles to breakfast at his Georgetown home and raised his guest's hopes higher than they had been at any time since the election.

"I want to ask you a hypothetical question," the President-elect said, knowing how tantalizing the question must have been. "If you were Secretary of State, what kind of an organization would you set up?" Bowles says he replied, "I think I'd start by asking Dean Rusk to become Undersecretary." Kennedy asked if Rusk wasn't the president of the Rockefeller Foundation. Rusk had not been on the list for Secretary until that point.

Four days later, at a meeting of the board of the Rockefeller Foundation in Williamsburg, Bowles, Bunche, Lovett, McCloy, and Rusk were among the trustees around a table when an urgent phone call came for Rusk. On his return, he wrote a note to Bowles that it was Kennedy, who wanted to see him: "What do you think he wants to talk to me about?" Bowles wrote back: "He's going to ask you to become Secretary of State."

The night before he saw Kennedy, Rusk spent the evening at Bowles's home asking about Kennedy—whom he had opposed for the nomination that spring, as chairman of the Stevenson for President Committee of Scarsdale, New York. After his meeting with the President-elect, Rusk called to tell Bowles: "Well, that's one possibility that we can cross off our list. Kennedy and I could not communicate. If the idea of making me Secretary of State ever actually entered his mind, I am sure it is now dead."

I was relieved by this news. On the 1957 trip with Bowles, we had joined forces with Rusk in India and spent some days together visiting Rockefeller Foundation population control projects in the Punjab. Rusk was intelligent, suave, and cautious. He seemed open-minded (except when he and Bowles were required to inspect displays of various contraceptive devices and the customary smiles of both men curled downward in disapproval until each resembled a scowling John Foster Dulles). Rusk had come a long way from Cherokee County, Georgia, but something seemed missing: insight? vision? a view of the world that went beyond the conventional wisdom? He had been Assistant Secretary of State for Far Eastern Affairs during the Korean War, but, as someone pointed out, practically no one remembered it. Rusk seemed to me a plausible Undersecretary, but not the right Secretary.

However, Bowles felt warmly toward him; so did Stevenson and, on the other side of the fence, Dean Acheson. Time was running out. The President-elect had been pleased by Rusk's quiet manner and apparent competence. He had read and liked Rusk's article "The President," in the 1960 spring issue of *Foreign Affairs*. It emphasized the President's central role, although it suggested leaving diplomacy to diplomats and looked askance at the idea that the State Department's role was to think up "new ideas"—not exactly the spirit of the New Frontier. The chief argument against Rusk was that in the inner circle, as Robert Kennedy noted later, "nobody knew Dean Rusk particularly well."

On December 9, according to Robert Kennedy's account, the President-elect was inclined to choose David Bruce, who was said to be "tough with the Russians." Robert urged his brother to call Robert Lovett, who he knew supported Rusk. "It was the conversation with Lovett that convinced him that Dean Rusk should be the selection," wrote Robert afterward. The next day the President-elect invited Rusk to Palm Beach.

On the evening of December 11, Kennedy called Bowles to say that he had asked Rusk to be the Secretary, that Stevenson would be the UN Ambassador, and that he wanted Bowles to be the Undersecretary. Resilient as ever, Bowles accepted and expressed confidence that the new foreign policy team would be effective.

In their first meeting after being appointed, Rusk told Bowles he wanted him to be his "alter ego" and to have the kind of relationship with him that Undersecretary Lovett had had with Secretary Marshall. He asked Bowles to take primary responsibility for finding and recommending the people to fill the major posts in the department and the more than a hundred ambassadorships. Thereafter, Shriver and I worked directly with Bowles on those positions.*

---

* On December 18 Bowles submitted to Rusk (and to the President and the talent search) a memorandum, "Considerations Regarding the Selection of Top Policymakers." It urged that in all top foreign policy posts, "with a minimum of exceptions, we bring in people from the outside who are unhampered by past loyalties and associations," and who would "have the capacity for fresh affirmative thinking, and for deal-

Mennen Williams had been picked and announced as Assistant Secretary of State for Africa even before Rusk was chosen. Noting the importance of Africa, Kennedy had called it "a position of responsibility second to none in the new administration." Though it was odd to appoint an Assistant Secretary before a Secretary, when Kennedy passed over the Michigan governor for Secretary of Health, Education, and Welfare he felt it important for Williams' pride to make public some high position for him. He had concluded that Governor Abraham Ribicoff of Connecticut would fare better in Congress with HEW's costly programs than the adamantly liberal Williams. After Kennedy had consulted Bowles about the African post for Williams, several of us assembled at Bowles's home for a long talk with Williams to convince him to accept the unexpected assignment.

Most people did not require long persuading. When Bowles suggested Edward R. Murrow for Director of the United States Information Service and the Voice of America, some of us doubted that CBS's leading commentator would leave his lucrative position of great influence, but Rusk and the President authorized Bowles to make the offer. In thirty seconds Murrow accepted, asking only, "When do I start?"

Clark Kerr, president of the University of California, was Bowles's strong recommendation for Assistant Secretary for Latin American Affairs, but the California Board of Regents was unwilling to give him leave. Bowles also failed to get Averell Harriman appointed Assistant Secretary for either European or Far Eastern Affairs. All three key posts went instead, on Rusk's urging, to career diplomats, about whom Bowles felt uneasy; Harriman became a roving Ambassador-at-Large. Bowles prevailed in a number of high-ranking appointments, and accident also played a part. Rusk and Bowles—and Kennedy—had agreed, for example, that the number three position in the department, the Undersecretary for Economic Affairs, would go to William A. Foster, a Republican business executive who had headed the overseas aid program under Truman. Kennedy approved and Foster accepted Bowles's offer. When Stevenson learned of the pending appointment he complained about it to Senator Fulbright. Fulbright happened to see Kennedy in Florida and protested: why give another top post to a Republican when an experienced Democrat like George Ball was at hand? To his consternation, Bowles had to withdraw the offer to Foster (who later became head of the new Arms Control and Disarmament Agency), and accept as his fellow Undersecre-

---

ing with the new powerful forces which are shaping events throughout the world." It proposed criteria for the selection of ambassadors and some immediate steps to reform the Foreign Service. See Chester Bowles, *Promises to Keep* (New York: Harper & Row, 1971), Appendix II, p. 605.

tary a sharp critic. Ball was overwhelmingly European-minded, with little sympathy for Bowles's special focus on Asia, Africa, and Latin America.

Kennedy did not switch to Ball in order to please Stevenson. To Shriver, the President-elect remarked that in terms of jobs in the administration, Adlai's close associates and supporters were doing better than many of their counterparts who had supported Kennedy. The lesson being taught, he said, was that if you want a top job it was better to work against Kennedy than for him. Moreover, those he did not know had an advantage over those whose faults he knew too well.

There were then some 135 American ambassadors. Whose resignations should be accepted, and who should be appointed in their place? Even before Rusk was selected, the issue of ambassadorships had erupted. There were seven newly independent African nations, each in need of an ambassador from the United States. Two weeks after the election, the outgoing administration tried to put through the appointment of seven senior Foreign Service officers for these posts. Thomas Farmer, a Washington attorney who was helping us in the talent search, learned of the effort and protested to Robert Kennedy, and I brought it to Bowles's attention. We argued that seniority should not be the criterion for those nations; they were not places for older, tradition-minded officers awaiting retirement at the end of their career. Bob Kennedy agreed that New Frontier-type ambassadors could deal best with the new African leaders, and the plan was delayed. Shortly after his designation as Undersecretary, Bowles directed that more appropriate envoys be found.

One of my assignments was to continue working closely with Bowles on ambassadorships. We had accumulated many promising suggestions, and Bowles himself drew on a decade of experience. To demonstrate respect for the Foreign Service, he decided that any ambassador who had performed effectively and who had served less than three years at his present post should be asked to remain. The three-year test still left more than half of the ambassadorships to be filled.

The most difficult task was making negative judgments about senior Foreign Service officers. From several high-level inside sources, men in whose judgment Bowles had confidence, we invited comments on the quality of those officers. To our surprise, from one of them we received a detailed, case-by-case list, which we went over with our informant. Negative insights are often the most certain; adverse allegations the most interesting. These discussions of "Mr. X's Shit List" were fascinating and influenced a number of decisions. Questions of due process can be raised, since the accused had no chance to reply; but throughout any talent search one seeks confidential opinions. For the sake of the informant's future career, the list's existence was a closely held secret. In addition, of course, Bowles reviewed the personnel files of each Foreign Service officer under consideration, and sought evidence of outstanding performance which should be rewarded. Assistant Secretary of State for Congressional Relations William Macomber, a Republican holdover in the State Department who worked with Bowles on ambassadorships, recalls how much attention was given to identifying good appointees of the outgoing administration who should be kept. According to Macomber, Bowles's ambassadorship to India had been considered such a success by all sides that he would have been continued in 1953 by Dulles and Eisenhower but for the insistence by Governor John Davis Lodge of Connecticut that this would build up a Democratic rival in state politics. Bowles did not want that kind of veto to disqualify excellent Republican ambassadors in 1961.

In this ambassadorial sifting and recruiting, the President-elect took strong interest. He was amused to learn that no one in the Foreign Service under fifty held the rank of career minister or ambassador and that under the existing promotion system the highest grade he could have expected at age forty-three was FSO 3, about halfway up the ladder. It was agreed that emphasis would be given to the promotion of outstanding young officers, and that efforts would be made to encourage the less effective of the older officers and those who seemed to be marking time to take early retirement.

As Bowles persuaded some thirty current or former ambassadors to retire, he was accused of bypassing the Foreign Service, yet after all of Kennedy's initial appointments were made, the proportion of ambassadorships held by the Foreign Service—more than three out of four—was a record high. But the profile was different. Most of the new ambassadors were younger, although George Kennan was an interesting exception. He was persuaded to return from retirement and become Ambassador to Yugoslavia, where he established a close and useful relationship with Tito.

Leon Poullada was an example of the kind of young Foreign Service officer Bowles sought to identify and promote. In 1957, as a junior embassy attaché in Afghanistan, Poullada had guided the Bowleses and me around Kabul. He spoke the language and knew the people and politics to an extent not then often found in Foreign Service officers sent to Asia and Africa. During the Depression, he had got his start in a CCC camp. He was a departure from the customary diplomat. Finding that Poullada's record was by all accounts excellent, Bowles secured his appointment as the first American Ambassador to Togo.

Kennedy himself proposed and appointed several of the most prominent ambassadors: John Kenneth Galbraith to India; General James Gavin to France; and David Bruce to Britain. Only one selection backfired: Kennedy promised the ambassadorship to Switzerland to Earl E. T. Smith, a Palm Beach friend, a Republican who had served as Ambassador to Cuba in the last years of Batista. Despite very negative reports on Smith's role in Cuba, Kennedy was determined to go ahead, but the Swiss sent word that he would not be welcome. Switzerland had just agreed to handle U.S. interests in Cuba, and Smith, who was an ardent foe of Castro, was anathema to the new regime. Kennedy was furious, and for a while the word was passed that members of the new administration should refuse to attend affairs at the Swiss Embassy.

In general the new ambassadorships were a source of pride for the President and for all of us. One of the most distinguished appointees, Edwin O. Reischauer, professor of Japanese history at Harvard, was almost blocked by senior Foreign Service officers. An argument against him was that he had a Japanese wife—in the end, she turned out to be one of the keys to his success. When Kennedy wavered, Senator Fulbright gave strong support and the appointment went through. The selection of the first Puerto Rican to become an Ambassador of the United States, Teodoro Moscoso to Venezuela, was a break in tradition suggested to Bowles by his friend Governor Muñoz Marín of Puerto Rico.

Three college and university presidents were on the list: John Badeau, of the American University in Beirut, to the United Arab Republic; Charles Cole, of Amherst, to Chile; and William Stevenson (Adlai's cousin), of Oberlin, to the Philippines. Harvard economist Lincoln Gordon went to Brazil. A former labor attaché in Mexico, Ben Stephansky, who was a scholar of Latin American revolutions, went to Bolivia. James Loeb, a newspaper publisher and founder of Americans for Democratic Action, became Ambassador to Peru. A Foreign Service officer who had served with distinction in Europe and survived an attack by Joe McCarthy, Fulton Freeman, went as Ambassador to Colombia. He succeeded, as Bowles predicted, in part because he was not a member of the department's old "Latin American Club" and was able to view Latin America from a fresh perspective. Philip Kaiser, Assistant Secretary of Labor in the Truman administration, went to the newly independent Senegal. William Atwood, an editor of *Look* magazine, who personally knew Guinea's first President, Sékou Touré, was sent as the ambassador to that new nation.

These and other choices were well received in the countries to which they were sent. Viewed all together they turned upside down the conventional concept of "political appointees." They certainly constituted a change in the spirit and style of American diplomacy.

Some Cabinet appointments flowed naturally out of the campaign. The outgoing governor of North Carolina, Luther Hodges, who had been a successful businessman before going into politics and had agreed, at Shriver's request, to head the Business for Kennedy section of the 1960 campaign, became Secretary of Commerce. To the incoming Governor of North Carolina, Terry Sanford, the propriety of his predecessor's appointment was not so obvious. During the campaign Sanford told Bob Kennedy that Hodges had given him trouble for supporting Kennedy before Los Angeles, and that "if I ever nominate or suggest Luther Hodges for any job, throw me out of your office." After the election, however, he came and did recommend Hodges, saying, according to Bob Kennedy, that "he wanted him out of the state of North Carolina and this was the way to get him out"—but also adding that Hodges was well regarded and had done a good job as governor.

Stewart Udall, the new Secretary of the Interior, was one of the few congressional colleagues of Kennedy (and one of the few Cabinet appointees) who supported him before the Wisconsin primary. Among conservationists, his selection was acclaimed. Robert Frost telegraphed Kennedy that Udall's appointment "reconciles me once for all to the party I was born into." The new Secretary of Labor, Arthur Goldberg, was also an early Kennedy supporter. Although he was not labor's choice, he had been a lawyer for unions and had strong labor ties. During the investigation of labor racketeering, he had worked closely with both John and Robert Kennedy.

According to Robert Kennedy (in his oral history), the President-elect first offered Abe Ribicoff the Attorney Generalship but "he turned it down because he said he didn't want a Jew putting Negroes in Protestant schools in the South." Bob Kennedy said the Connecticut governor wanted to be appointed to the Supreme Court when Frankfurter resigned and thought that as an Attorney General involved in civil rights "he'd build up so many enemies, create so much controversy about himself personally that he could never get approved." Instead Ribicoff became Secretary of Health, Education and Welfare.

Campaign ties led to the announcement of an offer that wasn't an offer. The elderly and no longer very effective Congressman William Dawson, dean of the black members, visited the President-elect during the transition period and afterwards announced that Kennedy had offered him the Postmaster Generalship but he had turned it down because of his age and health. We were surprised since Shriver had not recommended Dawson and he was not one of the black leaders we were urging Kennedy to appoint to any position. Bob Kennedy explained that the papers kept speculating that Dawson would get the post, so in order to put the matter gracefully to rest, with Mayor Daley's help he arranged this offer that Dawson had to refuse. A top officer of the Prudential Insurance Company, J. Edgar Day, who had been Insurance Commissioner in Illinois when Stevenson was governor, became Postmaster General.

The most embarrassing matter during the transition was the question of whether Robert Kennedy would become Attorney General. Soon after we started the search, Shriver asked me to help with recommendations for the Justice Department. The chief advice I received, from a diverse group of leading lawyers and law teachers, was to urge the President to take the Justice Department out of politics and make the Attorney General his most nonpolitical appointment. In one sense, that is what he finally did, but when I first heard that he was considering his brother, I was appalled. I wanted the Attorney General to be one of the most experienced and respected lawyers in the land. No one could make that case for the thirty-four-year-old Robert Kennedy. Nor did he seem to have the fair and thoughtful cast of mind required of the nation's chief legal officer. He would hold the operating power in most federal policy on civil rights and his reactions during the campaign left me dubious about how well he would use such power.

About this time, Ted Kennedy, then twenty-nine, breezed into my office with a question he said Sarge (or "Saage," as Ted and his brothers pronounced it) told him to ask me: "Do you think it would be a good thing for me to go to Africa?" Senator Frank Church had invited him to come along on a Senate Foreign Relations subcommittee tour of African countries. I had drafted one of John Kennedy's first major talks on Africa in 1959, but had never been on that continent except for Egypt, and envied Ted his chance. After I recommended the trip, Ted said he'd better hurry and get his passport; the other senators had left and he'd catch up with them in Dakar. Gregarious and adventurous in the campaign, Ted was warmer and more political in the older Boston Irish way than his elder brothers, but for a moment he reminded me of the day in 1946 when John Kennedy swept onto the scene at Clare Luce's, with a bevy of young women but without a serious idea in evidence. They really are late bloomers, I thought to myself.

Then I remembered a 1957 prediction in *The Saturday Evening Post*; the article had reported that fervent Kennedy admirers "confidently look forward to the day when Jack will be in the White House, Bobby will serve in the Cabinet as Attorney General, and Teddy will be the Senator from Massachusetts." My God! I thought, maybe it's all going to happen!

My fervor for Kennedy did not then extend to either of his younger brothers, and I continued to argue with Shriver that Bob's appointment as Attorney General would be indefensible. A few days later I was relieved when the President-elect called and asked for our recommendations for Attorney General. The next day, however, when Shriver presented our best list, Kennedy said, "Why give me these? Bobby will be Attorney General." At that point, though I could hardly believe that Kennedy would finally dare to do it, I returned to assembling suggestions for the other major Justice Department positions. A few days later, Kennedy called and asked, "Don't you have some more names for Attorney General?" Bobby himself was declining, on grounds of lack of law practice and the President's vulnerability in having his brother in so controversial a post, especially in civil rights.

It went back and forth like this for weeks. On December 1, when Stevenson was wavering about accepting the Ambassadorship to the United Nations, Kennedy decided to ask if Adlai would be interested in the Attorney Generalship. The question was presented through Bill Blair, but Stevenson said no, he preferred foreign affairs.

Among the two brothers and their father, the argument apparently raged about the right role for Bobby (as the President-elect insisted on calling him, to his younger brother's discomfort). At different times we heard that Bob (as we were supposed to call him) was being considered for Undersecretary of Defense or Assistant Secretary of State for Latin America, but having the President's brother and closest confidant as deputy or assistant to someone else was probably too much to ask of any member of the Cabinet, and too contradictory a relationship for either brother to enjoy. Before McNamara was appointed, they toyed with the idea of asking Eisenhower's Secretary of Defense, Tom Gates, to stay on for a year or so, with Bobby as Undersecretary until the time was ripe for him to take over the Defense Department. But they feared this would build Gates up to be a Republican candidate for governor of Pennsylvania.

A White House assignment, which many of us thought most natural and fully defensible, Bob considered unnatural and insufferable. "For brothers—or at least for the two of us," he told Arthur Schlesinger, "we had to have our own areas. I had to be apart from what he was doing, so I wasn't working directly for him and getting orders from him as to what I should do that day. That wouldn't be possible." On the other hand, as Robert explained in his later oral interview, the Justice Department was not a wholly congenial prospect. "I had been chasing bad men for three years and I didn't want to spend the rest of my life doing that." Justice Douglas encouraged him to return to Massachusetts, strike out on his own, and run for governor in 1962.

The President-elect was ambivalent, too. Later he told Clark Clifford that he had "very serious reservations" but that his father had been "absolutely determined" that Bobby become Attorney General. Joseph Kennedy's line was: "Damn the torpedoes, full speed ahead!" Eunice Shriver, in a light moment at Christmas 1959, is said to have said, "Bobby we'll make Attorney General so he can throw all the people Dad doesn't like into jail. That means we'll have to build more jails."

Not wanting to lose his brother's talents, John Kennedy sought to find a way to tap and further test the extraordinary executive abilities Bob had demonstrated in the campaign. He relished the idea of an Attorney General whom he could fully trust and a member of the Cabinet to whom he could confide anything. Finally, the President-elect had the courage of his clan. He told Bob that he needed "somebody who's going to tell me the unvarnished truth, no matter what."

Bob at last agreed, and they tried to joke their way through the barrage of criticism. When asked how he would announce the appointment, John Kennedy said, "I'll open the front door of the Georgetown house early some morning, about two o'clock, look up and down the street, and, if there's no one there, I'll whisper, 'It's Bobby.'" In fact they walked out the door in the midday sun, after the elder brother told the younger, "Damn it, Bobby, comb your hair." According to Bob, "I brushed my hair and we went outside and announced it." Robert was said not to like the President's wisecrack that he named his brother Attorney General to give him "a little experience before he goes out to practice law."

After this appointment, Shriver presented a full file of recommendations that became part of the Attorney General's own all-out hunt for talent. Archibald Cox, who was asked to be Solicitor General when Paul Freund declined, was on our list; he had served ably during the campaign as chief of research. Byron White, the Rhodes Scholar from Colorado who had headed Citizens for Kennedy, was not among the names we submitted, but was on the President's list and the Attorney General's. In our clashes over civil rights during the campaign, White had come across to me as stubborn and humorless, in contrast to others such as Griffin Bell of Georgia, with whom I was also often in dispute but whom I enjoyed and liked. White was chosen as Deputy Attorney General (and, two years later, became Kennedy's first appointment to the Supreme

Court). He was responsible for finding some of the outstanding men Bob brought into the Justice Department. Seasoned lawyers agree that the top group around Robert Kennedy may have been the best ever assembled by an Attorney General.

The appointment that gave me the most pleasure—and some pain—was Burke Marshall as Assistant Attorney General for Civil Rights. This was the job I had wanted; Burke was the man I recommended as the best one to fill it. We had worked together at Covington and Burling, taught together a corporation law course at Howard University Law School, and participated for more than a year in a small seminar that read most of the volumes in Toynbee's *A Study of History*. In the seminar as elsewhere, Burke earned a reputation for wisdom by saying almost nothing—but listening so well that when he merely asked, "Why?" it made other members try to think hard before replying. Although he had never been involved in the civil rights effort, I talked with him often about issues before the Civil Rights Commission and he usually had penetrating questions and sometimes important insights. The idea of a court-appointed, federal voting registrar to overcome denials of the right to vote came spontaneously from him during a luncheon we had with the *New York Times* Supreme Court reporter, Anthony Lewis. Marshall exuded fairness, thoughtfulness, and responsibility, and instilled a sense of confidence and readiness to reason in others.

These were some of the arguments I gave Shriver, when he asked me why I had written such a glowing recommendation of Marshall for a job that he thought natural for me. He insisted on adding his nomination of me to that list I was submitting, which included Professor Louis Pollak of the Yale Law School and several others.

In *Robert Kennedy and His Times*, Arthur Schlesinger quotes Robert Kennedy as saying that of all his appointments, the Assistant Attorney General for Civil Rights was "the major one that I worried over" because the "fellow that should naturally have been appointed was Harris Wofford." However, he considered me too committed to civil rights. Schlesinger reports that "Byron White, who had decided during the campaign that Wofford was too much a crusader, now proposed Burke Marshall" and Wofford "also graciously recommended him." It is true that White opposed me and supported Marshall, but he had not known Marshall and was responding to the recommendation I had made.

While Bob Kennedy was trying to decide, his chief assistant, John Seigenthaler, asked me to have a drink with White in order to show him that I didn't have crusader's horns. The encounter was disastrous. Just back from teaching a weekly Notre Dame law course on professional responsibility, I told how we had spent the entire session on the propriety of Bob Kennedy's call to the Georgia judge requesting Martin Luther King's release from jail. The class was divided on the question of whether he should be disbarred for such behind-the-scenes intervention in a matter before the court. White asked me what I thought. Still in a bantering mood and citing the Canons of Professional Ethics of the American Bar Association, I said I agreed with the majority of the students: reprimand, yes; disbarment, no. White was not amused. He commented sourly, "You might be interested to know that I recommended to Bob that he call that judge."

The Assistant Attorney Generalship was settled, I think, when Bob and Burke met. Both shy, they sat looking at each other during long silences. In the oral history accounts, there are two versions of this meeting. At the time, I was told by several people that at the end of the Kennedy-Marshall meeting, partly because of those mutual silences, they knew they were meant for each other. Ed Guthman, the Pulitzer Prize-winning newsman who became Bob's chief of public information, heard a different story, which he tells in his book *We Band of Brothers*:

> Marshall was so self-effacing and so laconic that when he came for an interview with the equally laconic Attorney General, the meeting was notable only for long periods of dreadful silence. When it was over, Marshall . . . left believing that he had blown his chances. Bob was not impressed and doubted that he ever could establish a relationship with Marshall. They were to become the closest of partners and the closest of friends, deeply trustful and respectful of each other.
>
> "I picked him on his reputation," he explained. "I asked a dozen people, and they all said Burke was the best young lawyer in Washington."

In any case, sometime before the inauguration, a warm and gentle Robert Kennedy called to explain to me that he had decided upon Marshall. He emphasized the problem of dealing with the chairman of the Senate Judiciary Committee, Senator Eastland of Mississippi, not only in getting the nomination confirmed, but in continuing relations over the appointment of judges and future legislation. Identification with the civil rights movement would be a great liability for the Assistant Attorney General. Marshall's lack of involvement was a major asset, not only with Congress but with public opinion. I agreed with his assessment, and said that if I needed a lawyer, Burke was the first one I would go to.

As Bob talked, I realized that the liability he mentioned extended to my relationship with him and with White. If they viewed me as a crusader, and did not think I could be committed and critical at the same time, they would regularly discount my judgment—perhaps discounting it more, the more I pressed and at the most crucial moments. With stormy

94

times coming in civil rights, it was essential that the head of the Civil Rights Division have the complete confidence of the Attorney General. It was also fair that Bob did not have such confidence in me since I then did not have it in him.

Afterwards, Shriver and I joked that we were rapidly working ourselves out of any job in the new administration. One by one the people we most respected, often at our initiative, were being appointed to key posts, and the relatively few jobs that interested either of us were being filled.

Late on the afternoon before the inauguration, Adam Yarmolinsky and I delivered the files of the talent search to the White House. Observers of past administrations assured us that no such search—going outside the circle of party patronage on such a scale—had ever been done before. A continuing search for the best men and women for future agency, ambassadorial, and sub-Cabinet appointments would thenceforth go on primarily within the departments and agencies, with White House supervision and intervention. The new chairman of the Civil Service Commission, John Macy, with New Frontier spirit, agreed to continue the process, drawing on our files and leads. In due course, Ralph Dungan in the White House became the President's chief talent scout.

It is accurate to say "men and women," although in the light of the women's revolution of the 1970s our hunt was backward and had little to boast about in the recruiting and placing of women. We talked of finding women, and pointed to Esther Peterson's appointment as Director of the Women's Bureau and Assistant Secretary of Labor for Labor Standards. But, except for secretaries, there was no woman on our talent search staff, and none on the new White House staff or in the Cabinet or heading an independent agency.

Chuck Stone, editor of the Washington *Afro-American*, wrote an editorial charging Shriver with discrimination against black women. Robert Weaver had been made head of the Housing and Home Finance Administration, which was slated to become a Cabinet department. Thurgood Marshall was being advanced for a federal judgeship, there were black men as ambassadors and sub-Cabinet officers, but no black women in major posts. Shriver did not think it very funny when I said that Stone was wrong; our prejudice was against not black women, just women. He insisted that he, at least, had looked far and wide for appropriate women.

In his oral history interview, Louis Martin did not blame Shriver for the lack of women appointed but pointed to "the Irish Mafia" and the Kennedys' "typical Irish attitude": "They see women as more concerned with the home." Nevertheless, even if we in the talent search did not have that attitude, I know how much more would be done today to find and propose women, and how much more successful the search would be. Indeed, the "we" doing the searching would include women.

It was easy to take pride in many of the appointments, and as the new appointees started working together, they seemed a remarkably congenial group. Were they too congenial, too much in the same mold? Was there among them a single independent-minded character, like the cantankerous Harold Ickes in Roosevelt's Cabinet? Larry O'Brien may have been right that political factors should have been more heavily weighed. Would a more political Secretary of State, from the Senate (like Fulbright or Humphrey) or from state governments (like ex-governors Bowles or Stevenson), have been better than the unpolitical foundation executive Kennedy picked? The President had drawn heavily on the Eastern Establishment, perhaps more than was appropriate for the New Frontier. Kennedy wanted a "ministry of talent" and talent there was, in abundance, but toward what end?

In a Kennedy presidency there was a good chance that, as Norman Mailer had predicted before the election, we as a nation would become "at last, again, adventurous." But where would the adventure lead, and by what compass?

From time to time, usually in late hours when work kept us overnight at the Mayflower Hotel, Shriver and I would raise such questions. He would regularly read in his bed long after midnight, turning from the endless memos of the talent search to something philosophical, religious, or literary. Stirred by a passage in Saul Bellow or a verse in a poem, he would read it aloud, and a conversation would spring up until sleep put it out. Often it would continue first thing in the morning when Shriver would take me along to mass, his common routine (which he thought good for my Episcopalian soul).

Not many outside his family saw this side of Shriver. Superficially he gave the impression that one was not virtuous unless exhausted by work, but those who worked and traveled with him discovered that meditation and philosophical thought were never far from the surface. His pace was too fast, though his enthusiasm and good humor generated energy and excitement in those he didn't wear out. Yet just as you would think he will never stand still and listen, he would ask a penetrating question opening new lines of thought and action. He persistently tested whether a course was right or wrong by measures of both principle and practicality.

Had Kennedy picked many people who would go beyond pragmatism to questions of principle? In foreign policy and civil rights, the configuration of people in policy-making positions seemed promising, but there would be many divergent views and conflicting pressures and the President himself would make the difference. Around him in the White House would be the two groups at the center of the campaign, the so-called Irish Mafia of O'Donnell, O'Brien, and company and the Sorensen, Feldman, Goodwin team of lawyers and speechwriters. Salinger was a colorful, ebullient, unideological character in his own right, and Ralph Dungan and Fred Dutton would be significant independent forces. Arrogant, articulate, liberal Arthur Schlesinger was to be there with a roving assignment. When he said he wasn't sure what he would be doing as Special Assistant, Kennedy replied, "Well, I am not sure what I will be doing as President either, but I am sure there will be enough at the White House to keep us both busy." Because Rusk declined to offer State Department posts to either McGeorge Bundy or Walt Rostow, as Kennedy had suggested, they came to the White House as the President's advisers on foreign policy and national security, where they would often have more influence than Rusk. Jerome Wiesner, who became the President's adviser on science and technology, and Carl Kaysen, Bundy's deputy, were to play particularly valuable roles. It was a high-powered staff, but taken all together it made me uneasy.

In one way or another they all seemed to me too much like Kennedy —cool, skeptical, pragmatic. A LEADER LIKE ROOSEVELT was the caption of our main civil rights campaign brochure, and the more I saw of Kennedy, the truer that seemed. But FDR had Eleanor, and Jacqueline Kennedy was not her equivalent. Mrs. Roosevelt had a conscience as overdeveloped as her husband's may have been underdeveloped, and she constantly nagged him to consider moral questions. In their time together, Kennedy's wife tried to divert him from politics and stir his underdeveloped artistic tastes, but probably not very often his conscience. Shriver was hardly like Eleanor Roosevelt, but I could see why he was considered the "house liberal," or worse, by some of those around Kennedy. He seemed close to the President, if not to some of his aides, and could speak up to him, when necessary; I thought Kennedy would do well to have Shriver near at hand, and hoped he would be appointed to the White House staff.

That was not to be. There was one position we had forgotten. The talent search had barely succeeded in making sufficient recommendations for the posts already waiting to be filled; we never got around to thinking about the person who might best organize the one new agency Kennedy had promised to create: the Peace Corps.

There was no excuse for forgetting it. Kennedy and the talent search received more letters from people offering to work in, or to volunteer for, the nonexistent Peace Corps than for all the existing programs of the United States government put together.

After the inauguration, Shriver called me: "You thought you were going to have a vacation? The President just asked me to set up a task force to see whether the Peace Corps idea really makes sense. When shall we have our first meeting?"

Soon afterward, Robert Troutman, Griffin Bell's colleague in the Kennedy campaign in Georgia, came by, covered in post-inaugural snow, to wish Shriver well and to concede that the King affair had come out all right. "But I hope all you bomb-throwers will now be corralled in one place, like the Peace Corps," added Bobby Troutman, in his friendly Southern drawl, "so all your energies can be directed overseas instead of toward Georgia."

Meanwhile, unknown to us, the day before the inauguration the "War Corps" had presented Kennedy with the first critical tests of his presidency. In a final meeting with President Eisenhower before he took office, Kennedy was told that American military intervention might be necessary in Laos and that military action was recommended in Cuba. Eisenhower said that Laos was the key to all Southeast Asia; that if the Communists took Laos, they would bring "unbelievable pressure" on Thailand, Cambodia, and South Vietnam. As to Cuba, Eisenhower remarked that we were "helping train anti-Castro forces in Guatemala" and that it was "the policy of this government" to aid the anti-Castro guerrillas "to the utmost." He recommended that "this effort be continued and accelerated."

The next day on the steps of the Capitol, framed by the sunlit snow and blue sky, John Fitzgerald Kennedy in strong voice sent the word forth "that the torch has been passed to a new generation of Americans, born in this century, tempered by war, disciplined by a hard and bitter peace, proud of our ancient heritage, and unwilling to witness or permit the slow undoing of those human rights to which this nation has always been committed, and to which we are committed today at home and around the world."

Seated in the open mall in front of him, I listened carefully for those last words. In the draft I had seen the day before, I had been delighted by Kennedy's support of the United Nations as "our last best hope," by his pledge to enlarge the fields "in which its writ may run," by his call for "not a new balance of power but a new world of law," and by his promise "to those peoples in the huts and villages of half the globe struggling to break the bonds of mass misery." We would offer our best efforts to help people help themselves, he said, "not because the Communists may be doing it, not because we seek their votes, but because it is right." That was the view of the world I had hoped for. Nevertheless, in the priority he gave world affairs, there was no reference whatsoever to the struggle for equal rights within America. When we called this to Kennedy's attention almost at the last moment, he added two words, to affirm America's commitment to human rights "at home" as well as around the world.

"All this will not be finished in the first one hundred days," Kennedy had concluded. "Nor will it be finished in the first one thousand days, nor in the life of this Administration, nor even perhaps in our lifetime on this planet. But let us begin."

Not long after taking the oath, Kennedy began to carry out his commitment at home. As the United States Coast Guard marched by the inaugural stand, the President asked why there were no Negroes. When told there were no Negroes in the Coast Guard Academy, he directed that action be taken immediately to remedy that. The next time they paraded before him he wanted to see a contingent that was more representative of America. Using the White House switchboard for the first time, Richard Goodwin conveyed Kennedy's message to the Coast Guard, and thought: "With a telephone like this, we can change the world."

Later, my wife and I trudged through snow drifts in formal evening clothes to the Inaugural Ball in the armory, where the President's friend Frank Sinatra (not yet barred because of reputed Mafia ties) sang the campaign song, "High Hopes." John and Jacqueline Kennedy seemed to have a special grace. For a brief and shining moment, one could believe that Robert Frost was right; in his inaugural poem he had acclaimed "a Golden Age of poetry and power / Of which this noonday's the beginning hour."

In the early hours of the morning, after an unexpected stopover at Joseph Alsop's house on the way home from the ball, John Kennedy went to sleep—in Lincoln's bed. It had begun.

II

Popular Protest
and Public Power:
Civil Rights

*Nonviolence in its dynamic condition means conscious
suffering. . . . It is possible for a single individual to defy
the whole might of an unjust empire . . . and lay the
foundation for that empire's fall or its regeneration.*
                                        —*Mahatma Gandhi*

4 · Martin Luther King, the Bus Boycott, and Civil Disobedience

The government of the United States is propelled by three engines—the legislative, executive, and judicial—but before John Kennedy became President, it was operating, in civil rights, on only one engine, the judiciary. The issue did not fully engage Kennedy either, until the movement for civil rights and the violence used in combating it brought the matter to a head so forcefully that he could not put it aside.

It is not surprising that the President had an inadequate sense of the breadth and depth of the problem. Prejudice and discrimination were irrational, he felt, but many immigrant groups had overcome similar barriers, and he was sure Negroes would do so, too, in due course, with appropriate help. Knowing the people of Boston, however, he feared a white backlash if he helped too much or moved too fast. Looking ahead, he saw Cuba, Berlin, Southeast Asia, and the domestic economy as the urgent priorities, and did not foresee that events in the American South would overtake him and make civil rights a central concern of his administration and of the country.

Of all the events that led to this change in the nation's agenda, none was more important than the year-long Montgomery bus boycott of 1955–56—and the civil disobedience that precipitated it and grew out of it. The demonstration of the practicability of a new method for social change began an era in American politics.

Before Martin Luther King, Jr., led 50,000 Alabama Negroes in nonviolent direct action, the civil rights movement had only one main cutting edge: litigation. With NAACP lawsuits in the 1940s and 1950s successfully striking down segregation in one area of public life after another, black Americans had come a long way up from Booker T. Washington's program of self-improvement. But as massive white Southern resistance mounted, it became clear that the law needed help. Courageous litigants and lawyers, together with the Supreme Court and all the lower court orders in the land, were not by themselves enough to bring about the far-reaching changes sought.

Adding the new dimension of civil disobedience to the popular struggle and bringing the other two branches of the federal government into action made major progress toward racial integration possible—and necessary. An understanding of how those two essential and complementary developments came about, or began to come about, in the South in the late 1950s is crucial to an understanding of the critical events of the 1960s that brought civil rights to the center of the American stage.

At the Atlanta airport in December 1957, the twenty-eight-year-old Negro Baptist minister looked at two signs, "Men" and "Colored." He went into the men's room. Although none of the white men paid attention to the well-groomed Negro, a black attendant became alarmed. "Colored men don't come in here," he said. The minister did not reply. The attendant shuffled over and tapped him on the shoulder. "You go in the colored room across the hall," he said. The minister continued with his business. Finally he turned and asked the attendant, "Do you mean that every time you need to go to the bathroom you go out of here and all the way to that other room?"

"Yes, suh, that's the place for colored," the attendant replied.

Martin Luther King, Jr., walked out in exasperation and said to me, "That's the way most of the Negroes of Montgomery acted before the boycott."

We were flying to Montgomery, where King was to preside at the first anniversary celebration of the boycott—a three-day Institute on Nonviolence and Social Change—and I was to conduct a seminar on Gandhi. He told me about the crucial role a wiry old Pullman porter, E. D. Nixon, had played in starting the boycott.

Nixon was a local organizer for the NAACP who had greatly impressed me when I interviewed him in Montgomery for a law school paper in 1952. King told me that after the arrest of a respected Negro seamstress, Mrs. Rosa Parks, who had refused to move to the back of the bus to make way for white passengers, Nixon had telephoned the young minister to see if for once the church might do something. King, like other ministers, had hesitated at going through with a boycott until the unschooled porter said, "The time has come when we's either going to be men or boys. If we's going to be men, then let's be men."*

King told me that's when he decided to go ahead, come what may.

Saying he would rather live one day as a lion than a thousand years as a lamb, Nixon had personally escorted hundreds of Negroes to registration offices, often facing physical threats; sometimes he carried a gun. When I questioned him about the issues of discrimination under the Federal Railway Labor Act, he queried me about Gandhi, whom I had studied in India. He particularly appreciated Gandhi's dictum that "when

---

* Lively accounts of E. D. Nixon and Rosa Parks are given in Milton Viorst's *Fire in the Streets* (Simon and Schuster, 1979), and Howell Raines's *My Soul Is Rested* (Putnam, 1977).

there is only a choice between cowardice and violence, I would advise violence." When we parted, I told him he was a Gandhi-with-gun.

Martin Luther King, Jr., liked that kind of fighter. He said his father had some of the same characteristics, though the respectable preacher never carried a gun and had no interest in becoming—or seeing his son become—any kind of Gandhi.

"When I was a boy I had to sleep with a mule," the elder King would tell his son. "When I went to school I smelled like a mule, and I was teased for smelling like a mule. My father was a sharecropper and I came from nowhere. I swore to myself that when I grew up and had children they would have all the things I had not had and would never smell like a mule." He also swore that someday he would own "a brick house . . . as fine as any brick house" and become a director of a bank.

After leaving the farm, he worked his way through college, married the daughter of a successful minister, and as pastor of Atlanta's thriving Ebenezer Baptist Church before long bought a fine brick house and became a bank director—and was able to support Martin, Jr., through his doctorate at Boston University. From then on, Daddy King (as his family and friends came to call him) started pressing his son to look out for his financial future and to achieve security through sound investments in stocks and bonds.

If Daddy King had had his way, Martin, Jr., would have married a daughter of one of Atlanta's leading Negro families, not Coretta Scott, a singer from a backward Black Belt town in Alabama (and graduate of activist Antioch College); he would have accepted a call from his father's prosperous church and not gone to Montgomery, the onetime capital of the Confederacy and continuing bastion of white supremacy; and in October 1960 he would certainly not have been sitting in Rich's department store with a group of militant young people. He would never have become a turning point in a presidential campaign because he would never have gone to jail.

No doubt Martin, Jr., accepted the call to the smaller Dexter Avenue Baptist Church in Montgomery partly in natural rebellion; sons are sharp to see the faults of their fathers. Yet he greatly admired his big, robust, commanding father, whom he considered fearlessly honest. While a little boy he went with Daddy King to a downtown shoestore where they were ordered to move from their seats in the front of the store, to the rear. "We'll either buy shoes sitting here," his father retorted, "or we won't buy shoes at all." Twenty years later, Martin, Jr., still remembered his angry father muttering, as they walked out of the store, "I don't care how long I have to live with this system, I will never accept it."

Rather than accept insults, Daddy King refused to ride the segregated city buses. When a policeman accosted him for accidentally driving through a stop sign and said, "All right, boy, pull over and let me see your license," he replied, "I'm no boy." Pointing to Martin, Jr., he said, "This is a boy. I'm a man."

Yet courageous as he was, Daddy King became terrified about his son during the bus boycott, after the younger King's home had been bombed. When Martin, Jr., and a hundred others had been indicted for an illegal conspiracy, his father asked him to meet with a group of Atlanta Negro leaders, who tried to persuade him not to return to what looked increasingly like a long term in jail and possibly death in Montgomery. When Martin, Jr., remained adamant that he must go back, his father broke into tears. Yet characteristically, according to Martin, Jr., his father then insisted on accompanying him on the drive back to an uncertain fate.

Martin, Jr., told the court he would rather go to jail than pay a fine, and was then sentenced to 386 days. To black supporters he said, "If we are arrested every day, if we are exploited every day, if we are trampled over every day, don't ever let anyone pull you down so low as to hate them. We are seeking to improve not the Negro of Montgomery but the whole of Montgomery." To those who had bombed his home, he warned, "Kill me, but know that if you do you have fifty thousand more to kill."

"All men are created equal," wrote Jefferson, the slaveholder, knowing that he was setting up a tension between that avowed truth and American reality. Years later, looking at the continuing gap, he said, "I tremble for my country when I reflect that God is just." The Constitution embedded the contradiction in Article I: in determining the number of a state's representatives in Congress, a Negro slave was to be counted as three-fifths of a person.

Negro spirituals and blues have recorded the plight of an uprooted people, but in song, drama, and fiction, black and white Americans have been able to laugh at themselves and the contradictions in which they are caught. With his acute sense of irony and interest in history, John Kennedy could—and did—laugh at aspects of the American racial predicament, but most of the time he preferred to put the whole problem out of mind. History was not to let him laugh long or avoid an early confrontation as President.

Kennedy was, of course, not alone among Presidents or among the American people in not seeing the centrality of race. It is not correct to say, as Archie Bunker does, that until "Eleanor Roosevelt discovered the colored . . . we didn't know they were there." There were the abolitionists and there was the Civil War, and the American Negro community was growing like Topsy. But when Woodrow Wilson in World War I and Franklin Roosevelt in World War II boldly proclaimed the rights of man and vowed to defend and extend them everywhere in the world, they seemed unconcerned that the rights of colored Americans were still far from established at home. It took the threat of a wartime march on Washington by the Brotherhood of Sleeping-Car Porters' A. Philip Randolph and Eleanor Roosevelt's prodding to get the President in 1941 to issue an Executive Order calling for fair employment practices in defense and government work. In 1948 Harry Truman finally desegregated the armed forces, and in 1957 Dwight Eisenhower reluctantly ordered troops to Little Rock to enforce a gradual plan for school integration ordered by a federal court. For the most part, however, neither the Executive Branch nor the Congress took much initiative in civil rights.

When the Supreme Court in 1954 ruled that segregation of public schools was unconstitutional, the President of the United States was asked if he had any advice to give the South. Eisenhower replied, "Not in the slightest." He grumbled, "I don't believe you can change the hearts of men with laws or decisions." He told newsmen he had not even disclosed to his wife whether he thought the Supreme Court decision to be right or wrong. The last thing in the world Ike wanted was to get involved in racial controversies. For three years he took no action to deal with the most vexing issue facing the country; not once did he speak to the people about the great issues involved—until Governor Orval Faubus of Arkansas misused the National Guard to block nine Negro students from enrolling in Little Rock's Central High School, and the Negroes had been driven away by a howling, violent mob. Even then, while swearing to enforce the law, Eisenhower expressed sympathy for "the strong emotions on the other side, people that see a picture of a mongrelization of the race." Having refrained from using his vast prestige to give moral leadership when it might have prevented violence, the President at the last minute was forced to send a thousand paratroopers to protect the nine students with bayonets.

"In this and like communities," Lincoln said, "public sentiment is everything. With public sentiment, nothing can fail; without it, nothing can succeed. Consequently he who molds public sentiment goes deeper than he who enacts statutes or pronounces decisions. He makes statutes and decisions possible or impossible to be executed."

Unlike Eisenhower, Lincoln was not one to underestimate or undermine the educational effects of the law, even if the law and its enforcement alone were not enough. Nor did he minimize the President's opportunity and responsibility to mold public sentiment. But he also knew the power of the people that had shown itself in the abolitionist movement, and then in the rise of the Republican Party. When he met Harriet Beecher Stowe he said, "So you're the little woman who wrote the book that made this great war!" He knew how much *Uncle Tom's Cabin* had done to stir sympathy for the slaves and antipathy to the slave-holding South.

A century after the antislavery crusade reached its climax, a popular movement demanding action for civil rights by all parts of the federal government was gathering momentum. The first thrust came in 1910 when a biracial group founded the National Association for the Advancement of Colored People and began to press for congressional and presidential action. Since Presidents were unresponsive and filibusters continued to block legislation against lynching, discrimination in employment, denials of the right to vote, and segregation in public institutions, the NAACP under W. E. B. Du Bois, Walter White, Roy Wilkins, and Thurgood Marshall concentrated more and more on litigation.

Case by case, often at great risk, and in the face of professional and physical intimidation, civil rights attorneys obtained court orders declaring various kinds of racial segregation unconstitutional. Finally in *Brown v. Board of Education* in 1954 the Supreme Court unanimously overturned the rule of "separate but equal" altogether.

The difficulty of the problem of enforcement, particularly in the absence of assistance from the President and Congress, should have been expected. For no prejudice seems so long-standing, so deeply rooted, or so widespread as racial bigotry. It is not only in English that the very words "light" and "dark" are synonyms for good and evil. In India, the discrimination against darker-skinned people was recorded thousands of years ago and institutionalized in caste; Nehru pointed out that the root of the word for caste, *varna*, meant "color." The outcastes, or "untouchables," whom Gandhi called *Harijans*—"children of God"—are dark-skinned descendants of the original Dravidians who were taken over by the light-skinned Aryans invading from the North. The Arabic word for slave means "dark ones." In America, the accident of geography concentrated slavery in the South, but as Negroes moved North and West white fears, hostility, and feelings of superiority were everywhere aroused.

By 1955 it was becoming clear that without some new strategy the peaceful revolution required by the Supreme Court would not succeed. To mold public sentiment, something or someone able to go deeper than decisions or laws can go was required. At just that point Martin Luther

King, Jr., a young preacher from Boston University, appeared on the scene in Montgomery, Alabama.

To appreciate what King accomplished in Alabama, it is necessary to have a picture of what he found there in 1954. A personal account of Alabama-before-King may help set the stage.* Since World War II, the political scene and public sentiment in Alabama had been of special interest to me. As an eighteen-year-old Air Force volunteer in 1944, I was disappointed to be sent to Craig Field, Alabama; Selma was too distant from the Nazis I wanted to fight. But the thought of returning to family roots in the Deep South intrigued me. My great-grandfather, Colonel Jefferson Llewellyn Wofford, had led Confederate infantry in the last battle of the Civil War at Blakeley, Alabama; it was on his lawn in Lexington, Mississippi, in 1860, that his friend Jefferson Davis had given his first speech in favor of secession. (My great-grandfather opposed secession and as a delegate to the Democratic Convention of 1860 had refused to join the Southern walkout, but like Robert E. Lee had reluctantly fought for the Confederacy after his state voted to secede.)

Stationed outside Selma for a year and a half, I came to feel very much at home there and to think I knew the community well. Yet I often wandered down Selma's sleepy Broad Street without once going the two blocks over to the unpaved roads and dilapidated quarters where the Negro majority of the town's 20,000 citizens lived. On many Sundays I enjoyed warm Southern hospitality, and rode horses along countless country lanes, without once talking to any Negro except my friends' servants. I went to theaters, churches, restaurants, parks, the hotel, and the public library without reflecting on the absence of Negroes.

That special blindness may have come from my first six years growing up in Johnson City, Tennessee, but later life in Scarsdale, New York, was not so different—occasionally on the train to Grand Central Station I would look out the window around 125th Street and wonder what life was like in those dingy slums and on those dirty streets. Yet in a family whose ancestors were accustomed to slaves, I was often tended by Negro cooks, and was close to several of them.

One summer when I was about eight years old, at a family barbecue on an East Tennessee farm a distant relative taunted me, "Little Harris, Jr., you've been up North two years now—I suppose you think the nigras

---

* Another account of the racial conditions in Alabama in the mid-fifties was presented in the Montgomery hearings and the reports of the Commission on Civil Rights. See appendix, pp. 467 ff.

and us is equals." When I said yes, he went on: "Pretty soon I guess you'll decide that the monkeys and us is equals." Having been reading the Doctor Dolittle books, I argued that someday we might learn their language and treat animals better, too. I can still see him roaring with laughter, with his red face and big belly, holding a beer can and calling out to everyone, "Listen to this—Little Harris, Jr., has been up North for two years and thinks us and the monkeys and the nigras is all equals."

In 1950, stirred by studying in India, I enrolled at Howard University Law School in Washington, D.C., because it was a center of the civil rights law I intended to practice, and because I realized I had never lived and worked among Negroes in circumstances where we were on an equal footing. I was Howard's first white law student since the days when women suffragists attended, unable to get degrees elsewhere. My parents were terribly upset, fearing for my career. It was a shock to my grandmother in Tennessee, but as an active churchwoman she braced herself and sent me an Episcopalian prayer against race prejudice. For my other grandmother from Little Rock, it was the end of the world. Ironically, she was the one who started my interest in India and Gandhi and first encouraged me to break out of the family's Republican fold. She was a devoted Democrat who adored both Franklin and Eleanor Roosevelt. She was also an inveterate traveler who took me around the world for six months when I was twelve. But to stop me from enrolling in a predominantly Negro university she pleaded, "You can go there to teach them, to help them, but you can't go and be a student with them." When her arguments failed, she literally collapsed and my father and I had to carry her upstairs while she shouted, "If God made them equal, I hate God! I hate God! I hate God!"

In the summer of 1951, I went back to Alabama to escort a political leader of India through the South. With his skin color and my status at Howard, I wondered what kind of reception we would get. When my Indian friend and I reached Montgomery, there was a dispute among the waiters at the restaurant, but we were finally admitted. "I knew he wasn't no colored man," the waitress explained to me afterwards. "We're getting good at spotting foreigners. Besides, no colored man would come in here."

Fortunately my closest friends outside Selma, two farm families who had taken me in like a son during the war, were not unduly disturbed about Howard, and they enjoyed Rammanohar Lohia, a Ph.D. from the University of Berlin who had been a leading follower of Gandhi. They arranged for him to address an overflow audience at the Dallas County Experiment Station. "He's the smartest man that has ever been here—no one could hold a candle to him," said our hostess. "It's the first time we ever had a brown-skinned man talk to us." They had been charmed by his championship of a farmers' civilization based on little village republics, and his faith that those who see the dawn and feel the seasons change are closer to the secret of life than city folk. They even tolerated his talk about Gandhi's way of nonviolent direct action to bring about changes in society, including the ending of caste and color discrimination.

"Man has thought twice in our century," Lohia said, "once with Einstein, then with Gandhi. Einstein's thought transformed understanding of the physical world; Gandhi's thought transformed understanding of the political world."

Afterwards Dr. Lohia asked if he could meet some Negro leaders. With a drawl and a half smile, our host said, "Down here in Alabama there are just nigras—no nigra leaders." Nonviolent action had turned some Indians into leaders, Lohia replied. "Why don't you talk to our nigras about all that," my friend said, with warm Southern hospitality, but added, "Come on and try—and I'll shoot you."

Later we did meet some Alabama Negroes. "Why not a little jail-going?" Lohia asked them after they had described the daily indignities they faced. "Resist some of this directly, nonviolently, and go to prison if required."

A prominent Negro educator replied, "No, we're not like India. Here we have the law and Constitution on our side. Besides, we're too weak a minority in America, just thirteen million. It can never happen here."*

The next year, when I went back to Selma and Montgomery to do research on a law school paper, "The Status of the Negro in Dallas County" (including Selma), it still seemed as if it would never happen there. "Are you always on the side of the minority?" one of my Alabama white friends asked. If so, I said, I would be on the side of the whites, since we were then in one of the 191 counties in the South where Negroes were a majority—and we were all part of the white minority in the world.

During that 1952 field study I began to discover the other city and county I had lived in but not known, and some of the men and women I had lived among but not seen. The director of the Dallas County Chamber of Commerce told me, "Selma is nigger heaven." When I met the leading Negro businesswoman, Mrs. Amelia Boynton, she responded,

---

* Another development which Lohia urged, and which he was told would never happen, was American Negro identification with Africa and active support for African freedom. A prominent Southern Negro said, "Dr. Lohia, I am no more interested in Africa than in Argentina or Australia." Lohia replied, "Well, I am."

"Then God keep me from heaven." She told me how she was conducting her own private boycott of white businesses where she was first-named. People were beginning to respect her dollars, but she said she could count on the fingers of one hand those fellow Negroes willing to stand up for their rights in Selma.

"You just don't know our niggers," my white host contended. "All the civil rights of the North won't ever mean as much to them as one nigger Saturday night in the South." His wife, a kind woman who stays with her maid when she is sick, said, "We in the South are the only ones in the United States who *love* the colored people. You champion them as a race and from a distance, but we like them as individuals." A Negro sergeant, back home from the Air Force, said to me, "It is a heart-touching thing when a man calls you a nigger. It just sets you on fire."

From behind his desk, a leading white businessman said, "You can't swallow Christianity with this sort of thing, if you let yourself analyze it. But when I get on a bus, I just hold back from sitting down with a Negro. You can sit on a tack and say it doesn't hurt, but you just don't do it." One worried Negro woman warned me that she thought her people were on the verge of a plunge into hate. When asked if she could forgive white people, she replied, "I have to, don't I, to be a Christian. I guess I'd never get to heaven if I knew half the things these white people say."

Despite assurance that they knew their "nigras," my white friends questioned me closely each night to find out what they were saying to me. A black schoolteacher later told me the story about the young Negro hired to serve at a white family's table. "What do the white people talk about?" her parents asked at the end of the first day. "Well," she reported, "they spend most of their time talking about us." As I was leaving, with my briefcase crammed with such notes, Amelia Boynton, the businesswoman, said, "Fear is the key to it all—once we lose our fear, we'll be O.K."

In Montgomery it was the women who first lost their fear, Martin King told me in 1956 when we met in Washington, D.C., during the early months of the bus boycott. The nearly two hundred members of the Women's Political Council had worked boldly with E. D. Nixon and attorney Fred Gray to strike against discrimination wherever they could. Most Negro ministers, King said, had been apathetic or intimidated, like most white ministers. They were busy "preaching God and raising their salaries," according to the head of the Women's Council. Then Rosa Parks changed all that simply by saying no and going to jail rather than moving to the back of the bus.

I told King that I had ended my 1952 law paper with the presumptuous line that what the Black Belt needed was "a Negro with some of Gandhi in him," and King recalled the talk I had given in October 1955 at Hampton Institute, Virginia, making the same point. He had read that talk shortly before the boycott, and been struck by the challenge from Gandhi that I cited. In 1935, Howard Thurman, a Negro minister and philosopher, dean of the chapel at Howard and then at Boston University, had gone to Gandhi and asked him to come to America to help the Negro fight for civil rights. Gandhi said that he had to make good the message of nonviolence in India first, but added that "it may be through the Negroes that the unadulterated message of nonviolence will be delivered to the world."

After that Hampton talk urging a Gandhian strategy for civil rights was widely circulated among Negro leaders, I had received many replies saying such a course was impossible. Nixon himself said sadly that there were only a handful of Montgomery Negroes who would fight for their rights either nonviolently or violently. The respected dean of Howard University, William Stuart Nelson, who had known and revered Gandhi and tried to spread his message, wrote to me that he had about given up hope. Everyone seemed to be saying that the American Negro did not have the Gandhian dimension in him.

Martin King laughed his low, slow laugh and said, "Yes, I would have said the same—before Rosa Parks sat anchored in her seat on that bus." He liked to believe that she was "tracked down by the *Zeitgeist*." She had thought about Gandhi, and discussed the idea of civil disobedience at an earlier seminar at the Highlander Folk School in Monteagle, Tennessee (where I had also taken Rammanohar Lohia in 1951), but King was sure that the soft-spoken seamstress had not planned to cause any trouble when she headed home after a long day's work. Then the driver ordered her to get up and give her seat to a white passenger and join the Negroes standing and jammed together in the rear, something she had done many times before. For some reason, she explained later, "This time I just didn't move." When the driver threatened to call the police, she said, "Then just call them."

"It's a sudden little spark like that that starts great conflagrations— when the tinder is ready," King said. He believed it was truly the spirit of the times that moved in her, then in E. D. Nixon, and, in response to their action, in King himself. Still, it would have been just a one-day boycott, King told me, but for the surprising popular response. On December 5, Martin and Coretta King rose at five-thirty for what they later called "the day of days." They waited for the first bus to pass to see how many had responded to the call to boycott that had gone out from a dozen pulpits and from the Women's Political Council during the weekend. The first bus, usually filled with Negro domestic workers, came around 6 a.m. "Darling, it's empty!" Coretta cried out. In fifteen minutes the next one came: empty. Instead of the 60 percent cooperation King had hoped for, it was almost 100 percent.

Later in the day Mrs. Parks was convicted of disobeying the segregation law and fined ten dollars; the city hoped this would end the matter, but young Attorney Gray, the first Negro lawyer in Montgomery, announced that the case would be appealed to the Supreme Court if necessary. Negro leaders met and decided to organize the Montgomery Improvement Association to plan the next steps, and King was elected president. That night King was uncertain whether they were ready for a long struggle and considered calling off the boycott before it fizzled; the Women's Council had only proposed a one-day protest, and it might be wise to stop while they were well ahead. King and his close friend, the Reverend Ralph Abernathy, agreed they would be guided by the turnout and spirit at the public meeting scheduled for that evening. As King approached the church for the meeting, he was caught in a traffic jam of Negroes from all over Montgomery; loudspeakers were being put up on the sidewalk for the several thousand who could not get in. The church had been filled for hours. As the congregation started singing "Onward, Christian Soldiers," King turned to Abernathy and said, "Heck, man, we're gonna boycott!"

"There comes a time," King said in his talk that night, "that people get tired. We are here this evening to say to those who have mistreated us so long that we are tired—tired of being segregated and humiliated." *Amen!* the congregation chanted. "But in our protest there will be no cross burnings. No white person will be taken from his home by a hooded Negro mob and brutally murdered. There will be no threats and intimidation.

"Once again we must hear the words of Jesus echoing across the centuries: Love your enemies, bless them that curse you, and pray for them that despitefully use you. If we fail to do this our protest will end up as a meaningless drama on the stage of history. If you will protest courageously, and yet with dignity and Christian love, when the history books are written in future generations, the historians will have to pause and say, 'There lived a great people—a black people—who injected new meaning and dignity into the veins of civilization.' "

Then by a standing, cheering, unanimous vote, a resolution was adopted that called for Negroes to refrain from riding the buses until (1) courteous treatment by the bus operators was guaranteed; (2) passengers were seated on a first-come, first-served basis—Negroes seated from the back of the bus toward the front and whites seated from the front toward the back; (3) Negro bus operators were employed on pre-dominantly Negro routes. The demands were moderate, even conforming to the separate but equal doctrine, but the method of mass non-cooperation was rightly viewed by the white people of Montgomery as revolutionary.

For the next twelve months some 50,000 Negroes in that city "walked with God"—or rode in car pools in automobiles driven by the better-off members of the community who seldom, if ever, used the buses. In great church meetings, they prayed for those who opposed them and rededicated themselves to the methods of nonviolence. In the Gandhian tradition, King engaged in negotiation and was open to compromise, and when the city decided to break the boycott by arrests, he was the first to go to jail.

From our first meeting I wanted to help King in any way I could. He complained there were no Southern black lawyers who would help him go to jail, and not use all the tricks of the lawyer's trade to keep him out of jail. Even courageous Fred Gray in Montgomery considered it against his professional principles to refrain from any proper legal move to save his client from prison.*

I felt a strong pull to leave Washington law practice and simply offer my services to King, but even then, before black separatism or chauvinism had shown its strength, I doubted the usefulness of a white interloper. Or was that a rationalization for my own fear, especially the fear of being laughed at? If King had asked me to join him full-time I suspect I would have gone, but already he was being plagued by offers of assistance from people all over the world. Even the shrewd and intelligent help of Bayard Rustin verged on a kind of manipulation I disliked. Steeped in Gandhian lore, with extraordinary personal experience in nonviolent action, Rustin seemed ever-present with advice, and sometimes acted as if King were a precious puppet whose symbolic actions were to be planned by a Gandhian high command.

Soon after the boycott ended, I started urging King to go to India. Getting away from the pressures upon him from all sides and talking with some of the key people who had worked with Gandhi while they were

---

* NAACP lawyers complained that King underestimated their role. At the time of King's arrest during the 1960 election, they worked night and day on the necessary court motions to secure his release. When public attention became focused on the telephone calls of John and Robert Kennedy, NAACP legal defense chief Thurgood Marshall commented wryly: "They tell me that everybody got King out of jail but the lawyers." In 1980, Fred Gray and another NAACP attorney were the first two blacks to be nominated as Federal District Judges in Alabama.

still alive would give him valuable firsthand information and a broader perspective. He liked the idea but wanted a formal invitation. In the fall of 1957 I helped Chester Bowles make some of the initial arrangements in India and drafted a letter from him to King about a possible trip. Bowles commended "adaptations . . . of the Gandhian techniques which amount to no more or no less than Christianity in action" as "the only practical way out of our present dilemma." Indicating that he was ready to visit India, King wrote to Bowles on October 28, 1957:

> It is my hope that as the Negro plunges deeper into the quest for freedom and justice, he will plunge even deeper into the philosophy of nonviolence. The Negro all over the South must come to the point that he can say to his white brother: "We will match your capacity to inflict suffering with our capacity to endure suffering. We will meet your physical force with soul force. We will not hate you, but we will not obey your evil laws."

The Indian trip did not come to pass for sixteen months—not until King had completed his book *Stride Toward Freedom: The Montgomery Story,* and was stabbed, almost fatally, by a deranged woman in Harlem while autographing copies. Feeling special identity with Gandhi, who was killed by a fellow Hindu, King accepted an invitation from the Gandhi Memorial Foundation. Through the singer Libby Holman Reynolds, who greatly admired King, I was able to secure a grant of $5,000 from her Christopher Reynolds Foundation to pay the traveling expenses of Martin and Coretta.

On arriving in New Delhi, King said, "To other countries I may go as a tourist, but to India I come as a pilgrim. This is because India means to me Mahatma Gandhi." For four hours he talked with Nehru about the problems of Gandhian action. The Indian Prime Minister lived up to his reputation for candor, and said of Gandhi, "You know, I did not always agree with him." Indeed, after independence Nehru dismayed Gandhi by announcing that there was no room for civil disobedience in a free India. Gandhi's last fast was in part directed against the policies of Nehru's government.

In meeting the veterans of the Indian independence movement, King was struck by their endurance and the "Long March" mentality they had maintained. In contrast to his few days in jail, some of them had spent ten years or more in prison. After four weeks on the subcontinent he came home resolved to have patience for a long struggle, and "more convinced than ever before that nonviolent resistance is the most potent weapon available to oppressed people in their struggle for freedom."

Coretta King says that after this trip her husband constantly pondered how to apply Gandhian principles in America. He even considered the idea of changing his style of dress to a simpler one, but "decided that since his main purpose was to attract people to the Cause, unusual dress might even tend to alienate followers." He worried about owning a car and a house, but concluded that in America one had to have certain things.

Before and after the India trip, King and I shared Gandhian stories and talked late into the night about effective American adaptations. He asked me to work with him on his book about Montgomery, especially in the sections spelling out his case for nonviolent action. The collaboration increased my respect for his thoughtful, philosophical mind and his serious search for practical wisdom.

We had come to Gandhi by somewhat similar routes, each having read and reread Thoreau's *Essay on Civil Disobedience* while in college in 1946 (King entered Morehouse College when he was fifteen years old). In 1950, while at Crozer Theological Seminary, King had gone into Philadelphia to hear a sermon on Gandhi by Mordecai Johnson, president of Howard University, and been so electrified that he bought and read a half dozen books on Gandhi's life and works. During that same period I had been reading all of Gandhi's writings in English and, after returning from India in 1950, often listened at Howard University to talks on nonviolence by Mordecai Johnson. In *Stride Toward Freedom*, King wrote:

> Prior to reading Gandhi, I had about concluded that the ethics of Jesus were only effective in individual relationships. Gandhi was probably the first person in history to lift the love ethic of Jesus above mere interaction between individuals to a powerful and effective force on a large scale.

After Gandhi's death, the whole man seemed to have gone through a prism and come out divided into various beams: the pacifist Gandhi, the ascetic Gandhi, the vegetarian and faddist Gandhi, the religious Gandhi, the political Gandhi. It was Gandhi the political artist that had primarily drawn me to India, and nonviolent direct action as a powerful new form of political persuasion was the Gandhian beam King was following. More and more King was coming to believe, with Gandhi, that the art of politics involved the skillful dramatic use of symbolic acts. The Salt March that so stirred King was high drama. The pictures of the Mahatma with his walking stick gaily leading his followers 170 miles to the sea had moved hearts and minds with a force beyond that of any speech. Gandhi recognized the political leader's role as actor on a large stage, and identified himself with Charlie Chaplin, the little man who stood up to the great

Leviathan. When Gandhi journeyed to England in 1930, Chaplin was at the top of his list of those he wanted to meet; there is a photograph of the Mahatma and the comic artist laughing heartily together.

King acknowledged that a successful artist in political drama needs to be ready for both comedy and tragedy. When he opened the 1957 Institute on Nonviolence and Social Change, he argued for the "tremendous educational and transforming possibilities" of nonviolent direct action, and quoted Gandhi:

> Things of fundamental importance to people are not secured by reason alone, but have to be purchased with their suffering. . . . The appeal of reason is more to the head, but the penetration of the heart comes from suffering. It opens up the inner understanding in man.

Then in words sometimes used to describe the culmination of a comedy, King argued that the end of nonviolent action is redemption and reconciliation. "The aftermath of nonviolence," he said, "is the creation of the beloved community, while the aftermath of violence is tragic bitterness." The audience said *Amen!*

"Is that true?" I asked in the morning seminar on Gandhi that I led in a corner of Ralph Abernathy's Baptist church during that 1957 Institute. "Isn't it an unhappy fact that often the aftermath of nonviolence may be violence?"

"That's a fact!" said a Negro woman seated in the seminar circle. "Too true!" said another. Two-thirds of the thirty-five or forty participants that morning were women, most of them rather large and emphatic people. My question released a flood of reminiscences about the boycott. They talked about the awful night in the eighth week of the protest when King's house was bombed. (It happened on January 30, 1956—the anniversary of Gandhi's birthday.) In the midst of one of the evening mass meetings, word was brought to the church that the front of the Kings' home had been blown up, with Coretta and their baby inside. King rushed home to find them alive; Coretta had run to the back of the house when she heard a strange thud on the front porch. For weeks they had been receiving telephone threats on their lives; after one especially angry call, King had been unable to sleep and had gone into his study to pray for strength; Coretta had known such fear since her childhood.

The seminar argued about the stand King had taken. Finding infuriated Negroes outside his house with guns, he had spoken to them from the wreckage and said, "If you have weapons, take them home. We must meet violence with nonviolence. Remember the words of Jesus: 'He who lives by the sword will perish by the sword.' We must love our white brothers, no matter what they do to us." Coretta King recalls the crowd singing "My Country, 'Tis of Thee," but also remembers how angry they were. Two nights later a stick of dynamite was thrown at the home of E. D. Nixon.

Later some members of the Negro underworld had sent word that although they knew Dr. King believed in nonviolence, they didn't, and neither did a lot of whites; so they intended to keep him safe. For a while he went along with having armed men hidden around his yard. Then one night, a white Western Union boy was almost shot by the volunteer guards as he stepped into the bushes to relieve himself. King called off the guards, saying that if that one boy had been shot, all the good of the peaceful protest would have been lost overnight.

Most of the members of the seminar admired King but doubted that they would have had that kind of courage. At a mass meeting he had said, "If one day you find me sprawled out dead, I do not want you to retaliate with a single act of violence," but a big, rough-talking man in the seminar said that when King was sprawled out dead, "That's when I climb off the nonviolence train."

"If nonviolence provokes violence, why is it worthwhile?" I asked. "Are you sure there is some good that comes from it that is worth the suffering?" I reported Thurgood Marshall's comment: "All that walking for nothing! They could just as well have waited while the bus case went up through the courts, without all the work and worry of the boycott."

"He wasn't here—he didn't know what it did *for us*, how proud we were that we walked all the way," said one of the participants. Another said they all stood straighter because of what they had done; if they had just let the lawyers do it, and waited for the Court, it would not have been the same. This way it wasn't just a few judges giving their opinions from on high; it was also 50,000 people speaking with their prayers and their feet.

On the other hand, a more critical member of the seminar said, "Let's face it. The Court saved us, just in the nick of time." After forty-five weeks, people were getting tired of walking and the city was about to enjoin the car pool. While King had been before a city judge, facing an injunction about to be handed down against him and others, the proceedings were interrupted by word that the Supreme Court had just declared the Alabama bus segregation law unconstitutional. The mayor had rushed out in consternation, while a triumphant Negro shouted, "God Almighty has spoken from Washington, D.C.!" Eight thousand Negroes had gathered the next night to celebrate. The most moving moment, according to Coretta King, was when Robert Graetz, the one local white minister who had supported the boycott, read from Paul's Letter to the Corinthians:

> When I was a child, I spoke as a child, I understood as a child, I thought as a child; but when I became a man, I put away childish things. . . . And now abideth faith, hope, love, but the greatest of these is love.

"At those words," says Coretta King, "the whole audience rose to their feet shouting, cheering, waving their handkerchiefs. They knew they had come of age."

"And even then we didn't stop walking," said a member of the seminar, recalling that great night. Since the Supreme Court's mandate would take a month to reach Montgomery, the Negroes decided to keep off the buses right to the end. She told of a grandmother who waved the car pool on, saying, "I'm not walking for myself but for my children and my grandchildren."

"But has all your loving reached the white citizens and really moved their hearts?" I asked. In the Indian independence struggle, I reported, Jawaharlal Nehru contended that he never saw so much hate as that in the eyes of the troops who were beating him with clubs, while he was turning the other cheek.

"We can't tell what's going on in white people's hearts," a woman replied. "But we know it changed *our* hearts: we aren't afraid any more." She told about the Ku Klux Klan march through her neighborhood, as a last effort to intimidate Negroes from integrating the buses, even after the Court had spoken. The hooded white men expected frightened Negroes to get off the streets and close their shutters. Instead, when the carloads of Klansmen came, they found porch lights on, doors open, and people in the streets, waving and laughing. Treated like a circus parade, the robed white men soon drove away.

"It wasn't our loving or our praying or our walking that got to white people," a young businessman said. "It was our efficiency—when we organized a car pool for more than fifteen thousand people each day—that's what took them by surprise and won us some respect."

Seminar members recalled the funny situations that occurred during the repeated practice sessions held in churches to prepare for a proper return to the buses. Sometimes people playing the parts, both of whites and of Negroes, carried their acting too far, and went beyond the threshold of nonviolence. Printed instructions advised:

> Remember that this is not a victory for Negroes alone, but for all Montgomery and the South. Do not boast! Do not brag!
> Be quiet but friendly; proud, but not arrogant; joyous, but not boisterous.

Be loving enough to absorb evil and understanding enough to turn an enemy into a friend.

If cursed, do not curse back. If pushed, do not push back. If struck, do not strike back.

When the day came—December 21, 1956—King got up to take the 6 a.m. bus. "I believe you are Reverend King, aren't you," the driver said with a cordial smile. "We are glad to have you this morning." It reminded Coretta King of Stanley's greeting to Livingstone.

On most buses, Negroes sat in vacant seats freely. In a few cases there were complaints. One rider said, "I would rather die and go to hell than sit behind a nigger." One Negro woman was slapped by a white man as she got off the bus. "I could have broken that little fellow's neck all by myself," she said, "but I left the mass meeting last night determined to do what Reverend King asked." In another bus a white man, finding himself behind a Negro, said, "I see this sure isn't going to be a white Christmas." A *New York Times* reporter said the Negro smiled and said, "Yes, sir, that's right," and everybody laughed.

For a while everything went smoothly, despite the Montgomery City Commission's statement that it would "not yield one inch, but will do all in its power to oppose the integration of the Negro race with the white race in Montgomery, and will forever stand like a rock against social equality, intermarriage, and mixing of the races under God's creation and plan." Then three days after Christmas buses were fired on throughout the city; a Negro woman was hit in the leg. Ten days later, while Abernathy and King were in Atlanta launching the Southern Christian Leadership Conference, to carry the strategy of nonviolence to every Southern community, bombs did severe damage to Abernathy's home and the home of the white minister, Robert Graetz. Two Negro churches were nearly destroyed.

After one more round of bombings two weeks later, sentiment in the white community had clearly turned. Business leaders, the white press, city officials, and even the usually silent white ministers called for an end to violence. Seven white men were arrested and prosecuted for the bombings (and ultimately acquitted). Soon desegregation of buses was an accepted fact of life.

Had the nonviolence worked? Or was it the violence that had finally moved the whites? That was a central argument in the 1957 seminar in Montgomery. "Nonviolence doesn't always work," an older Negro said. "There's nothing people dislike more than other people doing good against them." A minister replied that it shouldn't be disheartening that whites were upset: "We've put them on the moral spot, we've disturbed their consciences. No one likes that."

Afterwards, the organizer of the Institute, the debonair Reverend Mose Pleasure, Jr., said to me that he had been reading about Gandhi but hoped we wouldn't carry him too far. "Those fasts and that vow of celibacy are downright un-American," Reverend Pleasure said, knocking the ashes of his cigar. "I'm working for civil rights so we can enjoy the good things of life, not renounce them." As we were walking out of the church, an old woman thanked me for the seminar and added, "Gandhi's all right, but we get this straight from Jesus Christ."

Before the final session of that 1957 Institute I called my two closest white friends from years past. "Things have changed," said a warmhearted white woman who still lived on a farm outside Selma. "We used to think nothing could change Alice," she reported, referring to their family servant, an uneducated Negro who before had been Exhibit Number One of the Negro's incapacity for anything different. "Then some mornings Alice would come in sullen and wouldn't talk. We'd know that an NAACP had talked to her the night before." Finally Alice had departed for Detroit, to join her children.

Despite my ties to King, that friend still hoped I would come by for a visit. But my other good friend from another farm near Selma had since moved to Montgomery and refused to see me while I was having anything to do with Martin Luther King. "Things are serious now, son," she said grimly. "There's no playing around with this problem any more, you have to be on their side or ours. This is dynamite, man."

Six years before, she had delighted in Rammanohar Lohia's talk of Gandhi, and nothing ever seemed to daunt her sense of humor. Now she was in dead earnest: "King's no Gandhi. He's nothing but a demagogue and a hypocrite, stirring up trouble for his own profit."

That was what a lot of Englishmen in India had said to me about Gandhi, I replied.

"Oh, you don't know King like we do," she said.

"Have you ever heard him talk?" I asked.

"No, but we know him down here, we know all about him. There's just no Christianity in him."

That night King gave the closing sermon at the Institute. A large, enraptured woman in the pew next to me whispered, "When I hear Dr. King, I see angels' wings flying around his head."

"There are three ways by which an oppressed people can respond to injustice," King said. "One is by acquiescence, but that involves acceptance of evil. Another is by violence, but as Christians we should not obey the old law of an eye for an eye. The way we must rise up is through nonviolence.

"To our white brothers, we say, 'In winning the victory we will not only win freedom for ourselves, but we will so appeal to your heart and conscience that you will be changed also.' The victory will be a double victory."

In winning their nonviolent victory in Montgomery, King and his colleagues served notice on the rest of the nation that a new response was required. King said to me that he never felt more a partner in the making of American law than when he was sitting in jail. At the time of his first arrest during the bus boycott, his primary partner in testing and changing segregation laws was the federal judiciary. But soon after the Montgomery boycott, President Eisenhower proposed to Congress a civil rights bill that included the establishment of a Commission on Civil Rights. As King's Southern Christian Leadership Conference confronted massive white resistance with nonviolent action, the leaders of Congress began to respond.

In the appendix I tell the story of how the Senate Majority Leader, Lyndon Johnson, in 1957 brought about the enactment of the first Civil Rights Act since Reconstruction, and how the Commission on Civil Rights set up under that act thereafter became, unexpectedly, the chief partner of Martin Luther King and the civil rights movement. On the Commission staff in the first years of its work, as counsel to Father Theodore Hesburgh, a key member of the commission, I saw the six commissioners—three conservative Southern white lawyers, and three Northerners, including a black lawyer and a priest—struggle with their consciences, like the nation in microcosm. By a combination of deliberation and accident, with men responding to facts and doing their duty, the commission developed into an extraordinary catalyst for further presidential and congressional action in the sixties. Its hearings in the Deep South and around the country and the findings and recommendations in its reports played a major part in molding public sentiment. If the law needed King's help and that of black citizens claiming their rights, they and the President and Congress needed the Commission on Civil Rights as an official goad and guide.

Expressing amazement that three Southerners and three Northerners had been able to reach so much agreement on the facts and on recommendations concerning the state of civil rights in 1959, Eisenhower said that the commission "holds up before us a mirror so that we may see ourselves, what we are doing and what we are not doing, and therefore makes it easier for us to correct our omissions." King and his colleagues in nonviolent action had been holding up a similar mirror, and the nation was beginning to see.

5 · Kennedy Action and Inaction: "One Stroke of the Pen"?

When President Kennedy met with members of the Civil Rights Commission, two weeks after the inauguration, he assured them he would issue the Executive Order Against Discrimination in Federally Assisted Housing they had recommended in 1959. He also said he would see to it that the Executive Branch did everything in its power to achieve equal access to voting, employment, education, and public accommodations. Taking seriously Kennedy's campaign words that "the challenging, revolutionary sixties . . . demand that the President place himself in the very thick of the fight," the commissioners had rolled into one ball a number of their past proposals and urged him to begin his administration with one inclusive proclamation on equal opportunity in all federal programs and all parts of American public life—a second Emancipation Proclamation at the end of the Negro's first century of freedom.

"When our next President takes office in January, he must be prepared to move forward in the field of human rights in three general areas: as a legislative leader, as Chief Executive, and as the center of the moral power of the United States." That was John Kennedy's campaign promise in September 1960. Did he fulfill that promise? Critics charge betrayal, and attribute lives lost, the rise of black separatism, and much of the anger and subsequent cynicism of the late sixties to non-performance of the promise.

For nearly five hundred of Kennedy's thousand days in office I was his adviser on civil rights and coordinator of federal policies in that field, and thereafter I followed events carefully, though from afar in Africa. There were high points and low points, the lowest of which, for me, were the occasions when the President delayed signing the order against discrimination in housing. As pens marked "one stroke of the pen" poured into the White House mail room in a campaign to remind him of his promise, Kennedy said, "Send them to Wofford!"

What disappointed me most was not so much the President's recurring decision to wait, for which he had reasons I understood, as the way he made the decision—each time hurriedly, at the last minute, in response to Southern political pressures without careful consideration of an overall strategy. The worst point in the process came during a hastily convened session of representatives of the departments and agencies involved. The

President turned to a spokesman for the Attorney General who was not from the Civil Rights Division, and asked, "What does Justice say?" I hoped to hear some wisdom from one of the nation's leading attorneys. Instead this high official answered: "You tell me how you want it to come out, boss, and I'll tell you what the law is."

Then there was Kennedy's call to me during the Freedom Rides when he said, without any of his customary humor, "Stop them! Get your friends off those buses!" He felt that Martin Luther King, James Farmer, Bill Coffin, and company were embarrassing him and the country on the eve of the meeting in Vienna with Khrushchev. He supported every American's right to stand up or sit down for his rights—but not to ride for them in the spring of 1961.

The highest point for me came in a personal encounter when the President said, very seriously, with uncharacteristic gentleness and warmth, as I left for a new assignment in Africa in August 1962, "It will take some more time, but I want you to know that we are going to do all these things." He was referring to a list I had prepared of difficult civil rights actions awaiting his decision, including the still postponed housing order. As we parted he smiled reassuringly and repeated, "You will see, with time I'm going to do them all." He did not have much time.

One of the most instructive moments, which vividly conveyed the President's relative isolation, came during the Freedom Rides. Members of the Peace Corps' National Advisory Council were waiting for the President in the Cabinet room. A number of them, especially Harry Belafonte, Eugene Rostow, Benjamin Mays, and the first Peace Corps General Counsel, Morris Abram, were vigorously critical of the President for not speaking out in moral terms in support of the black and white riders who had been brutally attacked in Alabama. When they kept telling me what to tell Kennedy, I said they would be talking to him face to face and should tell him themselves, straight. "Don't think you've done anything by pressing me," I warned. "He knows what I think and has my draft of what he should say on his desk. Put it to him strongly yourselves if you want to get it across."

The President entered, mingled informally with the group of about twenty, sat down and talked about the Peace Corps, answered questions, and then lingered for a few minutes of conversation. No one brought up the Freedom Riders. As he turned to leave, I decided to smoke out my colleagues before they lost their chance.

"Mr. President, Harry and Gene and Dr. Mays have been telling me what they feel about the Freedom Rides. Would you have a minute?"

Kennedy wheeled around and said, "Sure." In the initial silence some of the most articulate men in America were tongue-tied. Then Harry Belafonte, in very low key, in his quiet, hoarse voice, said, "Mr. President, I know how much you're doing in civil rights. I deeply respect your leadership in civil rights. I trust you in civil rights. And I know all these other things are going on. But perhaps you could say something a little more about the Freedom Riders." Someone else took time to pay another tribute to the President, then Rostow, dean of Yale Law School, spoke more crisply, though also very respectfully, about the need for moral leadership on the substantive issue of equal access to public facilities.

Kennedy asked if they had seen his statement in the morning papers. To my surprise, they hadn't; he said he thought it would satisfy them. They thanked him profusely and left. When they read his statement, they were still dissatisfied—it was limited to a plea for law and order.

As we walked toward the White House gate, it was my turn to berate them for not making their points more strongly. I knew why they had been so mild; the sense of respect for the presidency had often, in Kennedy's presence, come over (or overcome) me. A guard came running up to summon me to the President's office.

"Who the hell was that man with Harry Belafonte?" Kennedy asked. When I said it was Gene Rostow, the law dean brother of his foreign policy adviser, Walt, he asked, "Well, what in the world does he think I should do? Doesn't he know I've done more for civil rights than any President in American history? How could any man have done more than I've done?" He went on in irritation, and then sat down and more calmly discussed what he would say in a further stronger statement.

Perhaps they had conveyed their feelings more effectively than I thought. A photograph of the encounter with Kennedy shows Benjamin Mays scowling at the President and Harry Belafonte looking angry, so their looks may have said more than their words. But what struck me was how little direct heat he must get to have reacted so keenly—how sensitive he was to criticism about his moral leadership. As I saw how stung he had been by a few restrained remarks, I realized how seldom even such an open, candid, and informal President received critical comments straight.

One of the funny moments in my White House career involved our high-level effort to integrate restaurants along Route 40 in Maryland and Delaware. When the ambassador from the newly independent African republic of Chad presented his credentials in the first days of the administration, he told the President (according to the translator, Pedro Sanjuan), "I was thrown on my rear end as a result of entering the Bonnie Brae restaurant over on Route 40." Kennedy asked Sanjuan to see that something was done to stop such incidents. With sixteen African countries having just received their independence, scores of black diplomats and their families would be facing similar indignities. As head of the African Subcommittee of the Senate Foreign Relations Committee, Kennedy had been aware of a number of earlier affronts based on color.

To deal with the situation, the State Department was persuaded to set up a special section, under Sanjuan (who had been a key organizer of Kennedy's presidential campaign among Hispanic Americans and was the new Assistant Chief of Protocol). Project number one was ending discrimination in eating places on the southern half of the road between New York and Washington. It was an extraordinary operation, unlike anything the Protocol Office had ever before undertaken, but Angier Biddle Duke, the new Chief of Protocol, rose to the occasion, as did the Secretary of State. Dean Rusk stressed that the only way to stop insults to foreign diplomats who were colored was to stop discrimination against all persons of color, for "we cannot solve this problem if it involves a diplomatic passport to claim the moral rights of American citizens."

At Sanjuan's energetic initiative, I would send—and sometimes go and personally read—strong messages from the President to various meetings with Maryland restaurant owners. Since the messages were clearly in line with Kennedy's policy, I never checked them with him. Within nine months, thirty-five out of the seventy main roadside establishments had voluntarily desegregated, and a state law was about to be enacted. Then to our dismay, another African ambassador was refused service—even a glass of water—and the incident made headlines in the morning papers in Washington and around the world.

Angier Biddle Duke called to tell me about a disconcerting phone conversation he had just had with the President. Kennedy had reached him very early that morning, obviously upset about the incident. "Can't you tell them not to do it?" the President had asked. When Duke, with considerable pride, started to describe how much progress had been made in integrating Route 40, and how many speeches he and Sanjuan had made in Maryland, Kennedy interrupted to say, "That's not what I'm calling about. Can't you tell these African ambassadors not to drive on Route 40? It's a hell of a road—I used to drive it years ago, but why would anyone want to drive it today when you can fly? Tell these ambassadors I wouldn't think of driving from New York to Washington. Tell them to fly!"

Kennedy hung up, leaving his Chief of Protocol in doubt about the

President's commitment to the campaign we were so diligently waging in his name all up and down Route 40. "Are you sure the President is fully behind our efforts?" asked Duke.

One of the last encounters I had with both Kennedy and Martin Luther King had left me, too, with similar questions about the President. It was during one of the recurring crises of civil rights, when King was in trouble and wanted greater presidential intervention, in Georgia and on all civil rights fronts. Kennedy asked me to bring King up to his residential quarters, so we went over to the tiny elevator in the center of the White House; instead of going up, it went down to the basement, and Jacqueline Kennedy entered. She had soot on her face and was dressed in jeans. When I introduced them, she said, in her unusual voice, "Oh, Dr. King, you would be so thrilled if you could just have been with me in the basement this morning. I found a chair right out of the Andrew Jackson period—a beautiful chair." King replied in his benign, slow way, "Yes—yes—is that so?"

At the top, Jacqueline Kennedy said, "I've just got to tell Jack about that chair." Then on second thought she excused herself, saying, "But you have other things to talk to him about, don't you?"

When she left, King said, "Well, well—wasn't that something!"

At first I had been amused by her choice of small talk, when King obviously had so much else on his mind. Yet after the elevator ride, he was more relaxed, so she may have contributed to one of his most successful talks with Kennedy. Unlike the President's relations with Whitney Young and Roy Wilkins, which were easy and sophisticated, there was always a strain in his dealing with King, who came on with a moral tone that was not Kennedy's style and made him uncomfortable.

This time, in his study next to the Lincoln bedroom, Kennedy was at his best; so was King. The President candidly explained how he felt limited by the federal system in what he could do to protect civil rights workers in the South and why he was postponing the Executive Order on housing and efforts to get new legislation—what the bills were that he wanted to get through Congress first, the number of Southern senators and representatives he needed to overcome the conservative-Southern-Republican coalition, the problems of re-election for certain Southern moderates, and so forth, in remarkable detail. He was equally precise in affirming his intention in due course to do most, if not all, of what King sought.

King came to our home for dinner that night, and we took a walk. After a while he said, somewhat sadly, "In the election, when I gave my testimony for Kennedy, my impression then was that he had the intelligence and the skill and the moral fervor to give the leadership we've been waiting for and do what no other President has ever done. Now, I'm convinced that he has the understanding and the political skill but so far I'm afraid that the moral passion is missing."

Memory dims his exact words, but those were about the terms in which he gave me his interim judgment that Kennedy grasped the problem and analyzed the politics well but lacked the necessary moral thrust. He put it as a question and asked what I thought about Kennedy's convictions and commitment.

Leaving aside ambition to be elected and re-elected, which Kennedy presumably associated with the common good, no one who worked with him could doubt his determination to bring the maximum intelligence to bear on all the issues vexing the country. But he made it difficult for anyone to be sure of the depth of his understanding or the extent of his vision. About the most important things, he was a man of few words— even with those closest to him.

Looking back on his own and his brother's approach to the status of the Negro, Robert Kennedy in 1964 conceded that before 1960 "we didn't lie awake nights worrying about it." After the administration began, he says, they still didn't talk much about civil rights, except for saying—when faced with cases of white segregationist obstruction— "Aren't they bastards!" According to Robert Kennedy, when they were dealing with some outrageous racial situation, the President would not show emotion but his attitude would be: "It was just silly and it didn't make any sense and it wasn't helping the country, so why don't you do something about it?"

In *A Thousand Days*, Arthur Schlesinger says that Kennedy began his presidency with a "terrible ambivalence about civil rights" but that "ever since he became President" he "had prepared the ground" for the strong position he finally took. "He had quietly created an atmosphere where change, when it came, would seem no longer an upheaval but the inexorable unfolding of the promise of American life." In *Kennedy*, Theodore Sorensen contends that he was the first President with convictions on equal rights, and the one "who finally brought" the issue "to the attention of the nation." Through "a long and difficult Presidential journey," Kennedy is said to have moved from being a senator who was "mildly and quietly in favor of civil rights legislation as a political necessity consistent with his moral instincts," to becoming a President who "was deeply and fervently committed to the cause of human rights as a moral necessity inconsistent with his political instincts."

Such claims infuriate the critics who blame Kennedy for arousing false expectations by his campaign oratory and personal charm, then as

President for failing to speak up or take action until forced to do so, for delaying major intervention until civil rights workers had been killed, and for trying to control and divert and finally to claim the civil rights movement. "Faced with a social movement and a moral crisis that transcended the ordinary boundaries of American politics," Kennedy is seen by one angry writer as a pragmatist without moral convictions who continued "to play politics as usual" and failed in his "responsibility to educate" until seven-eighths of his time in office had passed.*

From the following firsthand account of a substantial part of Kennedy's difficult presidential journey in civil rights, grist can be found for the mills of both these contending positions. Instead I hope there emerges a more accurate, if more complicated, judgment—not a compromise between extremes, but a significantly different conclusion about Kennedy's character and approach, and about the political process.

One of the many things about Kennedy and civil rights I will never know for sure is whether my White House assignment resulted from his meeting with the Civil Rights Commissioners on February 7, 1961, or was already set in his mind and just not conveyed to me during his first two weeks in office.

Between the election and the inauguration, Kennedy gave only passing attention to civil rights. That subject was conspicuous by its absence from the list of planning task forces announced by the President-elect. In December he sent word to me to delay further the publication of the far-reaching recommendation of the October Conference on Constitutional Rights. However, he asked me to prepare for him a confidential memorandum with suggestions for civil rights strategy in 1961. I submitted a thirty-page memorandum but heard nothing from him, except in reference to talent search matters, until after he met with the Civil Rights Commission in February.

Before seeing the President, commission chairman John Hannah and Father Hesburgh discussed with me the points they were going to make. Last on their agenda was to stress that a President needs a key staff aide for civil rights. They had sorely felt the lack of anyone around Eisenhower with sustained interest and authority in the field. They hoped I would fill that role.

After explaining that I had just agreed with Sargent Shriver to stay

---

* Bruce Miroff, *Pragmatic Illusions: The Presidential Politics of John F. Kennedy* (New York: David McKay Company, 1976), p. 224. A more affirmative balance was struck in a detailed, critical appraisal by Carl Brauer: *John F. Kennedy and the Second Reconstruction* (New York: Columbia University Press, 1977).

with him in organizing the Peace Corps, I told Hannah and Father Hesburgh that in my memorandum to the President I had recommended Louis Martin for the White House staff "since the Negro community is a particularly complex, isolated and politically important one, and since a sensitive Negro is able to hear and sense the mood of his community better than a white man." The October Conference had urged the appointment of a White House coordinator for all pertinent federal policy, but appreciating the power and special position of Robert Kennedy and the ability of Assistant Attorney General Burke Marshall, I had suggested to the President that the Justice Department could well be the best center for overall civil rights coordination. Hannah and Father Hesburgh said that the White House made more sense to them, and went off to see the President.

An hour or so later, Hannah called. "Either the President was putting us on, or you are—or there is a failure of communication," he said. "Kennedy seemed to agree with most of our recommendations but when we came to the point about a White House assistant on civil rights, he looked us in the eye and said, 'I already have a special assistant who is working full-time on that—Harris Wofford.' We told him that when we last saw you, you were getting established in an office at the Peace Corps. He said, 'That's only temporary.' "

There was barely time to consult my wife by telephone before Ralph Dungan called from the White House to say the President wanted to see me right away. Two or three times in the seventeen days since the inauguration, the President's secretary, Evelyn Lincoln, had telephoned to say they were running behind schedule and the President wondered whether I could come over to entertain some waiting group or person connected with civil rights. I wondered whether he had really wondered or she had turned to me on her own, but in a large venture when you wonder what the chief executive is thinking about you, the best guess is that he isn't. So I would hurry over and talk with Roy Wilkins or whoever was there until the President was ready. Kennedy would nod to me warmly when I took the visitor into his office, then I would return to the rump encampment, still without furniture, a block away, where the Peace Corps was being planned.

This time I was the one kept waiting in the outer office. My old friend Thomas Hughes, then still the chief assistant to Undersecretary of State Chester Bowles, happened also to be waiting. Hearing the Hannah story, Hughes relished the President's—and my—predicament. Just when I finished giving Hughes the case for sticking with the Peace Corps—an embodiment of ideas he, Bowles, and I had long shared—a solemn-looking man in a dark suit, carrying a book, interrupted us.

"Are you Mr. Wofford? Please raise your right hand and repeat after me."

"What for?" I asked.

"I'm supposed to swear you in," he said.

"But I don't know what the job is, and I haven't talked to the President yet," I said.

"That's not my problem," he said. "I don't know about you, but I take my orders from the President, and I was asked to come up and swear you in immediately. So here's the Bible—please raise your right hand and repeat the oath of office."

"Do you know what the office is?" I asked.

"That doesn't matter," he said. "The President knows. All you do now is swear to uphold the Constitution. Is there anything wrong with that? Please do as the President requests and raise your right hand and repeat after me . . ."

It was the simplest and shortest of all the swearing-in ceremonies that Tom Hughes—or I—ever attended. Then the door opened to the Oval Office, and the President waved for me to come in.

The President was standing by the large floor windows, scanning a memorandum in his hand; his figure made a striking silhouette. On entering, one knew that this was the political center of the nation. The quiet of the place suggests that the President—and for a brief moment, his visitor —may be in the eye of a storm.

It is a common experience for a sense of respect, if not awe, to fill a visitor in the Oval Office. The brace Kennedy wore for his back and the pain he bore from his war injury somehow made the burden he was carrying seem heavier, and the grace with which he carried it greater.

The very elliptical shape of the room itself might make a mathematical imagination see an analogy to the office of the President in our constitutional system: an ellipse is a plane curve such that the sums of the distances of each point in its periphery from two fixed focal points are equal. Coming into the Oval Office with a focus on civil rights, I recognized how many pressing problems were on the President's periphery, and how difficult it must be to deal with them all equitably, if not always equally or equably.

"What's this about your going to the Peace Corps?" he asked. "Sarge can't have everyone. I need you here to get this civil rights work on the tracks at the White House. We've got to do these things we promised we were going to do. You ought to have the best office that's left. I'll back you up."

That was the way he talked. In his crisp, wry style, thoughtfully, but not wasting time—he spoke elliptically long before occupying the Oval Office—he said he had appreciated and was in general agreement with my December civil rights memorandum, which he waved in his hand. He wanted me on his staff to help him carry through the proposed course of executive action, and coordinate federal policy along the lines of my memorandum. I would report directly to him.

As for the suggestion of appointing Louis Martin, he considered him a very fine fellow but needed him as a key man at the Democratic National Committee; we could call on him informally as much as we wished. He was happy to hear that Assistant Attorney General Marshall was someone I respected. He would go along with the Civil Rights Commission's and my recommendation, and nominate for commission staff director Berl Bernhard (another outstanding attorney, whom I had helped bring on the commission's legal staff in 1958). So we should all be able to work together and get things done in a careful and effective way, without too much fanfare. The President added that I should call on him when needed—"just get on the telephone"—but otherwise go ahead and do what seemed necessary and appropriate.

When I reminded him that he had first enlisted me to work on Asian and African matters, and explained that the Peace Corps was an idea that had been close to my heart for ten years, he said that Shriver could have part of my time. He would leave the division of time to my judgment, so long as I kept my civil rights constituents happy. To my prediction that federal civil rights policy would be centered on Robert Kennedy and the Justice Department, he said the White House could not escape its responsibility.*

Kennedy did not then, or ever, take the time to talk through the issues, or to look ahead and set long-term priorities. He certainly wanted to do enough so that the civil rights constituency was not too unhappy, and beyond that he wanted to make substantial headway against what he considered the nonsense of racial discrimination. Before the President was called away to a meeting on an urgent foreign policy issue, he did emphasize that the strategy for 1961 would be "minimum civil rights legislation, maximum executive action." He said we would meet again soon; meanwhile I should work with Sorensen's office and the Justice Department on the appropriate executive orders, and do whatever else made sense. "You're the expert," he said with a grin. "Get going."

---

* Unknown to me, Byron White had been urging that the White House be the coordinator of overall federal action on civil rights, so that the Department of Justice could remain an objective enforcer of the laws. However, Robert Kennedy, according to Burke Marshall's oral history interview, did not favor such direct White House involvement and thought that Justice's Civil Rights Division was the appropriate agency.

When Kennedy had gone, I told Kenny O'Donnell that the President was now an honest man in saying he had a Special Assistant for Civil Rights. O'Donnell explained that there was no line of command and there would be no staff meetings. All the Special Assistants or other top staff men (fifteen or twenty altogether) were spokes on a wheel. At the hub was Kennedy.

Once a week the key administration men on civil rights met in my office to share information and discuss strategy: Burke Marshall from Justice; Berl Bernhard from the Civil Rights Commission; Louis Martin from the Democratic National Committee; John Feild, who had become the director of the President's Committee on Equal Employment Opportunity; and others from time to time. To assist with the fact-finding necessary for overall coordination of federal policy, William Taylor, an imaginative and persistent attorney on the Civil Rights Commission's legal staff, was informally assigned to my office.

In our first meeting it was encouraging to hear from Marshall how Robert Kennedy was responding to the immediate test facing him on school desegregation in New Orleans. In December I had reported to him and the President that "supporters of the school system there say that Presidential support of the school board is desperately needed. They want both eloquent and symbolic public support and strong behind-the-scenes efforts to persuade the Governor and Senators to let that token desegregation take place." Coming into office, the Attorney General found that Louisiana officials were withholding state funds from the recently desegregated schools. Before the election, Judge Skelly Wright had requested federal marshals to enforce his desegregation order; Eisenhower's Department of Justice had denied the request and asked for a delay until after the election. Judge Wright had complied, and then still found the Justice Department standing by while screaming mobs closed down two of the three affected schools.

After careful deliberation with Burke Marshall (but without consulting the President), Robert Kennedy made the basic decision that henceforth the department should accept full responsibility for enforcement of school desegregation orders. Marshall told us that after reviewing the confidential files on past experience in school cases, he had concluded that "some, if not all, of the violence and law enforcement problems were caused—or at least were not averted—by reason of a failure of the Justice Department to recognize explicitly and give effect to this responsibility."

"We'll have to do whatever is necessary," Robert Kennedy had said, and then he telephoned state officials to warn that if they continued to refuse to pay teachers' salaries, he would ask the court to hold them in contempt and to put the state Superintendent of Education in jail. Marshall started court proceedings and the state yielded. After working with Robert Kennedy under the pressures of the New Orleans case, Marshall told us he had no doubt about the Attorney General's readiness to do his duty in civil rights, no matter how painful politically.

The President was also prepared to add his public support. He paid tribute to the principals, officers of school boards, and teachers who were making peaceful integration possible in New Orleans and elsewhere. "This is no time for schools to close for any reason, and certainly no time for schools to be closed in the name of racial discrimination," the President said in a message that I did clear with him. Referring to the schoolchildren and parents of both races, "who have been on the front lines of the problem," Kennedy said that, "in accepting the command of the Constitution with dignity, they, too, are contributing to the education of all Americans."

Kennedy made several strong statements on school desegregation during 1961—the first such presidential endorsements. When he heard that Prince Edward County, Virginia, had closed its public schools to avoid integration, he shook his head with incredulity. He strongly backed the initiative by the Attorney General and Marshall to make the federal government an active party in a suit to reopen the schools, and also their efforts to provide interim classes for Negro children until the lawsuit was successful. In another precedent-setting case, the Justice Department brought a suit to extend desegregation to a new parish in Louisiana, when that district assisted another parish's plan to evade integration.

Behind the scenes, the Attorney General's chief Southern aides, John Seigenthaler of Tennessee, Ramsey Clark of Texas, and Louis Oberdorfer of Alabama, met with Southern officials and community leaders to lay the groundwork for first-step desegregation in Atlanta, Dallas, and Memphis that fall. "I'd go in, my Southern accent dripping sorghum and molasses, and warm them up," Seigenthaler recounted. Then Marshall would tell them what the law was. We all drew on our contacts in the critical cities.

On the front of voting rights, it was no surprise that the Civil Rights Division at Justice promptly expanded and intensified investigations (under way soon in sixty counties) and in some of the most deeply resistant areas suits were brought to require the registration of blacks. When the Attorney General had taken Marshall in to see Senator Eastland, he had joked that this was the man who would integrate Mississippi; within a few months four voting rights suits were begun in Mississippi, the first in the history of that state.

In one of our early White House sessions on civil rights, Marshall reported that success in litigation was not enough in Haywood and Fayette counties, Tennessee. In these Negro-majority districts, the right of Negroes to register was finally being won (in 1959 not one black had been on the rolls in Haywood County), but in retaliation those who registered were being evicted from their tenant farms. Leaders of the registration drive were being denied credit by local banks and merchants, their insurance policies were canceled, and they lost their jobs. The Justice Department had secured an injunction against such intimidation, but many of the poorer victims were living in a Tent City and lacked adequate food. We decided to enlist the help of the Departments of Agriculture, HEW, Commerce, and Labor. The Agriculture Department, with its network of white Southern extension agents and its dependence on congressional appropriations, preferred to get a presidential order rather than act on its own. So we arranged for the President to write to the department, and before long surplus food was being provided directly to some 14,000 people in those two counties.

Since Kennedy has been blamed by so many critics for not seeking legislation during his first year, and in some writings I have been exonerated as a civil rights activist who was outflanked and overruled, the record should be set straight. The 1961 strategy of "minimum legislation, maximum executive action" made sense because of the 1960 election returns. The Democrats had lost twenty-one seats in the House of Representatives and two in the Senate; on most controversial social and economic issues, the Republican-conservative Southern Democratic coalition could probably muster a majority in the House, and successfully invoke a filibuster in the Senate. The strategy for 1961 that I proposed to Kennedy did not call for new civil rights legislation, other than an extension of the Civil Rights Commission, passage of an anti-poll tax constitutional amendment (already supported by two-thirds of the senators), and, most important, a change in the Senate rules on cloture. Though the platform had proposed action to end literacy tests, I thought that before plunging into a major battle for a new voting rights bill, there was every reason to test and use to the full the powers given by Congress in 1957 and 1960. "If after a year of bringing many varied voting suits throughout the black belt no real breakthrough on Negro voting has occurred, then it would be the time to go to Congress to ask for legislation," I had written the President in December.

That December memorandum was my semi-mandate from the President, and the initial touchstone for our ad hoc White House coordinating committee. "If the full power of the Federal Government can be brought to bear on this problem with intelligence and consistency, the racial bottleneck in our national life can be broken in one decade," the memorandum had stated as an overall objective. For the coming four years, it outlined a set of regional goals:

The Deep South. The barriers to Negro voting should be broken everywhere, so that at least another million Negroes are registered. . . . This requires action in some 100 rural counties which are the stronghold of disfranchisement.

Footholds of token school desegregation should be established in each Deep Southern state so that the solid front of massive resistance is broken. This should include the admission of Negroes to institutions of higher education in each state.

Steps should be taken toward employment and upgrading of Negroes in the Federal Service, on Federal Government contracts and on Federal grant-in-aid projects.

The Upper South, Southwest, and Border States. Here, as in most large cities in all parts of the South, the right to vote is practically established and the few remaining pockets of voting discrimination can be eliminated. School desegregation must be extended throughout whole school systems and the present spots of token desegregation steadily converted into full-scale desegregation.

Equality of job opportunity must be vigorously promoted on all government contracts and grant-in-aid projects, and throughout the Federal Service in the region. Probably only token progress can be made toward integration in federal housing programs in this region.

The rest of the country. Here the main thrust must be toward equality of job opportunity and integrated housing. This alone can overcome the growing *de facto* school segregation. The Northern vicious circle of Negro slums taking over the central cities, with white suburban nooses tightening around an expanding, demoralized Negro population, is as explosive as any Southern school crisis. The present rising tensions can lead to serious race riots. Vigorous and effective enforcement of provisions against discrimination in government employment or government contract employment and in federally assisted housing is possible here and necessary.

Thus each region could be prodded to advance a stage during Kennedy's first term, and the pressure would be national, not focused on the South alone. The approach was designed to build the precarious coalition between Northern Democrats and moderate Southern Democrats that Kennedy needed to get programs through Congress and to be re-elected. Increasing the Negro vote in the South would strengthen the hand of white moderates, whose congressional support was essential for the passage of the social or economic measures necessary to overcome the legacy of poverty into which a large proportion of Negroes had been born. Seeking enactment of new programs in employment, education, housing, and health and at the same time strong executive action against racial discrimination, would require "artful balancing," but could succeed, I had suggested, "if pursued with the combined consummate political skills of the next President and Vice-President." Victory in 1960 had required both Kennedy's civil rights campaign and Lyndon Johnson's presence on the ticket. This winning combination needed to be continued.

"Your strong civil rights stand and . . . the nomination of LBJ," I had written Kennedy, "administered a mild and useful shock treatment to white Southerners, Northern liberals, and Negroes. If you had retreated from either your civil rights stand or your choice of LBJ, the contradictions could have blown up your campaign." Johnson's nomination and the call to Mrs. King were examples of the kind of symbolic actions needed "to shock and reshape the thought patterns and the political patterns of this problem."

In contrast to those advising Kennedy to divert Johnson from the field of civil rights, and not appoint him to head the proposed Presidential Committee on Equal Employment Opportunity (a strengthened successor to the Committee on Government Contracts that Vice-President Nixon had chaired), I urged that the new Vice-President be seen "as an essential ingredient, a major creative factor," and argued that "the more of the load of civil rights that Johnson will carry, the better."

Much of the strategy suggested in the memorandum could be accomplished, or at least begun, by presidential leadership, without new legislation. Since the votes to break a Senate filibuster against any major civil rights bill were not there, an unsuccessful attempt to do so would endanger all the rest of the administration's program, including measures of great importance to most blacks. It would demonstrate the President's weakness at a time when he needed to build strength.

Civil rights groups that had operated so long in the absence of presidential action would initially greet such a decision against early legislative efforts as a sellout, I predicted to Kennedy. But "*if* you go ahead with a substantial executive action program," then "after they have tasted the fruits of executive action, they will know the barrenness of their legislative lobbying, and see that the logic of such executive action will lead to complementary legislation—and lead there sooner than a party-splitting legislative battle at the beginning of your administration." The memorandum warned Kennedy, however, that the executive action would have to be bold and prompt, for "no one can predict when the Negro cup of bitterness and skepticism is going to overflow."

Even before the inauguration, a test was facing Kennedy during the opening days of Congress in early February. The Democratic platform had called for a change in the Senate rules to enable a majority, instead of two-thirds, of the senators to end a filibuster. Civil rights forces were far short of the votes for majority cloture, but a 60 percent cloture rule seemed attainable—if Kennedy took steps to secure the missing three votes. Such a three-fifths rule for limiting debate would lay the groundwork for future civil rights legislation. In my memorandum I had listed ten Democratic senators open to presidential persuasion. "A call from you or Johnson could swing more than three of these," I had written. I argued that "if there is to be no civil rights legislation this session, some such civil rights victory is wanted. You or Johnson need only give the signal."

The opposite signal was given. There was no presidential pressure whatsoever to secure the extra votes for a change in the Senate rules. Kennedy did not want to risk a break with the Southern leaders who controlled a number of key Senate committees. Instead he supported an effort to change the composition of the powerful House Rules Committee, which was important to the prospects for his whole legislative program, but had less bearing on civil rights.

Kennedy's assessment may have been right, but it seemed to me that he was unduly inhibited in dealing with the Senate, perhaps because he had never mastered its inner politics while a senator. You worry most about what you know best, an old hand in Washington, Averell Harriman, had noted. As the former Ambassador to Moscow, Harriman worried most about how to deal with the Russians; I was concerned most about the civil rights leadership and the Negroes who had voted for Kennedy; the President feared the power of the senatorial club he knew well but in which he had always been something of a junior member.

In private talks with a number of civil rights leaders during these first months in office, Kennedy defended his position with relative success. Before seeing King or Roy Wilkins, or delegations such as the Civil Rights Commission, he would call me in to learn what was on their agendas and discuss what he should say. Such preliminary briefings became the main occasions for discussing civil rights. Unless I thought someone would greatly appreciate seeing the President alone, I would stay through the meeting, and sometimes talk with the President for a few minutes afterwards. He invited frank exchanges but his candid account of facts as he saw them often left visitors so impressed, sometimes so dazzled, that they had little to say.

"If we go into a long fight in Congress it will bottleneck everything else and still get no bill," Kennedy told King. The President assured civil rights leaders that the steps he and the Attorney General intended to take would do far more good than any currently possible legislation, and he invited their collaboration.

Top Negro leaders were privately persuaded to go along with the new course, although they were not prepared to speak up as its proponents. However, there was a letdown in the civil rights movement generally. Clarence Mitchell, the outspoken Washington representative of the NAACP, and long-time Kennedy critic, charged that the New Frontier looked "suspiciously like a dude ranch with Senator James O. Eastland as the general manager." It seemed time to make a public case for the new approach. In a speech to a large conference of civil rights activists in March 1961, I suggested that we had all learned too well the habits of opposition, and urged that we be "on guard to avoid a tendency to prefer a long, loud fight for a congressional civil rights bill rather than to win a quiet, steady campaign for effective executive action."

This course had plenty of built-in contradictions. The need for enactment of vital economic measures might have to be weighed against proposed executive actions to advance civil rights. The weighing process, I recognized, would sometimes be painful.

The immediate pain I had in mind was a delay in the Executive Order against discrimination in housing. "By one stroke of the pen," Kennedy had said, that order could, should, and would be signed. I had urged him to do it in the first days of the new administration, but congressional leaders advised that doing so would jeopardize the nomination of Robert Weaver as head of the Housing and Home Finance Agency. Weaver was Kennedy's top black appointment to date, so a temporary delay was agreed to. Then, after Weaver's nomination, there was the matter of the housing bill itself, which required Southern support for passage. On the ground that the bill was of vital importance to low-income Negroes, among others, a further delay was decided upon. With each delay, the pressures against its issuance increased and the order became more controversial. One of the obstacles in the course of executive action is that the same forces determined to block legislation will also use all their congressional leverage to prevent a presidential action they dislike.

Meanwhile, civil rights organizations began to accept the new challenge. Assuming that the housing order would soon be signed, they started calling for other actions. The NAACP and the Southern Christian Leadership Conference both submitted long detailed proposals; the

Southern Regional Council, headed by Harold Fleming, prepared an excellent study, "The Federal Executive and Civil Rights." Delegations started visiting federal departments and agencies. During this period the President seemed pleased by his artful balancing and confident that he could stay ahead of the pressures.

On fronts other than Congress and housing, the first hundred days were full of action for equal rights. At his first Cabinet meeting, Kennedy discussed his impromptu Inaugural Day order for the integration of the Coast Guard; he asked each Cabinet member to examine the situation and take affirmative action to recruit Negroes. Undersecretary of State Chester Bowles soon reported that there were only 15 Negroes out of 3,674 Foreign Service officers. Robert Kennedy found only 10 out of the more than 950 attorneys in the Justice Department in Washington, and 9 out of 742 lawyers in the U.S. Attorneys' offices around the country (though all 56 department messengers were black). While blacks comprised about 13 percent of the more than 2 million federal employees, we knew there were relatively few in the upper grades paying from $9,000 to $18,000 a year. The written reports we required showed how few they were: out of 6,900 employees in GS-12 to GS-18 in the Agriculture Department, 15 were blacks; out of 69,955 in Defense, 444. Above GS-12, there were two Negroes in the General Services Administration and five in Treasury. In all the federal Civil Service there was only one Negro in each of the two top ranks.

On March 6, 1961, the President issued Executive Order 10925, establishing the Committee on Equal Employment Opportunity with wide coverage and strong enforcement powers—and with Lyndon Johnson as chairman. It combined two previous ineffective committees, one on employment within the government and one on private employment under government contracts. Affecting more than 20 million workers employed by some 60,000 government contractors, the committee was the nucleus of the FEPC promised in the Democratic platform.

"From this time forward," Kennedy told the committee at its first meeting, "the committee will exercise the great powers given to it by executive order to remove permanently from government employment and work performed for the government every trace of discrimination because of race, creed, color or place of national origin." To my delight, the President accepted in the draft for his remarks, and stated to the committee, the far-reaching principle the Civil Rights Commissioners had urged him to state: "that federal money should not be spent in any way which encourages discrimination, but rather should be spent in such a way that it encourages the national goal of equal opportunity."

On April 1, all government departments and agencies were formally directed to report to the committee plans and recommendations for ending discrimination in employment. For the first time a racial employment census was undertaken in all parts of the government. (This required the overcoming of resistance by civil rights groups who had long sought to prevent bias by prohibiting any racial questions on employment forms.) That same day anti-discrimination directives were issued by the U.S. Employment Service and the Bureau of Apprenticeship and Training. Local employment offices were prohibited from accepting "whites only" job orders, and a long process of persuasion and pressure was begun to open union apprenticeships to blacks. On April 10, the Postmaster General ordered non-discrimination in the construction of postal facilities and in all leased properties. On April 18, a White House memorandum directed all departments to cease sponsoring discriminatory employee associations or recreational activities. This chronology in one area indicates the pace of early executive actions.

Kennedy was particularly pleased with major black appointments, and kept pressing departments for more. In July, Louis Martin released with pride the names of 47 Negroes selected for high-ranking positions. The new chairman of the Civil Service Commission, John Macy, agreed to undertake recruiting of Negroes for all parts of the government, and to work with each department as "positive measures" were initiated to make up for the past discrimination. The President's aim was "to see that employment breakthroughs occur for qualified Negroes in all regions, in all departments and at all levels." Roy Wilkins said that it became a joke around Washington "that Kennedy was so hot on the department heads . . . that everyone was scrambling around trying to find himself a Negro in order to keep the President off his neck." "Hot" may have been too strong a description, but Kennedy clearly thought the appointment of outstanding Negroes would speak louder than words and be good public education in integration with few bad political repercussions.*

The President's warm support of efforts to overcome employment discrimination came to include a program about which Wilkins and other NAACP leaders were dubious. They were looking forward to at least one government contract being canceled with a major employer, and the

---

* Breakthroughs did not come easily. Noticing almost no black employment in federal agencies in Birmingham, Alabama, where a new federal office building was opening, Macy ordered that Civil Service examinations be given at a nearby Southern black college. When no one passed, Macy went himself to administer the test, to ensure impartiality, and still all failed. Inadequate educational background and possible cultural bias in the questions continued to be a major obstacle.

Lockheed Corporation seemed the likely candidate. A complaint was filed showing manifest discrimination in that company's plant at Marietta, Georgia. The Equal Employment Opportunity Committee investigated promptly and, in late May, with the intervention of committee member Robert Troutman of Atlanta, negotiated a settlement that was to set a new pattern. Lockheed agreed to a "Plan for Progress" under which it would recruit, employ, promote, and train minority group members, not only in the Marietta plant but throughout the company's operations.

At a White House signing, the President hailed the agreement as a "milestone in the history of civil rights," and, with Johnson, he supported Bobby Troutman in launching an effort to persuade all major contractors to adopt similar Plans for Progress. The program soon came under fire from civil rights forces and from some members of the committee's staff, including its executive director, John Feild. They wanted early strong enforcement of the executive order rather than mediation.

Bobby Troutman was an ebullient, controversial character who epitomized the ironies in the politics of civil rights. As a Southern campaign operator for Kennedy, he had tried to block proposals of our Civil Rights Section, urging that ties with King be played down. After the election he agreed the call to Mrs. King had been worthwhile and boasted about the Negro and white vote together carrying Georgia by the largest percentage of any state. I was surprised—and, on balance, pleased—that he wanted to serve on the Equal Employment Opportunity Committee. A funny man, full of jokes, Troutman could bluff his way into almost any office. Evelyn Lincoln would let him in to see Kennedy because she knew the President found him entertaining; Troutman also drew on their old personal ties as schoolmates at Choate. When I was away, to my secretaries' irritation, Troutman would drop by, ease his way into my office, and use it and our White House phone as his base.

With White House leverage, Troutman parlayed Plans for Progress into a major venture. Despite mounting criticism from the committee staff, Johnson backed the effort since it was so much in line with his own approach. In May, he and the President met first with executives of the fifty leading corporations doing business with the government, and then with labor leaders, asking them all to take affirmative initiative so that the committee would not need to become "a police agency." Johnson's chief assistant, George Reedy, advised the Vice-President that Plans for Progress had the advantage of so involving the committee "in constructive activities that the temptation to the committee staff to become a cop with a night stick chasing down individual cases would be held to the minimum." Moreover, since such agreements were voluntary, the extension of coverage beyond workers on government contracts to millions of other employees of the participating companies could not be legally challenged. The committee's own authority had never been tested in court, and in the absence of congressional support there was reason to fear such a test.

Within a few months, twenty-five of the fifty largest contractors had signed detailed plans; in a year the list of signers passed fifty, and efforts were under way to secure similar agreements with labor unions. Meanwhile, after six months, committee investigators found substantial progress in Lockheed's Georgia plant—where some 200 Negroes had been hired, many in skilled crafts or supervisory, administrative, and professional jobs. In all of Lockheed's plants, black employment had increased by 1,000 (26 percent). Not all companies fulfilled their promises, and many more never agreed to any plan. Troutman finally resigned from the committee to put an end to the feuding about his freewheeling role. In retrospect a good case can be made that early action to cancel at least one contract, for failure to comply, would have produced much more voluntary compliance, but the President believed the Plans for Progress that were negotiated vindicated his support.

Kennedy also supported the committee's effective but bureaucratically burdensome program that became known as "affirmative action." Though the committee staff never became "a cop with a night stick," it insisted on compliance reports and acted vigorously on the 600 complaints filed with it in its first nine months.

The President liked to hear of "firsts" in Negro employment in private industry, and enjoyed reading and commenting on reports of positive results inside the government. During the first year, in the Labor Department, for instance, the number of black employees holding jobs in grades 12 and above increased from 24 to 41; in Agriculture, from 15 to 46. At a Cabinet meeting in late 1961 Kennedy went around the table, department by department, asking for factual evidence of gains in minority group employment, not just generalizations. At first, some officials gave the President progress reports only in percentages, but specific numbers were insisted upon when we called his attention to the fact that one agency's 250 percent increase in Negroes GS-12 and above meant an increase from 4 to 10; in another, the proportional increase was vast— from none to one. Even the small gains, however, were a signal that the doors of opportunity were opening.

The mechanism through which many of these and other actions were initiated or promoted was an unusual body called the Subcabinet Group on Civil Rights. Meeting monthly at the White House, the group became an open conspiracy (though never much publicized) to invoke the full power of the Executive Branch against racial discrimination in all parts of American public life. At times this required concerted efforts to evoke the President's power—and even to try to change his mind.

In the President's name, the Subcabinet Group was first convened on April 14, 1961, in the Cabinet room by Fred Dutton, an enterprising California lawyer, then Kennedy's Secretary to the Cabinet. Dutton had asked all the departments and other major federal agencies to designate representatives at the Assistant Secretary level who would meet regularly "to survey civil rights aspects of public programs . . . and coordinate these on a government-wide basis."

Unknown to me, a week after I joined the White House staff Dutton had proposed to the President this "special interdepartmental program" as "an additional string in our civil rights harp." The musical metaphor may have been apt—at least no trumpet was intended. Dutton's memorandum stressed that the departments and agencies would work together *quietly* with an approach that would be "economic and social in nature rather than legalistic" and "anticipatory rather than only after-the-fact." As an example of what could be done, he suggested a concerted effort to make "showcase progress" in several selected Southern cities by getting the U.S. Commissioner of Education, other parts of HEW, the Commerce Department, the U.S. Employment Service, and the FBI to work behind the scenes with local community leadership, particularly with powerful government contractors, to prepare the way for successful school integration. The President gave Dutton a green light to go ahead.

When our small ad hoc coordinating committee heard about the proposed Subcabinet Group, some at first considered the move a threat to our role—a bureaucratic maneuver by Dutton to "get civil rights under his wing." As one who had enjoyed the creative chaos of the Kennedy presidential campaign, I saw it as a promising new way of releasing and enlisting extra energy for civil rights. "If it gets more horses on the track, it will be good," agreed Louis Martin, never one to succumb to bureaucratic paranoia. In fact, Dutton only intended to launch the project; he immediately turned over the chairmanship of the Subcabinet Group to me, and our problem was to keep his attention and claim as much of his time as possible.

Often a committee amounts to less than the sum of its parts; the reverse was true of the Subcabinet Group. Consisting almost entirely of new Kennedy appointees, most of whom were personally committed to civil rights, it took on a collective force of its own. Some of its members, like Hyman Bookbinder at the Commerce Department, Jack Conway at the Housing and Home Finance Agency, James Quigley and Lisle Carter at HEW, and Adam Yarmolinsky at Defense, had backgrounds in the field. For others, including the representatives from Agriculture, the Atomic Energy Commission, the Federal Aviation Agency, and the General Services Administration, it was all relatively new. But together a common purpose took hold and individuals found themselves and their agencies doing more than they had expected.

The dynamics of the Subcabinet Group worked to put pressure on any agency that was dragging its feet. Sometimes the representative of a department would catch the spirit, and would report fully the problems he faced and welcome (or even invite) White House intervention. More often, he would point to shortcomings in other agencies and support remedial measures by others, but be less forthcoming about his own. The thrust of the group as a whole, however, was almost always toward action.

Above all, the group tried to see the administration's civil rights policy as a whole, and to recommend what we thought that policy ought to be. Since the President had given little specific direction, we did not sit around trying to guess what he would desire. Where there was a clear mandate, such as in federal employment, we moved as fast and far as we could. In areas where there was no specific mandate, but no reason to believe Kennedy would oppose action, we went ahead, reporting to the President or going to him for authority when it seemed necessary. His attitude was that we had a mandate to do anything we could get away with without causing him undue political trouble. When we knew that the President was opposed or hesitant, as he was about early issuance of the order on housing or about legislation, we kept appraising the problem and from time to time would give him our best advice, even though he didn't enjoy hearing it.

Reflecting on this period, Robert Kennedy indicated in an oral history interview in 1964 that he sometimes worried whether the advice I would give "was in the best interest of President Kennedy" or of "a group of Negroes or a group of those who were interested in civil rights." Anthony Lewis, the interviewer, who knew me well, felt obliged "in fairness to history" to comment that there wasn't any question about my loyalty to President Kennedy. Robert Kennedy readily agreed and added kind words about my work, but in fairness to him there were interesting questions about dual and triple loyalties for many of us in the Subcabinet Group.

An unsympathetic observer listening to parts of our meetings might have said, "My God, they're not loyal to the President—they're plotting how to get him to do things he may not wish to do." Most of us would have answered that persuading the President to do more in this area than he might otherwise have done was one of the ways we were most loyal. He was concerned about many areas and depended on us for our best views of what he ought to do in civil rights. If freedom is the recognition of necessity and the ability to do what you ought to do, as fathers of Kennedy's church have said, then we were adding to the President's freedom.

For me there was never a conflict between what I thought good for Kennedy and good for civil rights—or for the country. Nor did it ever seem a disservice to press advice that was contrary to the President's prevailing view or the views of those closest to him, including Robert Kennedy. Nonetheless, the Subcabinet Group no doubt stretched the conventional definition of employee loyalty. There we would be at the Cabinet table, planning how to persuade the President or how to build pressures for action on some pending matter. It was the kind of ferment a President needs around him if he is to be responsive, and we thought we were doing our part to help him become a great President. Our best ally (and defense) was his own self-image; he saw himself as a strong President, open to criticism and prepared to give courageous moral leadership.

When he gave us any words to go on, we took them and moved; sometimes even a nod was good enough. At the first meeting of the Subcabinet Group, Dutton cited Kennedy's statement to the Equal Employment Opportunity Committee that "federal money should not be spent in any way which encourages discrimination," and asked agencies to take action to bring their activities into line with this principle. Following up, in a memorandum on the President's behalf, I requested "that each department or agency (a) survey and specify the degree and location of any such discrimination in its operations, facilities, services or programs, including grant-in-aid programs, (b) appraise the agency's present power to take action in regard thereto, and (c) make departmental recommendations." Written reports were to be submitted within two months.

As the reports came in, Dutton and I were struck by how few questions were raised about the power to take action and by how many good proposals were made that could have been carried through long ago. With the adroit help of Bill Taylor from the Civil Rights Commission, we encouraged departments to implement their affirmative recommendations, and when the submission of facts seemed insufficient or remedial proposals inadequate, we goaded them to do better. We did not take many issues to the President because when things were going well, he didn't want to be bothered, and we wanted momentum to develop before anyone, including the President, had second thoughts about the program.

Some steps were taken speedily and quietly. Secretary of Interior Stewart Udall issued a regulation ending all segregation in national parks; other agencies followed suit. Sometimes threats to cancel leases and concessions had to be made, but before long lunchrooms and public facilities in federal government buildings throughout the South were desegregated.

In one of the first meetings of the Subcabinet Group we took up protests about the practice of army military police ordering Negro personnel to leave a restaurant when requested by the manager. On Adam Yarmolinsky's recommendation, Secretary McNamara determined that military police should never again be used to enforce segregation, that legal advice should be provided by the services to any serviceman in difficulty with local authorities on this issue, and that in areas where local facilities were not available to blacks, such facilities should, so far as possible, be provided on base for all servicemen. This was an important change of policy and practice that I do not think was ever reported in the press.

Similarly without any fanfare, in response to a study for the Subcabinet Group, Secretary Ribicoff directed that the HEW financing of language and guidance and counseling institutes under the National Defense Education Act be conditioned on an agreement by all participating universities that the institutes would be conducted on a non-discriminatory basis. Although more than 150 presidents of colleges and universities throughout the country were informed, there was no outcry. Six Southern institutions withdrew, but the great majority of participants in the South as elsewhere accepted the new terms calmly, including the Universities of Mississippi, Florida, Tennessee, Kentucky, and North Carolina and seventeen other Southern institutions.

Some steps were taken speedily but not so quietly. In early 1961 it was brought to our attention that the official Civil War Centennial Commission, set up by Congress to mark appropriately our "supreme national experience," was about to commemorate the firing on Fort Sumter in a segregated local hotel which would exclude Negro participants. I called the commission's chairman, Major General Ulysses S. Grant III, to get him to work out alternative non-discriminatory arrangements and found that he and the majority of the commissioners did not seem to recognize that it was Lee who had surrendered to Grant at Appomattox. Out of deference to his Southern colleagues, President Grant's grandson talked in terms of the War Between the States, and felt that states rights required the commission to respect South Carolina's policy of segregation. Unless forced by the President, the commission would not budge. Finally, Kennedy signed a telegram to Grant requesting that the affair be moved to the desegregated facilities of the Charleston Naval Station and, faced with the loss of federal funds, the commission surrendered to the Union.

Before long, Grant was replaced on the commission by historian Allan Nevins (who had written an introduction to Kennedy's *Strategy of Peace*). Arthur Schlesinger says the President was "very angry" about the Charleston situation; I found him irritated that he had to go public and offend South Carolina's governor, congressional delegation, and white citizens, but otherwise amused by the poetic injustice of it all.

No matter how Kennedy felt, in the Subcabinet Group we treated his telegram as a clear precedent against participation by federal officials in public meetings or conferences held in segregated circumstances. As a result, not long afterwards, Negro attorneys attended the dinner of the Atlanta Bar Association for the first time; the speaker, Secretary of State Rusk, a native son of Georgia, had explained and insisted upon the administration's new policy. Thereafter, from time to time, alert colleagues in the civil rights movement would warn us when the President or some other official was about to find himself in a segregated facility; it would be integrated, at least for that occasion, or plans would be changed.

Washington, D.C., itself remained one of the most embarrassing centers of racial discrimination; blacks were excluded from choice residential areas, from the main private clubs, from white barbershops, and from other business and recreational facilities. D.C. IS A HARDSHIP POST FOR NEGRO DIPLOMATS ran the headline for a detailed Washington *Post* account of the difficulties African embassy officials and their families faced in the city.

Members of the Subcabinet Group assisted the State Department's special section under Pedro Sanjuan in persistently pressing realtors, banks, zoning commissions, and barbers to cease racial discrimination. The Washington press helped. So did Secretary of State Rusk, who refused to sign a racially restrictive covenant on his new home. Robert Kennedy, Angier Biddle Duke, George Cabot Lodge, Charles Bartlett, and others resigned from the Metropolitan Club when it continued to exclude Negroes, and the President endorsed their action. When Arthur Krock protested that the rules of his club were none of the President's business, and then protested the administration's closed door to Moïse Tshombe, the secessionist leader of the Congo, Kennedy said he would give Tshombe a visa if Krock would give him dinner at the Metropolitan Club.

Some proposed steps were not taken, or were long delayed. Yarmolinsky and Assistant Secretary of Defense Carlisle Runge, for instance, agreed in principle with a Civil Rights Commission recommendation that the National Guard should be integrated in every state, but defense appropriations and the very existence of the National Guard in some Southern states seemed in jeopardy if that action was ordered forthwith. Outside pressures from civil rights groups had to mount, and a Presidential Committee on Equal Opportunity in the Armed Forces had to be appointed and make a report to the President before the Guard was integrated. The committee was headed by Gerhard A. Gesell, a tough-minded Washington attorney under whom Burke Marshall and I had both worked for several years.

So many civil rights efforts were proceeding smoothly during the spring of 1961 that we did not worry much when the issue of legislation was handled with unnecessary clumsiness by the White House press office. Carrying out their campaign assignment from Kennedy to prepare a legislative package incorporating the civil rights plank of the Democratic platform, Senator Clark and Congressman Celler were ready by early May to introduce the bills. Kennedy agreed that they be introduced, but he made it clear he would not seek their passage in 1961. On the other hand, we did not expect him to disavow them, and I don't think he intended to. Yet on the day after their introduction Pierre Salinger disassociated the administration from the bills and, to make matters worse, indicated that there had been "very little pressure" for civil rights legislation. Since the President and many of us had done our best to persuade civil rights groups not to press for legislation, this was a low blow.

The matter of the Clark-Celler bills was overshadowed by what happened just before and after their introduction on May 8. On the sixth of May, in a Law Day address to the University of Georgia, Robert Kennedy gave a major statement of the administration's position on civil rights. It was his first formal speech as Attorney General. After months of turmoil, the university had finally admitted two Negroes, one of whom was in Kennedy's audience; the Attorney General's coming was a sign of support for the moderate white administrators and state officials—and the Negro students—who had prevailed.

It was a bold talk, beyond anything said in the South by any Attorney General since Reconstruction. Kennedy straightforwardly expressed agreement with the Supreme Court in *Brown* v. *Board of Education* but added that his personal belief was not what mattered; it was the law. The Attorney General called for "amicable voluntary solutions" and pledged his best efforts to achieve these, but added: "I say to you today that if the orders of the court are circumvented, the Department of Justice will act. We will not stand by and be aloof. We will move." He also decried Northern leaders who opposed discrimination in the South but practiced it in their own lives. To his surprise, and to the delight of Griffin Bell, who made the arrangements, the students gave him an ovation.

The editor of the Atlanta *Constitution*, Ralph McGill (whom Kennedy had confidentially consulted on what he should say), wrote, "Never before, in all its travail of by-gone years, has the South heard so honest and understandable a speech from any Cabinet member." The NAACP expressed its "profound appreciation." Georgia-born Louis Martin, who had seen an advance draft, wrote Kennedy that it was "a peach of a speech," and said that "congratulations are pouring in from brothers everywhere, here and abroad. If you keep this up, one of these days I might be able to go back home."

While Louis Martin was writing that, others—black and white—were in buses heading for Georgia and on into Alabama and Mississippi to integrate the waiting rooms, washrooms, and eating places at every stop —or, if blocked, to demonstrate that despite the law segregation was still the rule. The violence and passions that erupted around the Freedom Rides brought a quick end to the optimism generated by the Attorney General's reception in the Deep South.

Robert Kennedy complained that he didn't know they were traveling down there until a mob overturned and burned a bus in in Anniston, Alabama, on May 14. In an April meeting with the Attorney General, Martin King and other civil rights leaders had pointed to the failure of the Interstate Commerce Commission to enforce Supreme Court decisions against segregation in terminals and other facilities serving interstate commerce. They had been dissatisfied with Kennedy's explanation that the ICC was a very slow-moving and very independent agency, but they did not advise him that the Congress on Racial Equality (CORE), a militant pacifist organization, committed to Gandhian action, was then preparing to launch an interracial group on a dramatic and dangerous ride through the South. "Our philosophy was simple," James Farmer, the director of CORE, said later: "We put on pressure and create a crisis and then they react."

The immediate reaction by the Attorney General was to try to find ways to save the Riders' lives. By the time a second bus had picked up those not hospitalized in Anniston and reached Birmingham, a larger mob, led by members of the Ku Klux Klan, was waiting with pipes, chains, and baseball bats, if not guns. One of those in the forefront of the assault was a paid FBI informant in the Klan, Gary Rowe, Jr. Days in advance, Rowe had reported the plans to his FBI "handler," and the Birmingham FBI office had sent a teletype message to J. Edgar Hoover warning that the local police and the Klan were plotting an ambush. Hoover was told that Birmingham's police chief, Eugene ("Bull") Connor, had promised the Klan fifteen to twenty minutes to attack the Riders, whom he wanted beaten until "it looked like a bulldog got a hold of them." Hoover did not inform the Attorney General, and took no action to prevent the violence.*

Afterwards, without giving details of his own part, Rowe described how the CORE group were all beaten so badly that he couldn't see their faces through the blood; he noticed FBI agents "taking movies of the beatings." The governor of Alabama, John Patterson, had washed his hands of responsibility, saying: "The people of Alabama are so aroused that I cannot guarantee protection for this bunch of rabble-rousers." Police Commissioner Connor, known for his vow that he would never let "niggers and whites segregate together in Birmingham," explained that his policemen could not be on hand to protect the Riders because it was Mother's Day and he had let them go home.

Covering the scene for CBS News, Howard K. Smith reported that "the riots have not been spontaneous outbursts of anger but carefully planned and susceptible to having been easily prevented or stopped had there been a wish to do so." Alerted to the plans the day before, he had watched the gang of thirty heavyset men in sports shirts assemble and wait. After describing the contradictory and misinformed reactions of many well-intentioned Southern whites, Smith concluded that "a job of explanation" was necessary: "If the confusion in the Southern mind is genuine and not willful, laws of the land and purposes of the nation badly need a basic restatement, perhaps by the one American assured of an intent mass hearing at any time, the President."

The President tersely called for law and order, and John Seigenthaler was sent to Alabama to represent the President and Attorney General. Seigenthaler arrived in time to escort the first group of wounded

---

* Not until 1980, when *The New York Times* acquired a confidential 1979 Justice Department report on the role of Gary Rowe did Burke Marshall learn that Hoover knew the plans for the attack on the Freedom Riders in advance. Marshall was stunned and is sure that he and the Attorney General would have taken prompt action. "In hindsight," the 1979 Justice Department stated, "it is indeed unfortunate that the bureau did not take additional action to prevent violence, such as notifying the Attorney General and the United States Marshals Service, who might have been able to do something."

and shaken Riders from the bus terminal to the airport, and flew with them to safety in New Orleans. He had to hurry back, for James Farmer was arriving at the Alabama border with a new group, joined by a contingent from Nashville, including student sit-in leaders James Lawson, John Lewis, and Diane Nash; Lawson, who had studied with Gandhi during three years as a student missionary in India, said they would go by bus all the way to New Orleans, by way of Alabama and Mississippi, or die trying.

As these events unfolded, the President was busy preparing for his forthcoming encounter with Khrushchev and concentrating on the impending Berlin crisis; he did not appreciate the crisis CORE had deliberately precipitated in Alabama. It was then that I received the angry phone call; the voice was familiar, but the tone urgent and sharp.

"Tell them to call it off!" John Kennedy said. He wanted me to do something right away to get the Freedom Riders off those buses. "Stop them!"

"I don't think anybody's going to stop them right now," I said. He was not satisfied, but even his brother and the ever-persuasive Burke Marshall found that the Freedom Riders were adamant.

The Attorney General wanted, if at all possible, to get state and local police to carry out their responsibilities, and avoid the use of federal force, but Governor Patterson, an early Kennedy supporter, would not even answer his phone calls. At a press conference Patterson said the Freedom Riders had asked for trouble, and "the State of Alabama can't guarantee the safety of fools." The President himself called the governor and finally, on May 19, after the Riders had been beleaguered in Birmingham for several days and the Attorney General was assembling a large force of federal marshals, Patterson returned Robert Kennedy's call. In a meeting with Seigenthaler he promised to protect the Riders when they proceeded to Montgomery and on toward Jackson, Mississippi.

Just as the way seemed open, so that the ride could be finished and done with as far as the Attorney General was concerned, he learned that the Greyhound Company could find no drivers to drive the bus. Exasperated, he called the company superintendent in Birmingham, and told him to get in touch "with Mr. Greyhound" since "under the law they are entitled to transportation" and "the government is going to be very upset if this group does not get to continue their trip." So "somebody better get in the damn bus and get it going and get these people on their way." He added, to his great regret, a misleading statement: "We have gone to a lot of trouble to see that they get to this trip and I am most concerned to see that it is accomplished." The driver was found, but the transcription of the conversation, from a Greyhound tape, convinced many Southerners that the administration had actually instigated the rides.

Convoyed out of Birmingham by the state police, with sirens going and armed troopers on guard, the Reverend Fred Shuttlesworth, King's militant colleague in Birmingham, said, "Man, what this state's coming to! An armed escort to take a bunch of niggers to a bus station so they can break these silly old laws." As he had boarded the bus, with state troopers lined up with rifles, Shuttlesworth had walked back and forth, as if he were reviewing an honor guard, and then exclaimed, "Now we're gonna assault Mississippi!" Then he led the Riders in singing, "He's Got the Whole World in His Hand—He's Got Governor Patterson in His Hand—He's Got Bull Connor in His Hand!" Shuttlesworth was quoted as saying, "We're gonna make a steer out of Bull."

Governor Patterson was not in anyone's hand; he broke his word: state police left the bus when it reached Montgomery and the Riders were assaulted again. From a phone booth, John Doar, Marshall's chief deputy, directly described the scene to the Attorney General: "The passengers are coming off. . . . There are no cops. It's terrible. . . . People are yelling 'Get 'em, get 'em.' It's awful." Seigenthaler went to the defense of a girl being beaten and was clubbed to the ground; he was kicked while he lay there unconscious for nearly half an hour. Again FBI agents present did nothing, except take notes. The Attorney General ordered 500 marshals to Montgomery and put Byron White in charge. Fifty were there in time to protect Martin King when he arrived at the airport to address a mass meeting that evening.

Not enough marshals were on hand to assure the safety of the nearly 1,500 people in the First Baptist Church against a huge, howling mob. From this pulpit, King said, "We hear the familiar cry that morals cannot be legislated. This may be true, but behavior can be regulated. The law may not be able to make a man love me, but it can keep him from lynching me." For a few hours that night even that claim was in question.

This was one of several nights to come that Robert Kennedy stayed awake worrying about Negroes. Marshall secured an injunction against further violence from federal judge Frank Johnson, but it was not obeyed. At about 4 a.m. Kennedy talked again to King by telephone; still trapped in the stifling hot church, with traces of tear gas coming in the windows, King complained that the Attorney General was not doing enough. "Now, Reverend," Kennedy said, "you know just as well as I do that if it hadn't been for the United States marshals you'd be as dead as Kelsey's nuts right now." That ended that conversation, but there were harder words to come.

The governor belatedly sent in the National Guard and the mob was driven back so that at dawn people could leave the church. With the help of Senator Eastland (who Kennedy said always kept his word, and was easier to deal with than the "so-called liberals"), Mississippi officials finally assured Marshall and Kennedy that there would be no violence— but the Riders would be arrested when they reached Jackson. The Attorney General had told Eastland that "my primary interest was that they weren't beaten up." That was not King's primary interest, and he disliked the implicit deal. Marshall argued that there was a vital "difference between winding up in jail and winding up at the mercy of a mob." On May 24, twenty-seven Freedom Riders, led by James Farmer, dined in the white cafeteria at the Montgomery bus terminal, and then under police escort traveled in two buses to Jackson, where they were arrested and jailed in an orderly fashion.

Thinking "that people were going to be killed" if Riders kept coming into Alabama and Mississippi, and that "they had made their point," the Attorney General publicly called for a "cooling-off" period during which further Freedom Riding would be delayed. He had been urging this privately from the beginning. Farmer rejected it, saying Negroes "had been cooling off for a hundred years" and would be "in a deep freeze" if they cooled any further. Then to Kennedy's consternation, in a long telephone conversation King turned down an arrangement by which those arrested could be released on bail.

"It's a matter of conscience and morality," King explained to him. "They must use their lives and their bodies to right a wrong." Like many others in authority stung by the gadflies of civil disobedience, Kennedy reacted coldly: "That is not going to have the slightest effect on what the government is going to do in this field or any other. The fact that they stay in jail is not going to have the slightest effect on me." King said perhaps it would help if students came down by the hundreds of thousands. "The country belongs to you as much as to me," Kennedy said. "But don't make statements that sound like a threat. That's not the way to deal with us." King restated his case: "You must understand that we've made no gains without pressure and I hope that pressure will always be moral, legal, and peaceful." He argued that the "creative and nonviolent" approach "can save the soul of America." Kennedy contended that the problem wouldn't be solved "but by strong federal action." King said, "I'm deeply appreciative of what the administration is doing. I see a ray of hope, but I am different than my father. I feel the need of being free now!"

After an hour on the phone, alternately with Kennedy and Marshall,

King said to his friends in Montgomery, "You know, they don't understand the social revolution going on in the world, and therefore they don't understand what we're doing."

After his conversation with King, Robert Kennedy telephoned me. "This is too much!" he said. "I wonder whether they have the best interest of their country at heart. Do you know that one of them is against the atom bomb—yes, he even picketed against it in jail! The President is going abroad and this is all embarrassing him."

Even as we were talking another group of seven Freedom Riders, led by Yale chaplain William Sloane Coffin, Jr., and John Maguire of Wesleyan, was coming into Montgomery under National Guard protection. Burke Marshall had telephoned to urge Coffin to reconsider his Alabama trip, but Gene Rostow had countered with different tactical advice. "Never forget," the dean of Yale Law School told Coffin, "that Meade missed his moment of truth at Gettysburg when he failed to pursue a retreating army." Coffin was not one to miss his moment of truth. Robert Kennedy wisecracked that "those people at Yale are sore at Harvard for taking over the country, and now they're trying to get back at us."

As a rock smashed against Ralph Abernathy's car, in which Coffin was sitting, being driven away from the Montgomery bus station, a reporter called through the window, "Reverend Abernathy, President Kennedy is about to meet with Premier Khrushchev. Aren't you afraid of embarrassing him with these demonstrations?" Abernathy replied in his slow voice, "Man, we've been embarrassed all our lives."

Worried about what to do himself but sure of what the President should do, Bill Coffin toward midnight went to a phone booth and put through a collect call to the White House to his fellow member of Skull and Bones, McGeorge Bundy, the President's chief aide on foreign affairs. The President should follow De Gaulle's example, Coffin said: go to the people and ask for understanding. (In seeking to end the war in Algeria, the French President had gone on television, thrown out his arms, and almost shouted, "Français, françaises, aidez-moi!") "Couldn't Kennedy do the same?" Coffin asked. "A little moral suasion would clear up the confusion in the country."

Getting a frosty reception, Coffin used his dime again and called me collect; the White House operator found me at home. Coffin says I was "both awake and far better informed" (as I should have been, given my job and Bundy's), but that though I listened to his suggestion with sympathy, I explained why I doubted the President would take further action.

Before Coffin and his colleagues decided whether to go on to Jackson, King said, "Let's have a word of prayer," and he got down on his knees. They all followed, and afterward King said for them to sleep on it. The next morning the Riders went to the bus station to resume their journey but were promptly arrested and jailed. After putting up bail they went back to Yale and other northern climes.

It all may indeed have been too much, for public sentiment seemed strongly against the continuation of the rides. "Nonviolence that deliberately provokes violence is a logical contradiction," said an editorial in *The New York Times*. In a June Gallup poll, 63 percent of those questioned disapproved the rides while 70 percent approved Kennedy's action in sending marshals to protect the Riders, including 50 percent of those polled in the South. Nevertheless, although King himself finally reluctantly recommended "a temporary lull," the rides continued and ended only after some 250 arrests and convictions in Jackson.

It would be inaccurate, however, to conclude that the rides and the jail-going were having no constructive effect. Two weeks after the first violence in Alabama, the Attorney General petitioned the Interstate Commerce Commission to issue regulations requiring the end of segregation in all interstate terminals. Under heavy administration pressure, the ICC issued the order on September 22, and the Justice Department took steps, city by city, to bring down all segregation signs in railroad and airport as well as bus terminals. By the end of 1962, CORE was satisfied that the immediate aims of the Freedom Riders had been achieved: segregation in interstate travel had been ended.

CORE and King failed, however, in their effort to force the President, by the logic of events, to speak out in moral terms. Kennedy knew better than to echo former President Truman's remark that the Freedom Riders ought to stay home "and attend to their own business" instead of "stirring up trouble" like the antislavery agitators who "did their part in bringing about the Civil War." But he was irritated by their tactics and preoccupied with planning his coming trip to Europe; they had already changed his domestic agenda and produced an intervention in the South he had hoped to avoid.

So the President refused their request that he personally welcome the Freedom Riders back to Washington. He rejected a statement I urged him to make at the time of the petition to the ICC and would not include in his June State of the Union address a paragraph on the subject that Marshall and I proposed. He did not say anything on the substantive issues until a press conference on July 19, and then said little more than that he believed "that everyone who travels, for whatever reason they travel, should enjoy the full constitutional protection given to them by the law and the Constitution." No doubt he thought the Attorney General's actions had spoken louder than words, and he feared a white backlash in the South.

With evident relish, in his State of the Union address on the eve of his departure for Europe, the President sought to lift the nation's sights from its domestic troubles to a new and faraway target. To face "the extraordinary challenge . . . of extraordinary times," he proposed "a major national commitment" to "go to the moon." "Achievement in space," he said, "may hold the key to our future on earth."

In the Civil Rights Commission's Second Report to the President and Congress that was just going to press, Father Hesburgh could not refrain from a rejoinder. Though he favored the exploration of space, the president of Notre Dame added this note to the report: "Personally, I don't care if the United States gets the first man on the moon, if while this is happening on a crash basis, we dawdle along here on our corner of the earth, nursing our prejudices, flouting our magnificent Constitution, ignoring the central moral problem of our times, and appearing hypocrites to all the world."

At the June 1961 meeting of the Subcabinet Group on Civil Rights, Jack Conway, Deputy Administrator of the Housing and Home Finance Agency, remarked that the idea of nonviolent direct action against segregation had caught fire among the young generation and the pace of progress would now have to be increased. The Assistant Postmaster General, Richard Murphy, said the movement would grow and counsels of caution or efforts to "cool off" the situation were futile. It was agreed that if federal agencies took the initiative and used their full power to protect and promote equal rights, the necessity for popular pressure could be removed or at least reduced. Burke Marshall said that he and the Attorney General were encouraging vigorous voting registration efforts and thought "it would be valuable if some of the present energy were channeled into this vital work."

Various critics, then and later, saw in this a devious stratagem to divert the civil rights movement into a less embarrassing area and to destroy the direct action movement represented by the Freedom Riders. King has also been accused of going along with this strategy simply in order to get money that was held out to his organization as bait. That is a distortion of the facts.

The adverse public reaction to the rides no doubt reinforced the President's and Attorney General's emphasis on voting rights, always their preference and priority. Behind the scenes we did work actively to encourage private donors to provide large sums to support nonpartisan voter registration. But the strategy was not suddenly discovered or imposed by the Kennedys.

In King's first major foray North, in the 1957 Prayer Pilgrimage for Freedom, he had stirred more than 15,000 people in front of the Lincoln Memorial with his refrain:

> Give us the ballot. Give us the ballot and we will no longer have to worry the federal government about our basic rights. . . . Give us the ballot and we will fill the legislature with men of goodwill. Give us the ballot . . .

Afterward, he had launched a Crusade for Citizenship to register five million Southern Negroes; it had floundered, but the plan was still close to King's heart. He had had enough doubts about the tactics of the Freedom Riders so that he never rode himself. Instead, King got the Southern Christian Leadership Conference to start planning for a registration drive. Later in the summer of 1961, when the SNCC students were torn by the question of whether to turn away from direct action to the voting drive, many of them felt King was being "co-opted by the Kennedys." For King, the fact that the new administration and private foundations would support a registration drive only provided additional reasons to do what he thought the civil rights movement should do anyway.

It was a strategy I fully supported. In the first paper on civil rights I gave Robert and John Kennedy in 1959, I argued that a shift of focus to the clear-cut issue of voting rights would be "politically right and psychologically healthy." "The Solid South is split on this issue," I wrote. "The wedge of the Constitution must widen that split at just this point." So I was delighted to work with Burke Marshall in persuading friends in the Taconic and Field Foundations and in the Stern Family Fund to give private leadership and money to this effort. Steven Currier of the Taconic Foundation and the Potomac Institute played a central part in bringing private donors and civil rights leaders together, and providing the initial funds. At the Attorney General's request, the new Voter Education Project, headed by Wiley Branton, was given prompt tax exemption. Andrew Young was enlisted to administer the first large grant.

Then, as registration drives began in rural Black Belt counties and intimidation or violence—including murders—occurred, a more serious charge was made: that the administration had promised but failed to give protection to ensure the safety of registration workers. There were some arrests and prosecutions, but often these resulted in acquittals by white juries. "If we are murdered in our attempts, our blood will be on your hands," one young activist in Georgia warned Robert Kennedy.

It is true that in September 1962 the President said:

They deserve the protection of the United States Government, the protection of the state, the protection of local communities, and we shall do everything we possibly can to make sure that protection is assured and if it requires extra legislation and extra force, we shall do that.

But the limits on what the federal government could do, without new legislation, had been apparent during the Freedom Rides. In our June Subcabinet Group meeting, Burke Marshall had pointed to the Justice Department's inability to prevent the police in Mississippi from arresting the Riders, and outlined the frustrations of the federal system. "The legal limitations of the federal system are not understood by the civil rights leaders," he had said to us. "The effect of that lack of understanding on their part and a corresponding lack of ability to act effectively and immediately on our part is going to create a series of problems over a long period of time until the segregation is eliminated."

His prediction proved to be accurate. Hundreds of times a year, he was to complain later, he had to explain to people calling for federal action that "we do not have a national police force, and *cannot* provide protection in a physical sense for everyone who is disliked because of the exercise of his constitutional rights." The argument led to a bleak conclusion in a candid talk he gave at Fisk University in late 1961:

> There is no substitute under the federal system for the failure of local law enforcement responsibility. There is simply a vacuum, which can be filled only rarely, with extraordinary difficulty, at monumental expense, and in a totally unsatisfactory fashion.

This was the paradox at the center of the administration's voting rights strategy. On a progress report, President Kennedy wrote, "Keep pushing the cases." The Attorney General did. As the Justice Department brought more and more voting cases (including 30 in Mississippi), more young registration workers went into hostile areas. Robert Kennedy wanted the registration drive to gain momentum, since the cases would come to nothing unless blacks sought to register, yet he was worried, and Marshall was worried, that things would get out of control, especially in Mississippi, and that violence on a large scale might occur.

That concern made Kennedy and Marshall especially cautious about anything that might stir up further white antagonism, and they thought new investigations or hearings in the Deep South by the Civil Rights Commission would do just that. This was the only good reason for the conflict that developed between the Justice Department and the commission. When bureaucratic warfare between Burke Marshall and commission staff director Berl Bernhard first broke out, I couldn't believe it; it couldn't happen between friends of such obvious goodwill and common dedication. I did my best to get them to relax and enjoy their overlapping roles, but before long the Justice Department was just as opposed to the commission as it had been under Eisenhower. Part of the problem was the competitive nature of all bureaucratic beasts, but the basic cause of the clash was the different missions of the commission and the department. The strong personalities and convictions of both Robert Kennedy and Father Hesburgh were also important factors in the clash.

In an early meeting with the commissioners, Robert Kennedy urged that they leave voting rights to him. "You're second-guessers," he told them. "I am the one who has to get the job done." They reminded him of their statutory duty to investigate complaints of denials of the right to vote, and contended that their hearings and reports were a way to educate the public. He saw such intervention as a duplication of effort and a source of confusion. The commissioners said litigation would not be sufficient; they thought that legislation striking down literacy tests, or using the completion of sixth grade as a criterion for literacy, and enabling federal registrars to be appointed was necessary. The Attorney General felt new legislation was not necessary or politic and said, "I can do it, and will do it, in my way, and you're making it more difficult."

The commissioners saw themselves as a conscience for the nation, or, as Father Hesburgh put it, a "burr under the saddle of the administration." Robert Kennedy saw them as a runaway grand jury that might suddenly at a critical juncture propose something he didn't want proposed, or turn and criticize him in a sensitive situation. The creative chaos he espoused had its limits, and one of them was his desire for overall control. His effort to bring the commission under control turned the commissioners against him, and made them more independent than ever. Berl Bernhard said he had never seen anyone so angry at the commission as Robert Kennedy—not even John Patterson or George Wallace. I said that Attorney General Rogers had also seemed on the edge of apoplexy in 1959 about the commission's first report and subsequent criticisms of Rogers' proposed voting rights bill. Unfortunately the animosity went down in the ranks. An attorney in the Civil Rights Division at Justice gave his case against the commission: "It's easy to play Jesus and it's fun to get in bed with the civil rights movement, but all of the noise they make doesn't do as much good as one case."

The first impasse came over the access to files. The Attorney General was forcing the FBI to undertake investigations in Black Belt counties. The commission was willing to refrain from its own investigations in counties already being investigated if it could review the files and satisfy itself that nothing further needed to be done. Though Kennedy and Marshall seemed agreeable to this, the FBI files were never made available. Finally Marshall conceded his inability to give the files. Hoover considered the commission an unwitting tool of King and the civil rights movement. The commission accepted Hoover's offer to assign an FBI liaison officer to work with it daily, but this only resulted in the FBI knowing everything about the commission's work, without the commission getting any more information from the FBI.

The commission was also assured that FBI agents in the South had been ordered to cooperate with its investigations, but Bernhard recalls how cold, distant, and proper they were. He knew how closely they worked with white police officials. During a ride with an FBI agent from Jackson to New Orleans at a time when violence was in the air, Bernhard felt queasy and unsafe. "If we who were also in the government didn't feel the FBI men were our friends," he thought, "how must blacks feel?"

The worst disputes between the commission and the Justice Department came over the holding of hearings in Louisiana and Mississippi. By the spring of 1961, after long investigations, the commission had subpoenas out to registrars and witnesses all over Louisiana. Unknown to the public, Governor Earl Long had opened the door to the evidence the commission needed to prove massive discrimination against Negroes, and the hearings were likely to have considerable impact.

"You're here to help niggers vote," Earl Long, the son of Huey Long, told Bernhard in a private meeting. "And I'm for you because they're my niggers and I want their votes." He said that his foe, Leander Perez, the boss of Plaquemines Parish, was a crazy character who kept Negroes from voting there and ran it as if it were another country.

"Now, we're never gonna talk about my helping you," the governor said, "but I'm gonna get my state registrar to give you the records you need, and after you talk to him, you remember, you never saw me."

The packet of information on the parishes gave the details on just how and where Negroes were kept from registering.

Literally on the eve of the hearing, at about 1 a.m. the Attorney General called Bernhard in New Orleans. "Do you know what you're doing?" Kennedy asked. "If you continue with your hearing and make race a big issue, DeLesseps Morrison will lose the primary election for mayor and you will have destroyed one of the truly moderate politicians in the South. I want it called off—now!"

Bernhard argued back, but Kennedy just repeated, "You tell the commission to call it off. Get in touch with them now, and call it off." Dean Storey, who was to be chairman of the hearing, agreed to talk with the other commissioners, and at about 2 a.m. telephoned Bernhard to say the hearing should be postponed. To Bernhard's protest, the former president of the American Bar Association explained, "We just can't ignore the request of the Attorney General of the United States when he thinks our timing would be harmful."

Bernhard reported the news to the Attorney General and asked what reason he should give the press the next morning. "If you're not smart enough to give a good reason," Kennedy said, "I don't know why my brother nominated you. And remember you never talked to me."

At the press conference Bernhard reported a temporary postponement due to commission chairman Hannah's trip to Nigeria and Father Hesburgh's travel schedule which made a quorum impossible. A few months later the hearing was held, successfully. Not long afterward more or less the same sequence of events began in connection with the commission's long-prepared hearings in Mississippi. Three times the commission scheduled Mississippi hearings and three times Robert Kennedy forced a cancellation because of pending litigation. The lawyers on the commission deferred, reluctantly, to the chief legal officer of the nation, but the commissioners concluded that he was trying to avoid any additional confrontation with the white Southern power structure. Father Hesburgh wrote me that he was deeply disappointed by "the Administration's stance on Civil Rights progress versus practical politics." Commission documents on police brutality made Father Hesburgh's "blood run cold" and he felt like giving "a loud blast from my moral soul"; in the next commission report he publicly blasted the Justice Department's policy of non-intervention and called for protection of civil rights workers by the federal government.

When I heard how Father Hesburgh had stood up to the Attorney General in a direct confrontation, I recalled his earlier encounter with agents of the United States government. While representing the Vatican at the International Atomic Energy Agency, he had developed a close rapport with the chief Soviet delegate; when they met in Vienna they embraced warmly. A worried State Department officer tapped Father Hesburgh on the shoulder and drew him aside. "We have strict instructions not to have our pictures taken smiling with any Russian," the American Foreign Service officer said. To which Father Hesburgh replied, "My friend, you and I take our instructions from different quarters."

Robert Kennedy, on his side, had become convinced that the commission was "not objective," that in its fervor "it was almost like the House Un-American Activities Committee investigating Communism." Ironically, at the same time he was developing this anti-commission position his own anger about discrimination and ardor about civil rights were mounting. "The more he saw," Burke Marshall said, "and this was true of me as well, the more he understood. The more you learned about how

Negroes were treated in the South . . . the madder you became." By early 1962, according to Marshall, "he was so mad about that kind of thing it overrode everything else."

The same feelings led the commission, after two years of frustration with the administration, to override the Attorney General and the President and publish a special report on the situation in Mississippi. Summarizing its investigations, the commission reported that citizens were being "terrorized because they sought to vote" and recommended that the President order greater efforts to protect citizens exercising their rights and "consider seriously" whether federal funds should not be withheld from the state until it "demonstrates its compliance with the Constitution and laws of the United States."

Disapproving this approach, fearing a congressional outcry, and hoping to get the commission to reconsider, the President called Hannah and Bernhard to his office. He was surprised to learn that the commissioners, including two white Southern members, were unanimous and firm. The balance within the commission had shifted after Governors Battle and Carlton and George Johnson were replaced by a moderate Southern political science professor, Robert Rankin from Duke University, the dean of Harvard Law School, Erwin Griswold, and NAACP attorney Spottswood Robinson III. At the prospect of a Virginia Negro, Robinson, replacing the former segregationist governor, Senator Talmadge had warned Congress that this was "like making a tomcat custodian of a canary bird."

Kennedy was irritated to learn that Dean Griswold had been a strong champion of the controversial proposal to cut off aid to Mississippi.

"Who the hell appointed Griswold?" Kennedy asked.

"You did," said Bernhard.

"Probably on the recommendation of Harris Wofford," the President replied.

By then I was in Addis Ababa. I had left the White House staff in mid-1962 primarily because of the affirmative pull of the Peace Corps, and of Africa, but there were also negative reasons. Roy Wilkins sensed some of them when he wrote me that my White House assignment would "curl the hair on a bald-headed man."

What Kennedy liked best in my role, and I liked least, was my function as a buffer between him and the civil rights forces pressing for presidential action. In fact, it was good neither for him nor for civil rights leaders. What they conveyed to me lost its freshness and impact when passed on secondhand to the President, and yet they felt that by talking with me they were getting through to him. Usually their points were in line with views I had already given the President, which he didn't want to hear ten times a week. Telling him what somebody else said, especially when it reinforced my own position, had far less effect than Kennedy's hearing it directly. I constantly told King, Wilkins, and others, "Keep asking to see the President, that's what counts."

On the other hand, the guardian of the presidential gate, Kenneth O'Donnell, would plead: "We have to save the President's time—does he have to see King now?" When the interval between visits by civil rights leaders seemed too long, Louis Martin would help by saying to O'Donnell, "The brothers are getting restless, you better let them in."

Another reason for my decision was a sense that the time had come for a black Assistant to the President for Civil Rights. "Wofford Go Home" was the caption of an editorial by Chuck Stone in the Washington *Afro-American*. He had been particularly offended by my wearing a Confederate general's uniform to a high-spirited New Frontier costume party.* Kennedy should get a true champion of civil rights, he urged, like Congressmen Adam Powell, Charles Diggs, and William Dawson. Those who knew Dawson's opposition to current civil rights campaigns laughed at that nomination, but the rise of black consciousness, with its new form of black patronage, was indeed at hand. The idea of a Civil Rights Section for the 1960 campaign, in which blacks and whites worked together, instead of an all-Negro section (as there had been before under Dawson), had been an innovation. But we were now coming full circle. "White liberals in the movement are going to be eaten up or pushed aside," a black friend predicted. That didn't worry me personally, since there were other things I wanted to do in my life, but it was late for a white man to be a President's Special Assistant for Civil Rights.

Underscoring these thoughts was a discovery about myself: I was too often amused at the ironies around me, and too prone to take the long view, to be fully effective with all the earnest people for whom each day and hour was a moment of truth. Studying and working with blacks on a regular basis had dissolved most of my self-consciousness about that relationship, and I found myself increasingly irritated by the patronizing attitude of many white liberals, who seemed to be moved primarily by a guilty conscience. When asked to graph the rise of Robert Kennedy's civil rights consciousness after becoming Attorney General, Burke Marshall shot his arm straight up. My own graph would show something of a level

---

* Aside from its obvious upside-down relation to my civil rights assignment, the uniform was a token of my great-grandfather, a reluctant Confederate officer. See page 109. Chuck Stone was not amused.

line during the decade since I helped organize Howard Law School pickets to integrate the lunch counter in Hecht's department store in downtown Washington in 1951. One of the ties that I enjoyed with John Kennedy was a sense of the comedy of politics, but I began to think that the joshing might be letting him off too easily on civil rights. In any case, I got tired of his accosting me with a grin and asking, "Are your constituents happy?"

Helping to persuade me that in good conscience I could leave the civil rights front was the fact that though the President might be "the vital center of action in our whole scheme of government," as John Kennedy had said when he launched his campaign in 1960, the Attorney General was clearly the vital center of action in civil rights. By late November 1961, the Executive Order on housing had been fully processed and agreed to in a final form. The President was expected to sign the order over the Thanksgiving weekend at Hyannis Port. On that assumption I had written him a cover memorandum saying that once his "good weekend's work" was done, he might be ready to let me move from the domestic to the international front. When he came back, the President told me that the order would be delayed again, at least until the spring primaries were over. He had made that decision walking the beach with his brother.

If everything else had been moving, the further delay in the order would have been a small matter, but this was the period in civil rights in which the President seemed to be suffering from the "slows" (as Lincoln once said of McClellan). At just this juncture, Shriver persuaded me to undertake a six weeks' mission arranging for Peace Corps projects in Africa and negotiating with the new governments of Togo and Nyasaland (Malawi). On my return in January 1962, I wrote the President that ending discrimination in America would do more to promote good relations with Africa than anything else, but that "the greater problem of integration is *our* integration into this largely colored world."

> The American Negro is going to make it, sooner or later, with more or less anguish. He has the strength—and has on his side the Constitution, the Federal Government, and the national conscience. Whether we, the Western minority, make it in this new world is the more interesting question.

I asked him to let me follow that logic and shift to "the big integration," presumably working with the Peace Corps. I urged him to bring Louis Martin to the White House in my place, "for we are heading into stormier weather with Negro leadership in view of the rising disappointment over our current slower strategy."

Beyond a friendly grumble that Shriver shouldn't raid the White House, Kennedy didn't respond. In March, I wrote again asking permission to accept Shriver's request that I become the Peace Corps' Special Representative for Africa and first director of a large new Ethiopian program. The Peace Corps had from the beginning seemed to me the liveliest embodiment of the New Frontier. "The spirit of your administration and your spirit," I explained to Kennedy, "make me want to go and work on a frontier of my own."

At last, in April, Kennedy called me over to his office, and asked whether I wouldn't rather be an ambassador to one of the countries in Africa that interested me if I was determined to leave the White House. The Assistant Secretary for Africa, Mennen Williams, had suggested the same possibility, and I told the President I would like to do that when it seemed appropriate to him, but the Peace Corps assignment was challenging for the time being. Kennedy asked when the incumbent American ambassador in Addis Ababa was due to leave and said he would like me to move into that post, after a year or two, if that was appealing; he thought it would be a signal of the importance placed on Peace Corps experience. He said Lee White of Sorensen's staff would take over the civil rights portfolio when I left.

Then, looking at a memorandum I had sent him, he circled the sentences that began: "You know the big steps which I believe you should take. They have been sufficiently outlined: the executive order on housing, integration of the National Guard, an executive order conditioning aid to higher education on nondiscrimination. . . ." This was when he gave me the assurance that with time he would take all the steps listed. In May we exchanged warm letters, in which I expressed confidence that he would "continue to make history in civil rights," and in August my family and I left for Addis Ababa.

Thus it was from thousands of miles away that I followed the travails and triumphs in civil rights of John Kennedy's last fifteen months. First came a fall and winter of discontent, with the Battle of Ole Miss, when despite the most active attempts to negotiate by the Attorney General and Marshall, the President had to send hundreds of marshals and then thousands of troops to Oxford, Mississippi, to save the life, and assure the registration in the university, by court order, of James Meredith. A black Air Force veteran, Meredith had written to the university for an application the day after Kennedy's inauguration, stirred by the new President's commitment to civil rights.

The Attorney General, the President, Burke Marshall, and others stayed up all night on September 30–October 1, seeking to get the governor to do his duty and advising Nicholas Katzenbach in Oxford not to order the federal forces to shoot unless absolutely necessary. For the first time, Kennedy went on the air in a nationwide appeal on civil rights. From an African perspective, Kennedy's actions and words were particularly impressive: if Meredith had been killed or driven out of the university it would have undermined America's standing everywhere, but most critically in Africa and Asia. The all-out federal effort to support one black citizen strengthened Kennedy's—and our country's—reputation overseas.

In America, however, many civil rights leaders were disappointed by the President's talk; its emphasis was almost entirely on law and order. Moderate white opinion throughout most of the South, however, rallied against the belligerence of the state of Mississippi. Yet the Mississippi State Senate passed a resolution conveying its "complete, entire and utter contempt for the Kennedy administration and its puppet courts."

Far from the judges being puppets, Kennedy's Southern judicial appointments were becoming another source of growing discontent within the civil rights movement. Kennedy was following a strongly entrenched tradition in deferring to senators of his party; contrary to the constitutional theory, the senators usually initiated the nominations for federal judges in their states "with the advice and consent of the President." As chairman of the Judiciary Committee that controlled the number—and the confirmation—of new judges, Eastland carried special weight. When he nominated his friend William Harold Cox, Roy Wilkins protested, but the American Bar Association gave Cox an "exceptionally well qualified" rating. The president of the ABA, Bernard G. Segal of Philadelphia, warned Robert Kennedy that though Cox was certainly qualified as a lawyer, his racial attitudes were another matter. Segal urged Kennedy to talk with Cox and put the question to him straight. Kennedy did, and was assured by Cox that when he put on the judicial robe he would put his personal views aside and adhere to the Constitution. The Attorney General pressed him on whether that meant he would follow the Supreme Court's interpretation of the Constitution, and Cox said yes. Kennedy reported to Segal that Cox had told him, "When I ascend to the bench my bible will be the writings of those nine men in their black robes in that marble palace in Washington."

Soon Judge Cox was blocking the Justice Department's voting investigations in Mississippi. Later in court he was to call some litigants, who were seeking the right to vote, "a bunch of niggers . . . acting like a bunch of chimpanzees." Bayard Rustin charged the President with being a smart, two-faced politician who says to Negro leaders, "I want to help you get

168

money so Negroes can vote," and then "turns and bows to the Dixiecrats and gives them Southern racist judges who make certain that the money the Negro gets will not achieve its purpose."

Not until the transcripts of the oral history interviews with Robert Kennedy were opened in 1979 did I learn how he felt about all this. Of Judge Cox, he said: "I was convinced that he was honest with me, and he wasn't." He regretted several Southern appointments (though not Griffin Bell in Georgia, whom he considered "an awful good fellow"). He was proud of the selection of Thurgood Marshall for the Federal Court of Appeals and of ten other black judges. Most surprising to me was the discovery that Robert Kennedy had wanted his brother's first appointment to the Supreme Court, in 1962, to go to a Negro, Federal Court of Appeals Judge William Hastie.

"I thought that it would mean so much overseas," Robert Kennedy said. But he made the mistake of going up to the Supreme Court and asking Chief Justice Warren about it. Warren "was violently opposed" to Hastie because, the Chief Justice told Kennedy, "he's not a liberal, and he'll be opposed to all the measures that we're interested in." Such prior consultation with a Chief Justice may have been unprecedented and seems inappropriate; Robert Kennedy says he didn't do it again. His brother suggested Byron White—who turned out on the bench to be more of a supporter of civil rights than I had expected, although he is at least as conservative judicially as Hastie is likely to have been.

Four months after I left, the President finally signed the Executive Order on housing. Former colleagues in the White House and the Civil Rights Commission wrote to congratulate me, although they regretted that the order's scope was more limited than the commission had recommended. The order had been so long delayed and then so narrowed that it had little immediate impact on anyone. The commission had originally proposed it as more of a symbolic action and statement of intention by the President on behalf of the federal government than a readily enforceable code. After all the procrastination the symbolism was weak: people sensed the President's heart was not in it. In the 1960 campaign, Kennedy had liked to recite Lincoln's words on signing the Emancipation Proclamation:

> If my name goes down in history, it will be for this act. My whole soul is in it. If my hand trembles when I sign this proclamation, all who examine the document hereafter will say: "He hesitated."

Kennedy always added, "But Lincoln's hand did not tremble. He did not hesitate. He did not equivocate." That could certainly not be said of

Kennedy and the housing order. Sorensen in his *Kennedy* told how the President equivocated to the last minute:

> His desire was to make a low-key announcement that would be as little divisive as possible. He found the lowest-key time possible on the evening of November 20, 1962. It was the night before he and much of the country closed shop for the long Thanksgiving weekend. The announcement was deliberately sandwiched in between a long, dramatic and widely hailed statement on Soviet bombers leaving Cuba and another major statement on the Indian border conflict with China.

As a final footnote, when Robert Kennedy's oral history interviews were made available, I learned that in the earlier period of delay the President kept muttering and kidding about how in the world he had ever come to promise that "one stroke of the pen."

In late February 1963, we read in the Ethiopian press that President Kennedy had asked Congress to enact a civil rights law, and that he had gone beyond legalities to say of racial discrimination, "Above all, it is wrong." It turned out that Louis Martin had asked for the inclusion of those words which Kennedy had hesitated so long to say as President: "The basic reason" for achieving true equality of opportunity "is because it is right."

Despite the strong rhetoric, the bill itself was weak, and disappointing to civil rights leaders. Letters from home disclosed the mounting disaffection in the movement, especially among the young activists. After a meeting with the President on policy toward Africa, a delegation of Negro leaders, including King, were encouraged about African policy but discouraged about the cautious approach to civil rights at home. One of them commented: "We've gotten the best snow job in history. We've lost two years because we admired him."

In early April we received an article King had written for *The Nation* warning the administration it was at "a historic crossroad." Civil rights "no longer commanded the conscience of the nation," he wrote. "In fairness it must be said that this Administration has outstripped all previous ones in the breadth of its civil rights activities," but now "its moral commitment and with it its political fortunes" would be determined:

> The Administration sought to demonstrate to Negroes that it has concern for them, while at the same time it has striven to avoid inflaming the opposition. The most cynical view holds that it wants the votes of both and is paralyzed by the conflicting needs of each. I am not ready to make a judgment condemning the motives of the Administration as hypocritical. I believe that it sincerely wishes to achieve change, but that it has misunderstood the forces at play.

Then over shortwave radio in Addis Ababa we learned in rapid succession that King was leading his forces into nonviolent action to end segregation in Birmingham, Alabama, known as the most segregated city in the South; that Marshall, the Attorney General, and the President (and members of the Cabinet, especially Robert McNamara and Douglas Dillon) were responding with extraordinary efforts to achieve a satisfactory settlement; that corporate leadership was being effectively engaged by the administration; that Martin King and hundrds of others had been jailed (and Coretta King had received another call from the President); that finally in early May, on Easter morning, thousands of children had marched against Bull Connor's police and more than 900 were arrested; that the television pictures of unarmed black men, women, and children being beaten by nightsticks, bitten by police dogs, and knocked over by water from high-pressure hoses had horrified the country, and that again, more than ever before, the issue of civil rights was commanding the conscience of the nation. In the mail came more detailed accounts—and the text of King's *Letter from a Birmingham Jail*.

The road not taken! For the first time since going to Africa, I felt the pull of Washington—and even more of Alabama. There may be more light at the periphery than at the center, I had said when I left. Now the President was at last in the thick of the fight and King was proving the power of nonviolence on a large scale—and I was far from the "historic crossroad."

In the next few months so much came together: the Birmingham agreement, promising a substantial breakthrough, that coincided with Bull Connor's departure from office; the bombings of the home of King's brother and a Negro motel; the showdown with George Wallace at the University of Alabama; the President's far-reaching message to Congress on civil rights; the March on Washington; and, throughout, the active intervention and outspoken leadership of Robert and John Kennedy.

It could have gone the other way, with everything falling apart. On May 13, 1963, Louis Martin warned Robert Kennedy that "the accelerated tempo of Negro restiveness and the rivalry of some leaders for top billing coupled with the resistance of segregationists may soon create the most critical state of race relations since the Civil War." On May 24, Robert Kennedy had an explosive meeting in New York with a group assembled by James Baldwin, whose best-selling book, *The Fire Next Time*, was explaining to whites the appeal of the Black Muslims and the Negro temptation to violence. "For the horrors of the American Negro's life," Baldwin had written, "there has been almost no language." After nearly three hours as the target of attacks, led by a young Freedom Rider invited by Baldwin, Robert Kennedy left the meeting angry and shaken.

"They don't know anything," he said. "They don't know what the laws are—they don't know what the facts are—they don't know what we've been doing or what we're trying to do. You couldn't talk to them as you can to Roy Wilkins or Martin Luther King. . . . It was all emotion, hysteria. They stood up and orated. They cursed. Some of them wept and walked out of the room."

Kenneth Clark later said that he and Harry Belafonte and other people in the meeting did not come to Bob Kennedy's defense (which infuriated him) because they "were trying to say that this was an emergency for our country, as Americans." Though Clark said it was *the* most dramatic experience" he had ever had, he thought it "never got over" to the Attorney General. He was probably wrong. After his first reaction to events, Robert Kennedy tended to brood about them; his friends say he pondered long and hard the meaning of the drama in that room—and in the country.

During this period the administration decided to go all-out, with an effort to get strong new civil rights legislation and to mobilize the economic and political leadership of the country for racial change. Kennedy's Southern Secretary of Commerce, Luther Hodges, agreed that the President should address the nation, but urged him to limit his appeal to the case for law and order. Kennedy acknowledged that his proposed action might lose him the 1964 election, but, according to Hodges' recollection, said, "There comes a time when a man has to take a stand . . ."

Most of all, Kennedy's brother urged him to take his stand. According to Burke Marshall, "every single person who spoke about it in the White House—every one of them—was against President Kennedy sending up that bill; against his speech in June; against making it a moral issue; against the March on Washington." Marshall said that the "conclusive voice within the government" was Robert Kennedy. "He urged it, he felt it, he understood it. And he prevailed. I don't think there was anybody in the Cabinet—except the President himself—who felt that way on these issues, and the President got it from his brother."

Robert Kennedy himself discounted most of the dramatic accounts of how the President finally made his choice at that crossroad on June 11: "He just decided that day. . . . He called me up on the phone and said that he was going to go on that night." During the day, faced with overwhelming federal force, Governor Wallace had backed down at Tuscaloosa and let two Negro students register. Kennedy thought the moment was right to go beyond anything he had said as President, and to ask the country and Congress to go beyond anything it had done since Reconstruction. He almost went on the air without a text, and Burke

Marshall, who was with him as he waited before the microphones, thinks that if he had given the talk extemporaneously, it would have been as good or better; but Sorensen's draft arrived just in time. Ever the faithful speechwriter, Sorensen said afterward that the speech "had been in preparation by the President himself for some time," and that it "drew on at least three years of evolution in his thinking" and, among other things, "on at least three months of revolution in the equal rights movement."

Kennedy apparently took pride in the decision to go ahead. Sorensen reports that while the President himself "did not indulge in comparison, he was not averse to those who called his speech and bill 'the Second Emancipation Proclamation.' " This time his hand had not trembled.

Listening to his talk by shortwave, I felt a thrill run down my back. "One hundred years of delay have passed since President Lincoln freed the slaves, yet their heirs, their grandsons, are not fully free," said Kennedy. "Now the time has come for this nation to fulfill its promise. We are confronted primarily with a moral issue. It is as old as the scriptures and is as clear as the American Constitution." It was the speech I had long wanted him to give, and this time the bill he sent Congress provided for large new steps in ending discrimination in all public accommodations and in public education, as well as in voter registration.

The President did not stop with one strong speech. He called meeting after meeting in the White House, usually with the Attorney General and the Vice-President at his side, with leaders of the main sectors of American society. More than 1,600 educators, lawyers, business executives, governors, mayors, editors, Negroes, Southern whites, clergymen, labor spokesmen, Republicans and Democrats came to hear personal appeals. Louis Martin played a key part in organizing a citizens' lobby for the bill. The Attorney General, Marshall, and the President worked ceaselessly with congressional leaders and the civil rights movement to shape the best bill that could be passed. (On June 12 Kennedy had called Eisenhower to get his help, but the former President did not favor passing a "whole bunch of laws.")

It was not surprising to learn that John Kennedy had some second thoughts. Robert Kennedy later said that in a semi-jocular fashion the President would ask him "every four days, 'Do you think we did the right thing by sending the legislation up? Look at the trouble it's got us in.' "

Robert Kennedy himself wavered, and wondered whether the controversial and sweeping public accommodations section—affecting restaurants, hotels, theaters, and stores—should be cut. Louis Martin later told me how he "bucked up Bobby" in a strategy discussion that was about to compromise. There was a restaurant near his home whose manager refused to serve blacks, and Martin told the Attorney General: "If that man shuts the door on my daughter, I'm going to shoot him." The easygoing Martin added: "If I, an old man, who wouldn't shoot anyone, feel that way, what about the kids?"

At first the President thought the proposed March on Washington would antagonize Congress, but in an encounter with King, A. Philip Randolph, James Farmer, and others, he finally agreed—and said publicly—that it was in "the great tradition" of American protest. King had pointed out to him that the timing of a protest always seemed wrong to people who were affected, and that some had even thought the Birmingham movement ill-timed. "Including the Attorney General," said Kennedy with a grin. They were, however, dissuaded from carrying through a sit-in in the congressional galleries, and at the last minute at the Lincoln Memorial John Lewis was persuaded to modify his text, which had originally included a threat that next time they would "march through the South, through the Heart of Dixie, the way Sherman did." On August 28, 1963, when Kennedy met the leaders at the end of the massive, triumphant march, he greeted them with King's refrain, "I have a dream."

At the American Embassy in Addis Ababa, I watched a special film of the March with a group of Peace Corps and Ethiopian friends of Ambassador Edward Korry. Again I felt the awful frustration of distance as we saw a quarter of a million people, black and white together, moving down the Mall, through the heart of Washington to the Lincoln Memorial.

Two weeks later a bomb killed four little girls attending Sunday school in Birmingham's Sixteenth Street Baptist Church. Again the President spoke strongly to the nation.

After that we heard little for a while about racial matters. A mid-fall Harris poll estimated that Kennedy had lost some 4.5 million white voters because of civil rights. Since another Harris poll showed Kennedy with about 90 percent of the Negro vote in a race against either Rockefeller or Goldwater, a projected increase of 580,000 Negro voters, the balance was not encouraging. (After the President's June speech, Gallup had found that 36 percent thought he was pushing integration "too fast"; 32 percent "about right"; and 18 percent "not fast enough.")

During the fall the Justice Department reported that nearly 200 communities in the South and border states—40 percent of cities or towns in the region with a population over 10,000—had responded to the President's appeal by desegregating at least some public facilities. In Congress, after tense negotiations and compromise, support was growing for a bipartisan bill that went even further than Kennedy had proposed, but not so far as to have no chance of passing the Senate.

On November 21, as Kennedy was leaving for a visit to Texas, the news came that the bill—stronger than any that had ever passed Congress—had been reported favorably out of the House Judiciary Committee and was ready to be sent to the floor by the House Rules Committee. In his last press conference before the trip, a high-spirited Kennedy gave his judgment that "by the time this Congress goes home" a civil rights bill—along with measures on education, health, and taxes—would be enacted. "However dark it looks now, I think that 'westward, look, the land is bright,' " he said, and predicted that "by next summer it may be."

Who, above the age of consent on November 22, 1963, does not remember where he was when he heard that President Kennedy had been shot? In our home on a mountain outside Addis Ababa the shortwave radio brought us the news from Dallas. Peace Corps Volunteers throughout Africa later told how their students had come to class weeping, or otherwise showing that they shared in what was a worldwide mourning. Learning belatedly that Emperor Haile Selassie was flying to Washington for the funeral, I hurried to the airport to talk my way aboard his special plane, but the Ethiopian Air Lines jet was just lifting off the field. Off and on for days and nights we listened to the radio. We heard Lyndon Johnson tell a joint session of Congress and the people that passage of the Civil Rights Act would be the most fitting memorial to John Kennedy. Later I read in Coretta King's memoirs how the King household had received the news, and how they had sat by their television, "hoping and praying that John Kennedy would not die."

> We felt that President Kennedy had been a friend of the Cause and that with him as President we could continue to move forward.
> Then it was announced that the President was dead. Martin had been very quiet during this period. Finally he said, "This is what is going to happen to me also. . . ."

Watching Kennedy's funeral was for Coretta King like "steeling myself for our own fate." Then their six-year-old son Marty asked, "Daddy, President Kennedy was your best friend, wasn't he . . . ?" Coretta King replied, "In a way, he was."

What is the truth about John Kennedy and civil rights, and about his relationship with Martin Luther King? This much seems clear to me: Kennedy was no hypocrite nor did he play politics as usual with civil rights. He was an extraordinary politician, and learned through politics in the best American tradition of learning by doing.

Was Kennedy's "whole soul" ever in civil rights, as Lincoln said his was in the Emancipation Proclamation? Even Lincoln delayed that proclamation so long and then limited its scope so shrewdly that abolitionists considered him a traitor to their cause, and he clearly weighed it in the balance against other heavy concerns, like winning the next battles in a war that was above all to save the Union.

Kennedy liked the comparison with Lincoln, and on the centennial of the Emancipation, in commending a hundred-year history by the Civil Rights Commission, wrote that the Proclamation "was only a first step— a step which its author unhappily did not live to follow up." Unhappily, we will never know how well Kennedy would have followed up his own great—and late—initiative in civil rights.

Was it really so late? I thought so then, but looking back across two decades the whole of Kennedy's thousand days seems almost like a flash of lightning. Kennedy was probably wrong in delaying his Executive Order on housing. If he had signed it promptly, as promised, I think it would have done more good and caused less trouble. But this was just one of many issues. Would it have been better, all around, if his bold legislative proposals and dramatic moral leadership of 1963 had come sooner? After his brother's death, Robert Kennedy said of the civil rights situation in 1961 and 1962, "There wasn't anything he could do then. . . . Nobody was ready." That isn't quite true, but William Sloane Coffin was even further from the truth when he said, in the midst of his 1961 Freedom Ride, that "a little moral suasion" from the President "would clear up the confusion in the country." The confusion was too deep. It may well be that the President was right, in the long run, to let things ripen as they did. "Events have controlled me," Lincoln once said, but he waited on Emancipation and other great steps, to be sure that his action was what the occasion truly called for.

"We're in this up to the neck," Kennedy had said to King and other civil rights leaders before the March on Washington. That was his language of commitment, not unlike FDR's, but a far cry from Lincoln's talk about his "whole soul."

Arthur Schlesinger has written of Kennedy that "only the unwary could really conclude that his coolness was because he felt too little. It was because he felt too much and had to compose himself for an existence filled with disorder and suffering." Perhaps, but over time I concluded that Kennedy's coolness was because he was cool. Fortunately the coolness in his soul was warmed by a comic spirit. Kennedy would surely have laughed at Schlesinger's unmitigated romanticism about him.* Yet I do not doubt that John Kennedy felt much that he did not put into words.

To the suggestion that President Kennedy didn't recognize the fundamental civil rights crisis in the country until he was forced to respond to Birmingham, Robert Kennedy said "hogwash." Martin King himself came to see much more in Kennedy's "ability to respond to creative pressure" than mere political calculation and crisis-management. Kennedy "frankly acknowledged that he was responding to mass demands" but did so, according to King "because he thought it was right to do so. This is the secret of the deep affection he evoked. He was responsive, sensitive, humble before the people, and bold on their behalf."

John Kennedy might have responded to questions about his timing by reading his favorite passage from Ecclesiastes, adding the lighter ending he once used:

"To every thing there is a season . . .

A time to be born, and a time to die;
a time to plant, and a time to pluck up that which is planted . . .

A time to weep, and a time to laugh;
a time to mourn, and a time to dance . . .

A time to keep silence, and a time to speak . . .

A *time to fish and a time to cut bait*."

---

* In an oral history interview, Robert Kennedy said the President "thought Schlesinger was a little bit of a nut sometimes."

6 · Marching to Montgomery

"Is it a sickness or a death in the family?" the United Airlines agent in Atlanta asked. Citing an "emergency," I had requested special help to get a late-night connection to Selma, by way of Montgomery, and the agent wanted more information.

"A sickness," I said, not feeling far from the truth.

"I hope it turns out all right," he said, in a deep Southern accent.

"So do I."

Thirty-six hours before, on Sunday, March 7, 1965, Alabama state troopers and white civilian "volunteers" deputized by Dallas County Sheriff Jim Clark had attacked an unarmed band of some 500 blacks marching across the Edmund Pettus Bridge to assert their right to vote. With tear gas and clubs the marchers were blinded, beaten, and dispersed. Martin Luther King had issued a call for clergymen and others from all over the country to join Alabama Negroes Tuesday morning, March 9, for a fifty-mile protest march to the state capitol in Montgomery.

It was a call I couldn't refuse. While working for the Civil Rights Commission or President Kennedy I had not been free to join King in public protests. Now back from two years in Africa, I knew afresh that America's relationship with the world depended on how speedily and fully we ended racial discrimination at home. Though I was still a government official, as Associate Director of the Peace Corps I was in an agency that prided itself on crossing conventional bureaucratic lines.

The Conference of Returned Peace Corps Volunteers—"Citizens in a Time of Change"—had just concluded in Washington, D.C. A thousand former Volunteers had come in surprising numbers from all parts of the country. At the request of Volunteers from Ethiopia, Harry Belafonte —arm in arm with Chief Justice Warren, Sargent Shriver, Secretary of Defense McNamara, and Vice-President Humphrey—had led the assembly in singing "We Shall Overcome." Together we had resolved to bring insights learned abroad into action in America. As we were leaving the State Department auditorium, we heard the news from Selma. Without asking him, I knew Shriver would respect my journey, whatever the criticism from some circles.

My wife was another matter; she did her best to prevent my going straight from the frying pan of night-and-day organizing of the Returned

Volunteers Conference into the fire of a five-day march. Though she agreed that the new politics of walking had come a long way in the ten years since 50,000 Negroes of Montgomery voted with their feet for an end to bus segregation, she considered it a romantic indulgence for me to insist on participating firsthand—and by foot.

Her arguments were still ringing in my ears when I landed in Atlanta. Noticing an unusual number of white and black men with clerical collars, I found they were all heading to Selma. Since my arrival at that airport with King in 1957, there had been one change: the sign on the door of the only washroom, for a black or white man, read "Men."

Sometime after midnight, the bus passed Craig Air Force Base, and I could see in the distance the well-lit flight line where in 1944, along with other new aviation cadets, I had been impressed with a sign on the control tower: "There is no place on earth more than 36 hours away from Craig Field." Now satellites measured the earth in minutes, and Ranger 9 was about to be shot to the moon. Just down the road was the Edmund Pettus Bridge, where the first marchers had been gassed and beaten thirty-six hours before—an event immediately televised or radioed to the whole world.

Thousands of Selma blacks and out-of-town visitors were leaving a late mass meeting at Brown's Chapel when I arrived. Outsiders were directed to private Negro homes or to motels; the streets were deserted in the white section, except for hundreds of extra state police cars parked for the night. I found a place to sleep on the floor of a room in the Holiday Inn, along with nine Episcopalian ministers.

Early the next morning, March 9, Mrs. Amelia Boynton, the insurance agent who had been so much alone in the fight for civil rights in Selma during the 1950s, greeted me at Brown's Chapel. "You've come back! After all these years, you've come back! And look at what's happened—look at the thousands of our people here in the street." She recalled our 1952 discussions about jail-going and Gandhi. "Just think what's happened in Selma!" she said. She told about the first voter registration clinic, when only one person showed up. Then some young civil rights workers came from outside and stayed for many months. Soon after receiving the Nobel Peace Prize in Oslo, King had come with some of his staff to join the efforts started by the Student Nonviolent Coordinating Committee (SNCC). Mrs. Boynton's office became their headquarters. King had decided that Dallas County, in the heart of the Black Belt, was the right target for an all-out assault on black suppression—and that such a dramatic and dangerous assault, well reported by the press and television, was the way to stir national support for stronger voting rights legislation and further federal intervention. "We are going to bring a voting bill into being in the streets of Selma," King said.*

The church meetings addressed by Martin and Coretta King drew large congregations, and in February King and Abernathy led 250 blacks and 15 whites from Brown's Chapel to the Selma courthouse to demand the registration of Negroes. Sheriff Jim Clark arrested them all; the two leaders, refusing to post bail, stayed in jail five days.

During that time Malcolm X came to town and so roused a Negro mass meeting with exhortations to violence that Coretta King was summoned by Andrew Young to deliver the gospel of nonviolence. Afterwards, according to Mrs. King's account, Malcolm said he was sorry not to be able to see Martin in jail, but hoped she would give him this message: "I want Dr. King to know that I didn't come to Selma to make his job difficult. I really did come thinking that I could make it easier. If the white people realize what the alternative is, perhaps they will be more willing to hear Dr. King."

While Coretta King thought the Black Muslims represented "The Hate That Hate Produced," as a television documentary had put it, she was encouraged by Malcolm's break with Elijah Muhammad and his turn toward internationalism after a pilgrimage to Mecca. She sensed he was reaching for something better than black racism. Eighteen days later, just before the events of March in Selma, Malcolm X was killed in Harlem. Had he lived, he might well have been on the march to Montgomery.

Amelia Boynton would have welcomed him, I think; she wanted all the company she could get. She was proud that already during the demonstrations there had been some 2,000 arrests, but she knew what it meant to be outnumbered. On "bloody Sunday," when she and 500 others started marching toward Montgomery, a state trooper's club hit her in the back of the neck and she fell to the ground, just across the bridge. While she was regaining consciousness, she heard someone ordering her to get up and run or she would be tear-gassed. Then the tear gas can was dropped next to her head. To a mounted posse, Sheriff Clark shouted, "Get those goddamn niggers! Get those goddamn white niggers!" and the horsemen charged with bullwhips. "Deputies," using electric cattle prods, chased the marchers still on their feet all the way back to Brown's Chapel.

Back on her feet, Mrs. Boynton was ready to march again, though her eyes were still red from the tear gas. This time there were thousands

---

* In his comprehensive study, *Protest at Selma: Martin Luther King, Jr., and the Voting Rights Act of 1965* (Yale, 1978), David J. Garrow contends that Selma was chosen because a confrontation there was certain to be dramatic and dangerous, and thus assure a national audience.

of others with her, including people from far away: Emily Taft Douglas (wife of Senator Paul Douglas), Mrs. Harold Ickes, Bishop John Wesley Lord, Bishop James Pike, and several hundred priests, ministers, and rabbis. Mrs. Boynton said it made her feel good to see them here, and it made her feel better about the government to think that a Peace Corps official could just take leave and come join the march.

As we were reminiscing and everyone was milling around, word spread that federal judge Frank Johnson had issued a temporary injunction forbidding the march until Governor Wallace's request for a permanent injunction could be heard. This was the judge who in 1958 had compelled state circuit judge George Wallace to produce voting records after he had refused to obey the Civil Rights Commission's subpoena. Now that same Judge Johnson, a courageous upholder of the Constitution, was telling us not to march to Montgomery.

Disputes raged around the field outside the church as the march leaders met in a secret hideaway to decide what to do. Many of the black students were shouting "March!" and were in fact lining up to begin. "We've been under an injunction for two hundred years," said one Negro minister to the impatient group. I argued that it was important for federal courts to be on the side of civil rights and for civil rights workers to stay on the side of the federal courts. Diane Nash, one of the militant young leaders of the Student Nonviolent Coordinating Committee and an organizer of the 1961 Freedom Ride from Nashville, replied heatedly: "As far as I'm concerned, the federal government *is* the enemy." Nothing I said dented her bitterness about lack of FBI and Justice Department protection in the Deep South during the "Freedom Summer" of 1964.

Seeing an unnecessary, confusing, and dangerous confrontation coming between the marchers and federal law, I decided to try to find King and make the case for some immediate protest short of violating the injunction against marching to Montgomery. We might march, I thought, but not to Montgomery until Judge Johnson or a higher court lifted the injunction. Andrew Young, who was trying to keep the throng calm, finally agreed to take me to King.

King listened to the alternative I proposed, and when I said we would all come back for the march when the injunction was lifted, he asked, "Do you think people really would?" He had been stung by charges that he had lost his nerve and compromised too much in suspending the struggle in Albany, Georgia, and that he had not come to Selma to lead the ill-fated Sunday march. Our discussion was interrupted by the arrival of the head of the Federal Community Relations Service, former Governor Leroy Collins of Florida, and the Assistant Attorney General for Civil Rights, John Doar.

Half an hour later, King and Ralph Abernathy came out saying, "We march." There were cheers as King was escorted back to the church. We walked together and he said quietly, "This was a prayerful decision. Sometimes you don't know whether you are making the right decision or not, but you have to decide. We have to march today." Then he added softly, "But we may not march very far."

Into Brown's Chapel we poured, and King was introduced as "a man whose address is the whole world." King said we would march peacefully in obedience to a higher law. Wondering whether we should be marching in the face of the temporary injunction and whether we had a good claim that the injunction was unconstitutional, I wanted at least that case to be stated, so I wrote the key words of the First Amendment on the yellow pad I was carrying, and passed the note up to King. He was climbing higher and higher on the rungs of the Gospel, defending our right to march with eloquent lines from the Bible; then, looking at the yellow sheet, he added, "And we march in the name of the Constitution, knowing that the Constitution is on our side. The right of the people peaceably to assemble and to petition the Government for a redress of grievances shall not be abridged. That's the First Amendment."

Once I had wondered whether Bob Kennedy should be disbarred for telephoning a judge about a case before the court; now I worried whether the professional legal ethics I had taught at Notre Dame permitted a lawyer to march in these circumstances. Why did the first occasion to practice civil disobedience have to come in connection with a temporary injunction that was not so clearly unjust? Nevertheless, it had come, and in the heat of the church meeting I decided the grievances to be redressed were great enough to claim the protection of the First Amendment against any injunction.

Several thousand would-be marchers were assembled outside the church. As King stepped out to lead them forth, Governor Collins came up for a final whispered conference, then gave a friendly wave to the crowd. "God bless you all!" he said, and we were off.

Down Sylvan Street, then across to Broad Street, we marched silently, two abreast. Watching from windows or the sidewalk were hundreds of white citizens. At the foot of the Edmund Pettus Bridge a deputy United States marshal stopped us to read the court order against a march to Montgomery. Then we moved up the long bridge. At the top we saw behind us a line of marchers about a mile long; ahead we saw a thin blue line of state troopers and a great mass of police cars blocking the road.

We proceeded steadily down the bridge toward the troopers. Soon they were lining both sides of the road with their billy clubs on display, and we were approaching the solid human wall across the road. We passed the billboards ("Chick-n-Treat: Home of Big Mickey-Burger" and "Free-Cash with Stamps") where the beatings and gassing had occurred two days before. As we got closer to the troopers, I thought we were about to experience a repeat performance. This is what King meant by not marching very far! Governor Collins was standing by a car, watching nervously.

From a loudspeaker a command came to halt and disperse. We stopped and King said that some of the religious leaders of the nation would lead us in prayer. First, Ralph Abernathy led us in singing "We Shall Overcome." Then we knelt on the pavement. In his prayer, Methodist Bishop Lord of Washington, D.C., compared us to the exodus from Egypt and asked God to open the Red Sea and let us through.

Just as the bishop finished his prayer, the loudspeaker started ordering state troopers to pull to the side of the road. Miraculously, it seemed to us, they moved aside and the road to Montgomery lay before us. At that point, as we surged forward, King faced us and said, "Back to Brown's Chapel!" One of his aides—I think it was Andy Young—started singing "We Love Everybody," while King began leading the line back to Selma.

Even as those of us toward the front turned and followed King, I doubted that the rest of the line would go with us. But the song caught on, and Andy Young stood in the middle of the road turning the line back toward Brown's Chapel. Soon we were all singing: "We love everybody." The most repeated verse was:

> *We love Governor Wallace,*
> *We love Governor Wallace,*
> *We love Governor Wallace—in our heart.*

Even the troopers had their turn as we passed them along the road:

> *We love the state troopers,*
> *We love the state troopers,*
> *We love the state troopers—in our heart.*

Among the marchers there was a sense of relief, even of a kind of triumph, mixed with considerable consternation. "We do what our leader says," said a Negro minister. "I feel I've been misled," said a white minister. Several young blacks agreed.

"All I can say is, 'Thank the Lord!'" said a white Catholic priest. He had expected King to lead him into the clubs of the troopers, not back to the church. As he prayed, this priest had asked for guidance. To go forward into the troopers seemed to him a kind of violence in itself, and that would surely be a violation of the federal injunction. But at that point, it would have taken far more courage to have deserted the march, even on grounds of conscience, than to have fallen under the billy clubs.

For Bishop Lord it had been a tumultuous moment. When the troopers cleared out of the road in the midst of his prayer, it seemed as if the Red Sea were indeed parting once again for a new Moses. Then, having wrought this miracle, he felt betrayed when King turned the line back to Selma.

Why did the troopers suddenly clear the road? Because they trusted the word from Governor Collins that King was going to turn back? Or because they wanted to embarrass King and divide his followers? Or did they hope the march would proceed so that King and the marchers would certainly be found guilty of contempt by Judge Johnson?

Back at Brown's Chapel, King reminded the would-be marchers that the principle of nonviolence required them to stop rather than use force against a human wall of troopers. This is what he had told Governor Collins, who was then able to assure the Alabama officials that the march would turn back.

"Why didn't we just sit down in the highway and wait till the injunction was lifted?" a young Negro called out in the chapel. King gave no answer to that, but vowed that the march would take place as soon as the court permitted it. He asked everyone to come back when that happened. Meanwhile, he asserted, the march through Selma and beyond the point of Sunday's violence—250 feet closer to Montgomery—was the greatest civil rights demonstration that had ever taken place in the Black Belt of the South.

Later, Bishop Lord said to me, "I guess this was the only way King could have kept us out of a federal jail. I suppose if he had let the word out that he intended to turn back, half the line would have rebelled and marched on to Montgomery."

One of those who might have marched on, James Forman, the head of the Student Nonviolent Coordinating Committee, insisted on speaking at the end of the meeting. "I've paid my dues in Selma, I've been to jail here, I've been beaten here," he said. "So I have a right to ask this: Why is it that there was violence on Sunday and none on Tuesday? Why is it that when we were just a bunch of kinky-haired, broad-nosed Negroes we were beaten and tear-gassed, but when all these good white people were here nothing happened? You know the answer. They don't beat white people. It's Negroes they beat and kill."

A Selma Negro answered him: "That's right. They didn't beat us today because the world was here with us. But that's what we want. Don't let these white people feel that we don't appreciate their coming.

We've paid our dues, all these years, and it's too late for us to keep paying them all by ourselves."

That night the Reverend James Reeb, a white Unitarian minister from Massachusetts, father of five children, was attacked by white men on the streets of Selma, and paid his dues in full. "White nigger!" one of them snarled, while clubbing him unconscious.

Before leaving town—and before learning about Jim Reeb's death —I talked to one of my old white friends who lived on a farm outside Selma.

"Maybe the best thing is for our Negroes to move North," he told me. "We really don't need them any more. We can mechanize our farms. Of course, if they keep going North we'll soon have a mongrel race, and you know history shows that when nations become mongrelized they fall and never rise to power again."

Thousands of Negroes had left Dallas County, but most had stayed —finally staking their claims as citizens. Not for a century had Selma been so shaken from its slumbers; not since its first occupation by Federal troops in the spring of 1865. In the Battle of Selma, on April 2, 1865, 1,500 Confederate troops and 2,500 civilian volunteers were quickly defeated by a larger Union force. But it took four days for the conflagration on Broad Street to be extinguished. How long would it take this time for the fires to go out? What would Selma be like then?

Six days later, stirred by the violence and nonviolence in Selma, and responding to a wave of indignation that swept the nation, the first Southern President since the Civil War told a joint session of Congress that "this time, on this issue, there must be no delay, or no hesitation, or no compromise." Speaking "as a man whose roots go deeply into Southern soil," Lyndon Johnson, on the evening of March 15, 1965, said to a hushed chamber:

> Rarely, in any time, does an issue lay bare the secret heart of America itself. The issue of equal rights for American Negroes is such an issue. And should we defeat every enemy, and should we double our wealth and conquer the stars and still be unequal to this issue, then we will have failed as a people and as a nation. For with a country, as with a person, "What is a man profited, if he shall gain the whole world, and lose his own soul?"
>
> At times, history and fate meet at a single time in a single place to shape a turning point in man's unending search for freedom. So it was at Lexington and Concord. . . . So it was last week in Selma, Alabama.
> What happened in Selma is part of a far larger movement which

reaches into every section and state of America. It is the effort of American Negroes to secure for themselves the full blessings of American life.

Their cause must be our cause, too. Because it is not just Negroes, but really all of us who must overcome the crippling legacy of bigotry and injustice.

And we shall—overcome!

Most of the members of the Senate and House of both parties rose to applaud. Johnson then called for the prompt enactment of the most far-reaching right-to-vote bill ever seriously considered by Congress. It included our controversial 1959 Civil Rights Commission recommendation for temporary federal voting registrars—the central proposal to come out of the commission's 1958 hearings in Alabama. In a two-and-a-half-hour meeting with the President on March 5, Martin King had urged him to give priority to the registrar plan and make sure that it passed this time. I recalled Roy Wilkins' confidential prediction in 1960 that of all the candidates Lyndon Johnson would actually *do* more for civil rights than anyone else.

Johnson himself said to Congress that "the real hero of this struggle is the American Negro." The President asked: "Who among us can say that we could have made the same progress" but for the Negro's protests "designed to call attention to injustice, designed to provoke change, designed to stir reform?" He had invited Martin Luther King to be his special guest in the Senate gallery, but King was in Selma conducting a memorial service at the courthouse for the Reverend James Reeb. King and his colleagues in Alabama listened—along with an estimated 70 million Americans—as the big man from Texas, with a Southern drawl, gave the ultimate commitment of federal power and moral leadership to the Negro's cause.

It was the first special message on a domestic bill that a President had delivered in person since Harry Truman went to Congress for help in breaking a nationwide railroad strike in 1946. Instead of going at the customary hour of noon, Johnson asked for an unusual night session so that most people would be home to see it on television.

"It's the violence that did it, it's always the violence, not the nonviolence that gets action," complained a skeptical Negro who was watching with me. "It's only when we are bombed or killed that the country listens or does anything."

A few days later, Judge Johnson ruled that King and his colleagues had a constitutional right to march. When Governor Wallace vowed further resistance, President Johnson federalized the Alabama National Guard and ordered 4,000 regular army troops to keep the peace. The march to Montgomery would now proceed, protected by the President of the United States, with a new civil rights bill promised at the end of the road.

On March 21, when I reached Selma, the march had already crossed the bridge and passed the point at which we had turned back twelve days before. As I trotted along the highway, a white man called out from his car, "Hurry up, or you'll miss your march!"

Hundreds of cars full of curious white people were crawling along the one open side of the road. Many displayed Confederate flags. Some had signs painted on them: "HAVE FUN—COME TO SELMA—COONSVILLE, U.S.A." "NIGGER, GO HOME!" "GO HOME, SCUM!" "OCCUPIED SELMA."

Army MPs were lined along the road, keeping the traffic moving. Air Force helicopters circled the fields and woods. Justice Department officials were riding or walking alongside. Burke Marshall joined me and walked along for half a mile until we reached the tail of the line; he had resigned as Assistant Attorney General for Civil Rights, but the President had asked him to go to Alabama to assist with the protection of the march.

Also walking along was the SNCC leader John Lewis, who had led the march on Bloody Sunday and been badly beaten. Despite the angry dissent of some of his young colleagues who wanted to be more "revolutionary," Lewis had thrown himself into the registration drive, contending that campaigns to win the right to vote in the Black Belt had as large an impact as—and required no less courage than—the earlier sit-ins and Freedom Rides. Sheriff Clark had helped him prove his point. Lewis told me that a recent trip to Africa had given him a new perspective, in which he felt more American and attached more importance to the attainment of political power.

It was a sunny day and this time the marchers were in festive mood. Different parts of the long line were singing different songs. The one the Dallas County students liked best began:

> *I'm gonna March when the spirit say March,*
> *I'm gonna March when the spirit say March,*
> *And when the spirit say March, I'm gonna March,*
>   *oh Lord,*
> *I'm gonna March when the spirit say March.*

And it ran on, verse after verse: "I'm gonna Sing when the spirit say Sing," "I'm gonna Love when the spirit say Love," "I'm gonna Vote when the spirit say Vote," "I'm gonna Die when the spirit say Die."

Soon Selma was in the distance and the last welcoming billboard signs were moving out of sight. "VISIT BEAUTIFUL CALVARY CHURCH." "NEED MONEY? SEE US. COMMERCIAL SECURITIES COMPANY." "STANDING ON OUR HEAD TO GIVE YOU A BETTER DEAL—FORD-TURNER."

Late in the afternoon we passed Craig Field, where extra troops could be seen waiting in trucks. A newsman reported on the progress of Ranger 9.

"An American rocket is going to the moon, and we're marching to Montgomery. Glory, glory, hallelujah!" exulted an old Negro minister, who was already limping along and admitted he wouldn't make Montgomery on foot. "But I'll be there for the last mile to see Brother Wallace," he said.

One of President Johnson's appeals to Governor Wallace, I had learned from Burke Marshall, had been in terms of the new age we are entering: the world of the year 2000, when men would be on the moon and exploring space. He had tried to get the Alabama governor to think in that perspective. What would people say then of Johnson and Wallace and the march to Montgomery?

Whatever people say in the year 2000, Johnson would have been happy to hear what the people on the march were saying about him. King told the marchers that "never has a President spoken so eloquently or so sincerely on the question of civil rights." A militant Negro lawyer said to me, "When I heard him saying, 'We shall overcome,' I just couldn't believe it. Why, if he had asked me, I would even have advised him, 'You better not say that. That's going too far.' He's with us—he's really with us!"

The students were singing again:

> Oh, which side are you on, man,
> Which side are you on?

At King's side were the Deputy Secretary-General of the United Nations, Nobel Peace Prize winner Ralph Bunche; the nation's top civil rights leaders; delegates from Canada and Britain; and, most prominent of all, the clergy, hundreds of Protestant, Catholic, and Jewish leaders. One of the latter, Rabbi Abraham Joshua Heschel, had such an imposing mien and such an impressive beard that an onlooker shouted, "Why, there is the Lawd!"

As Air Force helicopters hovered overhead, with water trucks and carriers for press and television crews in front of us and mobile toilets following in the rear, I kept recalling the joke about Gandhi by Sarojini Naidu, one of his devoted lieutenants, a poet who was to become governor of India's largest state. Waiting for a special third-class car to be brought from miles away so the Mahatma could travel like the poor, she said, "If Gandhi only knew how much it costs us to keep him in poverty!"

The only near-violence that day came when a white man's horse, tied to a road sign, panicked at the noise of a helicopter, uprooted the sign, and galloped wildly toward the marchers with the sign bouncing and hitting him. "You see, even the white man's horse is crazy down here," a Selma Negro said.

About eight miles from Selma, we turned off the highway to a side road, and then over a hill to a field near a Negro church. Several thousand marchers were taken back to Selma. For those who wanted to go on to Montgomery, tents were erected, food distributed, and bedrolls spread out. Most of us were too tired to talk, but the students sang on and on into the night:

> *Many good men have lived and died,*
> *So we could be marching side by side.*

At noon on the second day the first crisis came: how to reduce the number of marchers to the 300 permitted by Judge Johnson for the twenty-two miles of two-lane highway through Lowndes County. Blisters had thinned the numbers, but there were still several hundred too many.

"Why don't all the whites go back?" a white woman asked.

"Because the white people are part of our protection," Andy Young replied. "And because this is not a Negro movement. It's for Negroes and whites together." Most of the Negroes applauded.

Finally, to accompany the main group of marchers—the Negroes from Dallas County—twenty-two representatives of organizations throughout America were selected. Then the rest of us waited tensely while Andy Young read the names of ten of us, who were designated "special guests of Dr. King."

"We shall overcome," we sang as the reduced band marched onto the narrow highway into Lowndes County. Although four out of five of the county's citizens were Negro, no Negro was registered to vote—until March 15, when on the eve of the march the county board announced it had started processing two Negroes. "We are not afraid—we are not afraid—we are not afraid—today," ran the song. "Black and white together . . . today."

Up front, the yellow sun helmet of Len Chandler, a black folk singer, bounced back and forth between two large flags. The Stars and Stripes and the blue flag of the United Nations were being carried by Negro high school students from Selma.

Scattered groups of white people watched silently at crossroads. Then a waving black family of seven or eight, sitting on the broken-down porch of an unpainted shack, gave us our first welcome. The grandmother was clapping ecstatically. A reporter went up to ask if any of them had ever tried to register to vote. They said they would be thrown off the land if they did.

In front of one sagging old mansion with pillars a white family stood, together with an old black woman who appeared to be their cook or nurse. At first, only her eyes popped with excitement. As marchers waved to her, she began hesitantly waving her forefinger; soon she was waving openly as we passed by.

From overhead came a flutter of yellow sheets, dropped by a small plane. Addressed to "White Citizens of Alabama," the slips called for "Operation Ban": "Selective Hiring, Firing, Buying, Selling—An Unemployed Agitator Ceases to Agitate." At the bottom was the informative note: "This message was brought to you by the world's smallest air force—Confederate Air Force."

The road went through wooded and swampy areas where Spanish moss hung from the trees. "Is it true alligators and snakes are in there?" a white minister asked. "That's what they say," replied Mrs. Boynton. "But if you ask me, most of them are two-legged."

We passed a large billboard with a picture of Martin Luther King purporting to show him at a "Communist training school"—actually the Highlander Folk School in Monteagle, Tennessee (where I had taken the Indian leader Rammanohar Lohia in 1951).

In the late afternoon, Coretta King joined the march. She had grown up near here, in Marion, Alabama, and had been delighted that the movement was at last coming close to home. Her parents had attended the church mass meetings. All their pleasure soured when the nephew of one of her best friends in high school was shot while trying to protect his mother during a protest march in Marion. The streetlights had been turned off suddenly, and the marchers were attacked by police and other white men. Aside from the great personal sorrow, the death of Jimmy Lee Jackson stirred old fears that Coretta had shared when we first met in the fifties. But "on this great day," she assured me, she felt no fear, "even in the midst of Lowndes County!"

Not having talked with her since I left for Africa in 1962, I was relieved to find that in no sense—except for her resentment of J. Edgar Hoover—did she view the federal government as an enemy, and that she did not begrudge Robert Kennedy and Burke Marshall the relatively conservative position they had taken in 1963 on the matter of federal protection for civil rights workers. She understood the problem, she said, and had the greatest respect for them—and for John Kennedy. Looking back and weighing everything, she was glad Negro votes had been a key to his victory, and proud that she had been a part of it.

In the sunshine, miles out in the country, conditions were good for quiet conversation, but for the constant noise of the Air Force helicopters. Even more disruptive was a noisy overheating hearse that followed alongside. It had been turned into an ambulance, which a few badly blistered marchers needed.

For a while another vehicle was slowly accompanying us. Former Governor Collins leaned out the car window. "You won't believe it," he said, "but I'd rather be walking." I could believe it, because even as governor of Florida in the fifties he had wanted Eisenhower to take action in the South and had offered, to no avail, to work with him in breaking the white massive resistance. Now, as the first head of the Community Relations Service created by the Civil Rights Act of 1964, he had been working, night and day, behind the scenes to make the peaceful walking possible. President Johnson himself had taken an active interest in the logistical problems of the march; reviewing the preliminary plans, he pointed out that provision should be made for the transportation of Dallas County marchers back to Selma after they reached Montgomery.

The farther we went, the greater the Negro response. At crossroads or at Negro stores and churches, large clusters of people were waiting. King and Abernathy would step aside to shake hands. "See you in Montgomery!" marchers would cry. When the roadside response was hesitant, the marchers would call, "Get your courage up!" One old man was carried from his porch in a chair, so he could wave us on.

The Kings were driven back to Selma for the night. There had been a rumor of an assassination plot, and Martin had been persuaded to keep an important speaking engagement Tuesday in Cleveland. Coretta went to Atlanta to see the children. They would rejoin us two days later. It was not a very Gandhian action, but King's journeys had included seven Southern prison cells, including Selma's, so who were we to judge? Besides, we were on U.S. Highway 80, not on the road from Ahmedabad to the Indian Ocean. American priorities and symbols are different. Still, King's departure dampened spirits, even more than the rain that began to fall.

"Lift 'em up and lay 'em down, we are coming from Selma town!" sang out a black marcher when heavy rain, most of the third day, started to slow our pace. The downpour and the absence of the Kings and Ralph Abernathy (who also left to make a speech) did not seem to diminish our reception by Negro bystanders, who were increasingly outspoken and confident.

"What do you want?" someone in the march would shout, and people along the road would join in shouting back: "Freedom!"

"When do you want it?"

"Now!" came the answer.

"Where are we going?"

"Montgomery!"

Before long, a copy of the *Alabama Journal* went from hand to hand. An editorial entitled "Dr. King's 'Gandhi' Humbug" ridiculed the march, comparing it unfavorably to the Salt March. The latter, it noted, covered 241 miles and took twenty-four days. Gandhi was marching against the whole panoply of British power, not "pampered" by federal troops, and he never left his followers to make a speech. At the end, thousands of Indians, in small disciplined groups, walked wave on wave into the troops, and without raising a hand, were knocked unconscious. This was a far cry, the *Journal* said, from the "theatrical sham" taking place in Alabama, led by a "vaudeville Gandhi."

The *Journal's* criticism was taken as a challenge. "We can do that, too," a young Negro said as he read the editorial. "We'll go to Wallace and he can knock us unconscious, wave upon wave, if we have to—wave upon wave!"

Andy Young and the Reverend James Bevel, wearing a skullcap and overalls, were leading us. Young's constant good humor and common sense were contagious; I understood better why Burke Marshall, who had worked with him in many tense situations, considered him so wise and trustworthy. Young told me how much he had come to like working with Marshall and Bob Kennedy. But there was no monopoly on the spirit of leadership. At one stop, an old Alabama Negro minister suddenly started praying in a booming voice: "Oh, Jesus of Nazareth, go with us on this pilgrim journey. Lead us out of Egypt. Like Moses did, Martin Luther King and the Reverend Abernickel are leading us out of Egypt land."

Some of the high school students from Selma snickered at the mispronunciation of the absent Abernathy's name. But an older Selma civil rights worker, Mrs. Marie Foster, a dental hygienist, turned on them: "Don't you make fun of him! It isn't pronunciation that counts."

Mrs. Foster and Mrs. Boynton, sloshing along in the mud, then started defending the high school students. "These kids are the great ones," Mrs. Boynton said. "They've taken everything. They were ahead of their parents and their teachers. They've gone to jail. They've been beaten. And now look at them march, and listen to them sing." We had no choice but to listen—or to sing with them:

> *Before I'll be a slave,*
> *I'll be buried in my grave—*
> *And go home to my Lord and be free.*

> *Before I'll be afraid,*
> *I'll be buried in my grave—*
> *And go home to my Lord and be free.*

Walking alongside us, soaked in rain, was the Assistant Attorney General for Civil Rights, John Doar. Mrs. Boynton and Mrs. Foster agreed that they would like to run him for President. "Give us a few more years and we'll have the vote—then John Doar will sweep the Black Belt," Mrs. Boynton said.

John Doar was asked why army and National Guard troops, stationed at regular intervals, almost invariably faced in toward the marchers instead of out toward the woods or fields from which any attack would come. Doar departed and in a few minutes the U.S. troops were facing outward.

Alabama state troopers, who had attacked the marchers two weeks before, were also out in force, directing the traffic, making sure that no one stepped over the middle white line. State trooper cars all carried Confederate flags as a front license plate. Troopers were heard shouting "nigger" while giving directions.

Meanwhile, a marcher with a transistor radio, a tall young Negro assistant district attorney from Contra Costa County, California, gave us regular bulletins on the progress of another journey. From the firing of the Gemini space shot at Cape Kennedy that morning, at just about the time we started marching, Henry Ramsey followed Grissom and Young in their flight, orbit by orbit. We also learned that Ranger 9 had crashed with remarkable precision near the center of the moon.

"Keep your eyes on the prize," sang the students.

> *I've never been to heaven, but I think I'm right,*
> *You won't find George Wallace anywhere in sight.*
> *Oh, keep your eyes on the prize.*

To some unresponsive Negro bystanders the students sang another favorite verse of the song "Which Side Are You On?"

> *All you Uncle Toms,*
> *With all your excess fat,*
> *Come and join the march*
> *And we'll get rid of that.*

In the late afternoon, the rain stopped and on the hill ahead we could see the four-lane highway starting again. "Land of milk and honey!" cried out the old minister who had prayed for us earlier.

But we could not reach it right away. Our scheduled campsite, several miles nearer Montgomery, was completely under water. So we had to stop after only eleven miles and camp in a higher field. The mud was so thick we expected our sleeping bags to sink, but to our amazement the straw mixed with it and the plastic we put around it kept us afloat.

In the crowded men's tent, the exhausted "special guests" and older Alabama Negroes were trying to sleep, but the high school students were still full of song and jokes. Suddenly a sleepy white man stood up and yelled, "You goddamn kids, shut up! You are ruining my march."

The students sang back, quietly:

> I'm gonna Cool it when the spirit say Cool it,
> I'm gonna Cool it when the spirit say Cool it—

Unfortunately the man continued to shout angrily, "The worst thing about this march is each night with you!" To which the students responded, even more softly:

> And when the spirit say Cool it, I'm gonna Cool it, oh Lord,
> I'm gonna Cool it when the spirit say Cool it.

This was the second time the question had arisen of whose march it was. Earlier, the students had been skipping from their assigned rows and moving toward the front. The plan was for the outside representatives and special guests to come second in line, after the march leaders, and the Reverend Bevel wanted to keep it that way. As the students pushed through our ranks, Bevel kept sending them back, saying, "The dignitaries march first." To the mud-covered, unshaven "dignitaries" this description gave a special lift.

From the transistor radio came news that a resolution of the Alabama legislature had charged the marchers with free love, constant fornication, and a trail of sex orgies. Several nuns in the march joked about their lost reputations. John Lewis replied to the press, "These white segregationists always think about fornication. That's why you see so many shades of brown on this march."

My thoughts went back to my grandmother from Little Rock, who had often driven this road with me during some months she lived in Selma while I was stationed at Craig Field. "Lust," she feared, was at the bottom of all white men working for Negro rights. She told of their Little Rock minister who had preached brotherhood and then was discovered with a Negro mistress. "When he died, he was buried in a Negro cemetery!"

Whatever lust may have been in our hearts, and without discounting human ingenuity, even in rain and mud, I had seen no sign of the activities alleged by the legislature; piety seemed to me much more our problem. I almost welcomed the wild charge as an antidote to the sentimental-izing carried on by a few of the marching outsiders. One white woman went on interminably about the wonderful quality of the Negro high school classes she had visited in Selma. "Such bright and interested students! Such dedicated teachers—you can see it in their eyes!" she said. She was sure the level of learning was higher than in her own children's suburban school. She sounded like some Peace Corps Volunteers during their first week abroad.

Moving again on the four-lane section leading into Montgomery, we were joined by dozens, then hundreds and thousands of new marchers, as cars and buses unloaded faraway delegations. Two former Peace Corps Volunteers—Roger Landrum and Ernie Fox—and a Peace Corps Representative, Murray Frank, back from Africa, joined me with word that a number of others were on their way. Their special train from Washington had been stalled in Atlanta for lack of a crew willing to take them on to Montgomery.

During the morning, Martin and Coretta King and Ralph Abernathy rejoined the march. "We have a new song to sing tomorrow," said King as we halted in front of the Montgomery airport. "We *have* overcome."

As we crossed the city line, a downpour of rain drenched us again. But there was a song for Montgomery: "Oh, Lord, Kumbaya—Oh, Lord, come by here." There was even a touch of Sargent Shriver on the road-side—a new billboard: "HELP SOMEBODY BE SOMEBODY—VOLUNTEER FOR VISTA, THE DOMESTIC PEACE CORPS."

When we reached our camping ground inside Montgomery, in the compound of St. Jude's Catholic school and hospital, a loudspeaker asked the 300 who had walked all fifty miles to assemble in a muddy field. We were given bright plastic orange jackets to wear, the kind some-times used by traffic policemen.

"These orange jackets will assure you first preference on everything —dinner, seats tonight at the Belafonte show, beds, front positions in the procession tomorrow," one of the march organizers said. We were all "dignitaries" now.

The irony of marching in the name of King's "redemptive suffering" and ending in the "first preference" orange jackets was compounded by what then happened. "First preference" to dinner turned out to mean standing among a thousand others in front of the usual food truck, trying to catch a stale cheese sandwich as it came through the air. "First prefer-ence" to seats at the evening show did at first mean space to sit in the mud in front of the makeshift platform. But the space was short-lived as over 20,000 people pressed upon us. We escaped just before we would have been trampled, bright orange jackets or not. At this point, with dozens fainting in the dark and the crowd nearly out of control, we were called into service as marshals.

"Orange jackets, please link hands and push this crowd back," someone shouted over the loudspeaker. For the next hour and a half, we engaged in a constant battle to keep the crowd off the platform and give the engineers a chance to fix the lights. Finally, two hours late, the thirty artists from New York and Hollywood were able to proceed.

Harry Belafonte presented a remarkable assembly, including Leonard Bernstein, Ralph Bunche, Sammy Davis, Jr., Mike Nichols and Elaine May, Nina Simone, James Baldwin, Anthony Perkins, Floyd Patterson, Peter, Paul and Mary, Shelley Winters, Odetta, Billy Eckstine, Pete Seeger, Alan King, and Dick Gregory. In the middle he persuaded Coretta King to read Langston Hughes's poem "Mother to Son."

Dick Gregory produced wave upon wave of laughter as he punctured some of the poses of both blacks and whites. "Now don't you believe that Communist propaganda about the great experiment of a Russian spaceman climbing out of his rocket," Gregory said. "What really happened is that they had engine trouble and the radio told them they were to make an emergency landing. 'We're going to put you down in Selma, Alabama,' their radio orders said. That's when that Russian decided to climb out."

That was about when I decided to go to my tent, claim a piece of plastic for the soggy ground, and crawl into my sleeping bag, exercising an orange-jacket priority to a "bed." Odetta's last song was still singing in my head when one of the young volunteer marshals started shouting, "A girl has had her jaw broken, our security has broken down, we've got to move you out of here." After an hour's wait we were packed in trucks and carted around the Negro section of Montgomery looking for a Negro church with some floor space left. Finally, they found a church able to take us in. We filled the pews and stretched out up the aisles and under the pulpit. The orange jackets made good pillows.

At dawn, church women arrived to cook us a send-off breakfast of eggs, grits, and fried chicken. Then we joined thousands of lined-up marchers and waited for hours, and the streets around the St. Jude compound were clogged with still more people coming to join the final four-mile procession to the state capitol. Flags and signs were carried by hundreds of separate delegations. A dozen or more former Peace Corps Volunteers and staff made their own sign: *The Peace Corps Knows Integration Works.* Finally Dr. King arrived with a new group of prominent people who had flown in during the night.

"All you dignitaries got to get behind me," called out Profit Barlow, a seventeen-year-old orange-jacket student from Selma. With the help of the parade marshals, the orange jackets generally succeeded in forcing the newcomers to fall in line behind them. One man was pulled out of the front ranks because his shoes were shined. "There's no mud on those shiny shoes, how did he get in there?" an orange jacket called to a marshal. "I didn't see you fellows in Selma and I didn't see you on the road to Montgomery," said Profit Barlow. "Ain't nobody going to get in front of me but Dr. King."

NAACP chief Roy Wilkins caught this mood quickly and walked back to a place behind the orange jackets. "You fellows deserve to go first," he said. Some of us urged him to go back up front, but it was a day for symbolic acts and his was appreciated.

At last a prayer was said, and, singing "We Shall Overcome— Today," the line began to move. For a mile or more the street rose, so that we could look back to the end of the march. But there seemed to be no end. As far as we could see, the marchers kept coming out of St. Jude's. In the Negro part of town tens of thousands lined the way, waving and singing, many of them then joining the march.

Tears were streaming down the face of a Negro woman from Montgomery marching next to me. "This is the day! This is the day!" she kept saying.

In the white sections many thousands were on the street or at windows, but were generally quiet. There was one elderly white couple, however, leaning out of a fifth-story window, shouting openly and wildly gesticulating. They were thumbing their noses, putting their fingers over their heads as horns, and thumbing from their ears with such frenzy and leaning so far out the window that we thought they might fall. It struck most of us as funny, and we waved up to the couple. But a one-legged white marcher from Saginaw, Michigan, Jim Leather, who had come all the way on crutches, was infuriated. He stopped and started shaking a crutch at them. The marchers behind him gently pushed him on, before the television crews could catch this angry encounter.

Then King led us into Confederate Square. There, in the middle of town, a symbolic center of the old South, a little after high noon, we stopped and sang:

> *Deep in my heart, I do believe*
> *We have overcome—today.*

More solemnly, we started marching up Dexter Avenue, past the church where King had served during the boycott, to the state capitol. Up this broad avenue had gone Jefferson Davis's inaugural parade; then in

1955 and 1956 fifty thousand Negroes had walked for 381 days to end segregation on the city's buses.

At the steps of the capitol, we stopped before a line of armed Alabama state police. Looking back, we saw the square full of marchers, and all the way up the hill behind them they were still coming, as far as we could see, for a mile or more—forty or fifty thousand people, no one could count them all. Looking up to the capitol dome, we saw, on the one mast towering over the scene, two flags: the Alabama state flag and, above it, the Stars and Bars of the Confederacy. The Selma students were carrying the only flag of the United States in sight.

Then, from the podium erected in the street, speaking to the largest assembly for civil rights in the history of the South, Andrew Young said:

> This is a revolution—a revolution that won't fire a shot.
>
> Some of us are rich, most of us poor; some of us are old, most of us young; some of us are officials of the government of the United States, in the Peace Corps, most of us are private citizens.
>
> We come to claim representation in the government of Alabama.
>
> We come to ask the right to vote *now*.
>
> We come to warn that someday some of you in the State House are going to be in the cotton patch, and some of us in the cotton patch are going to be in the State House.
>
> We come to love the hell out of the state of Alabama.

Next Ralph Abernathy said, "Let's begin by rising to our feet and facing the flag at the front of our march, not the flag of the Confederacy up there, but our flag, the flag of the United States of America. Mrs. Martin Luther King will lead us in singing our national anthem."

For about two hours dignitaries marched to the podium for two-minute (usually it turned out to be five- or ten-minute) nonviolent shots at Governor Wallace. The governor was against outsiders, Ralph Bunche noted. "But no American can ever be an outsider anywhere in this nation," said the Deputy Secretary-General of the United Nations in his dispassionate voice. "I belong here because my mind and conscience tell me as an American this is where I ought to be. This is an all-American attack on an all-American problem."

Then Mrs. Amelia Boynton of Selma read the proposed petition to Governor Wallace. The marchers roared their approval. Newsmen reported that Wallace and other state officials listened to the proceedings in their offices, and that the governor several times peeked out of his window to watch.

At the end of the line of speakers came Mrs. Rosa Parks, the Montgomery seamstress who nine years before had been arrested for refusing to move to the back of the bus. Introduced as the woman who started all this, she spoke briefly of the bus boycott and then said there were others who could say it all better.

"Now we're ready for 'de Lawd,' " one of the students said. There was a touch of derision in his words, but to most of the assembly that afternoon there was music in the name of Martin Luther King. "As God called Joshua to lead His people across the Jordan," said Ralph Abernathy, "so also He called Martin Luther King to go to Montgomery and tell Pharaoh Wallace, 'Let my people go.' "

"Last Sunday more than eight thousand of us started on a mighty walk from Selma, Alabama," King began. "We have walked on meandering highways and rested our bodies on rocky byways. Some of our faces are burned from the outpourings of the sweltering sun. Some have literally slept in the mud. We have been drenched by the rains.

"Our bodies are tired, and our feet are somewhat sore," King said. It reminded him of what a seventy-year-old Negro woman had said during the bus boycott, when one day she was asked while walking if she wasn't tired. She had replied, "For a long time my feet's rested and my soul's been tired. Now my feet's tired, but my soul is rested."

Coretta King's father, who had suffered the burnings of Klansmen, said to her, "This is the greatest day for Negroes in the history of America."

As we headed for home that evening, we were happy, and the airport was full of celebration, like a festival after an Easter sunrise service.

The peculiar revolution that King had been leading since the bus boycott had come a long way, in rain and shine. It had helped elect one President and had received unprecedented endorsement from the next. It had changed the laws of the land and moved the minds and hearts of many people.

The next morning, back safely with our families and friends, we learned that during the night one of our companions in Montgomery, Viola Liuzzo, a white woman from Detroit, had been shot and killed on Highway 80 while driving one of the student marchers back to Selma. The television news showed Mrs. Liuzzo's husband and children, and then replayed the last words Martin King had spoken the day before. The film showed the sun setting on the Alabama capitol as King said:

My people, listen! We are still in for a season of suffering. . . . There are still many jail cells waiting for us, many dark and difficult moments. But we will go on with faith in the power of nonviolence.

Our aim must never be to defeat or humiliate the white man but to win his friendship and understanding. The end we seek is a society at peace with itself. That will be a day not of the white man, not of the black man. That will be the day of man as man.

You are asking today, "How long will it take?" It will not be long. How long? Not long, because no lie can live forever. How long? Not long, because you still reap what you sow. How long? Not long, because mine eyes have seen the glory of the coming of the Lord. He is trampling out the vintage where the grapes of wrath are stored. He has loosed the fateful lightning of his terrible swift sword. His truth is marching on. . . . Oh, be swift, my soul, to answer Him. Be jubilant, my feet. Our God is marching on.

Glory, glory hallelujah!
Glory, glory hallelujah!
Glory, glory hallelujah!

7 · MLK, RFK, LBJ, and the FBI: Matters of Life and Death

On April 4, 1968, at the Atlanta airport, Coretta King got the call that she says she had subconsciously been waiting for all her life. Her husband "had felt a mystical identity with the spirit and meaning of Christ's Passion," and she felt it somewhat strange, yet somehow appropriate that his death should come in the week before Easter.

Before going to Memphis, in his last sermon at the Ebenezer Baptist Church, Martin King had spoken of his own death, saying, "I don't want a long funeral"; he asked for it to be said only that "Martin Luther King, Jr., tried to give his life serving others . . . tried to love somebody . . . tried to be right on the war question." The funeral with its many eulogies was far from short, but he would have approved the long march. For hours it wound halfway across Atlanta, black and white together, from all over the country, a hundred thousand or more, following the casket on a flatbed farm wagon drawn by a pair of mules. "We marched at his funeral," Coretta King explained, "because Martin had spent so much of his life marching. . . . This was his last great march."

For many of us the march through Atlanta was the culmination of the politics of walking. As we moved up a long slope toward Morehouse College, fifteen, twenty abreast, we could look back a mile or so upon a sea of people that stretched beyond the horizon, and memories went back to other marches in Montgomery, Albany, Birmingham, Washington, D.C., Selma, Chicago, rural Mississippi, and Memphis. The maxim of more than twelve years seemed to have been: when words are weak, walk!

Walking as a form of political action has been a special phenomenon of the twentieth century. From Gandhi's first great South African march into the Transvaal and his later Salt March in India, to Mao Tsetung's Long March, to American marches for women's suffrage, peace, and civil rights, it has been a powerful method of getting attention. It is a manifestation of politics as drama, in which citizens can themselves act on the public stage. For Martin King marching was also a form of liturgy —a way of making words become flesh.

When the news of his death came, I was at Dartmouth College, attending a conference on innovation in higher education. We stopped the meeting and hurried to the nearest television set, just in time to see Robert Kennedy speaking from the back of a truck to a large group of

Indianapolis blacks. His face was in anguish, and a cold wind was blowing, as he told them Martin Luther King had been murdered. There were cries of disbelief and horror as he went on to ask "what kind of a nation we are and what direction we want to move in."

To those who were black and tempted to be filled with hatred, he said he had had a member of his family killed and felt in his own heart that same kind of feeling. "You can be filled with bitterness, with hatred, and a desire for revenge," he said. "We can move in that direction as a country, in great polarization—black people amongst black, white people amongst white, filled with hatred toward one another. Or we can make an effort, as Martin Luther King did, to understand and to comprehend, and to replace that violence, that stain of bloodshed that has spread across our land . . . with compassion and love." He seemed almost unable to go on, but finally said, "Let us dedicate ourselves to what the Greeks wrote so many years ago—to tame the savageness of man and to make gentle the life of this world."

The Indianapolis police chief had warned him not to go into that black ghetto that night as the bearer of such news. It was a meeting arranged by John Lewis, who was now campaigning for Kennedy for President; thanks to the schedule set by the former SNCC leader and Freedom Rider, millions of black people and a hundred million other Americans (before the evening was over) were able to hear from the one man who could best put such a death in perspective. Once, eight years before, also in connection with Martin King, I had half joked that the Kennedys never showed their passion; through television, we were now privy to the passion of Robert Kennedy. Even a roomful of Gene McCarthy partisans, who were still angry about Kennedy's late entry in the race, were deeply moved; we had all been witnesses to a great and genuine grief that we shared. Such a death breeds an extraordinary sense of community.

Then we watched television as parts of King's sermon the night before were repeatedly rerun. On the evening of April 3 King had told his Memphis congregation about the threats of "what would happen to me from some of our sick white brothers," and about the pilot that morning who had announced over the public address system that the plane's delay had been caused because Martin Luther King was aboard and they had "to be sure that all of the bags were checked." In his last public words, King said:

"But it doesn't matter with me now. Because I've been to the mountaintop. . . . I would like to live a long life. Longevity has its place. But I'm not concerned about that now. I just want to do God's will. And He's allowed me to go up to the mountain. And I've looked over. And I've seen the promised land. I may not get there with you. But I want you to know tonight, that we as a people will get to the promised land. And I'm happy tonight. I'm not worried about anything. I'm not fearing any man. Mine eyes have seen the glory of the coming of the Lord."

Our sixteen-year-old daughter, Susanne, went with me to the silent memorial march in Memphis, and then, on April 9, to Atlanta for the funeral. Like the television programs replaying high points of the drama enacted by King during more than twelve years on the national stage, I found my mind (on my forty-second birthday) running backward over the events of those years. Most of the cast of characters were there. At Harry Belafonte's suggestion and in his company, Coretta King had gone to Memphis to lead the march her husband had scheduled. Robert Kennedy had placed a plane at her disposal, and with Ethel and Jacqueline had come to Atlanta. He had asked Burke Marshall to help Mrs. King make arrangements for the funeral; Louis Martin was on hand. Rockefeller had provided another plane, and had come too. Richard Nixon, Hubert Humphrey, Eugene McCarthy, and hundreds of other public figures were there, with the notable exception of Lyndon Johnson. The President had just announced that he would not run again; he proclaimed a day of national mourning for King, but could not bring himself to go to Atlanta for the funeral of the man who had done so much to turn opinion against the war in Vietnam and thus bring down his presidency.

How had it all come to this?

A moment after King fell to the floor of the motel balcony, Andrew Young and companions were photographed with their arms pointing out to the source of the shot. After a long hunt James Earl Ray, a white ex-convict, was caught and pleaded guilty. But Benjamin Mays, in the final burial eulogy in Atlanta, pointed to a different cause of King's death. "Make no mistake," he said, "the American people are in part responsible. . . . A century after Emancipation, and after the enactment of the Thirteenth, Fourteenth, and Fifteenth amendments, it should not have been necessary for Martin Luther King, Jr., to stage marches in Montgomery, Birmingham, and Selma, and go to jail over twenty times."

Mays meant more than a general historical indictment. "The assassin heard enough condemnation of King and of Negroes to feel that he had public support," the long-time president of Morehouse College added. "He knew that millions hated King."

Among those millions was the Director of the Federal Bureau of Investigation. On the memorial march in Memphis and during the long day in Atlanta, for the first time I heard associates of King express their suspicions that somehow J. Edgar Hoover was directly or indirectly involved in King's death. Since then, as evidence of Hoover's and the FBI's extraordinary campaign against King has come to light, those suspicions have grown.

Berl Bernhard, who had discovered Hoover's implacable hostility to King firsthand, from the Director's lips and from FBI memoranda sent to the Civil Rights Commission, told me his awful conviction, which he has not shaken to this day, that Hoover somehow was behind King's murder. At the funeral in 1968 that possibility seemed farfetched to me. I had known of Hoover's general antipathy to the civil rights movement and his allegations that one of King's closest associates was a Communist; indeed, I had been directly and painfully involved in the matter of that adviser's ties to King. But I found it almost impossible to believe that the man who for so long stood as the embodiment of law and order could in any way have encouraged or incited the assassination of an American citizen revered by so many millions.

Then in 1976 Senator Frank Church's Select Committee to investigate abuses in government intelligence activities disclosed the FBI's concerted counterintelligence program (known by the acronym COINTELPRO) that sought, in Hoover's words, to "expose, disrupt, misdirect, discredit, or otherwise neutralize" King and his Southern Christian Leadership Conference (SCLC). "Neutralize" is a word that in foreign covert operations might include murder, and William Sullivan, head of the FBI's Domestic Intelligence Division, testified to the Church committee that counterintelligence was "a rough, tough, dirty business," that "no holds were barred," and that techniques used against Soviet agents were "brought home against any organization against which we were targeted." Walter Mondale pressed the question:

> *Senator Mondale.* Would it be safe to say that the techniques we learned in fighting . . . true espionage in World War II came to be used against some of our own American citizens?
> *Mr. Sullivan.* That would be a correct deduction.

It was no deduction but a fact, admitted by the FBI and shown in documents supplied by the Bureau, that King was an American citizen against whom rough, tough, dirty tactics were used. The Church committee's 103-page "Dr. Martin Luther King, Jr., Case Study" summarizes the evidence of the tactics used in the FBI's "war" against King. Since the committee was limited by the FBI's own file search and testimony, and since covert actions are by their nature undocumented, it is likely that only the top of the iceberg of the COINTELPRO against King and the SCLC has been (or ever will be) disclosed.

In 1979 further evidence of Hoover's obsession with King and his determination to rid the country of his influence was presented in the hearings of the House Select Committee on Assassinations. "We were operating an intensive vendetta against Dr. King in an effort to destroy him," testified Atlanta FBI agent Murtagh. FBI section chief Brennan, conceding that the effort "to remove him as a civil rights leader" was "an abuse of power," told how one agent "jumped for joy" when King died and had said, "They got the son of a bitch." Another agent said he knew people in the FBI who might well have been involved in aiding the assassination. "It could have happened," he said. "I hope it didn't."

We must all hope it didn't. But the country must deal with the ugly fact, uncovered by the Church committee, that in a number of cases involving so-called black nationalist groups other than the SCLC, FBI COINTELPRO campaigns did include deliberate efforts to "intensify the degree of animosity" toward targeted groups and "turn violence prone organizations" against the targeted leaders. In connection with the campaign against the Black Panther Party, the Church investigation found that "although the claimed purpose of the Bureau's COINTELPRO tactics was to prevent violence, some of the FBI's tactics against the BPP were clearly intended to foster violence, and many others could reasonably have been expected to cause violence."

For example, the FBI sent an anonymous letter to the leader of a Chicago street gang, the Blackstone Rangers, falsely informing him that the Chicago Panthers had "a hit out" on him. The stated intent of the letter, according to the Chicago field office's memorandum to FBI headquarters in 1969, was to induce the Ranger leader to "take reprisals against" the Panther leadership. In a similar action in California, after the FBI claimed credit for inciting "shootings, beatings and a high degree of unrest," a local FBI office wrote headquarters that it was seeking to bring two rival factions together "and thus grant nature the opportunity to take her due course."

Letting nature take its course is hardly an adequate description of the elaborate steps the FBI took to bring out the worst in human nature. Even while Huey P. Newton was in prison and Eldridge Cleaver was out of the country, the FBI sent them a barrage of anonymous letters designed to provoke a fight between them and among their followers, and destroy the Panthers. In measuring the effectiveness of the COINTELPRO against the black nationalists, the head of the Bureau's Racial Intelligence Section did not claim direct credit for the factionalism that disrupted them, but said, "We hope that it did play a part. Maybe we just gave it a nudge."

Would the FBI go to these lengths to destroy the nonviolent King?

Did it give a "nudge" to his assassination? The 1979 investigation of the House Committee on Assassinations could not prove any direct connection between the FBI determination that King was "the most dangerous Negro" in the country and the killing. But its report points to evidence of a conspiracy to kill King that may have involved white hate groups and the underworld, and by 1968 the FBI had an extensive network of paid "informants" in both the Ku Klux Klan and the Mafia. Robert Kennedy had pressed Hoover to infiltrate both those targeted groups with the vigor and skill the FBI used to penetrate the Communist Party, but the role of these informants involved more than Kennedy imagined.

One of them, Gary Rowe, testified before the Church committee that he had himself gone with other Klansmen and "beaten people severely . . . with blackjacks, chains, pistols." In addition to joining in the attack on the Freedom Riders in Birmingham in 1961, he was in the car from which the shots came that killed Mrs. Viola Liuzzo after the Selma march in 1965 (and one of those charged with the murder alleged that Rowe actually fired the gun). Only when the Klan promoted Rowe to an Action Group squad leader did the FBI tell him he would have to resign that position or be taken off the FBI payroll. "He couldn't be an angel and be a good informant," said his FBI "handling agent."

Did some violence-prone FBI informant, encouraged by an aggressive "handling agent" who wanted to please his boss and rid the country of a living menace, conspire to kill King? We will probably never know. The chairman of the House investigation of King's assassination, Representative Louis Stokes of Ohio, summarized the evidence pointing to a conspiracy and the evidence of the FBI's campaign against King, and concluded that though no direct connection could be proved, the actions and attitudes of the FBI and its Director had encouraged someone to pull the trigger.

The story of how Hoover and the FBI helped create the climate that invited King's assassination is probably the single most disturbing story of the 1960s, or perhaps of any decade in American history. It is the story of a rogue elephant trampling on the rights of American citizens, but for the most part not being seen and with almost no one daring to bring it under legal control. The reports of the Senate and House committees ought to be read in full, but the outline of the plot—so far as it is yet known—can be briefly told.

Hoover's enmity to King began in the late 1950s but only came into public view a few days after Robert Kennedy resigned as Attorney General—which was also shortly after it was announced that King would receive the 1964 Nobel Peace Prize. As King was preparing his acceptance address, he read that the Director of the FBI had said to a group of women reporters that Martin Luther King was the "most notorious liar in the country." When criticized for this attack, Hoover replied, "I haven't even begun to say all that I could about that subject."

Hoover's charge was supposedly a reply to King's criticism of FBI agents in the South, but no one who knew Hoover's pent-up feelings about King doubted that it covered what the Director considered a multitude of sins. "King is no good," Hoover had written privately in February 1962. By May of that year he had included King among those to be rounded up and detained in a national emergency. In October 1963 he secured authorization from the Attorney General for the FBI to maintain a wiretap on King's home telephone, ostensibly in order to ascertain whether King was being influenced by Communists. Later that month Hoover circulated to various government officials a memorandum on King that an aide advised him could be taken "as a personal attack" and might "startle the Attorney General." Hoover replied, "We must do our duty."

When Robert Kennedy learned of the distribution outside the department of a document he considered unfair and misleading, he ordered the recall of all copies. This did not stop Hoover. In a few days John Kennedy was dead, and most of Robert Kennedy's limited control over Hoover was gone. Thereafter, the Attorney General was away from the department much of the time, grieving, and Hoover immediately reestablished the direct relationship with the President that had been unbroken from 1924 through 1960. In the last months of Kennedy's tenure at the Justice Department, he and Hoover did not speak to each other.

In December 1963, the FBI's Domestic Intelligence Division held a nine-hour session that resulted in a secret program to help the country see King "as being what he actually is—a fraud, demagogue and scoundrel" and thus "take him off his pedestal and . . . reduce him completely in influence." When this is done, "and it can and will be done, obviously much confusion will reign," wrote William Sullivan, who proposed that the FBI therefore identify "the right kind of a national Negro leader" who "could at this time be gradually developed so as to overshadow Dr. King and be in the position to assume the role of the leadership of the Negro people when King has been completely discredited." Hoover's aide proposed a particular Negro to replace King. Hoover wrote on the memorandum: "I am glad to see that 'light' has finally, though dismally delayed, come to the Domestic Int. Div. I struggled for months to get over the fact that the communists were taking over the racial movement but our experts here couldn't or wouldn't see it."

Hoover was referring to an earlier memorandum from Sullivan that had concluded that the Communists had failed "dismally" in efforts over many years to influence American Negroes. An angry Hoover had stopped speaking to Sullivan. Before long, Sullivan (who wanted someday to become Director) saw the light and reported: "The Director is correct. We were completely wrong." No longer limited to "legalistic proofs," Sullivan said that "in the light of King's powerful, demagogic speech yesterday [the "I have a dream" talk at the Lincoln Memorial], we must mark him now, if we have not done so before, as the most dangerous Negro of the future in this Nation from the standpoint of communism, the Negro and national security." Later, to the Church committee, Sullivan testified: "Here again we had to engage in a lot of nonsense which we ourselves really did not believe in. We either had to do that or we would be finished."

Hoover stated his goal in a 1964 memorandum to FBI agents: "taking such action as is appropriate to neutralize or completely discredit the effectiveness of Martin Luther King, Jr." The Atlanta FBI office responded with a list of actions. It included steps to widen any rift between King and Roy Wilkins, "furnishing to friendly newspapers on an anonymous basis, certain specific leads"; investigating "twelve key [SCLC] employees . . . to obtain some weakness that could be used for counter-intelligence activities"; "injection of false information with certain discontented [SCLC] employees"; sending letters to SCLC's financial donors, written on SCLC stationery fabricated in the FBI laboratory and bearing Dr. King's signature, stating that the IRS was checking SCLC's tax records, which would "eliminate future contributions"; placing a pretext call to an SCLC creditor to impress him with the "financial plight" of the SCLC so that he would "be incited into collection efforts." Hoover expressed "the Bureau's gratitude" to the Atlanta agents for their "aggressive imagination."

Hoover's own imagination was ever at work. Following an off-the-record briefing he gave the House Appropriations Committee, congressmen were alarmed by his allegations about King and tried (unsuccessfully) to get the USIA to withdraw its film of the March on Washington (which we had been so glad to see at the U.S. Embassy in Addis Ababa). Hoover gave a special commendation and monetary award to an agent who persuaded Marquette University in Milwaukee not to give King an honorary degree. Senator Leverett Saltonstall was not so successful; at the FBI's instigation he tried to get Springfield College to uninvite King, but the president, Glenn Olds, refused (the FBI did not want to approach Olds directly because of his "close association with Shriver"). When FBI agents, even with the promised help of Cardinal Spellman, failed to dissuade the Vatican from giving King an appointment with the Pope,

Hoover wrote, "Astounding . . . I am amazed that the Pope gave an audience to such a ———— [excised by FBI]."

In January 1964 (if the FBI's admission tells the whole story) the first of many microphones were hidden in King's hotel rooms, and the alleged evidence of sexual misbehavior was reported to President Johnson's assistant, Walter Jenkins. According to a memorandum by Hoover's assistant, Cartha DeLoach, "Jenkins was of the opinion that the FBI would perform a good service to the country if this matter could somehow be confidentially given to members of the press."

Later in 1964, after the Nobel Prize for King was announced, Hoover secured White House approval from Bill Moyers to send to members of the National Security Council an expanded version of the memorandum on King that Robert Kennedy had ordered recalled. Materials alleging Communist influence and improper sexual activity were shown to selected journalists and to some of Hoover's friends in Congress—and sent to United States ambassadors in European countries that King might visit on his trip to the Nobel ceremony.

Next, according to the Church report, Sullivan prepared, at Hoover's direction, a composite tape of alleged scandalous conversations or sounds recorded in King's hotel rooms. A copy was mailed to Mrs. King with an anonymous letter for her husband: "King, there is only one thing left for you to do. You know what it is. You have just 34 days. . . . You are done. There is but one way out for you. You better take it before your filthy fraudulent self is bared to the nation." Coming shortly before the Nobel award, the thirty-four days may have been timed so as to scare King away from Oslo. Some of King's colleagues, and apparently King himself, took it as a heavy-handed effort to drive him to suicide. Sullivan indicated to the Church committee that the tape was sent as a device to break up King's marriage, which Hoover thought would help discredit him.

The riots in Watts in the summer of 1965, Chicago in 1966, and Detroit and Newark in 1967, and the new slogan of "Black Power" being raised by Stokely Carmichael and other young militants, along with the separatism of the Black Muslims, gave Hoover a new opportunity. In the summer of 1967 the FBI launched a full-scale new (but, of course, secret) counterintelligence program designed to disrupt, discredit, and otherwise neutralize "Black Nationalist–Hate Groups." Over the objections of at least one FBI specialist the Southern Christian Leadership Conference, which had stood steadfast against separatism and violence, was listed (along with CORE, SNCC, and the Nation of Islam) as a "black nationalist–hate" organization that Hoover said was to receive "intensified attention." In early 1968, Hoover wrote his agents that one of the goals of the COINTELPRO should be to "prevent the rise of a 'messiah' who could unify and electrify the militant black nationalist movement." Malcolm X "might have been such a 'messiah,'" but, with him gone, Hoover warned that "King could be a real contender for this position. . . ."

In the last months before the assassination King was planning a Poor People's March on Washington for mid-April. King warned that "mass civil disobedience" would be part of the new struggle. From the President on down, Washington was worried, and no doubt Hoover and the FBI further intensified their COINTELPRO, in the name of preventing the violence they predicted the demonstration would produce.

"There was a real fear of Martin coming to Washington with thousands of people to disrupt the life of the government," said Andrew Young, explaining his suspicions that the FBI might have taken more extreme measures to prevent the march. Things said in the capital, including remarks in the *Congressional Record*, led Young to "think that there would possibly have been people in the federal government somewhere that made a decision that Martin had to be stopped."*

A few days before King's death, a Domestic Intelligence Division memorandum reported, with implicit pleasure, that "acts of violence and vandalism broke out including the breaking of windows in stores and some looting" during King's Memphis march for the sanitation workers; this demonstrated, as the FBI had wanted to have demonstrated, that acts of so-called nonviolence advocated by King cannot be controlled." Hoover agreed that this point should be made "to cooperative news media sources." In the light of the FBI's proven efforts to provoke violence among the Black Panthers and other targeted groups, so that they would neutralize and discredit, if not kill, themselves, one has to wonder whether the FBI itself, through its secret agents and paid informants, incited the violence in Memphis that drew King back to the Lorraine Motel for a second march.

Even King's going to the Lorraine Motel raises another doubt about the FBI's role (although that hotel, owned and operated by Negroes, was clearly King's preference without any outside influence). One is haunted by the Church committee's discovery that on March 29 the Domestic Intelligence Division recommended that a cooperative news source be given the following article to print:

---

* One memorandum, for example, was found describing a plan approved in March 1968 to mail an anonymous letter to a civil rights leader in Selma, designed to turn him against King. It is not known how many other undiscovered letters of this kind were sent.

Martin Luther King, during the sanitation workers' strike in Memphis, Tennessee, has urged Negroes to boycott downtown white merchants to achieve Negro demands. On 3/29/68 King led a march for the sanitation workers. Like Judas leading lambs to the slaughter, King led the marchers to violence, and when the violence broke out, King disappeared.

The fine Hotel Lorraine in Memphis is owned and patronized exclusively by Negroes, but King didn't go there for his hasty exit. Instead King decided the plush Holiday Inn Motel, white owned, operated and almost exclusively patronized, was the place to "cool it." There will be no boycott of white merchants for King, only for his followers.

The FBI memorandum proposing the planting of this article has a notation "handled, 4-3-68." That was the day before King was murdered on the balcony of the "fine Hotel Lorraine." A bullet ended the life of the second potential "messiah" on the list of those whose "rise" Hoover most feared, but death has never been a foolproof way of disposing of messiahs.

Aside from the possible link between the FBI's acknowledged "character assassination" and the actual killing, what was the effect of all this on King—and on the civil rights movement? "It was a great personal suffering," Andrew Young told the Church committee, "but since we don't really know all that they did, we have no way of knowing the ways that they affected us." However, there was "no question" but that for King "it was a great burden to be attacked by people he respected, particularly when the attacks engendered by the FBI came from people like Ralph McGill."

The editor of the Atlanta *Constitution*, one of the most influential moderate voices in the South, had been given derogatory information about King as part of the FBI's effort to undermine a civic banquet planned upon his return from the Nobel ceremony. Sullivan reported that McGill had taken the information to a banker who was helping to finance the banquet and who "said he would contact some other bankers also involved and see if support could be quietly withdrawn. . . . McGill said he would do what he could to encourage key people to limit their praise and support of King as much as possible. McGill also told me that he is taking steps through [a Negro leader] to get key Negro leaders to unite in opposition to King and to gradually force him out of the civil rights movement if at all possible." Hoover reported this progress directly to Bill Moyers in January 1965.

Sullivan's memorandum is no proof that McGill said or did any or all of what was reported. His close friend and colleague on the *Constitution*, Eugene Patterson, a long-time member of the Civil Rights Commission, vows that McGill was appalled by Sullivan's approach and continued his support of King, and that Sullivan's account was a self-serving lie. That Sullivan would lie to Hoover is indeed a further danger inherent in the world of covert operations.

Andrew Young also described how the FBI's efforts "chilled contributions": "There were direct attempts at some of our larger contributors who told us that they had been told by agents that Martin had a Swiss bank account, or that Martin had confiscated some of the monies from the March on Washington for his personal use. None of that was true." One of King's legal counsels who was involved in fund raising for SCLC said that the rumors of poor financial management and Communist connections "stayed in the political bloodstream all the way through to the time of Dr. King's death, and even after."

On another front, to what extent did the counterintelligence program against King create dissension in Negro leadership or undermine his various nonviolent campaigns? Chicago is now cited as a place where King failed because the white power structure did not respond adequately and Negroes turned to violence. His effort had begun well in 1966, with Negroes hopes high and the powerful Catholic Archbishop of Chicago joining King in a press conference where agreement on civil rights goals was announced and priests and nuns were called upon to participate in the SCLC campaign. With Archbishop Cody's strong influence among whites, including Mayor Daley, the police, and business leaders, indications pointed to a major success. A special FBI agent was promptly sent to brief Cody and reported back that the Archbishop "will do everything possible to neutralize King's effect in this area." As the white power structure turned away, whites in the streets turned violent and the police gave inadequate protection. King was hit by a rock, and fell to his knees; after the riot on West Sixty-third Street he said, "I have seen many demonstrations in the South, but I have never seen anything so hostile and so hateful as I've seen here today."

What else did the FBI do to disrupt King's efforts in Northern cities, in the final Poor People's Campaign, in the Mississippi march after the shooting of James Meredith, even back in Albany, Georgia? In all those places, events got out of control, and there were provocations or instances of black violence that deeply disturbed King and set back his movement. Were any of these instigated by the FBI?

King tried to keep himself and his colleagues from catching the paranoia of which they were targets. As they began to assume that the FBI was bugging just about every place King went, he would joke about it, according to Andrew Young, and "when somebody would say something a little fresh or flip, Martin would say, 'Ol' Hoover's gonna have you in the Golden Record Club if you're not careful.' " But there was a chilling effect in the knowledge that the strategies they talked about in their meetings or on the telephone were known to the government with whom they were dealing—that such inside information would probably be in the hands of the President himself.

Why did Hoover conduct this vendetta?

Three reasons have usually been given in defense or explanation: he was responding to King's criticisms of the FBI; he was concerned about King's association with alleged Communists; and he became convinced that King's sexual behavior was immoral. William Sullivan conceded that these were factors, and stressed that Hoover was "very distraught" by King's criticisms, but said that "behind it all was the racial bias, the dislike of Negroes, the dislike of the civil rights movement." Hoover's assistant said, "I do not think he could rise above that."

By all accounts, with each passing year Hoover became more and more infuriated by any criticism. Ever since the Civil Rights Commission began its investigations, the FBI's performance in the South in racial matters had been an object of increasingly critical public and private comment. Although Robert Kennedy sparred with the Civil Rights Commission, he and Burke Marshall were themselves questioning the FBI's ability in civil rights, and pressing Hoover to appoint Negro agents and to act with far greater diligence. They found that only 48 out of 13,649 FBI employees were black and none of these was an agent with responsibility. Hoover may well have viewed King as a source of this odious interference, for King had freely vented his case against Southern FBI agents to me and many others from 1957 on, and some of this must have reached Hoover's ears.

King was, in fact, one of the sources of information about the FBI that I passed on to the President and Attorney General shortly before the inauguration in 1961. The FBI has been a "bottleneck," I wrote Robert Kennedy in January; it "has, or uses, few if any Negro investigators. White FBI investigators, who often have a Southern accent, run into great resistance from skeptical, fearful Negroes." Hoover would not co-operate, I added, until convinced that "our new Attorney General is just as serious about conspiracies against civil rights as about the Communist conspiracy."

As Robert Kennedy and his colleagues began to insist that the FBI investigate violations of civil rights in the South, and even drafted long detailed guidelines listing precisely what questions should be asked local officials or Negro witnesses, Hoover's frustration mounted. King, with his close connections to the Kennedys, was an easier target than the Attorney General, yet damage to King was also a blow to John and Robert Kennedy.

King's bold criticism of the FBI no doubt was like a red flag to an angry bull. Almost no one of equivalent stature had ever taken Hoover on as King did when the press reported, in early 1964, that the FBI Director had asserted that "Communist influence does exist in the Negro movement." Affirming that the SCLC was "unalterably opposed to the misguided philosophy of communism," King challenged Hoover "to come forward and provide real evidence." He added:

> It is difficult to accept the word of the FBI on communist infiltration in the civil rights movement, when they have been so completely ineffectual in resolving the continued mayhem and brutality inflicted upon the Negro in the deep South. It would be encouraging to us if Mr. Hoover and the FBI would be as diligent in apprehending those responsible for bombing churches and killing little children as they are in seeking out alleged communist infiltration in the civil rights movement.

The other red flag to Hoover was his oldest foe, the "Red" menace itself. The Church report suggests that Hoover's crusade against King started in 1962 after what its documents show as the first FBI allegations of Communist infiltration of the SCLC (in a January 1962 FBI report to Robert Kennedy), and went into high gear only after Kennedy authorized the wiretap in late 1963. But Hoover's antipathy to King and the civil rights movement, and his allegations of Communist connections with them, began well before the Kennedys had come on the scene.

As far back as 1957 the Director had told Eisenhower's Cabinet that the "crusade for integration" was creating an "explosive resentment" in the South, that it had raised "the specter of racial intermarriages," and that it was the object of Communist infiltration. I know as a fact that as early as 1957 and 1958 King's close associate Stanley Levison, whom Hoover contended was King's chief link to the Communists, was under at least telephonic surveillance. Taking into account Hoover's hatred of Communists and adding a strong measure of racial bias, one can imagine that from the time he knew of King's ties to Levison, King was on his enemy list. If those ties were not the first cause of Hoover's hostility, they were certainly a contributing and continuing factor.

Putting together the unauthorized and illegal trespasses and use of microphones by the FBI over many years, as documented in the Church report, and my own experience in connection with Levison, I have long suspected that King was a target of wiretapping and other counterintelligence actions from his emergence in 1956. In his posthumous 1979 book, *The Bureau: My Thirty Years in Hoover's FBI*, William Sullivan admits that "we had been tapping King's telephone since the late 1950s." Sullivan says that when he took over the Intelligence Division in 1961 Hoover told him that "he wanted it proved that King had a relationship with the Soviet bloc" and "he wanted evidence developed that would prove that King was embezzling or misusing large sums of money. . . ." Although "no damning information on him had been unearthed," Sullivan says "Hoover was monomaniacal about that case. . . . Many of us, myself included, sent Hoover memos that would echo his attitude toward King just to get him off our backs. . . ."

Thus, it seems likely that the request for permission to tap King's phone in 1963 was primarily an effort by Hoover to get Robert Kennedy on the record, and thus to add to whatever other information he had in his files on the Kennedys. Sullivan writes that "Hoover was desperately trying to catch Bobby Kennedy redhanded at anything," and that he "was always gathering damaging material on Jack Kennedy." The number-two man in the FBI was sure that Hoover "was saving everything he had on Kennedy, and on Martin Luther King, Jr., too, until he could unload it all and destroy them both."*

What, if anything, did Hoover and the FBI surveillance get on King?

Was Levison a Communist, who lied to and misled King about his party connection? Was there that one grain of true perception in Hoover's paranoia about King being under Communist influence? When I was being cleared for an administration post in the first weeks of 1961, the Attorney General asked Sargent Shriver to query me about Stanley Levison. I had forgotten the name, but when Shriver said that the FBI field investigation disclosed a dozen or more phone calls to or from Levison in the late fifties and I discovered that the number for some of the calls was King's office, I finally recalled a quiet and thoughtful man with whom I had been in touch when I was helping to arrange King's trip

---

* According to Sullivan, Hoover blamed himself for John Kennedy's becoming President. In the early days of World War II, the FBI Director discovered that young Jack Kennedy, a naval officer, was involved with a glamorous Scandinavian woman whom Hoover believed to be a Nazi spy. A transfer from Washington to active sea duty was arranged, and Kennedy ended in PT-109, without which Hoover doubts that Kennedy would have been President. "They shagged my ass out of town to break us up," Kennedy told Robert Donovan, author of *PT 109*.

Hoover's antipathy to the Kennedys did not stop with John and Robert. Sullivan reports that on the Director's orders FBI agents circulated the story of Edward Kennedy's suspension from Harvard for paying someone to take an examination, and although there was no federal jurisdiction Sullivan says Hoover sent an FBI team to investigate the accident at Chappaquiddick (allegedly on orders from President Johnson).

to India. Levison had also called me on behalf of King when I was helping to edit the story of the Montgomery bus boycott, *Stride Toward Freedom*. Whoever had listened to the phone conversations could verify their substance, I told Shriver; they would indicate that Levison was devoted to King personally and to the idea of nonviolence.

During my first days on the White House staff, a confidential luncheon meeting was arranged at the Mayflower Hotel for Robert Kennedy, Burke Marshall, Martin King, Andrew Young, Louis Martin, and two or three others of us to talk about the future course of civil rights in the new administration. King brought Stanley Levison, who found himself sitting next to the Attorney General. While Kennedy was at the buffet table, I told him that the man about whom he and Hoover had been so concerned was at his right.

Sometime after that Burke Marshall came to ask me, on behalf of the Attorney General, to talk with King and urge him to break his ties with Levison. Marshall could not himself verify the charge that Levison was an active Communist agent, with Soviet connections, but insisted that if you believed the FBI at all, you would have to believe that there was a basis for serious concern. I agreed to inform King but said that since my own experience with the FBI involved a matter in which an FBI informant had the facts turned upside down, I would also add that skeptical note. Marshall stressed the political damage to King and the civil rights movement if the charge about Levison was made public, and I well knew Hoover's ability to leak what he wanted to leak to the press and to Congress.

King seemed depressed and dumbfounded when I talked with him about Levison; he could not believe it, and said he had far more reason to trust Levison than to trust Hoover. Later, the astute anti-Communist Bayard Rustin was to reinforce King's judgment, pointing out that Levison's positions on a number of issues were contrary to the Communist Party line. Hoover's hand was strengthened, however, in the spring of 1962, when the Senate Internal Security Subcommittee, probably triggered by Hoover, called Levison into executive session. After stating, "I am a loyal American and I am not now and never have been a member of the Communist Party," Levison denied the committee's right to ask about his political beliefs and pleaded the Fifth Amendment to further questions, including Eastland's direct query: "Isn't it true that you are a spy for the Communist apparatus in this country?"

As John and Robert Kennedy became committed to an all-out effort for civil rights legislation in 1963, the potential embarrassment of a public scandal led them both to urge King to break with Levison. After the President met with civil rights leaders before the March on Washington, he took King into the Rose Garden and, according to King, warned him that the FBI considered Levison "a conscious agent of the Soviet conspiracy," that he, King, was "under very close surveillance," and that "if they shoot *you* down, they'll shoot *us* down too—so we're asking you to be careful."

King finally agreed, with Levison's consent, to break their ties; they did not meet again for about a year. By the fall of 1963, however, King had started telephoning Levison to check matters they had been working on; with this information from the FBI's standing tap on Levison, Hoover, in turn, pressed Kennedy to authorize a wiretap on King himself. Later, after Robert Kennedy's death, Hoover was to say that the Attorney General had initiated the idea of that tap, but Hoover's deputy Sullivan said, "Bobby Kennedy resisted, resisted, and resisted tapping King. Finally, we twisted the arm of the Attorney General to the point where he had to go. I guess he feared we would let that stuff go in the press if he said no." On October 21, Kennedy signed the authorization, insisting that at the end of thirty days—November 20—the results should be evaluated to see if the tap should be continued. After the President's assassination, the distracted Attorney General apparently did not deal with the matter again.

Reviewing a number of authorizations for wiretaps, the new Attorney General, Nicholas Katzenbach, found that the taps on King had disclosed nothing to warrant their continuation and canceled them in 1965. William Sullivan, who was responsible for supervising and summarizing the electronic surveillance, later admitted that he had seen no evidence in them, or from other FBI sources, that Levison was a member of the Communist Party. Ramsey Clark, who as Attorney General supposedly saw all the evidence Hoover had to offer, concluded that the allegations about Levison were false. After his own inquiry, Arthur Schlesinger came to the same conclusion. Before Levison's death in 1979, Robert Kennedy's former aide John Seigenthaler, now publisher of the Nashville *Tennessean*, wrote him a letter of apology for having believed the charges.

What about the allegations of sexual misbehavior that Hoover spread so widely? Did the microphones or wiretaps catch King in behavior he wouldn't want his wife, or the public, to know about? Was the so-called composite tape sent to Coretta King genuine?

Two friends of mine in the government to whom Hoover delivered his damning material say there was nothing but Hoover's word to connect the alleged sounds and actions to King. When the tape was belatedly discovered in a pile of mail, long after the thirty-four-day ultimatum had expired, King asked Andrew Young and several other colleagues to listen to it with him. "It was a very bad-quality recording," Young told Howell

Raines, in his book, *My Soul Is Rested*; it seemed to have been made at the Willard Hotel and was "basically just a bunch of preachers that were relaxin' after a meeting." Toward the end, Young said, "there was a recording of somebody moanin' and groanin' as though they were in the act of sexual intercourse, but it didn't sound like anybody I knew, and certainly not Martin."

If the allegations against Levison or the tapes of King were false, did Hoover know that, or were they concocted by his agents to please him and better serve his purposes (which they knew so well)?

Whatever the degree of the FBI's responsibility for the climate that encouraged the assassination, there is a more important question: How did it happen that so many abuses of power, and such a concentration of power in one man and one agency, could take place—and continue? Why did Presidents or Attorneys General fail to stop it?

The first answer given to the Church committee by some officials was that they did not know what was going on.

If the documents given the committee are complete, the FBI's most detailed report of counterintelligence tactics was given the President and Attorney General in 1958, in connection with the COINTELPRO against the Communist Party. There is no record of any response from the White House or Justice Department. Hoover sent a less detailed report to Robert Kennedy just before he took office, also focused entirely on the Communist Party—to which there was no reply.

In 1965 Hoover informed the White House and the Attorney General that the Bureau was "seizing every opportunity to disrupt the activities of Klan organizations." Attorney General Katzenbach appreciatively replied that "perhaps at some point it may be possible to place these achievements on the public record, so that the Bureau can receive its due credit." The Bureau interpreted this response as approval of its whole range of COINTELPRO covert actions, although Katzenbach testified that he had never heard the term "COINTELPRO" and that "it never occurred to me that the Bureau would engage in the sort of sustained improper activity which it apparently did." The Church report noted that "the absence of disapproval has been interpreted by the Bureau as sufficient authorization to continue an activity (and occasionally, even expressed disapproval has not sufficed to stop a practice)."

In 1967 Hoover sent Attorney General Ramsey Clark an account of the Ku Klux Klan investigation that included the goal of "neutralizing it as a terrorist organization." The Bureau considered "neutralize" a key word that gave notice of manifold counterintelligence techniques. A sentence, buried in the report, did give a clearer indication of some of the kinds of actions under way: "We have found that by the removal of top Klan officers and provoking scandal within the state Klan organization through our informants, the Klan in a particular area can be rendered ineffective." Did those phrases put the Attorney General on notice? "No," said Ramsey Clark. "I either did not read them, or if I did read them, didn't read them carefully."

The lack of disapproval, or care, was no doubt partly related to the particular targets—the Communist Party and the Ku Klux Klan—against which it was easy to tolerate extreme measures. Hoover, it seems, never reported to his superiors the existence of a COINTELPRO to neutralize or remove King, or the nature of most of the techniques used against him—with one major exception: he did repeatedly report the alleged results of electronic surveillance. Even there, he never indicated the material came from illegally hidden microphones. Before Sullivan gave the first material from the microphones to Walter Jenkins in the White House, he raised the question whether it should be shown to Attorney General Kennedy, who might have perceived and stopped the bugging. "No," wrote Hoover on the memorandum. "A copy need *not* be given the A.G."

Did anyone in the White House ever question the propriety of the FBI's disseminating that type of material? Bill Moyers testified that "there were comments that tended to ridicule the FBI's doing this, but no." He himself, one of the most sensitive and sensible men in government, a champion of civil liberties, said, "I never questioned it, no." He thought the allegations about personal behavior were "spurious and irrelevant" but a "natural" fallout of an investigation of the Communist allegations.

It was the fear that a naïve black preacher was being duped by a Communist that concerned Johnson, Moyers explained to me in 1980. He remembers the President saying: "If I get in bed with Martin Luther King and it is discovered that a Communist is in bed with us, Jim Eastland will have a field day." Johnson wanted to take precautions against such an exposure. According to Moyers, Johnson was always walking a tightrope in his relations with Hoover. He recognized the damage Hoover could do if he was bridled too tightly—or if he was given too free a rein. John and Robert Kennedy walked the same tightrope.

Katzenbach testified that in the first days after Robert Kennedy left the Justice Department, Ben Bradlee of *Newsweek* told him that one of his reporters had been invited by the FBI to listen to some interesting tapes involving King. Shocked by this news, the new Attorney General and outgoing Assistant Attorney General Burke Marshall flew to see President Johnson at his ranch in Texas to urge him personally to order

Hoover to stop immediately. Johnson seemed sympathetic but, according to an FBI memorandum published in the Church report, what the President actually did was to tell Bill Moyers to warn the FBI that Bradlee was not to be trusted.

When Marshall warned Moyers that the FBI was leaking information concerning King to the press (and Moyers told the FBI White House liaison about this charge), Hoover wrote that "Marshall is a liar." In fact, Marshall says one of Hoover's aides telephoned him to say, "The Director wants you to know that you are a goddamned liar."

If no one outside the FBI was questioning and checking its covert activities, was there any process of self-control within the Bureau? Sullivan testified:

> Never once did I hear anybody, including myself, raise the question, is this course of action which we have agreed upon lawful, . . . is it ethical or moral? We never gave any thought to this realm of reasoning, because we were just naturally pragmatists. The one thing we were concerned about [was] will this course of action work, will it get us what we want . . . ? I think this suggests really in government we are amoral.

To the degree that this testimony reflected the state of thinking within the FBI, the feud between the Bureau and King seems preordained. In his first significant writing, an article in the Morehouse College student journal published in his senior year, King attacked his fellow students' emphasis on utility at the expense of morality. "The function of education," he wrote in 1948, "is to teach one to think intensively and to think critically. But education which stops with efficiency may prove the greatest menace to society. The most dangerous criminal may be the man gifted with reason, but with no morals."

A government intelligence (and counterintelligence) agency, with efficiency but no morals, had indeed become a menace. The crux of the "command and control" problem was revealed in the testimony of one former Attorney General that he was too busy to know what the Bureau was doing, and by another that as a matter of political reality he could not have stopped it anyway. The FBI had found that by invoking the specter of Communism it could do practically anything it wanted to do.

There was another large political reality that gave added support to Hoover's campaign against King: the war in Vietnam, President Johnson's determination to win it, and his fury toward anyone who opposed him. If King had not attacked Johnson's policy in Vietnam, beginning in 1965 shortly after the Selma march, the White House might well have taken action to check, if not wholly stop, Hoover's vendetta. Bill Moyers testified that by about the spring of 1965 Johnson "seemed satisfied" that Hoover's "allegations about Martin Luther King were not well founded." Johnson disliked the civil rights demonstrations King organized as much as John Kennedy had—they upset his national agenda for "reconciliation"—but he considered himself even more committed to civil rights than his predecessor. To Hoover's consternation, Johnson was initially determined to maintain cordial relations with King.

Then King started criticizing the war, and before long he was being viewed as an enemy by the new President, as well as by the Director of the FBI. "Johnson, as everybody knows, bordered on paranoia about his enemies," Bill Moyers told the Church committee. Thus, when King died, the President who had done more than any other public official to achieve the passage of the three main civil rights bills of the twentieth century, did not want to go to the funeral of the man who had done more for civil rights than any other private citizen in American history. One of Johnson's aides told me that the President would not go to Atlanta because of his fear that he would be booed, or insulted, or treated as second to Robert Kennedy—or assassinated—by those who opposed the war in Vietnam.

There was a special sadness in this estrangement. But for the war, Lyndon Johnson would probably have been one of the great heroes of the American Negro.

Johnson and the civil rights leadership, including King, had started off so well together in 1963. After a fifty-minute meeting with the new President on December 3, 1963, King had been "very impressed" by Johnson's "awareness of the needs of civil rights and the depth of his concern." Father Hesburgh told me that the Civil Rights Commissioners had a similar early meeting, at which Johnson stretched out on a couch, saying he was worn out dealing with the British all day, and with the members sitting around him told how the test of his presidency would be how much he could do for the poor, and particularly for the Negroes, Chicanos, and Puerto Ricans.

To Johnson's dismay, and to a chorus of criticism in the press, King decided in the summer of 1965 that he could not "sit by and see war escalated without saying anything about it," and declared that "the long night of the war must be stopped." After all he had done for civil rights, the President considered that statement the height of ingratitude. In August, when King, Wilkins, Whitney Young, and James Farmer came to the White House for the signing of the 1965 Voting Rights Act, Johnson's coolness to King was evident.

Most civil rights leaders opposed King's action. His father and long-time advisers such as Bayard Rustin also thought the civil rights movement would be damaged by any connection with the anti-war movement. Stanley Levison warned that SCLC might go bankrupt. Friends argued that in the light of Johnson's civil rights actions, this was the time for a grateful pause.

As the pressures against his position grew, King wondered whether he had indeed damaged the civil rights movement. The President requested King to see United Nations Ambassador Arthur Goldberg before making any further attacks on American policy; Goldberg, in turn, assured King, Andrew Young, and Bayard Rustin that the United States was committed to peace and that a very early settlement could be expected. For a while King refrained from further active opposition (although his wife participated fully in the growing anti-war movement).

King's silence did not assuage Johnson. As plans were made for a major June 1966 White House Conference on Civil Rights, the President's aides, citing FBI reports, refused clearance for an invitation to King. Berl Bernhard and others preparing the assembly of more than a thousand leaders involved in civil rights informed the White House that there would not be a conference without Martin Luther King.

In the end, King was, of course, invited and the conference held, although he was given no role in it. The administration arranged that no anti-Vietnam resolution could be considered. Whitney Young told the press that the "Negro was more concerned about the rat at night and the job in the morning" than about Vietnam.

Finally, with the war continuing, King decided to break "the betrayal of his silences" and accept the co-chairmanship of the Clergy and Laymen Concerned About Vietnam, and in the spring of 1967 resumed a full attack on Johnson's policies in a speech at the Riverside Church in New York and in subsequent talks and writings. "We are committing atrocities equal to any perpetrated by the Vietcong," King said. "The bombs in Vietnam explode at home—they destroy the dream and possibility for a decent America." This time he did not draw back from the war's connection with the rights of the poor, including most Negroes, who were being sent to fight and die "in extraordinarily high proportions to the rest of the population."

Behind the scenes, still largely unknown to King, Hoover stepped up the FBI's campaign of vilification; what King felt was the public attack on him which was worse than anything he had experienced. *Life* magazine wrote that King "goes beyond his *personal right* to dissent when he connects progress and civil rights here with a proposal that amounts to abject surrender in Vietnam, and suggests that youths become conscientious objectors rather than serve." The only black senator, Edward

Brooke of Massachusetts, opposed him, and Carl Rowan, former head of the United States Information Agency, published a devastating, many-sided attack in the *Reader's Digest* entitled "Martin Luther King's Tragic Decision."

Andrew Young told the Church committee that King "sat down and cried at the *New York Times* editorial about his statement on Vietnam, but this just made him more determined." King did not realize the extent of FBI efforts to influence the media against him, nor can we ever know for sure how many of the writers criticizing him were the recipients of briefings by the FBI.

Six days after King's Riverside Church talk, the FBI had sent an expanded monograph against King to the White House and circulated it inside (and probably outside) the government. The FBI noted that King's remarks were "a direct parallel of the communist position on Vietnam" and further proof that he "has been influenced by communist advisers." Hoover directed that "friendly" reporters be furnished questions that would embarrass King. An editorial in a Negro magazine, which criticized King for his stand on Vietnam, was given to "friendly news sources" in order to "publicize King as a traitor to his country and his race" and, according to the FBI covering memorandum, "to reduce his income."

It cost King a lot to be able to claim for his eulogy that he "tried to be right on the war question."

What was the role of Robert Kennedy in these matters?

Historians reviewing the record will not find a simple answer. In his 1964 oral history interview, opened to scholars in 1979, Kennedy admitted that Levison was the reason he and the President and the Department of Justice were "so reserved" about King during 1963, which he was sure King had felt. On the other hand, Kennedy in retrospect indicated that his own strategy toward Hoover may have been a serious mistake. "I think he's dangerous," Robert Kennedy said. He was sure his brother would have replaced Hoover before he left office, but they thought it important "that he remain happy and that he remain in his position because he was a symbol and the President had won by such a narrow margin." They thought they could control him and deal with him "at an appropriate time"; meanwhile it was "better if we had him on our side."

It is difficult to calculate the price paid for not replacing Hoover at the beginning of the administration, or soon afterwards. Of all the delays in civil rights I suspect it was the most damaging. In retrospect I recognize that the fear of Hoover, distrust of what the FBI would do, and a desire to get Hoover and the FBI on their side pervaded John and Robert Kennedy's approach to civil rights at some of the most critical moments.

In the larger picture, the wiretap on King was a minor matter. Robert Kennedy himself may have regarded it as such, since electronic surveillance did not shock him; beginning with his investigations of organized crime, labor racketeering, and the Teamsters he had shown few civil liberty scruples about tapping phones or taping conversations. It is noteworthy that he approved the wiretap authorization without consulting his closest adviser, Burke Marshall; he may not have wanted to hear any libertarian objections. After his dramatic meeting with the group James Baldwin assembled in 1963, the FBI had sent Kennedy reports on those present. Kennedy must have found some of the FBI material amusing (he sent the dossiers to Marshall with the note: "What nice friends you have"), but such secret reports do not seem to have been offensive to him, and were certainly standard operating procedure for the Justice Department.

King himself did not hold the FBI's electronic eavesdropping against Robert or John Kennedy. When President Kennedy took him into the Rose Garden to talk confidentially about Levison and the FBI surveillance, King came back to Andrew Young reporting that the President was afraid to talk in his own office and, laughing about it, said, "I guess Hoover must be bugging him too."

In *Why We Can't Wait*, King wrote that, despite his long-standing rule against endorsing candidates, "had President Kennedy lived, I would probably have endorsed him in the forthcoming election." Stanley Levison, who had reason to resent what had happened to him, took a similar tolerant view, saying he could really understand their position. "They were so committed to our movement, they couldn't possibly risk what could have been a terrible political scandal. When I realized how hard Hoover was pressing them and how simultaneously they were giving Martin such essential support, I didn't feel any enmity about their attitude toward me."

Much more serious than the matter of wiretapping was the charge that in the name of a false concept of federalism, Robert Kennedy had failed to protect civil rights workers in the Deep South, with a consequent loss of lives and, among many blacks, a loss of confidence in the federal government and in white society generally. That argument is made in vivid detail by Victor Navasky in his book *Kennedy Justice*; Burke Marshall gave his answer in his earlier eloquent *Federalism and Civil Rights* (with a foreword by Robert Kennedy). To have indicated that federal protection would be available to any civil rights worker anywhere would have encouraged people to get killed, Marshall believed. To have tried to make such protection available he thought would require a vast and pervasive federal police force. He feared that the development of the FBI into such a force would undermine the foundations of American federalism and freedom. The Civil Rights Commission and many others were unconvinced.

"Everyone agrees that the states have the first responsibility," Commission Staff Director William Taylor conceded. "But how do you get them to exercise it? By telling them you don't have the power? Our theory is you tell them, 'If you don't do it, we will.' " In fact, in area after area, the Justice Department finally moved in when local authorities failed to act; not until the FBI was driven to establish a Mississippi office and sent a substantial number of agents there, did the state police begin to respond adequately. "History has borne out that Robert Kennedy's tactics were wrong," says Taylor.

History seldom gives such a clear verdict. Navasky concludes that Kennedy made a Faustian bargain, in which he allowed the FBI to grow in power and gave up any serious effort to control Hoover, in return for Hoover agreeing that the FBI would join in the effort to secure civil rights and to prosecute organized crime. Yet to have done what Taylor, Navasky, and the civil rights movement wanted would have meant a far larger expansion of the FBI, the only federal agency potentially able and conceivably authorized to provide regular protection. Knowing what Kennedy knew then, and what we know now about the FBI's tendency to abuse power, one might well draw back from that course.

At the time, I favored earlier and more extensive FBI intervention; I did not see why FBI agents could not have been ordered to make arrests when they witnessed attacks on civil rights workers, and in many other ways to have acted to prevent mob action or local police violations. Today I suspect that Kennedy and Marshall may in fact have been pressing Hoover for action in the South to the maximum they thought he could tolerate. That practical limitation on federal power, which could not be included in their public explanations, must have been a source of special frustration for the Attorney General and his colleagues. To a generation that had grown up hearing that the FBI could do anything in war and peace, the apparent failure of the Attorney General to demand that it do something about the widespread intimidation and violence against civil rights workers caused increasing distrust. It also took a considerable toll in the disillusionment that set in among young black and white activists.

"Not protecting the kids was a moral shock," said Harold Fleming, who had played a key role in organizing the Southern voter registration drive. "To have the FBI looking out the courthouse windows while you were being chased down the street by brick throwers deeply offends the sensibilities. So people wept and cursed Robert Kennedy and Burke Marshall more than the FBI, whom they never had any confidence in to begin with." But Fleming urged the disillusioned to recall their illusions:

> Project yourself back to '61 or '62. There was a totally unjustified euphoria. The climate of expectation was created not by the Kennedys with an intention to deceive, but by the ethos of the movement. The feeling was: After Ike, at last we'll have an activist Administration. We were all unsophisticated about power. We thought it was there to be used. This was exciting. We didn't know about the inhibitions of power. . . . So SNCC & Co. weren't given pledges. But they assumed—everybody overestimated the capacity of the Administration to intervene in an unlimited way. And everybody underestimated the prospective need for intervention.
>
> The sense of betrayal which came later was the inevitable hangover from the binge. Nobody would ever forgive the Kennedys for playing politics because they weren't supposed to on this front. The very fact that there was a sense of partnership had much to do with it. We all thought we were *part* of the Administration—which is absurd.

During the early skirmishing in the South the administration's tactics were no doubt often disappointing but when the major battles began the Attorney General and President responded with all the force necessary. "There was a war on, and they were our allies," recalled the long-time American Civil Liberties Union lawyer Charles Morgan, Jr., a white Southern veteran of the struggle in Birmingham and many other places. "That's the most important thing."

Whether that was the important thing or there were other, deeper perceptions about Robert Kennedy, there was no doubt about the affection for him, and the faith and hope in him, shown by a hundred thousand Negroes and by most of their leaders at Memphis and Atlanta in April 1968. Along with the two widows, Coretta King and Jacqueline Kennedy, the person at the center of attention at the funeral and on the march was Robert Kennedy. He was like a lightning rod in an electric storm: black leaders headed for him, children were drawn to him, people along the way reached out to touch him.

Walking behind him, I talked with battle-scarred veterans of the Freedom Rides, Selma, and Mississippi "freedom summers"; many of them had been bitterly critical of John and Robert Kennedy for their refusal to provide federal protection with the speed or on the scale they had expected, and for their delay in seeking strong civil rights legislation and signing the Executive Order on housing. Some of them said that for a time they had blamed Robert Kennedy and his brother for having lost a historic opportunity, and for driving a whole generation of young blacks into cynicism and separatism, if not violence. But listening to the reminiscences being exchanged along the funeral route, I found that much of that argument had been washed away by subsequent events, and that for almost all of them Robert Kennedy had emerged as the one point, the central person, around whom black and white, young and old civil rights workers were ready to rally. According to Roy Wilkins, the rank and file of Negroes in the South and the leaders who lived there, in contrast to the young militants who came from elsewhere, never lost faith in either President Kennedy or his brother.

As for Robert Kennedy's own reflections on the frustrations of federalism, when Anthony Lewis asked him whether he still thought the federal system of state and local responsibility wise, Kennedy said he thought it was, though for periods of time "it's very, very difficult." Looking at it from the perspective of a hundred years, he told Lewis in 1964, "I think that it's well that all of the great power is not centered in Washington with the federal government." More might have been accomplished with a dictatorship, or if large numbers of federal agents had been sent to patrol Mississippi, but, he said, "I think that it comes back to haunt you at a later time. . . . Now, maybe it's going to take a decade; and maybe a lot of people are going to be killed in the meantime, and I think that's unfortunate. But in the long run I think it's for the health of the country."

On the question of federal intervention both sides were right, and there was no good answer. Since lives were at stake, and lost, it was the most tragic dilemma of civil rights in the 1960s. To the extent that Robert Kennedy did force the FBI to intervene in civil rights, and thus expand its role in American political life, it did come back to haunt him, Martin Luther King, and the country.

Haunting Martin King in his last years was not only the war in Vietnam and the FBI's secret war against him, but also the recognition that despite all the legal and political victories the majority of blacks were still sunk in poverty, and that angry young blacks were turning to violence and separatism. King was not surprised that the achievement of civil rights had led to the even harder struggle for economic rights, but he was depressed by the disillusion and despair spreading among blacks of all ages, and the indifference among the majority of whites. And the final irony of this decade of nonviolent action is that it ended in so much bloodshed. Nothing would have appalled King more than the riots in sixty-three cities that erupted after his assassination. Robert Kennedy and Lyndon Johnson, who both believed so strongly in the political process and the rule of reason, looked out of their windows in the Capitol and the White House and saw Washington burning.

Johnson's first thought was to use King's death as the occasion for another major civil rights address to a joint session of Congress, this time calling for a massive effort to improve life in the inner cities, to be paid for by transferring funds from the Defense Department and the Highway Trust Fund, and by new taxes. In her book *Lyndon Johnson and the American Dream*, Doris Kearns describes how for three days she and a small group under Secretary of Labor Willard Wirtz worked late into the night on the message, while smoke spread over the Washington sky and armed soldiers patrolled the riot-torn streets. Meanwhile, Johnson became convinced that "the riots had destroyed whatever sense of injustice, compassion, or guilt King's death had produced," and concluded that neither the Congress nor the country was ready to take further action to help Negroes.

In Atlanta the mood of the marchers was very quiet, as if we were in in a lull after (or before) the storm. There was grief, but little gloom, and a sustaining sense of history on the march. When we sang, "Mine eyes have seen the glory of the coming of the Lord," we remembered King's thirteen years in public action. Some of his achievements were certainly marching on: integrated buses, trains, airports, restaurants, stores, public places all around us; millions of new black voters and thousands of black officeholders, in the South as in the North; and most of all, so many Negroes themselves walking with their backs straighter. It was not hard to believe that, as King had predicted, when the history books were written, historians would say that in this decade the black people of America had "injected new meaning and dignity into the veins of civilization."

The funeral was naturally a time when much was claimed for King. On the other side of the ledger, the violent words and actions of many young blacks made everyone draw up a balance sheet in his own mind. Although King was an ordained minister and drew much of his power from preaching, from 1955 until his death he was primarily a political person, so it is his politics that must first of all be appraised.

King gave American politics a large injection of nonviolent direct action, a relatively new ingredient. It is a strong medicine, and it may be that one or two ounces, properly administered, will cure, while ten ounces might kill. It is a form of shock treatment and therefore dangerous. King saw and accepted the danger. He knew he was playing with fire, but called it (in his last talk at Memphis) the "fire that no water could put out." By its very nature civil disobedience increases tension in the community, but King believed this was "a type of constructive, nonviolent tension which is necessary for growth." In his *Letter from a Birmingham Jail* he explained:

> Nonviolent direct action seeks to create such a crisis and foster such a tension that a community which has constantly refused to negotiate is forced to confront the issue. It seeks so to dramatize the issue that it can no longer be ignored. . . . Just as Socrates felt it was necessary to create a tension in the mind so that individuals could rise from the bondage of myths and half-truths to the unfettered realm of creative analysis and objective appraisal, so must we see the need for nonviolent gadflies to create the kind of tension in society that will help men rise from the dark depths of prejudice and racism to the majestic heights of understanding and brotherhood.

King's hyperbole makes him sound like a naïve optimist or mere romantic, but the doctrine from the Birmingham jail was a hard one, rooted in a realistic view of human nature. To the Grand Inquisitor's question to the returned Christ, "Dost thou know that . . . the very people who have today kissed Thy feet, tomorrow at the faintest sign from me will rush to heap up the embers of Thy fire? Knowest Thou that?"—King would have answered that he knew. "Reason is darkened by sin," he once wrote. The suffering of nonviolence was necessary because lesser means would not suffice to break the bondage of myths or penetrate the depths of prejudice.

Did the thirteen years of marching, jail-going, suffering, and dying suffice? Did it help people rise, if not to the majestic heights, at least to the first foothills of understanding and brotherhood? To listen to the young men shouting "Black Power!" as King had to do on the march in Mississippi, or "Burn, Baby, Burn!" which he heard in Watts, how could he help but be discouraged? Then in his last days in Memphis, his plans for the sanitation workers' march were challenged by leaders of a teen-age gang called the Invaders. "If you expect honkies to get the message, you got to break some windows," one of them declared. Another said, "Man, you know, we want to get something done. I mean all this stuff about marching downtown, all these bourgeois wanting to march downtown and get their pictures on national television doing their civil rights thing, man, that's nothing." During the march windows were broken and rioting begun, thousands of nonviolent demonstrators were dispersed, and a boy was shot to death.

Martin King was more depressed than any of his colleagues had ever seen him before. "The way it should be presented," Stanley Levison called from New York to suggest, "is eight thousand people showed magnificent discipline, and maybe thirty or forty lost their heads—but look at the eight thousand." Levison says that King's reply came with such muffled slowness that it could have come from another galaxy: "Yes, Stanley, but we'll never be able to get that story through." His aides said that he couldn't sleep and agonized over the march as though he had committed the violence with his own hands. Ralph Abernathy had never before found him in such a state, and was worried, but King told him, "I'll pull out of it, Ralph."

For a month, according to some of his friends, King had not seemed to be quite himself; Andrew Young says that during this period King's "faith was draining because even people inside the organization were running around the country spouting talk about violence." More damaging "was the flak we were getting from friends. They kept telling him he was failing."

King's biographer David Lewis, turning to the tradition from which his subject had drunk deeply as a philosophy student, considers this the moment when King was personally confronted by the distinction Kierkegaard made between a knight of faith, who had the capacity to transcend his adversity by a leap of faith, and a tragic hero who was flawed by the incapacity to carry through such an act.

If something like that inner struggle was taking place, I am sure it did not revolve simply around doubts about the philosophy or strategy of nonviolence, or about his ability to transcend the difficulties of taking the struggle into the secular cities of the North and West. To be sure, he was being taunted by his critics and had been booed by young militants. Adam Clayton Powell was calling him Martin "Loser" King, and Roy Wilkins was saying that the impending Poor People's March to Washington should be called off since Memphis indicated that King could not prevent violence. Eldridge Cleaver's *Soul on Ice*, which ridiculed King's program as self-flagellation, was a best seller, and Frantz Fanon's *The Wretched of the Earth* and other books were persuading some people that letting out black rage in violent rebellion (or even just terrorism) against whites was therapeutic. King's own last book, *Where Do We Go from Here? Chaos or Community?* got little attention; the most serious review, by Andrew Kopkind in the *New York Review of Books*, had put it down as an irrelevant middle-class tract. Kopkind wrote that King "has been outstripped by his times" and that instead of sighing that the world was not ready for him it would be "more accurate to say that King is not ready for the world." Yet King never showed any sign of wavering in his basic approach.

"Even if every Negro in the United States comes to think that Negroes ought to riot," King had said in the violent atmosphere of Chicago, "I'm going to stand as that lone voice and say, 'it's impractical, it's unsound. . . .' " When young blacks in Watts said to him, "We won," he asked, "How can you say you won, when thirty-four Negroes are dead, your community is destroyed, and whites are using the riots as an excuse for inaction?"

It would be wrong, however, to picture King as primarily standing firm against a violent tide during his last years and months. He was one who responded to events constructively (as John Kennedy did in his way), and the riots stirred King to turn his attention and imagination to the black poor in urban ghettos. He realized they had been ignored as the civil rights movement had focused on desegregation and voting rights in the South. He girded for the new battles and particularly enjoyed the marching clothes—denim overalls—that he donned for the Poor People's campaign, which identified him with the workingman.

In a conversation with me in the winter of 1967–68, King told me he wanted to explore the possibilities of a deliberate, peaceful black exodus from a slum that was unsafe and beyond repair, to be followed by the actual burning of that slum (after public notice and care to prevent any human injuries). We agreed that would be quite a symbolic action! He noted with interest that toward the end of their independence struggle, some leading Gandhians in India had adopted the rule of nonviolence to persons but destruction to property. Yet he also knew that the magic of nonviolence could easily go wrong. Already a "blow their minds" approach among some wilder ones had led to a "piss-in" designed to provoke Alabama police, and to plans for blocking the Triborough Bridge and bringing traffic in New York to a halt at the opening of the World's Fair. King seemed confident that he could contain the craziness before it produced a white backlash, and from everything he said I concluded that he was looking forward to the challenges of a new decade. For the road ahead, he told me, we would all need to develop a "Long March" mentality.

What then accounts for the agony he seemed to be suffering in his last days? After talking with some of his associates and reading what his wife and others have written, I think he must have been wrestling with a different and deeper fear than political failure. Three weeks before this he had surprised his wife with a gift of artificial red carnations. "They're beautiful and they're artificial," she said; it was so unlike him to choose artificial flowers, something he had never done. "Yes," he said, "I wanted to give you something that you could always keep." During these last weeks Andrew Young noted with alarm that Martin had developed the habit of looking about him as though he expected to see an assailant. In his final sermon at the Ebenezer Baptist Church he had shocked his congregation by dwelling very personally on "that something we call death," and proposing his own eulogy ("I want you to be able to say that day, that I did try to feed the hungry . . . that I did try to clothe those who were naked . . . that I tried to love and serve humanity").

After the violence in Memphis his depression deepened—and then almost miraculously, his friends said, somehow lifted. The morning after his worst despair, he called a press briefing in which, according to Coretta King, he restated his total commitment to nonviolence and "poured out his soul." One of his young colleagues, Bernard Lee, commented, "Martin must be called to do what he is doing. He could not have changed as he did in one night if God had not put his hands on him." Ralph Abernathy said to Coretta King, "I saw a quality in Martin I hadn't seen before—a kind of lion quality." One of the newsmen asked, "Dr. King, what has happened to you since last night? Have you talked with someone?" King said, "No. I haven't talked with anyone. I have only talked with God." It was after this that he told the Memphis congregation, the night before his death, that he had been to the mountaintop and was not fearing any man.

Earlier in his life, King had said, "If you are cut down in a movement that is designed to save the soul of a nation, then no other death could be more redemptive." But most of the time his recurring talk about the redemptive power of suffering had an abstract ring. After he was struck by a rock in Chicago, and had fallen to his knees, it sounded real when he said to his worried friends, "I have to do this—to expose myself— to bring this hate into the open." He knew that the final test of the theory of nonviolent action he espoused—as of the faith he professed—was "that something we call death," and quoted Gandhi's affirmation that the non-violent soldier's last resort in place of the sword was to give his own life. Still, another side of his soul asked that the cup pass from him.

This natural human ambivalence comes through clearly in Andrew Young's account in *My Soul Is Rested* (a moving collection of oral histories by Howell Raines). "Martin never had that kind of messiah complex," Young said. "I'm convinced that Martin never wanted to be a leader; he just did not wanna assume the leadership of the entire Southern struggle or of the entire national struggle." Young said that most of the other SCLC leaders "were driven, ambitious sorta guys. Martin never was, and they were always pushin' him, trying to generate ambition for him." It was at the time of Birmingham, Young thinks, "that he kinda decided that he wasn't going to be able to escape that, that he was going on."

From more distance and less firsthand evidence, I have a different guess. I think the little boy whose favorite hymn was "I Want to Be More and More Like Jesus" grew up with an unusually strong messiah complex that he wrestled with to the end. He did not show the ambitions of politically driven men because he was driven by the highest ambition of all. It was not for nothing that young militants behind his back called him "de Lawd" or that some women in his congregation called him affectionately "LLJ," for "Little Lord Jesus."

Nor was it only in Birmingham that Martin King decided that "he was going on." In 1959, for example, in his farewell sermon to his church in Montgomery, he wept as he told the congregation, "I can't stop now. History has thrust something upon me which I cannot turn away from."

Nor was the month before Memphis the only time he had a premonition of death. Not only did he predict his own fate when Kennedy was killed, but later, on the way to the march to Montgomery, he told Abernathy, "Ralph, I thought I would have been assassinated in Mississippi, but it did not happen. So it will probably come to me over here in Selma." And he had already faced it more directly, when the mad black woman in Harlem stabbed him and he lay with the blade next to his heart, knowing that if he sneezed, he would die.

The dangers he faced were far more than physical. He believed that martyrdom could be redemptive but he knew that either to seek it unduly or to unduly seek to avoid it would be "reason darkened by sin." His fear for his life was very real and grew as the threats (and Hoover's persecution) increased, but so was his fear for the state of his soul and that fear, too, may have grown as he found simple people treating him more and more like a messiah. On occasion, after a speech in which he had been carried away to a point that verged on megalomania, I would tease him about his sounding like the Second Coming. When I cited Mark Van Doren's remark to Thomas Merton that anyone can become a saint if he wants to badly enough, King paused and then in his pondering way said, "Yes—yes—that *is* something to think about." We once joked together about messianism being the last worst sin.

In a healthy mind like Martin King's, messianism inevitably involves a strong sense of one's own shortcomings or, King would say, sins. David Garrow, author of *Protest at Selma*, concludes, after much new research in the late seventies, that in his last years King was burdened with a sense of guilt. Whether the sins that darkened King's reason were any of those alleged by Hoover, or were other superficial matters such as the expensive suits he wore while refusing to buy a new family car or spend money on their home, or were deeper questions, only Martin knew. But close friends noted that he brooded about whether he was at bottom a hypocrite who lacked the courage of self-control and true dedication. The redemption he half sought through suffering seems to have been personal as well as political.

In any case, in early April 1968, after coming down from the mountaintop Martin Luther King showed a special zest for life. In the sermon the evening before his death, he told of the white girl in ninth grade who wrote to him after the stabbing in Harlem to say, "I'm so happy that you didn't sneeze." King told that last Memphis audience that he, too, was "so happy that I didn't sneeze" because if he had he would not have been around for the sit-ins, the Freedom Rides, and all the marches. He went on to put it in more cosmic terms:

> If I were standing at the beginning of time, with the possibility of a general and panoramic view of the whole human history up to now, and the Almighty said to me, "Martin Luther King, which age would you like to live in?"—I would take my mental flight by Egypt through, or rather across the Red Sea, through the wilderness on toward the promised land. . . . I would move on by Greece, and take my mind to Mount Olympus. And I would see Plato, Aristotle, Socrates, Euripides and Aristophanes assembled around the Parthenon as they discussed the great and eternal issues of reality.
>
> But I wouldn't stop there. . . . Strangely enough, I would turn to the Almighty, and say, "If you allow me to live just a few years in the second half of the Twentieth Century, I will be happy." Now that's a strange statement to make, because the world is all messed up.
>
> But I know, somehow, that only when it is dark enough, can you see the stars. And I see God working in this period of the Twentieth Century in a way that men, in some strange way, are responding—something is happening in our world. . . . Now, I'm just happy that God has allowed me to live in this period, to see what is unfolding.

It was good to learn that after the sermon the preachers did some relaxing in the Lorraine Motel, and that in Martin King's last hours, as he looked forward to a supper of soul food (with the chitlins, pig's feet, and potato pie he liked), he shared a platter of catfish with his best friend, Ralph Abernathy, eating from the same plate. He joked with his companions and had a little pillow fight before going out on the balcony. From the courtyard Jesse Jackson introduced him to Ben Branch, the musician for that night's rally. "Ben, be sure and sing 'Precious Lord, Take My Hand,' " King said. "Sing it real pretty."

How do you measure whether a death is redemptive?

In his last words to his Atlanta congregation, King almost sang forth his own test: "If I can do my duty as a Christian ought, if I can bring salvation to a world once wrought, if I can spread the message as the master taught, then my living will not be in vain." His master, he pointed out, was an itinerant preacher who "was thirty-three when the tide of public opinion turned against him. They called him a rabble-rouser. They called him a trouble-maker. They said he was an agitator. He practiced civil disobedience; he broke injunctions. And so he was turned over to his enemies. . . . Nineteen centuries have come and gone, and today, he stands as the most influential figure that ever entered human history."

In his own time, King's life affected the lives of the American people as much as any other man—some would say more than the actions of Presidents and Acts of Congress put together. Others thought that with his death an epitaph could be written for nonviolence in America. "When white America killed Dr. King last night she declared war on us," said Stokely Carmichael. The SNCC leader added, "It would have been better if she had killed Rap Brown . . . or Stokely Carmichael. But when she killed Dr. King, she lost it." Rap Brown said that "violence is as American as apple pie." Another Black Power advocate, Floyd McKissick, said, "Dr. Martin Luther King was the last prince of nonviolence. Nonviolence is a dead philosophy, and it was not the black people that killed it."

For a time those three and many others of their persuasion (aided and abetted by the media which for a time featured them) did their best to make those prophecies self-fulfilling. At King's funeral we could not know how long it would be before the bitterness, separation, and violence, too, would pass away. But if death does not necessarily redeem, it at least encourages a longer perspective. For me, thinking about the meaning of King's life and death brought into focus the whole panorama of the politics of civil rights during a decade of extraordinary turmoil and progress.

About the time King began, an astute white Southern scholar, V. O. Key, concluded in his major study, *Southern Politics*, that "the conversion of the South into a democracy in the sense that the mass of people vote and have a hand in their governance poses one of the most staggering tasks for statesmanship in the Western world." By 1968 that task was almost accomplished.

To enfranchise the Southern Negro and end segregation in American public life required a combination of government and non-government forces; not a partnership, but, after much struggle, a coming together of many political factors. In addition to civil rights organizations, major roles were played by the news media, business corporations, labor unions, educational institutions, foundations, political parties, the legal profession, and the nation's religious bodies. Statesmanship in civil rights involved the mobilization, over time and despite great inertia, of many such principalities and powers that operate between the individual and the state, and through which Americans govern themselves and are governed in some of the most important areas of their lives.

In a mass society, for example, the means of mass communication are an indispensable part of our self-government. If the news media had not carried into American homes the scenes of black children, Freedom Riders, and other protesters being hosed, beaten, bitten by dogs, and stuck with cattle prods, the conscience of the nation might never have been massively stirred. On the other hand, from the bus boycott to King's death the performance of the media was as mixed as that of the Executive and Legislative branches of the government. Some of the marches and most of the violence were covered vividly, but the sermons and hymns at the church meetings, which could have conveyed much of the spirit of the movement, were almost never shown, and in the years after Selma, King was given relatively short shrift while the cameras zoomed in on, and built up, the rioters and the angry young men proclaiming "Black Power." At first nonviolent direct action and civil disobedience seemed ready-made for television, but violence proved to be even more appealing to a mass audience (or to the programmers who made that judgment). Even the violence, however, was part of the process of persuasion under way. As Kennedy told the leaders of the March on Washington, they ought to thank Bull Connor for the help he gave their cause with his shocking incivility.

No summary of factors and forces should omit the women and children. The black women of the South were the mainstay of the movement, marching and singing behind their preacher-men, and the children were often at the front. Thurgood Marshall and Malcolm X both were caustic about the use of children in place of men at Birmingham, while King was in jail; but Marshall himself and NAACP attorneys and parents started that tradition when they made children parties to the school desegregation suits, long before the nine Negro children braved the mob outside the high school at Little Rock in 1957. It may be that the sight of those children, and the ones that followed them elsewhere in the South, including the four little girls who were killed in the Birmingham Sunday school, did more to move the hearts of white Americans than all the other symbolic and substantial acts of the movement put together. Cynical observers have instead argued that it was the young *white* people getting beaten on the Freedom Rides and murdered in Mississippi that finally made the nation pay attention.

The framework for all these actions was American law, which itself had a pervasive and profound effect. In his first book, *Stride Toward Freedom*, Martin King emphasized that "the enforcement of the law is itself a form of peaceful persuasion." He liked to quote Justice Brandeis:

Our government is the potent, the omnipresent teacher. For good or ill, it teaches the whole people, by its example. . . .

Brandeis had added a warning:

> If the government becomes a law-breaker, it breeds contempt for law: it invites every man to become a law unto himself. To declare that in the administration of the criminal law the end justifies the means . . . would bring terrible retribution.

Despite the lawbreaking by the FBI and Southern police, the potential of the law for good is a central fact in the story of civil rights. The major campaigns of the movement aimed at the enactment of some new federal law, and at critical points the campaigns might have collapsed without new momentum from favorable decisions by federal courts. Above all there was the Supreme Court. "Today we are witnessing a massive change," King had said, looking back on the case of *Brown* v. *Board of Education.* "A world-shaking decree by nine Justices of the United States Supreme Court opened the Red Sea, and the forces of justice are crossing to the other side."

Some conservative commentators think that if Martin King and John Kennedy had not, in their separate but stimulating fashions, raised expectations so high around the year 1960, the gap in American law and politics between promise and fulfillment would not have been so great and progress could have been more orderly, if somewhat slower. As one who on occasion assisted the pen of both men and urged Kennedy to make some of those promises, I still think the tension produced by that gap was creative. It was the kind of spark-gap that moves American history.

Without any words from King or Kennedy the world was closing in on white America. The colored majority of the human race, with a growing numerical majority in the United Nations, would not have left us in peace with all our prejudices showing. Kennedy's chairmanship of the Senate African Subcommittee made it clear to him, without any Special Assistant for Civil Rights, that a segregated Route 40 leading to the capital of the United States was an anachronism that could not have been ignored—or simply flown over.

The agenda and timetable were not within anyone's control, for as King said in his last sermon,

> something is happening in our world. The masses of people are rising up. And . . . if something isn't done, and in a hurry, to bring the colored peoples of the world out of their long years of poverty, their long years of hurt and neglect, the world is doomed.

"Doom" may be too apocalyptic, but the twin problems of race and poverty were—and are—deep and darker than any of the simple solutions proposed. Thurgood Marshall thought that almost alone lawsuits would suffice to secure civil rights: if King had just waited for the Court to hand down its decision on bus desegregation there would not have had to be all that walking. In *Kennedy Justice*, Victor Navasky suggests that if Robert Kennedy had just ordered the FBI to arrest Sheriff Clark and the state troopers when they seized Negroes lined up to register at the Selma courthouse in 1963, "perhaps there never would have been a need for Dr. King's famous march two years later to *force* the government to act." From the opposite perspective, Malcolm X had all along contended that what blacks needed was to fight, not to undergo King's demeaning Christian "kneeling-in and crawling-in." William Sloane Coffin prescribed a little more moral suasion from the President.

The mystery of how the minds and hearts—and feet and votes—of people are moved, on issues of fundamental importance where prejudices or differences of opinion are deep-rooted, remains one of the great questions vexing our republic, to which there is no easy answer. Our written Constitution was designed to contain the conflicting energies of states, classes, and factions and to transform the heat from the ensuing friction into light, so that reason might rule. Out of the checks and balances, the division and separation of power, this federal system is supposed to generate the consent of the governed. The spirit of our laws and the larger "constitution" of our pluralist society seek the same result. The principle of a tyranny is fear, says Montesquieu; of a republic, it is learning.

Thanks to Martin Luther King and John and Robert Kennedy, and Lyndon Johnson; to Father Hesburgh and the Civil Rights Commission; thanks to the NAACP lawyers, the children, and the whole civil rights movement; and finally to all three branches of the federal government; and thanks to all that walking and voting and singing and suffering, and to the tapping of America's religious and political tradition—and to all the deaths—somehow in some strange way the nation learned.

"Underneath everything," a black friend said to me while we were grieving over the lost lives, "this is a time of progress. The only way we make real progress in civil rights is through people thinking about the problem. Now when I go down the street and a white man looks at my black face I know he is thinking about civil rights—and the United States Constitution."

The progress was no less real and lasting because there soon set in an era of "benign neglect," and because before long a black man could go down most streets without anyone thinking about his rights or about the Constitution. One odd measure of the progress was that the time came when if anyone thought of black men in connection with the Constitution, it was to contend that they had become the unconstitutional beneficiaries of "discrimination in reverse."

Reflecting the new times, David Lewis, in his critical biography, mocks Martin King's "joyous expectancy that, by putting on walking shoes, by singing to the courthouse, by suffering for a season in jail or out of work, not only would Pharaoh's social system change but its heart would change as well." Lewis conceded that for nearly a decade "the scenario of a morality play . . . tended to satisfy the majority of American blacks," but he welcomed the new era in which blacks would break loose from "the exploitable limitations of compromise and gradualism" that "inhered" in the doctrine of nonviolence. Yet King's story, if it did not convert his skeptical biographer, did win his grudging admiration and wonder. To imagine such a "morally autonomous man," who had learned so much, "surviving the electoral summer of 1968," he concluded, "raises plausible speculations whose promise and pain are stupefying."

Neither King (nor Lewis), nor the Kennedys and Johnson, nor the nation or any of us, learned enough. But during that intense decade, people in all parts of the country, and in all walks of life, thought about the rights of Negroes and the requirements of the Constitution. Has any other nation fought so hard or argued so freely about a fundamental question of human need and national purpose? Looking far back, the fighting included the bloodiest civil war in modern history, as well as the early eras of civil disobedience and other nonviolent actions by the abolitionists of the nineteenth century. On a larger stage, history was made again by the twentieth century movement for civil rights that culminated in a nonviolent struggle without precedent in any democratic nation-state.

No one should be so bold as to say simply, "Our system works!" but the story of civil rights from the early 1950s to the late 1960s can encourage all of us to affirm, "Still it moves." Compromise is inherent in a federal constitutional system, and speed inevitably has to be deliberate. Though the Supreme Court, as the "living voice of the Constitution," will occasionally goad us to do what we ought to have done without any goading, on issues that divide us deeply the Constitution and the Court will slow us down until there is a large measure of public consent. Sometimes, as Robert Kennedy said, it is very, very difficult.

III

The Politics of Service and Social Invention

*I didn't dream that in this remote corner of the world . . .
I would discover what life is really all about, sharing
yourself with others.*

> —Lillian Carter, writing in 1968
> as a Peace Corps Volunteer in
> India, on her seventieth birthday

8 · The Peace Corps: "Hijos de Kennedy"

Of all the social inventions of the sixties, the Peace Corps has been the most successful. It is John Kennedy's most affirmative legacy. In accepting the presidential nomination, Kennedy promised "invention, innovation, imagination, decision"; in establishing the Peace Corps, he kept his promise. Through this novel and anti-bureaucratic bureaucracy, the idea of voluntary service was revived in American life and applied as a new form of politics on the world stage. By their full-time service of two or more years, some 80,000 Peace Corps Volunteers have been educated about the human condition and about America's relationship with the Third World in an unusual university in dispersion. Millions of people in Asia, Africa, and Latin America have been taught, tended, organized, irritated, charmed, and otherwise stirred to claim their rightful place in the twentieth century.

When Kennedy proposed the Peace Corps in the last days of the 1960 campaign, Eisenhower derided it as a "juvenile experiment" and Nixon charged that it would become a form of "draft evasion." Few expected that many young people of the supposedly "apathetic generation" would volunteer—or that those who did would really contribute to the development of poorer nations or to better understanding between those nations and the United States. Ridiculing the idea of a "Kiddie Korps," Robert Ruark asked what "a crew-cut product of togetherness could teach a Masai." The Daughters of the American Revolution at their 70th Continental Congress warned against a "yearly drain" of "brains and brawn . . . for the benefit of backward, underdeveloped countries." Worse still, as they saw it, in the Peace Corps young Americans would be "living under abnormal conditions . . . and not with fellow-compatriots in barracks, as is customary in the armed forces." With Volunteers thus "separated from the moral and disciplinary influences of their homeland," the DAR saw only dire and "serious consequences."

Yet young people in large numbers did respond to Kennedy's call, and before long, critics became converts. Returning to the United States a few weeks before Kennedy's assassination, Ruark conceded that "wherever I've been in the world over the last six months . . . all I've heard is praise for the Peace Corps' solid, helpful work and generally fine projection of the best American image with the downtrods." In a cover story during the program's third year, *Time* concluded that the Peace Corps was "the greatest single success the Kennedy administration has produced." Most members of Congress, Republicans and Democrats alike, seemed to join in this judgment as they authorized the Peace Corps' growing annual budgets, with majorities second only to those for the Defense Department.

Overseas observers were also impressed. Arnold Toynbee concluded that "in the Peace Corps, the non-Western majority of mankind is going to meet a sample of Western man at his best." The historian predicted:

> If the Peace Corps makes even a partial success of its job, it may achieve for America, and for the Western World as a whole, the one thing that we need above all. It may help us to break down the psychological barrier that now insulates us from the great majority of the human race.

According to the Foreign Minister of Thailand, Thanat Khoman, the Peace Corps was "the most powerful idea in recent times." He said that many Thais thought of the United States "as a wealthy nation, a powerful nation, endowed with great material strength and many powerful weapons. But how many of us knew that in the United States ideas and ideals are also powerful?" Through the Peace Corps, people were learning or rediscovering this about America. And this, he said to Americans, "is the secret of your greatness."

The Peace Corps' extraordinary success took Kennedy as well as the country by surprise, and with pride he claimed it as his own. In his last State of the Union address he said that no amount of dollars given in foreign aid could win a war against poverty in the world since "in the end the crucial effort is one of purpose, requiring not only the fuel of finance but the torch of idealism." He was therefore pleased to report that "nothing carries the spirit of American idealism and expresses our hopes better and more effectively to the far corners of the earth than the Peace Corps."

In the midst of the pervasive skepticism of the seventies, those encomiums from the sixties have an odd ring. As the eighties begin, with opinion polls showing an unprecedented lack of American confidence in public institutions of all kinds, and particularly in government programs, the questions arise: What was the Peace Corps' secret? What was the political process that made it different from so many other bureaucratic failures?

No Peace Corps adventure was more dramatic than the Volunteers' role during the revolution in the Dominican Republic in 1965. Reporters on the scene described how rebel soldiers waved the Volunteers through their battle lines, while resisting the Marines sent in by Lyndon Johnson. Identifying with the poor with whom they lived and worked, the Volunteers refused to leave their posts. The rebels called them *hijos de Ken-*

nedy and did everything they could to protect these "children of Kennedy."

John Kennedy would have liked that, whatever he might have thought about the decision to send in the Marines. In fairness to history, however, the Volunteers were not just his progeny and the Peace Corps is not simply a Kennedy (or Shriver) success story. Indeed, at a critical point in the birth, Lyndon Johnson was the midwife who assured the new program's independence and integrity when Kennedy would have let it become submerged as a subsidiary of the long-established and very bureaucratic foreign aid administration. And well before the intervention of either Kennedy or Johnson, Senator Hubert Humphrey, Representative Henry Reuss, and others were seeking to be parents of a Youth Peace Corps or Point Four Youth Corps. Before them, several private programs in the 1950s served as prototypes and provided stimulus to the quantum jump in volunteer service represented by government's decision to create and fund a Peace Corps.

Thus, like civil rights in the early 1960s, the Peace Corps was an idea that had long been in the air, and diverse factors from public and private sectors were converging in its behalf. Yet from the moment Kennedy called on Americans to "ask not what your country can do for you—ask what you can do for your country," the Peace Corps became identified with him. With that call to service as his main theme, the Peace Corps was a natural corollary. Just as it had been the one innovative idea in his campaign, during his thousand days in office it was his primary specific answer to those who asked what they could do for their country.

Success has a hundred fathers, while failure is an orphan. That aphorism (used by John Kennedy in other contexts) applied to the Peace Corps, whose alleged "first proposers" are legion. In a later campaign for the Pennsylvania governorship, Milton Shapp claimed that he had put the idea in Kennedy's head, and through Ted Sorensen the then Philadelphia businessman had indeed suggested something like a Peace Corps. Through Robert Kennedy, a talk along the same lines by General James Gavin also reached the presidential candidate in the fall of 1960. Sorensen listed six additional sources in Kennedy's mind: the Mormon Church's requirement of full-time voluntary service (often overseas) by its young people; other voluntary service efforts; an editorial Kennedy had read years earlier; the suggestions of some academic advisers; the legislation previously introduced in Congress; and, finally, the response to a spontaneous late-night challenge he issued to Michigan students three and a half weeks before the election.

The legislation which had brought the idea to Kennedy's attention was introduced by Congressman Henry Reuss. Following a 1957 visit to

Indochina, the Wisconsin Democrat proposed a Point Four Youth Corps that would enlist young Americans, "neither busybodies nor misfits," for service "in far-off places, at a soldier's pay," and give new human thrust to the program of technical assistance announced in the fourth point of President Truman's 1949 inaugural address. In Cambodia, Reuss had talked with a team of four young American schoolteachers going from village to village setting up elementary schools, on behalf of UNESCO. "So many villages want us, and we are so few," they told him. In early 1960, Reuss succeeded in getting Congress to initiate a non-governmental study of the "advisability and practicability" of such a venture; the study was undertaken by the Colorado State University Research Foundation.

Meanwhile, a Youth Peace Corps was proposed in the spring presidential primaries by Senator Hubert Humphrey, who had also been championing the idea for several years. In June 1960 he recommended to the Senate "the formation of such a corps now, rather than waiting for a study."

Kennedy was aware of and sympathetic to these proposals. In February 1960 he had expressed interest when students on the televised "College News Conference" asked him about the idea. Later he discussed it with staff members and with both Chester Bowles and Humphrey. Congressman Reuss and Michigan University professor Samuel Hayes, an early advocate, were asked to prepare position papers on the idea, and Archibald Cox at Harvard was told to discuss it with the Kennedy Cambridge group and send back any specific suggestions. Kennedy may also have known about the enthusiasm for a Peace Corps among the leaders of the Young Democrats, who listed it in their campus talks and in their literature as one of the things to expect from a new Democratic administration. On the campaign trail in September, his running mate, Lyndon Johnson, spurred on by his young aide, Bill Moyers, had also called for a "volunteers for peace" program that would "offer our young people an opportunity to serve humanity in the remote stretches of the world."

In early October a "Message of Senator John F. Kennedy to the Nation's New Voters" was sent out by the Young Democrats, in which the candidate supported the proposition (attributed to Humphrey and Reuss) "that some appropriate way be found to . . . utilize the services of those properly trained, on the new frontiers of the underdeveloped world —which are in fact the new frontiers of humanity—to aid in building dams, teaching schools, operating hospitals, establishing irrigation projects, and to generally help other people to help themselves." As one who had been involved with the idea for more than ten years. I was elated when this mimeographed message was distributed to our Civil Rights Section of the campaign, but I noted that Kennedy had hedged in promising only that, if elected, he "would explore thoroughly the possibility" of such a "Youth Peace Corps."

Then on October 14 we learned that at the University of Michigan, in extemporaneous remarks in the middle of the night to some 10,000 people who had waited until 2 a.m., Kennedy had asked students if they would volunteer for overseas constructive service, and had received an ovation. Later I arranged to hear the tape of that initially little-noticed talk on the steps of the Student Union. The thrust of the Peace Corps idea was there, but Kennedy's questions gave no clear sense of the program. "How many of you are willing to spend ten years in Africa or Latin America or Asia working for the U.S. and working for freedom?" he asked. "How many of you [who] are going to be doctors are willing to spend your days in Ghana? Technicians and engineers, how many of you are willing to work in the foreign service, and spend your lives traveling around the world? On your willingness to do that . . . will depend the answer whether we as a free society can compete."

Why did Kennedy put those questions that night in Ann Arbor? The best guess anyone on the staff could give was that it was his immediate way of responding to the attack from Nixon earlier that evening in their third television debate. The Republican candidate had said that he did not mean to suggest that the Democratic Party was a "war party" but noted that no Republican had led the country into war in the past fifty years and "there were three Democratic Presidents who led us into war." Stung by Nixon's words, Kennedy may have remembered the idea of a Peace Corps and spoken as he did in order to counteract the image of a Democratic war party. Despite the strong favorable response, however, Kennedy gave no signal that he wanted to develop the theme in any of his remaining major speeches or in the final television debate.

On the contrary, at that point in the campaign, Kennedy was on a very different track in foreign policy. Most of the time Nixon was attacking Kennedy and the Democrats for being soft on Communism, and Kennedy was concentrating on proving his toughness. As Nixon accused him of being willing to surrender the offshore islands of Quemoy and Matsu to Communist China, Kennedy became increasingly bellicose about Cuba.

When Kennedy went so far as to suggest support for the armed overthrow of Castro, liberals and editorial comment generally censured him. The widespread negative reaction made him particularly receptive to anything which would show him as a man of peace. Thus, in a roundabout way, the competition over who was the most militant anti-

Communist led Kennedy into a political situation which called for a constructive proposal like the Peace Corps.

Meanwhile, in Ann Arbor, the students who had been most stirred by Kennedy's Peace Corps remarks were taking steps to show that their response was serious. In the aftermath of the emotional surge caused by Kennedy, many of them had listened to a long, thoughtful campus talk on the same theme by Chester Bowles. After hearing Bowles, two graduate students, Alan and Judy Guskin, wrote a letter to the editor of the *Michigan Daily*, asking readers to join in working for a Peace Corps. The Guskins' phone rang day and night with offers of help. Professor Hayes, who was writing a memorandum on the idea for the Kennedy staff, called to ask what they were up to. About 250 students and some faculty members attended a meeting and organized themselves into a group they called "Americans Committed to World Responsibility." Petitions designed as an answer to Kennedy's questions, saying that signers would volunteer if a Peace Corps were formed, spread faster and more spontaneously than anyone had thought possible.

The editor of the *Michigan Daily*, Tom Hayden (later leader of Students for a Democratic Society, and husband of Jane Fonda), had listened to Kennedy at the Student Union and followed the development of the student organization with amazement. It had been an era in which few young people had been politically active, and in which graduate students particularly were known for their political apathy. (That year Hayden's paper won a journalism award for its imaginative coverage and support of the Peace Corps movement.) Democratic National Committeewoman and UAW official Mildred Jeffrey learned about the student response from her daughter Sharon, who was studying at the university. An active colleague in our Civil Rights Section and one of those who brought Michigan Democrats into the Kennedy camp before Los Angeles, Millie Jeffrey decided to put the students in touch with the candidate's staff. The first staff man she called showed little interest, but she persisted. By then nearly a thousand Michigan students had signed the petitions, and she wanted Kennedy to know the hopes he had aroused among young people. She finally reached Ted Sorensen, who liked the idea of a major speech on the subject, and promised to tell Kennedy about the Ann Arbor petitions.

During these same hectic days Nixon was being urged to propose a Peace Corps. The Michigan students had been challenged to be nonpartisan by two popular faculty members, Elise and Kenneth Boulding, who were critical of Kennedy's cold war stances. If it was the Peace Corps, not Kennedy's candidacy, to which the students were devoted, they should press the idea with the Republican candidate, too, said the Bould-ings. Reluctantly—because by then their loyalties were in fact dual, to the Peace Corps idea and to a Kennedy victory—the Guskins and their chief colleagues agreed that their appeal should go to Nixon, too.

Soon after that, Nixon's train came through Ann Arbor, and the case for a Peace Corps was said to have been made to him by a university professor working in the Republican campaign. Senator Jacob Javits had already been urging Nixon to take up the plan, to no avail. As a con-gressman in the early 1950s, Javits had called for the United States to enlist a million young people to serve overseas in an "army of peace." The Michigan students were advised in late October that Nixon had rejected the proposal; the field was clear for Kennedy. Fortunately, Ken-nedy did not know this; at this time a memorandum by a member of the Kennedy staff reported rumors that Nixon was on the verge of proposing an overseas volunteer program for college graduates. That warning was a further spur to Kennedy to move out front with the idea before his opponent did.

On November 2 the Guskins were notified that at the Cow Palace in San Francisco that evening Kennedy was going to make a major address on the Peace Corps idea. Following it, the Senator would like to meet some of the Michigan students. Could they come to Toledo and deliver their petitions when he stopped on his way back to Washington? So in San Francisco, six days before the election, to a large and enthusiastic audience, Kennedy formally promised that if elected he would form a Peace Corps to supplement America's inadequate efforts in foreign aid with the talent of young volunteers who "could work modern miracles for peace in dozens of underdeveloped nations." As inspiration for the idea, he cited the work of Dr. Tom Dooley in Laos. For evidence that America was "full of young people eager to serve the cause of peace in the most useful way," he described the response of students at the University of Michigan.

Nationwide attention by the news media indicated that the proposal was making a strong impact. While Kennedy flew eastward, Judy and Al Guskin and other Michigan students drove in a caravan to meet him at the Toledo airport. As the students presented their petitions, Kennedy grinned at the long scroll of names, and sensed the students' discomfort when he started to put the petitions in his car. "You need them back, don't you?" he asked. He had guessed right; it was before the era of Xerox and they had not copied the names and addresses.

"How serious are you about a Peace Corps?" one of the students mustered the nerve to ask him. Al Guskin recalls Kennedy replying gaily, "Until Tuesday we'll worry about this country. After Tuesday—the world!" Sorensen or Richard Goodwin joked, "You'll be the first to go—that's a promise!" Some of them were; Judy and Al Guskin were among the first Peace Corps Volunteers sent to Thailand in 1961.

Almost everywhere Kennedy went in the last week of the campaign, he was asked about the Peace Corps, and in his election eve broadcast he repeated the proposal. Sargent Shriver and all of us in the Civil Rights Section were then working day and night to spread the story of Kennedy's call to Mrs. King among black voters, but our spirits had been lifted by the Cow Palace talk. On the civil rights front, we could not be sure whether the King affair would win him more votes than it lost him. We had no doubt, however, that the Peace Corps proposal would increase the turnout of young people for Kennedy, and there was no sign it would lose him any voters.

Like the call to Mrs. King, the Peace Corps turned out to be good politics—some say it surely won Kennedy more than the 120,000 votes that were his margin of victory, and thus ranks as one of the factors that made a difference. Also, like the King call, it was not the product of methodical calculation. In his 1961 book *The Peace Corps*, Charles E. Wingenbach says that "the evidence indicates that it was deliberately timed for maximum political appeal." What evidence? Sargent Shriver's later account of the Peace Corps' origin, in his 1964 book *Point of the Lance*, was much closer to the truth. Shriver concluded that the Peace Corps would probably "still be just an idea but for the affirmative response of those Michigan students and faculty. Possibly Kennedy would have tried it once more on some other occasion, but without a strong popular response he would have concluded that the idea was impractical or premature. That probably would have ended it then and there. Instead, it was almost a case of spontaneous combustion."

Fires go out, and campaign promises are often forgotten. Among the many task forces the President-elect formed before the inauguration, there was none on a Peace Corps. One of his Cambridge academic advisers, Max Millikan, director of the Center for International Studies at MIT, was asked to report to him on the idea, but in a note to Millikan's MIT colleague Walt Rostow, Kennedy indicated he was not sure it made sense. If Kennedy was cooling to the concept, or placing it far down on his list of priorities, people were not letting him or his staff forget it. Press Secretary Pierre Salinger found that the President-elect received more mail on the Peace Corps than any other subject. Over thirty thousand Americans wrote to support the idea. A Gallup poll released before the inauguration found that 71 percent of the American people favored a Peace Corps, and only 18 percent opposed it.

Again, students were in the forefront. In the first week after the election, Princeton was host to a conference on the subject. A Peace Corps Council was soon organized at Ohio State University. Five hundred Amherst students sent Kennedy a letter backing the idea. During the Thanksgiving weekend, a resolution supporting it was passed by representatives from a number of Eastern colleges. Student delegates from fifteen other colleges endorsed it during the New Year's holiday and the National Students Association gave Kennedy its enthusiastic proposals.

In early January, Max Millikan submitted a cautiously affirmative report, suggesting the more modest name International Youth Service Agency, and recommending a pilot operation as a carefully supervised part of the overall U.S. aid program. The President-elect, or whoever wrote on his behalf, adopted this subdued approach in a press release issued on January 9, 1961. Using the less ambitious name International Youth Service Agency, the Kennedy statement was designed to respond to the flood of letters and petitions. It conveyed Kennedy's continuing interest, but tried to lower some of the high expectations by warning:

> Because of the experimental nature of the program, and the limited information now available about needs, it should certainly be started on a small scale. . . . It should probably be possible to place several hundred young people in the first year or two, but there should be no pressure to achieve greater volume until there is sufficient experience and background study to give some confidence that expanded numbers can be wisely used.

If that small, slow, low-key beginning is what Kennedy really wanted, he made a mistake: a day or two after the inauguration he asked Sargent Shriver to report to him how the Peace Corps could be organized —and then to organize it. Shriver was delighted to do the report but told the President that he doubted it would be good for him to appoint another relative, or good for a new agency to fight charges of nepotism. Having crossed that bridge with Robert Kennedy, the President brushed aside Shriver's resistance and said, "Go ahead. You can do it."

Shriver liked to say that Kennedy picked him for the Peace Corps because no one thought it could succeed and it would be easier to fire a relative than a political friend. In fact, as Kennedy knew, the assignment was logical. Not only was Shriver a man of strong ideals, but he had proved himself as an effective manager of a major business undertaking, the Merchandise Mart, and as president of the Chicago Board of Education.

For three summers in the late 1930s, Shriver had been first a student member of, and then a group leader for, the Experiment in International Living in Europe. After visits to several Asian countries in the mid-

1950s he had proposed a plan of sending to Asia, Africa, and Latin America three-man teams consisting of vigorous and imaginative young labor leaders, businessmen, and politicians. As he outlined it, "They would offer their services at a grass-roots level and work directly with the people, contributing to the growth of the economies, to the democratic organization of the societies, and to the peaceful outcome of the social revolutions under way." Shriver had immediately seen the Peace Corps as a way of realizing, in a new form, this old idea.

Kennedy's experience with his brother-in-law in the campaign, where Shriver had been such an effective organizer, may have had the most to do with the appointment. The Peace Corps may itself owe much of its success to its birth in a political campaign. "The Peace Corps started out with, and has tried to keep, the momentum and unbureaucratic spontaneity of the 1960 campaign," Shriver wrote in *Point of the Lance*. Knowing that "American history is full of unfulfilled campaign promises," Shriver was determined to make sure that with this idea "the gap between promise and fulfillment became a creative 'spark gap.' "

The Millikan report, which Kennedy had given him, with its emphasis on slow development and the uninspiring goal of placing several hundred young people in the first year or two, was contrary to every bone in Shriver's body and every cell in his brain. It was just that kind of slowness—too little and too late—that he thought had earned a bad reputation for U.S. overseas aid efforts.

"We knew the Peace Corps would have only one chance to work," Shriver recognized. "As with the parachute jumper, the chute had to open the first time." But to succeed he thought it had to be a jump—indeed, a quantum jump, something new in its very size and thrust. If it were a cautious little experiment within the foreign aid program it could not hope to capture the attention and win the allegiance of prospective volunteers, the public at large, and the Congress.

Within hours of getting the assignment, Shriver was assembling a "President's Task Force" of, at first, about a dozen people to help him plan the Peace Corps. He asked me to coordinate the effort. Once again we were working night and day, as in the campaign and the talent search. One night at the height of the campaign Shriver had asked me, "When did you last have a thought—I mean when did you seriously think about an idea?" Only half joking, I said, "Back at Notre Dame when I was teaching law, before I joined you and your brother-in-law." But unlike those previous high-pressure ventures, where one could only think on the run, the Peace Corps was first of all an idea that had to be thought through.

An earlier Shriver came to the fore, the one I had encountered in

1959 when he carefully outlined and analyzed the racial problems of the Chicago school system and prodded and probed me to see if I had any useful ideas about what could be done. For four weeks in the task force sessions and in meetings with others who might throw light on the Peace Corps, Shriver questioned, sharpened the issues, and pitted contending positions against each other until he felt he understood. "I use not only all the brains I have, but all I can borrow," he said to one session, quoting Woodrow Wilson. By February 28, Shriver's report was on the President's desk.

For me it was also an old dream coming true. In the late 1940s, I had joined a group of Student World Federalists in proposing a peace force of volunteers to serve overseas in community development projects. In the early 1950s I had collaborated with Douglas Kelly in organizing the International Development Placement Association. Its aim was to locate assignments in the developing nations for young Americans who would work in local conditions, and to recruit qualified volunteers for these assignments. IDPA proved that the assignments were waiting and young Americans were ready, but that the placement and recruiting was unduly costly when done on a small scale. After four years the chief donor ran out of funds, and the placing of teachers in Africa, one of the most promising of IDPA projects, was turned over to the African-American Institute. In 1957 I had visited sites in India where privately supported volunteers from the United States and Europe were working with a Gandhian organization called the Shanti Sena, or Peace Army, and we had talked about ways to promote such volunteer service on a large scale. In the late fifties I was in touch with Justice Douglas and Walter and Victor Reuther, who advocated similar plans.

Each member of the task force brought special experience. From the International Cooperation Administration came James Grant. From the private sector there were Gordon Boyce, who headed the Experiment in International Living, and Albert Sims, of the Institute of International Education, who had worked with Shriver on the student airlift from Kenya, which the Kennedy Foundation had funded in 1960.

Max Millikan was not invited because Shriver thought we could best deal with the Millikan report afresh, without the author present—and because he found the report so uncongenial. Indeed, during the first weeks, he would give copies to prospective colleagues, and anyone who fully agreed with its approach was likely to be scratched from the list.

Soon Shriver had another paper to use as a litmus test. In the first days of February, copies of a "think piece" on the Peace Corps, by an experienced but maverick young administrator in the foreign aid administration, reached our makeshift office in the Mayflower Hotel. Contrary to the conventional wisdom of his fellow professionals, Warren W. Wiggins contended that a Peace Corps would only make sense if it were large-scale and designed to have substantial impact. A little Peace Corps would be a minor public relations gesture, he argued, but a big Peace Corps could make history.

From his work in the Philippines, Wiggins was convinced that 5,000 volunteer teachers might make a major contribution to the educational, social, and economic development of that country. He advocated beginning with just a few countries but with dramatic projects requiring thousands of volunteers in each. In his paper, "The Towering Task," titled after a passage in Kennedy's State of the Union address, Wiggins took seriously the President's statement on world development: "The problems . . . are towering and unprecedented—and the response must be towering and unprecedented as well."

When I read Wiggins' paper in the middle of the night before the first enlarged task force meeting in early February, I disagreed with the Philippines proposal but was struck by how much he was talking Shriver's language. At 7 a.m. I called Shriver to suggest that we invite Wiggins to our session that morning. "You're late," laughed Shriver. "I read the paper last night, too, and sent him a telegram about 3 a.m. Track him down and make sure he comes."

Wiggins came, and stayed to become a main organizer of the Peace Corps, second only to Shriver. In their book *Keeping Kennedy's Promise*, two Peace Corps veterans, Kevin Lowther and C. Payne Lucas, blame Wiggins for persuading Shriver to press for too rapid growth and to play what they call a "numbers game" of constant expansion. In their reconstruction of history, "the task force was groping" and "lacked a clear and galvanizing statement of purpose" until Shriver read Wiggins' paper and "instantly embraced its vision of the Peace Corps as a major force for world progress and sent for Wiggins by telegram an hour later." The embrace was instant and the telegram was sent; however, for the fast start, the big goals, and the drive toward operations in many countries, Shriver deserves the primary blame—or credit.

Before Wiggins appeared, we had already been galvanized and the proposed program's purposes had come into clear focus. Already, too, Shriver had advised Kennedy to return to the ambitious name Peace Corps, rather than International Youth Service Agency, and not to limit it to youth. In his State of the Union address, the President had adopted both of these recommendations, stating his intention to form "a National Peace Corps, enlisting the services of all those with the desire and capacity to help foreign lands meet their urgent needs for trained personnel."

Some of the credit or blame for the pressure for rapid motion should also go to the President himself. After the State of the Union address, he kept asking Shriver if the report was ready, and when the Peace Corps could start. In a month he had his answer.

In two other ways Kennedy influenced the shape of the new program. In response to Republican criticism, the President's first concern was that the Peace Corps be tough and effective in order to answer those who called it "Kennedy's Kiddie Korps" and "a haven for draft dodgers." This led to an early decision that, contrary to the Cow Palace talk, draft exemption would not be sought for Peace Corps Volunteers. Volunteers might be temporarily deferred while overseas, but on their return they would be subject to local draft board action.

The second point was implicit in the emphasis on a *National* Peace Corps in the State of the Union address, probably a word that was added at Sorensen's instigation. Later, in *Kennedy*, Sorensen explained that Peace Corps backers had "threatened to dissipate its momentum by talking, even before it was started, of a UN peace corps," which he considered bad politics.

In the task force we had indeed explored such a possibility, and one member who was familiar with the Red Cross recommended that movement as a model. From the moment a young Swiss, Henri Dunant, conceived the idea on an Italian battlefield and wrote his book *A Memory of Solferino*, proposing that all countries organize trained volunteers to help care for wounded combatants in time of war, the Red Cross had been international, although the initial International Committee in 1864 was all Swiss. The American Red Cross was chartered by Congress, but was part of an international organization.

That approach was appealing to Shriver, but he was sure that the President and the dominant mood of the country expected first of all a *United States* Peace Corps. On the other hand, the United States could claim no monopoly on the idea, and by then several countries had already started small volunteer service programs abroad. The task force particularly benefited from the experience of the largest of these, the British Voluntary Service Overseas, a private organization which since 1958 had sent more than 160 volunteers to teach or work in agricultural extension and various kinds of community development in British territories or Commonwealth countries.

Although the task force did not propose UN management or control of the whole program, it did decide to recommend that one of the channels for Peace Corps Volunteer service be through the UN and other international agencies. The report to Kennedy also suggested that in presenting the Peace Corps to other governments and to the UN, the United States "propose that every nation consider the formation of its own peace corps and that the United Nations sponsor the idea and form an international coordinating committee." In his report, Shriver stressed the hope that Peace Corps "projects will be truly international and that our citizens will find themselves working alongside citizens of the host country and also volunteers from other lands."

In Kennedy's Cow Palace talk he had used the example of a young Russian sanitation engineer and nurse studying Swahili and African customs in order "to live their lives in Africa as missionaries for world communism." He added that in Moscow, Peking, Czechoslovakia, and East Germany hundreds of scientists, physicists, teachers, engineers, doctors, and nurses were in training for overseas work. Such a challenge, Kennedy said, "can only be countered by the skill and dedication of Americans who are willing to spend their lives serving the cause of freedom." The question for our task force was: Should the Peace Corps be understood by Americans, and presented to the world, as a way to counter Communism?

We recognized that Congress and the country were accustomed to cold war rhetoric, and Kennedy often enough reverted to it. But all of us with experience in the developing nations knew how little the contest between the United States and the Soviet Union, or between the Free World and Communism, as Americans liked to put it, interested people in what was beginning to be called the Third World. To the extent that they were treated as pawns in the cold war, it irritated them. Most of all, however, the American preoccupation with Communism amused them.

A recurring joke, with many variations, told about the Prime Minister of Monaco (or of some other country) coming to Washington for foreign assistance and being asked about his Communist problem. When he replied proudly that there were no Communists in his country, his high American official host said in embarrassment, "Then we can't help you. Congress would never vote the aid unless there is a Communist threat." On the Prime Minister's way home, he stopped in Paris and asked his friend the French Foreign Minister for a favor: "Lend us some of your Communists, to start a riot or two and get on American television." The Frenchman replied, "I'm sorry, we want U.S. aid, too. We need every Communist we've got."

The presumptuousness of the Peace Corps would cause some amusement anyway, and probably some irritation, but the new program was an opportunity to show other peoples that Americans were interested in them for their own sakes. An emphasis on countering Communism would negate that spirit and undermine the Volunteers' claim to be working for peace. Dean Rusk advised us that "the Peace Corps is *not* an instrument of foreign policy, because to make it so would rob it of its contribution *to* foreign policy." The Secretary of State hoped that Volunteers would help non-Communist nations succeed in their development and in the process promote goodwill toward the United States, but he thought avowed competition with the Russians or Chinese would be counterproductive.

"It is important," Shriver's report to Kennedy concluded, "that the Peace Corps be advanced not as an arm of the Cold War but as a . . . genuine experiment in international partnership. . . . If presented in this spirit, the response and the results will be immeasurably better."

Kennedy understood and accepted this approach, although his natural competitiveness repeatedly asserted itself. When speaking about the Peace Corps, Kennedy would say—extemporaneously, when it was not in his text: "I want to demonstrate to Mr. Khrushchev and others that a new generation of Americans has taken over this country, . . . young Americans [who will] serve the cause of freedom as servants of peace around the world, working for freedom as the Communists work for their system." He did not see this as a necessarily hostile competition, for Kennedy admired the Communist capacity to mobilize popular idealism. "Each weekend ten thousand teachers go into the countryside to run a campaign against illiteracy," the President remarked to Arthur Schlesinger about Cuba. "A great communal effort like this is attractive to people who wish to serve their country."

In urging that the Peace Corps be viewed not as a propaganda venture we were going against another tendency that came naturally to Kennedy —and to most Americans. He, like many others, had been disturbed by *The Ugly American,* and in his Cow Palace speech had referred to the 1958 book by Eugene Burdick and William Lederer which had given shocking examples of how Americans should *not* act overseas. Kennedy wanted the world to see a better brand of American. That was obviously part of the motivation behind the Peace Corps, but it seemed important to us that promoting American policy or producing pro-Americans not be among the program's purposes.

When the late George Sokolsky warned in the *Saturday Review* that before going overseas in the Peace Corps, Volunteers should know how to present "an ideal that will . . . make it possible for a person to look toward Washington as a Moslem does toward Mecca," Shriver replied, "Our purpose is peace—not salesmanship. If Peace Corps Volunteers ever did seek to persuade people to 'look toward Washington as a Moslem does toward Mecca,' they would be laughed out of any country I have ever visited. If they even secretly harbored this hope, it would corrupt their approach to their mission. Their mission is not to convert, but to communicate."

To counteract the temptation to a public relations approach, our task force emphasized the reciprocal learning that would come through the Volunteers' service. "The Peace Corps is in fact a great venture in the education of Americans and of people in the newly developing nations," our report stated

Dean Rusk had pointed out that foreign affairs had no natural constituency in America; one of the by-products of the Peace Corps, he suggested, would be to build such a constituency. In the Senate, Kennedy had seen how domestic interest groups so often skewed American world policy, and how few citizens there were with international perspectives and interests. In concluding his report to the President, Shriver stressed the Peace Corps' potential role in changing this:

> The letters home, the talks later given by returning members of the Peace Corps, the influence on the lives of those who spend two or three years in hard work abroad—all this may combine to provide a substantial popular base for responsible American policies toward the world. And this is meeting the world's need, too, since what the world most needs from this country is better understanding of the world.

The education of Americans was important, and one of the ways the Peace Corps might contribute to peace, but the program would obviously stand or fall on whether it would do what Kennedy had promised: "help foreign lands meet their urgent needs for trained personnel." If Volunteers did not succeed in doing that, they would not long be welcome in foreign lands.

The feasibility study commissioned by Congress in 1960 had resulted in encouraging findings (published later that year as the book New Frontiers for American Youth). In every country the Colorado State University team visited, it had found a need for trained personnel and a receptivity to the coming of Peace Corps Volunteers. More than 50 percent of the requests in Africa and Southeast Asia were for teachers, especially in countries where the language of instruction at the elementary, secondary, or university levels was English. In Latin America the felt need for teachers was relatively small, but there was a desire for American Volunteers to work in a variety of community development projects. Health, agriculture, construction, and public administration were some of the other fields in which Volunteers were wanted in a number of countries.

In most developing nations, expert technicians were concentrated in the capital city or other metropolitan centers. As one foreign observer told the Colorado team, "Our technicians won't work in the villages or rural areas—they haven't yet learned the dignity of labor." The best way of learning techniques of problem-solving and institution-building, said another observer, would be working side by side with Peace Corps Volunteers. Along with their teaching or other special skills, Volunteers could contribute a "do-it-yourself" attitude and their restless organizational abilities.

The Peace Corps would constitute a new form of overseas work. Volunteers would *not* be missionaries, business representatives, government officials, intelligence agents, or researchers. Nor would they be high-level experts or advisers. They would go in a new capacity—to teach or build or work in the communities to which they were sent, serving local institutions and living with the people they were helping. Without any aspersions on the 33,000 Catholic and Protestant missionaries then said to be overseas or the businessmen, government officers, and scholars working abroad, Peace Corps Volunteers would be different: they would go with a different purpose, operate in a different relationship to their host country colleagues, and presumably return with different results.

Development planners began describing Volunteers as "middle-level manpower," but that was an inadequate term for this new kind of overseas American. The Volunteers would break the pattern of government aid experts who too often operated at too high a level. With national variations, there was a commonly told story—about the "Point Four bull"—that made the point. When the prize American bull, sent by the U.S. aid program, was put in the pasture with the cows, he just looked around. When asked why he didn't do something, the bull replied, "I'm an adviser."

Recruiting, selecting, and training effective Volunteers was the first critical problem. Would the flood of interest diminish to a trickle when it came time to sign up for two years overseas with no salary except living allowances and a seventy-five-dollar-a-month post-service stipend (the terms our task force recommended)? A large pool of applicants would be necessary if the best talent was to be found. We hoped that once the Peace Corps was a going concern, much of the training for it would be integrated within the four-year college curriculum for students interested in joining after graduation. Standards would be set for language study and courses on the history, economics, politics, and culture of the area to which the student would like to go, along with training in particular skills, such as teaching. But in the beginning, with the cooperation of universities and private agencies, the Peace Corps would need to arrange intensive training programs that would vary in length from six weeks to several months.

We recommended that "wherever feasible" the overseas projects themselves should be administered through contracts with colleges, universities, and other educational institutions. Warren Wiggins and others on the task force who had faced the high overhead costs and what seemed the grant-seeking greed of academia in U.S. aid programs were skeptical, but Shriver and others of us were persuaded that the potential gain was worth the risk. Part of the gain was political: some fifty-seven universities were already working in thirty-seven countries on development or educational projects under contract with the aid program; they were a constituency the Peace Corps needed, and if ignored could become a formidable opposition. As the first draftsman and last editor of the report to the President (except for Shriver, who worked through the nights honing every part of it), I was no doubt responsible for some of the weight given to this approach.

In several sessions, Father Hesburgh had argued the case for what Notre Dame and other universities could do. They could recruit on the spot, from among their own students, and provide faculty for training programs or for overseas supervision. They could develop area studies and research to assist the Volunteers and draw on what the Volunteers had learned. The Peace Corps in turn could help universities by giving new purpose to students during their years of study. Father Hesburgh reported that students were studying their Spanish more seriously in anticipation of a university Peace Corps project in Latin America. University involvement could help American education expand its horizon—its research and its curriculum—to the whole world. "The Peace Corps will help them with this transformation," the report stated. "As a high education venture, the Peace Corps' proper carriers are our traditional institutions of higher education. It is time for American universities to become truly world universities."

The task force also proposed that private agencies such as CARE, the Experiment in International Living, and the American Friends Service Committee receive grants to administer the work of Peace Corps Volunteers overseas, and that Volunteers should be assigned to United Nations technical assistance programs. Then, our report added, there would be "some projects of a size or complexity or novelty or urgency which cannot be carried out, or carried out well, through any of the above channels"—and which would need to be administered by the Peace Corps staff. Those experienced with the expansive appetite of government agencies, and those of us who knew Shriver, should have realized that such direct Peace Corps-run projects would grow to become the dominant model.

A clear statement of purpose was also required. From the first sessions several purposes had been articulated and some discarded, and Shriver welcomed hard argument among the contending viewpoints. Providing trained manpower for development? Promoting mutual international understanding? Creating goodwill toward America? Educating the Volunteers and their fellow citizens?

Some members of the task force insisted that Shriver and the President choose a single purpose or at least settle for a main one. Shriver found the tension between competing purposes creative, and thought it should continue. "Peace" was the overriding purpose, and the process of promoting it was necessarily complex, he said, so the Peace Corps should learn to live with the complexity. Finally we agreed on three propositions about the program.

> It can contribute to the development of critical countries and regions.
> It can promote international cooperation and goodwill toward this country.
> It can also contribute to the education of America and to more intelligent American participation in the world.

On February 28, Shriver submitted his report to the President. "The Peace Corps can either begin in very low gear," he wrote, "with only preparatory work undertaken between now and when Congress finally appropriates special funds for it—or it can be launched now and in earnest by executive action." Applying the theory of executive action developed for civil rights, we found that the President could allocate sufficient funds from existing Mutual Security appropriations to permit a number of substantial projects to start right away. That would make it possible to have several hundred Volunteers in training during the summer, and not to lose the chance to recruit the most qualified people from the graduating classes of 1961.

There was no doubt about Shriver's own preference. "Having studied at your request the problems of establishing a Peace Corps," he said in the opening line of his report to Kennedy, "I recommend its immediate establishment." Though he thought we had sufficient answers to justify going ahead, he said that many of the questions "will only be finally answered in action, by trial and error."

The President was ready. On March 1 Kennedy issued an executive order creating the Peace Corps on a temporary basis, and sent a message to Congress recommending the establishment of a permanent Peace Corps. "Although this is an American Peace Corps," he concluded his message, "the problem of world development is not just an American problem. Let us hope that other nations will mobilize the spirit and energies and skill of their people in some form of Peace Corps—making our own effort only one step in a major international effort to increase the welfare of all men and improve understanding among all nations."

The Peace Corps was alive, but in danger.

Thousands of handwritten applications were pouring in to the new office—before an application form was printed, before there were even desks on which to place the mail. Shriver was on the telephone hunting for top staff and interviewing prospects. Wiggins was in charge of developing overseas programs. Morris Abram, our intermediary after the arrest of Martin King, had agreed to come from Atlanta to be the first general counsel. Meanwhile William Josephson, Wiggins' close colleague from the aid program, was aboard as special counsel. A brilliant, suspicious, tenacious lawyer from New York, Josephson was immediately drawn into a fight with the established federal bureaucracy to win the necessary freedom of action for the new agency.

The first sign of danger came one day in the White House mess when I ran into Ralph Dungan, whom the President had just asked to coordinate a high-level task force on the reorganization of American overseas assistance programs. Since early February, when I had become Special Assistant to the President, I had been shuttling between the Executive Office Building, attached to the White House, and Shriver's headquarters a block away. Noting my dual duties to the Peace Corps and civil rights, Dungan warned me that, of course, the Peace Corps would be a subdivision of the proposed new Agency for International Development (AID). "Not if Sarge has anything to say about it," I said, laughing at the tug-of-war I saw coming, which I felt sure Shriver would win. With the opposite assumption, Dungan smiled and said that Sarge could talk all he wanted, but the President was determined to bring all the fragmented components of overseas aid together in a comprehensive program; that was the only efficient way to do it, and the Peace Corps would be no exception.

When Shriver went to Dungan's task force, he found some of the nation's leading experts on foreign aid—such as John Kenneth Galbraith, Henry Labouisse, and Lincoln Gordon—lined up in favor of the new plan. They showed him a big chart for the new super-agency, with control lines to the major operations involving billions of dollars, and over in a small section on the far right were programs called "resources," under which were little boxes for Food for Peace and the Peace Corps.

Afterwards Shriver described to us the scheme as he foresaw it working: AID country directors all over the world would make plans for development assistance to their countries, with Harvard and MIT economists working with their slide rules to determine what ought to be done in Ethiopia or Brazil. Requests would come to Washington for millions of dollars in aid or loans, so much surplus food, and a certain number of Peace Corps Volunteers. George McGovern, who headed Food for Peace, would send the food; Shriver, the Volunteers. The Peace Corps would be like a depot or a warehouse. Peace Corps staff would have little place or power in the field since AID representatives were already there and knew the countries. The Peace Corps would be reduced to recruiting, selecting, and training Volunteers to meet the country programs set by the AID director.

This might sound efficient, but it would doom the Peace Corps, Shriver thought. However, he had failed to make a dent in the thinking of Dungan's task force. "There are about twenty people in Washington who have our concept of an autonomous Peace Corps," he said in uncharacteristic dejection, "and twenty million public administration experts who want a tidy organization chart."

If the twenty include the President of the United States, it will be all right, we said. Shriver was about to depart on a crucial trip around the world, to see various Presidents and Prime Ministers who had expressed an interest in the Peace Corps, so he left with Wiggins and Josephson a strong position paper in favor of the Peace Corps' independence, to be used in the final meetings of Dungan's task force. If they were still unconvinced then it was to be taken directly to the President, with a note from Shriver.

We were all riding high then, and could not believe that Shriver's appeal would not prevail. Washington was rife with stories about how the new Peace Corps was beating the bureaucracy. When Shriver said he wanted fifty people on his staff within the first month, Chris Weeks, from the Bureau of the Budget, thought he was crazy; the Bureau hadn't yet allocated the Peace Corps' first $500,000. The government's usual lethargic pace was broken and Shriver got his staff. A General Services Administration budget manager came, on loan, to maintain government fiscal regulations. Briefly he tried sending around memorandums saying, "There will be no more overtime unless it is authorized at least three days in advance." At a time when almost everyone was working overtime, that rule did not last long.

"You guys had a good day today," a management consultant said one evening. "You broke fourteen laws." But he promised to straighten out the paper work and urged us on: "Keep it up, we're making progress." With this élan and the momentum under way, and with Shriver's special ties to Kennedy, we were confident that the Peace Corps' special identity and autonomy would not be taken away.

We were much too confident. Dungan's task force overruled Shriver and, without waiting for Shriver's return from overseas, the President agreed that the Peace Corps should be included within AID. Dungan told Wiggins and Josephson that the decision was final, and they cabled Shriver, who was then in New Delhi. The President had approved my going on this first exploratory mission, so I was with Shriver in the 110-degree Indian heat as he tried to figure out what could be done.

One last resort suddenly came to his mind: Call Bill Moyers and ask him to urge Lyndon Johnson to intervene with Kennedy. Moyers had left Johnson to become the Peace Corps' congressional liaison (and later its Deputy Director) and, despite his irritation at losing Moyers, Johnson had become the chairman of the Peace Corps' National Advisory Council. Those are little stories in themselves.

The White House had tried to keep Moyers from shifting over to the Peace Corps. In the first weeks of Peace Corps planning, I had arranged a meeting between Moyers and Shriver after Washington attorney James Rowe, a long-time close friend of Johnson's, had called to say that the best man around the Vice-President, a twenty-four-year-old Baptist minister from Texas, wanted to work for the Peace Corps more than anything in the world, but that LBJ was never going to lift a finger to arrange it. "I can't imagine why," said Rowe in his bantering fashion, "but this young man, who ran Johnson's campaign staff and is as good as they come, has fire in his belly about the Peace Corps." Three times Rowe had heard Moyers tell Johnson that if they won the election he wanted to help organize the Peace Corps, and Johnson had promised to help him do it, but Rowe was sure that Johnson would never willingly let him go. "I'm too old for heroes," Rowe said, "but Moyers qualifies."

A few minutes after I had set a date for Moyers to see Shriver, Moyers called back in embarrassment to postpone it. He had promised to tell Kenneth O'Donnell if he contemplated any change of job, and O'Donnell had insisted that he see the President before seeing Shriver. In a few minutes O'Donnell called me to say Shriver couldn't have Moyers. "He's the only one on Johnson's staff we trust," O'Donnell said. "The President's going to tell him to stay there, and you can tell Sarge to keep his cotton-picking hands off Moyers." In fact, when Moyers explained to the President how much he wanted to be a part of the Peace Corps, Kennedy said that of course he should do it if Shriver made him a good offer. Shriver was delighted to win this little competition with the White House, but was not so pleased when he was told that the President wanted him to make Lyndon Johnson the chairman of the Peace Corps' Advisory Council. Since bipartisan support seemed essential, Shriver had thought Herbert Hoover would be a better choice, but for reasons Shriver didn't understand, the White House disapproved. Without that White

House-imposed switch, however, the Peace Corps would probably not have lived to become what it did.

In early May, before leaving on the overseas trip Shriver had seen Johnson to bring the Advisory Council chairman up to date on the disturbing proposal pending before the Dungan task force on AID. Moyers suggested to his former boss that the people who had been presiding over foreign aid pooh-poohed the idea that young Volunteers could contribute to a field which had been dominated by professional experts. Since they could not block the new President's special fancy outright, Moyers thought they were trying to do the next-best thing: absorb it. The result would be a stifling regulation and submersion of an idea which needed to be conspicuous in order to attract Volunteers and public support. The new wine should not be poured into an old bottle.

As they were stating their case, Johnson had interrupted Moyers and Shriver to make a more colorful argument, with all the hyperbole he loved, drawing on his own past battles with bureaucracy, and his experience as the Texas administrator of the National Youth Administration during the New Deal. "Boys," he said (as Moyers later remembered and wrote it down), "this town is full of folks who believe the only way to do something is their way. That's especially true in diplomacy and things like that, because they work with foreign governments and protocol is oh-so-mighty-important to them, with guidebooks and rulebooks and dos and don'ts to keep you from offending someone. You put the Peace Corps into the Foreign Service and they'll put striped pants on your people when all you'll want them to have is a knapsack and a tool kit and a lot of imagination. And they'll give you a hundred and one reasons why it won't work every time you want to do something different, or they'll try to pair it with some program that's already . . . provoked a suspicious reputation.

"Besides," the Vice-President added, "you don't have money to give out and all these other programs do, so you'll get treated like the orphan in a big family where your prestige depends upon your budget. And to top it off, they'll take your volunteers and make them GS ones and twos and you'll send little government employees marching off into the villages over there when you want those countries to accept you as American citizens and not employees of the Secretary of State.

"This boy here," said Johnson, pointing to Moyers, "cajoled and begged and pleaded and connived and threatened and politicked to leave me to go to work for the Peace Corps. For the life of me I can't imagine him doing that to go to work for the foreign aid program . . . If you want the Peace Corps to work, friends, you'll keep it away from the folks downtown who want it to be just another box in an organizational chart."

Pacing up and down in the heat of New Delhi, Shriver vividly re-called this conversation and put in a call to Moyers. It went through right away, and Shriver said that before they hung crape out the windows Moyers should go to Johnson and ask him to make one last personal plea to the President. Later we learned that Johnson responded immediately and made the case with such force that Kennedy finally agreed. The former Senate Majority Leader reminded the President of the foreign aid program's deep-rooted unpopularity in Congress and convinced him that the Peace Corps, with its fresh appeal, needed its special identity and a life of its own in order to have any chance to succeed. Buoyed by the good news, Shriver declared Lyndon Johnson "a founding father of the Peace Corps."

When we returned home at the end of May, we found there was a price to pay for the Peace Corps' newfound freedom. It took Shriver a few weeks to realize what was happening: Larry O'Brien and the White House congressional liaison staff were doing nothing whatsoever to pro-mote the Peace Corps Act, while they were going all-out to pass the bill for AID. In a White House meeting, Ralph Dungan, who had been angry at Shriver's end run through Lyndon Johnson, said to Wiggins and Josephson, "O.K., hotshots, you wanted to be on your own—you're on your own!"

Assuming that the President did not know about this non-coopera-tion of his staff, Shriver told his wife about the Peace Corps' legislative impasse. One day at Hyannis Port, Eunice Shriver decided to tell her brother and ask for help in Congress. After a talk with the President, she reported to her husband: "Jack feels that you and Lyndon Johnson demanded that the Peace Corps be separate and that therefore the two of you ought to get your damn bill through Congress by yourselves." She quoted him as saying that getting the AID bill passed was going to be goddamn difficult and he didn't want to have to turn around and then go to the Congress all over again to put the Peace Corps through. "If Sarge hadn't demanded that it be separate," Kennedy told his sister, "I would have only had to ask for a congressman's support once and we could have got AID and the Peace Corps together. But now I left it out there by it-self at their request—they wanted it that way, they didn't want me to have it in AID where I wanted it—so let them go ahead and put the son of a bitch through."

When he heard that, Shriver says he made a resolution right then: "By God, I will never ask anything from the White House as long as I live. I'll never ask a favor from the President—never." And he says he never did again—not even a light for a cigarette. (Shriver doesn't smoke, but enjoys his own brand of hyperbole.) The business of trading favors was bad enough among politicians, but it seemed even worse to him among brothers-in-law. Because of that family relationship, he says, he "never spoke one more word to President Kennedy asking him or anybody in the White House ever to do anything for the Peace Corps—ever again."

From that point on, says Shriver, "I really went to work. The one thing I was certain of—I was going to put the goddamned Peace Corps through the House and the Senate." After four months of hard work, with the help of Moyers, Johnson, Humphrey, Reuss, and others, the bill was put through. "And then we ran the Peace Corps without ever asking permission or getting clearance for anything from the White House."

Later, to some Peace Corps staff, the President said: "I do not think it is altogether fair to say that I handed Sarge a lemon from which he made lemonade. But I do think that he and other members of your staff were handed one of the most sensitive and difficult assignments which any administrative group in Washington has been given almost in this century." Kennedy paid tribute to Shriver's congressional work, calling him "the most effective lobbyist on the Washington scene."

Moyers and Shriver started most days on Capitol Hill by taking a legislator to breakfast, and then making another visit or two to congressional offices. At the end of the day they often resumed their Capitol rounds. "You know why I really voted for the Peace Corps?" a powerful member of the House Rules Committee explained. "One night I was leaving about seven-thirty and there was Shriver walking up and down the halls, looking into the doors. He came in and talked to me. I still didn't like the program but I was sold on Shriver—I voted for him." One by one, Shriver wooed and won over the early critics—Republicans like Senator Barry Goldwater, Congresswoman Frances Bolton of Ohio (who said the idea gave her shivers at first), and Southern conservatives. When traveling out of the country, from each stop Shriver would send postcards or notes to members of the Senate or House, with news of Peace Corps progress or words of appreciation for their backing.

The buttonholing, cajoling, and coaxing of Congress became for Shriver a labor of love. In the process he developed respect and affection for many of the members of Congress, which they reciprocated. When asked why there was so much congressional support, he gave the credit to the power of the idea and the responsiveness of politicians. "The philosophy of the Peace Corps really is the philosophy of America," he said.

"And when you cut down deep with honest politicians in the Congress, they understand that. And therefore they support it because it is a genuine American enterprise."

The Peace Corps would go only where needed and when asked, and Shriver promised critical congressmen that he would not fish for invitations. After the executive order of March 1, 1961, another wave of mail arrived from thousands of potential Volunteers wanting to know how to enlist. *Time* magazine reported March 10 that "the Peace Corps had captured the public imagination as had no other single act of the Kennedy Administration." But the returns from overseas were slim, and no major leader of the developing nations sent an invitation for the Peace Corps to come.

As the new agency sent 400,000 application forms to post offices, colleges and universities, and to more than 25,000 people who had requested information, we began to wonder whether the old adage about giving a party to which no one came was about to be reversed. How foolish we would all feel if we got hundreds of Volunteers ready with no place to go.

The first break came in Tanganyika, about to become independent (and change its name to Tanzania). Chester Bowles had a warm relationship with Prime Minister Julius Nyerere, and talked with him about the Peace Corps. (I was in one such conversation, and was struck by Nyerere's faith and hope in Kennedy and by his contagious laugh.) A fast-talking member of the Peace Corps staff sent to Dar-es-Salaam cabled that Tanganyika wanted twenty to thirty surveyors and engineers for a major road-building project. Could the Peace Corps provide them?

While recruiters and selection officers searched for surveyors and engineers, we wondered how to produce other solid requests, especially for liberal arts graduates (soon to be dubbed "B.A. generalists"), who were in the most plentiful supply. We particularly hoped for requests from India, the largest democracy in the world and leader of the neutral bloc, and Nigeria, the largest nation in Africa. We were not supposed to fish for invitations, but we tried to prime the pump of foreign interest.

When I found that the Ambassador from India, an old friend, was curious about the Peace Corps, we promptly arranged for him to come to dinner and talk with Shriver. B. K. Nehru was a thoughtful but usually pessimistic man who was Jawaharlal Nehru's cousin. As he left, the Ambassador said, "Am I correct, Mr. Shriver, in thinking that you would not be averse to an invitation from our Prime Minister for you to visit India and talk about your program?" In a few weeks the invitation came.

268

With the visit to Jawaharlal Nehru as the excuse, stopovers and meetings with heads of government were easily arranged for Ghana, Nigeria, Pakistan, Burma, Malaya, Thailand, and the Philippines.

When Shriver asked me to accompany him, I jumped at the opportunity; it was good to get away from Washington during the depression right after the Bay of Pigs. Also along was Franklin Williams, former California NAACP attorney and that state's assistant attorney general, who had run the black voter registration drive during the campaign. He was joining the Peace Corps staff to develop programs through the United Nations. To handle the press there was former Wisconsin newsman Ed Bayley (who complained regularly that Shriver ran the Peace Corps as if we were in the last stage of a presidential campaign).

"We've come to listen and learn," Shriver said upon landing in Accra. It was about all he could say: uncharacteristically, he had lost his voice, an embarrassment for a man who claims not to have been sick in bed for a day in his adult life.

With Kwame Nkrumah, the President of Ghana, called "Osagyefo," or "Savior," the most important thing was to listen. The then leading spokesman for African nationalism lectured Shriver on American shortcomings, some of which he had experienced as a student at Lincoln University, a black institution in rural Pennsylvania (where Franklin Williams had been his fraternity brother). Three weeks after the landing at the Bay of Pigs, Cuba was also much on his mind.

Nkrumah's response to the Peace Corps reflected his ambivalence toward the United States. He said, in about these words: "Powerful radiation is going out from America to all the world, much of it harmful, some of it innocuous, some beneficial. Africans have to be careful and make the right distinctions, so as to refuse the bad rays and welcome the good. The CIA is a dangerous beam that should be resisted. From what you have said, Mr. Shriver, the Peace Corps sounds good. We are ready to try it, and will invite a small number of teachers. We could use some plumbers and electricians, too. Can you get them here by August?"

English was the language of secondary and higher education in Ghana, and the country's development depended on having enough instructors who could teach in English. There were not enough Ghanaians yet able to do this. "Peace Corps Volunteers who will teach, but not propagandize or spy or try to subvert the Ghanaian system, will be very welcome," said Nkrumah. "I do not want them to teach the social sciences. There their biases would influence our young people." He preferred science and mathematics because those subjects did not lend themselves to politics or foreign influence. And he considered English safe.

Later we pondered Nkrumah's distinction between academic subjects and wondered whether in the long run science and mathematics didn't have the most profound revolutionary effect of all. What is more subversive of inherited superstitions, imposed ideologies, and ancient ways than the scientific process? What makes a modern mind and sharpens a free intellect more than mathematics? And in learning English, the language of Shakespeare and Milton, Locke and Lincoln, the King James Bible and the common law, students would be learning more than just a useful foreign tongue.

Nkrumah had teasingly pressed Shriver on another point: Why the one-way traffic? Didn't he want some young Ghanaians to volunteer for service to America? In the same half-serious spirit, Shriver had said yes, he would welcome and find assignments for thirty Volunteers from Ghana (about the number of Peace Corps Volunteers the Prime Minister had suggested). It was clear that some kind of reciprocity would help counteract the immodest benevolence and the condescension in the name Peace Corps.

Next stop was Nigeria, then in the first year of its independence. Shriver was warmly received by President Nnamdi Azikiwe, Prime Minister Tafawa Balewa, and leaders of the main regional governments, and the Peace Corps was readily seen as a way to help meet some of the country's vast educational needs. There were places in Nigeria's elementary schools for only 14,000 out of the more than two million eligible children. An official commission headed by Sir Eric Ashby had found, among other needs, a shortage of an estimated 7,000 man-years of teachers over the next ten years. Great oil resources were awaiting development, and the prospects for the future looked bright if Nigerians could be trained fast enough and educated well enough to know how to manage a complex economy and create a modern society. The government could build the schools, but for a while most of the teachers would have to come from overseas and speak English, the language of instruction. If Peace Corps Volunteers were qualified and behaved themselves, they would probably be invited in large numbers.

President Azikiwe ("Zik"), who had called on Nigerians to "go Gandhi" in their campaign for independence, was concerned that their British-style educational system was producing an educated elite alienated from the people. As the first Ibo to go to school in the United States, he had been impressed by Jefferson's ideas of education and by America's success, through the land grant colleges and universities, in shaping a curriculum appropriate to a new land. He wanted Peace Corps teachers to help Nigeria achieve a similar democratic system of education.

In Pakistan, we were not surprised that President Ayub Khan and his government, with so many military ties to the United States, also wanted Peace Corps projects. Rural public works and agricultural and community development were the primary assignments proposed. The village development center at Comilla, in poor and crowded East Pakistan (now Bangladesh), was a successful model of what could be done with good leadership. Aktar Ahmeed Khan, its director, a man of vision and compassion, was esteemed by many as a kind of Moslem Gandhi. Hard-working and friendly young farmers, sent by the government of Japan as part of that country's overseas aid program, were demonstrating in Comilla how to raise crop yields dramatically, by better seeds, irrigation, fertilizer, and skilled labor, without tractors or heavy equipment. For miles around, as far as we could see, the Green Revolution was a reality.

India was the hardest and most critical test of the trip—and with its half billion people and leading role in the Third World it was our chief objective. As an old India hand, I knew that the idea of an American Peace Corps coming to that ancient civilization would rouse the pride and sense of spiritual superiority of many Indians we would meet. On the other hand, Chester Bowles was still enormously popular there, the Community Development Program he had helped initiate and plan during his ambassadorship from 1949 to 1953 was in need of the energy and drive of outside volunteers, and he had urged his Indian friends, including Prime Minister Nehru and his daughter Indira, to receive us well and look favorably on President Kennedy's new venture.

From our first encounters in New Delhi, I found that Kennedy had stirred strong but mixed feelings. His youth, charm, and call to service, his concern for the progress of Asia, Africa, and Latin America, and his recognition of the right of India and other Third World nations to maintain their neutrality in the cold war were all appealing. Indians were glad the torch had passed to a new generation, but worried where and how Kennedy would carry it. The word that went forth from the new President's inaugural address, "to friend and foe alike," that America would "pay any price, bear any burden, meet any hardship, support any friend, oppose any foe to assure the survival and the success of liberty" had a disturbing imperial ring. American support for the invasion of Cuba had been even more alarming.

One thoughtful Indian friend had been struck by Robert Frost's prophecy that "young ambition eager to be tried" would usher in a new "Augustan age . . . of poetry and power." A passage in Frost's poem for John Kennedy's inauguration had particularly irritated my friend, who wondered if the Peace Corps had been conceived in its patronizing and imperial spirit:

We see how seriously the races swarm
In their attempts at sovereignty and form.
They are our wards we think to some extent
For the time being and with their consent,
To teach them how Democracy is meant.

Much of our talk in New Delhi and on a tour of rural projects in the Punjab was intended to convince Indians that Peace Corps Volunteers would not come in such a neocolonial spirit. American Volunteers might teach techniques of modern poultry production (the special assistance requested in the Punjab), but they would not have the presumption to teach democracy to a nation that since 1948 had been regularly holding the world's largest free elections. Many times, in different ways, Shriver said that by letting Americans participate in India's struggles they would be giving us a chance to find ourselves.

The Peace Corps' future in India was to be decided by Shriver's meeting with Nehru. Wearing his red rose, the Prime Minister received him wearily, as was his fashion, and slumped back in his chair, almost going to sleep during Shriver's description of the Peace Corps. Finally Nehru responded along the following lines:

> For thousands of years outsiders have been coming to India, some of them as invaders, sweeping down the plains of the Punjab to the Ganges. Many of them stayed and were assimilated. Others went home, leaving India more or less the same as it was before they came. India has usually been hospitable to these strangers, having confidence that its culture would survive, and that it had much to teach the newcomers.
>
> In matters of the spirit, I am sure young Americans would learn a good deal in this country and it could be an important experience for them. The government of the Punjab and the Minister for Community Development apparently want some of your Volunteers, and we will be happy to receive a few of them—perhaps twenty to twenty-five. But I hope you and they will not be too disappointed if the Punjab, when they leave, is more or less the same as it was before they came.

However patronizing or fainthearted, this permission to proceed was the green light Shriver needed. From then on the Peace Corps had Nehru's imprimatur, which helped open the door in a number of other Third World countries.

On reflection we realized how wrong Nehru's history was, at least about the effect of the British Raj. As Nehru's own life showed, when the British left, India was not the same as it had been when they came. "I have become a queer mixture of the East and the West," Nehru had written. And that is what India had become, with its reception and continuation of the British judicial system, common law, civil service, and parliamentary politics. But we, too, were wrong—in denying that the Peace Corps represented a new stage in the centuries-long colonial movement that was Westernizing the planet. Columbus never found his passage to India, but the West had finally done so on a large scale. Now more Americans would be on their way to speed up the process of modernization. Would India really be the same when they left?

The answer depended on another question, which was quietly put to Shriver by an Indian who made even more of an impression on him than Nehru. Ashadevi Aryanayakam, a close associate of Gandhi, who had long presided over the Mahatma's ashram called Sevagram ("Service Village"), traveled three days and nights on a train to talk with us about the Peace Corps. As a young woman she had left the elegant poet Tagore and his luxurious colony of artists to follow the ascetic (but resiliently gay) Gandhi in search of the poorest village in the poorest part of India. There they had tried to carry through, in one community, a social revolution.

"Yours was the first revolution," Ashadevi said to Shriver. "Do you think young Americans possess the spiritual values they must have to bring the spirit of that revolution to our country?"

She was a beautiful woman with a very low voice, and we had to lean forward to hear her words. "India should not boast of any spiritual superiority," she said. "There is a great valuelessness spreading around the world and in India, too. Your Peace Corps Volunteers must bring more than science and technology. They must touch the idealism of America and bring that to us, too. Can they do it?"

She brought us up to date on Gandhi's idea of a Shanti Sena—an army of peace volunteers—which the Mahatma's aging disciple Vinoba Bhave was still trying to implement, as part of his effort to collect gifts of land to be distributed to the landless. Her account of this Indian Peace Corps had interested Martin Luther King on his trip in 1959, and she had first discussed it with me when we met in Sevagram a decade before that. For the volunteer in a Peace Army, she said, "character or soul force must mean everything and physique must take second place."

Ashadevi had heard talk of a "new politics" in America, connected with Kennedy or the civil rights movement, but she thought the best source for a genuine transformation of politics was Gandhi. He had shown that when the well of words runs dry you must turn to work and to struggle. We talked about how the "seditious Middle Temple lawyer" (as Churchill described Gandhi) had combined three forms of action into a coherent strategy: the Spade, the Prison, and the Vote. The Vote stood for the usual Western politics of elections, parliaments, petitions, and laws. But in order for self-government—*swaraj*—to succeed, according to Gandhi, the Spade and the Prison had to be added.

The Prison was the course of civil disobedience which many in India, and Martin Luther King and others in America, were choosing. The Spade, in India, had been represented by a thirteen-point constructive program to end untouchability, promote Hindu-Moslem unity, form village cooperatives, improve agriculture, provide sanitation, teach children—and take better care of cows. For Gandhi, the Spade was in fact a spinning wheel, which symbolized India's determination to be self-sufficient. When he spun, he said he could hear "the music of freedom."

"It is the Spade that is most often missing, in India and perhaps also in America," Ashadevi said, "—the hard work that gets real things done." She told how Gandhi, at a great Congress Party assembly, had shocked educated and high-caste India by taking an untouchable sweeper's broom and cleaning a stinking latrine. When people said it was not proper work for him (or for them), he replied, "Why wait till the advent of *swaraj* for the necessary drain cleaning?"

"You see, Gandhi was the first Peace Corps Volunteer," said Ashadevi laughingly. For her, there were these three, the Vote, the Prison, and the Spade, but the greatest of these was the Spade.

Although at each stop the American ambassador had been cooperative, we encountered enough skepticism, if not underlying hostility, among U.S. Foreign Service officers and aid officials to know that many were lying in wait to say that they had always considered the Peace Corps a mistake. Some of that opposition did not surface until later. After retiring, career diplomat Elliot O. Briggs said that the Peace Corps was a movement "wrapped in a pinafore of publicity, whose team cry is: 'Yoo-hoo, yoo-hoo. Let's go out and wreak some good on some natives.' "

To the Senate Foreign Relations Committee, Shriver presented upon our return a quite different approach. At the heart of the Peace Corps, according to its director, was the spirit of volunteer service—"that quality in American life which de Tocqueville more than a century ago saw as the central source of American strength." At the start of his testimony, Shriver repeated the question put to him in India by Ashadevi. Could Volunteers bring with them the values and spirit of the American Revolution? "Our answer," Shriver said, "based on faith, was Yes."

By then that answer was based on more than faith. As a result of the new requests, including some from Latin America, the number of Volunteers needed for the first projects had grown from the first estimate of 300 to more than 3,000. With 12,000 applicants being processed for projects in eight countries and several thousand about to take the newly prepared Peace Corps test before being chosen to enter training, the

Peace Corps was a going concern by the time Congress acted on the legislation. Nkrumah received the first fifty-one Volunteers as he had hoped—in August. To the surprise and evident pleasure of the Ghanaian Minister of Education and other high officials welcoming them at the Accra airport, the first contingent of Peace Corps Volunteers expressed their appreciation by singing a song in Twi, the main language of Ghana.

In September 1961, as large bipartisan majorities in the Senate and House passed the Peace Corps Act and authorized $30 million for its first year, the omens looked promising. But Shriver reminded the staff of a proverb we had heard in Africa: "Until you have crossed the river, don't insult the crocodile's mouth."

Selection and training had gone relatively well—incredibly well, given the speed with which the staff and participating colleges, universities, and private agencies were working, and the pressures they were under to get the first thousand Volunteers overseas. The columnist Marquis Childs had written that "the ideal candidate for the Peace Corps must have the patience of Job, the forbearance of a saint, and the digestive system of an ostrich." Sometimes it seemed as if the Peace Corps' selection officers were using those criteria, as they "selected out" (in their bureaucratic euphemism) applicants and later trainees who, they thought, fell short of the very high standards Shriver and Congress had set. Peace Corps Advisory Council member David Riesman warned against seeking or expecting saints, since if there was one around, he or she wouldn't need the Peace Corps, and wouldn't fit readily within its structure. "You want healthy, representative Americans," Riesman said, "whose motives will be mixed, like most people's." That is what we got.

Their reasons for joining, as one Volunteer wrote, "were complex, profound and personal." A sixty-year-old teacher got tired of being asked why she had volunteered. When a newsman asked her why she would go to Africa after teaching school thirty years in Kansas, she replied, "Young man, have you ever taught school thirty years in Kansas?"

Paul Theroux, a Volunteer in Malawi (a Peace Corps program I had negotiated), was clearer about his reason for enlisting. After reading Conrad's *Heart of Darkness*, future novelist Theroux had put his finger on the title page and said, "When I join the Peace Corps I shall go *there*." But Conrad "ruined Africa" for Theroux, who found no "there" there—no crazed Belgians and "unspeakable rites." Instead of reacting to "the horror," as Conrad's colonial agent had, many Volunteers seeing their new lands were first of all moved by the beauty.

Not all of them, however. The first crisis came, in the fall of 1961, when a Volunteer in the initial contingent to Nigeria had to be hurried back to the United States because of an indiscreet postcard she had written home. Margery Michelmore was a *magna cum laude* graduate of Smith College who was able to say a lot—too much—in very little space. "With all the training we have had we were really not prepared for the squalor and absolutely primitive living conditions rampant both in the cities and the bush," she had written. "We had no idea what 'underdeveloped' means. It is really a revelation. . . . Everyone except us lives in the streets, cooks in the streets, and even goes to the bathroom in the streets."

A Nigerian student had seen the card before it left Ibadan and excitedly passed it around. Soon it was reproduced and angry protest meetings were held to demand that she go home. It became front-page news in Nigeria and around the world. Critics of the Peace Corps said, "I told you so."

On her card Margery had added that she was having "great fun" in the "fascinating" city of Ibadan, and that "once we got over the initial, horrified shock, it is a very rewarding experience." But, as the Nigerian Ambassador to the U.S. explained, "no one likes to be called primitive." After her exaggeration about a city where thousands of Nigerians had relatively comfortable homes and few lived on the streets (although open sewers openly arrived at were not uncommon), nothing would suffice to mitigate the student fury. An African friend of mine, who had been brought up by his father on the motto "Never trust a white man," said the incident showed how right his father was. Margery's rapid departure was the price necessary to enable her fellow Volunteers to stay and prove themselves more sensitive.

"I came to Nigeria with high anticipation, interest, and goodwill and I have been very happy here," she said on leaving for the States. At the New York airport a hand note of sympathy from President Kennedy awaited her. Through her tears she said she had learned a lot. "What?" asked a newsman. To write on her next postcard from a Peace Corps project, she said, only: "Having a wonderful time. Wish you were here."

She had also learned a lot about the problem of the integration of the wealthy white minority in a world in which the great majority is colored and poor, and had seen firsthand how explosive this problem is. The poverty of the Nigerians, their proud nationalism, their raw racial nerves, their determination to catch up, and the difficulty of closing the gap between rich and poor, black and white, American and African— these indeed were a revelation.

In the long run, Margery Michelmore's debacle added significantly to the Peace Corps' sensitivity and success. From the moment her postcard was in the headlines, every other Volunteer was on guard. It made more acceptable a somber section in the *Peace Corps Handbook* entitled "Living in a Goldfish Bowl." "Like the proverbial goldfish, the Peace Corps Volunteer will be 'in view' constantly," Volunteers were warned. "You never will have real privacy."

> . . . your every action will be watched, weighed and considered representative of the entire Peace Corps. . . . Basically, you are a guest in the host country. You must learn—and respect—the local customs, manners, taboos, religions and traditions, remembering always that the slightest "goof" will quickly be seen and talked of by many persons.

If Margery Michelmore had been able to stay and teach, at the end of two years she would have found, as her fellow Volunteers did, that the Nigerians were as forgiving of "goofs" as any other people. In the sweep of the land and amidst the gaiety of a people that at the first sound of music will dance the bouncing "Highlife," there was also plenty of privacy. *Nun onya ocka*—"Welcome, white man"—were the words that waving villagers cried to the first busload of teachers for the University at Nsukka. And then above the bush and plain there were the dome hills that reminded Volunteer Roger Landrum of the hills in Alan Paton's *Cry the Beloved Country*, that are "lovely beyond the singing of them." At the end of his first semester teaching, Landrum wrote:

> The *Harmattan* has begun to blow itself out, and each day our vision of the surrounding hills is clearer. Most of us feel very much at home now and are busy with our work. We are waiting to see what the rainy season will be like. When the new growth will come to the burnt hills, the grass will grow on campus, and we will be able to look back over a term of completed work.

On the departure of Landrum's group in the spring of 1963, the student newspaper wrote that when "President Kennedy's Volunteers arrived, the wounds were still fresh in the minds of Nigerians from Miss Michelmore's uncomplimentary remarks." The Volunteers had been met by a long line of students shouting that they were spies and chanting, in Ibo, "The elephant tramples everything in its way." But as time went on:

> Their devotion to duty, their simplicity, their good grace and ease, their complete lack of those "qualities" that are the preserve of master spies . . . all combined to effectively erase ill feelings the students nursed against the Peace Corps Volunteers on our campus.
>
> Now . . . we feel that no amount of praise showered on them for their work is too much. . . . To our Peace Corps friends about to leave us, we say: We are indeed sorry to see you go. We shall miss you and your services.

Some observers had said that the tide of Nigerian opinion turned favorable to the Peace Corps when one of the early Volunteers saved the life of a drowning Nigerian by mouth-to-mouth resuscitation. But, as Shriver commented, "dramatic incidents, even symbolic acts, do not count as much as the quiet work, the daily drudgery of Volunteers on the job."

By the time Margery Michelmore's colleagues returned, seven other groups totaling over 450 Volunteers had replaced them in Nigeria, or were on their way, at the request of the Nigerian government. The quality of the Peace Corps experience, and the measure of it, however, is not in quantity or in the reactions of governments and the press. "You Washington people have no idea what it is all about," one Volunteer said to me. "You have to go upcountry to find the hidden heart."

Meanwhile, in Washington, Peace Corps staff members were proud of a newspaper photograph showing the lights ablaze on the Peace Corps' seven floors, while other government buildings were dark, their employees long gone home. It was not a waste of fuel or human energy, for operations were expanding into seventeen countries the first year (and into twenty-nine more the second year), with the number of Volunteers increasing from just over 2,800 through June 1962 to 6,500 by June 1963.

As often as White House duties permitted, I attended Shriver's senior staff meetings, held two or three times a week when he was in the country. Unlike Kennedy's spokes-of-the-wheel theory, under which his staff reported directly but separately to him (when we could get to him), the operating principle at the Peace Corps was staff dialogue—by the constant circulation of memorandums but most of all face to face, around a table, with Shriver at the head. Sometimes there would just be Wiggins, Moyers, Josephson, Franklin Williams, Charles Peters (who set up an unusual deep-probing, hard-hitting system for evaluating programs), Joseph English, the chief Peace Corps psychiatrist, and perhaps Bill Haddad, a general troubleshooter; sometimes another dozen division chiefs, plus those especially involved in any issue on the agenda; sometimes a larger ring of staff would crowd into the room—but almost always there would be a hard-fought argument.

By those who liked this, and those who didn't, Shriver has been accused of administering through tension—pitting people against each other, as Franklin Roosevelt is said to have enjoyed doing during the New Deal. Instead of acknowledging a theory of creative tension (as Martin King did in making his case for civil disobedience), Shriver explained what he thought he was doing in other terms. "It isn't that I seek tension, but when some difficult new problem is coming up—let's say, whether we should go into a particular country—I often do not know enough to make that decision. I read a lot of reports but the way I most like to resolve a matter in my own head is to get conflicting points of view argued in front of me. Not just in front of me, but with maybe four or five close associates also involved in the argument. From that interplay I am able to make wiser decisions than if I had decided in a cool-nosed way, removed from the hurly-burly of human action and reaction."

One hotly disputed early decision involved a program I had negotiated with President Sylvanus Olympio of Togo, after I had driven every road in his small West African country, from Tsevié to Sokodé, Mango to Dapango. The program called for the Peace Corps to send volunteer doctors and nurses to provincial hospitals, where upcountry, outside the capital city, Lomé, there were altogether only nine doctors and very few qualified nurses. Several Peace Corps program officers vehemently opposed the project on the ground that "curative" medicine was counterproductive if not counterrevolutionary. They favored mass health education, eradication of malaria, and various forms of "preventive" medicine but considered hospital care for a relatively small number of individual patients a luxury Togo couldn't afford.

Joining the argument, Shriver recognized the contradictions and supported the Togo plan. "Taking modern medicine into a valley that has never had it could have a far-reaching impact," he said. "In some places the very idea that every human being has a right to decent medical care is profoundly revolutionary." The volunteer doctors and nurses would be spreading the news that the means exist to make such care available to everyone.

For Shriver, a more difficult political decision was to authorize Peace Corps assignments in birth control projects sponsored by host governments. After word spread of Volunteers distributing contraceptives, the Planned Parenthood movement wanted to give Shriver a special award for pioneering in the use of federal money for such a purpose. He declined the honor, but agreed with the staff consensus that this was important and appropriate work for any Volunteer willing to do it. Mrs. Lillian Carter was in the first group of Volunteers trained to disseminate birth control information in India.

Another early issue was what to do about the CIA. After lively staff discussion of the damage to the Peace Corps' reputation if a Volunteer or staff member were found to have been associated with the CIA, a policy of absolutely no ties with the CIA was adopted. The President informed the CIA and, as far as we could ascertain, the Agency kept its hands off the Volunteers and staff in the field and afterwards. As added protection, the FBI and Civil Service Commission were asked to let Shriver know if the background investigations of applicants as Volunteers, or for staff positions, disclosed any previous connection with intelligence work. Not only would no one with CIA ties be selected, but the ban extended to Volunteers' later careers, and beyond the CIA to the whole so-called intelligence community. Some former Volunteers and staff considered this an unfair limit on their subsequent freedom. Thomas Hughes called me in 1965 to complain that his Bureau of Intelligence and Research was blocked from hiring an outstanding man because of the sweeping Peace Corps policy. Since the State Department's bureau conducted no covert operations or espionage, Hughes thought it should be exempt, but Shriver would not permit any hole in the dike.*

Shriver was equally stubborn in opposing efforts to force the Peace Corps to conform to U.S. geopolitical strategy. Despite Rusk's position that the Peace Corps should operate apart from foreign policy, at one point pressures came from the State Department to send Volunteers to Algeria. It was proposed as a way to woo Algerian Prime Minister Ben Bella. After heated staff debate about the merits of the specific program, which was part of an AID project, Shriver decided the Peace Corps wouldn't cooperate. Complaining about the Peace Corps' "independence of strategic concerns," a department official wrote to McGeorge Bundy asking: "Shouldn't we quash this nonsense that PC independent of US policy interest?" In his memorandum, Harold Saunders added that the Bureau of the Budget "fully agrees Shriver needs a gentle straightening out." Bundy obligingly wrote Shriver a memorandum urging him to yield:

> I know you don't like to get into nasty international political considerations, but nevertheless there are only two or three countries in Africa that are as important. . . . As an entirely accidental benefit, I note that entry by the Peace Corps in Algeria might be mildly irritating to some of those in Europe who are giving us most trouble at the moment—but fooling aside, the real point is that Ben Bella is impressed with the Peace Corps, with you, and with the President. And a little help here might butter a lot of parsnips.

Shriver held his ground, and the Peace Corps stayed out of Algeria. That may have been unfortunate, since other reports confirmed that Ben Bella's interest in the Peace Corps was genuine. Whether or not Shriver was wrong about Algeria—an issue which divided the staff—his defense of

---

* The man Hughes wanted, William Miller, had served briefly on the Peace Corps staff in Iran. Later, ironically, Miller became the staff director of the Senate Intelligence Committee under Senator Church, and conducted the investigation that exposed the CIA activities discussed in chapters 11 and 12.

the Peace Corps' right to determine its program helped preserve its unprecedented freewheeling status within the government.

The dialogue on these and countless other issues, presided over by Shriver, was the closest to decision-making through a Socratic seminar that I have experienced in government. Except that after listening and questioning, proposing and prodding, Shriver would decide on a course of action, usually with a strong consensus behind him but sometimes in the face of strong opposition.

Another Greek model comes to mind: Alexander was said to have imagined at night, while drunk, but to have decided in the sober light of dawn. There was not much drinking at the Peace Corps, but sometimes the night work ended in a free-for-all, in which a new idea would take flight in Shriver's mind and he or his close associates would "shriverize" it. Used behind his back, that verb meant to escalate, to enlarge, to speed up, to apply greater imagination. Then a second Shriver would preside critically and thoughtfully at the next morning's staff meeting, when many a night flight was brought down to earth, punctured like a balloon, by sharp questioning.

Participation in the making of the Peace Corps was an intoxicating and illuminating experience. Shriver was not a tidy administrator, but he was a great executive. He did not delegate powers through an orderly chain of command, but he empowered people. He released their energies, backed their efforts, and drew on their insights. Wives of staff men tended to be jealous because Shriver harnessed their husbands' energies and loyalties—and weekends.

What Volunteers in the field found most unsettling and most resented was their publicity. The stories in the press (which, at first, they blamed on an oversell by Shriver or by what they called "Peace Corps Washington") were too glamorous, too glowing, too pat, drawing an image of Volunteers effortlessly spouting Pushtu, Swahili, or Tagalog and winning legions of friends while transforming economies. The day-to-day problems—the "dysentery and boredom," as one Volunteer put it—were seldom mentioned. Or as Volunteer Paul Theroux was to write in a poem:

> We are pure until faced with fruit
> but the seen shape takes away our history
> so we open our fat hands to a new world.

At the height of the public enthusiasm about the Peace Corps, Eric Sevareid commented dryly that "there is nothing so irresistible as pure intentions backed by pure publicity." More accurately, when there is undue publicity about purity, someone will find it irresistible to puncture the pretension. Peace Corps Volunteers were prompt to do it about themselves.

Exposing impostors, reducing would-be heroes to human size, and bringing people down to earth are among the functions of comedy. Bringing people together in some form of reconciliation and in a new recognition of reality, after unusual predicaments and usually some laughter, is another outcome of comedy. That dramatic form is especially appropriate for the Peace Corps' efforts to promote world peace and friendship. The very concept of American Volunteers going forth to do good in underdeveloped lands—and do good against people, as it must often have seemed—sets up an inescapable comic situation. Yet it is in the nature of comedy that the characters in it do not consider themselves comic. "Your sense of humor doesn't ignite until quite a lot later," wrote Paul Theroux later.*

As the first Volunteers began to write reflectively about their experience, most of them seemed to approach it seriously but not solemnly. "What we need is a philosophy—not of high adventure à la Conrad or Saint-Exupéry—but of dullness," wrote Kenneth Kressel from the Ivory Coast: "A philosophy which will satisfy our craving for accomplishment and a certain nobility while we are faced with tedium, fatigue and the desire to sit down and dream." From West Pakistan, Addis Palmer wrote:

> Some of the Volunteers are finding it very hard to keep from being depressed with the enormity of it all. None of us say how we really feel. We gripe and complain, laugh and poke fun, and yet each of us has another side sacred only to himself. Why are we embarrassed to express how we really feel? For fear we might sound corny and possibly be laughed at? We are such a cold culture outwardly, and yet we are the softest on the inside. How we should hate ever being found out.

Soon after returning from Nigeria, David Schickele described how the "favorite parlor sport during the Peace Corps training program was making up cocky answers to a question that was put to us seventeen times a day by the professional and idly curious alike: 'Why did you join the Peace Corps?' " He said: "It was less painful to be facetious than to repeat the idealistic clichés to which the question was always a veiled invitation." To his fellow Swarthmore alumni Schickele reported that during his two years teaching at the University at Nsukka he was "more alive

---

* Future novelist Theroux was sent home from Malawi and "terminated" as a Volunteer for getting involved in anti-regime politics in that country.

intellectually" than he had been in college because he had "worked much harder at Nsukka"; because "one learns more from teaching than from studying"; and because "it is always an intellectual experience to cross cultural boundaries." No intellectual understanding can exist without a sense of identification at some deeper level, he contended. That is what the Peace Corps accomplishes, he said, "when it is lucky":

> This to me is the meaning of the Peace Corps as a new frontier. It is the call to go, not where man has never been before, but where he has lived differently; the call to experience firsthand the intricacies of a different culture; to understand from the inside rather than the outside; and to test the limits of one's own way of life against another in the same manner as the original pioneer tested the limits of his endurance against the elements.

That was perhaps an impossible idea, surely impossible in the narrow scope of two years, Schickele conceded, but "it was an adventure just the same." John Kennedy would have approved that theme. We tend to inflict on others our own best experiences, and as an early traveler around the globe he wanted young Americans to profit by the experience of crossing cultural frontiers. He would have appreciated the words of a Volunteer in Ethiopia who wrote in 1964: "Whatever we were before, and none of us can quite remember, that's all gone. Peace Corps life tempers one by its sheer and irresistible intensity." Richard Lipez added: "We look forward to coming home, but missing will be the adventure, the thrill that none of us will ever be able to live again with such intensity, such freedom." In meeting their responsibilities in Ethiopia, Lipez said, "we found a kind of freedom greater than any we could have imagined."

And Kennedy would have enjoyed the stories of a Volunteer on the highland of Eritrea whose extracurricular assignment was to assist the village postmaster in a long-distance romance with a girl in Addis Ababa who read English but not Tigrinya. The Volunteer would write the postmaster's love letters, according to his dictation. With delight she had told me the last sentence in one letter. "And so," said the postmaster to his faraway friend, "I have loved you, I am loving you, and I will love you until my perpendicular is horizontal and I die."

If Volunteers overseas had to worry about goofs, the President of the United States had reason to be sympathetic. The White House is no goldfish bowl, but the President's own alertness and sensitivity were always on trial.

"And do you send all your Negroes to Howard for training?"

When John Kennedy asked that question, Warren Wiggins could not at first believe his ears. The President was about to go out into the Rose Garden to say farewell to several hundred Peace Corps Volunteers heading overseas. Wiggins had just explained that they had all trained in Washington-area institutions, such as Georgetown, George Washington, American, Catholic, and Howard universities. And the President, who had campaigned on the strongest civil rights platform in history, who would not have been elected but for a wave of black votes, had asked— in the summer of 1962—if the Peace Corps had segregated its black Volunteers and sent them all to the Negro university.

When Wiggins explained how inappropriate that would have been, the President readily said he understood. Never liking to be caught off base or uninformed, Kennedy seemed irritated as he came into the garden. This time it was a send-off for me, too, and I walked with him as he went down the long line of nearly three hundred Volunteers heading for Ethiopia, where I would be the Peace Corps representative. The contingent for Ethiopia was the largest to go at one time to any country. As he shook hands and wished them good luck, his humor quickly returned.

"Keep in touch," he said to me, grinning, "but not by postcard!"

9 · A War on Poverty and the Idea of National Service

From the moment he became President, Lyndon Johnson viewed himself as the legitimate custodian of John Kennedy's political will, and sought to use the moment of national unity produced by the assassination to advance some of his predecessor's most controversial proposals, beginning with civil rights. That "act of violence," Johnson wrote later, "shocked the nation deeply and created the impetus to send the country surging forward."

With the new President, in his first State of the Union address, having declared "unconditional war on poverty in America," with the Director of the Peace Corps appointed to organize that war, and with a "domestic Peace Corps" slated to be on the front lines, Washington in 1964 seemed full of promise for returning Peace Corps Volunteers and staff. Another encouraging sign for many of us was the key White House role of Bill Moyers, whom Lyndon Johnson had reclaimed from the Peace Corps in the first hour of his presidency.

If Washington lacked the special luster of John and Jacqueline Kennedy (whom Johnson said had made the White House a "great palace of light" that cast its reflection over the world), and Art Buchwald could no longer joke about little Caroline calling Lee Radziwill "my aunt, Princess Radish," the legends about Lyndon Johnson were lively enough to fill the cocktail conversation in the capital. His tall Texan tales, vivid, dirty anatomical analogies, and congressional arm-twisting were aspects of an extraordinary political personality. "He is a force of nature," said Bill Moyers, who knew how much good—or harm—that force could do.

At the time of the assassination, Moyers had been in Austin, making arrangements for President Kennedy's visit there. It was an unusual assignment for the White House to have given the Deputy Director of the Peace Corps, but the political skill and charm of the twenty-nine-year-old former aide to Johnson drew responsibilities to him like a magnet. Hearing that Kennedy was shot, Moyers chartered a private plane and reached Air Force One in Dallas just before his past and future boss was sworn in as the thirty-sixth President of the United States.

Thereafter, for almost four years, Moyers was at Johnson's side, as his Special Assistant and then Press Secretary. Some said he acted as Johnson's conscience; others, that he was a surrogate son. "If I had a boy, I'd like him to be like this young fellow," Johnson said of Moyers, according to Eric Goldman in *The Tragedy of Lyndon Johnson.* "He gets along with people. He can sit down with three people when they are miles apart in their thinking and get an agreement on what policy ought to be." Also, Johnson added, "That boy has a bleeding ulcer. He works for me like a dog, and is just as faithful."

While the Peace Corps was being launched and then while he visited us in Ethiopia in 1963, I had enjoyed Moyers' engaging humor and steady good judgment. It was hard to believe he suffered from an ulcer— until I saw the way Johnson commanded his every hour, keeping him at the office late at night to talk, telephoning to the White House limousine taking him home, summoning him to the ranch in Texas just as he was about to relax with his family. More and more, according to Goldman (who had become Johnson's White House "intellectual," his Arthur Schlesinger), the word was: "Better have Bill handle it." For me and others in the Peace Corps who greatly admired Moyers, his ascendancy was good news for the country.

For Shriver, too, this was an exhilarating time. On February 1, Johnson had appointed him to plan and direct the all-out campaign to end poverty in America that the President had promised in his January address to Congress. He was to do this as a Special Assistant to the President (with a seat at Cabinet meetings), while continuing as Director of the Peace Corps. "Sarge," Johnson had said, in giving him the White House title, "this thing can't survive less'n everybody knows when they're hitting it, they're hitting me. I'm your protection."

Describing his new assignment, Shriver said that the President wanted the War on Poverty "to proceed with the same sense of urgency, to gather the same kind of momentum, to tap the same volunteer spirit, to take the same basic approach to people and their problems at home as the Peace Corps has done overseas." Yet the two efforts were otherwise not the same. The antipoverty campaign would begin with nearly a billion dollars, ten times the Peace Corps' appropriation after four years of buildup. No one could predict the cost or time it would take to do what the Bible said could never be done. The effort to abolish poverty, Shriver said, would require "the broadest and most effective partnership of city, state and federal governments and of the people working together that this nation has ever seen."

Before Shriver was given this mandate, preliminary planning had begun, under the direction of Walter Heller, chairman of the Council of Economic Advisers. At the end of Johnson's first full day as President, Heller had come to report work done during the previous months in preparing an anti-poverty program for President Kennedy to present to Congress in 1964. Kennedy had given Heller "a green light to pull together a set of proposals" and the day before he left for Texas had definitely decided to include such a program in his forthcoming budget. Heller now needed to know what Johnson wanted. In recalling that moment, Johnson said he swung around in his chair and looked out the window at the lights burning "in the offices of grief-stricken men." Finally he "turned back and looked into Heller's eyes" and said, "Go ahead. Give it the highest priority. Push ahead full tilt."

Johnson's response surprised many who expected him to be more conservative than Kennedy, and more cautious in approaching Congress. But Johnson recounted in his memoirs how he weighed the prospects "for a revolutionary new program to attack one of the most stubbornly entrenched social ills in America." Thinking about the pendulum of social reform in America—how it swung over the years from creative activity to almost total inaction, and then back to action again—he knew three conditions were required for any great reform: a recognition of need, a willingness to act, and someone to lead the effort. Through the civil rights movement and the growing problems of the young, especially in the ghettos, "the need was more apparent every day." John Kennedy's death had "touched all our hearts and made us, for a while at least, a more compassionate people." And, he said, "when I looked inside myself, I believed that I could provide the third ingredient—the disposition to lead." He saw the "three conditions coming together in historic harmony." A War on Poverty, he concluded, was "my kind of undertaking."

In his inaugural address, Kennedy had said that "man holds in his mortal hands the power to abolish all forms of human poverty," but he hadn't done much about it. Kennedy's anti-poverty proposals had not been made public, or even shaped, and if he had lived his chance of getting any major new program through Congress in 1964 would have been slim. Johnson recalled his own slogan when he first ran for public office: "He gets things done." The new President resolved to go beyond anything Kennedy had done or imagined doing, and give the undertaking an unmistakable LBJ brand.

When Heller and Budget Director Kermit Gordon came to the ranch during the Christmas holidays with the outline for an initial pilot program in a limited number of "demonstration project" cities, Johnson told them to start thinking more ambitiously and come back with a new concept. "I didn't want to paste together a lot of existing approaches," he wrote. "I wanted original inspiring ideas." He was convinced it "had to be big and bold and hit the whole nation with real impact."

With that in mind, he chose Shriver as his "personal chief of staff for the War on Poverty," and told him to work fast. Johnson said he wanted "a strong man" and had been impressed by Shriver's executive ability, by his seemingly endless energy, and by the unusual measure of congressional respect he had earned.

During this period I was back from Ethiopia for some weeks to help Shriver (before our family's return later in the spring), and heard from him how convincingly, even movingly, Johnson talked about "his" war, the only war he wanted, to rescue the poor. He would go back to the Mexican-American children he had taught at Cotulla, Texas, who had come to school hungry. He had dreamed of finding a way to help them, and now he was going to do it. When the Civil Rights Commission met with him, Johnson told them, with intense feeling, that the test of his presidency would be what he did for the poor.

In his memoirs, Johnson recalled the work of Shriver's anti-poverty task force in the winter and spring of 1964:

> Their excitement was contagious. Hundreds of people—high school and college students, returning Peace Corpsmen, housewives, and even congressional wives—volunteered to work thousands of hours in every kind of capacity. . . . They went at it with a fervor and created a ferment unknown since the days of the New Deal, when lights had burned through the night as men worked to restructure society.

Johnson's—and Shriver's—exuberance no doubt annoyed and further depressed Robert Kennedy. Since the assassination he had been in deep gloom much of the time, brooding about his brother and the burden of his legacy. When I saw him that spring his melancholy mood made him seem, for the first time, vulnerable. At the signing of the Civil Rights Act of 1964, Martin Luther King was struck by the sadness in the Attorney General's eyes. Kennedy hung back and did not go near Johnson, until pushed forward. Only on the eve of the Democratic National Convention in August, when he went to New York to announce his candidacy for the Senate, did the shadows seem to lift from him. Once more he found himself in all-out political combat, and his life force returned.

In the first months of the new administration, Shriver had tried to encourage his brother-in-law to respond affirmatively to Johnson's initiatives, when they were in line with what John Kennedy had stood for, and to give the new President a fair chance. But Shriver found he was "walking into a buzz saw." At John Kennedy's funeral, the family had entrusted Shriver with a central role in making the arrangements, but his enthusiastic collaboration with Johnson now caused family friction. It was in sharp contrast to the "government-in-exile" spirit setting in among many in Robert Kennedy's inner circle.

The Attorney General was probably irritated when Shriver was appointed to direct a program that he saw as his special province. During the presidential campaign, especially in West Virginia, John Kennedy had called for "an economic drive on poverty." But in office it was Robert Kennedy who started doing something about it.

A few days after the 1960 election, Robert enlisted his schoolmate and good friend David Hackett (said to be the model for Phineas in John Knowles's A *Separate Peace*) to organize the new administration's efforts against juvenile delinquency. In May 1961, at the urging of the Attorney General, the President formed a Committee on Juvenile Delinquency and Youth Crime, with Robert Kennedy as chairman and Hackett as executive director. With $10 million a year, the committee sought to promote comprehensive community action to remove the causes of juvenile delinquency and crime. It emphasized the participation of the poor themselves in the planning and administration of programs to change the structure of institutions affecting youth. The largest and most controversial project it supported, Mobilization for Youth and Harlem Youth Opportunities Unlimited, operating in New York, initiated various efforts at preschool education, job training, neighborhood work, legal services, and day care for the poor.

Then in 1963, at the behest of Eunice Shriver, Robert Kennedy had taken up the idea of a domestic Peace Corps. In 1948 Eunice had herself worked in the Department of Justice as executive secretary of the National Conference on Juvenile Delinquency and later in Chicago had continued her involvement with juvenile delinquents. Concerned about the rise in youth unemployment and crime and impressed with the success of the Peace Corps overseas, she tried to get her husband to organize a national service corps. He told her to go and convince Jack. The President said it sounded good—"Why don't you call Bobby? See if Bobby could get it going." Bobby did.

With the help of Richard Boone (a friend of David Hackett's who was then with the Ford Foundation), a feasibility study was made, and after meetings with interested members of the Cabinet, a voluntary National Service Corps was proposed by President Kennedy. Robert Kennedy was its chief proponent and primary witness when it went to Congress.

Just as Peace Corps Volunteers served in Asia, Africa, and Latin America, so, the Attorney General said, "we are convinced that Americans are equally willing to take on the toughest jobs in this country, whether in a city slum, an Indian reservation or a mining town." The Service Corps would call on people "to invest a year of their lives, at no salary and under Spartan conditions, to help millions of their fellow citizens who, through no fault of their own, are denied the essentials of a decent life." The bill passed the Senate but not the House.

Robert and John Kennedy intended to renew the proposal for a National Service Corps and initiate other anti-poverty action in 1964. At a Cabinet meeting on October 29, 1963, the President had written, encircled, and underlined the word "poverty" on a yellow pad a number of times. In November, according to Schlesinger, the President had said to him, "The time has come to organize a national assault on the causes of poverty, a comprehensive program, across the board," and had suggested it would be "the centerpiece in his 1964 legislative recommendations."

No one can know how strongly, how successfully, or how soon Kennedy would have pressed for an anti-poverty campaign, or on what scale. In telling Heller to proceed with the planning of such a program, the President said (just before leaving for Dallas), "First, we'll have your tax cut; then we'll have my expenditures program." Whatever may have been the President's intentions, Schlesinger is probably accurate in reporting Robert Kennedy's view: "His brother's last wish had been a war against poverty."

When Johnson seized on the idea for the centerpiece of *his* administration, and escalated the poverty war into something bigger than John Kennedy had ever indicated, the Attorney General must have had mixed feelings. Sorensen, who had continued as the new President's Special Counsel but was close to Robert Kennedy, gave the impression, in December, that the Attorney General might seriously consider heading the poverty program. Whether or not Robert Kennedy would have agreed to any new Washington post (other than the vice-presidency), he must have been miffed when he was not asked, and bypassed in favor of his brother-in-law.

These were relatively minor matters, however, compared to the question of the vice-presidency, which was Robert Kennedy's recurring preoccupation during the first seven months of 1964. When Johnson deliberately began to float the idea that Shriver would be a good vice-presidential running mate, Robert Kennedy and some of his closest aides were said to be furious. They saw it as a ploy by the President to outflank the Attorney General and try to tap the well of Kennedy appeal through an in-law instead of the bloodline. Their anger increased when Shriver did nothing to stop the speculation.

Though immersed in launching the anti-poverty campaign, Shriver was naturally intrigued with the vice-presidential prospect. In the spring, at my initiative and the urging of the publisher Harper & Row, he agreed to let us put together and hurry into print a book of his speeches and papers. Organizing and editing the material took many nights and weekends of extracurricular time in my first weeks back from Ethiopia. By the summer of 1964, *Point of the Lance* was off the press. It included not only Shriver's main addresses and articles on the Peace Corps and plans for the War on Poverty, but statements on civil rights, education, health, world affairs, and "the soul of our nation." It was a good book of its kind, similar to John Kennedy's *The Strategy of Peace*. It was also rather obviously the book of a candidate or prospective candidate.

How long or how seriously Johnson entertained the notion of Shriver for Vice-President no one can be sure. When Moyers wrote a memorandum making the case for Shriver, Johnson said it made sense and directed that the idea be leaked to key journalists. The President himself began to build up Shriver, singing his praises and sending him on a special mission to see the Pope and visit the leaders of Israel and the Arab world. Then one day Moyers came on the intercom in the Oval Office while Kenneth O'Donnell was in the room with Johnson. Moyers reported that Shriver would be willing to run on the ticket and that Bob would not complain. O'Donnell interjected, "The hell he wouldn't!" Earlier, Schlesinger had warned Robert Kennedy that "LBJ might well prefer Shriver on the ground that Shriver would bring along Bobby's friends without bringing along his enemies." O'Donnell, who had stayed over in the White House at Johnson's request, was one of Bobby's most devoted followers and friends, and Johnson could foresee the storm from Bobby's camp if he were passed over and Shriver picked. Another spokesman for the Kennedys sent word to Johnson that Shriver's selection would tear the family apart; if a Kennedy were to be chosen, it had to be the elder brother. Whatever other appeal Shriver had, he was clearly no solution to what Johnson viewed as "the Bobby problem."

War against Bobby was not something Johnson would admit, perhaps even to himself in the beginning. Poverty was Public Enemy Number One. "This administration today, here and now, declares unconditional war on poverty in America," the President told Congress on January 8, 1964.

Johnson had personally chosen the term "war on poverty." He had considered "Point One" as a title, patterned after Harry Truman's Point Four program, but decided that didn't convey "the sense of drama and importance required."

For Shriver this was much more than a metaphor. If war is the extension of politics by other means, the crucial problems of peace, Shriver thought, required the application of some military means to political ends. "The problems are too large and too important to be left to normal political methods," he wrote:

> To eliminate poverty at home, and to achieve peace in the world, we need the total commitment, the large-scale mobilization, the institutional invention, the unprecedented release of human energy, and the focusing of intellect which have happened in our society only in war. We need what William James called "the moral equivalent of war."

Given that approach, Shriver could not accept the initial plans presented by Heller and Gordon, even though they had already been incorporated in the President's budget message. Searching for the "original inspiring ideas" that the President had demanded, they had turned to the work of the Attorney General's Committee on Juvenile Delinquency. There, in the program of community action advocated by Robert Kennedy's men David Hackett and Richard Boone, they thought they had found the answer. They adopted the concept of comprehensive planning by a novel combination of public and private forces within a community and the subsequent focusing of federal, state, and local resources and services as the central, if not the single, thrust of the proposed anti-poverty war.

"It will never fly," Shriver concluded after being briefed on the plan. He agreed with Secretary of Labor Wirtz (who was appalled by the omission of any job-creation program) that community action alone was not enough. A one-idea, one-title bill would be a letdown after all the expectations raised by the President. A war required an overall strategy and more than one front, and Johnson was right in saying that the initial program would have "to be big and bold and hit the whole nation with real impact."

So Shriver invited all interested government departments and agencies to submit their ideas. In night and day sessions for six weeks, he consulted more than a hundred mayors, governors, businessmen, labor leaders, community organizers, economists, foundation executives, and professionals in fields related to poverty, social services, and unemployed youth. And he read a mountain of books, articles, and memorandums, calling in the authors to help. Michael Harrington, whose 1962 book, *The Other America*, had helped awaken John Kennedy's concern for the poor, joined the planning group. So did Daniel Patrick Moynihan, Assistant Secretary of Labor, who argued for massive vocational training and remedial education for millions of demoralized young people born into the culture of poverty.

Out of this immersion in the problem, Shriver developed the six-title Economic Opportunity Act of 1964. It provided for the Neighborhood

Youth Corps that Wirtz had been urging, to fund local service jobs for young people, especially during the "long hot summers." It authorized a work-study program of assistance to young people working their way through school, a plan recommended by the U.S. Office of Education. It proposed a Job Corps, one stream of which would be conservation camps such as Senator Humphrey had imagined for the Youth Conservation Corps (which had passed the Senate but failed in the House). However (to Humphrey's displeasure), the larger part of the Job Corps would be centers for urban job training and remedial education. It offered special new assistance to small family farms and to small businesses in slums, to be administered by the Agriculture and Commerce departments. And the act included the two programs advocated by Robert Kennedy: Community Action and a National Service Corps (renamed Volunteers in Service to America: VISTA).

VISTA was almost taken out of the act when Robert Kennedy objected that a National Service Corps was his idea and it was already before Congress. Shriver agreed to drop it if the idea would fare better in Congress on its own. In fact, despite the Attorney General's strong testimony for it, Congress had passed a rider forbidding the expenditure of any funds to continue preparations for a National Service Corps. After checking with Larry O'Brien, Kennedy conceded that its best chance was as a part of the new anti-poverty package.

Advocates of Community Action, on the other hand, feared for a while that, in his enthusiasm for the Job Corps, Shriver would himself omit the other program the Kennedy group and early planners had proposed as the central strategy. According to one of them, the only reason Community Action survived was the Attorney General's direct intercession with Shriver. Shriver and his chief deputy on the planning task force, Adam Yarmolinsky (on loan from the Defense Department), deny that. They had sharply questioned the concept, as they had other proposals, and had concentrated on adding new elements, but Community Action had been an integral part of the Shriver bill from the first draft.

In that first draft was also the provision which was to cause so much controversy, the requirement of "maximum feasible participation" of the poor. That was a direct contribution from the Kennedy group. Out of his experience with pilot community action programs supported by the Attorney General's Juvenile Delinquency Committee and the Ford Foundation, Dick Boone kept pressing the point that the poor themselves must be involved in the planning, so that programs were not imposed on them by existing organizations, city hall, or the federal government. In the first brainstorming session on February 4, Yarmolinsky complained to Boone that he had used the phrase "maximum feasible participation" four or five times. "Yes, I know," Boone replied. "How many more times do I have to use it before it becomes part of the program?" The response was: "Oh, a couple of more times." Yarmolinsky says Boone did, and it did.

Also becoming parts of the program were projects Head Start (for preschool education and medical attention) and Upward Bound (to help teen-agers qualify for college). They fit what soon became the major theme for the whole campaign: special education and training to enable young people to get out of poverty by their own earning power.

To the extent he had to choose between preparing people for jobs or preparing jobs for people—or providing better social services for people unable to get or hold jobs—Shriver gave priority to preparing people for jobs. The President agreed. Drawing on his experience as Texas director of Roosevelt's National Youth Administration, Johnson said he "wanted to place heavy emphasis on efforts to help children and youth. They offered the best hope of breaking the poverty cycle."

Shriver put much of his hope in the plan for a Job Corps. "It will penetrate to the streets of every slum in the nation," he said. To the young men and women caught in the hard core of poverty—dropouts from school who were about to become dropouts from society—it would offer up to two years of hard work and good education "in an entirely new environment, where for the first time they will be given a full opportunity to develop as productive citizens." The Job Corps residential centers were to be "different from anything that has existed in American education before." They would be "communities of work and study" with the most effective modern teaching techniques, most appropriate curriculum, best possible teachers and counselors. The cost would be high, but Shriver believed the poor more than the rich needed such "public boarding schools—where special education will be offered those most in need of it."

In a showdown Cabinet meeting before the President sent his new program to Congress, Shriver's original plan for the Job Corps was curtailed. Working closely with Secretary of Defense McNamara, he had intended to locate most Job Corps centers in abandoned army camps, with the military establishment managing the housing, feeding, clothing, and medical care. The special education and job training would be run by universities or business corporations. The idea of contracting with profit-making enterprises had come under fire in the early planning, but Shriver had insisted that, as in war, business leadership was essential. The combination of military logistics and the business-academic training, he thought, would enable the Corps to begin on the largest practical scale in the speediest and most economical way, and in an environment that encouraged discipline. But in the Cabinet there was such vehement opposition to the military connection, from members who invoked horror stories about army basic training, that Johnson told Shriver to reduce the military flavor. This resulted in the loss of McNamara's direct involvement, which Shriver had counted upon, and of the military's large potential resources. It probably meant a smaller and less effective Job Corps.

Other parts of the proposed anti-poverty bill came under attack at the Cabinet meeting. Shriver had included a major public-employment program, strongly advocated by the Department of Labor, to be financed by an additional five-cent cigarette tax. But the President concluded that this would be inconsistent with the pending proposal for a tax cut, which itself was designed to generate jobs for the unemployed. Having lost that battle, Secretary of Labor Wirtz insisted that the Labor Department, not any new agency under Shriver, run the Neighborhood Youth Corps, the only remaining jobs program. The President agreed.

The most serious attack on the plan came from the Secretaries of Labor and HEW, who opposed creation of an independent new Office of Economic Opportunity to run the Community Action Program, Head Start, the Job Corps, and VISTA. They thought the major appropriate departments (such as HEW and Labor) would provide greater resources, experience, and assurance of continuity. Then Shriver would have time to coordinate all the programs and guide overall strategy. For the same reasons that Johnson had prevailed upon John Kennedy to create an independent Peace Corps, he decided that there should be an independent operational anti-poverty agency, headed by Shriver, who would report directly to the President. "The best way to kill a new idea is to put it in an old-line agency," he said. Moreover, he did "not intend that the war against poverty become a series of uncoordinated and unrelated efforts— that it perish for lack of leadership and direction."

One Republican opponent of the anti-poverty bill complained that doubters of the War on Poverty were "under the suspicion of being in favor of poverty." Many congressmen and their constituents were doubters, and a Gallup poll reported that 83 percent of the American people did not believe that a war against poverty could be won. In an audience with Pope Paul, Shriver said that people were quoting the Bible, saying, "The poor always ye have with you." Paul replied, "Tell them that they are also commanded by the Bible to feed the hungry and clothe the naked."

The Pope did not command many battalions among the conservative Southern Democratic–Republican coalition that opposed the program. The act would make Shriver a "poverty czar," congressmen protested. Shriver said that, knowing what happened to the czars, he had no such ambition; he would be a sergeant, serving the President and Congress. A more substantial criticism rose out of a different concern: despite the President's rhetoric, wasn't the program "a series of uncoordinated and unrelated efforts"? Instead of one "original inspiring idea," wasn't it a pasting together of a lot of approaches, which Johnson had said he didn't want?

Using a wartime analogy, Shriver said that since no one knew a single sure road to victory over poverty, several different but complementary ways had to be tried. The problem was like the one America faced in World War II when its survival depended upon splitting the atom before Hitler did. "Einstein knew more than anyone else, yet even Einstein could only say that it could be done," said Shriver. "So the Manhattan Project tried something new in our public life. With no time to waste, it experimented with several approaches simultaneously. It took two main routes, one the plutonium route, one the route of uranium, U-235, and it tried variations on each." In the War on Poverty there was no time to waste either, and thus he was proposing three main routes, with variations of each: education (Head Start, Upward Bound, Work-Study, the Job Corps), volunteer service (beginning with VISTA but going on to Foster Grandparents and other part-time and full-time volunteer programs), and community action. In community action, the same diversity of approach would take place at the local level, by trial and error.

The new anti-poverty efforts were part of a larger picture of existing or already proposed policies for economic growth and welfare: the tax cut, Social Security, housing programs, health care, minimum wages, unemployment compensation, area redevelopment, manpower training. But the Economic Opportunity Act would "provide a new focus on the hard-core poverty that these programs have not reached," and thus "give the whole national effort a new thrust." The new approaches, he said, "will not solve the problem, any more than the Peace Corps could alone accomplish America's overseas aims. They are just the first steps. But like the Peace Corps, they should set a new pace and a new pattern, and serve as a catalyst for the national commitment and the further federal, state, and local action that will be necessary."

Congress did not agree to try everything Shriver proposed. It struck from the bill grants and loans to marginal family farmers, tenants, and sharecroppers. A Mississippi congressman got through an amendment requiring a non-Communist oath from all members of the Job Corps. (It was the first time many high school dropouts in the Job Corps had ever stopped to think about Communism or what it means to take an oath.)

But after six months of hearings and debate, and never-ending lobbying by Shriver and the President, in September 1964 the bill passed the House by 41 votes, a more comfortable margin than anyone expected, and carried the Senate by nearly two to one.

A price was paid, however, for winning 60 out of 100 Southern Democrats in the House, or at least for eight of them. Larry O'Brien had warned that the bill would not pass unless they pulled "a magnificent rabbit out of a hat." At first the rabbit was Representative Phil Landrum of Georgia, an author of the 1959 Landrum-Griffin labor bill, and a conservative respected by his fellow congressmen. Johnson and Shriver persuaded him to sponsor the Economic Opportunity Act. Initially, George Meany and the top command of the AFL-CIO were incredulous and antagonistic; "Landrum" was a dirty word to them. Johnson said he knew Meany could be "counted on to put the interests of his country first," and got in touch with the AFL-CIO leader himself. "After all, it's the result we're after," the President said, and before the bill had passed Landrum and Meany were meeting together for friendly talks.

No compromise of principle was involved in enlisting Landrum, but the sacrifice of Adam Yarmolinsky, as the price for the support of eight Carolina congressmen, was a different matter. Just before the crucial vote in August, they gave Shriver an ultimatum: they would vote against the bill the next day unless they were guaranteed that Yarmolinsky would be excluded from any post in the Office of Economic Opportunity. Shriver had already asked Yarmolinsky to be his Deputy Director if the bill passed, and McNamara had agreed to the transfer. The conservative congressmen believed a completely inaccurate right-wing charge that Yarmolinsky was a subversive. Having first met Yarmolinsky when he was organizing an anti-Communist caucus in the American Veterans Committee after World War II, I knew how far removed he was from any sympathies for Communism. I presumed that Shriver would stand firm.

Meeting with the Carolina representatives, Shriver tried to delay, saying that only the President could decide who would be Deputy Director. The congressmen insisted on his putting the question to the President. After a call to the White House, an unhappy Shriver reported that the President did not object to his assuring them that Yarmolinsky would not be appointed. Again it was the result they were after. Johnson and Shriver did not know that the eight votes would prove to be unnecessary.

Yarmolinsky returned to the Defense Department (where he resumed dealing with the nation's top secrets), and remained a close colleague of Shriver's and an anti-poverty adviser, though he had no formal connection thereafter to the program he had helped design. What made the incident worse was the President's response at his next press conference to a question about why Yarmolinsky was leaving the poverty program. "No, your thoughts are wrong," Johnson said to the correspondent asking the question. "He is still with the Department of Defense." When pressed about Yarmolinsky having previously left the Defense Department to join Shriver, the President insisted, "He never left." So much for seven months of Yarmolinsky's life. The loss to the poverty program was greater than either Johnson or Shriver expected. It was a long time, if ever, before the right deputy was found, during a period when an effective second-in-command was urgently needed.

Cabinet critics were right in contending that Shriver would have little time to coordinate overall anti-poverty strategy while he was organizing three complex and demanding new programs: Community Action, VISTA, and the Job Corps. On the other hand, those institutional inventions—and others soon under way such as Head Start and Community Legal Services—were not likely to have been as innovative or to have had the initial appeal and thrust if they had been left to any of the slower-moving, established departments. It was a no-win situation, for without operating programs having budgets and growing constituencies of their own, Shriver would have lacked direct leverage and probably suffered the impotence of most "coordinators" imposed upon existing bureaucracies. Not having Yarmolinsky made it all the more difficult.

The President's duplicity and the surrender to the eight congressmen were a cloud no bigger than a man's hand, but Lyndon Johnson's hand was large and his reach long. The effects of his intervention were felt, for better and for worse, at the Peace Corps as it entered its third stage. After its initial planning and launching, and then the overseas experience, its next test was the homecoming of thousands of Volunteers.

During 1964 and most of 1965 the Peace Corps' deputy directorship was unfilled, too, because in his first moments as President, Johnson had swooped Bill Moyers into the White House, and it was not certain that he would not come back (perhaps as Director). Then the President appointed the chief of the Peace Corps' African division, Franklin Williams, as the American Ambassador to Ghana, and the Latin American chief, Jack Vaughn, as Ambassador to Panama (and before long the Assistant Secretary of State for Inter-American Affairs). One winter day, Richard Goodwin accompanied Shriver to the White House and met Johnson unexpectedly in the corridor. After an ill-starred two years in the State Department, Goodwin had gone to the Peace Corps and was beginning to play a key role there. Johnson quickly drafted him to write speeches, at first on a *sub rosa* basis because the former Kennedy speechwriter was so controversial (or because Goodwin *was* a former Kennedy speechwriter).

But the chief problem for the Peace Corps was Shriver's consuming new anti-poverty assignment, which should have taken, and almost did take, all his time. Johnson made a mistake in asking anyone to be chief of staff of a war on poverty in its crucial organizing stage and direct the Peace Corps, too. He overestimated even Shriver's executive abilities and energy, stretching him too thin. Shriver tried to make the best of his dual role by emphasizing the possible connections between volunteer service at home and abroad, and calling on Peace Corps veterans to enlist in the anti-poverty war. If Peace Corps Volunteers from the advantaged part of society, who had learned overseas how rich America was, and VISTA Volunteers would unite with the disadvantaged volunteers in the Job Corps, together, he said, they could become "a giant pincers movement converging in the great center which is smug and self-satisfied and complacent."

At the Peace Corps we tried to make the best of Shriver's absence by administering the agency, to the extent possible, by a kind of Quaker consensus among the several associate directors and the general counsel. Frequently we involved a much larger circle of staff colleagues. Needing to come to an agreement in order to act without going to Shriver, we tended toward the lowest—or least controversial—common denominator. Sometimes we achieved the "maximum feasible participation" of the staff, but seldom was it the optimum participation. We measured out our lives in committee meetings.

The experience made me doubt the wisdom of administration through participatory democracy, and appreciate more than ever the role of a chief executive. I realized how much I preferred the strong argument of a Shriver staff meeting, at the end of which everyone expected him— and respected his right as Director—to decide.

In the summer of 1964, when Johnson did not pick Shriver as his vice-presidential candidate, our disappointment at the Peace Corps was mitigated by the choice of Hubert Humphrey. After their sweeping election victory, Johnson asked Humphrey to take his place as chairman of the Peace Corps National Advisory Council.

In a letter to the Vice-President, released January 26, 1965, Johnson gave a new mandate to the Peace Corps. In four years, he said, "the Peace Corps has made history." For the next stage, he called for the doubling of the number of Volunteers, from 10,000 to 20,000, and other steps to "see that it continues to make history." He pointed particularly to the returning Volunteers, whom he called "a major new national resource." Noting that he had already selected people from the Peace Corps "more frequently than from any other government department or agency in order to staff this Administration," the President wanted "to ensure that this nation makes full use of former Volunteers."

There were already some 3,000 Volunteers back home, and tens of thousands were due to return during the rest of the sixties. Johnson looked forward to their further service "in all parts of our public life—in the War on Poverty and in the Foreign Service, in our work to promote human rights at home and in our overseas AID programs, in our school classrooms and in our universities, in our unions and in private enterprise." "For the Great Society," he said, "requires first of all Great Citizens, and the Peace Corps is a world-wide training school for Great Citizens."

Specifically, the President asked Humphrey and the Advisory Council to convene on or about March 1, the organization's fourth anniversary, a Conference of Returned Volunteers "to discuss their role in our national life" and meet with leaders of American education, business, labor, community action, and federal, state, and local government. Although Moyers and I had drafted this presidential letter to Humphrey, it could not go out without official Peace Corps concurrence. In the absence of Shriver and with no deputy director, the top Peace Corps staff had been sharply divided about whether to hold such a conference, and, if so, whether it should be small and controlled, or larger and open-ended.

Convening the Volunteers was another gamble. No group knew the Peace Corps' shortcomings more intimately and could describe them more colorfully. Many had experienced serious frustrations in their work overseas. Most were coming home with more critical perspectives on their own country. Inviting them to Washington to sound off within the hearing of Congress and the national news media was asking for trouble.

Yet they were a return on the investment—the product coming back. In speeches to Volunteers in training I had been saying that there was more light to be gained on the periphery than in the center of world power—not so much from the people of developing nations, who were no wiser than those in Washington, as from the Volunteers' distance and temporary detachment from the blinding dazzle of American life. Withdraw-and-return was the most creative rhythm in history, according to Toynbee. Why not see what, if any, insights the Volunteers had brought back?

Characteristically, when Shriver was called in to resolve the issue he decided to ask the President to send the letter to Humphrey—and to invite to the conference *all* returned Volunteers. Shriver noted that the

Peace Corps had spent time and money flying staff and outside consultants overseas to lead two-day Completion of Service conferences with each group of Volunteers before they returned. The results had been very worthwhile (as I had found leading such sessions in India, Malaysia, and Brazil). He thought there might be even more to learn from the Volunteers' reflections after they had been home for a while.

Working with a committee of fifty former Volunteers from the Washington area, Elizabeth Forsling Harris and I directed the conference planning. Discussion leaders and other special participants from the main sectors of American public life were invited, for twenty-four separate workshops. A detailed questionnaire went to 3,000 returned Volunteers—and an amazing 77 percent replied. Ninety percent of them wanted to attend the conference.

Other answers were also interesting. Eighty-five percent of the 2,300 who replied said they knew what careers they wanted, but half of them had changed their minds during their two years overseas. Many more wanted to enter some kind of international service, or to involve themselves in some form of attack on American social problems, than had planned to do so when they volunteered. About half wanted to be involved in the War on Poverty, and civil rights was a cause most intended to support. To get further training, more than half were back in school, mostly at the graduate level. Forty-one percent had already gone to work—one-third in teaching, one-third in federal, state, and local government, and the rest in business, foundations, the arts, and professions.

Only a handful were unemployed, and finding a job was listed as a problem by just 7 percent. Finding a job with the challenge they had known overseas was a problem for many. "The Peace Corps gives vent to potential," wrote one Volunteer. "Somehow, our society doesn't assign responsibility to potential." "In the United States it is no longer easy to score a 'first,' to do something which has never been done before," wrote an Ethiopian Volunteer. How do we find "a job or a life that comes close to providing the excitement, opportunity for achievement and responsibility that we felt overseas?" asked Philippines Volunteer Edith Barksdale.

With so much Volunteer interest in the conference, we raised funds from private sources to assist with the travel expenses for a cross section of 200. Another 800 came at their own expense—three times as many as we expected. So for three days in early March 1965, some 1,000 Volunteers met with 250 leaders of American society, discussing the potential role of ex-Volunteers in connection with (and their concerns about) local communities, primary and secondary education, colleges and universities, government, business, labor, international service, and foreign students.

The conference was a high-water mark of the Peace Corps, though we did not know then how far the water would later recede. It was the last large occasion that I know about when the spirit of Kennedy's New Frontier seemed alive and strong, despite the assassination. And—with one exception a week later, after the events at Selma—it was the last time the spirit of the Kennedy era would be joined with Johnson's call to a Great Society, a call that still in the spring of 1965 seemed full of promise.

The State Department's Diplomatic Reception Rooms had never seen anything like the opening buffet. Spirited reunions took place, with Volunteers from their respective countries forming circles on the floor, and Cabinet members, leaders of Congress, ambassadors, corporation presidents, labor leaders, and academics on the floor with them. Richard Rovere wrote in *The New Yorker* that the conference was "the most informal as well as the liveliest gathering ever to have taken place in that ungainly pile of concrete in the heart of Foggy Bottom." As opening speeches by Shriver and Humphrey evoked volleys of laughter, one journalist worried about everyone's safety on the ground that the State Department building was engineered to withstand everything but laughter.

Elated by the evening, the Vice-President remarked that Volunteers enjoy "what John Adams once characterized as the 'spirit of public happiness' "—a line for which he was pilloried a few years later. That first session ended in an overflowing State Department auditorium with Harry Belafonte linking arms with Chief Justice Warren, Secretary of State Rusk, Secretary of Defense McNamara, Shriver, and the Vice-President, and leading everyone in singing "We Shall Overcome." (It was the weekend of the first ill-fated march across the Edmund Pettus Bridge in Selma.)

The Volunteers' problems with their press image were not over, however. Contrary to their dominant mood, newspaper accounts portrayed them as a frustrated, discontented, unemployed lot, feeling sorry for themselves and unnerved by zip codes, digit-dialing, pop-top beer cans, and supercilious job interviewers. It was an easy, if inaccurate story, and the press ran with it. Reading such articles, Eric Sevareid wrote a column deriding "the returning Peace Corps boys and girls." He felt sorry instead for young Africans who had found their student years in America "enriching and exciting and returned to their home villages . . . and suffered profound 'cultural shock' as they saw through new eyes the boredom, triviality, prejudice and crushing conformity of tribal life."

In the first planning sessions on the Peace Corps, Shriver had interrupted anyone who called the prospective Volunteers "boys and girls." "They are men and women, or will be, in the Peace Corps," he said. If Sevareid had met the Volunteers, he would not have discovered upset boys and girls but men and women who were resilient, individualistic, cantankerous, and skeptical. After two years' work overseas they had more worldly wisdom than Sevareid suspected or the press conveyed.

"You had more guts than brains in calling this conference," a foundation executive said after an intense workshop on the second day of the sessions. "We're seeing the Volunteers as they really are, not as the romantic unknown quantity they were before." Resisting the "romantic mantle" being draped on the "small modest thing" the Volunteers had done, Harold Isaacs of MIT recalled the refrain from *Call Me Mister*: "You went into the Army a jerk and came out still a jerk."

The jerks among them might still be jerks, but the chief of psychiatry of MIT, Benson Snyder, was struck by what a growing experience the Peace Corps had been, "not in a Boy Scout way, but in a realistic, discouraged way." Richard Rovere found them "sharp, independent, and confident critics of American society" and reported that "most of the observers went away persuaded that the Peace Corps' impact on American life may in time be an immense one."

Since there was no typical Volunteer, it was difficult to predict what that impact would be. The most likely place to expect it was on American foreign policy and public opinion, especially in regard to the nations of Africa, Asia, and Latin America, where they had served. "I know Nigeria better than I know Kansas," said keynote speaker Roger Landrum. "The Volunteers in this room are personally concerned with the vital interests of the people of forty-six nations with which our country has had little contact—except for a few economic interests or where Communism scared us in. We are sons and daughters of America but we are in a sense also sons and daughters of a thousand towns and villages scattered around the world."

The primary experience, said former Volunteer Michael Sellon, was "becoming in mind and even more in spirit, those very people we had come to help . . . we *felt* like Dominicans, and *reacted* like Tanganyikans." The other people, said Anabel Leinback, "became our people." A paper by John Schafer from Ethiopia said Peace Corps Volunteers were spurred on "by a new kind of worldwide patriotism, a patriotism which involves feelings of universal rather than merely national brotherhood." Atomic Energy Commissioner Mary Bunting of Radcliffe summarized her main impression: "You went out ambassadors, and came back world citizens."

If Volunteers saw themselves as lobbyists on behalf of the countries where they had served (and many did), they were not uncritical of their host governments; indeed, in some cases they came back opponents of the regimes in power. Faults in America also loomed large from afar. At the same time many returned with more appreciation of the privilege of being an American. Despite the prospect of de facto segregation in the United States, a black Volunteer said, "After two years in Africa, all I can say is I'm very glad I was sold." Few black Volunteers would say that, but many said that the experience of working and living with white Volunteers, and seeing white and black staff working together, for the first time gave them hope for racial integration.

Political action, however, was a new prospect for most Volunteers. Many confessed that politics had not interested them much before the Peace Corps, but said they were jarred into it overseas. "The local people hold a Peace Corps Volunteer responsible for American affairs," said Landrum in his keynote talk. "That is a powerful teacher. My neighbors were black Africans and I couldn't defend Mississippi to them."

Some of the non-Peace Corps participants goaded the Volunteers to be politically bold. "No establishment ever welcomes the agents of change," said the former legal adviser to the State Department, Abram Chayes. "If you want to live on the commanding heights, you must seize them." Yet only six of the 2,300 Volunteers had indicated on the questionnaire that they wanted to enter politics. Hearing this, Humphrey urged Volunteers not to be Monday-morning quarterbacks. "If you think politics is a little dirty, why don't you get yourself a bar of Ivory Soap and get in and clean it up. . . . You don't really have to save the world, just start saving the home town."

Bill Moyers, representing President Johnson, called on the Volunteers "to pursue the ideals of a Joan of Arc with the political prowess of an Adam Clayton Powell." Ideas are arrows, he said, "but there has to be a bow—and politics is the bow of idealism." In "whatever bureaucracy you enter—determine to be an effective, efficient, courageous politician." A Volunteer, by definition and by experience, "has left the ranks of the bystanders and spectators to become a participant." People who took themselves lightly historically (and often took themselves bloatedly personally) were a major problem for democracy. Moyers warned that unless a person "takes himself seriously historically" he "will simply disappear into the bog of affluent living."

To such pep talk, the Volunteers responded with a modesty that at first surprised and frustrated those who hoped for them to be a great new political force. "The worst thing overseas was the idea we were bringing light to darkness," said one Volunteer. "It would be just as bad if we or anyone else thought we were bringing light to darkness at home." Instead, they first needed to "discover America," because, as another Volunteer remarked, when she left for Nigeria the only thing she knew about her home community was the fire station. Ethiopian Volunteers who were teaching in American schools had discovered that what they had considered Addis Ababa problems were also Chicago or Philadelphia problems.

After prodding Volunteers all day for radical proposals, discussion leader Abram Chayes said he finally decided that they were ahead of him—they were letting his words run off them like water off ducks, sensing that the old ideologies were irrelevant, and wanting to be practical. Adam Yarmolinsky, who led another of the group discussions, wrote Shriver afterward that the less idealized picture of the returned Volunteers —who combined "internal stability with constructive dissatisfaction"— was in fact "more encouraging than the preconceptions."

As "Citizens in a Time of Change" (the conference theme), the Volunteers were not drawn to direct party politics, but said they did want to engage in a simpler, perhaps more profound kind of politics—of work, not words; institution building, not electioneering. They were joining the largest party in the world, of non-party people, but not in apathy or in pursuit of merely personal pleasure. Their strongest spontaneous response was a standing ovation given to Sister Jacqueline Grennan, then president of Webster College, who had led a discussion on higher education. Volunteers should look upon the local communities and institutions they were now entering as their new underdeveloped countries, she advised. They should "case them" and go about understanding them as they had learned to do in their overseas assignments. And then they should learn the tactics of change and try to change them because they love them, since in loving them they must be committed "to be responsibly important" in their evolution.

"Stop focusing on us!" said a number of Volunteers. "Let's not talk about beautiful Peace Corps Volunteers," pleaded Myles Weintraub, an architect back from Tunisia, "but talk about beautiful societies and how we get there."

The Volunteers did not offer many new ideas about how to get there. They favored a proposal in the wind since the beginning of the Peace Corps—a Reverse Peace Corps to America (which Kwame Nkrumah had first suggested). A Volunteer back from Africa predicted that someday the pride of other nations would reject the Peace Corps unless two-way traffic was developed. In proposing an Exchange Peace Corps, one of the conference workshops pointed to the foreign students already in the United States as an immediate resource. A period of volunteer work in American society could give them the direct experience in another culture that Peace Corps Volunteers have abroad. They could teach Spanish, or the language, culture, and history of their part of the world, in American schools. Or they could work alongside VISTA Volunteers in community action, providing the stimulus of an "outsider." Even without a formal structure, Volunteers were urged to take special interest in (and provide volunteer opportunities for) the 25,000 foreign students from the countries where they had served.

To perpetuate and institutionalize the volunteer spirit, one conference workshop suggested the "tithing of time." Whatever jobs they took, former Volunteers should offer a number of days or evenings each month to voluntary service. To help them apply their energy and skills at home, Volunteers suggested internships for community service. They advocated special projects, such as the one at Cardozo High School in Washington, D.C., where twenty-six former Volunteers were teaching in a black high school, as part of a concerted effort to improve the curriculum. Bennetta Washington, the principal at Cardozo and newly appointed head of the Women's Job Corps, said: "We are searching for great teachers, and we think you are a reservoir of great teachers." If large numbers of Volunteers went into inner-city teaching, Mrs. Washington said, "we would not have so many bitter children in our country."

One of the outside participants smelled nostalgia in the air, and warned against fostering a "permanently adolescent Peter Pan in an ever-ever land of volunteerism." The Peace Corps was "professionalizing and legitimizing amateurism," he charged. To which another conferee replied, "Amateurism is the genius of America and God-given if we know what to do with it."

Like other participants, the Volunteers were of two minds about creating special new institutions for volunteering in America. Within the Peace Corps they had generally maintained an anti-bureaucratic, anti-staff attitude, and they still professed a pure individualism. They disliked the idea of "systems" they had to enter, and saw themselves as antibodies to the Organization Man. But they granted that it had taken a "Corps" to make possible their individual experiences and the freedom they had known overseas. Many of them agreed with one Volunteer that the Peace Corps was "prophetic of institutions and interactions to come." Their paradoxes were showing.

What the Volunteers seemed to be saying, according to scientist John Calhoun, was that the antidote to the Technological Society would be "something on the order of a universal Peace Corps." This was what Calhoun himself prescribed. Along with the "standardization, order, predictability, hierarchy, and minimum channels of communication" that go with technology, he said, we need a counteracting "process of programmed diversity, programmed uncertainty, sufficient unpredictability—just going to the threshold of chaos but not quite reaching it." From what he had seen at the conference he thought that was a good description of the Peace Corps.

In at least two ways uncertainty hung over the conference (or at least over the conference organizers). One was the President's unpredictability: first, he was coming to welcome the Volunteers—then he wasn't—then Secret Service men appeared in the auditorium, and we thought he was coming to close the conference. Though he had called it, and this was an audience of young people likely to be especially friendly, he could not bring himself to face them.

On the opening day, he had a good excuse; he spent more than two hours with Martin Luther King on the growing civil rights crisis in Alabama. But the rest of the weekend he was in the White House, off and on fretting over whether or not to greet the Volunteers. He was held back by the thought that these were "children of Kennedy," and might not like him, and by the fear that they might embarrass him with a protest about the mounting war in Vietnam.

His fears about an organized Vietnam protest were not unfounded. A few Volunteers had threatened to picket the White House. Until State Department guards tried to prevent them from circulating an anti-war petition in the building, they had not stirred much interest among other Volunteers. When that denial of the right to petition occurred, those of us in charge warned the State Department officers that we would move the meeting to another place if we could not get the ban lifted.

Finally we reached the Secretary of State's deputy, who immediately relaxed the ban, but by then the issue was whether the group of protesting Volunteers should use the Peace Corps name on their signs at the White House. Shriver made one point to them: Most of the Volunteers at the conference had opposed any organization of ex-Volunteers speaking in their name. Did they feel they had a right to use a name earned by such a large group with so many different views?

We did not know what they would do, but later the organizer of the dozen pickets who went to the White House said they had been persuaded. "We took all reference to the Peace Corps out of our signs," George Johnson told me. "We will send the petition from Yale Law School next week so nobody will know it came out of the conference."

This was the last time in the sixties, in my experience, when young people would show that spirit of compromise. Even then, if I had been in their shoes, I might not have forgone my Volunteer status in making such a protest. But it was only the first month of the bombing of North

Vietnam. Some of us who strongly opposed the escalation of the war (or any military involvement) hoped that reasoning and the logic of events would lead the President back from that course. Shriver and others of us with ties to the White House knew what fury would descend on the Peace Corps if the President were confronted by ex-Volunteer pickets.

George Johnson himself was more prophetic than any of us realized. In 1961, he had been chosen by his fellow Volunteers training for Tanganyika to speak for them at a ceremony on the White House lawn. Proud of a new full beard but anxious to represent the Peace Corps' first Volunteers well, he asked Shriver if he should shave it off for Kennedy. Knowing that Shriver did not want the first Volunteer seen on national television to be bearded, I listened carefully to the reply. "It's your beard, George," he said. When Johnson arrived in Washington from El Paso, he was clean-shaven—and made a strong and favorable impression on the President and the assembled press.

Four years later, George Johnson was still impressive, and was tentatively invited to give one of the Volunteer keynote addresses. When he made it clear that he would use the occasion to attack the war in Vietnam, the conference committee, after much dispute, disinvited him as a keynoter but agreed that he would be recognized from the floor and given time for his remarks. Shriver invited him to the podium, and the assembly, including many of the leaders of government, listened attentively.

"We joined the Peace Corps because it represented a new form of action," he said, and "was a personal affirmation of faith in the democratic ideal." What Volunteers did above all overseas, in all their various assignments, was to promote the process of self-government in other countries. Now, he contended, "we who sought to infuse others with the democratic ideal have an obligation. We must measure and challenge our own society." His challenge was threefold: full civil rights for black Americans; an end to poverty without a new form of "welfare colonialism"; and peace in Vietnam. To translate action abroad to action at home required "new forms of political action" which "the pressures of the sixties" were creating. He saw "techniques of direct action, of creative nonviolence, of mass organization" as "the beginnings of a new politics. They are stirrings of life in America. They are portents of change."

The thousand Volunteers were very quiet while Johnson spoke. To many of them, the tall young Yale law student sounded very radical. After the rest of the sixties and seventies, few would think so. But in March 1965 university teach-ins were just beginning and the waves of the Berkeley revolt had not really reached Washington. Even so, Johnson's remarks on Vietnam should not have shocked anyone. In retrospect, it is disturbing that so few public figures were then saying what he said.

"Not all the obstacles to a peaceful world lie in the Communist bloc," Johnson said. "Some of those obstacles are ideas and attitudes that are held by Americans. . . . There are, we are told, no simple answers, but the official cry for more bombs is not more complex than the call for withdrawal. Neither states our proper goal." Instead, he urged efforts to get a political settlement in which we could "rightly resist totalitarianism—but do it with methods that build, rather than destroy, the values that we seek to defend."

A few days later, Shriver received a letter from former Volunteer Al Ulmer. The day after the conference, Ulmer had driven Reverend James Reeb from the Montgomery airport to Selma. "You and many others at the conference mentioned the necessity of our working within the establishment," Ulmer wrote. "I am not sure I want to or even if I could if I wanted to, for the establishment here in the South is what we are fighting, not joining. . . . You asked at the conference what we were doing now that we were home. Well, last Monday night I took Reverend Reeb to Selma so that he could march in protest to voting discrimination and repeated police brutality. They say he is going to die tonight. . . ." Ulmer's letter ended: "We're outnumbered here and we need your help."

By the time Shriver read this, Reeb was dead. About that time I telephoned Shriver from Selma to explain why I had gone to join the march. He said he wished he were there, too. Instead, while King was in Selma conducting a memorial service for Reeb, on March 15 Shriver watched Lyndon Johnson go before a joint session of Congress to call for the Voting Rights Act of 1965 and to vow, "We shall overcome."

Whatever their impact on American society, returning Volunteers by 1965 were having a pervasive effect on the agency itself, where they were joining the staff in increasing numbers. Fresh from the front lines, they joined the chorus of evaluators who had been criticizing the lack of well-prepared assignments, especially in the more unstructured community development projects in Latin America. Like the hard-nosed journalists hired by Director of Evaluation Charlie Peters, most of the ex-Volunteers suspected and opposed a "numbers game." Instead of pressing for ever-greater numbers in a country, the former Volunteers wanted more careful advance field work so that specific jobs awaited each Volunteer. And they called for more realistic and effective training.

Shriver resisted advice to slow down, saying that the Peace Corps' numbers were "minuscule" compared to the needs abroad and to the potential pool of Volunteers. To correct shortcomings, he looked particu-

larly to the ex-Volunteers on the staff. He counted upon the veterans of
overseas service to shape better training programs and to work with host
country institutions in assuring worthwhile jobs for new Volunteers.

Like all members of the staff, former Volunteers would be limited to a
maximum employment of five years so that new Volunteers from the field
could take their places. By such turnover, Shriver hoped, the Peace Corps
would keep learning from experience while preserving its flexibility and
amateur spirit. At his insistence, this rule of in-up-and-out in five years,
known as the "five-year flush," was actually approved by Congress and
made a part of the Peace Corps Act.

Determined to prevent the burgeoning of a permanent, professional
bureaucracy, Shriver rejected repeated proposals for the appointment of
professional "programmers." Reading one such suggestion by an evalua-
tor of a purportedly unsuccessful project in Brazil, Shriver scrawled his
response to the notion of "programmers":

> They will be "experts." They will issue forth from a program "office."
> They will zoom around telling the overseas staff what is permissible—
> huge "program documents" will be prepared in the field at huge expense
> in time and money. Secretaries will type them with copies for five dif-
> ferent Washington offices, all of whom will have to "sign off." Reps
> will begin to display their program "submissions" to visitors instead of
> the PCVs. It will all be done to raise quality, maximize Vols' time and
> talent and save money. The Peace Corps will receive an award for clean-
> cut, hard administrative efficiency from Forbes Magazine and the direc-
> tor of the Peace Corps will move from his post to an exec V-P post in a
> large industrial concern in Dayton.

By the mid-sixties, the stream of volunteer service, in which the
Peace Corps had started, was becoming a river of broad dimensions. The
Peace Corps was the lead raft, but many other countries had formed,
or were forming, their own full-time volunteer programs. European and
Commonwealth countries were sending volunteers to the developing nations, while those nations were themselves organizing various forms of
domestic youth service.

Beyond being an example, the Peace Corps had actively sought to
spur this wider movement. In October 1962 it organized an International
Conference on Human Skills to assess the role of volunteer service in
nation-building. Under the chairmanship of Vice-President Johnson, high-
level representatives of forty-three nations assembled in Puerto Rico. In
inviting countries to the conference, President Kennedy had asked, "Is it
true, as we are beginning to suspect, that our joint economic development
efforts have been concentrated too heavily in the wrong place—that we

have been placing too much reliance on investment in things when perhaps we should be investing more in people?"

The delegates' answer was that volunteer service was not just a nice experiment in international brotherhood but was a dramatic world movement to disgorge and utilize the earth's richest resource—its people. The economists, development specialists, and other representatives found: "In the most practical sense, it can be demonstrated that investment in education and training yield at least as high a rate of return as direct investment in industry or agriculture, quite aside from its indirect benefits to the society and enriching value to the individual; and we are learning that virtually anyone can be trained and can benefit himself and society from that training."

Forty-one of the forty-three countries at the conference formed an International Peace Corps Secretariat (later renamed the International Secretariat for Volunteer Service), initially headed by Richard Goodwin. Before long, volunteers were serving abroad from eighteen developed countries, and the mobilization of youth in some form of service was on the agenda of almost every country where overseas volunteers were working.

"This is new and it is also very old," said Pablo Casals at the Puerto Rico conference. "We have, in a sense, come full circle. We have come from the tyranny of the enormous, awesome discordant machines back to a realization that the beginning and the end are man, that it is man who is important, not the machines; that it is man who accounts for growth, not just dollars or factories; and above all, that it is man who is the object of all our efforts."

As volunteer service spread, the United Nations gave official sanction to it, inviting Peace Corps and other nations' volunteers to work under the sponsorship of UN technical assistance projects. In 1965, the United Nations Secretary-General, U Thant, declared to the Social and Economic Council that he was "looking forward to the time when the average youngster—and parent or employer—will consider one or two years of work for the cause of development, either in a faraway country or in a depressed area of his own community, as a normal part of one's education."

Also in 1965, at the University of Kentucky, on George Washington's birthday, President Johnson urged the United States to apply the principle of the Peace Corps on a large scale inside America. He proposed that the nation "search for new ways" through which "every young American will have the opportunity—and feel the obligation—to give at least a few years of his or her life to the service of others in the nation and in the world."

At Bill Moyers' prompting, a number of us at the Peace Corps were working with key colleagues of Shriver in the Office of Economic Opportunity to propose steps that would lead toward such universal voluntary service by young Americans. "Universal" and "voluntary" seemed like a contradiction in terms, but Father Hesburgh pointed out that universal completion of secondary school was a national goal although school attendance after age sixteen was voluntary. Even the compulsory school attendance laws were enacted after the idea of everyone going to school had become overwhelmingly accepted and voluntarily acted upon. The goal of universal secondary education was adopted because people came to see its value. With growing national and international recognition of the value of voluntary service, and with the strong support of the President, we thought the time was fast coming when the case for a period of voluntary national service (sometime after high school) could be made successfully to millions of young people and their parents.

In the War on Poverty, despite Shriver's promise of a pincers movement by Peace Corps and VISTA Volunteers (most of them well-off and white) and Job Corps trainees (most of them poor and black), there was nothing bringing them together. The Job Corps experience, for all its valuable skill training and remedial education, was largely a segregated one, and not just because of the large concentration of blacks and Hispanic Americans. By the statutory definition of those to be helped, the Job Corps, like many anti-poverty programs, primarily involved the young who were least educated and most demoralized. For Job Corps trainees, the location of the residential centers was new, but most of the youth they found there were not unlike those they knew on their neighborhood streets. Thus the Job Corps was not the "entirely new environment" that Shriver had thought necessary to break the cycle of discrimination and poverty.

A large-scale national service program would be designed to enlist a cross section of young people, from city, suburb, small town, and farm, college-bound and those stopping with high school, rich and poor, black and white. The experience of such diverse young people living and working together would be different from anything most of them would have ever known. For the rich, it should enrich their lives, in ways Peace Corps service had done for most Volunteers. For some of the poorest youth, participation in national service could save lives. It would keep them from sinking into the ranks of the unemployed right away after leaving school. After a year or two of challenging and disciplined service, many of them should emerge with the hope, ambition, and sense of confidence necessary to cope in a difficult and demanding society.

The difference in psychological impact between participation in national service and being assisted by programs designed to help the poor would also be great. Having someone care about you is important and assistance is sometimes necessary, but having aid given you—being the object of charity—is not the best way to become self-reliant. Inevitably there is some wound to the pride in receiving aid, and such artful terms as "disadvantaged" do not remove the self-doubts about one's capabilities. Whatever the rhetoric about the Job Corps, the reality was that those who entered it were stamped in the public mind and in their own minds as being near the bottom of America's pool of talent.

The message of national service would be the opposite. "We need you, we need your service, we call on you to volunteer to help your fellow citizens and work on some of our country's problems," would be the primary appeal. That such work could also be designed as apprenticeship for later jobs, that the service should instill habits of responsibility—such as getting to work on time—which would be useful for the rest of one's life, would be beneficial by-products.

Those were some of the points our planning group on national service made to Shriver, Vice-President Humphrey, and the White House. A voluntary national service system that would grow in stages, from tens of thousands of volunteers to hundreds of thousands or more, seemed to us a major missing ingredient in the War on Poverty. Such a mobilization of youth, for one or two years' work in urban slums, poor rural areas, and national parks, in Head Start, housing rehabilitation, the delivery of health services, the care of the elderly, and various programs of community action, would give new momentum to the anti-poverty effort. One million National Service Volunteers, the number that might be expected to enlist each year once the program had proved itself, could provide the troops a War on Poverty required.

The idea, of course, was as old as William James, whose 1910 essay, "The Moral Equivalent of War," had proposed universal civilian service (at least for men). "The war against war is going to be no holiday excursion or camping party," James wrote. For the "war party" was right in believing that "a permanently successful peace-economy cannot be a simple pleasure-economy." "So far," the philosopher said, "war has been the only force that can discipline a whole community." But he believed that "strenuous honor and disinterestedness" (to which "priests and medical men are in a fashion educated") could be instilled, without war, if the way were found "to inflame the civic temper as past history has inflamed the military temper."

James proposed an "army enlisted against Nature," in which "our gilded youths" would "get the childishness knocked out of them" and "come back into society with healthier sympathies and soberer ideas." Then "no one would remain blind, as the luxurious classes now are blind, to man's relations to the globe he lives on, and to the permanently sour and hard foundations of his higher life"; ". . . injustice would tend to be evened out, and numerous other goods to the commonwealth would follow." The military passion was strong, he concluded:

> But who can be sure that other aspects of one's country may not, with time and education and suggestion enough, come to be regarded with similarly effective feelings of pride and shame? . . . Individuals, daily more numerous, now feel this civic passion. It is only a question of blowing on the spark till the whole population gets incandescent, and on the ruins of the old morals of military honor, a stable system of morals of civic honor builds itself up.

For those of us "blowing on the spark" there was a special pleasure, and irony, in learning of one inroad in what James would have considered the "war party." The Secretary of Defense was taking up the idea. Through Adam Yarmolinsky, we passed on to McNamara all our working papers. In a major address to the American Society of Newspaper Editors on May 18, 1966, the Defense chief proposed that we move toward universal national service "by asking every young person in the United States to give one or two years of service to his country—whether in one of the military services, in the Peace Corps, or in some other volunteer developmental work at home or abroad."

McNamara gave two reasons for such a move. First, "our security is related directly to the security of the newly developing world," and for the people of that world "security is development." Volunteer service overseas could speed up the necessary social and economic development of that critical Third World. Second, the growing inequity of the military draft was unacceptable. In deferring those in higher education, draft boards (with only 1 percent of their membership black) were conscripting a disproportionate number of the poor, including blacks. Just how to choose fairly those required to serve in the military when not all have to, McNamara left to a new Commission on Selective Service that the President was about to appoint. He also left open the question of whether "asking" all those not required for military service to serve in nonmilitary programs just meant a strong call to voluntary service or meant conscription of everyone.

Not knowing the President's determination never to be upstaged, our informal task force on national service was elated by the McNamara speech and the favorable public attention it got. Then Moyers let us know that it had set back, perhaps permanently, Johnson's plans to go forward with a commission to review the existing military draft and consider the alternative of offering young people options for non-military service. The President canceled his flight to the United Automobile Workers convention in California, where he was scheduled to announce his new approach toward draft equity, and it was not until July 2 that he finally appointed the National Advisory Commission on Selective Service.

Again our hopes were lifted when Burke Marshall was made the commission's chairman, and the President specifically asked the commission to explore the alternative of national service, with military and non-military options. Donald Eberly, the first International Development Placement Association teacher in Africa during the 1950s, Professor Morris Janowitz of the University of Chicago, and I worked closely with the commission in outlining possible structures for national service. The publicly chartered, privately based model of the Red Cross, once considered for the Peace Corps, was suggested, although federal funding seemed necessary. With foundation support, Eberly established a small Secretariat for National Service to stimulate further study and debate, and be of assistance to the President's commission. At Burke Marshall's request, Eberly prepared an eighty-page plan, and several of us testified before the commission.

During this period the President further encouraged the hope that a strong recommendation by the Marshall commission would lead to an administration bill establishing a system for national service. In signing the 1966 Peace Corps Act, Johnson restated his desire to "develop a manpower program for young people which could work at every level to transform our society," and lead to the day "when some form of voluntary service . . . is as common in America as going to school."

By March 1967, however, when the Marshall commission issued its report, we could read the writing on the wall: the day for large-scale voluntary service was not at hand. The commission suggested that the idea had merit and should be tested on a small experimental basis, but did not recommend it as an alternative to a draft. In retrospect, they were probably right in rejecting a link between non-military service and the draft. In peacetime, a civilian service alternative might make good sense, but in wartime it would appear to be a haven for draft dodgers. When no one is fighting, volunteer civilian service might be at least as arduous as military service. In time of war, the risk of death ruled out such a comparison. And though the President had not admitted it and Congress had not declared it, and most of us had not faced or foreseen its full consequences, America was above all at war.

Even before the commission's report, it had become clear that the day for national service would have to be delayed. The White House had made it clear to our task force at the Peace Corps, and to the Marshall commission, that because of the mounting costs of the conflict in Vietnam there would be no money for any such large new venture. Even though Johnson's attitudes and actions were sometimes like a roller coaster, there was no reason to expect another upward course on major domestic programs so long as the fighting in Indochina continued.

To the end, Johnson publicly maintained that "guns and butter" were possible. "I believe that we can continue the Great Society while we fight in Vietnam," he told Congress in January 1966. In his memoirs he says that "the dream of a Great Society at home and the inescapable obligations halfway around the world" were "two great streams in our national life" that "converged" and "were to run in confluence until the end of my administration."

To the extent that Johnson maintained or expanded domestic budgets while escalating the fighting in Vietnam—and avoided asking Congress and the country for new taxes—he has been blamed for the inflation that later burst out of control. However, the war itself was cause enough for inflation. And unlike World Wars I and II, Vietnam caused a depression of the national spirit in which no adventurous new ideas on the domestic front had much chance. Indeed, such opposition to the war was brewing among young people that even if the President and Congress had established a voluntary national service system, with no link to the military, it would have been swamped and sunk by the wave of student rebellion soon sweeping the nation.

Whether it was confluence or the submergence of the Great Society, war was the larger river we all finally realized we were traveling.

10 · The Great Society and Lyndon Johnson's Other War

In the summer of 1965, along with colleagues at the Peace Corps and various legislators, I went to the White House for the signing of the Peace Corps Act of 1965. Standing tall in the Rose Garden, the President first spoke quietly, benignly, paying special tribute to Shriver and Moyers. When he thought about those whom he trusted most, he said, those to whom he could turn for wisdom, right after Lady Bird, the ones he thought of were Bill Moyers and Sargent Shriver. His compliment was longer-drawn-out and more vivid, but that was its gist. A newsman who regularly covered the White House commented under his breath, "The second and third occupants of the bed shift with the occasion."

Then, using dozens of pens, Johnson signed the bill—one stroke (or half stroke) for each pen—and called out, "Everybody come up here and get a pen." So we lined up and he shook our hands in a double grip, sometimes grasping an arm or shoulder. "I know you've been a lot of he'p, a lot of he'p," he said as he drew me closer to give a short version of the famous Treatment. I didn't know whether he meant the draft of a civil rights talk I had done for him (at Moyers' request) or the planning for national service—or whether he meant anything in particular.

When we were about to depart, Johnson suddenly shouted, "Y'all come in here, right into my office. I want you to see what your President does!" As we crowded into the Oval Office, I remembered the sense of space, the quiet eye of the hurricane, that I used to feel on entering. The high French windows opening to the garden filled with flowers and the Great Seal of the United States woven in the rug were the same. But something seemed very different and jarring. Behind the President's desk, ticker tapes were tapping away with AP, UP, and Reuters bulletins, and there were three television screens. Even without the television going (usually all at once, I was told, for the evening news, so Johnson could follow how he was covered), the tapes were rattling.

Johnson's voice boomed out, "Bill, come over here to my desk and go through the papers on it so everyone can know what the President does." Moyers picked up a stack of papers and described several of the problems they represented. When he noted that the next item was a letter from a mother of a soldier killed in Vietnam, Johnson grabbed it from him and came out in front of his desk. His words went something like this:

"Believe me, my heart breaks when I read this mother's letter, and I want you to know there is nothing more important to your President than peace, there is nothing I spend more time on than peace. That's all we're fighting for in Vietnam. I lay awake nights asking myself if there is anything more I can do for peace. Just last Sunday at the ranch, I took Billy Graham and Bill Moyers down to the banks of the Pedernales and we sat there talking and thinking and praying for peace."

The President's eyes began to close and his arms went out and up as if for a laying on of hands. He waved and shook them, tremblingly, as he went on: "And I want you to know that no matter what my problems and my worries are, when I think of you, when I think of the Peace Corps, when I think of all those Volunteers around the world, helping the poor, healing the maimed and curing the blind, then my heart lifts up and I know that peace is on its way."

The content of what he said seemed less important than the peculiar, emotional, intense—afterwards, several used the word "crazy"—way he talked and seemed to get carried away. At points he was almost whispering, with his eyes squinting or shut, then, eyes bulging, he would rant and almost bellow. Whether Johnson mesmerized himself by his own act, I could not tell. Whether this was the kind of performance that supposedly cast a spell on so many other groups, I did not know. But it did not work with us that day.

Perhaps we were put off by the thought of the bombs falling in Vietnam while the President talked so wildly of peace, or by the knowledge that on the desk was the black box with the buttons by which this emotional and mercurial man could bring on a nuclear holocaust. Perhaps the banging ticker tape broke any potential spell.

Next to me, Peace Corps educational consultant John Seeley, with professional experience in counseling of the disturbed, shook his head. As we filed out, Seeley said, "Clinically, I'm alarmed."

Presidential aide Jack Valenti had just given an ardent defense of Johnson to the Advertising Federation of America, describing his "extra glands . . . that give him energy that ordinary men simply don't have." Valenti had said, "I sleep each night a little better, a little more confidently because Lyndon Johnson is my President." After our encounter in the Oval Office, I didn't.

Washington was rife with rumors about Johnson's instability and I was determined not to succumb to what seemed to me rampant paranoia about the President's state of mind. Moreover, there was the reassuring record of extraordinary accomplishments at home, if not abroad. A few weeks after signing the Peace Corps Act the White House was able to release a summary of 150 major presidential recommendations on which Congress had already acted favorably or was in the process of so acting. Thanks to "the landmark partnership" between the President and what the White House called "the Great Congress," legislation had been enacted that "broke a new trail in America."

In education, there was the breakthrough in aid to elementary and secondary schools; the plan for a National Teacher Corps to enable "teachers with a sense of mission" to serve in city slums and rural poverty areas; and the International Education Act (on which I had worked as a member of the President's Smithsonian Task Force). In health, there was Medicare for older Americans. In urban affairs, there was a new Department of Housing and Urban Development, headed by the first black member of the Cabinet; a Demonstration Cities program to attack urban blight; and an urban mass transit bill. On the environment, there were programs against air, water, and river pollution, and for highway beautification, new recreation parks, and solid-waste disposal. In consumer and citizens' protection, there was a truth-in-packaging bill, a highway safety program, and a child safety act. In civil rights there was the long-sought Voting Rights Act. In the War on Poverty there was the eleven-state regional Appalachian program and the expansion of Head Start. And there were Johnson's plans for the doubling of the Peace Corps, for utilizing returned Volunteers throughout the government and public life, and for moving toward large-scale national youth service.

Underneath the surface of these achievements, however, all was not well. Within months of declaring "unconditional war on poverty," the presidential resolve had diminished. Begun in 1964 as Point One of the Great Society, by 1965 it was being barely mentioned by the President, who no longer called it "my war"—it was the "poverty program." Johnson was embarrassingly silent on the subject during most of the congressional debates. In the critical second year of the effort, Shriver was left to defend and fight for passage of the necessary renewal legislation with almost no White House support. Within the administration, the President let the Budget Bureau cut the program for 1966–67 from the expected $3.4 billion to $1.75 billion, and Congress cut another $138 million— cuts which Shriver called "great and grave."

A political observer noted in late 1966 that Shriver was "left out in the cold—out in the desert where the ants can pick him to pieces." The picture was not that grim. With 113 Job Corps centers for some 40,000 trainees, with community action programs in nearly 1,000 communities, large and small, with VISTA Volunteers at 373 sites, and with 570,000 children in Head Start programs and 20,000 older students in Upward Bound, the anti-poverty landscape did not look like a desert. Nor was the climate all cold. Shocked by budget cuts, the growing constituency of those involved in these ventures, including many local officials and business, labor, and civic leaders, rallied to the defense. After this surprising mobilization of support and grueling months of congressional lobbying, Shriver secured a two-year authorization and a 1967–68 budget slightly above that of the previous year, though below what he considered the minimum necessary to maintain the momentum already achieved.

The new programs of the Office of Economic Opportunity were proving themselves, and their survival seemed probable, but the lack of presidential support for an overall administration-wide "war" meant that the whole endeavor was doomed to becoming the very "series of unco-ordinated and unrelated efforts" that Johnson originally said he did not want. When he appointed Shriver his "personal chief of staff," Johnson had said that the anti-poverty campaign could not survive unless everybody knew "when they're hitting it, they're hitting me." Everybody did begin hitting it, as the presidential protection disappeared.

It has been suggested that the President retreated from the program because so many people *were* hitting it. It was hardly the "historic harmony" he had hoped for. No doubt Johnson had an inordinate desire to be liked (or loved, as he put it), and the complaints from mayors, civil rights groups, and new activist organizations of the poor may have taken him aback. "The day the first letter of protest arrived at the White House from an aggrieved mayor was the day the administration began its retreat," according to the *Christian Science Monitor* correspondent covering the War on Poverty. As the Office of Economic Opportunity insisted upon participation by representatives of the poor in the local programs, letters and phone calls poured in from mayors. Then protests came from private groups as mayors resisted their participation. Congress added to the local controversies in 1966 by adopting an amendment specifying that "maximum feasible participation" meant that at least one-third of the local community action boards had to be representatives of the poor, chosen by the residents of poverty areas.

Not satisfied with this, spokesmen for the poor (sometimes self-appointed) demanded full control of the local projects, and more and more congressmen concluded, as one legislator said, that they were funding "a bunch of Boston Tea Parties around the country." Shriver replied that a War against Poverty would inevitably be "noisy, visible, dirty, uncomfortable and sometimes politically unpopular." Unlike the Peace Corps, it took place close to home. The Office of Economic Opportunity, he said, was not set up "to create community torpor or community apathy" but to "encourage at the local level the basic democratic processes which have made this country great."

On the public record, Johnson insisted that he had expected such heat all along. In his memoirs, he wrote that from the beginning anti-poverty planners "warned me of the risks—particularly the political risks . . . I was willing to take the chance. I realized that a program as massive as the one we were contemplating might shake up many institutions, but I decided that some shaking up might be needed to get a bold new program moving. I thought that local governments had to be challenged to be awakened. . . . But as I used to tell our critics: 'We have to pull the drowning man out of the water and talk about it later.' "

In fact, privately, Johnson talked about it a lot at the time. "Is OEO being run by a bunch of kooks, Communists, and queers?" he asked Shriver. He was tired of hearing mayors complain about the kind of local activist organizations they were being forced to deal with. "I thought we were just going to have the NYA [National Youth Administration]," he said to Bill Moyers. "I thought we were going to have CCC camps and I thought we were going to have community action where a city or a county or a school district or some governmental agency could sponsor projects." Inclusion of private "liberal outfits" perturbed him. "I'm against that. Now if we had 100 billion dollars we might need to but with all the government agencies in this country, I'd prefer that Dick Daley do it rather than the Urban League."

Many mayors had in fact become advocates of community action, and the program's rapid response to requests during the hot summers of racial disturbance in 1965, '66, and '67 converted others. Shriver's tour of Watts evoked remarkable community support, and national opinion surveys reported a gain in popular sympathy for the program. But the growing constituency did not bring back Johnson's support.

The President's turnabout has also been attributed to his angry reaction to the black riots in Watts and other Northern ghettos. The uprising and burning of Watts occurred one week after Johnson had signed the Voting Rights Act of 1965, which he viewed as "a triumph for freedom as huge as any victory that has ever been won on any battlefield." "How is it possible," he asked his aide Joseph Califano, "after all we've accomplished? Is the world topsy-turvy?" He was so horrified that he wouldn't take calls from the generals asking authority to fly in the National Guard. "He just wouldn't accept it," said Califano. Later, to Doris Kearns, Johnson said, "It simply wasn't fair for a few irresponsible agitators to spoil it for me and for all the rest of the Negroes, who are basically peace-loving and nice. . . . Spoiling all the progress I've made in these last few years."

The hundred riots that ensued in the next three years, taking 225 lives, wounding thousands, and doing billions of dollars of property damage, caused a white backlash. Opinion polls showed that in 1964 only 34 percent of American whites thought Negroes were trying to move too fast; two years later, 85 percent held that view. So a strong reaction by a political man like Johnson was predictable. But after his first fury passed, Johnson had second thoughts, and to Doris Kearns spoke more understandingly:

> As I see it, I've moved the Negro from D+ to C−. He's still nowhere. He knows it. And that's why he's out in the streets. Hell, I'd be there too. . . . No matter how well you may think you know a Negro, if you really know one, there'll come the time when you look at him and see how deep his bitterness is.

Johnson's hyperbole led some of his critics simply to conclude that he was hypocritical. In this view, the War on Poverty was an election gimmick that he pointed to proudly throughout the 1964 presidential campaign, then dropped like a hot potato. But no one I knew who worked closely with Johnson doubted the depth of his sincerity about race and poverty. Bill Moyers saw him weep as he watched the television reports from Selma. "My God, those are people they're beating," the President had said. It was hard for anyone to hear Johnson's address to the joint session of Congress after Selma and not believe he meant what he said:

> I do not want to be the President who built empires, or sought grandeur, or extended dominion. I want to be the President who educated young children to the wonders of their world. I want to be the President who helped the poor to find their own way and who protected the right of every citizen to vote in every election. I want to be the President who helped to end hatred among his fellow men and who prompted love among the people of all races and all regions and all parties. I want to be the President who helped to end war among the brothers of this earth.

When asked who wrote that speech, Johnson took out a photograph of the poor Mexican-American students he had taught in Cotulla, Texas, and said, "They did."

What undermined the War on Poverty and kept Johnson from being the kind of President he wanted to be, was one main thing: the Vietnam war. "Remember the dates!" Bill Moyers reminded me, years later, as I tried to unravel and understand what happened to Lyndon Johnson. Four days before Congress passed the Economic Opportunity Act in August 1964, Moyers pointed out, it had adopted the Gulf of Tonkin Resolution.

With only Senators Wayne Morse and Ernest Gruening voting No, and despite murky information about the alleged Vietnamese attack on two U.S. destroyers, Congress had rushed through, under presidential pressure, an open-ended authorization for the President to "take all necessary measures to repel any armed attack against the forces of the United States and to prevent further aggression." Then in February 1965, Johnson decided to bomb North Vietnam. McGeorge Bundy had reported that he and McNamara were "pretty well convinced" that the policy of not attacking North Vietnam "can only lead to disastrous defeat." Then, after a Viet Cong assault on an American barracks in South Vietnam, Bundy had telephoned from Saigon to say that he, Ambassador Maxwell Taylor, and General Westmoreland urged immediate U.S. air strikes against the North.

There was concern about the state visit to Hanoi of Soviet Chairman Kosygin, but, as Johnson later wrote, "If we failed to respond, we were 'paper tigers.' " After a long discussion, McNamara, his deputy, Cyrus Vance, George Ball, William Bundy, Douglas Dillon, Carl Rowan, and House Speaker John McCormack all concurred. In that meeting only Senator Mike Mansfield was opposed.

At a decisive National Security Council meeting on February 10, 1965, Humphrey was a minority voice, arguing against the bombing. Afterwards, Thomas Hughes, then Director of the State Department's Bureau of Intelligence and Research, urged him, as a last chance, to spell out his case directly to the President. Over a long weekend, Humphrey and Hughes prepared a memorandum which makes sad reading (in Humphrey's *The Education of a Public Man*). Writing as a long-standing ally of Johnson's, Humphrey bluntly presented the inescapable moral dilemmas, the political pitfalls of adopting the Goldwater and Nixon policy of "going North," the setback to other international policies such as arms control, and the popular dissension an expanded war would cause. "To sustain public support, American wars have to be politically understandable by the American people," the memorandum argued. This one would not be. It "is always hard to cut losses," Humphrey said, but, with the President's landslide electoral mandate, 1965 was the year to do so in Vietnam. Urging Johnson to apply on the world scene his "unrivaled talents as a politician" to achieve a settlement in Vietnam, Humphrey warned that a year from now, if the country was "embroiled deeper in fighting in Vietnam . . . political opposition will steadily mount" and "negativism and disillusionment" would spread.

The day after receiving the memorandum, Johnson ordered the bombing to begin. Publicly, Humphrey did not disclose his opposition, and even accepted White House deletion of peace-seeking passages in a speech he gave to the *Pacem in Terris* conference at the United Nations. Afterwards, his close friend former Senator William Benton said, "Hubert, that is the worst speech I have heard you give." Inside the White House, Humphrey also paid a price: he was henceforth excluded from most of the key decision-making sessions on Vietnam. Humphrey felt his ostracism in a variety of ways. For example, just as former Ambassador to Denmark, Eugenie Anderson, was about to be appointed director of the Foreign Service Institute, Johnson learned she was being backed by Humphrey and said, "She's not my choice. Take her name off the list."

Johnson himself paid a far heavier price for approving the "sustained reprisal" known to the inner circle by the secret code name Operation Rolling Thunder.

Hour after hour the President pored over the U-2 maps of North Vietnam, approving and disapproving targets, to prevent the escalation from extending too close to China or increasing so drastically as to provoke Chinese intervention. "I won't let those Air Force generals bomb the smallest outhouse north of the 17th parallel without checking with me," Johnson said. "The generals know only two words—spend and bomb."

As Johnson became absorbed with the battle reports from Vietnam, he lost interest in, or had no time for, the war against poverty he had started at home. The detailed attention that complex domestic campaign required was going into the checking out of the outhouses of North Vietnam. Heads of domestic departments such as John Gardner at HEW and Willard Wirtz at Labor felt this as much as Shriver, and came to realize that the President did not want to be bothered with their problems.

It was Vietnam that had become "his war," for which he would spend and bomb, and into which he would send half a million troops. As the bombers streamed north, Rowland Evans and Robert Novak reported in their *Lyndon Johnson: The Exercise of Power*, "the war that had been impersonal, distant, and secondary became for Lyndon Johnson the consuming passion of his presidency." It was "a war he had not started and could not end, a war that broke his consensus, alienated the liberal wing of his party, and threatened to undermine his higher purposes. . . ." Evans and Novak concluded that by the fall of 1966 the war was "the bone in his throat" and "the malignant cancer of the Great Society."

As Johnson became more embroiled in foreign policy and increasingly defensive about his overseas military action, pressures from both the White House and the State Department began to threaten the independence and integrity of the Peace Corps. In one country, an ambassador sent home a Volunteer who had written an editorial against the Vietnam war in the Volunteers' newsletter, as well as the Peace Corps Representative who had failed to censor him. This was a painful boomerang: in early 1961 I had been delighted by and informally involved in the successful effort of Chester Bowles (aided by Tom Hughes) to persuade Kennedy to strengthen the authority of our ambassadors over all parts of the missions in their countries. We had thought this would help ambassadors bring CIA operations in their countries under some control, but instead this authority was being used to curtail the freedom of speech of Volunteers.

At the Peace Corps we were relatively slow in feeling the effects of Vietnam, because we were not operating in that country or in Laos and Cambodia, and had our hands full in some fifty other countries. To some extent we had more freedom in other places because of the White House and State Department preoccupation with Vietnam. But in two countries where there were Volunteers—the Dominican Republic and India—the President intervened in ways that adversely affected the Peace Corps. Each case was a warning that American world policy was moving in a direction contrary to the Peace Corps' basic approach. Both events ended my hope that Johnson would come to understand world politics and bring reason to that arena, in the way he had learned to master the politics of the Senate.

Peace Corps Volunteers in the Dominican Republic had been overwhelmingly against the 1963 right-wing military coup that overthrew Juan Bosch's newly elected, leftist government (which had invited the Peace Corps to the country). By their life and work among the poor, they were doing their part to remove the stain of the United States' longstanding support for Rafael Trujillo's thirty-one-year dictatorship. From all sides they heard tales of Trujillo's cruelty and corruption and the vast fortune he had accumulated. When civil war broke out in 1965, most of the Volunteers, like most of their Dominican neighbors, sympathized with the "legitimatist" rebels seeking the restoration of a democratic regime. When Johnson sent in 500 Marines "to protect American lives" some Volunteers agreed that a rescue operation was necessary, but, as the American force was increased to 22,000 troops, most Volunteers opposed the continuing occupation—and the deception. Clearly it was not danger to American lives but fear of a radical regime that kept the troops there. It was the first such intervention in Latin America since the ill-fated U.S. occupation of Nicaragua in 1925.

News accounts of the role of the Volunteers and the reports by the Peace Corps chief for Latin America, Frank Mankiewicz, sent a current of pride through the agency's headquarters in Washington. *New York Times* correspondent Tad Szulc wrote about the Volunteers in his *Dominican Diary*:

> These brave young Americans had refused to be evacuated from war-torn Santo Domingo and had gone on working in the hospitals and elsewhere despite the fighting and the mounting resentment in the rebel zone against the United States intervention. . . . The volunteers were not supposed to discuss politics with newsmen, but privately they could not hold back their fears that the current U.S. policy was undermining their efforts to "build bridges" to the Dominicans.

The *Times* correspondent and Volunteers alike were upset by the simplistic briefings given by U.S. military officers, who would refer to the forces of the military junta as the "Friendlies" and those on the other side as the "Unfriendlies." During some periods of the fighting, the thirty-three-year-old Peace Corps Director in the Dominican Republic, Bob Satin, was the only U.S. official admitted in the rebel zone. Once while making arrangements for food distribution by the Volunteers, Satin brought about the release of three captured Marines.

Later, the State Department proposed that Volunteers be assigned to work with the U.S. Special Forces, the Green Berets, on helicopter missions around the country to inquire about the political views of the people. When the scheme was put to the Peace Corps, the answer from Mankiewicz, personally approved by Shriver, was: "Not only no, but hell no!"

The President, in turn, was furious when he read stories about the Dominican Volunteers' criticism of his policies. At one point, Mankiewicz dissuaded the Volunteers from sending an open letter of protest on the ground that it would only inflame Johnson while endangering the continued existence of the Peace Corps.

Johnson blamed the press for having misreported the Dominican events. Almost all the Volunteers and Peace Corps staff with experience there seemed to agree with *Times* correspondent Szulc's conclusion that "the original error of the U.S. was to misjudge the nature of the rebellion, largely because of the inability of U.S. diplomats in Santo Domingo to understand the forces at play." Instead of becoming "aligned with a popular democratic movement while using the leverage that the U.S. would then possess to root out the Communist influence . . . we closed all the democratic options to the rebels and placed the Communists in the role of being the only 'friends' of Dominican democracy." The press was, according to Szulc, "nothing more and nothing less than the Greek chorus of that tragedy."

Johnson, too, as I followed the events, was misunderstanding the forces at play. Finally, after months of skillful and painstaking negotiation by Ellsworth Bunker on behalf of the Organization of American States, a settlement was reached, U.S. troops were withdrawn, and a free election held. President Johnson wrote that this solution "demonstrated what I hope and believe the people of South Vietnam, and other beleaguered countries, will increasingly demonstrate," that "if they are given half a chance" they will "carry out their responsibilities as democratic citizens." That false encouragement to Johnson to continue the fighting in Vietnam was one of the worst results of sending troops to Santo Domingo.

The Peace Corps wanted to do more than bewail the fighting. A few weeks after the U.S. military intervention, an unusual proposal was made by the respected chancellor of the University of Puerto Rico. Jaime Benítez was then serving as an adviser to McGeorge Bundy, who was in Santo Domingo unsuccessfully seeking a negotiated settlement. The Dominican Republic would be better off, Benítez suggested, if the respective numbers of Peace Corps Volunteers and Marines on the island were reversed. The United States, "as the world's oldest democracy, the most powerful and the nearest," he said, is "called upon . . . to support the legitimate revindications of the other communities of America." "Unfortunately, it has not done so," Benítez said—except through the work of the Peace Corps Volunteers.

Benítez and Teodoro Moscoso, former U.S. coordinator for the Alliance for Progress, proposed that the Peace Corps send 1,000 Volunteers to the Dominican Republic. Though Shriver had opposed any kind of Volunteer involvement with the military or with intelligence work, he liked the idea of proving, on its own, that the Peace Corps "can make a difference." He approved an emphasis on health, since that could not so easily be attacked as cultural imperialism. Frank Mankiewicz was sent to Santo Domingo to lay the groundwork. Finding the country depressed and in no mood for a massive infusion of additional North Americans, despite the continuing popularity of the Volunteers, Mankiewicz scaled down the estimate of the optimum number of new volunteers to 250. Skepticism among Volunteers led to further reduction, until only sixty-five were sent.

"The Peace Corps *versus* the War Corps" was a heady thought, but it was a contest the Volunteers couldn't win. The effect of the United States' resort to force could not be counteracted so easily.

In India, the issue was not the use of U.S. military force, but Johnson's willingness to use American economic and technical assistance to bend others to his will. A few months after the Marine landing in the Dominican Republic, war broke out between India and Pakistan, and the flow of all aid to either side was suspended. Some 170 Volunteers for India, who had just finished training, had to be diverted elsewhere until conditions were safe. In the emergency, an old proposal of mine for training on Israeli kibbutzim was accepted. The Volunteers for poultry expansion in India, who had been in a training program at St. John's College, were sent to work on an Israeli agricultural settlement that specialized in poultry. For the first six weeks, I was delighted that we had bypassed the State Department's opposition to such involvement in Israel. The Volunteers were finding it an extraordinarily instructive experience. Even the tragic Arab-Israeli hostility had suggestive parallels with the recurring conflict between Pakistan and India.

Then in September 1965 the United Nations secured a cease-fire, and from New Delhi American Ambassador Chester Bowles sent word for the Volunteers to come as soon as possible. Their arrival was part of a scheduled buildup to more than 1,500 Volunteers in India. (If the Peace Corps had the Volunteers, Bowles thought 10,000 would not be too many for the largest democratic nation in the world. Among 600 million Indians, even such a vast Peace Corps contingent would amount to only one Volunteer for every 60,000 people; the equivalent ratio in the Dominican Republic was one Volunteer for every 5,000 Dominicans.)

But President Johnson refused to let the Volunteers fly on to New Delhi. He was angry that India would not yield on Kashmir, as he had demanded, and ordered the cessation of all U.S. aid, including the Peace Corps, until the Indian government gave in.

After letting a little more time pass for the President's temper to cool, we began to press the White House to lift the embargo on the Peace Corps. The Volunteers were forgetting the Hindi they had learned, and itching to get to the assignments for which they had been trained. Bowles kept repeating his pleas for their arrival, fearing that the withholding of Volunteers as a sanction would turn the Peace Corps, in Indian eyes, into a tool for political blackmail. Johnson remained adamant.

Remembering Nehru's condescension about the Peace Corps coming to India in the first place, I could not believe that Johnson would not see the error of his position, if someone would just present the situation to him straight. Shriver tried to, but got nowhere. Then Warren Wiggins sought the help of McGeorge Bundy, who saw the damage being done to the Peace Corps and to Indian-American relations. Wiggins reported that a discouraged Bundy had replied, "Warren, if you knew the mood the President was in you wouldn't ask me to do that." Bill Moyers told me that the President's state of mind made any further appeal impossible.

From Thomas Hughes in the State Department, I heard that a recent visitor to the White House said the President had grumbled that he wasn't going to listen any more to Hindu-lovers like McGeorge Bundy, Bill Moyers, and Dean Rusk, but was going to look for advice on that area henceforth to people like Clark Clifford and Arthur Dean (puzzling choices, since they had no special involvement in the area). Johnson reportedly said that he wouldn't let the Volunteers go to India until the Indian Prime Minister crawled on the floor and kissed his boot.

In Johnson's petulance, irrationality, and bad politics, we were seeing the other side of this "force of nature" Moyers had talked about: the harm he had warned it could do, if it went awry. Wiggins recalled an incident he had suppressed. In 1961, when he was in the White House with Vice-President Johnson, waiting to see Kennedy to argue that the Peace Corps should be independent, Johnson had started telling the President's assistant Ralph Dungan the way to operate foreign assistance. "Run AID the same way I ran the Texas Youth Conservation Corps. You put out the dollars to buy the votes. When you give AID dollars, you line up these countries to be on our side—to vote with us. That's the point of AID."

There was one extenuating circumstance. In the middle of the tug-of-war about India, Johnson had to have his gall bladder and a ureter stone removed. Some of his worst reaction had come after the operation, when he was weak and especially irascible. Weeks later, when his spirits improved (to the point where he was showing his scar to reporters), he relented, and let the Volunteers and flow of economic aid to India go forward.

Much as I wanted to hope that Johnson would change his mind about Vietnam, there were no signs of this, and Bill Moyers, though circumspect, seemed increasingly gloomy. From the beginning Moyers had been dubious about the military advice the President was getting, and took steps to provide an alternative view of reality. He developed a network of young officers in the Pentagon, State Department, and CIA who gave him assessments that differed from the prevailing views of the National Security Council. When he asked Johnson whether he wanted to see this information, the President said yes. After the Vietcong attack on Pleiku in February 1965, the President told Moyers to sit in on all Vietnam strategy meetings: "But don't open your mouth—just stay in the background, like a babe, and then afterwards tell me what you think about the politics of the situation." Soon, however, as Moyers continued questioning the decisions, Johnson got more and more irritated. "Here comes 'Stop-the-Bomb Bill,' he would say," with a cutting edge.

In early 1966, Moyers pressed unsuccessfully to get the President to ask for new taxes to pay for the war and check inflation but Johnson said no, the conservatives would use such a request to defeat the Great Society programs. Disturbed by the course of events, Moyers went to the Pentagon for a long, private talk with McNamara, who agreed that the war was destroying all their hopes. When Johnson learned of their meeting, he angrily told Moyers, "You're a staff aide to me, a flunky, and you're never to go see a cabinet member again without my telling you to." Moreover, the President thought McNamara was losing his nerve.

Seeing the handwriting on the wall, Moyers wrote the President that he wanted to leave the staff. On the day he announced his departure, he went to lunch with Robert Kennedy, to let his friend, the Senator from New York, know that he was going to New York to become the publisher of *Newsday*. When he learned of the luncheon, Johnson stormed around the White House, charging Moyers with "treason."

Though we kept in touch while he served Johnson, Moyers only gave unhappy hints about what was happening in the White House. Later he explained to me that almost to the end he kept hoping he would be able to influence the President's priorities and his approach to Vietnam. According to Mary McGrory, Moyers said more poignantly, "I thought I could make him more like me, but I left when I realized he was making me more like him."

Chester Bowles was not so circumspect. After talking to the President about aid to India, in the summer of 1966, Bowles told us that Johnson had taken up most of the time with "almost paranoic references" to Robert Kennedy, Senators Fulbright and Morse, and other critics of the war. Bowles concluded that Johnson was "headed for deep trouble."

In fact, of course, we were already deep in the trouble. The morning headlines and the evening television news did not let anyone forget Vietnam, but it became accepted as a fact of life. Just as a visitor in Asia gets inured to poverty—if he stays long enough, he begins to take beggars and hungry people for granted—so the bombing raids, free-firing zones, defoliations, and even American casualties and body counts became daily fare.

To White House visitors Johnson explained that his strategy was seduction, not rape—a slow moving in on North Vietnam, always being ready to draw back if China slapped us down. If it produced none of the results sought in Vietnam, the process seemed to work at home. The American people and Congress let it happen. Step by step, with very little political resistance, Johnson took America into a war that Congress was never asked to declare, and at first wasn't even asked to pay for.

Looking back, many of us in the administration realize that we were in the forefront of those being seduced. Our own respective assignments were constructive and consuming. There was all the good that could be done, through the Peace Corps or the War on Poverty, for example. Someone has called this the last, worst temptation—the temptation to serve. Anthony Lewis and James Thomson (a key aide to Bowles) have asked why so few exercised the power of resignation.* In retrospect, given my strong views about Vietnam, I wish I had used that power, for whatever it would have been worth, after that summer of 1965, or at least after Johnson resumed bombing in January 1966, following the thirty-nine-day Christmas pause.

The thought of resigning in protest occurred to me, but the words of Bill Moyers, which closed the Conference of Returned Volunteers in the spring of 1965, kept ringing in my ears. "The President is fond of saying that while the lightning is flashing and the thunder is rolling and the rain is falling, the grass is growing," Moyers had told us. "In the midst of international tensions, amidst the clamor of dangers, the work that you are doing is going on. Catalytic, yes; quiet, subtle, yes—nonetheless growing—growing, changing, serving, fulfilling. And that's true."

It was true. The significance and scope of the work, as we saw it in that year, are recorded in the special May 1966 issue of the *Annals of the American Academy of Political and Social Science*. Most of the articles, including mine, "The Future of the Peace Corps," convey the optimism we felt. Assuming that the war would pass, but the Peace Corps would be permanent, I looked forward to a further quantum jump in both overseas and domestic volunteering, in which volunteer service would become accepted as part of the definition of American citizenship, and an integral part of American higher education.

But the reverse of Johnson's saying was also true. While our grass was growing, Operation Rolling Thunder was dropping more explosives on Vietnam than the Allies dropped on Germany in all of World War II. Johnson knew this better than anyone, and was undoubtedly not exaggerating when he told us in the Oval Office that he was lying awake nights wondering what he could do to end the war. During the week of July 21, 1965, shortly before talking to us, he had spent more than fifty hours in meetings with his chief advisers on Vietnam, weighing the recommendation for a major new escalation that McNamara had brought back from Vietnam. He and General Westmoreland urged that in addition to continued massive bombing, American troops be sent into combat on a large scale, and be quadrupled—from 70,000 to 280,000. Reluctantly Johnson decided to go ahead, but not to do it by calling up the

---

* See James C. Thomson, Jr., "Getting Out and Speaking Out," *Foreign Policy*, Winter 1973–74, and Albert O. Hirschman, *Exit, Voice, and Loyalty* (Harvard University Press, 1970).

reserves, or asking Congress for new authority. That would only stir up further opposition, and set back the prospects for Great Society programs.

Those prospects were dimming faster than we knew, or than Johnson was willing to admit. The intensity he displayed at the signing of the Peace Corps Act must have reflected inner turmoil. That summer of 1965, Johnson told Doris Kearns seven years later, he felt he could "almost touch" his "dream of improving life for more people and in more ways than any other political leader, including FDR," and "was determined to keep the war from shattering that dream." He said he "knew the Congress as well as I know Lady Bird, and knew that the day it exploded into a major debate on the war, that day would be the beginning of the end of the Great Society."

Johnson forestalled congressional fiscal reaction by bookkeeping maneuvers within the federal budget that deferred payment on some defense costs, and by not asking for a tax increase. But Wilbur Mills, the congressional watchdog and sometime master of the federal budget, could see what was happening. By 1967, Mills served notice on the President that he had to make major slashes in domestic spending. "You have to go on TV," he wrote to Johnson, and explain to the people that "because of Vietnam we must cut domestic spending and pass a tax increase."

That was the last thing Johnson wanted to do. The War on Poverty and other Great Society programs were just moving out of low gear, and he knew they needed increased fuel to get into high gear. He agreed with Shriver's contention that the programs were like an airplane taxiing for a takeoff; they needed a great burst of energy and speed to get off the ground. But he also knew that defense spending for 1967 would be about $6 billion more than the $10 billion increase previously forecast and that inflation showed signs of getting out of control. Without disclosing any projections for defense costs, Johnson, unhappily, directed domestic programs to tighten their belts—just when they expected, and in many cases needed, major expansion.

Did Johnson foresee the consequences of what he was doing? His conversations with Doris Kearns, recorded in her *Lyndon Johnson and the American Dream*, suggest that he did, and that his agony on the Pedernales had been genuine. But in those amazing talks between a would-be teacher and his would-be student—which read like the last love story of a lonely political man—he still wanted to have it both ways. Johnson told her in 1970:

> I knew from the start that I was bound to be crucified either way I moved. If I left the woman I really loved—the Great Society—in order to get involved with that bitch of a war on the other side of the world, then I would lose everything at home. All my programs. All my hopes to

feed the hungry and shelter the homeless. All my dreams to provide education and medical care to the browns and the blacks and the lame and the poor. But if I left that war and let the Communists take over South Vietnam, then I would be seen as a coward and my nation would be seen as an appeaser and we would both find it impossible to accomplish anything for anybody anywhere on the entire globe.

Oh, I could see it coming all right. . . . Once the war began, then all those conservatives in the Congress would use it as a weapon against the Great Society. You see, they'd never wanted to help the poor or the Negroes in the first place. But they were having a hard time figuring out how to make their opposition sound noble in a time of great prosperity. But the war, oh, they'd use it to say they were against my programs, not because they were against the poor . . . but because the war had to come first. . . . Oh, I could see it coming. And I didn't like the smell of it. . . . So you see, I was bound to be crucified either way I moved.

Johnson had imagined the Great Society as his child, a daughter who would grow into a beautiful woman. She had begun to crawl, and he had hoped that she would begin to walk and then "she'd be off and running, all the time growing bigger and healthier and fatter. And when she grew up, I figured she'd be so big and beautiful that the American people couldn't help but fall in love with her, and once they did, they'd want to keep her around forever, making her a permanent part of American life, more permanent even than the New Deal." As he looked back, in his conversations with Doris Kearns, he didn't blame the war, or his own mistakes, for the Great Society's downfall, but Richard Nixon, who had come along and ruined everything. "There's a story in the paper every day about him slashing another one of my Great Society programs. I can just see him waking up in the morning, making that victory sign of his and deciding which program to kill." Johnson agonized as he saw the Great Society "getting thinner and thinner and uglier and uglier all the time; now her bones are beginning to stick out and her wrinkles are beginning to show. Soon she'll be so ugly that the American people will refuse to look at her; they'll stick her in a closet to hide her away and there she'll die. And when she dies, I, too, will die."

On the day after Nixon was inaugurated for a second term—the same day a cease-fire finally took effect in Vietnam—a new plan was announced for the further disbanding of the one time War on Poverty. The next day Lyndon Johnson died of a heart attack.

In a talk I was giving late in 1966, just before leaving the Peace Corps, I was boasting about the Volunteers' good record of health and safety. The mortality rates in the Peace Corps were lower than if one stayed at home. A woman raised her hand and asked, "What about the Volunteer in Ethiopia who was eaten alive by a crocodile?" I assured her that a lot of things happened in Ethiopia, but not that. Afterwards she showed me the clipping from that day's paper. Camping by a river in a remote province, a young Volunteer had gone swimming, and to the horror of his companions, what had looked like a passing log suddenly turned out to be a huge crocodile that pulled him under. For so many Indochinese and Americans the Vietnam war was that crocodile. It also swallowed and destroyed Lyndon Johnson—and his War on Poverty.

The Peace Corps itself survived, although after Nixon's election it was folded into the new Action agency, along with VISTA and several other components of the dismantled War on Poverty. Instead of increasing to 20,000 or more Volunteers, it fell back to about 5,000. Its identity and even its name were muted, but for the individual Volunteer the basic experience of teaching or otherwise serving in a town or village of Asia, Africa, or Latin America remained much the same. The Vietnam war, however—and then the disclosures about the CIA—made it more difficult to represent America overseas.

In Lyndon Johnson's memoirs, *The Vantage Point*, there is only one passing reference to the Peace Corps (on the page about Shriver's appointment as chief of staff in the War on Poverty). The man who was responsible for the Peace Corps' independence, who had proposed it even before Kennedy, who had backed it as chairman of its advisory council, who had convened the returned Volunteers and vowed that he would see that the Peace Corps "continues to make history," did not, or could not, deal with it when he came to writing the story of his administration. And Bill Moyers, his closest aide, the man he had recalled from the Peace Corps to be at his side during the most critical period of his presidency, was barely mentioned—beyond identifying him as one of those supporting the intervention in the Dominican Republic and the escalation of the war in Vietnam. After Moyers left the White House and became an outspoken critic of the war, for Johnson he became a nonperson. Photographs in which he appeared were removed from the collection of official pictures of the Johnson presidency.

When the news came of Johnson's death, Moyers was filming a tribal meeting of the Chippewa Indians for public television. An Indian pulled him aside and said: "A mighty wind has been stilled." Moyers recalled the day he had told Johnson he was determined to resign. After driving around the LBJ ranch for hours together, Johnson had finally said "Okay," and then added: "You were born over there with those Choctaw Indians. Bet you don't know where the word 'okay' came from?" Moyers didn't.

"Right from the Choctaws themselves," the President said. "It meant 'we can agree now, if you aren't so all-fired set on perfection.'"

Why wasn't Johnson the great congressional compromiser willing to compromise in Vietnam? The irony, Moyers says, is that he thought he was. After a secret American offer was rejected by Ho Chi Minh, Johnson said with sadness: "I don't understand it. George Meany would've grabbed at a deal like that." Half Texas hill country, half Washington, Johnson—according to Moyers—"was so much a creature of those places that he may have shaped the world in their image." Yet Johnson was also a man who could say: "The President's hardest task is not to *do* what is right but to *know* what is right." Regretting the break in their relationship, Moyers said in a reminiscence for *The New York Times*: "He died before the prodigal got home. But he did more for me than any man and I loved him."

IV
Conflicting Legacies:
An American Tragedy

I have been one acquainted with the night.

—Robert Frost

11 · From the Bay of Pigs to Vietnam

When asked to reflect on the policies that had led America into war, Lyndon Johnson shouted at Doris Kearns: "No, no, no! I will *not* let you take me backward in time on Vietnam. Fifty thousand American boys are dead. Nothing can change that fact." Yet Johnson's own poignant and most frequent explanation for the course he had taken pointed backward. Before and after he ordered the bombing, and all along the way as he committed nearly half a million troops, he would ask—sometimes proudly, sometimes plaintively: How could he have done otherwise, when "all the Kennedy men"—the best and the brightest—were advising him that escalation was necessary?

In 1979 I asked Senator William Fulbright to help me understand why Johnson followed this advice instead of that of such long-time Senate colleagues as Humphrey, Mansfield, and himself. The chairman of the Foreign Relations Committee said sadly it was because Johnson knew so little about the world—and *knew* that he knew very little. Fulbright had traveled with Johnson on his first trip to Paris, and described how green and ill at ease the Senate Majority Leader was—"Lyndon's eyes popped out." Fulbright said, "I've often wondered how history might have been different if Johnson had just studied overseas for a year or two on a Fulbright fellowship."

Away from the Senate and domestic politics, Johnson felt insecure and beyond his depth, and turned to the experts. For a while, Fulbright sensed that the President was wavering—was listening to him and Mansfield and worrying about continuing and extending the war. But finally Johnson had to choose, and he could not bring himself to believe that his long-time colleagues were wiser than the very impressive men from the foreign policy, intelligence, and military establishment whom Kennedy had assembled. "And they are very impressive, you know," added Fulbright, "when they are all together, with their charts and sophisticated arguments and the military brass behind them."

From White House arguments about Cuba and Vietnam, I knew how weighty and intimidating the geopolitical talk of the established experts can be. Critics who raise questions of morality or legality tend to sound soft and sentimental, and soon turn silent. I had expected that their experience in American politics had taught both Johnson and Kennedy to deal with such experts at arm's length. But I was underestimating the powers of persuasion of that military, foreign policy, intelligence

339

establishment, and overestimating the ability of political leaders to resist the domination of international affairs by the military mind.

With war the extension of politics by other means, in the cold war we were seeing the extension of the principles and practices of war into world politics. When applied figuratively to the War on Poverty or the Peace Corps, to suggest all-out effort, the military metaphor had value. But the habits that spread in international affairs during the years after World War II were war's rougher ones: the readiness to use any means, the reliance on force to attain any end, and the suspension of conventional morality for the duration. War has always justified lying, killing, and almost every crime prosecuted by the civil law. In the struggle against Communism, even when outright war was not taking place, the standard operating procedures of war became the rule, and war's most potent, unprincipled practices were always a temptation.

Faced with defeat in Vietnam unless more drastic means were used, Johnson was led into that temptation. The Joe McCarthy charges and all the Republican accusations against Truman and Acheson for "losing China" would be "chickenshit compared with what might happen if we lost Vietnam," he predicted. "This time," he told Doris Kearns, "there would be Robert Kennedy out in front leading the fight against me, telling everyone that I had betrayed John Kennedy's commitment to South Vietnam. That I had let a democracy fall into the hands of the Communists. That I was a coward. An unmanly man." He reported that during his last years as President: "Every night when I fell asleep, I would see myself tied to the ground in the middle of a long, open space. In the distance, I could hear the voices of thousands of people. They were all shouting at me and running toward me: 'Coward! Traitor! Weakling!' They kept coming closer. They began throwing stones. At exactly that moment I would generally wake up . . . terribly shaken."

Johnson's limited perspectives and his manifest psychological need to demonstrate manliness made him especially susceptible to the military mind. Inside the astute political man was a trigger-happy Texan boy who liked to make his guests prove their manhood by shooting deer. In his extravagant words and excessive actions he came to embody what Fulbright called "the Arrogance of Power." In the crunch, he naturally turned away from a fastidious ex-Rhodes Scholar like Fulbright or a former professor of Far Eastern history like Mansfield or a big-hearted populist like Humphrey and succumbed to the apparent practicality and power of the Pentagon.

Why Johnson felt he had no choice is the first question in going backward in time on Vietnam, but it is not the hardest or most important

340

one. So long as Vietnam is relatively fresh in popular memory, people may reject a recurrence of the flamboyant LBJ brand of military-minded machismo. But the historical, political, and psychological errors that drew the United States into Vietnam are still deeply ingrained in the American mind.

The fear of being soft, the determination to be tough, the resolve never to be a coward was a prominent, sometimes dominant, strain in the sons of Joseph Kennedy—as in the foreign policy thinking of many Americans. What is painful for many of us to recall, and much more difficult to understand, is the legacy that Kennedy bequeathed to his successor—the mounting military involvement in Vietnam and armed intervention and covert action in Cuba. It was the worst possible precedent for Johnson, and the one he was least able to handle.

John Kennedy was no provincial. His major interest had long been world affairs; he had no reason to be intimidated by the military. How could Kennedy, and the brightest men around him, have led us further into Vietnam? Why did Kennedy go along with the abortive incursion into Cuba and the prolonged secret CIA war against Castro called Operation Mongoose?

It is not easy to come to terms with failure. It was not easy for John Kennedy to acknowledge the mistakes that produced the fiasco at the Bay of Pigs in April 1961, the first major defeat in his life. Indeed, instead of renouncing the strategy and tactics of the CIA and the military planners that had led to the disaster, he applied much the same approach to Vietnam—albeit with a determination to be far more efficient. Instead of turning to those few who had opposed the resort to armed force in Cuba, he proceeded to replace the one top adviser who had clearly opposed the plan.

Publicly, the President gracefully accepted responsibility for the Bay of Pigs, saying that "victory has a hundred fathers and defeat is an orphan." But privately he lashed out at Chester Bowles for allegedly leaking to the press his opposition to the Cuban invasion—and for not being aggressive enough at White House councils in proposing alternative ways to bring about Castro's downfall.

Reflecting the President's anger, Pierre Salinger accosted me in a White House corridor the day after Castro had captured more than 1,000 survivors of the CIA's Cuban brigade. "That yellow-bellied friend of yours, Chester Bowles, is leaking all over town that he was against it," Salinger almost shouted. "We're going to get him!"

"Why don't you get those who got us into this mess?" I replied. Bowles flatly denied the leak, and James Reston told me his source for the story that infuriated Kennedy was Rusk, but it was a minor point.

The important question, I told Salinger, was why had the President not taken Bowles's advice—or Fulbright's—or Stevenson's—but followed instead the lead of Allen Dulles and Company? This made no dent on the President's Press Secretary, who roared down the hall cursing the "jelly-bellied Chester Bowles."

It was the ninetieth day of the new administration, and I asked myself: How could Kennedy have gone so wrong before the end of his first hundred days? Then, as the President turned more and more to his brother, and together John and Robert Kennedy committed themselves to counter-insurgency, covert action, and increased military effort as the way to counteract the Cuban defeat and to win in Vietnam, I wondered what whirlwind they would reap.

The first inkling most of us had of a possible attack on Cuba came ten days before Kennedy's inauguration. On the front page of *The New York Times* of January 10, 1961, a large headline proclaimed: U.S. HELPS TRAIN AN ANTI-CASTRO FORCE AT SECRET GUATEMALAN AIR-GROUND BASE. The detailed story was even more alarming. I talked to Chester Bowles, already designated as Undersecretary of State, to see what he knew about it; he knew nothing whatsoever. We agreed that Kennedy should be alerted to stop any American military involvement that might be afoot.

The news stirred a concern that had grown in my mind during the 1960 campaign, as Kennedy seemed to relish taking rhetorical shots at Castro and competing with Republicans over who would take the strongest action against the new Cuban regime. I was most disturbed by the statement issued in Kennedy's name in the final weeks before the election, calling for the United States "to strengthen the non-Batista democratic anti-Castro forces in exile, and in Cuba itself, who offer eventual hope of overthrowing Castro." He charged that "thus far these fighters for freedom have had virtually no support from our Government."

What made the matter worse for me was the discovery that the statement was prepared as a rejoinder to Republican criticism of a passage on Castro I had drafted for Kennedy's book *The Strategy of Peace*. The controversial words, taken out of context, seemed to recognize Castro as part of the revolutionary tradition of Simon Bolivar. In his book *Kennedy*, Sorensen reported that the Senator "regretted the implication, was angry he had not caught it and was embarrassed by the Republican attacks on the passage; nevertheless, he refused to disown either the words or the junior staff member who had written them from a wholly different perspective." The passage in question, which served as the introduction to the Senator's speeches on Latin America, read:

Just as we must recall our own revolutionary past in order to understand the spirit and the significance of the anticolonial uprisings in Asia and Africa, we should now reread the life of Simon Bolivar, the great "Liberator" and sometime "Dictator" of South America, in order to comprehend the new contagion for liberty and reform now spreading south of our borders. . . .

Fidel Castro is part of the legacy of Bolivar, who led his men over the Andes Mountains, vowing "war to the death" against Spanish rule, saying "Where a goat can pass, so can an army." Castro is also part of the frustration of that earlier revolution which won its war against Spain but left largely untouched the indigenous feudal order. . . .

Whether Cuba would have taken a more rational course after his victory had the United States Government not backed the dictator Batista so long and so uncritically, and had it given the fiery young rebel a warmer welcome in his hour of triumph, especially on his trip to this country, we cannot be sure.

But Cuba is not an isolated case. We can still show our concern for liberty and our opposition to the *status quo* in our relations with the other Latin American dictators who now, or in the future, try to suppress their people's aspirations. And we can take the long-delayed positive measures that are required to enable the revolutionary wave sweeping Latin America to move through relatively peaceful channels and to be harnessed to the great constructive tasks at hand.

Since that was the approach I thought—and hoped—Kennedy would follow, I did not like him being pushed in the other direction. The statement calling for U.S. support to Cuban freedom fighters had been drafted by Dick Goodwin after Kennedy had gone to sleep and released by Sorensen without waking the exhausted candidate. "It was, in all candor, a vague generalization," Sorensen wrote, "thrown in to pad out an anti-Castro 'program.'" Nevertheless it sounded serious and James Reston called it Kennedy's first major blunder. In the fourth TV debate Nixon said it was "the most shockingly reckless proposal ever made . . . by a presidential candidate." Such United States intervention, the Vice-President said, would be "condemned in the United Nations" and be "an open invitation for Mr. Khrushchev . . . to come into Latin America and to engage us in what would be a civil war and possibly even worse than that."

The ironies and illusions of politics! Both the passage in the book and the statement of rejoinder, for which Kennedy was criticized from different quarters, were written by others and published without his careful checking or approval, and Nixon's response was wholly deceptive. Unknown to us at the time, within the secret councils of the Eisenhower administration the Vice-President was himself a strong proponent of the very proposal he publicly attacked as "shockingly reckless." Nixon used extreme language in denouncing Kennedy because he mistakenly thought Kennedy had been briefed by Allen Dulles on the CIA plan for military action, and had knowingly endangered the operation in order to win votes.

The New York Times and the liberal press notwithstanding, Kennedy probably did win votes by seeming to be harder on Castro than Nixon. From the questions asked in campaign meetings, there appeared to be more popular antipathy to Castro than to Khrushchev. The tough line on Cuba may have been another of the factors that turned enough votes to Kennedy to assure his 100,000 margin of victory. Kennedy's own wry comment to Goodwin and Sorensen was: "If I win this election, I will have won it myself, but if I lose it, you fellows will have lost it."

In the language of the CIA, one who is fully informed about a secret plan is "witting." Others may have unwitting roles to play (and some may know part but not all and be half witting). It was after the election that Kennedy became witting.

On November 27 in Palm Beach, CIA chief Allen Dulles and Richard Bissell, his deputy in charge of covert operations, briefed the new President on their plan for a Cuban landing by some 1,500 CIA-trained and -armed Cuban exiles. In the Oval Office the day before the inauguration, Eisenhower commended to his successor this effort to overthrow Castro. He stressed that it was the new administration's responsibility to do whatever was necessary to make it successful. But for most of us in the new administration, Cuba was far from our minds. At a post-inaugural costume party when Robert Amory, the CIA deputy director for Intelligence, arrived dressed in green battle fatigues and beard as Fidel, we all laughed. Only the witting few knew what it portended.

Undersecretary of State Bowles, UN Ambassador Stevenson, and even Ted Sorensen were not among the few to be informed. It was explained that Bowles was excluded from the inner circle because everyone knew what his position would be, and his long arguments against the operation would be boring.

In late March, Bowles found out the details by accident. In Rusk's absence from the country on a trip to Asia, he was Acting Secretary of State and had to be invited to National Security Council meetings. At one such White House session, Dulles and Bissell went over the Cuban plan. Bowles was appalled, and thought that Dulles "should have been thrown out of the office" for proposing such a venture. But he did not speak up against it: Bowles decided it would be better tactics to get Rusk, who was about to return, to lead the opposition. He also feared being labeled "soft" and wanted to have his arguments well honed before he took on the top men of the CIA.

Without disclosing the details, Bowles told me the issue and asked for ideas on a memorandum he was writing to Rusk. In the paper handed to the returning Secretary of State, Bowles contended that in sponsoring the Cuban operation, "we would be deliberately violating the fundamental obligations we assumed in the Act of Bogotá establishing the Organization of American States. The Act provides: . . . 'The territory of a State is inviolable; it may not be the object, even temporarily, of military occupation or other measures of force taken by another State, directly or indirectly, on any grounds whatever. . . .' "

Moreover, Bowles predicted, "under the very best circumstances . . . this operation will have a much more adverse effect on world opinion than most people contemplate." The best of circumstances were not likely, however, for "as the venture is now planned, the chances of success are not greater than one out of three. . . . If it fails, Castro's prestige and strength will be greatly enhanced."

Since Bowles thought Rusk's voice would carry more weight with Kennedy than his, he urged the Secretary to "personally and privately communicate your views to the President . . . I think you can kill this thing if you take a firm stand on it." If the plan was still not stopped, Bowles asked to be immediately informed so he could take his objections directly to the President.

Four days later, Rusk reported to Bowles that the plan had been greatly modified and that it would not be necessary for Bowles to see Kennedy. The scale of the action had been so reduced, according to Rusk, that it would resemble other guerrilla operations that had attracted little attention; he doubted that it would even make the front page of *The New York Times.* "Don't worry about this," he said. "It isn't going to amount to anything."

Bowles, and those of us close to him, were relieved. Although Rusk had not shown Kennedy the Bowles memorandum, he knew that an equally strong case against the plan had been submitted by Senator Fulbright. While flying to Florida for Easter, Kennedy had read the Fulbright memo—without comment to the senator, who was sitting with him on Air Force One. The rumored invasion was illegal, immoral, and impractical, the memo argued. It would be "of a piece with the hypocrisy and cynicism for which the United States is constantly denouncing the Soviet Union." U.S. military intervention would undo "the work of thirty years in trying to live down earlier interventions." Fulbright recommended restraint, for the Castro regime "is a thorn in the flesh; but it is not a dagger in the heart."

On the way back to Washington, Kennedy asked Fulbright to accompany him to the State Department that afternoon for a critical session on the Cuban plan. Fulbright soon found himself in the midst of Bissell, Rusk, McNamara, the Joint Chiefs of Staff, and others concerned with the project. Kennedy went around the room, asking top officials to answer yes or no to the landing. Only Fulbright spoke out clearly against it; he felt the President was using him "to voice his own doubts."

After that April 4 session there was no turning back, although Kennedy did not give Bissell the final green light for the initial air strikes against Castro's air bases until April 14, three days after the first troopships had left Nicaragua and only one day before the pre-invasion air raids were to take place. He had warned Bissell, "Dick, remember I reserve the right to cancel this right to the end."

During this period the White House worked frantically to prevent the press from publishing the plans. *U.S. News & World Report, The New Republic,* and *The New York Times* all had the story in remarkable detail. *U.S. News* understood "the delicacy of the situation" and did not intend to disclose military secrets. Gilbert Harrison, publisher of *The New Republic,* presented a difficult problem to Schlesinger, who had himself been opposing the operation. He sent over proofs of what Schlesinger found to be a "careful, accurate and devastating" article and asked if there was any reason not to print it. Schlesinger showed it to Kennedy, feeling "defeated by the moral issue" of whether the government should seek "to suppress the truth." Kennedy said he hoped Harrison could be persuaded not to publish it. Harrison agreed, as a "patriotic act," according to Schlesinger.

The New York Times was more stubborn. Based on what Rusk had told him, Bowles assured James Reston there would be no U.S.-backed invasion, but Tad Szulc's Cuban informants in Miami spoke emphatically otherwise. Reston went to see Allen Dulles, who denied CIA involvement but seemed to Reston to be "lying like hell." Szulc checked with his friend Don Wilson, deputy director of the U.S. Information Service under Ed Murrow. Shocked, Wilson hurried to Murrow, who was also in the dark; together they went to see Dulles, who smiled, puffed on his pipe, and said he was sorry he simply could not discuss the subject. McGeorge Bundy then called Murrow to the White House to explain the operation. Murrow said it was a terrible idea, unworthy of the United States, and that the U.S. role would be discovered. But when Bundy said nothing could stop the operation now, Murrow and Wilson decided to be "good soldiers."

Nothing could stop the *Times* from printing its story, however, except possibly the President himself. Kennedy talked with the publisher,

Orvil Dryfoos, discounting the imminence of an invasion, saying he had not even given orders to release fuel for the operation. Dryfoos worried about the paper's responsibility for national security—and for the lives of the Cuban rebels who might die on the beaches because of a premature disclosure. Editor Turner Catledge decided they would print the story, but water it down and play it down. References to the CIA and the timing of an invasion were deleted, and an unsensational headline about the training of anti-Castro units substituted. Even so, the President was furious.

On the day the troopships sailed, Reston, in a page-one story in the *Times*, reported a "sharp policy dispute" within the administration "about how far to go in helping the Cuban refugees to overthrow the Castro government." The "conflicting concepts of policy and morality have raised a flurry," wrote Reston. In fact, it was Reston who was trying to raise a flurry. Kennedy by then had silenced most of the critics within the government, or disarmed them by a firm public announcement that "there will not be, under any circumstances, any intervention in Cuba by United States armed forces." On April 14 Reston wrote a strong column against U.S. support for an invasion, reminding readers of the avowed American effort "to put some kind of ethical base under the new world order," wondering what Kennedy would do if the invaders got in trouble once they landed, and declaring the whole venture "very wrong" and an "absolute violation" of American principles.

Ted Sorensen only learned of the plan during these last days of the countdown. When he went to the President, Kennedy made it clear he didn't want to hear any more criticism. "I know everybody is grabbing their nuts on this," he said. Sorensen concluded that Kennedy, unlike the critics, was not going to be chicken. To Richard Goodwin, who opposed the plan, the President said, "Well, Dick, we're about to put your Cuban policy into action."

Robert Kennedy had not been briefed until that final week, when Bissell came to see him at the President's request. The CIA planner assured him the chances of success were about two out of three and that failure was almost impossible because if Castro was not overthrown the invaders would become guerrillas and be a major thorn in Castro's side. Afterwards, the Attorney General told Schlesinger "he was performing a disservice" in bringing the issue back to the President and that henceforth "he should remain quiet" and everyone should make "all efforts to support him."

Schlesinger finally fell into line. He wrote a new memorandum talking optimistically about the need for an astute and aggressive U.S. Ambassador to Havana to "make sure that the new regime gets off on a socially progressive track." Hedging his bet, he also recommended that if the invasion failed "we will have to be prepared to show that the alleged CIA personnel were errant idealists or soldiers of fortune working on their own." Above all, the President's reputation must be protected as "one of our greatest national resources." He advised: "When lies must be told, they should be told by subordinate officials." He endorsed "Rusk's suggestion that someone other than the President make the final decision and do so in his absence—someone whose head can later be placed on the block if things go terribly wrong."

So it happened, and things went terribly wrong. On the Friday that Kennedy gave Bissell the final go-ahead, Bowles told me he was writing a letter that he would deliver to the President. The next morning, Saturday, April 15, as Bowles prepared to leave for the White House, the news came that planes had struck the Cuban bases.

Only six B-26s, with American-trained Cuban pilots, were used because Kennedy had turned chicken (as the CIA and the Cubans would put it), or prudent. When he called Bissell to approve the strikes, he asked how many planes would be involved. When he learned there would be sixteen, the President said he didn't want it on that scale. "I want it minimal," he ordered. Bissell was so pleased that the President had not canceled the whole venture that he did not argue; he sent word that only six should fly.

Much more serious a reduction of the original plan was the decision by the President against an all-out surprise air attack simultaneous with the landing. Kennedy said it would be "too much like a World War II invasion," and too easy to tie to the United States. The President had understood the dilemma, that the smaller the political risk, the greater would be the military risk, and vice versa. On the assurance that the men could become guerrillas, he opted for the smaller political risk; and he spent much of the time in this last meeting before the landing questioning the "noise level" of the air strikes. General David Gray, who was the Pentagon's liaison to the project, urged McNamara and the Chairman of the Joint Chiefs, General Lyman Lemnitzer, to stress the "absolute necessity" of air supremacy, but this point was never clearly made. Gray pleaded with the CIA to arrange a full-scale military briefing for the President, but it was never done. It was the CIA's show, and Pentagon interference was resented.

When the wire services reported the air attacks in Cuba, Adlai Stevenson was preparing for UN debate on a long-standing Cuban complaint about U.S. plans of aggression and intervention. After the Cuban Foreign Minister reported strikes by "United States aircraft," an emergency session of the UN was called. In Washington, the State Department drafted a statement for Stevenson to read denying the Cuban charges. The planes were said to be "Castro's own," flown from Cuba by defectors from his air force; the UN was promised that the United States would "do everything it possibly can" to make sure "no Americans participate in any actions against Cuba." Assured that it had been carefully checked, Stevenson read the statement to the UN with conviction, and even flourished a photograph of one of the planes that landed in Florida with Cuban air force markings, which Stevenson said "everyone can see for himself."

The CIA propaganda chief, Dave Phillips, who was watching Stevenson on television, first thought: What a smooth, smooth phony this is! Then he realized that Stevenson didn't know the U.S. statement was a lie. Sixteen years later Rusk said, "I thought I was giving Stevenson the truth." Stevenson, who felt he had been "deliberately tricked" by his own government, considered it the "most humiliating experience" in his public life.

Kennedy was angry, because he had asked that Stevenson be fully informed so that nothing said at the UN would be less than the truth, even if not all the truth. Nothing should jeopardize the "integrity and credibility of Adlai Stevenson," he had said. From Stevenson's point of view, his integrity and credibility as Ambassador to the UN had been jeopardized by the fact that the President had not sought his advice on the project in the first place. At least the timing of the invasion might have been changed so that it did not coincide with the long-scheduled date for the UN debate on the Cuban item about alleged U.S. intervention.

Kennedy soon had far more than the UN embarrassment to regret. The advance air strikes on Saturday had not wiped out Castro's air force; a second strike was scheduled for Sunday, although the President and Rusk had understood there would be no such further air action until the invasion on Monday. With the negative UN reaction, the President and Rusk ordered the Sunday attack canceled, and required that Monday air attacks not begin until the beachhead was secured and the planes could be portrayed plausibly as Cuban-based.

Bissell and the acting CIA Director, General Charles Cabell, had protested that the cancellation would be very serious, and Rusk had accurately conveyed their case to the President, but the Secretary of State recommended that in view of Stevenson's problems in New York the raids not be reinstated. If Dulles had not been in Puerto Rico giving a speech, in order to show that nothing unusual was happening, he might have persuaded Kennedy; or Bissell might have done so, had he insisted on speaking to him. But General Cabell concluded he could not argue with the Commander in Chief and Bissell acquiesced; he was still afraid Kennedy might cancel the whole operation.

Since it was a CIA show, no one told the Joint Chiefs about the cancellation until 2 a.m. as the ships were moving close to the Bay of Pigs. "Pulling out the rug" like that, General Lemnitzer said, was "unbelievable . . . absolutely reprehensible, almost criminal." Sensing disaster, he ordered the Navy to prepare to give U.S. air cover at dawn. At 4 a.m. Kennedy was awakened with the request to approve American jet intervention from the nearby carrier *Essex*; it was too late for the exiles' planes to get there and the B-26s would not have been able to bring down Castro's fighters anyway. Kennedy held to the rule he laid down against direct U.S. military intervention, and ordered the carrier to move further out to sea and keep at least thirty miles from the Cuban shore. And there it sat, with seven U.S. destroyers, while five merchant ships and two landing craft carried the Cuban brigade into the Bay of Pigs.

The next three days saw 1,500 Cubans take, hold, and lose the beaches along the bay, fighting every step of the way, bravely, under repeated attack from Castro's air force, which dominated the sky. Contrary to the President's orders, a key American CIA agent led the Cuban frogmen ashore and fired the first shots into a Cuban army jeep. The CIA had promised its Cuban recruits that there would be complete air cover, by their own CIA-supplied B-26s, and above and beyond them by an American air "umbrella." As the air strikes were canceled and the navy jets prohibited from combat, a sense of betrayal spread, first among the CIA and navy men on the scene, and then among the Cuban invaders.

In New York the CIA's secret public relations man was awakened by a call from Howard Hunt, who dictated "Bulletin No. 1" to be released in the name of the Cuban Revolutionary Council. "Before dawn, Cuban patriots in the cities and in the hills began the battle to liberate our homeland from the despotic rule of Fidel Castro," it read. It had to be taken to one of the Cuban leaders to be translated into Spanish; he was puzzled that it was in English, if drafted by the Council chairman, as Hunt had pretended. The Council itself, which the CIA had put together with great difficulty, was flown to Miami and held incommunicado. The members, who had been given no details on the landing, pleaded to be allowed to join their forces on the beachhead, but were kept virtually as prisoners, pending the outcome of the invasion.

In Washington, the CIA cover story worked at first. Reston wrote in the *Times* that no invasion had occurred, but a landing by 200–300 Cubans, primarily to supply the anti-Castro underground. By dawn on the second day the President learned from Dulles and Bissell the dimensions of the pending catastrophe. The brigade was encircled and doomed unless the President ordered the Navy to intervene directly, and, as General Lemnitzer concluded, "It was a question of whether or not the Navy could save it if you sent them in."

Assigned to the CIA command post, Walt Rostow found an unshaven Bissell and his demoralized associates demanding that the President send the Air Force in. Rostow realized that they had never believed Kennedy would stick to his rule. "It was inconceivable to them that the President would let it openly fail when he had all this American power." The admiral commanding the Navy off Cuba kept pressing Kennedy for permission to take action, and had a stricken look when the President instead lifted one of the magnetic destroyer models and moved it further out to sea. Kennedy wanted it beyond the Cuban horizon.

That Tuesday night, in the midst of the annual Congressional Reception in the White House ballroom, Robert Kennedy interrupted Jacqueline Kennedy and Senator Smathers of Florida on the dance floor. To the senator who had often led the anti-Castro chorus, he said, "The shit has hit the fan. The thing has turned sour in a way you wouldn't believe!"

At midnight, the President, Vice-President, Secretaries of State and Defense, all in white tie, and members of the Joint Chiefs in dress uniform, met to hear Bissell's reports of Cubans dying on the beaches and a Revolutionary Council leader threatening suicide in Miami. The operation could be saved, Bissell argued, if the President would unleash the jets on the *Essex*. Kennedy said no, he had warned them "over and over again" he would not commit U.S. forces to combat. Robert Kennedy suggested that the President would have sent the jets in if it had been clear that it would make the difference. But the President had made a public promise against such direct intervention and Rusk urged that he not become a liar.

The argument raged until 2:46 a.m., and finally the President authorized a flight of six unmarked navy jets to protect the brigade's B-26s from Nicaragua, but they were not to attack ground targets. Rusk questioned this deeper commitment, but Kennedy said, "We're already in it up to here," bringing his hand up to his nose. Afterwards, Ken O'Donnell talked with the President in the Oval Office; he had "never seen him so distraught." He was "as close to crying" as O'Donnell had ever seen him. About 4 a.m. Kennedy went outside and walked by himself around the White House grounds for forty-five minutes.

In Cuba, Castro was exuberant, glad to be in battle again, certain of victory unless the "madness" of the landing by the outnumbered exiles was a prelude to an all-out assault by the United States. The Bay of Pigs was an area he knew and loved, a favorite fishing place where he went on weekends to "Fidel's key." It was far from the hills where invaders could disappear and become guerrillas. He moved fast, directing troops to contain and surround the rebels and push them back into the sea, and sending his fighter planes to blow up the supply ships and strafe the beaches.

At a funeral for the victims of the Saturday bombings, Castro told ten thousand cheering supporters, "The United States sponsored the attack because it cannot forgive us for achieving a Socialist revolution under their noses. . . ."

Five days later, while U.S. navy ships and frogmen were trying to rescue the remnants of the Cuban brigade, Castro went on television for four hours to describe his victory. All over Cuba people gathered to hear Fidel. Even his foes had to acknowledge the sense of triumph that swept the majority of their fellow citizens. "Imperialism examines geography, analyzes the number of cannons, of planes, of tanks, the positions," Castro said. "The revolutionary examines the social composition of the population. The imperialists don't give a damn about how the population . . . thinks or feels."

That same Thursday, April 20, John Kennedy asked Richard Nixon to the White House, to bring him up to date. It had been "the worst experience of my life," he told his recent rival for the presidency. "What would you do now in Cuba?" he asked Nixon. "I would find proper legal cover, and I would go in," said Nixon, who had been the first high U.S. official to decide that Castro should be overthrown, after meeting the Cuban leader in 1959. Kennedy said there was "a good chance that, if we move on Cuba, Khrushchev will move on Berlin. I just don't think we can take the risk."

Allen Dulles had told Nixon that soft-liners had "doomed the operation to failure" by the last-minute "compromises" but that "it took great courage for the President to go forward with the plan." Nixon, however, thought Kennedy had turned chicken when he canceled the air strikes and when he let the operation fail.

When a student had asked Professor Henry Kissinger what he thought about the invasion, Kissinger had told his Harvard class, "Well, as long as we're there, I don't think it would do us any good to lose." Called in only after the attack had begun, Robert Kennedy tended to agree with that judgment, and with his brother's comment, "I'd rather be an aggressor than a bum." The President had made that comment when collapse seemed imminent and he was considering whether to go in. In the last hours of the battle, while the President was out of the room, Robert Kennedy, in anguish, had told the top planners and advisers "to act or be judged paper tigers in Moscow."

Seeing that everyone was "numb" and that Rusk just pounded the arm of the President's empty chair, Walt Rostow took the Attorney General aside and said that "if you're in a fight and get knocked off your feet, the most dangerous thing was to come out swinging." This was a "time to pause and think."

That is what the President did. While Castro was proclaiming his victory John Kennedy walked with Ted Sorensen on the White House lawn. He recognized that the Bay of Pigs had been the worst defeat of his career, and that he had handed his critics a stick with which they would forever beat him. He asked Sorensen (whose advice he had not sought beforehand): "How could I have been so far off base? All my life I've known better than to depend on the experts. How could I have been so stupid, to let them go ahead?"

From beginning to end this whole venture was a case study in how not to govern and how not to deal with world affairs. At the time, I was in constant touch with Bowles, but otherwise followed events as a bystander. From my window I watched key officials hurrying in and out of the White House, and saw the President's lights burning late. When I could, I questioned the participants. Then and over the years as I probed the meaning and implications of Kennedy's decisions, it became clear that undue reliance on the experts was only one of the ways—and not the most important one—in which the President was "so far off base."

When I read the inside accounts by Sorensen and Schlesinger, the findings of General Taylor's study of the Cuban fiasco, the disclosures of Senator Church's Select Committee on U.S. intelligence activities, the transcripts of oral histories by Robert Kennedy and other participants, and then Peter Wyden's comprehensive book, *Bay of Pigs*, I realized what a weight was on the President's mind during those first months while I was pressing him for action on civil rights. Kennedy's shortness of attention and temper in regard to the Freedom Riders during the spring of 1961 was no doubt caused in part by his preoccupation with Cuba. "It even had a great physical effect on Jack," wrote Robert Kennedy, who noticed that his brother "kept shaking his head, rubbing his hands over his eyes." The President "was more upset this time than he was any other," for he "felt very strongly that the Cuba operation had materially affected . . . his standing as President and the standing of the United States in public opinion throughout the world. . . . The United States couldn't be trusted."

Sorensen and Schlesinger present the Bay of Pigs as an aberration which Kennedy corrected and did not repeat. Subsequent CIA and military actions in Cuba and Vietnam and the President's action against Bowles suggest otherwise. Kennedy's own words about the debacle acknowledge nothing more than a failure of intelligence: the faulty intelligence on Castro's air force and army, on Cuban public opinion, and on the terrain around the Bay of Pigs provided by the CIA; the inadequacy of the analysis of the battle plan by the Joint Chiefs; and his own failure to see through the puffery of the plan's proponents and get the facts. He was killed before he had shown in Indochina either greater intelligence or wisdom.

Whether or not the Bay of Pigs "made the President a different man" in any fundamental respect, as Robert Kennedy believed it did, it remains the prototype of what was wrong with America's approach to the world during the cold war—and in the administrations of John Kennedy and Lyndon Johnson. It is a failure that needs to be well analyzed.

To find out what went wrong, Kennedy asked retired General Maxwell Taylor to head a board of inquiry. On that board and in all future relations with the CIA, the Attorney General, at his brother's request, played a leading part.

After six weeks of intensive investigation, Taylor and Robert Kennedy attributed much of the basic misjudgment in not stopping the project to the inexperience of the new administration and to the confusion in government during the changing of the watch. Taylor surmised how John Kennedy must have felt about the legacy that Eisenhower had dumped in his lap: "The greatest military man in America, the President of the United States, got this thing going and gave it to the CIA. Why should I, a young President who doesn't even know the telephone numbers in the White House, rush in and try to challenge the basic assumptions?" Moreover, Robert Kennedy pointed out, his brother had relied uncritically on the CIA, military, and State Department experts in large part because he hadn't had a chance to work with them and learn how to measure their advice. And the new Kennedy advisers—including the Secretaries of State and Defense—didn't yet know him or each other very well. They were a green team and it had come upon them too soon, with too much momentum to stop.

"It was Eisenhower's plan, Eisenhower's people all said it would succeed," said Robert Kennedy. If his brother "hadn't gone ahead with it, everybody would have said it showed he had no courage. . . ." Allen Dulles himself conceded afterwards that he had repeatedly implied that if Kennedy backed out, he would appear less zealous than Eisenhower in the fight against Communism. The CIA chief regretted having done so. "I should have realized that, if he had no enthusiasm about the idea in the first place, he would drop it at the first opportunity rather than do the things necessary to make it succeed."

On the other hand, Maxwell Taylor concluded, the failure had not come from Kennedy's cancellation of the air strikes or other modifications made as a result of the change of administrations. With 200,000 troops and militiamen, Castro could not have been defeated without direct American military intervention, and the American role could never have been kept secret. Therefore, Taylor's report concluded that the Eisenhower administration should have assigned the project to the Defense Department as an overt mission of the armed forces, or, "failing such a reorientation, the project should have been abandoned."

Part of the confusion came from John Kennedy's spontaneous, unsystematic, ad hoc form of decision-making. Robert Kennedy defended the President's unstructured approach to the critical General Taylor, saying, "My brother doesn't think the way you do. He thinks about issues and people." But many of the people involved in the deliberations did not think the President's way of jumping from point to point and ignoring all chains of command produced the right choices. Rusk's usual reticence was reinforced when he found junior officials at a table with him and the President went around the room asking everyone's opinion, with no deference paid to the Secretary of State.

The crucial meeting of April 4, to which Kennedy had unexpectedly brought Fulbright, came under special fire. The CIA's William Bundy (McGeorge's brother) thought the senator's presence turned the critical strategy session into a "charade," forcing Executive Branch officials to feel they had to line up loyally behind the plan. Assistant Secretary of Defense Paul Nitze was disgusted that at the last minute, because of Fulbright, the focus was on the morality of the invasion. The real issue, he thought, was not "should" but "would it succeed?" and he did not get the opportunity to give his own judgment that the odds were less than fifty-fifty for an early success. When Kennedy asked him to vote yes or no, Nitze was unhappy with himself: "I should have had the guts to give a complicated answer." When Latin American adviser Adolf Berle started to give a long reply, Kennedy asked him just to vote, and the old New Dealer said, "Let 'er rip." Though the result was what Bill Bundy wanted, he said to himself, "This is not the right way to do it."

Later, during the first critical hours when the invasion was failing, Kennedy still did not ask the right questions, according to Assistant Secretary of State Harlan Cleveland, who was the liaison to Adlai Stevenson. The President would ask a "very specific question about some little piece of the jigsaw puzzle" but he gave no sense of having a view of the whole puzzle. Cleveland, an experienced administrator, was impressed by how fast Kennedy recovered psychologically and was able to reinstill confidence, but thought it was obvious that the President's main prior executive experience had been as commander of a PT boat.

A PT boat commander thinks in terms of the immediate action, and learns to respond with great speed and skill to unexpected dangers; he is not responsible for overall planning or long-range goals. The Bay of Pigs experience should have somewhat shaken the President's conviction, born in PT boat 109 in the Solomons and strengthened in each of his election campaigns, that the finest strategies are usually the result of accidents.

Another source of confusion was the self-deceiving nature of covert action and of the twilight world of the CIA. Neither an armed force proper nor a true civilian agency, operating in peace as if in war, the CIA was a secret state of its own.

"The emphasis on utmost secrecy did not permit the usual staffing," Admiral Arleigh Burke, who had been in charge of naval operations, told the Taylor board of inquiry. That was an understatement. Not only was the venture kept from obvious potential critics such as Bowles and Stevenson, it was kept from the regular planning staffs of the Army, Navy, Air Force, and Marines, and from the director of the State Department's Bureau of Intelligence and Research. A former OSS man who had fought with Merrill's Marauders in the China-Burma theater, the department's intelligence chief, Roger Hilsman, accidentally got wind of the plans for the Cuban brigade. When he asked Rusk to let his office study whether there were realistic prospects for a popular revolt against Castro, without which the invaders would have little chance to win, the Secretary said, "I'm sorry, but I can't let you. This is being too tightly held."

It was so tightly held by the CIA that the President wasn't informed of significant facts, large and small. Contrary to Kennedy's orders, Bissell had authorized bombing missions by half a dozen American pilots (from the Alabama National Guard and from the CIA itself), and four were killed. Kennedy did not learn the truth until almost two years later when Republican Senator Everett Dirksen of Illinois discovered and disclosed the facts. On instructions from the CIA, the President's Air Force aide, General Godfrey McHugh, had written the mother of one of the dead fliers that "neither the CIA nor any other government agency possesses the slightest pertinent information on your son's disappearance." Kennedy called McHugh at midnight and asked, "Godfrey, how could you do this to me? The whole Senate is after me! And how could you lie to that poor woman?" McHugh had not known the truth either.

So pervasive was the deception that Bissell never saw fit to correct the President's impression that if the first assault failed, the brigade could melt into the mountains and be a thorn in Castro's side. With the brigade all ready to go, Kennedy thought it better to "dump" them in Cuba "where they want to go," than to try to bring them back to the United States, where they would be a thorn in his side. It was on this assumption that Kennedy had scaled down the operation to what he considered a large-scale infiltration instead of an invasion. With swamps and open fields for miles around the Bay of Pigs and the mountains eighty miles away, that was never a realistic assumption.

Bissell was convinced that the logic of events would force the President to give the necessary direct military help, if the CIA could just land the brigade on the beach. Meanwhile he had to keep Kennedy's intentions and his own contingency plans secret, especially from his own men and from the Cuban exiles, who were being promised complete air cover. So there was misunderstanding up and down the line. When the President publicly pledged that no U.S. forces would be used, CIA man Howard Hunt did not take him seriously. "The statement was, we thought, a superb effort in misdirection," Hunt wrote, after he had gone on from his work as political action chief for the Cuban brigade to his no more successful efforts at Watergate.

Secrecy may lead to disastrous consequences, but it is very seductive, especially in high places, where it generates an aura of power. After the Bay of Pigs, Kennedy commented that he found it easy to overrule people pressing for action in domestic politics, "but you always assume that the military and intelligence people have some secret skill not available to ordinary mortals." In fact, Kennedy was not so awed by the military, having seen firsthand in the Navy that the admirals were ordinary mortals, and he backed McNamara strongly in asserting civilian control over the Pentagon. But the CIA was another thing, and the

Director of the CIA and his chief of covert operations, with more secrets in their heads than any other men in America, used their power with great skill.

In early 1961, Dulles and Bissell moved rapidly to demonstrate their power and skill to the key Kennedy men. The CIA Director invited some dozen White House aides close to the President to a dinner and long evening at Washington's little-known Alibi Club with the top ten CIA men. After most had relaxed with several cocktails, the inside stories of past secret exploits were recounted; it was heady wine. Bissell was asked to introduce himself and talk about his work. "I'm your man-eating shark," he said. CIA man Robert Amory thought that Bissell had set just the right note, that it was good to have got "a head start on State," and that Dulles had been correct: the New Frontiersmen would respond best to a "New Yorkerish type of précis."

Speed was certainly one of the skills Kennedy appreciated. He liked shortcuts. Before long McGeorge Bundy reported to Amory that the President had said, "By gosh, I don't care what it is, but if I need some material fast or an idea fast, CIA is the place I have to go. The State Department takes four or five days to answer a simple yes or no." This was music to CIA ears, as Peter Wyden wrote: "Eisenhower's cumbersome coordinating committees were scrapped. The intelligence business was fun again."

In sensing the Kennedy inner circle's penchant for a "New Yorker-ish type of précis," the top CIA men were closer to the mark than they ever were in staking out Castro. Hyannis, Harvard, Yale, and George-town were easier for them to understand than the Sierra Maestra. The style, taste, prejudices, and presumptions of the set most immediately around Kennedy, and of the President himself, made them especially susceptible to a CIA "intellectual" like Bissell.

Six feet three inches tall, considered by many to be a genius and by others a walking computer, with restless energy, intellectual curiosity, and physical daring, Richard Bissell was a natural and unusual leader whom people of diverse views looked up to and listened to with awe. During the 1960 talent search his name kept being suggested for key posts, with liberals and conservatives alike treating him as the epitome of the brightest and best for whom we were hunting. Under his driving, brilliant leadership, the U-2 had been built in two years and at 70,000 feet was photographing minute details of Soviet missile sites. When a U-2 was shot down over Russia in May 1960, government spokesmen lied about it, on Bissell's assurance that the pilot could not survive. Briefly Bissell's reputation was clouded when Gary Powers did survive and

Eisenhower decided to admit the deception and take responsibility for the aerial espionage. Khrushchev broke up a summit meeting over Eisenhower's admission. Then in August, under Bissell's direction, an American reconnaissance satellite was put in orbit, and his star was high again as he began planning to overthrow Castro.

When Chester Bowles was appointed Undersecretary of State, I was not surprised that his first thought was to get Bissell to become the Deputy Undersecretary for Political Affairs. When we came back from our ten-week trip to Eastern Europe, the Soviet Union, Afghanistan, Pakistan, and India in 1957, Bissell was high on Bowles's list to see. They had been friends and sailing companions since the 1930s, when Bissell had taught economics at Yale and later, in the 1940s, served Bowles as an assistant in the wartime Office of Price Administration. Through the years Bowles had kept in regular touch with the brilliant economist and political analyst. He admired Bissell's work on the Marshall Plan and understood why in the early 1950s his impatient, imaginative, and tough-minded friend would find greater scope with fewer bureaucratic or congressional limitations in the CIA. With its flexible and largely secret budget, the agency could always "find the money."

"I admire and believe in the use of power, when it's available, for purposes that I regard as legitimate," Bissell said. Since Bissell seemed to agree with Bowles's views on India and the developing nations, and on many other foreign policy issues they discussed, Bowles assumed that most of the purposes for which Bissell used power were legitimate. Indeed, many of the CIA's covert operations in other countries supported, financially and otherwise, the anti-Communist left and progressive political forces Bowles favored. Bissell was interested in Bowles's proposal. It would be a new challenge and he was already all but at the top of the CIA. With a vigorous young President, perhaps he could help shake up the State Department and get foreign policy moving out of its ruts. Thinking that Bissell would be skillful in dealing with the old Foreign Service hands, Bowles went to great lengths to convince Dulles to let his deputy go.

It would have been an interesting alliance. Dulles had said Bissell was busy on a project and couldn't be spared just then, but Bowles thought that in due course the appointment would go through. Then the President informed him that he couldn't have Bissell because before long he was going to take Allen Dulles's job. When Bissell learned of this conversation, he gained an even greater vested interest in making the Cuban project a success. His chance of heading the CIA and having all that power to use for purposes he regarded as legitimate depended on the outcome at the Bay of Pigs.

At first, Bowles was delighted that he might have an ally at the top of the CIA. Then two months later he was horrified to hear Bissell brief the National Security Council on plans for the Cuban invasion. That the worst proposal he had ever heard was coming from the man he considered the best in the CIA added to his shock, and contributed to his silence that day. His respect for Bissell was one of the reasons he did not insist upon taking the fight against the Cuban landing directly to the President, in a personal confrontation.

Bowles's recommendation of Bissell may also have been a factor in Kennedy's own response to the plan for the Bay of Pigs. That even the liberal Chester Bowles so respected Bissell enhanced the CIA planner's reputation. The President knew that Joseph Alsop revered his close childhood friend and Groton classmate (although Alsop also saw Bissell as "a terrific dominator" who ran his friends' lives if they let him). Anyone championed by both Alsop and Bowles couldn't be all wrong. Moreover, both Bundy brothers and Walt Rostow had been Bissell's admiring students at Yale. Rostow said, "Part of my growing up was learning to articulate differences with this most articulate man that has ever been." That turned out to be part of Kennedy's growing up, too.

The President had much in common with the CIA's chief of covert operations. Bissell represented part of what Kennedy enjoyed and wanted to be. As a student at Yale, Bissell became the leader of what one colleague called "a brilliant coterie of iconoclasts, loud in speech, brutal in analysis, enthusiastically uninhibited in their attack on the old tribal gods." They were rebels who "placed a special trust in the intellect" and believed that "by taking thought they could evolve a new and better world." Bissell's style was witty, terse, and elegant, his view of the world hard-nosed and ironic, and he got things done. Bissell and other leaders of the intelligence community meshed better with the Kennedy men than with their Republican predecessors, who tended to be less sophisticated and more inhibited by middle-class morality.

When I was told that Bowles was not brought into the councils on the Bay of Pigs because he would be boring, I began to comprehend the kind of closure at the center of what from a distance seemed such an open New Frontier. The President was open to any view, any analysis, any person, no matter how iconoclastic, with one limitation: Kennedy did not want to be bored.

Man-eating sharks, brutal analysis, and covert action were not boring. Lectures about morality, legality, and principles were. The secret use of power (to overthrow Castro or Diem) was not boring. The public support of Nehru or Nyerere was. Foreign aid and even perhaps the

Peace Corps were boring. The CIA was not. Chester Bowles was often boring. Richard Bissell never was.

The witty, rough, sardonic language that Kennedy liked was stimulating, but the degree to which this style dominated the White House and became the common denominator of those to whom the President listened was self-defeating. Ted Sorensen, perhaps the most earnest and least cynical of the President's close colleagues, saw Kennedy as having won an inner struggle between the lure of luxury and statesmanship. In the White House that struggle seemed to me to be continuing, in new forms: it was a luxury to insist on not being bored.

Years later, while reading S. P. Rosenbaum's book *The Bloomsbury Group*, I noted Leonard Woolf's remark that in Bloomsbury "one hesitated to say anything true or profound unless it was also amusing." Looking back on the heady days when many people were afraid of Virginia Woolf and their clever, irreverent, self-centered set, Leonard Woolf did not think so well of this trait. "In my experience," he said, "what is amusing is very rarely true or profound, and what is true or profound is hardly ever amusing."

In the Kennedy White House there was the same hesitation about saying anything unless it was amusing. That syndrome inhibited questions of principle and purpose, and strengthened the hand of those who knew how to talk about power with wit and sophistication. In silencing potential critics and giving short shrift to the more profound questions, this frame of mind contributed to the bad intelligence the President blamed for his mistake in approving the Cuban landing.

At the critical meeting of April 4, when the consensus was reached to go ahead, Rusk had brushed aside the fundamental moral and legal issues by arguing that success would be self-legitimizing, like Castro's own victory or the American Revolution. Equally proud of his pragmatism, the CIA's Bill Bundy dismissed Fulbright's concern about the political factors—of international law and public opinion—thinking to himself, "Damn it to hell, these are bridges we crossed long ago." The bridges had been crossed without anyone in the inner circle pressing the most important questions.

If the Bloomsbury syndrome was a factor in the "groupthink" that led to the Bay of Pigs, in other ways the Kennedy set was the opposite of Bloomsbury. There was nothing effete about John and Robert Kennedy's approach to politics. They were attracted to those who talked tough and were not afraid to use power. Bissell had these qualities in abundance. Schlesinger tells how the President and his chief national security advisers sat "transfixed" in the Cabinet Room while Bissell, pointer in hand, explained how the invasion would go. They were "fascinated by the workings of this superbly clear, organized and articulate intelligence." In retrospect, the project's manifest lack of clarity suggests that the fascination with Bissell must have had some source other than his sheer intelligence.

Part of the explanation may lie in Kennedy's yearning for adventure, a vicarious form of which was his fondness for James Bond stories. (It was said that the President once asked the CIA to help him meet an 007-type agent, and a pistol-carrying, martini-drinking adventurer was found and sent over to the White House.) Bissell did not carry guns, but dealt boldly with far more sophisticated methods of destruction and was at the center of the government's most dangerous adventures. Bissell was like a character out of literature, a figure larger than life, engaged in plots more important than any James Bond fantasy.

In his heyday, the CIA's chief of covert operations was something like the Grand Inquisitor of Ivan Karamazov's imagination. He stood at the command post of a secret order prepared to pay any price, bear any burden, meet any hardship, use any force, commit any crime to advance the interests of the United States or to save mankind from Communism. His reconnaissance satellites were circling the globe, seeing everything that moved; his agents were at work on every continent, supporting America's friends, opposing its foes. Like the Spanish Inquisitor, he had taken the sword of Caesar and accepted lying and deception, death and destruction, in order to accomplish the purposes he considered legitimate. And he, too, dared the moralists to judge him, for he had joined what Dostoevsky called "the clever people."

John Kennedy was never one to pose as a messiah—or a moralist. He listened—too long—to the chief of covert operations as if Bissell were not an ordinary mortal. Then finally Kennedy's strong sanity and sense of balance prevailed, and he parted company with that "most articulate man that has ever been." At some point, perhaps when the Cubans were dying on the beach and Bissell was asking him to go to war against Castro, Kennedy saw through the "secret skill" of the CIA's master planner, and turned back from what he finally realized was madness.

After the debacle, the President decided that Bissell must go, but he carried through the firing gently and with respect. He explained to Bissell: "If this were the British government, I would resign, and you, being a senior civil servant, would remain. But it isn't. In our government, you and Allen have to go, and I have to remain." In a public ceremony, Kennedy bestowed on Bissell the Medal of Freedom, the nation's highest civilian honor.

Four years later, the former chief of covert operations declared himself "on balance, unregenerate." In his first public defense Bissell told the Washington *Evening Star* in 1965 that "if we had been able to dump five times the tonnage of bombs on Castro's airfields, we would have had a damned good chance."

How far did Kennedy and Bissell part company? How much did the President learn from the whole experience? Did he ever come to agree with the point made after the invasion had failed by a member of Stevenson's staff, Clayton Fritchey? "Mr. President, it could have been worse." Kennedy wanted to know how, and seemed taken aback when Fritchey replied, "It might have succeeded."

Machismo was not a minor factor in Kennedy's makeup and it must have hurt him to know that the Cuban "freedom fighters," the CIA and navy participants, and millions of Americans considered him a coward. When the American who went ashore and fired the first shots at the Bay of Pigs found out that it was the President who said no to the air strikes and to further U.S. military intervention, he was "absolutely shocked." Having voted enthusiastically for Kennedy, Gray Lynch said it was like "finding out that Superman is a fairy."

But the one acting like Superman was Bissell, not Kennedy. Except for his letting Bissell go ahead at all, Kennedy at each critical point resisted pressure for escalation. If Kennedy lacked courage, it was first of all when he agreed to the project, fearing (as Lyndon Johnson was to fear in an Asian context) that if he didn't proceed he would be called coward, traitor, weakling, and that Nixon would be there saying he had betrayed Eisenhower's commitment to liberate Cuba.

When a Gallup poll two weeks after the invasion showed that support for the President had gone up to an unprecedented 82 percent, Kennedy dismissed it, saying, "It's just like Eisenhower. The worse I do, the more popular I get . . . If I had gone further, they would have liked me even more."

Kennedy seemed to be gaining respect for a new form of courage, the courage of self-restraint, including the courage to refrain from unwise gutsy action even if this opened you to the charge of cowardice. He also indicated a greater openness to public challenge from the press. To the *New York Times* publisher Dryfoos, whom he had urged to squelch the story of the invasion plan, he said afterwards, "I wish you had run everything on Cuba . . . at the time." To *Times* editor Catledge, he said, "Maybe if you had printed more about the operation you would have saved us from a colossal mistake."

As the fighting on the beach was coming to an end, the President said, "It's a hell of a way to learn things, but I have learned one thing from this business—that is, that we will have to deal with CIA." To save himself from future colossal mistakes, he vowed henceforth to involve his brother Robert in all critical foreign policy, intelligence, and defense decisions. He could expect the "unvarnished truth" from his brother, who would not be afraid to ask the experts the toughest questions. "I made a mistake in putting Bobby in the Justice Department," he said. "Bobby should be in CIA."

If only the Cuban story could end here, with a wiser and better advised President going on to more constructive efforts in the world. But Robert Kennedy's own machismo then came into play in American foreign policy with a vengeance, and the President's competitive instincts drove him to seek other, more sophisticated ways to destroy Castro. Throughout 1961 and most of 1962, they, too, on the question of Castro remained on balance unregenerate.

One indication of the President's and Robert Kennedy's response to all this was the downfall of Chester Bowles. A generation later, it is difficult to recall what Bowles represented to many Americans. Not only had he been right about the Bay of Pigs; for more than a decade he had been laying the foundations among the public for a new foreign policy that would point in the opposite direction from the CIA's action in Cuba. Along with Justice Douglas, Bowles had opposed the CIA intervention in Iran to overthrow Prime Minister Mossadegh and bring back the Shah. Although the Kennedys (and Nixon) tended to view the former governor, ambassador, congressman, and OPA chief as a liberal ideologue, in his talks around the country and through his writings Bowles had been able to reach beyond the liberal Democratic constituency to appeal to a wide cross section of Democrats, Republicans, and independents. For many of them, as for me, Bowles's standing within the administration was a test of the President's intentions in foreign policy.

The week after the defeat at the Bay of Pigs, Bowles attended a meeting of the National Security Council at the President's request. It was "the grimmest gathering in my experience in government," Bowles said afterwards. He found the thirty or so highest officials of the government "emotional, almost savage" in their response. "The President and the U.S. government had been humiliated and something must be done" was the consensus.

The militant "get Castro" mood alarmed Bowles, who noted that Robert Kennedy and Lyndon Johnson, as newcomers to the foreign field, were easy targets for the "military-CIA-paramilitary type answers" that predominated in the discussion. Afterwards, "as a friend," Bowles asked to speak to the President, who had appeared to be the calmest man in the meeting. He urged Kennedy to resist the pressure to retaliate and not to let the situation "deteriorate into a head-to-head personal contest between the President of the United States and Fidel Castro."

At a second National Security Council meeting three days later, Bowles argued against proposals that the United States should move directly against Castro. Such an invasion, he contended, would "compound the disaster" and "even if it succeeded, Castro would emerge as the hero in what would surely be viewed throughout the world as a struggle between David and Goliath." He felt his argument was brushed aside.

At the third meeting, however, the invasion was dropped. The emphasis was on clandestine harassment and possibly economic sanctions against nations such as Mexico and Brazil which had voted in the UN to condemn the United States. The President vetoed the sanctions, saying that we had no alternative but to live with the humiliation our error had created and respect the attitudes of other nations who had disagreed with our actions.

Later that day Bowles found that the State Department cable drafted for the guidance of all U.S. embassies misrepresented the President's decision and seemed to instruct American envoys to bring pressure on their host governments to cut relations with Castro and sever trade with Cuba. Bowles got Rusk to change the wording to reflect the President's more moderate views.

Encouraged by the President's attitude, Bowles recommended a drastic reform: the dismantling of the CIA and absorption of its noncovert functions by offices directly responsible to the State Department. Soon after the inauguration, he had proposed a more limited reorganization of the CIA, but the Bay of Pigs experience convinced him that a complete change was required. The President, however, was not prepared to take on the CIA in a major political battle, and since he was no more affirmative toward the State Department than toward the CIA, he was unlikely to see their combination as any gain.

The President's and the department's leadership were on trial throughout the spring of 1961 on the issue of Laos, where another Cuban situation, or something worse, was developing. Between Kennedy's election and his inauguration, the Far Eastern Bureau of the State Department and the CIA helped to engineer a rightist coup against the neutralist regime of Prince Souvanna Phouma. In the first discussions of Laos within the new administration Bowles urged steps toward neutralization

365

but found a surprising consensus in favor of military intervention if necessary to save the American-backed regime.

At a White House meeting in mid-March, Bowles pressed the Pentagon for their contingency plans in case the Chinese came in to prevent an American military presence just south of their border. In response, he was shown a study which concluded that the Chinese could be kept out of Southeast Asia by 300,000 U.S. troops plus assistance from our allies, but admitted that at some stage nuclear weapons would probably be required. If this occurred, the scenario continued, the Russians could be expected to introduce their volunteers supported by nuclear weapons.

The thought that America should attempt to "save Laos" by a nuclear attack struck Bowles as preposterous. With the support of Ambassador-at-Large Averell Harriman, he pushed hard for an alternative: American support for the neutralist Souvanna Phouma.

The pendulum swung back and forth between military intervention in Laos and a political solution. To show that his restraint in Cuba during the invasion did not mean the United States was going to abandon its friends in Laos, the President, over Bowles's opposition, ordered American military advisers in Laos to wear military uniforms instead of their previous inconspicuous civilian clothes. Then in May quiet British-Soviet negotiation produced an agreement on a cease-fire and the convening of a fourteen-nation conference at Geneva to seek a political settlement. Hard-liners contended that the Soviets had agreed to compromise because of the threat of U.S. force. Bowles believed that their readiness to negotiate more likely arose from Moscow's and Hanoi's unwillingness to see Laos "saved" by Chinese intervention. Kennedy was said to have wryly asked how we could expect to stop Communism with U.S. troops in Laos if we couldn't do so in Cuba. Harriman was sent to Geneva with instructions not to come back without a settlement. The accords finally reached bought time for the people of Laos, but before long the growing war in South Vietnam spilled over and the Ho Chi Minh Trail through Laos became a major military problem.

During this period there were other pressures for U.S. military intervention, which Bowles helped to resist. On May 30, 1961, the Dominican dictator Trujillo was assassinated with U.S. assistance (which Bowles approved) to those planning the coup, and there was fear that if the United States didn't move in to establish a pro-American regime Castro would take over. On the more critical military front in Europe, Khrushchev began challenging Kennedy in Berlin, and the case was made in high policy-planning circles that to underline American firmness (especially after Cuba) the President should send heavily armored convoys up the Autobahn to Berlin. Bowles attacked this as a provocative game of Russian roulette.

Looking back on the first six months of the Kennedy administration, Bowles was uneasy. American armed forces had not been sent into action in Cuba, Indochina, the Dominican Republic, or on the Autobahn, but all of these affairs were cliff-hangers. He was concerned about the narrow perspectives of the "military mind," and the undue influence military leaders had on primarily political questions. But that did not fully explain the tendency of the Democratic administration to reach for military answers to political problems. Bowles thought "militarized liberals" were in part a reaction to years of being charged with softness on Communism. However, a larger reason for the narrow escapes, he began to fear, was the new administration's—and Kennedy's—lack of "a genuine sense of conviction about what is right and wrong." After one particularly disturbing White House session, Bowles wrote in his journal:

> Anyone in public life who has strong convictions about the rights and wrongs of public morality, both domestic and international, has a very great advantage in times of strain, since his instincts on what to do are clear and immediate. Lacking such a framework of moral conviction or sense of what is right and what is wrong, he is forced to lean almost entirely on his mental processes; he adds up the plusses and minuses of any question and comes up with a conclusion. Under normal conditions, when he is not tired or frustrated, this pragmatic approach should successfully bring him out on the right side of a question.
>
> What worries me are the conclusions that such an individual may reach when he is tired, angry, frustrated or emotionally affected. The Cuban fiasco demonstrates how far astray a man as brilliant and well-intentioned as President Kennedy can go who lacks a basic moral reference point.

From Bowles's standpoint, Kennedy was soon to go further astray.

In late June, Bowles gave Rusk a detailed, well-argued memorandum reviewing their first six months and proposing new directions for American foreign policy. Reading it nearly twenty years later in Bowles's book *Promises to Keep*, I feel as I did when he showed it to me in draft form: What a different history there might be if American foreign policy would ever really go in the direction he pointed!

Although Rusk may not have disagreed with Bowles's specific prescriptions for China, Southeast Asia, Southern Africa, or Latin America, the whole approach was the antithesis of how the Secretary operated. According to Samuel Lewis, a perceptive young Foreign Service officer,

Rusk was an orderly "staff man" who believed in the organization over which he presided, trusted the experts who made it up, and was conscious "of the limited power of men to alter broad courses of events." In contrast, Bowles was impatient with the career staff's endemic caution, and confident of "the power of talented men to make a real imprint on the tides of history if they boldly strike out to do so."

In his memorandum to Rusk, Bowles had said that "there are two ways for the State Department to deal with the President. One is to find out where we think he is going and to help him get there. The other is to determine what we think is right for him to do, and then vigorously and thoughtfully to present our case, even though he may disagree with it and even though our views may on occasion bring us into conflict with the Pentagon and other agencies. This latter approach is, I believe, the only responsible course." It was a course that Rusk was probably constitutionally unable to take.

Bowles's effort boomeranged. In early July, Rusk told his Undersecretary: "Last night, I was thinking of the frustrating job you have and how unhappy it must make you." Instead of responding to the memorandum on new directions, Rusk asked, "Why don't you free yourself from the department and take on the job of roving ambassador?" When Bowles asked him to say frankly whether this was his or the President's idea, Rusk said it was Kennedy's.

The President promptly invited Bowles to lunch, took him for a swim in the White House pool and then upstairs to the family quarters, and outlined his thinking. According to Bowles, Kennedy said that he might have made a mistake in not making Bowles Secretary of State, and that if he had done so, things might have been different. However, Rusk was Secretary, and the department had not come through with the new policy approaches the President had wanted. This called for some changes. While he knew the shortcomings of the department could not reasonably be blamed on Bowles, the Undersecretary was the logical target. He asked Bowles whether he would like to go as Ambassador to Chile. Bowles said he wasn't interested in an embassy, but would like to come back and tell the President in detail what he had been trying to do in the State Department and what he thought the problems were. They agreed to meet again the following week.

When Bowles described these conversations to me, I was astounded. That he should be the scapegoat for the department's weaknesses, which he was trying more than anyone else to overcome, seemed too absurd to believe. Vividly remembering Pierre Salinger's fury against Bowles at the time of the Cuban invasion, I could not help thinking that Bowles's opposition then was a major factor behind this action ten weeks later.

Press accounts had described Robert Kennedy as angrily accosting Bowles at a White House meeting, jamming his fingers into Bowles's stomach, and saying that Bowles may have been against the landing once but he better damn well be for it now. Bowles said there had been no such physical assault but that Bob's anger had been made very clear. It seemed to me the kind of case Bowles had rightly feared: in the aftermath of a humiliating defeat, tired, angry, frustrated people, without a basic moral reference point, were striking out at the wrong target.

What made it so confounding was the President's own strong and convincing statements agreeing with Bowles's basic approach. In a blow-by-blow account to Adlai Stevenson (then in Italy), Bowles wrote of the luncheon with Kennedy that "I have never heard the President talk as thoughtfully and passionately on foreign affairs. He said precisely the things you and I have been advocating for years, and he said them well." Stevenson, by telephone, and others of us close to Bowles in Washington, including Abram Chayes, Thomas Hughes, James Thomson, Mennen Williams, and Orville Freeman, urged Bowles to stand and fight and not quietly resign and take an ambassadorship. I wrote and hand-delivered the following memorandum to the President on July 15:

> Since one of the obligations of loyalty to you is to speak plainly about matters that seem important, I must give you some of the reasons why I believe that firing Bowles would be a serious mistake.
>
> 1. *It would be a setback to the United States in the world.* Bowles is the chief symbol of a policy of supporting the developing nations, of sympathizing with independence forces, and of respecting uncommitted countries. He is understood to be the one high Department official who opposed the Cuban invasion. For his to be the first head to fall in the aftermath of Cuba . . . would be a bad sign to many key people in Africa, Asia, and Latin America.
>
> 2. *It would be a setback politically at home.* The firing of any top and symbolic figure is an important act. For the first such act of your Administration to be the firing of Bowles would be a signal to all his friends in the country—and to the supporters of Stevenson, Humphrey, Williams, and Reuther—that you are turning away from them and their view of the world. . . . There is a feeling among them that there is little new, aside from the Peace Corps and our position on Angola, and that the Democratic foreign policy is in danger of being merely a more elegant version of John Foster Dulles. . . .
>
> 3. *It would be a setback in the State Department itself.* In symbol and in fact Bowles is the central figure in the Department who has been trying to introduce new ideas, people, and procedures. A fair appraisal of the last six months would give Bowles a great deal of credit for most of the encouraging things done in and by the Department—and credit for blocking some of the potentially disastrous things. . . .

To such efforts the resistance of old-line Foreign Service Officers and old-school, Europe-first policy makers was to be expected. These are the same people who attacked you—on much the same grounds—in 1957 when you proposed this approach in your Algerian speech.

To cut down the one person in the Department who has been doing his best to reform the Department is the wrong therapy, if reform is what you want. All the wrong forces in the Department and in the Foreign Service will be reinforced—and most of the New Frontier type people will be dismayed. To cut Bowles down in the name of more vigorous action to reform the Foreign Service, when the chief opposition to Bowles is because he has been too vigorous in his efforts of reform, makes even less sense.

4. *It would be a setback for you in your efforts to devise a new foreign policy.* Rather than conclude that you can do without Bowles, I would think that the events of the last six months—Cuba, Laos, Angola, Berlin —would convince you that you need him more than ever in your policy planning. You need someone who, from the time he wakes up in the morning until he goes to sleep, knows that the Cuban invasion is wrong and that our new position on Angola is right . . . someone who, if given a chance, will argue strongly from this special view of the world. If Bowles goes, I don't know who else you have at the top level ready or able to do this. I do not mean that you should always take Bowles' advice—but it needs to be there steadily and to be heard.

I knew this was not a memorandum the President would like. In a personal addendum, I emphasized that although Bowles was "one of the men who, after you, and along with Sargent Shriver, I would go through fire for," my chief concern was not for Bowles but for "the unfortunate public effects such an action would have." I was for firing people, even close friends, when called for, but this was "the wrong firing, at the wrong time, of the wrong views, in the wrong Department." Kennedy skimmed through the memorandum, nodded, and said he would read it; in two days he was to see Bowles again and decide what to do.

During those days, newspapers carried front-page stories about Bowles's impending resignation. The President's close friend, columnist Charles Bartlett, asserted that numerous Foreign Service officers were angry at Bowles because so many senior men had been asked to retire, and that they were "in short, after his scalp." Joseph Alsop and Rowland Evans joined the fray: "highly placed White House spokesmen" were said to charge that Bowles was at home only with "big thoughts," and "members of Kennedy's political staff" were said to carry a grudge against him because of his refusal in 1960 to campaign against Humphrey in Wisconsin. At a Georgetown dinner, McGeorge Bundy said to the State Department's legal adviser (and fellow Harvard faculty colleague), Abram Chayes, that no one in the White House knew precisely who was responsible for the lack of direction and initiative in the State Department but that changes would have to be made, and "you can't change Rusk." To fire Rusk after only six months would reflect on the President's judgment in picking him; that left Bowles the natural one to go. Arthur Schlesinger was to write that Bowles was "the hapless victim of the conditions which he had diagnosed better than anybody else."

At a party with several Foreign Service officers, one of the department's most respected "old hands" told me that the trouble with Chet Bowles and Soapy Williams was that when they saw a band of black baboons beating tom-toms they saw George Washingtons. Another said that Bowles wanted our diplomats to put on sarongs and make love to the natives. A journalist with close ties to both the CIA and the White House announced that they need not worry about Bowles since his days in the department were numbered. The older Foreign Service officer raised his glass and toasted: "One down and Williams to go!"

Bowles's supporters were also galvanized and Kennedy received a wave of calls and letters from rank-and-file Democrats around the country as well as from leaders such as Stevenson and Walter Reuther. An editorial in the Washington *Post* on the "first full-scale internal political hurricane of the Kennedy Administration" commended Bowles for his work as an experienced executive "in straightening out the administrative jungle of the State Department" and listed a number of substantial achievements. The *Post* concluded that "his most grievous offense is that he is still Chester Bowles. It is pretty hard for him not to be that."

When Bowles returned to Kennedy on July 17, he showed the President several basic foreign policy memorandums he had written, including his warning against the Cuban landing. Saying that none of these had reached him, Kennedy read them, conveyed strong interest, and said that Bowles should proceed with his plans for a series of meetings with American ambassadors in Africa, the Middle East, and Asia. On his return they would continue their discussions about the department; meanwhile, the President said he would make a public statement confirming that Bowles was staying on as Undersecretary.

Pierre Salinger's press briefing, however, was far from reassuring. Saying that Bowles's resignation was "not currently expected," Salinger muttered off-the-record to at least one newsman that he might not be around for very long. But on Bowles's return in late August, he found Kennedy warm, friendly, and full of good questions; the President asked him for a private memorandum outlining the changes he would recommend in the department. For a while there was no further talk of his displacement as Undersecretary.

Then a widely syndicated column by Joseph Alsop stirred the issue again. Kennedy and Rusk were ridiculed for allowing themselves to be manipulated by Bowles and a lot of "wild liberals." Alsop added that the President "would have made no audible protest if Bowles had suddenly decided to join a community of Indian swamis on his recent visit to his favorite subcontinent."

Knowing Alsop's influence with both John and Robert Kennedy, I feared the column's effect. Robert Kennedy seemed particularly drawn to Alsop's approach. The President's attitude toward Bowles's old foe was ambivalent. Commenting on what Schlesinger called "the Achesonian Joseph Alsop and the anti-Achesonian Walter Lippmann," John Kennedy had said shortly after the Bay of Pigs, "I like them both, but I agree more with Lippmann than I do with Alsop." McGeorge Bundy commented: "That's exactly what Joe is afraid of."

The President probably agreed more with Bowles than with Rusk, which is what Alsop also feared. Kennedy "liked Bowles, liked most of his ideas and liked most of his personnel recommendations," and "felt the men recommended by Bowles had done better than Rusk's," wrote Ted Sorensen later. "Kennedy was not motivated by any criticisms that Bowles was too 'soft,' or too naive, or had attempted to clear himself of responsibility for the Bay of Pigs failure." The Undersecretary had amassed a powerful coalition of determined opponents, but "the Foreign Service cliques, the CIA professionals, the Pentagon generals and the right-wing editorials were all opposed to Bowles for the wrong reasons." For the President, according to Sorensen, it was just a matter of "better matching men and jobs."

This account omits the role of Robert Kennedy. From the time he entered the White House discussions on the second day of the Cuban invasion, he was infuriated by Bowles's lack of anti-Castro militancy. After the debacle, Bowles presented to the National Security Council a restrained department paper on Cuba that Bob Kennedy called "a disgrace." When a new Cuba task force, led by Maxwell Taylor and Robert Kennedy, took as their basic premise that "there can be no long-term living with Castro as a neighbor," Bowles was an obvious dissenter. In June the Attorney General had still not discarded the idea of sending in troops. "Maybe that is the answer," he wrote. "Only time will tell." He proposed that John Connally become the Assistant Secretary for Latin America: "Not an expert in the field but at least he is a man of action." As for Bowles, the Attorney General concluded that he must be removed from his key post. After Bowles, as acting Secretary of State, in Rusk's and the

President's absence in Europe, blocked a plan the Attorney General favored for an immediate, limited military intervention in the Dominican Republic to assure a friendly regime there, Robert Kennedy called Bowles a gutless bastard.

When the President didn't remove Bowles in July, Robert Kennedy (unknown to any of us at the time) kept pressing the point. After receiving a glowing account of Bowles's performance at the conference of American ambassadors in Africa, the Attorney General wrote his brother that "this is the kind of thing Bowles should be doing all the time." On Thanksgiving weekend, 1961, the President made his move. The "Thanksgiving Massacre" occurred swiftly. A few hours before Salinger was to announce sweeping changes in the State Department, Bowles was informed by Rusk that George Ball would take his place, and he would be offered an ambassadorship.

Bowles's first reaction was that he should leave the administration. "A complete break would set me free to spell out publicly the weaknesses in our foreign policy and in our State Department organization, the dangers of our increasingly military-oriented approach," he wrote. That was exactly what Kennedy feared. To prevent it, the President asked Sorensen to stand by with a political fire extinguisher and "hold his hand a little, as one 'liberal' to another." In *Kennedy*, Sorensen describes how late that Sunday afternoon he found Bowles alone in the all-but-empty State Department building, determined to "resign and speak his mind." The President's emissary "shared his grief . . . admired his efforts. It grew darker and darker, but neither of us moved to turn on the lights." Sorensen convinced Bowles that in spite of everything the President genuinely wanted him to stay on as a roving ambassador. Bowles said he could only consider that if he had specific responsibilities for the formulation of foreign policy, working directly with the President. Sorensen telephoned Kennedy and a proposal was made which Bowles finally accepted: he would become the President's Special Representative and Adviser for Asian, African, and Latin American Affairs. When Bowles spoke with the President, he expressed his concern whether there was enough personal rapport to make the new post worthwhile. He was not "the tough, terse, yes-or-no type" that the President apparently found it easiest to work with, he said, and there was nothing he could do to become one. Kennedy discounted that problem, assuring Bowles that he was the strongest asset the administration had in those three crucial regions of the world, and that he was indispensable.

From his session with Sorensen, Bowles went to Abram Chayes's home, where several of us joined him to try to make sense of the events.

The politics of the moves were obvious: by elevating Averell Harriman to Assistant Secretary for the Far East—the post that Bowles had for months been urging for him—and by appearing to give Bowles a significant new role, the liberal opposition was neutralized. By removing Bowles from the department, the old guard was mollified, and during the flux the White House men—Richard Goodwin, Walt Rostow, and Fred Dutton—were inserted in high positions without immediate Foreign Service opposition.

Bowles's weakness as Undersecretary, which called for this change, according to Sorensen, was that he "preferred exploring long-range ideas to expediting short-gap expedients." When he learned that Bowles had agreed to the shift, the President (who, Sorensen says, "looked with some amusement on my assignments as a missionary to liberals") congratulated him: "Good job, Ted—that was your best work since the Michigan delegation."

Perhaps my ties to Bowles distorted my vision (as I think Sorensen's ties to Kennedy distorted his), but I saw more in these events than the right matching of men and jobs. To the extent that Kennedy considered more expeditious management of short-gap expedients the main problem of the department, this for me was a measure of the inadequacy of his basic analysis. The failure of decision-making about the Bay of Pigs was not so much in the short-gap expedients as in the longer-range strategy. The same was to be true of Vietnam.

The record shows that most of the thinking about the changes in the department focused on how to get "action," not on what the action should be. The inertia, the almost feudal division of power among the regional bureaus, the tendency to support the status quo were indeed built-in, long-standing problems. John and Robert Kennedy had been brought up by their father to look down on these aspects of the department. When he heard his sons talking about their plans for its reform, Joseph Kennedy told them he had heard much the same kind of talk from Franklin Roosevelt. "He lamented the State Department. He talked about razing the whole thing and starting from scratch. He didn't do a damn thing about it, and neither are you."

With the State Department shake-up, Joe Kennedy's sons thought they were finally taking control. But, as Schlesinger notes, they were soon complaining that "nothing improved." Sorensen conceded that "even after the personnel changes" it was never clear to the President "who was in charge, who was clearly delegated to do what, and why his own policy line seemed consistently to be altered or evaded." One reason was that neither the Secretary nor, with Bowles gone, the Undersecretary was deeply committed to what the President probably meant by his "policy line." Another was that the President was so preoccupied with short-gap expedients that his longer-range policy line was not very clear.

One bright spot emerged: Averell Harriman. His success threw light on Bowles's failure. Deaf and in his seventy-first year, he was able to work with Kennedy better than anyone else in the department, and was more successful than any other Kennedy man in changing department policy. "I've learned," he said later, "that you have a split second" when the President is looking around the room at a time of decision. "You can't wait." With admiration, Schlesinger described how the wise old man would seize those split seconds, and if he dissented, would say so in a few blunt sentences. "Mouth open, and I bite," said Harriman. The White House nickname for Harriman was "the crocodile."

In contrast to Harriman, Bowles was not only prone to longer exploration of issues but to long explanations. Kenneth Galbraith, then Ambassador to India, thought that Bowles's trouble was his "uncontrollable instinct for persuasion which he brings to bear on the persuaded, the unpersuaded and the totally irredeemable alike." Kennedy could not stand hearing something he thought he already knew. He also disliked discussion of principles and morality, which he considered appropriate for the public platform, not for the inner councils of state. Unlike most of the witty people around Kennedy, Bowles did not cover his convictions with a veneer of cynicism. There was hardly any discrepancy between what he said in public and what he said in private.

Born with the idea of a republic in his head, Bowles was one of Mark Twain's true Connecticut Yankees. Put him down in Cuba or Indochina and his moral compass would swing around and say no to military intervention. Kennedy was skeptical of such a compass. Fed by his Irish and Catholic roots, Kennedy saw the world as tragic and comic. Bowles was ever an optimistic Unitarian and liberal humanist.

An encounter between Bowles and Albert Schweitzer in the 1950s reflected Bowles's distance from any darker vision. On the famous missionary's birthday, Bowles had traveled on a pilgrimage to Schweitzer's remote hospital settlement at Lambaréné in Equatorial Africa. He was disappointed to find no black African doctors and to hear the man who had given much of his life to serving Africans argue that it would be a long time before they would be ready for such advanced training.

When Bowles decried the effects of colonialism, Schweitzer emphasized how much good it had done for the natives. When Bowles pointed out how much profit the British had made out of India and other colonies, Schweitzer asked, "Why shouldn't they be well paid for all the suffering they endured?" Bowles said he was more concerned about ending the suffering of the poverty-stricken villagers of Asia and Africa and told Schweitzer about the community development program in India. The old man said it didn't interest him very much since "all my strength comes from the misery I see," and he spoke of "the brotherhood of those who bear the mark of pain." When Bowles quoted Jefferson on the value of self-government, Schweitzer said, "I prefer Schopenhauer."

For those of a tragic persuasion, it was easy to smile at Bowles's unshakable faith in democracy and progress. Because his convictions led him to focus on what people thought and felt, he had the ability that Castro said was missing in "imperialists": Bowles was able to assess more accurately the prospects for a revolution against Castro and the power of nationalism than those who concentrated mainly on military factors. In the twenty years after World War II, half the people of the world had changed their form of government even though the conventional forms of power—weapons, troops, industrial production, technology, communications, and the political apparatus—were on the side of the status quo. Citing Gandhi's India, Mao's China, and Castro's Cuba, Bowles argued that material power was likely to come out second best in a contest with ideas which move men to great efforts and sacrifice. In the National Security Council, under Kennedy as under Eisenhower, the dominant voice seemed always to be asking cynically, like Stalin, "But how many divisions has the Pope?" Yet on issue after issue Bowles turned out to have been more realistic than the realists.

Bowles's downfall was brought about by a convergence of factors, not the least of which were his formidable foes among the covert operators in the CIA, who had special access to the President and Attorney General and to people close to them, like Joe Alsop. Given his vulnerability, it was much easier to get Bowles than to get Castro. One has to wonder what would have happened if Kennedy had let Bowles get Bissell as the Deputy Undersecretary of State in January 1961. Working with Bowles, Bissell could have done the bureaucratic in-fighting the Undersecretary drew back from, and provided the President the quick, sharp short-gap expedients he required. Removed from command of the Bay of Pigs operation, Bissell's all-out personal commitment to its success would have been reduced, and the operation might have been canceled. Later Bowles said to Bissell, "If you'd taken that job, I'd have saved you and you'd have saved me."

In 1962 and early 1963, as the President's Special Representative and Adviser on Asian, African, and Latin American Affairs, Bowles tried to challenge the shared assumptions of the set around Kennedy, and lift sights from short-range expediencies.

On military aid, Bowles sought to persuade the Shah of Iran and Emperor Haile Selassie to cease their military buildup and concentrate resources on economic and social development. However, the Pentagon continued to offer them planes and guns. The President seemed to agree with Bowles, but the flow of arms was not checked. "Any thought that this Administration is tough-minded in the administration of our military assistance program is a serious mistake," Bowles wrote. "I do not know of any national leader who has come to Washington and asked for arms who has not gone home with more than he expected to get, regardless of the legitimacy of his claim."

Bowles urged a "two nation" policy for China and Taiwan. The President expressed interest, and for a time supported the idea of offering to sell wheat to China. However, it became clear that any relaxation of the policy of hostility toward the Peking government would have to await a resounding re-election victory in 1964.

There was one notable victory for the views Bowles championed: the President decided to stand by the UN effort to achieve a united Congo. Despite strong opposition from the Joint Chiefs of Staff, the Defense Department, and the European Bureau of the State Department, the course advocated by the African Bureau, led by Mennen Williams and his adroit deputy, Wayne Fredericks, prevailed after hard arguments at the White House chaired by the President. Bowles had returned from the Congo in late 1962 with recommendations for full American support of the UN troops defending the Congolese central government against the Katanga secessionists under Moïse Tshombe. European and American mining interests exerted great pressure to desert the UN effort. Williams, Fredericks, Bowles, and their allies were outnumbered within the government but they worked carefully, fought tenaciously, and argued effectively, and carried the day with Kennedy.

On another African issue—the financing of Ghana's Volta Dam— Kennedy made a hard decision, against his brother's advice, to support the Williams-Fredericks-Bowles position. Because of Nkrumah's anti-American posturing, Robert Kennedy wanted the United States to withhold previously promised aid to the proposed TVA-on-the-Volta. The President decided to continue with the commitment to the Volta Dam since it would help the Ghanaian people long after Nkrumah was gone. "The Attorney General has not yet spoken," John Kennedy noted, after giving his views, "but I can feel the cold wind of his disapproval on the back of my neck."

African policy, on balance, was a source of satisfaction to Bowles—and to Kennedy. There was a recurring tug-of-war over Angola and Portugal, with Kennedy wanting to support Angolan independence but the Pentagon insisting that the renewal of the treaty for our base in the Azores required support for Lisbon. To the consternation of Stevenson, Bowles, and John Kenneth Galbraith, Kennedy asked Dean Acheson to negotiate with the Portuguese dictator. "A libertarian may properly disapprove of Dr. Salazar," Acheson had written, "but I doubt whether Plato would." Having called Stevenson's mission at the UN "the department of emotion," Acheson was in no mood to serve a policy that sought to strengthen the UN's role in guiding African colonies to freedom. Galbraith warned Kennedy against trading in our African policy "for a few acres of asphalt in the Atlantic," and added that Acheson was able, "but I cannot think he is capable of loyalty. He . . . wants a policy that serves his ego, not your needs." Bowles told Kennedy "it would be unthinkable to modify an effective policy in a key continent to fit the eighteenth-century views of the Lisbon Government."

Kennedy vacillated, but aside from this Portuguese problem he supported the African bureau's and Bowles's approach. When Assistant Secretary of State for Africa Williams was criticized for saying that Africa was for the Africans, Kennedy defended him readily at a press conference: "I don't know who else Africa should be for." (Later, in his annual Gridiron remarks, the President said that Williams had asked to stay in Africa a few more weeks but he had replied, "No, Soapy, Africa is for the Africans."

On Vietnam, for a while, Bowles thought his influence—along with that of the more commanding General Douglas MacArthur, whose support he had enlisted—might count with the President. During the 1950s, Bowles had developed a surprising accord with MacArthur on Asian policies, and he was hopeful that the General's visits with Kennedy in 1961 would strengthen the President's resistance to further military involvement in Vietnam. Robert Kennedy, who heard the General, seemed to take seriously MacArthur's warning that "we would be foolish to fight on the Asiatic continent and that the future of Southeast Asia should be determined at the diplomatic table." Maxwell Taylor noted that it made "a hell of an impression on the President . . . so that whenever he'd get this military advice from the Joint Chiefs or from me or anyone else, he'd say, 'Well, now, you gentlemen, you go back and convince General MacArthur, then I'll be convinced.'"

But in fact it was Maxwell Taylor who was in the ascendancy, due in large part to Robert Kennedy's enthusiasm for the former war hero, after whom he named his newborn son. In April 1961, when the Pentagon had wanted to send 3,600 combat troops to Vietnam, the President had compromised on 100 military advisers and 400 Green Berets. As the Defense chiefs pressed for more in the fall of 1961, the President sent Taylor and Walt Rostow, both known to be strong advocates of counter-insurgency, on an investigating mission to Vietnam. Their choice, instead of Harriman, Schlesinger, or Bowles, reflected the President's desire to have no further setbacks in the contest with Communism. "There are limits to the number of defeats I can defend in one twelve-month period," the President explained to John Kenneth Galbraith, who also opposed escalation. "I've had the Bay of Pigs and pulling out of Laos, and I can't accept a third."

Taylor and Rostow returned with recommendations for the immediate dispatch of American helicopters, B-26s, military advisers, training experts, and some 8,000 regular ground troops, and accepted the possibility that as many as six full divisions, or 200,000 men, might eventually be required. Bowles renewed his proposal for an internationally guaranteed neutralization, urging that the Geneva negotiations on Laos be expanded in an effort to agree on a plan for all of Indochina and possibly Thailand, Malaysia, and Singapore. Averell Harriman, head of the U.S. negotiating team, reacted favorably and thought some such plan might be feasible.

The alternatives were actively argued within the State Department and the White House. The President seemed to consider neutralization a good goal, but one for which the time was not ripe. The President decided to go the military route, but only partway: he would increase the number of U.S. military advisers and the counter-insurgent Green Berets but not, for the present, introduce regular combat troops. The dominant view was that "the Communists must be taught a lesson."

In May 1962, as American casualties began to mount, Bowles returned from a visit to Southeast Asia and urged the President to undertake an "agonizing reappraisal." He pleaded with Kennedy to spell out in a major address a comprehensive proposal for peace, independence, neutralization, and economic development of the whole region. This time, the President not only agreed that the time was ripe for such a move, but seemed enthusiastic. Bowles was asked to draft a "Peace Charter for Southeast Asia" and to visit capitals in the region to secure advance support. Bowles expected opposition from the military, CIA, and parts of the State Department, but thought the President was finally committed to a peace effort.

Then, shortly before Bowles was to depart for Asia, a State Department memorandum directly attacked the new approach as "unrealistic, impractical and premature." It closed with the proposition that was to become the official American dogma for the next six years: "The primary problem we must recognize is that the Hanoi Government has not yet been given adequate reason to call off its aggression in South Vietnam." In response, Bowles predicted that if we did nothing to achieve a negotiated peace, "we may be forced within the next year or so to choose between committing more and more American troops and material . . . or withdrawing in embarrassed frustration."

On the ground that the timing seemed to be "inopportune," Rusk decided to delay the Bowles mission from September to October. By October, the Cuban missile crisis prevented its consideration. In November, the future Chairman of the Joint Chiefs of Staffs, General Earle Wheeler, declared that "the essence of the problem in Vietnam is military," and further escalation was under way. In the spring of 1963, Bowles wrote Kennedy on Vietnam once more, saying he hesitated "to play the role of Cassandra again," but "if this course is pursued, the Southeast Asia situation will ultimately have a serious impact on the Administration's position at home and abroad." He recalled the costly, losing French effort to defeat Ho Chi Minh in the early 1950s, opposition to which had first brought Kennedy and Bowles together, and said:

> Nine years have passed and now it is we who appear to be striving, in defiance of powerful indigenous political and military forces, to insure the survival of an unpopular Vietnamese regime with inadequate roots among the people. And now, as in 1954, many able US military authorities are convinced that the situation is moving in our favor and that victory can be foreseen within two to three years. I wonder if these assurances are not based on a dangerously false premise, i.e., that the Communists will not embarrass us by upping the military ante.

Visiting Vietnam again in the summer of 1963, Bowles was so disturbed by what he saw that he sent a private cable to the President urging him to send someone in whom he had personal confidence to make a fresh and independent analysis. Bowles suggested he consider Thomas Hughes, whom Kennedy had recently appointed as the State Department's Director of Intelligence and Research. High-level meetings were held on Bowles's cable, but nothing came of it. In his notebook, Bowles predicted that for our failure in Vietnam we would "pay a heavy price."

No one enjoys a Cassandra, and it became clear that Kennedy did not welcome Bowles's voice in his inner councils. In December 1962 Bowles had written the President that he wanted to resign his post because of the continued domination of foreign policy by European-oriented people who gave no priority to "outlying areas" where most of the human race lives. "Over and over again," Bowles said, "we have passed up opportunities to take the initiative and to help shape the course of events—rather than be controlled by them." In response, while persuading Bowles to become once again the Ambassador to India, Kennedy said the record would show that he had come down on Bowles's side of the intra-administration debates more often than not. Bowles agreed that "when forced to act in response to specific crises, we have often ended up at the last minute doing the right thing—thanks largely to your own personal insights." But he asked why it had to be like a Western movie in which the bad guys seemed to be winning until the last moment, when the tables suddenly turned and the President saved the day.

Bowles does not emerge as a pure hero. When he had the chance, in a critical National Security Council meeting on the Bay of Pigs, he didn't speak up and fight; he decided to wait.* And he did not later demand to see Kennedy to make his case; the President could not have refused him a hearing, if he had used his political capital for that purpose, instead of sending Rusk into battle armed with a memorandum. From years of working with Bowles, I believe he had an unwarranted inferiority complex about his own education that inhibited him in dealing with the best-educated and brightest of the Kennedy circle. He had gone to the former Sheffield Scientific School at Yale, and always regretted not having taken the full liberal arts program. Instead of going to graduate or professional school, he went into the advertising business, aiming to make a million dollars and enter public service. Though he was phenomenally successful in radio promotion of famous brands, introducing singing commercials and slogans that sold products to people, he was always embarrassed about his business background. Whether because of this or the "Bloomsbury syndrome" or other reasons, he was never at his best with Kennedy and his men. With them, as David Halberstam put it, he became "a curiously heavy figure," and knowing that he was not as facile as the lean, swift men around Kennedy he "became even more awkward."

Nevertheless, Kennedy's inability to bring out the best and draw on the wisdom of Bowles was the President's loss. That he could not get the benefit of such a mind, that it took man-eating sharks and crocodiles to get through to him, demonstrated a flaw in the President's own intelligence at least as great as the failure of the outside intelligence provided

---

* His defeat for re-election as governor of Connecticut in 1950 and severe attacks by Nixon, McCarthy, and others left him with a strain of caution, as in 1957, on an overnight train in Soviet Asia, when he heard me tell a Russian engineer that I favored U.S. recognition of Peking. Leaning out of his upper berth, he warned: "Watch out! They may quote you!"

him by the CIA, the Pentagon, or the State Department. He badly needed someone close to him who had "a basic moral reference point."

Fortunately for the public, Franklin Roosevelt was married to Eleanor, whose strong convictions about what was right and wrong bored him, who pestered him to do what she believed was right, and from whom he fled when he heard her voice coming down the White House corridor. But he couldn't send her off as Ambassador to India—where Kennedy sent Bowles in the summer of 1963.

After Nixon's election, Bowles resigned, came home, and, in his last months of good health, wrote his memoirs. At a State Department ceremony in July 1969, he was given the Award for Distinguished Service and the former Secretary of State gave the last toast. Dean Rusk spoke graciously of the freshness of Bowles's mind and the fact that he had more ideas in a day than most people have in a year. "Chet Bowles," said Rusk, "has contributed many ideas which are now an integral part of American foreign policy. In regard to the many more ideas of his which were not accepted—only the historians can determine who was right and who was wrong."

In his own writing, Bowles left no doubt about the ways he thought Rusk had been wrong. As for Kennedy, Bowles said he had a "deep conviction that if he had lived, he would have recognized the folly of our Southeast Asian policy, reversed our course of action and thereby altered the course of history." Some might say that this optimism merely measured Bowles's incorrigible naïveté. Yet his belief came from experience: in so many previous showdowns, Kennedy had finally come down on the side of restraint.

Shortly before leaving for Delhi, Bowles had a last encounter with Kennedy that gave him special encouragement. During a luncheon at his home with Soviet Ambassador Dobrynin, Bowles realized that the Ambassador was conveying a new willingness by the Kremlin to reach an agreement on a nuclear test ban. Bowles went straight to the President to report the possible breakthrough. Kennedy's reaction was wholly positive. If the Russian leaders were really ready to agree, he would fight to win approval of a test-ban treaty in the Senate, however politically difficult. "It may sound corny," the President said, "but I am thinking not so much of our world but the world that Caroline will live in."

"Had Kennedy lived," Bowles wrote in his memoirs, "I believe he would have become identified as a world leader whose thinking was not only pragmatic but increasingly guided by liberal principles which distinguished between what is right and what is wrong—and who was no longer embarrassed to say so." That had happened finally in civil rights and he thought it would have happened in foreign policy.

In the 1970s, Bowles became increasingly disabled with Parkinson's disease. In 1978, Indian Prime Minister Morarji Desai went to Bowles's home on the banks of the Connecticut River to pay a special tribute. "Chet, you are the best," he said. "Of all the ambassadors America will ever send, you are the best." By then Bowles was barely able to speak audibly, an ironic fate for someone so often criticized for talking too much. Under heavy medication, he had two recurring hallucinations. One was that dark-skinned, little Third World people were chasing him because their revolution had gone wrong. The other was that lawyers and experts, like those who dominated the State Department, were surrounding him and driving him into a corner in his own living room. "You know, they are 80 percent right in their facts," Bowles mustered the strength to whisper to his daughter Sally, "but in the end they're wrong."

In *The Best and the Brightest*, David Halberstam portrays Bowles as the hero of the early days of the New Frontier, and his downfall as a turning point: the "litmus test." If—by some measure of very high IQ, or of wit, cleverness, and the ability to amuse—the chief foreign policy advisers of Kennedy, who prevailed over Bowles, were the brightest, they were certainly not the best.

12 · The Agony of Robert Kennedy

The Robert Kennedy who in 1967 wrote *Thirteen Days: A Memoir of the Cuban Missile Crisis*—and who by then had become a committed force for reason, restraint, and peace not only in Cuba but above all in Vietnam—seemed to me a fundamentally different man from the one I had known in 1955 and 1960 and after the Bay of Pigs in 1961. After that fiasco, the Attorney General said that President Kennedy had become "a different man." He meant this in procedural terms, in the way the President dealt with his advisers. From his inauguration to his assassination, indeed from his election to the Senate to his trip to Dallas, John Kennedy's course was a natural progression. He learned and improved and became a wiser President, but did not fundamentally change. It was Robert Kennedy who seemed to move by epiphanies.

Malcolm X's taunt on the assassination of John Kennedy—"The chickens have come home to roost"—may have had more meaning and caused more pain to Robert Kennedy than any of us imagined at the time. Not because Malcolm knew anything special about the killer or killers, but because of what the Attorney General knew. It put into words a thought Robert Kennedy must have dreaded. Was he, to some significant extent, directly or indirectly, responsible for his brother's death?

Given the facts known to Robert Kennedy, but only to a few people in the CIA, the FBI, and the Mafia—and to Castro—and maybe not known fully by any of them, he could not have avoided asking himself some, or all, of the following questions:

> Had he and his brother, by unleashing the forces of counter-insurgency against Castro, started a process that led finally to the President's own assassination?
>
> By pressing the CIA to use any means short of war to destroy the Cuban regime, had they encouraged the unholy alliance with the Mafia and the other organized efforts to kill Castro?
>
> By pursuing a campaign against the Mafia, including the very Mafia leaders with whom the CIA had contracted for Castro's murder, had he incited them to conspire to kill the President?
>
> Was the President's own relationship with a woman closely connected with the CIA's Mafia conspirators in any way involved in his death at Dallas?
>
> Had the President and his advisers created an avenging monster in their midst, by arming, sending into battle at the Bay of Pigs, and seeming to desert the CIA's Cuban brigade?
>
> Was Lee Harvey Oswald a witting or unwitting agent of others with

the motive and means to conspire to kill John Kennedy? Of Castro, who knew of U.S. attempts to kill him? Of anti-Castro Cubans who felt betrayed? Of the Mafia leaders who saw themselves being persecuted and prosecuted? Of some wild men in the CIA whose plans were being foiled?

Was Oswald in his madness—even if he acted entirely on his own—a receptacle for the hostility toward the President being generated by these powerful forces? And, aside from what actually stirred Oswald to shoot, was there some terrible justice—what Lyndon Johnson in his worst moment called "divine retribution"—in an organizer of a Fair Play for Cuba Committee striking down John Kennedy?

Given the nature of the facts Robert Kennedy had learned before and after the assassination, he would not have wanted the Warren Commission or any other public body to pursue these questions. This must be one of the reasons, if not the main one, for his non-cooperation with further investigation of the assassination. The impact of these facts on Robert Kennedy must have been profound, and played a part in the extraordinary change that took place in him, first marked in the Cuban missile crisis, then even more notable after the assassination, and finally culminating in his campaign for the presidency.

For twelve years I resisted the temptation to indulge in conspiracy theories about the assassination. I was satisfied with the Warren Commission's finding that Oswald fired the only shots and that he did it entirely on his own. It was reassuring that Robert Kennedy, other members of the family, and those closest to John and Robert Kennedy seemed content to let the matter rest and opposed any reopening of the case. If Oswald did not represent a classic case history of American violence, familiar in the stories of the West, he was an example of the random, all too common, psychotic behavior of our stressful, mixed-up, modern mass industrial society. The murder reflected the alienation of the lonely crowd in twentieth-century America, but had little relevance to the actions of the Kennedy administration or the character of John and Robert Kennedy. Like Malcolm X, Chief Justice Warren, and millions of Americans, my first reaction to hearing the news that a white man in Dallas had been arrested for the shooting was to assume that he must have been a Ku Klux Klansman or some kind of Southern racist. Then we learned that Oswald was pro-Castro, that he had settled for a time in the Soviet Union, and that he had tried to kill the anti-integrationist General Walker. Oswald appeared, instead, to be some kind of fanatic of the left.

I was intrigued to learn from Priscilla McMillan, who had known Lee Harvey Oswald in Moscow and who had studied all the available evidence of his ideology for her book, *Marina and Lee*, that there might in fact have been a twisted racial factor in the murder. She found that Oswald had been upset by Kennedy's delay in fulfilling his promises on civil rights, but in the end she concluded that his resentment of the government's anti-Castro campaign was a much larger factor in making John Kennedy the target of his uncontrollable rage. For that campaign Robert Kennedy bore a major responsibility.

When I left for Africa in mid-1962, the Attorney General was the driving force behind the clandestine effort to overthrow Castro. From inside accounts of the pressure he was putting on the CIA to "get Castro," he seemed like a wild man who was out-CIAing the CIA. I also heard accounts of how avidly he was advancing counter-insurgency as the answer to the Communists in Vietnam. During this period Robert Kennedy would import Green Berets for weekends at Hyannis Port. They would demonstrate their prowess in swinging from trees and climbing over barricades. Sargent Shriver reacted against these paramilitary displays by staying away. When Eunice called to him to come out and watch the Green Berets, he said he did not like the children watching—it was not a good influence.

Robert Kennedy's growing influence in foreign policy did not then seem to me good for the country or the world. Yet not long afterward, in the missile crisis of October 1962, the Attorney General emerged as the strongest force within the administration for a negotiated settlement and the one who from the first moment raised the moral questions. After his brother's murder, peace became his consuming passion. When I returned from Ethiopia in the spring of 1964, I was fascinated by the change in him and wondered about its cause. Grief still seemed to grip Robert Kennedy throughout that spring. It was "almost as if he were on the rack," said his friend John Seigenthaler. He was largely withdrawn, taking long walks, tending his family, and turning to the ancient Greeks for solace. At Easter, Jacqueline Kennedy gave him her copy of Edith Hamilton's *The Greek Way* and remembers how he would disappear with it and "be in his room an awful lot of the time . . . reading that and underlining things." Among his underlinings in that book and others by Edith Hamilton, Arthur Schlesinger found: "The antagonism at the heart of the world." "To the heroic, desperate odds fling a challenge." "Having done what men could, they suffered what men must."

At first I could not believe that Robert Kennedy, who called anyone unwilling to attack Castro a "gutless bastard," who was always saying "Don't sit there thinking, do something!" was reading *The Trojan Women* and pondering the horrors of war. I learned that Richard Goodwin had sent him William Arrowsmith's translation of *Thetis and*

Achilles, and that he had asked for more Arrowsmith translations of the Greek plays. When I heard that Robert Kennedy was quoting Thucydides on the tragedy of the young Athenians who sailed to their deaths on the disastrous expedition to Sicily, I wondered if I had given a history of Greece to the wrong Kennedy.

After the Bay of Pigs, when the dust seemed to settle and tempers cooled, I had presented John Kennedy with Stringfellow Barr's *The Will of Zeus,* a dramatic rendering of the tension in Greek history between the myths of Achilles and of Odysseus. In Barr's account, the story of Achilles is that war—of grief and wrath and death—where glorious and lionlike courage proved inadequate to the human problem. But the ship and the oar symbolized Odysseus, not the sword or the shield. Throughout most of his voyage Odysseus "was busy less with either vengeance or glory than with solutions to hard and dangerous problems." He loved his queen, Penelope, yet he lay with the nymph Calypso; he let the sea bear him "to strange places where he could learn the world beyond beloved Ithaca," and it "taught him, and therefore changed him." He lived to reach home, and alone earned Homer's highest epithet, "wise." "Wisdom brought him a sense of proportion" that went along with his seaman's humor.

As the President was leaving for Thanksgiving weekend 1961 at Hyannis Port, I recalled to him General Marshall's comment that when he needed light on the cold war, he went to Fire Island and read Thucydides. Reading Barr's book, I wrote in a covering note, made me think of the President's task "of moving America toward the spirit of Odysseus."

It was during that Thanksgiving weekend that the President fired Chester Bowles as Undersecretary of State and during the same cold and windy days that he decided to delay for the third time the signing of the Executive Order against discrimination in housing. Even in those moments when his actions were most disappointing to me, he seemed to have in him far more of the wily and resilient Odysseus—the adventurer and learner—than the impetuous and angry Achilles.

Robert Kennedy, on the other hand, as I had known him, seemed very much an Achilles, impulsive, arrogant, and battle-prone. I was wrong. Instead of rising from his grief and rushing into battle, like Achilles, instead of resuming his course "cool, poised, resolute, matter-of-fact, debonair" as his brother (quoting Winston Churchill) prescribed in adversity, Robert Kennedy returned to action slowly and painfully. In a walk with him, from the Justice Department up to the Capitol, where he was to testify on civil rights one crisp sunny day in the spring of 1964, I found him gentle, thoughtful, vulnerable, and open to ideas in a way I had not seen before.

The agony he was undergoing marked a contrast between him and his dead brother. I could not imagine John Kennedy sinking into such long, dark melancholy for any reason. The quotation that Jack Kennedy, the war hero, had written in his 1945 notebook about a young man dying in battle "debonair and brilliant and brave" (from John Buchan's *Pilgrim's Way*) reflected his approach to life and death. The President liked to recall Robert Frost's words, "I have been one acquainted with the night." "What a terrific line," he said to Schlesinger while flying to Amherst to honor the old poet in late October 1963. But he was not one to be daunted by the night. He was an "enjoyer," who fretted when things went wrong or were going too slowly, but did not look back. He pushed ahead with zest to the next experience, the next encounter. "He lived at such a pace," Jacqueline Kennedy was to say, "because he wished to know it all." In one of his last press conferences, he repeated his favorite definition of happiness (from Aristotle)—"full use of your powers along lines of excellence"—and said that he found "therefore, the presidency provides some happiness." Gaiety was the key to his nature, said his friend Chuck Spalding: "It was like a lot of flags on a ship with Jack, easy and bright."

Robert Kennedy joshed, too, under fire, but he was a brooder. He, too, became acquainted with the night, but his response, unlike his brother's, was to "feel the giant agony of the world" (from Keats's "The Fall of Hyperion," used as the epigraph of *Thirteen Days*). John Kennedy could say (quoting Franklin Roosevelt) that Lincoln was "a sad man because he couldn't get it all at once. And nobody can." But as he tried to get as much as he could, there seemed to be little sadness in him. There was a lot in Robert. After the death of his brother, it welled up, and what poured out seemed just a token of the flood he was holding back within himself. One could only watch and wait for him to return to action, and wonder where his mental wanderings had taken him. Once in his meditations he scrawled on a yellow sheet: "All things are to be examined & called into question—There are no limits set to thought."

At the time, the depth and length of Robert Kennedy's melancholy suggested that there was something more on his mind than even the loss of a brother and President. My curiosity led me to press Burke Marshall for any clue, and especially to inquire if the Attorney General, with access to the FBI's investigation, thought there was more to the assassination than a mad, lone gunman. Marshall then and in the years to come made it clear that Robert Kennedy opposed all such further inquiry; it was just too painful for the family. They apparently agreed with what Anthony Lewis later wrote: "The search for conspiracy only increases the elements of morbidity and paranoia and fantasy in this country. . . . It obscures our necessary understanding, all of us, that in this life there is often tragedy without reason."

That was my view, too, until 1975 when the Senate Select Committee to investigate U.S. intelligence activities disclosed a set of facts about the CIA's plots to kill Castro that made paranoia seem like true perception. From the findings of the Senate committee, we could begin to understand the burden of knowledge—even of guilt—that Robert Kennedy was carrying in the last years of his life. Together with the findings of the House Select Committee on Assassinations in 1979, these facts can account for the grief beyond ordinary grief with which Robert Kennedy wrestled for long months and years. They do not prove that John Kennedy was killed as a result of a conspiracy, but they do suggest that it was not a tragedy without reason.

Robert Kennedy must have considered the story those facts told to be worse than the most terrible fiction. Adding to his burden was the obligation he felt to keep all the key facts secret from most, if not all, of his family and friends, and to try to withhold them forever from the people of this country and the world. Those secrets provided motives for Castro, or the Mafia, or the CIA's Cuban brigade, or some people in the CIA itself to have conspired to kill the President, yet to preserve the good name of John Kennedy and of the government of the United States they had to be kept from the Warren Commission and from the eyes of history. Also weighing on Robert Kennedy's mind must have been the risks of blackmail against the government and the family of the murdered President which threatened to make a special hostage of the Attorney General.

From the reconstruction of the record made possible by the Senate and House reports, and from everything we know about the character of Robert Kennedy, I believe that the shock of these discoveries and his realization of what violence, crime, and secret conspiracies can lead to were significant factors in his transformation. Thus, in order to understand Robert Kennedy and his times, the truth about these stories must be sorted out and the painful facts faced. That is what I believe Robert Kennedy did.

It is a fact, now known to the world, that the government of the United States, beginning under Dwight Eisenhower (if not before) and continuing under John Kennedy and Lyndon Johnson (if not their successors), sought through the CIA to assassinate leaders of foreign governments. The Senate Select Committee in 1975 found concrete evidence of at least eight plots involving the CIA to assassinate Fidel Castro from

1960 to 1965 and also of at least one abortive plot in 1960 to kill Patrice Lumumba of the Congo. The Inspector General of the CIA reported that "it is likely that at the very moment President Kennedy was shot, a CIA officer was meeting with a Cuban agent . . . and giving him an assassination device for use against Castro." A section of the CIA was responsible for developing the capability for disabling foreign leaders, including assassination. This capability was called "executive action."

Political assassination, by agents of kings, emperors, dictators, and ambitious office-holders or office-seekers, is as old as Rome, but there is no evidence that any executive of the United States authorized it until World War II. Allen Dulles, then a top agent of the OSS (the wartime predecessor to the CIA), encouraged German generals to try to kill Hitler, and most people later, when they learned about it, wished the plot had been successful. During the cold war, the CIA, under Dulles, made the same case for the elimination of anti-American dictators. A quick killing would be more effective and more humane, CIA planners argued in the inner circles of the "intelligence community," than letting people suffer all the casualties of a civil war or revolution.

According to the testimony of CIA officials, the first U.S. resort to assassination of a foreign leader was initiated in 1960, when Richard Bissell, in the belief that he had the explicit backing of Allen Dulles and at least the implicit approval of President Eisenhower, undertook to bring about the murder of Patrice Lumumba, Prime Minister of the newly independent Congo.

After Allen Dulles reported that Lumumba "was a Castro or worse," Eisenhower had expressed what one memorandum summarized as "extremely strong feelings on the necessity for very straightforward action" against Lumumba. "Straightforward" appears to be a euphemism. The official note-taker at the National Security Council meeting testified to the Senate committee that though he could no longer remember the exact words by Eisenhower, "they came across to me as an order for the assassination of Lumumba." Security Council staff member Robert Johnson said he remembered "that moment quite clearly because the President's statement came as a great shock." Bissell testified that when Dulles had said that "planning for the Congo would not necessarily rule out 'consideration' of any particular kind of activity which might contribute to getting rid of Lumumba," this was a "prime example" of the circumlocutious manner in which a topic like assassination was discussed by high officials. To Bissell it "obviously" meant "that if it had to be assassination, then that was a permissible means."

On August 26, 1960, Dulles had cabled the CIA Congo station: "IN HIGH QUARTERS HERE IT IS THE CLEAR-CUT CONCLUSION THAT IF [LUM-

UMBA] CONTINUES TO HOLD HIGH OFFICE, THE INEVITABLE RESULT WILL AT BEST BE CHAOS AND AT WORST PAVE THE WAY TO COMMUNIST TAKE-OVER. . . . CONSEQUENTLY WE CONCLUDE THAT HIS REMOVAL MUST BE AN URGENT AND PRIME OBJECTIVE AND THAT UNDER EXISTING CONDITIONS THIS SHOULD BE A HIGH PRIORITY OF OUR COVERT ACTION." The cable authorized the expenditure of up to $100,000 "to carry out any crash programs." In September a CIA scientist was sent to the Congo with biological materials that would transmit a fatal indigenous disease. The scientist testified that his instructions were for the materials to be used against Lumumba.

Bissell was frustrated by the refusal, on moral grounds, of one trusted agent to participate in the killing. Believing that "murder corrupts," Michael Mulroney, a senior officer, said no to Bissell. He argued that if Lumumba had to be eliminated, the Congolese government or military should do it, which appears to be what happened (after CIA urging). To the Senate committee, Mulroney explained that on reflection he concluded, "We have too much of the 'good German' in us, in that we do something because the boss says it is okay." His colleagues were "not essentially evil people. But you can do an awful lot of wrong in this."

There was, however, at least one agent in the Congo with no such moral scruples. Known by the code name WI/ROGUE, he was an essentially stateless soldier of fortune, "a forger and former bank robber," according to the CIA Inspector General. The CIA had hired him as "a general utility agent" who "would try anything once." It provided him with plastic surgery and a toupee, and slated him to be trained in "medical immunization." The CIA's African Division recommended him in the following terms:

> He is indeed aware of the precepts of right and wrong, but if he is given an assignment which may be morally wrong in the eyes of the world, but necessary because his case officer ordered him to carry it out, then it is right, and he will dutifully undertake appropriate action for its execution without pangs of conscience. In a word, he can rationalize all actions.

The Senate committee could not find out just what WI/ROGUE did in the Congo, although at one point he tried to recruit another agent for what he called an "execution squad." The station chief denied that WI/ROGUE was ever assigned to kill Lumumba, and attributed his talk to his "freewheeling" nature. The chief "found he was rather an unguided missile . . . the kind of man that could get you in trouble before you knew you were in trouble."

Richard Bissell was himself the kind of man who got the country in trouble before anyone in charge knew it. On July 21, 1960, a CIA cable to its Havana chief said: "POSSIBLE REMOVAL TOP THREE LEADERS IS RECEIVING SERIOUS CONSIDERATION AT HQS." The Havana agent said he "swallowed hard" when he read the further inquiry about "arranging an accident" for Raul Castro and the offer of $10,000 to a particular Cuban "after successful completion."

That plan was dropped, but the CIA's Technical Services Division was busy preparing other anti-Castro actions: chemicals to be put in Fidel's shoes that would cause his beard to fall out and damage his macho image in his own country and the rest of Latin America; drugs, similar to LSD, to be sprayed in the broadcasting studio so as to make the Cuban leader sound incoherent on the air—and various techniques for assassination.

The records of the CIA's Office of Medical Services indicate that on August 16, 1960, a box of Castro's favorite cigars was received with instructions to treat them with lethal poison. The cigars—contaminated with a botulinum toxin so potent a person would die after putting one in his mouth—were delivered to an unidentified person on February 13, 1961. The records available to the Senate committee do not show whether an attempt was made to pass those cigars to Castro.

Then, also that August, while Kennedy was calling for more vigorous action against Castro and behind the scenes Nixon was pressing the CIA to proceed with the Cuban landing before the election, Bissell was adding "another string to our bow." He and a close CIA colleague agreed that the most effective way to eliminate Castro would be by an arrangement with organized crime. Castro had closed the gambling casinos and driven the Mafia out of Cuba, which had been a very profitable place. If Cubans hired by the Mafia killed Castro, the motive would be obvious if they were caught, and the tie to the U.S. government might never be known. The Mafia was proud of its reputation for the sealed tongues of its assassins, or its ability to kill the assassins before they could talk.

So, in the summer or fall of 1960, agents of the CIA enlisted Mafia leaders John Rosselli and Sam Giancana to find one or more Cubans who would kill Castro. The CIA's middleman was Robert Maheu, an ex-FBI agent who had been on CIA retainer after he became a private investigator, but the Mafia men insisted on meeting a CIA official who would assure them it was a government project. The CIA remained deeply involved, providing the poison to be used and the cash offer for the killing (said to have been $150,000).

The Rosselli and Giancana efforts continued at least until the Bay of Pigs, after which Bissell says he called them off. Before Bissell left the CIA in February 1962, however, he had helped establish the new "executive action capability" within the agency, which was planning how to assassinate foreign leaders. Bissell briefed McGeorge Bundy on the new "capability," and the White House aide offered no "impediment." In April 1962, the chief of that executive action program delivered more poison pills to Rosselli, allegedly with the approval of Bissell's successor, Richard Helms. Rosselli testified that he told the CIA officer that the Cubans would try to kill Ché Guevara as well as Fidel and Raul Castro, and the CIA man approved. The CIA officer says he terminated the operation in mid-February 1963, but Rosselli testified that he never informed his Cuban agents that the $150,000 offer for Castro's assassination had been withdrawn.

Even after this, other CIA assassination plans proceeded through agents unconnected with the Mafia. On November 22, 1963, a poison pen was being delivered to a highly placed Cuban official working with the CIA—at the same hour Kennedy was riding through Dallas. The CIA files note that the would-be assassin was promised "everything he needed, telescopic sight, silencer, all the money he wanted," but "the situation changed" when they "left the meeting to discover that President Kennedy had been assassinated." Because of Kennedy's death, the CIA report says primly, "it was decided that we could have no part in the assassination of a government leader." The Cuban agent was not informed of this, however, until November 1964. CIA cables in early 1965, in fact, show that guns with silencers and "three packages of special items" were sent to this same Cuban agent, but that contact was ended with him in June 1965 "for reasons related to security."

Thus, while President Kennedy was proclaiming "executive action" as a constructive theme of his administration, in the creation of the Peace Corps and in other fields as well as civil rights, someone (presumably Bissell) used this phrase for the CIA's most destructive actions, including murder. Those of us setting out to prove the benign uses of executive action in civil rights never imagined the abuse of that power then also under way in the same President's name.

Did President Kennedy approve of these assassination efforts? We may never know for sure whether any of the three Presidents whose administrations made such attempts were aware of the plans. Bissell's self-serving testimony that Eisenhower and Dulles did not know details, but implicitly approved the aim of killing Lumumba or Castro, is not necessarily any more reliable than Allen Dulles' assurance to his fellow members of the Warren Commission that the CIA had submitted all evidence pertinent to Kennedy's assassination. In fact, despite his sworn duty on the commission, Dulles had withheld the potentially most crucial evidence: the story of the CIA's and the Mafia's attempts to kill Castro, which provided Castro (and, in a roundabout way, the Mafia) with a motive to kill Kennedy.

The CIA was so entangled in euphemisms and double talk about its covert operations that it isn't even clear whether its director, Allen Dulles, ever authorized the assassination plans. Bissell testified that Dulles was told about them "in somewhat circumlocutious terms." The CIA Inspector General reported that the briefing of Dulles "deliberately avoided the use of any 'bad words.'" Instead of "assassination," the "descriptive term used was 'an intelligence operation,'" and instead of specifying Maheu to Rosselli to Castro they talked of "from A to B to C." Instead of saying, "Yes, do it," Dulles merely nodded. Yet Bissell testified that he was sure Dulles understood the nature of the effort and approved.

With that shadowy authority, Bissell and his successor, Richard Helms, proceeded, and did not consider it necessary to brief the new head of the CIA, John McCone, or to seek renewed approval from him after he replaced Dulles in November 1961. McCone testified that he did not learn about the plans until August 1963, when he was told they had been terminated (which was evidently not the case). The man in charge of the murder plots, William Harvey, testified that he and Helms decided it was inadvisable to inform McCone. There was "a very pregnant possibility" of the United States government "being blackmailed either by Cubans for political purposes or by figures in organized crime for their own self-protection." Therefore, it might be necessary for McCone to be in a position to deny any involvement. Bissell explained to the Senate committee that covert operations should be carried out "in such a way that they could be plausibly disclaimed by the U.S. government."

There were reasons beyond the doctrine of "plausible deniability" for keeping McCone in the dark, and beyond Helms's explanation that McCone "was relatively new to the organization and this was, you know, not a very savory effort." Helms's executive assistant said that McCone had a fatherly feeling about John Kennedy, "a very protective sense," and "would have immediately said Jesus, this is a no-win ball game." And he believed that "as an individual, he would have found it morally reprehensible."

In August 1962, in the special task force on Cuba, McCone did hear a suggestion that the assassination of Castro should be studied, and he reacted sharply against it. He said the idea should be stricken from the record since no one should ever think that it had received serious consideration. The CIA chief told William Harvey (who directed the CIA's Mongoose projects against Castro as well as the assassination plotting) that "if I got myself involved in something like this, I might end up getting myself excommunicated." Unless McCone committed perjury, his sworn lack of knowledge is a strong indication that neither John nor Robert Kennedy was informed, at least during McCone's tenure. For anyone in the CIA to tell the President or the Attorney General but not his own chief makes no sense.

With such obfuscation at the highest levels within the CIA, it is not likely that there was ever clear authority for the assassination plans from President Kennedy. Bissell testified that the need for "plausible deniability" applied even more strongly to Presidents, and that Dulles would have desired "to shield the President" by intimating "that something of the sort was going forward, but giving the President as little information about it as possible" so that Kennedy could, if he chose, cancel it, or, by saying nothing, allow it to continue.

There is evidence, however, that the idea was on Kennedy's mind. On November 9, 1961, the President talked for more than an hour in the Oval Office with *New York Times* correspondent Tad Szulc, who had held a series of long conversations with Castro after the Bay of Pigs. Szulc testified that the President asked, "What would you think if I ordered Castro to be assassinated?" Szulc replied that Castro's removal would not necessarily change the Cuban system and that the United States should not be party to murders. According to Szulc's notes on the conversation, "JFK then said he was testing me, that he felt the same way . . . because indeed U.S. morally must not be a party to assassinations. JFK said he raised question because he was under terrific pressure from advisers (think he said intelligence people, but not positive) to okay a Castro murder. He [said] he was resisting pressures."

If George Smathers is to be believed, much the same conversation took place between the President and the Florida senator, a militant enemy of Castro. When Kennedy asked Smathers what reaction there would be throughout South America were Castro to be assassinated, the senator said the President would be blamed for it and it would work to his great disadvantage. Smathers testified that the President agreed and said he completely disapproved of the idea. But Cuba remained a sore subject, for one night at dinner when Smathers was pressing him about Castro, the President said, "Dammit . . . I don't want you to talk to me any more about Cuba." And with his fork Kennedy angrily hit and cracked his plate.

All administration officials and Kennedy advisers who testified to the Senate committee, except Bissell, said they believed Kennedy did not know of the plots and would have disapproved. Ted Sorensen said that "such an act was totally foreign to his character and conscience, foreign to his fundamental reverence for human life and his respect for his adversaries, foreign to his insistence upon a moral dimension in U.S. foreign policy and his concern for this country's reputation abroad, and foreign to his pragmatic recognition that so horrendous but inevitably counter-productive a precedent committed by a country whose own chief of state was inevitably vulnerable could only provoke reprisals and inflame hostility."

Unfortunately, part of the price paid for the CIA's secret operations is that John Kennedy's responsibility may never be ascertained or his reputation cleared. Since the assassination plots were the most closely held secret within the government, only Dulles or Robert Kennedy (once he knew) was likely to have told the President, and they were dead by the time of the Senate investigation. If the President was just testing Szulc and Smathers, once they indicated their disapproval it is not likely that he would have said anything on the other side. Did he raise the question with others (especially Robert Kennedy), and did anyone respond to the idea favorably? If so, what did the President say then?

Henry II's query about Thomas à Becket is the nearest any witness says the President got to proposing the assassination of Castro: "Who will free me from this turbulent priest?" After Kennedy's death, it was reported that a CIA official, Tracy Barnes (Bissell's deputy for the Bay of Pigs), claimed to have heard the President use that line in connection with Castro. For the CIA that would have been authority enough—nor would it have been beyond the CIA to fabricate such a self-serving report. Thomas Powers's *The Man Who Kept the Secrets* concludes that it was not the CIA director or the office boy but the President who ordered Castro's assassination. But Richard Goodwin argues that Kennedy would not have raised it with a reporter if he were going to do it, and says that after the Szulc conversation, Kennedy commented, "If we get into that kind of thing, we'll all be targets."

If the President was "under terrific pressure . . . to okay a Castro murder," did he take sufficient steps to make sure the CIA knew that he prohibited murder? In a public talk in November 1961, Kennedy said, "We cannot, as a free nation, compete with our adversaries in tactics of terror [and] assassination." In the spring of 1961, after the CIA had given weapons to Dominican rebels who sought to "neutralize" Trujillo, the President had secretly cabled the U.S. consul in Santo Domingo (and sent a copy to the CIA): "U.S. AS A MATTER OF GENERAL POLICY CANNOT CONDONE ASSASSINATION." But the record shows no specific clear directive against killing Castro (and despite the President's statement of policy, the Dominican rebels, presumably with guns from the CIA, assassinated Trujillo). With "terrific pressures" on him to approve

396

Castro's assassination, a strong counter-command was called for, if he was determined to stop it. Again Dulles and the Attorney General were the ones he would most naturally have spoken to, and their lips are sealed.

After the Cuban missile crisis in October 1962 presidential approval of killing Castro would have been most unlikely. Such actions would have violated the spirit of the agreement with Khrushchev, and would surely (even if plausibly denied by the United States) have precipitated a crisis in American-Soviet relations. Moreover, by the fall of 1963, Kennedy was looking favorably on the normalization of relations with Castro, and had authorized William Atwood, a Special Adviser to the United States delegation to the United Nations, to meet with Cuban officials and push for "an opening toward Cuba." In fact, as the CIA's poison pen was being delivered to its Cuban agent, a French journalist, with Kennedy's personal encouragement, was meeting with Castro to explore a possible rapprochement between the United States and Cuba; their talk was interrupted by the news of Kennedy's assassination.

This was not the first time one arm of the United States government was working against another arm, and the CIA's secret operations were belatedly discovered to be contradicting White House policy. In the midst of the missile crisis, when the President was seeking a peaceful settlement and trying to measure his response so as not to provoke a nuclear war, Robert Kennedy had "a terrible experience." Word reached him, from a man about to leave on a sabotage mission in Cuba, that the CIA (without McCone's knowledge) was in the process of sending ten commando teams to the island, and that three had already left. Whatever other destruction the commandos might have brought to Cuba, their actions could have blown up the delicate negotiations with Russia.

Although the Attorney General had approved the idea of commando landings, the timing appalled him and he was "furious" at such a "half-assed operation." Orders were given to call off all "sabotage or military operations." Assassination efforts were not included in the ban, but witting CIA officers must have realized that their plans would no longer be authorized. Yet they continued to conspire, if not with the Mafia, with their other chief would-be assassin in Cuba.

How much did Robert Kennedy know about the assassination plots, when did he learn it, and what was his reaction?

In 1967, when Drew Pearson and Jack Anderson wrote a column reporting that the CIA may have conspired with the Mafia to murder

Castro and that "Bobby, eager to avenge the Bay of Pigs fiasco, played a key role in the planning," Kennedy told his aides, "I didn't start it. I stopped it." The record available to the public, however, is not so clear.

The Attorney General certainly didn't start it, and before the Bay of Pigs he apparently had little to do with the CIA or Cuba. But in the aftermath of the invasion, he became the President's representative in Operation Mongoose, the CIA-led, interdepartmental secret campaign against Castro. He persuaded his brother to issue a top-secret order "to use our available assets . . . to help Cuba overthrow the Communist regime." In January 1962, Robert Kennedy assembled the Mongoose planners at the Justice Department and said that the operation had "top priority"; he urged that "no time, money, effort—or manpower . . . be spared." How could he be sure that his pressure had not encouraged the CIA to reactivate or intensify its assassination efforts?

His involvement may have gone deeper. At least one of those familiar with his role in Operation Mongoose thinks that his fascination with violent counter-insurgency and his frustration with Castro would have invited the assassination planners to make him privy to their plots (even as McCone's aversion to unsavory operations may have led them to keep him in the dark). Since the cost of the various expeditions of sabotage sponsored by Mongoose was excessive, in comparison to any damage they did in Cuba, the CIA planners needed an ally. They had one in the Attorney General. A rationale for Operation Mongoose was always inadequate, according to a non-CIA participant in the planning, but it was approved because of the Attorney General's insistence. In retrospect, that official thinks Mongoose made sense only as a cover for the attempts at murder. The assassination plotters needed just such a large unchecked budget, repeated landings of sabotage teams, and secret agents.

If Robert Kennedy understood and supported this secret plan within the larger covert operation, he himself may have been the source of "terrific pressure" for the assassination. Nothing in the testimony before the Senate committee suggests that the circumlocutious and evasive leaders of the CIA would have put such direct pressure on the President. Then who did? "Terrific pressure" is what anyone, including his brother the President, would have felt if he tried to resist a course strongly advocated by the Attorney General.

The President may have given in to the pressure—or not signified sufficient opposition, so that the CIA plotters, with or without the Attorney General's blessing, may have felt justified in going ahead. Or the plotters may have gone ahead on their own, unauthorized by either the President, the Attorney General, or the new agency chief. Or the President and Attorney General may never have finally decided, and the plotters, encouraged by Robert Kennedy's all-out anti-Castro attitude, continued (until 1965) on the course Bissell started in 1960.

Again, those close to Robert Kennedy who care most about his reputation cannot believe that he would tolerate murder. Schlesinger writes that no one who knew Robert and John Kennedy believes "they would conceivably countenance a program of assassination"—they were "so filled with love of life and so conscious of the ironies of history." But in an account of Operation Mongoose, Schlesinger concedes that in late 1961 and the first part of 1962 the Attorney General "wanted to do more, the terrors of the earth. . . ." McNamara testified that approval of assassination would have been "totally inconsistent with everything I knew about the two men," but in other testimony admitted "we were hysterical about Castro at the time of the Bay of Pigs and thereafter."

If it is conceivable that for some period of time the Attorney General countenanced the killing of Castro, his attitude must have changed in May 1962 when he learned of the CIA's murder contract with Sam Giancana and John Rosselli. Giancana had been one of Kennedy's major targets in the McClellan committee investigations of the connections between the criminal syndicate and labor unions in the late 1950s, and on becoming Attorney General, as part of a stepped-up drive against organized crime, Kennedy had singled out the Chicago racketeer and successor of Al Capone for intense investigation. The two Mafia men represented what the Attorney General considered the worst forces in the United States—*The Enemy Within,* as he titled his 1960 book.

Kennedy could blame himself for not having stopped the CIA's dealing with the Mafia a year before. In May 1961, Hoover had sent the Attorney General a summary of a CIA statement admitting it was using Giancana as a line to underworld agents in Cuba who might help the CIA's clandestine campaign against Castro. "None of Giancana's efforts have materialized to date," the CIA statement said, but "several of the plans are still working and may eventually pay off." No details were reported, the CIA security chief had explained, since this is "dirty business" and even he himself "could not afford to have knowledge of the actions. . . ."

On Hoover's cover memorandum, Kennedy wrote that he hoped the investigation of the circumstances involving Giancana would "be followed up vigorously." But there is no indication that he himself pursued it in the top-level planning sessions for Operation Mongoose that he attended with CIA leaders. He must have been torn between his desire to destroy the Mafia and his determination to get Castro. He may have concluded that Giancana's role was limited to helping the CIA recruit

399

agents in Cuba, and that the "dirty business" was limited to the various efforts which he knew were under way—and which he was ardently encouraging—to disrupt the Cuban economy, embarrass Castro, and undermine the Cuban regime, short of another invasion.

In fact, if Hoover and Kennedy had been working together efficiently, the head of the FBI would have called the Attorney General's attention to a report he had sent to Bissell, in October 1960, that Giancana was boasting to friends that he had met with an assassin who was soon going to poison Castro. Then Kennedy could have put the two reports of 1960 and of 1961 together and realized that Giancana's "dirty business" with the CIA might be to murder Castro. But the facts apparently did not come together until the CIA had to tell Kennedy about the arrangement in order to stop him from prosecuting Robert Maheu for a wiretap installed (with the CIA's probable connivance) on comedian Dan Rowan's Las Vegas telephone. Sam Giancana had apparently insisted on the tap as a condition for staying in Miami to work on the assassination, because of concern about a girlfriend reportedly having an affair with Rowan.

When two top CIA officials, on May 7, 1962, came to Robert Kennedy to plead with him to drop the prosecutions because Maheu, Giancana, and Rosselli were under contract with the United States government to murder Castro, the Attorney General must have been horrified. Whatever question there may be about his general attitude toward assassinating Castro, no one can doubt Kennedy's deep and abiding hatred of organized crime.

The CIA's general counsel, Lawrence Houston, who briefed Kennedy, testified that he assured the Attorney General the Mafia plots had been called off after the Bay of Pigs (and that he himself believed that to be so). Therefore, the situation only called for Kennedy to react to something that was finished. Houston recalled that at the end of the briefing Kennedy said "in very specific terms that if we were going to get involved with Mafia personnel again he wanted to be informed first."

That sounds like a peculiarly restrained response, but Houston testified that behind the words the Attorney General seemed upset. "If you have seen Mr. Kennedy's eyes get steely and his jaw set and his voice get low and precise, you get a definite feeling of unhappiness," the CIA counsel said. Two days later Kennedy advised Hoover, according to the FBI Director's memorandum of conversation, that he had been "considerably disturbed" to learn of a CIA proposition to Giancana, offering $150,000 for the killing of Castro. Hoover said Kennedy agreed with him that this showed "horrible judgment in using a man of Giancana's background for such a project," and the Attorney General stated he had "issued orders to CIA to never again in the future take such steps without first checking with the Department of Justice."

Running through Kennedy's head when he heard the CIA briefing and when he talked to Hoover was something the CIA men may not have known—but Hoover knew—that made the story even worse.

Ten weeks before, Hoover had reported to the Attorney General that a woman with whom the President had some kind of continuing relationship was also in close contact with Rosselli and Giancana. Just what the FBI disclosed about the President's role we do not know, but the 1975 Senate committee found that official telephone logs showed seventy instances of calls between the woman and the White House. The last occurred on March 22, 1962, a few hours after Hoover apparently discussed her Mafia ties with John Kennedy, at a private lunch.

Although the Senate committee did not give the name or even indicate the gender of the President's "close friend" (except to note that it was not Frank Sinatra, who also had close ties with Rosselli and Giancana), the press soon identified her as Judith Campbell Exner. She held a press conference and later published a book, *My Story* ("as told to Ovid Demaris"), to proclaim and describe in vivid detail almost simultaneous love affairs with John Kennedy and Sam Giancana, between late 1960 and mid-1962.

According to her account, she met Kennedy at Las Vegas in February 1960, through their mutual friend Frank Sinatra (with whom she says she had had a brief affair). Thereafter, on many furtive occasions, in Los Angeles, Miami, New York, and Washington (in the White House), she had come at Kennedy's call and had sexual relations with the Democratic candidate and subsequent President. A few weeks after her relationship began with Kennedy, Frank Sinatra, at a party of his clan in Miami, introduced her to Sam Giancana, who proceeded to pursue her as avidly as Kennedy did. She says she often went straight from one to the other, and that Kennedy would send her one dozen red roses while Giancana sent her five dozen yellow roses (which she understood to represent jealousy).

Again according to her, these were two separate, accidental, very human love affairs. Because of her "feelings for Jack," she kept Giancana waiting for a year and a half before they "became intimate." When Giancana was "happy-high" with drink, he would ride her about the Kennedys: "It was obvious that he didn't like them." Yet after Kennedy's election, in which the narrow margin of 9,000 votes in Chicago proved to be decisive, Giancana often told her, "Listen, honey, if it wasn't for me your boyfriend wouldn't even be in the White House." Giancana was the acknowledged boss of the Chicago criminal syndicate. He had been a prime suspect in numerous murders, controlled a reputed $2 billion in annual revenue from gambling and other rackets, directed thousands of agents, and by the time of the 1960 election was working with the CIA to kill Castro.

Looking back, Judith Exner asked herself, "Was Sam using me because I was the President's girl?" Indeed, she began to wonder whether Sam had arranged to meet her "accidentally on purpose." "When I think of it now," she wrote in 1976 of Giancana's pursuit of her, "I realize it was all too ideal, all too studied and planned . . ." She thought that "it's possible that Sam got exactly what he wanted from our relationship. Now that I know of his involvement with the Central Intelligence Agency, it is possible that I was used almost from the beginning." Nevertheless, it had seemed to her a case of passion. "Before we were intimate he would kid me about Jack," she wrote, but afterward "it wasn't funny anymore." Noting Giancana's growing irritation with Kennedy in 1962, she knew her relationship with the President "was eating away at him" and she "could tell by his silence that he didn't like it."

She had also first attributed the Kennedy relationship to great passion, but finally came to see that she was just another element in his life. "There was a niche for each one: his career, his Presidency, his political party, his family, his children, his wife, or perhaps the image of the First Lady, me, his cronies, and so on down the line." Later she concluded Kennedy was "a pretty fair actor" and that despite his protestations she was too far down the line.

How much, if any, of this is true? Judith Campbell Exner's story cannot simply be taken at face value. By the time she told it, the President and the two Mafia men had all been murdered, so no one could readily disprove her allegations. She could have concocted all or most of the tale in order to make her book a best seller. Claims of sexual adventures (especially those made by one of the avowed adventurers) should at least be substantially discounted.

The President's friend and aide David Powers said, "The only Campbell I know is chunky vegetable soup." And Kennedy's long-time secretary, Evelyn Lincoln, denied arranging the meetings, as Mrs. Exner had alleged, and ridiculed her as a campaign worker who pestered Kennedy, but whose calls were not put through. However, the unsworn testimony of a faithful friend or secretary must also be taken with a grain of salt. "Whatever I do or say, Mrs. Lincoln will be sweet and unsurprised," Kennedy once said to Sorensen. "If I had said just now, 'Mrs. Lincoln,

I have cut off Jackie's head, would you please send over a box?' she still would have replied, 'That's wonderful, Mr. President, I'll send it right away. . . . Did you get your nap?' "

Yet the matter cannot be put to rest with a dose of skepticism about all parties and a sense that where there was so much smoke there must have been some fire. There are more insidious possibilities, some of which Robert Kennedy must have pondered with anxiety and anguish. What if the woman's association with two of the most powerful and ruthless Mafia men and with the President of the United States was not accidental at all? It is possible that she was an agent employed by organized crime and that the seduction of John Kennedy was her assignment.* (We can carry that thought forward and wonder if in the late 1970s she was commissioned by the Mafia to defame John Kennedy in order to diminish another Kennedy's prospects for election.)

The worst strategies may also be the result of accident. Having learned from Sinatra about the woman's relations with the President, Giancana may have recruited her (or used her without her knowledge), to get the maximum blackmail on John Kennedy. A chilling possibility is that Giancana really did direct the vast Chicago criminal syndicate to provide votes (or stuff ballot boxes) in order to secure the election of a man over whom he would have the double blackmail of sex and the CIA assassination plot—a President from whom he might demand protection from prosecution (as well as otherwise influence through their mutual friend Frank Sinatra). It would be one of the great ironies of history, but not one Robert Kennedy would have enjoyed, if, out of these strange circumstances and with such a sinister purpose, organized crime was yet another factor making the difference in the razor-close election of 1960.

By the time CIA officials disclosed to him their murder contract with Giancana and Rosselli, the Attorney General must have talked with the President about the FBI's report on Judith Campbell. How candid John Kennedy would have been with his brother on such a matter is unknown. In explaining to Ben Bradlee why he considered Robert so great, the President said, "First, his high moral standards, strict personal ethics. He's a puritan . . ." That side of him may have diminished their rapport on matters outside politics and the family. Schlesinger says that Robert was not often asked to the White House on purely informal

---

* Though she was housed, transported, and given lavish gifts by Sam Giancana, Judith Campbell claimed not to be in his employ; but she admits she was on his side. "Sam was my friend and . . . he had my loyalty."

occasions, after working hours, because "at the end of a long day, he was often too demanding, too involved in issues . . . Teddy made the President laugh. Bobby was his conscience."

Yet the President listed "a real sense of compassion" as another of Robert's great qualities, and it may have included an understanding that John Kennedy needed a release from political and family pressures. One of the Attorney General's closest friends, responding to my questions about Judith Campbell Exner's book, said that Robert Kennedy was not surprised or shocked by his brother's "acquaintance with the night."

What surely shocked the Attorney General was the recognition, as he put the facts together, that his brother and the government of the United States were entangled with the most evil forces he could imagine, and that Sam Giancana, John Rosselli, and their like held an enormous power to blackmail not only John Kennedy and his family but any government of the United States. The Mafia leaders were privy to what may have been the worst national secret in the history of the United States, and the most embarrassing personal secret about John Kennedy. Nothing could damage the reputation of the United States government and of the Kennedy administration more than disclosure that it had conspired with organized crime to murder the head of a foreign government. Nothing could damage the personal reputation of John Kennedy more than detailed and public allegations of a sexual liaison, while in the White House, with a woman who at the same time was having an affair with a notorious Mafia chieftain.

The potential for blackmail extended beyond Giancana and Rosselli and their co-conspirators; it included Judith Campbell and those close to her, and any number of CIA and FBI agents who knew some or all of the facts. (FBI Special Agent Dodge, according to Judith, questioned one of Giancana's girlfriends about her, and was told, "If you want to know anything about Judy Campbell, I know she just came back from the White House. Why don't you go ask the President?") J. Edgar Hoover himself and future directors of the FBI who learned the facts from their predecessors or from the secret dossiers would also be able to hold these stories as a threat over John and Robert Kennedy as long as they lived.

Lurking in the background was also the mysterious Howard Hughes, for whom Maheu also worked while he was helping the CIA deal with Giancana and Rosselli, and whom Maheu apparently kept informed about the CIA assassination plot, if not about the Giancana-Campbell-Kennedy triangle. The ties between the Hughes empire, the underworld, and Las Vegas were being investigated by the Justice Department in Robert Kennedy's drive against organized crime. So Hughes, too, had reason to want embarrassing information about the Kennedy administration to use for protection, or for other, more aggressive purposes.

Aside from moral issues, the morass of potential blackmail in which the Attorney General found himself must have appalled him, and added to the revulsion he felt. How could the CIA and John Kennedy have been so stupid? How could they have thought that these actions could be kept secret when criminal characters were involved? What could they or the Attorney General do to extricate themselves and minimize the risk of exposure?

During the late spring and early summer of 1962, I would see the Attorney General and the President huddled in the Oval Office or walking together in the Rose Garden. Now I know one of the hardest subjects they had to discuss. If the President confessed to even one-tenth the relationship with Judith Campbell that she claimed, he had been bold and reckless in his personal life. Whatever John and Robert Kennedy said to each other about all this, the Attorney General apparently decided that he could not succumb to the threat of blackmail and would continue his all-out effort against organized crime, including Sam Giancana.

It was a bold course. While the President dropped his contacts with Judith Campbell, the FBI intensified its surveillance of her and Giancana, presumably seeking evidence to prosecute Giancana. "I was followed, hounded, harassed, accosted, spied upon, intimidated, burglarized, embarrassed, humiliated, denigrated and . . . finally driven to the brink of death" (through a suicide attempt), wrote Judith Campbell of those years. Her reaction was: "Okay, Sam, I'm with you. If you have to fight them, I'll fight them, too."

The pursuit of Giancana, which seemed to be persecution to him, was so extreme that in June 1963 he secured a temporary injunction from a federal district judge in Chicago, who ordered the FBI to cease its harassment. "How would you like it if you were on the eighteenth hole trying to line up a putt, and there were six FBI agents watching you?" Giancana's attorney asked the court. The judge required the FBI to let another group of golfers play between them and their quarry, and to park a block away from Giancana's home, but the injunction was soon set aside by the Court of Appeals and the close night-and-day surveillance continued. "They can't do this to me," Giancana was reported to have said to Edward Bennett Williams, whom he wanted to retain as his lawyer. "I'm working for the government."

Going to court for the injunction may have been Giancana's way of warning Robert Kennedy to lay off or suffer the consequences of full disclosure. Before filing suit, he had sent word to the Attorney General: "If Bobby Kennedy wants to talk to me, I'll be glad to talk to him, and he knows who to go through." The intermediary pointed out how close Giancana was to Frank Sinatra. By then the Kennedys had broken their ties to Sinatra because of his underworld connections.

Although the CIA involvement kept Robert Kennedy from prosecuting the Maheu-Giancana wiretap of 1961, the Justice Department moved vigorously on other fronts against the Mafia and especially Giancana. "Bobby pushed to get Giancana at any cost," said William Hundley, who headed the Organized Crime Section at Justice—but who did not know the cost the Attorney General realized he might have to pay.

No one can know how much all this contributed to the change in Robert Kennedy's attitude and approach that manifested itself so dramatically and decisively a few months later in the Cuban missile crisis. One of his most trusted friends, with whom I tested this theory that the CIA-Mafia-assassination-and-sex entanglement had a profound effect on the Attorney General's thinking, says it fits the facts and may be the key to the puzzle. As Justice Douglas had noted after their Russian journey in 1955, important insights penetrated Bob Kennedy slowly—but they penetrated. It had happened after the meeting with James Baldwin and the angry black intellectuals. Is it not likely that it happened in an even more intense way in the months after that day in May when he learned from the CIA about its contract with Rosselli and Giancana?

On the other side, Burke Marshall does not think the CIA–Mafia–Castro plot or the Mafia–Campbell–Kennedy triangle were paramount matters on Robert Kennedy's mind. However, the fact that Kennedy never discussed these questions with Marshall may be an indication that they were so disturbing that he would not share them even with a friend in whom he confided so many other things.

The threat of nuclear war was itself a profound enough problem to cause the Attorney General to restrain or reverse his tendency to resort to force in world affairs. But the change in him seems to have been evident even before the facts about the Soviet missiles were fully analyzed. By all accounts, including his own (in his memoir, *Thirteen Days*), from the moment he walked into the White House deliberations on the missiles, he was the chief opponent of the proposed surprise attack on Cuba. We now know that he was carrying into those October meetings whatever lessons he had drawn from the secrets he had learned that spring.

At one point, early in the missile crisis, Robert Kennedy stood almost alone against the hysteria of those who wanted an immediate air strike. Listening to the Joint Chiefs proposing war, he passed a note to the President: "I now know how Tojo felt when he was planning Pearl Harbor." He also was experiencing something of what Bowles had felt during the planning of the 1961 Cuban invasion and in its aftermath. But for the President's caution then, Bowles had said, 90 percent of the top policy makers would have gone to war against Castro. This time the President had Robert Kennedy to hold the line. Afterwards the Attorney General noted that among the ten or twelve "bright and energetic people" participating in the discussions were "the most able in the country, and if any one of half a dozen of them were President, the world would have been very likely plunged in a catastrophic war."

Dean Acheson, who had been called into the deliberations, argued that it was a clear test of wills with Khrushchev and that the missile bases had to be cleaned out by an air strike, the sooner the better. Despite his wish never to be on the other side of an argument with Acheson, whom he considered more lucid and convincing and brilliant than anyone he knew, Robert Kennedy challenged the former Secretary of State. "I said we were fighting for something more than just survival and that all our heritage and our ideals would be repugnant to such a sneak military attack," he reported later. Douglas Dillon, who had favored an air strike, was moved by Robert Kennedy's "intense but quiet passion" and felt he was "at a real turning point in history."

Robert Kennedy saw to it that they "spent more time on this moral question during the first five days than on any single matter," and in the end the President decided on the course of negotiation his brother recommended. Acheson withdrew in defeat, remarking later that Robert Kennedy was "moved by emotional or intuitive responses more than by the trained lawyer's analysis." In fact, the one who insisted that the principles and precedents of international law be considered was not Dean Acheson, the experienced international lawyer, but Robert Kennedy, who had never practiced law until he became Attorney General. Abram Chayes, the State Department's legal adviser in 1962, tells in his book, *The Cuban Missile Crisis*, how Robert Kennedy immediately asked the Department of Justice for an "international law work-up" and how he never let the legal points be forgotten.

Demonstrating the lawyer's negotiating art at its best, Robert Kennedy had the insight, when they were faced with two conflicting messages from Khrushchev, the first favorable and the second unfavorable, to urge the President to reply affirmatively to the first and ignore the second. With the Russian Ambassador he negotiated the tacit compromise calling for U.S. missiles to be removed from Turkey after Russian missiles were taken out of Cuba. With Sorensen's help, he drafted the presidential reply to Khrushchev that broke the deadlock.

Robert McNamara, in noting that a man's character is best shown when exposed to danger, said that in this period of the greatest strain he had ever operated under, he "came to know, admire and love Robert F. Kennedy," who remained throughout "calm and cool" and combined "energy and courage, compassion and wisdom." British Prime Minister Harold Macmillan, who had been kept intimately informed of events, said that "the way that Bobby and his brother played this hand was absolutely masterly. . . . What they did that week convinced me that they were both great men." The President, in the midst of the crisis, said, "Thank God for Bobby."

"Bobby best understood things by feeling and touching them," said Richard Boone, his aide on plans for a National Youth Service Corps. That explanation of how the Attorney General developed a deep concern about poverty applied equally to his understanding of the needs of people around the world. Traveling in Asia with his brother in 1951, he had felt the power of nationalism and, like his father and brother, he had an almost instinctive Irish-American anti-colonialism. Those feelings were reinforced on Robert Kennedy's first trip to Africa, in 1961, and, in 1962, during his travels to Japan, Indonesia, India, Europe, and Brazil.

In addition to missions for the President he had to accomplish with heads of state, at each stop the Attorney General gave priority to meetings with young people. In Tokyo, he faced thousands of students shouting Marxist and anti-American slogans, and, after the microphone had been disconnected, carried on with a bullhorn, answering questions with a directness that took the crowd by surprise, and in the end won an ovation. The news accounts of his talks made him sound like Chester Bowles, as he proclaimed that this was the century of "the awakening of peoples in Asia and Africa and Latin America—peoples stirring from centuries of stagnation, suppression and dependency."

When Schlesinger drafted a speech for him to give in Berlin, at the end of his Asian journey, the Attorney General rejected its standard cold war rhetoric, finding it "a strictly conventional damnation of the Communists." After returning from Brazil in December 1962, Kennedy wrote: "Far too often, for narrow, tactical reasons, this country has associated itself with tyrannical and unpopular regimes that had no following and no future. Over the past twenty years we have paid dearly because of support given to colonial rulers, cruel dictators or ruling cliques void of social purpose."

Foreign Service officers, Robert Kennedy wrote to the President in 1962, "must be made to meet with representatives of all kinds of groups, because more and more the people themselves are determining their country's future and policies." He urged his brother to say to the Foreign Service: "Innovations, imagination, yes, even revolutionary concepts are essential . . . *It is your responsibility not just to carry out policies that have been established but to suggest and come forth with new ones.*"

To get more innovation and imagination in developing a new policy on major problems the Attorney General proposed that the President utilize "the best minds in Government . . . in times other than deep crisis and emergencies." In a memorandum to the President in March 1963, Robert Kennedy wrote: "You talk to McNamara but mostly on Defense matters, you talk to Dillon but primarily on financial questions, Dave Bell on AID matters, etc. These men should be sitting down and thinking of some of the problems facing us in a broader context." He put an asterisk after "best minds" and a handwritten footnote: "ME."

A Socratic approach to administration was not the President's style, and he never tried, in any sustained way, to get the best men around him to do the long-range thinking the Attorney General proposed. Indeed, once, when James Reston asked him what long-range goals he had that he wanted to accomplish, John Kennedy looked blank and answered in platitudes. But he came to count upon Robert Kennedy to help him break out of the confines of narrow, tactical responses to urgent situations.

The realization began to dawn upon those of us who had wished John Kennedy had an Eleanor Roosevelt or some person of strong conscience by his side that he had one in Robert. The Attorney General may have felt the responsibility of his role as the President's goad and conscience, for even in the midst of the tremendous pressures of administering the Department of Justice and advising the President on all fronts, he deliberately tried to stretch and broaden his own mind. This was a new undertaking and underneath the arrogance of his ideology of action he was intellectually insecure—but curious. He tried to hide his nervousness. When he met with the Supreme Court law clerks, Peter Edelman, Justice Arthur Goldberg's clerk, and later a Senate aide to Robert Kennedy, noted that "all the time that this tough guy was answering questions . . . his hands were shaking under the table and were knotted up with one another."

The power he was wielding combined with a recognition of how little he knew seems to have driven Robert Kennedy to want to read, question, and learn more than he had ever done before. As his brother and leaders of the government began to look to him not just for executive action but for wisdom, I think he came to understand that his wisdom consisted in knowing what he did not know, and taking it as a mandate to learn. Whatever the motivation, the self-education that Robert Kennedy pursued in the 1960s was a matter of will and disciplinary resolutions.

While shaving in the morning, the Attorney General would listen to long-playing records of Shakespeare's plays, and at night he would read, more than at any time before. Between Christmas 1962 and Easter 1963, he read (according to what he told Fletcher Knebel) at least ten books, including Barbara Tuchman's *The Guns of August*; S. F. Bemis' *John Quincy Adams and the Foundations of American Foreign Policy*; Alan Moorehead's *The White Nile*; Barbara Ward's *The Rich Nations and the Poor Nations*; Herbert Agar's *The Price of Union*; and Knebel and Charles Bailey's *Seven Days in May*. He also resolved to spend time with some of the best minds he knew for discussions in a broader context.

After participating in a ten-day Aspen seminar on readings that raised large philosophical and political questions, he and Ethel asked Schlesinger to organize a series of evenings that would continue the seminar process in Washington among leading members of the administration. Instead of the Aspen format of conversation about a common text, the Hickory Hill meetings, held every month or so during 1962 and 1963, featured speakers, such as Isaiah Berlin, Al Capp, and John Kenneth Galbraith, followed by a lively question period that was often led by Robert Kennedy.

In the summer of 1963, he arranged for about fifteen student leaders from around the world to be brought to Aspen for a two-week session on America and the world. Stirred by encounters with young people during his overseas trips, he wanted to talk with them at length, face to face. Eric Sevareid and Ambassador Charles Bohlen participated, but were on wavelengths too different from the students' to communicate much. According to the seminar leader, Washington attorney and former St. John's College tutor Harvey Poe, it was Robert Kennedy, listening and questioning, day after day, who reached the students, and whom they felt and touched, too.

Young people became one of his central concerns. When the Iranian ambassador persuaded Dean Rusk to send certain Iranian students in American colleges back to Iran, at the request of the Shah, Robert Kennedy turned for advice to Justice Douglas, who knew Iran. Douglas said they would probably be going back to face firing squads. After further investigation, Kennedy finally reported to Douglas: "I just told Rusk to go chase himself." In 1963 when asked to prosecute American students who went to visit Cuba, he refused, saying: "What's wrong with that? If I were twenty-two years old, that is certainly the place I would want to visit." If he had not been born rich, he would have been a revolutionary, he once said. To an interviewer who said he belonged in the hills with Castro and Ché, he said, "I know it."

As the Peace Corps Representative to Africa, I followed with increasing pleasure the role of Robert Kennedy in American policy-making for that continent. After his 1961 opposition to aid for Nkrumah's Ghana, which the President fortunately overrode, the Attorney General became a staunch supporter of the efforts of Mennen Williams and Wayne Fredericks to promote African independence and development. Kennedy was appalled when George Ball replied to his call for involvement with the revolution in Zanzibar that it was foolish to waste our time, since "if God could take care of the little swallows in the skies, He could certainly take care of a little country" like Zanzibar. On November 20, 1963, the Attorney General wrote Bundy of his interest in developing the "policy of the United States toward the individuals and organizations which are attempting to gain independence in Mozambique, South Africa, Angola and Rhodesia." Contrary to State Department protocol, he himself had received the leader of the Mozambique struggle. "These areas are going to be extremely important to us in the future," he contended. By "a concentrated effort with students and intellectuals," he thought, "we could head off some of the problems that are undoubtedly going to appear on the horizon in the next year or so."

On the horizon instead was the Texas School Book Depository and the grassy knoll in downtown Dallas.

"God, it's so awful. Everything was really beginning to run so well." Those words of Robert Kennedy, as he went into the Lincoln bedroom to try to sleep for a few hours on the night of November 22, were echoed by most of us, but for the President's brother they had a weight beyond measure. His friend Charles Spalding heard him, behind the bedroom door, sob and say, "Why, God?" The questions that had faced him before, after the disclosures in the spring of 1962, must have all come back.

That very day he had been meeting with federal attorneys from around the country to plan the next stage of the drive against organized crime. Had his all-out efforts to destroy the Mafia, including Sam Giancana and those who thought they had bought protection by working with the CIA to kill Castro, caused them to kill the President? Or was it the result of his drive against Jimmy Hoffa and the Teamster leader's criminal connections? Could it even be something as absurd as Sam Giancana's jealousy over Judith Campbell? Was it Castro's retaliation, or that of anti-Castro Cubans? Could a fanatic CIA cold warrior have used "executive action" against a President who was moving for peace?

"There's so much bitterness," Robert Kennedy said to his aide, Ed Guthman, as they paced the lawn at Hickory Hill after J. Edgar Hoover

411

had, unsympathetically, told him the President had died. "I thought they'd get one of us but . . . I thought it would be me." He did not then indicate who he suspected the "they" were, but a few days later he said to Arthur Schlesinger that Oswald might have been part of a larger plot organized by Castro or by gangsters.

Also on Kennedy's mind was the CIA. Much later, he told his long-time colleague in the drive against organized crime, Walter Sheridan, that at the time of the assassination he had wondered about the possible involvement of CIA agents. Sheridan recalls Kennedy saying that he had asked his close friend CIA Director McCone "if they had killed my brother, and I asked him in a way that he couldn't lie to me, and they hadn't."

Among the gangsters, with ties to the Mafia, who might have insti-gated the assassination was Jimmy Hoffa, who was then being prosecuted by the Attorney General in a trial set for January. Very soon after the assassination Kennedy asked Walter Sheridan how Hoffa had reacted. Reluctantly, his aide reported that the union leader had been enraged to hear that the Teamsters' flag in Washington had been lowered to half-mast, and had said to a reporter, "Bobby Kennedy is just another lawyer now." The secretary-treasurer of Teamsters Local 901, Frank Chavez, wrote the Attorney General that he intended to raise money from union brothers to "clean, beautify and supply with flowers the grave of Lee Harvey Oswald."

Since the fall of 1962, Robert Kennedy had believed that Hoffa was considering his assassination. According to a key Hoffa aide, whose testi-mony the FBI confirmed by a lie detector test, that summer the Teamster leader had discussed using a lone gunman without any ties to the union, equipped with a rifle with a telescopic sight, to kill the Attorney General. Hoffa had even noted the desirability of doing it while Kennedy was riding in a convertible, somewhere in the South. The Louisiana Teamster official to whom he had proposed this had a criminal record and close ties to the Mafia syndicate based in New Orleans (with Cuba in its domain). Struck by the coincidence in details, and perhaps with knowl-edge of Oswald's time in New Orleans before the assassination, Robert Kennedy took confidential steps shortly after the President's death to look into the possible involvement of the Teamsters or organized crime.

Kennedy knew how difficult it would be to prove any such con-spiracy. Two months before his brother's assassination, he had testified to a Senate committee that in murders ordered by organized crime the leaders "have insulated themselves from the crime itself": "If they want to have somebody knocked off, for instance, the top man will speak to somebody who will speak to somebody else who will speak to somebody else and order it. The man who actually does the gun work . . . does not know who ordered it."

How soon, if ever, did Robert Kennedy see transcripts of the FBI's wiretaps of Mafia conversations before and after the President's murder? The evidence from electronic surveillance supplied to the 1979 House Select Committee on Assassinations, which the FBI should have shown to the Attorney General, conveyed the bitterness and anger with which organized crime leaders viewed the Kennedy administration. There were extensive and heated discussions about the difficulties the Kennedys were causing them. In 1962, a New York Mafia member said, "Bob Kennedy won't stop today until he puts us all in jail all over the country." That same year, Philadelphia boss Angelo Bruno told an associate, Willie Weisburg, who had urged that the Attorney General be murdered, that Kennedy's successor might be worse, but by mid-1963 Bruno's mood had changed; because of Kennedy's anti-Mafia pressure, he was angrily making plans to leave America. In October 1963, in response to a Mafia member's remark that the President "should drop dead," New York leader Stefano Magaddino exploded, "They should kill the whole family, the mother and father too."

After the President's assassination, the FBI's electronic surveillance found Mafia leaders relieved and elated. "Good!" exclaimed one of Bruno's men. "It's too bad his brother Bobby was not in that car, too."

Three days after the murder, in response to an aide who remarked that Oswald was an anarchist or Communist, Sam Giancana replied admiringly, "He was a marksman who knew how to shoot." On December 3, 1963, in a conversation with Sam Giancana about the assassination, a Mafia lieutenant predicted hopefully that "in another two months from now, the FBI will be like it was five years ago. They won't be around no more. . . . They're gonna start running down Fair Play for Cuba, Fair Play for Matsu. They call that more detrimental to the country than us guys."

That leaders of organized crime desired and approved the assassination was no proof that they planned it. Yet Robert Kennedy knew that the prompt killing of Oswald by Jack Ruby, a shady character with ties to both Teamster and Mafia agents, fit the traditional pattern of underworld murders. Manipulating Oswald by playing on his hostilities and fantasies, anyone planning to kill the President could have found him an ingenious cover—although an unreliable one who would have to be disposed of promptly.

Presumably the Attorney General soon learned, as the FBI did, that Ruby had been friendly years before in Chicago with two professional killers for organized crime, who in 1963 were associated with Sam

Giancana. Kennedy must also have learned, as the Warren Commission did, that Ruby had gone to Cuba in 1959 to visit one of his close friends, a gambling casino operator associated with the Mafia chieftain in Cuba, Santos Trafficante (who was the agent Giancana had enlisted for the CIA to kill Castro). Ruby's Havana friend later visited him in Dallas, and Castro let Trafficante out of jail to return to the United States. The Attorney General should also have found out from the FBI about Ruby's long-distance calls in the month before the assassination to various persons associated with Giancana or Hoffa, including a man whom Kennedy had once described as one of Hoffa's most violent lieutenants. According to Ruby's sister, another man he called was one of his old friends who was a professional executioner for Giancana.

Kennedy's suspicions were also inevitably drawn to Castro, who, he had reason to believe, had learned of the CIA's efforts to kill him. On September 7, 1963, Castro had told an Associated Press correspondent that "Kennedy is the Batista of our time, and the most opportunistic President of all time." He warned: "We are prepared to . . . answer in kind. United States leaders should think that if they assist in terrorist plans to eliminate Cuban leaders, they themselves will not be safe."

Kennedy knew that although the CIA's assassination plots were kept secret at the top, at the bottom Giancana (and probably others) had talked loosely in underworld circles. Trafficante himself, some suspected, had made a deal with Castro and was keeping him informed of the CIA plot. Moreover, Castro was attributing more to the CIA than it may have deserved (in 1975 he told George McGovern of twenty-four alleged CIA attempts on his life from 1960 to 1965, most of which the CIA denied).

Unknown to Kennedy, in early September 1963, the CIA's chief prospect for the Castro assassination, an unstable heavy drinker, had asked to meet the Attorney General; some in the agency suspected he was a double agent, trying to entrap the United States, but Richard Helms decided that a CIA official should meet the Cuban and speak in Robert Kennedy's name. Had Castro learned of this session with what the Cuban believed was Robert Kennedy's "personal representative"? "For three years, we had known there were plots against us," Castro told the House Assassination Committee in 1979.

There was at least one other group with the motives and means to kill the President. Despite Oswald's own left-wing past, Robert Kennedy could not discount the possibility that anti-Castro Cubans had conspired with the disturbed young man for their own purposes, perhaps posing as agents of Castro. The Attorney General was aware of the growing hostility and sense of betrayal among the Cuban exiles, especially those the CIA had armed, some of whom were still encamped near Miami. An anonymous sheet had circulated among Cubans in Miami saying that they would return to their island only "if an inspired Act of God should place in the White House within weeks a Texan known to be a friend of all Latin Americans." At a meeting of anti-Castro Cubans and right-wing Americans in a Dallas suburb on October 1, a vehement Cuban had said, "We're waiting for Kennedy the 22d. We're going to give him the works when he gets in Dallas." Though neither of these inflammatory attacks was apparently linked to the assassination, they reflected an angry mood that had worried the Attorney General. In June 1963 the Bay of Pigs brigade leaders had protested to the CIA that only a massive American invasion would overthrow Castro, and Helms had warned Kennedy that the Cubans were "disheartened in that they do not foresee such an invasion." "Disheartened" was an inadequate description; the more militant guerrilla bands were festering with frustration and hatred.

Some of this bitterness in the air among diverse men of violence came together, if only in Oswald's twisted mind, and struck down John Kennedy. For once in his life there was nothing Robert Kennedy could see to do or say about it. There was no way of getting to the bottom of the assassination without uncovering the very stories he hoped would be hidden forever. So he closed his eyes and ears to the cover-up that he knew (or soon discovered) Allen Dulles was perpetrating on the Warren Commission, and took no steps to inform the commission of the Cuban and Mafia connections that would have provided the main clues to any conspiracy.

Deputy Attorney General Nicholas Katzenbach, to whom all dealings with the commission were left, says that Robert Kennedy "never really wanted any investigation." In a memorandum to Bill Moyers in the White House, Katzenbach stressed two points: "1. The public must be satisfied that Oswald was the assassin . . . 2. Speculation about Oswald's motivation ought to be cut off. . . ." Hoover, who also knew and withheld information about the assassination plots, told another key Johnson assistant, Walter Jenkins, "The thing I am most concerned about . . . is having something issued so we can convince the public that Oswald is the real assassin."

Friends of Robert Kennedy like to believe that he refused to involve himself in the problem of who had murdered his brother because, as Schlesinger wrote, "investigation would only protract the unbearable pain." It may be that the Attorney General's non-cooperation and withholding of information was itself a source of additional, almost unbearable pain. Above all, his brother once said of him, he could be counted upon to give "the unvarnished truth," but in this situation he was putting his brother's and the country's reputation above the truth.

Late in the night, three years later, in P. J. Clarke's saloon in New York City, he wondered aloud to Schlesinger how long he could continue to avoid comment on the Warren Commission report, which he believed was a poor job and which he could not endorse. But according to Schlesinger's journal, Kennedy said he was still "unwilling to criticize it and thereby reopen the whole tragic business." The next year, when the New Orleans district attorney, James Garrison, claimed he had discovered a conspiracy to kill John Kennedy involving the CIA and various underworld characters, Robert asked Frank Mankiewicz whether he thought Garrison had anything. When Mankiewicz started to tell him, he said, "Well, I don't think I want to know."

In his official capacity as Attorney General, as well as in an extraordinary personal relationship, Robert Kennedy was his brother's keeper. If his brother's death—in Oswald's mind or through a larger plot—was somehow connected with the extreme efforts to get Castro, which the Attorney General had encouraged, with his own drive to destroy the Mafia, or with the President's relationship with a Mafia woman that the Attorney General had not stopped in time, then the assassination was both a personal and an official failure. Since he dared not unravel these things himself, he could only hope that some of the worst possibilities would be disproved by others.

The report of the French journalist Jean Daniel, who was seeing Castro when the news came of Kennedy's assassination, must have brought some relief. Daniel, who had interpreted the President's remarks to him a few weeks earlier as an olive branch for Castro, found the Maximum Leader interested. In a six-hour talk, through most of one night shortly before the assassination, he talked about Kennedy and asked Daniel to go over again and again Kennedy's statement that he had "approved the proclamation which Fidel Castro made in the Sierra Maestra," that he understood the "economic colonization, humiliation and exploitation" in the old regime, and that it was "as though Batista was the incarnation of a number of sins on the part of the United States. Now we shall have to pay for those sins."

Castro commented: "Kennedy . . . still has the possibility of being, in the eyes of history, the greatest President of the United States, the leader who may at last understand that there can be coexistence between capitalists and socialists. . . . He would then be an even greater President than Lincoln." There was a tough note, too, though also relatively encouraging, when Castro added, "Personally, I consider him responsible for everything, but I will say this: he has come to understand many things over the past few months."

At the word of Kennedy's death, Castro had seemed shocked and saddened, and said repeatedly, *"Es una mala noticia"*—"This is bad news," and added, *"Voilà,* there is the end to your mission of peace." It did not seem like the conversation of a man who had been plotting the death of John Kennedy.

There was one ominous note. In pressing Daniel for information about President Johnson, Castro asked, "What authority does he exercise over the CIA?" This caused Schlesinger to wonder whether Castro had been able to exercise complete authority over his own CIA.

Robert Kennedy did not live to hear Castro's explanation, in 1978, to the House Assassination Committee, of his September 1963 warning that Cuba was prepared to answer in kind any plans to eliminate Cuban leaders. That was not meant as a threat of retaliation, said Castro, but "a warning that we knew," and that such plots "set a very bad precedent, a very serious one—that could become a boomerang against the authors of those actions." For Cuba to have been involved in Kennedy's death would have been "insane," he said. "That would have been the most perfect pretext for the United States to invade our country which is what I have tried to prevent for all these years."

If Castro's words to Daniel helped to reduce Kennedy's concern that his Operation Mongoose and its secret corollary had boomeranged against his brother, Lyndon Johnson's did just the opposite. In the spring, just as Robert Kennedy was beginning to emerge from his brooding, he learned of a remark Johnson had made to Pierre Salinger which he considered "the worst thing that Johnson has said," and in Schlesinger's opinion was what made the gulf between the two "ultimately impassable." That Johnson said it to Kennedy's close friend and former aide meant that he intended it to reach Kennedy, perhaps as a warning.

"When I was young in Texas, I used to know a cross-eyed boy," Johnson said, as Robert Kennedy later recounted it. "His eyes were crossed, and so was his character. . . . That was God's retribution for people who were bad and so you should be careful of cross-eyed people because God put his mark on them. . . . Sometimes I think that, when you remember the assassination of Trujillo and the assassination of Diem, what happened to Kennedy may have been divine retribution."

Kennedy had reason to believe that Johnson had more in mind than Trujillo and Diem. Within hours of Johnson's becoming President, J. Edgar Hoover had established the direct access to the Oval Office that he had enjoyed with every President until Kennedy. (Hoover later boasted that he didn't speak to Bobby Kennedy the last six months he was in office.) The Attorney General had to assume that the FBI Director had disclosed to Johnson whatever damaging information he had on the Kennedys, including the story of Judith Campbell and the Mafia-CIA conspiracy to kill Castro.

Later, after Kennedy had publicly broken with Johnson, the President played his Cuban card (which some think he did not learn about until 1967, when he asked the CIA for an official secret report on its assassination plots). To Leo Janos of *Time* (and to others), Johnson said in confidence that the Kennedy administration "had been operating a damned Murder, Inc. in the Caribbean." To Howard K. Smith, he said, "Kennedy was trying to get Castro, but Castro got to him first." The newsmen did not print or broadcast these charges until after Johnson had died, but what the President was saying got back to Robert Kennedy, and intensified the pain that kept falling, drop by drop, upon his heart.

Even without the shadow of the assassination and the threat of blackmail, the relationship between Robert Kennedy and President Johnson would have been insufferable for both of them. To Johnson, the Attorney General was "that little runt" who "acted like *he* was . . . some kind of rightful heir to the throne." The President told his aide from Princeton, historian Eric Goldman, "That upstart's come too far and too fast. He skipped the grades where you learn the rules of life. He never liked me, and that's nothing compared to what I think of him." In an oral history interview, Kennedy said that Johnson was "mean, bitter, vicious —[an] animal in many ways." He found that "he lies all the time . . . even when he doesn't have to lie."

They were at their worst with each other, and nothing their mutual friends did made it any better. Bill Moyers, who admired them both, got caught in the cross fire, and became suspect by Johnson as a secret Kennedy man. A complete Kennedy man, Kenneth O'Donnell, who continued in the White House with Johnson for some months, was appalled by the vicious circle. "These two men just didn't know each other; and they built up this picture of each other which was just incredible." It was not all Johnson's fault, by any means. Robert Kennedy did not give an inch to him, let alone walk the extra mile.

Castro was right; John Kennedy's death was the end of any mission of peace. The new President, Bundy reported to his White House staff on national security just before Christmas 1963, "does not want to appear 'soft' on anything, especially Cuba." Soon the test of Johnson's toughness was Vietnam. But perhaps the most immediate trial of strength was with

Robert Kennedy. He delighted in telling reporters how he had broken the news to the Attorney General that he would not be Vice-President, and Kennedy had gulped, with "his Adam's apple going up and down like a yo-yo."*

To ensure against a Kennedy coup at the 1964 Democratic convention in Atlantic City, the President arranged for the film on John Kennedy to come after the nominations, and he had the FBI there in force, and in secret, to report to him on potential trouble, especially from Robert Kennedy or Martin Luther King. The FBI's William Sullivan later conceded that the primary purpose of the FBI surveillance was to provide Johnson with political information, particularly "in reporting on the activities of Robert Kennedy." The FBI agent in charge of the wiretap on King's hotel room and the other snooping said he gave Walter Jenkins and Bill Moyers forty-four pages of intelligence data and advised them constantly by telephone. To Moyers, whom he called the "Bishop," the FBI man wrote, "I'm certainly glad that we were able to come through with vital tidbits . . . which were of assistance."

Robert Kennedy's chief activity was to introduce the film on his brother—and to stand at the rostrum as the delegates and gallery greeted him with a spontaneous, continuous ovation that lasted more than twenty minutes. Watching him from the floor, I felt the surge of sympathy and memory that swept the hall, and was moved, as I had never been before, by this eldest-surviving son of Rose and Joseph Kennedy who stood there, smiling sadly. Finally, when he was able to speak, he closed with some lines from *Romeo and Juliet* that Jacqueline Kennedy had given him:

> *When he shall die,*
> *Take him and cut him out in little stars,*
> *And he will make the face of heaven so fine*
> *That all the world will be in love with night,*
> *And pay no worship to the garish sun.*

In the next few years a new perception of Robert Kennedy grew in me, as he ran for the Senate from New York, as he became the senator for the young and the poor, the black and the brown, the sick and the old, as he started on the hard climb to the presidency.

---

* When Johnson went on to ask Kennedy to manage his presidential campaign, both men must have recalled the day four years before when Robert Kennedy tried to get Johnson to withdraw from the vice-presidential nomination and take the chairmanship of the Democratic National Committee instead. Kennedy reported that Johnson "shook and tears came into his eyes, and he said, "I want to be Vice-President. . . ."

"I have absolutely no presidential ambitions, and neither does my wife—Ethel Bird," he said at the Women's National Press Club in January 1965. Yet his ambition was obvious, part of both the "Good Bobby" and the "Bad Bobby," and as Jules Feiffer said at the end of his famous cartoon, "If you want *one* Bobby to be your President you will have to take both . . . for Bobbies are widely noted for their family unity."

In these years we had only occasional contact, but I began to realize that I wanted him to be President more than anyone I had ever supported. The several Bobbies were coming together, at least in my mind, to make one of the most appealing and promising men in the history of American politics.

Others were discovering the "new Bobby," too. Norman Mailer, who met him only once, was excited by Kennedy's "admixture of idealism plus willingness to traffic with demons, ogres, and overlords of corruption." Somehow "he had grown modest as he grew older," and had "come into that world where people live with the recognition of tragedy." James Stevenson of *The New Yorker* found that Kennedy's new "toughness seems largely directed toward himself, inward." There was a mystery about him that made Galbraith suggest that "he was the least known public figure of our time," and Adam Walinsky, his Senate aide, said, "There were things he carried around in his head that were unimaginable, things that he just had to live with all by himself." But beyond his romantic qualities—that led Alice Roosevelt Longworth to say, "Bobby could have been a revolutionary priest"—there was his willingness and ability to use power practically in the political world. "As I look back on the sixties," Michael Harrington later wrote, "he was the man who actually could have changed the course of American history."

There was a new reflective quality that friends and at least one former foe found in him. Berl Bernhard told me how Bob Kennedy's old animosity toward the Civil Rights Commission seemed to have washed away. "What were we always fighting about?" Bob called out to him one day from the bathtub, as he was getting ready to make a speech arranged by Bernhard. "Oh, yes, you were 'second-guessers'—you were 'irresponsible,' " Kennedy said, mocking himself. "And then there was always Father Hesburgh coming around the corner telling me what I was doing wrong." Kennedy's early critic and later good friend Anthony Lewis said: "Most people acquire certainties as they grow older; he *lost* his. He changed— he grew—more than anyone I have known."

Many remained skeptical about the genuineness of his turn to peace and populism. He was just following the election returns from New York, and adjusting to his new constituency, it was frequently said. Others suggested that he had put on and worn for so long the mask of a progressive that he acted like one. Once while some critics of her brother were doubting his bona fides, Eunice Shriver cut short the questioning of Robert Kennedy's motives. "What difference does it make, why waste time arguing about that? What counts is that all that energy, all that power, all that ability is being used for peace and for civil rights and for the poor."

For whatever reasons, something else was happening within the family. Robert Kennedy was passing Sargent Shriver on the left, as the director of the War on Poverty staunchly defended the soundness of the programs he had started, and the senator from New York sharply questioned their adequacy. For Shriver, who had endured the slings and arrows of his young pro-McCarthy brother-in-law during the fifties, when Robert and his friends considered Eunice's husband too liberal ("the house Communist"), the switch in positions was difficult to take. For Kennedy, nothing that Shriver or Johnson could do would seem enough. It was one time when family loyalty broke down, to the disservice of both Shriver and Kennedy—and Johnson—each of whose effectiveness would have been greater if they could have all worked together.

In foreign policy, however, there was no way for Johnson and Kennedy to have worked together for long. Johnson sent the Marines into the Dominican Republic and elsewhere in Latin America backed down on the Alliance for Progress, just as Kennedy was deepening his conviction that military intervention was wrong and proclaiming (in Lima, Peru, in 1965) that "the responsibility of our time is nothing less than a revolution . . . peaceful if we are wise enough; humane if we care enough; successful if we are fortunate enough." And most serious of all their differences was the growing division over Vietnam.

Vietnam became the fire in which the President was determined to prove that he was made of steel. For Kennedy it was the crucible in which he found a new kind of courage—the courage to appear soft. Robert Lowell complimented him for learning "how to be brave without becoming simple-minded." In February 1967, as Kennedy was preparing a major Senate speech against the war, the poet congratulated him for "putting into practice that kind of courage and ability that your brother so subtly praised in his *Profiles*."

Kennedy became haunted by the pictures of the dead and the dying, the burned and the homeless in Indochina. And he believed that his brother would have adhered to General MacArthur's advice against a land war in Southeast Asia. Before his death, John Kennedy had told Senator Mansfield that he had been right about withdrawal, "but I can't do it until 1965—after I'm reelected." In mid-November 1963 he told Senator Wayne Morse that his criticism of the administration's Vietnam policy was right and that he was "in the midst of an intensive study which substantiates your position." Robert Kennedy, in his own way, continued that study, and became convinced that Johnson should stop the bombing and start negotiating a political settlement. When Johnson chose the opposite course, Kennedy said "we are headed straight for disaster."

With the strong feelings he had about the war, Robert Kennedy's reluctance, until 1967, to lead a public campaign against the President's Vietnam policy was curious. In January 1966 he spoke somberly in the Senate against Johnson's decision to resume bombing, after the Christmas halt, warning that it might "become the first in a series of steps on a road from which there is no turning back—a road which leads to catastrophe for all mankind." But there were long silences, when he said nothing publicly about the war, and anti-war leaders chastised him for his reticence. When he was practicing for a "Face the Nation" interview, Schlesinger asked him about John Kennedy's responsibility for the war, and he thought a moment and said, "Well, I don't know what would be best: to say that he didn't spend much time thinking about Vietnam; or to say that he did and messed it up." Schlesinger remembers him thrusting his hand to the sky and saying, "Which, brother, which?"

Part of his reticence no doubt was related to this ambivalence about his brother's—and his own—responsibility for American involvement in the war. In 1967 Jack Newfield found Kennedy "finally prepared to admit to himself that strange prophets like Chester Bowles, I. F. Stone, and those angry, panicked kids in SDS had been right all along, and that he, his brother, and their friends had been tragically wrong."

Then, in February 1967, in a private meeting with Johnson, he made his strongest plea to the President, to negotiate for a cease-fire with all elements in South Vietnam participating in the choice of a new government. "There just isn't a chance in hell that I will do that, not the slightest chance," Johnson replied (according to Kennedy's later account to Frank Mankiewicz). In such oral history, recollections may be inaccurate, but in explaining Kennedy's actions the important thing is what he heard and remembered Johnson saying. "I'll destroy you and every one of your dove friends in six months," Johnson was reported to have said. "You'll be dead politically in six months."

That threat must have had alarming overtones for Kennedy. Based on what we now know that Johnson knew and could use against Kennedy, a good guess is that the whole CIA-assassination-Mafia mess had played some part in holding the impassioned senator back from all-out opposition to the President. An all-out Johnson campaign to undermine Robert Kennedy might not have destroyed him politically, but it could have damaged his brother's place in history and the country's confidence in its leaders' integrity.

The past was an albatross Kennedy could not shake off, but neither could Kennedy avoid the public confrontation. Just as he had stepped up his pursuit of Giancana, Rosselli, and the Mafia after facing the blackmail they held over him in 1962, he now decided to take on Johnson openly, on the Vietnam issue, come what may. "I can testify that if fault is to be found or responsibility assessed, there is enough to go around for all—including myself," Kennedy said to the Senate in opening his major address against the war on March 2, 1967. But he asked his fellow citizens to picture the "horror" of the "ever-widening war" as "a mother and child watch death by fire fall from an improbable machine sent by a country they barely comprehend." After he finished, Senator Henry Jackson read a letter from the President defending the bombing, and said that Kennedy's proposals would leave the United States in a position of weakness. Nixon commented that Kennedy's speech "had the effect of prolonging the war by encouraging the enemy."

Even with the gauntlet down on the war, Kennedy tried to avoid a direct challenge to Johnson's renomination. Underneath the surface of his public calm about his decision not to seek the Democratic nomination, strong currents were swirling. One night he said to Schlesinger, "How can we possibly survive five more years of Lyndon Johnson? Five more years of a crazy man?" Yet he continued to resist the appeal from Allard Lowenstein that he run for President.

Late in the fall of 1967, my wife and I were among a few friends who had dinner and a talk with the senator at the Long Island home of Bill and Judith Moyers. Clare came prepared to urge him to be the first to enter the New Hampshire primary. At one point, he turned to her and, probing with his sad blue eyes, asked, "Do you think I should run?" To my amazement, after a few moments when they both seemed deep in thought, she shook her head, and said, "I don't know—I want you to, but I don't know." Afterward, she could not explain her hesitation, except that some sense of fear made her want to protect him.

Kennedy's own answer to the question that evening, as I remember it, was: "I would like to run, and the country cannot afford four more years of Johnson and the war, but if I do it, it will become so personal, he will make it so very personal, that the big issues might be lost. If I just fight on the issues, it will be harder for him to make it personal."

Later Moyers told me that Kennedy had asked him if he would leave his job as publisher of *Newsday* and join him in a presidential race. If Moyers and Robert McNamara would manage his campaign, Kennedy said, he would run. In February 1968, while Senator Eugene McCarthy was running in the New Hampshire primary (but before his near-victory that demonstrated how vulnerable Johnson was), my wife and I were on the deck of Robert McNamara's ski lodge in Aspen. A phone call came from Robert Kennedy. After a long conversation, McNamara returned to say that Kennedy was agonizing about entering the race, and sounded as if he was going to do it, contrary to the advice of most of his friends, including McNamara. Neither Moyers nor McNamara felt able to join the campaign, but a few days before the New Hampshire vote, Kennedy made up his mind to run.

The final turning point appears to have been his trip to California, in early March, to be with Cesar Chavez when the union organizer broke a fast of penance for violence in the farm workers' strike. At the mass, Kennedy shared the communion bread with Chavez, whom he called "a hero of our times." Chavez and the people crowding to see and touch Kennedy treated him as a hero, too. "You could see the blood," Chavez said of Kennedy's hands, which had been scratched by those reaching out to him. "Let me say to you that violence is no answer," said Kennedy. Chavez had written some words but was too weak to read them himself. Kennedy listened intently as the words were read:

> When we are really honest with ourselves, we must admit that our lives are all that really belong to us. So it is how we use our lives that determines what kind of men we are. It is my deepest belief that only by giving our lives do we find life. I am convinced that the truest act of courage, the strongest act of manliness, is to sacrifice ourselves for others in a totally nonviolent struggle for justice. To be a man is to suffer for others. God help us be men.

Afterwards, flying East, Kennedy said, "Yes. I'm going to do it." Still friends tried to dissuade him, but former Congressman Stewart Udall said "he really wasn't listening to us. . . . He was on fire." Udall "got the feeling that it was like a Greek tragedy in the sense that events themselves had been determined by fates setting the stage, and that there was really little choice left."

In the caucus room in the Old Senate Office Building, where I had seen John Kennedy launch his campaign in 1960, I watched a second Kennedy start down the long road. He conveyed a sense of relief and relish to be in the fray. To those who advised him to support McCarthy until that campaign ran out of steam and then pick up the pieces, he said McCarthy was not someone he could support for President and "Kennedys don't act that way." To Jack Newfield, he explained: "Not to run and pretend to be for McCarthy, while trying to screw him behind his back, that's what would really be ruthless. . . . It is a much more natural thing for me to run than not to run. When you start acting unnaturally, you're in trouble. . . . I'm trusting my instincts now and I feel freer."

There were three who did not feel freer.

In the very hour of euphoria, Gene McCarthy saw his campaign collapsing, and his victory being stolen by the latest leader of a clan he had long disliked. He and his partisans, who included so many of the young whom Robert Kennedy especially hoped to rally, turned angrily on the new candidate and raised the old charge of ruthlessness.

For Lyndon Johnson, his worst nightmare was coming true: "Robert Kennedy had openly announced his intention to reclaim the throne in the memory of his brother. And the American people, swayed by the magic of the name, were dancing in the streets." That was hardly an accurate description, for the initial response to Kennedy's entry in the race was mixed, with widespread criticism in the press. But as Kennedy began winning primaries, the tide seemed to be turning his way.

Jacqueline Kennedy, however, feared the worst. She had been surprised and pleased to find that William Manchester, the author of *Death of a President* who had felt so mistreated by her and Robert Kennedy, had come out for him and called him "genuinely humane" and "the least understood man in the presidential arena." She wrote Manchester that he had given Bobby "what he was pleading for . . . a wiping off of the blackboard of the past—a faith in now." But her own faith was shaken. "Do you know what I think will happen to Bobby?" she said to Schlesinger. "The same thing that happened to Jack. . . . There is so much hatred in this country, and more people hate Bobby than hated Jack." She said she had told Bobby this, "but he isn't fatalistic, like me."

Martin Luther King was the next to be struck down by hate. When Kennedy heard the news, he shrunk back, according to one newsman, "as though struck physically," and said, "Oh, God. When is this violence going to stop?"

At Martin's funeral in Atlanta, Kennedy asked me if I would come to California and campaign for him in the primary, and I said of course I would. When I got to Santa Barbara, Scott Buchanan and Stringfellow Barr, founders of the great books program at St. John's College, had their questions ready. "What is Bobby up to?" asked Buchanan. "Just what he said," I replied, "—trying to save the soul of the country." Barr said, "Can he save his own soul?"

Part of the case I made then and would make again, now with more evidence, is that Robert Kennedy had come to see that the Enemy Within America was the enemy within him, and that he had done as well in taming the savageness in men and in himself as anyone I knew. In his last talk with Kennedy, in the spring of 1968, Moyers had commented: "When I arrived in Washington I had far more energy than wisdom." Kennedy replied: "Same here." Reminiscing over dinner at the Caravelle in New York, they each regretted having come late to their judgment about Vietnam. Quietly Kennedy added: "I have myself wondered at times if we did not pay a very great price for being more energetic than wise about a lot of things, especially Cuba."

After King's death, Kennedy had said, "You know that fellow Harvey Lee Oswald, whatever his name is, set something loose in this country." There was hate all around, to an extent I had not known before. It was many years before I read of the 1968 remark about Kennedy made by the FBI's Clyde Tolson, J. Edgar Hoover's chief companion: "I hope that someone shoots and kills the son of a bitch." But the evening of June 4, after I had returned from campaigning in California, Clare and I were at a dinner party in New York City and found more hostility to Robert Kennedy, among highly literate, usually liberal people, than we had imagined existed outside of extremist hate groups. We went home depressed and turned on the television to hear the returns from California. The victory was reassuring, and we liked Bob's light touch in his thanks to campaign workers—and the confidence with which he said we can end the divisions and violence within the United States.

At St. Patrick's Cathedral during the night as Robert Kennedy's body lay at rest, the diverse men and women who stood vigil or sat thinking in the pews gave evidence that he was able to bring people together. Mayor Richard Daley and Tom Hayden were both weeping. In *Robert Kennedy: A Memoir* Jack Newfield recalled the line from Pascal in Camus's *Resistance, Rebellion and Death*: "A man does not show his greatness by being at one extremity, but rather by touching both at once."

13 · Chicago 1968 and the End of an Era

Spending the night in a Chicago jail was hardly the way I expected to mark the nomination of Hubert Humphrey. It may have been as good a way as any, however, to celebrate the end of an era. Sitting on a bench in a crowded cell, with a clogged toilet in the middle of the floor and a portable radio blaring the speeches from Convention Hall, I had a sense that the curtain was finally coming down on the decade of Martin King and John and Robert Kennedy.

There we were in the Cook County central jail on Thursday night, August 29, 1968, some seventy-nine Kennedy, McGovern, and McCarthy campaign workers, delegates and Democratic Party officials, ministers, priests, and rabbis, newsmen, and even a few Republicans. One of the latter was a barkeeper near Lincoln Park who had joined the protest march in anger at the police clubbing kids. "Eight cops beating one kid, is that law and order?" he said. Shaking his head, somewhat dumbfounded to be in prison, he half laughed. "What will my wife think? I'm not even a Democrat!"

Imagining the conversation that would occur when I tried to explain my whereabouts to my wife, at home in Old Westbury, New York, I doubted I could make her believe the sights I had seen: policemen beating protesters after their arrest, swinging clubs indiscriminately at anyone on the streets who looked young and radical, attacking reporters and cameramen covering the story, chasing bystanders into hotel lobbies, and hitting victims until they fell unconscious and bloody.

Bill Moyers, his wife, Judith, Adam Yarmolinsky, and I had separately run into similar violent encounters as we tried to go a few blocks across town early Wednesday evening, August 28. Meeting later, we compared notes and then watched other similar scenes on television. Something, we felt, had to be done to register opposition to such a police riot—something by those of us at the convention, and not just the war protesters in the park. We decided to call on colleagues at the convention —especially those who had been connected with John and Robert Kennedy—to join in a silent vigil the next noon, in front of the Conrad Hilton Hotel, standing on the edge of Michigan Avenue between the park protesters and the police.

The Massachusetts delegation agreed to co-sponsor the call, and then our Peace Corps colleague, Frank Mankiewicz, of Robert Kennedy's former staff, added his name; a number of us spent much of the night mimeographing and distributing the announcement. "We do this to put the force of conscience against the tear gas, bayonets, machine guns, billy clubs and barbed wire," it read. "Our protest will be entirely peaceful. We will not return violence with violence. We call upon Mayor Daley and the citizens of Chicago to put an end to this use of armed force."

By a series of accidents, that strategy of peaceful protest led the next night to the Cook County lockup. In our cell were twenty-five delegates—a *New York Times* correspondent, Tom Buckley just back from Vietnam; a syndicated columnist, Murray Kempton; a Republican barkeeper; and a college president (the present writer). As we listened on the radio to Humphrey's acceptance address, tears were streaming down our faces, not because of his words, although there was sadness in them, but because of the tear gas blowing in from the streets below.

The last thing I intended to do when I went to Chicago was to join the "park people" in any form of civil—or uncivil—disobedience. After the funeral of Robert Kennedy, I had reconciled myself to the nomination of Hubert Humphrey. Remembering the man he had been before becoming Johnson's Vice-President, I hoped for his emergence with new vitality and vision. Eugene McCarthy seemed to have no chance to win the nomination or the election, and I agreed with Robert Kennedy that McCarthy would not be a good President. Johnson's withdrawal, however, in recognition of the rising opposition to his war policy, had opened the way for Humphrey to run on a platform promising peace. The proposed disruption of the Democratic convention by the Yippies and militant peace protesters, led by Tom Hayden and other SDS leaders, seemed to me to play into Nixon's hands. Moreover, Daley was an effective mayor and did not deserve to be goaded into an angry reaction.

In early August, at the Vice-President's request, Bill Moyers and I had prepared a joint draft of an address accepting the Democratic nomination; we spent a weekend finding words that Humphrey might use to bridge the gap between the old and the new politics, between the young and the older generation, between the protesters against the war and those who wanted (but did not know how) to get out of Vietnam with honor. Although our draft dealt respectfully with the good Johnson had done at home, it was above all a declaration of independence.

Moyers had left the White House in December 1966 to become the publisher of *Newsday* in Garden City, New York; coincidentally, I had gone to nearby Old Westbury a month before to organize a new experimental college of the State University of New York. We both wanted to move Humphrey to a stronger anti-war position. Moyers felt the Vice-President had been led into support of escalation in Vietnam, as he himself had been, by the military argument that with this additional bombing or these additional troops the war would be ended in a few months. When the time estimated for victory kept being extended—by six months to a year, and then an indefinite number of years—Moyers climbed off the military wagon. He wanted to do whatever he could to help Humphrey do so too, knowing how pervasive, overwhelming, and demoralizing Johnson's influence had been on the Vice-President.

Humphrey's humiliation, if not emasculation, was witnessed by his former aide Tom Hughes, to whom the Vice-President would confide his troubles. One morning the Vice-President told him about the unexpected visit Johnson paid to the Humphreys' apartment the previous evening. Muriel and Hubert were doing the dishes when the President and Lady Bird arrived. The conversation was said to have gone something like this:

"Lady Bird can help dry the dishes, but I want Hubert to give me the speech," the President said.

Taking a seat at the kitchen table, Johnson explained that people told him Humphrey gave the best speech of anyone in the administration on why the United States was fighting in Vietnam, and he had come to hear it. Humphrey started to summarize briefly what he had been saying around the country, when the President interrupted.

"That's not what I mean," said Johnson. "I want you to give me that speech, right here in this kitchen."

So Humphrey gave the speech right there. He must have felt something like Khrushchev, when Stalin ordered his companions in the Kremlin to dance the gopak. As Khrushchev said, they danced the gopak. No doubt Humphrey delivered an abbreviated, somewhat subdued version of his talk: during his four years under Johnson his spirit had been subdued and his stature—if not his speeches—reduced.

Nevertheless, there was reason to hope that if the convention, with Humphrey's support, adopted a platform promising an end to the war in Vietnam, and if a Vice-President were nominated who represented what Robert Kennedy had stood for, the party could unite to defeat Nixon. A number of us who had worked with Sargent Shriver in the Peace Corps or the War on Poverty thought a Humphrey-Shriver ticket would be a good and winning combination. In the weeks before the convention, Humphrey had indicated that Shriver was on the list of those he was seriously considering for the vice-presidency. Since Shriver was then in Paris as the U.S. Ambassador (working closely with Averell Harriman and Cyrus Vance, who were there conducting peace negotiations), several of us decided to go to Chicago to uphold his interests—and our interest in his nomination.

Not having missed a Democratic convention since 1944, I would have gone anyway without the Shriver mission, like a moth to a quadrennial flame, and Moyers would have covered it for *Newsday*. But together with Peace Corps Advisory Council member and New York delegate Don Petrie, the Peace Corps' former general counsel Bill Josephson, and War on Poverty veterans Bill Mullins and Adam Yarmolinsky, we went as an open conspiracy to promote Shriver's selection.

We were a curious crew, and a campaign for the vice-presidency, except when the presidential candidate genuinely leaves the choice to the convention as Stevenson did in 1956, is a peculiar enterprise. The first night in Chicago, seeing a big poster, "HAYS FOR VICE-PRESIDENT" (probably Wayne Hays, I guessed), I knew we were playing one of the funnier roles in a convention. Thanks to Don Petrie, the Lazard Frères executive who helped build Avis into Number Two, most of us were ensconced in the Union League—my first such experience (Petrie claims he was the first Democrat in Chicago to be accepted as a member).

From our lines to the Humphrey camp, we learned that Shriver's name had survived the first cut, from a list of ten to seven, and the second cut, to a list of five. Then to our surprise, at a breakfast with Humphrey on Wednesday, August 28, Mayor Daley urged Shriver's selection. Before that, Daley had appeared to be going along with a last-minute move to draft Ted Kennedy for President, although Kennedy representatives were not sure whether the mayor's encouragement was a way to entrap the senator into accepting the vice-presidential nomination. If so, it is too bad he didn't succeed. A Humphrey-Kennedy ticket would probably have won. Kennedy could have insisted upon a peace platform as a condition for acceptance and given Humphrey the leverage to liberate himself from Johnson's policies. Then there would have been no Chappaquiddick, no Watergate, no need to impeach Nixon, and peace in Vietnam could have come four years sooner.

Instead, Kennedy adamantly said no to the vice-presidency, and Daley advanced Shriver as a way to incorporate the Kennedys in the campaign and help carry Illinois. While Daley was making this pitch to Humphrey, the Chicago *Daily News* carried a long favorable feature on Shriver headed "Half a Kennedy to Run for VP?" and the Chicago *Tribune*, in reporting Daley's move, speculated that Steve Smith (who was there representing Ted Kennedy) was "mainly interested in the possibility of Shriver's nomination for Vice-President." Having sensed some brother-in-law rivalry between Shriver and Smith in years past, and knowing that the line of family succession ran from elder to younger brother (not brother-in-law), I doubted that Smith's interest in the Shriver possibility was affirmative.

In a midnight call from Humphrey's suite, Walter Mondale told me that Kennedy family opposition to Shriver's nomination was weighing heavily against his selection. At the time, I suspected that Larry O'Brien, Pierre Salinger, or Kenneth O'Donnell had spoken in the family name (perhaps without prior authority). However much the former Palace Guard want a restoration on their own terms, I said to Mondale, they have no monopoly on the Kennedy legacy. Shriver was a man in his own right who could evoke some of the Kennedy mystique, draw on thousands of former Peace Corps Volunteers and anti-poverty workers, and help reach the young and the black and the poor better than anyone other than Ted Kennedy. Besides, I added, Mondale knew Ted Kennedy well enough to know that Ted was too decent a man to block his brother-in-law's selection.

From Hyannis Port, Ted Kennedy (after finally deciding to discourage the "Draft Kennedy" movement) did telephone Humphrey on Wednesday to assure him of his support. People close to Humphrey told Moyers and me that the senator had vetoed Shriver as Vice-President. Later Mondale would say only that Ted was "cool" to it.

In any case, for the second time Shriver had reason to believe that a brother-in-law had put his future political interests above Shriver's immediate opportunity. Later, when I pressed Shriver for his reaction, he was philosophical and practical. He recognized that if he had become Vice-President he might have been seen as an obstacle or at least an embarrassment to a subsequent presidential nomination for Ted. "In politics, when men are playing for such stakes," he reasoned (and rationalized),"you can't count on personal ties, and shouldn't take these things personally." In the Kennedy family, as no doubt in others, there was one law for blood brothers and another for brothers-in-law.

If Humphrey had picked Shriver, that week and the ensuing campaign might have ended differently. Listening to radio reports and our telephoned accounts, Shriver was appalled by the police violence. Unjustified violence by those armed to uphold the law seemed the worst kind of violence. However much it might offend Daley, he felt that the Democratic nominees would have to speak out strongly against the police behavior, and undertake some symbolic action of sympathy for those abused. "The test is what Humphrey does now," said Shriver from Paris. "He has about eighteen hours until his acceptance speech to show where he stands on all this."

To be ready in the event Humphrey called him, Shriver, with the advice of Harriman and Vance, had prepared an outline of what he would urge Humphrey to say and what he himself would insist upon doing, if nominated, to reach out to those who had been beaten and jailed and to the whole peace movement. From four thousand miles away, Shriver was able to see more clearly the significance of what was happening than Humphrey in his busy suite on the twenty-fifth floor of the Hilton. Some tear gas had been drawn into the Vice-President's suite through the air-conditioning ducts, but otherwise the Vice-President had been too engrossed in meeting visiting delegations and party leaders to notice the bloody encounter below on Michigan Avenue; when he looked out the window there was a lull in the fighting and it didn't seem very serious.

In an interview after the worst police beatings in front of the Hilton, Humphrey primarily criticized the protesters and defended the police; he would not turn his back on Dick Daley. Muriel Humphrey said the protesters were "noisy and rude" and had received too much attention; she and her husband knew the different views of most young Americans "by talking with young executives and young Jaycees." The Humphreys had missed most of the carnage, and had bitterly resented the networks interrupting the nominating speeches and the balloting with films of the violence in the streets, during the very hours of the triumph Hubert had sought for so many years. Later—too late to give the kind of acceptance speech the crisis called for—he appreciated the dimensions of what had happened. "Chicago was a catastrophe," he wrote afterward. "My wife and I went home heartbroken, battered and beaten. I told her I felt just like we had been in a shipwreck."

Meanwhile, back at our base in the Union League Club the Shriver contingent had also been playing the old politics of behind-the-scenes maneuver. A wide range of party leaders had been enlisted to support our vice-presidential candidate, but the battalions that Humphrey felt most came out of the South (another old story in the Democratic Party), and above all Humphrey feared the hot breath of Lyndon Johnson. Apparently, almost to the end, he wondered whether Johnson was plotting to come to the convention and seek renomination. Some close to Johnson said that if the Russians had not invaded Czechoslovakia, there would have been an August summit meeting in Geneva (as Johnson had planned); from a triumph at the summit, the President would have flown to Chicago, claiming the nomination for the same reason he had renounced it, to make peace.

Instead, the Russians sent their tanks into Prague, the National Guard took over the streets of Chicago, and Johnson resolved to prevent Humphrey from disowning him or the war in Vietnam. The President began complaining that Humphrey "cries too much." Johnson's most potent agents were leaders of Southern delegations, who threatened revolt if Humphrey accepted a peace plank satisfactory to the Kennedy, McGovern, and McCarthy delegates. Party rules were being changed to make state delegations more representative, and the black vote was beginning to make itself felt in the choice of Southern delegates, but John Connally and his allies still wielded great power. After meeting with a group led by Connally, and pondering an ominous warning from Johnson against going soft on Vietnam, Humphrey finally backed away from compromise with Kennedy, McGovern, and McCarthy forces on the platform.

By Thursday morning, August 29, we had learned that Shriver was off the vice-presidential list (along with Governor Richard Hughes, who had been vetoed by the Southern delegation), and that the choice would be between Senators Fred Harris and Ed Muskie. While Moyers had strong indications that Muskie would be picked, Fred Harris to the last minute expected to be the one, and kept pressing Moyers to help him draft his acceptance speech.

By this time, the politics of the vice-presidency had lost most of its interest for me. With the defeat of the peace platform and Humphrey's failure to say or do anything strong about the violence in the streets, Shriver himself had become increasingly skeptical of the value of being on a Humphrey ticket.

Meanwhile, the story in the streets was finally getting through to us. Monday night, Bill Mullins, en route to Hugh Hefner's continuous *Playboy* convention party, had happened upon the scene at Lincoln Park as police were beating some young people to bloody pulps. This caused Hugh Hefner to go down to the sidewalk as an observer and get clubbed himself. Tuesday, in the press and on television, we discovered the large scale of the violence. The Chicago *Daily News* attacked the "rising number of cases of deliberate savagery by police." A young business executive on his way to buy a Pierre Cardin suit told me how he had been trapped in a section of Old Town. Blocking the exits, police drove the people up and down the street, grabbing and beating whomever they caught, including the executive.

Then Wednesday evening, as we watched the usually moderate Senator Abraham Ribicoff charge Chicago police with using "Gestapo tactics," the consciousness and conscience of most of us at the convention came to a boil, one way or another. On the floor Daley half rose, shaking his fist and shouting (what those nearby said were obscenities) at Ribicoff. Looking down from the rostrum, the senator replied, "How hard it is to accept the truth!"

It was at this point that we issued our call for a vigil in front of the

Hilton to begin Thursday noon. Second thoughts about the prudence of Moyers' co-sponsorship led us to persuade him to withdraw his name; aside from compromising the reputation he was just beginning to build as a journalist, he feared that joining the vigil would probably have caused Captain Harry Guggenheim, the owner of *Newsday* and an unreconstructed cold warrior, to disown and discharge him. (The rupture came before long anyway, for other reasons, but Moyers continued his career as a journalist in television.)

Events were outrunning us. At the convention, while we were spreading word about the vigil the next noon, some delegates organized a procession with candles, from Convention Hall to the park where the peace protesters were tending their wounds. Hundreds joined and walked the several miles downtown. It was a beautiful sight as the candlelight parade approached Grant Park at about 2 a.m. From the Conrad Hilton a bell rang out in time to "America the Beautiful." A Bennington College student who had been feeling "abandoned, surrounded, but not frightened," in the midst of thousands of protesters who were sitting on the ground in the park, awaiting a new onslaught from the police, described her reactions:

> Then the grown-ups came, hordes of them, it seemed, carrying candles. We hadn't dared believe the reports of delegates marching from the amphitheater. But they were there. There was a cheer; it didn't just shout but welled up, grew and grew as realization came. We stayed seated, but how can I explain that yell? It wasn't just "hooray"—something more. It was, to me, almost a prayer of thanks because the grown-ups had come and no one was going to hurt us any more. Whatever happened before or will happen ever, nothing will shake my faith in those few hours. The candlelit delegates filed into the crowd on pathways cleared for them, winding through, they were hugged and blessed and loved at every footstep. It sounds corny, it sounds really corny, but it was corny. It was the corniest thing I ever saw. True goodness almost always reads as melodrama. I only know that walking back to the car after the grand night, at 6 a.m., I passed close to the National Guard first line, and noticed an old friend from high school, standing, bayonet in his hand, and eyes full of tears.

After that we knew our vigil would be an anticlimax. Indeed, I feared we might be giving a vigil to which no one would come, yet there was no good way to call it off without diminishing the message we wanted to convey. The press had been notified, so we resolved to be there at noon and hope that our ranks would be significant enough to make it worthwhile. Just before twelve I counted only a half dozen ready to cross Michigan Avenue and stand between the young people in the park and the National Guard patrolling the streets. For the first time I faced the worst fear in such a venture: the fear of being ridiculous. Just then Senator Ribicoff came up, looked at his watch, and said in matter-of-fact fashion, "It's noon, where's the vigil?"

Deciding to inform the commander of the National Guard about our plans before we took up posts facing the troops on the other side of the avenue, I went out in the street and was immediately surrounded by troops who took me to the commander. He thanked me and said it was the first time anyone had told him in advance what they were up to. If our peaceful vigil didn't include bottles being thrown at his men, he guaranteed courtesy from the National Guard. He gave a helpful suggestion: if we would line up at the edge of the sidewalk, we would find it kept our line straighter. The flurry caused by my armed escort led to the report by friends watching out of Hilton Hotel windows that I had been arrested at twelve noon and the vigil broken up.

As Senator Ribicoff, Adam Yarmolinsky, Pierre Salinger, Michael Novak, Sam Beer, Lester Hyman (chairman of the Massachusetts delegation), and I lined up, several former Peace Corps Volunteers and a number of Massachusetts delegates joined; the company was just large enough not to be ridiculous. For most of the time there were twenty-five or thirty delegates and party officials. Charles Evers of Mississippi stood for about two hours. Rafer Johnson and Norman Mailer joined the line briefly. Mailer fidgeted, asked when the speeches would begin. When informed it was to be a silent vigil, he said, "But there's a microphone over there, why don't we say something?" Soon Mailer disappeared "to get some more delegates," and in a few minutes we heard him addressing the crowd in the park.

Ribicoff left soon, too, but he will always occupy a warm spot in my memory. His participation had come as a welcome surprise. As governor of Connecticut, he had undermined Chester Bowles's prospects for the Senate in 1958, and in the Kennedy Cabinet he had played an undistinguished role. In his own first race for the governorship in 1954 he had used a slick refrain that went something like: "There comes a time when a man must have the courage to put principle above party, and whatever the consequences to me, whatever the price I will have to pay within the party, I must speak candidly and say I cannot defend Alger Hiss." Or, to other audiences, he would say he could not support everything advocated by Adlai Stevenson. Yet in Chicago on August 28 and 29, 1968, Abe Ribicoff was ready to be ridiculous at high noon on Michigan Avenue.

At about three-thirty, rather than peter out, we ended the vigil—in response to a call from the Wisconsin delegation to march to Convention Hall in further protest against the police behavior. Just then Gene Mc-

Carthy brushed by the troops and crossed the boulevard, heading toward the people in Grant Park and the ever-waiting loudspeaker. I listened as he addressed his several thousand supporters as "the government and people in exile." He said he would rather read poetry with his friends in the park than be witness to events at Convention Hall. He asked them to join him in "wandering in the wilderness."

As the college students who had stayed "Clean with Gene," the bearded Yippies of the "Youth International Party," and the Kennedy and McGovern delegates who had joined the gathering gave McCarthy a long, warm ovation, I looked up and saw some fifty men and women around a large banner, "RETURNED VOLUNTEERS." The group included Volunteers from VISTA and the American Friends Service Committee, but turned out to be led by former Peace Corpsmen. They told about their week of Vietnam protests and police beatings. Suddenly someone ran up to report that the march to the convention led by the Wisconsin delegation had just been stopped by troops. "Come along," said Gerry Schwinn, a returned Peace Corps Volunteer from Nigeria, who was then an organizer of Biafran relief. "It's our turn to march." He and his friends lifted their banner high and started down Michigan Avenue.

"Join us," they said to me, and—warily—I did, finding myself walking next to Gilbert Harrison, publisher of The New Republic. I had seen nothing to keep me from joining them, but reports of provocation from people in the park—taunting of police, hurling of epithets, throwing of bottles—had made me skeptical about some of the protesters' professed commitment to nonviolence. Someone had set off a stink bomb in the Hilton, and its stench, along with lingering tear gas, pervaded that central headquarters of the convention all week. Tom Hayden and other organizers of the mass protests had made ambiguous threats to disrupt the convention, and their rhetoric on the loudspeaker in the park seemed to invite violence against them. Some of my friends had heard demonstrators chanting, "Fuck you, LBJ!" and the Black Panther-coined cry of "Pig!" was used by some as a sure way of enraging the police. I wanted no part in that, so I listened with care to everything the Peace Corps Volunteers leading the march said on their bullhorns.

The primary issue for me that day was the excessive use and abuse of force by the police, which was worse than anything I had seen in Selma. Before our eyes, Chicago police had acted as judge, jury, and punishers. Threatened by massive confrontation and alarmed by rumors of impending violence against Humphrey and of plans to put LSD in Chicago's water supply, Daley needed to have the police, and probably

436

the National Guard, on hand in large numbers. But by running amuck, the police did just what the most violent radicals needed in order to radicalize others. An angry physician, who had been hit by a policeman while wearing his white coat and red cross, said he had assisted in a number of peace demonstrations, including the 1967 march on the Pentagon, and had never experienced anything like Chicago: "The injuries are incomparably worse," he said. Even Spiro Agnew said Daley's men had been "needlessly rough." And Perle Mesta canceled her long-heralded Democratic unity party because of the beatings she had seen—a British woman member of Parliament had been Maced outside the Hilton, and Winston Churchill, the grandson and journalist, had been attacked.

The Peace Corpsmen kept the several hundred marchers on the sidewalks, obeying traffic lights, until the police blocked the way and started preparing to use tear gas. We were advised to sit down and put wet handkerchiefs over our mouths. Someone started the chant "The Whole World Is Watching!" which everyone picked up while television cameramen and reporters forced their way through police lines. Once or twice someone shouted "Pig!" at policemen wearing gas masks (which make them look pig-like), but others told them to shut up. Paul Cowan, a correspondent for the *Village Voice* and former Peace Corps Volunteer in Ecuador (who later wrote the book *Making of an Un-American*), told me that during the demonstrations all week there had been tension between those who treated the police as "pigs" and those who wanted to appeal to them as human beings. Cowan preferred the approach demonstrated by people in Prague who had risked their lives trying to talk to invading Russian troops.

After unsuccessful negotiation with the police and National Guard, the Peace Corpsmen led the march back toward the Hilton. Each time we passed a large group of police, the Volunteers started the chant "More Pay for Cops!"

Filing back into Grant Park in the last rays of the sun, the marchers heard Dick Gregory at the loudspeaker, introducing the Deputy Superintendent of Police. There were jeers from the several thousand people now assembled. "Give him a chance," said Gregory. "Let's respect him for coming here and talking to us directly. That's what we've been asking for all week." There was strong applause, and the superintendent said, "We have intelligence information that this group is here to destruct the city. Our objection is to your moving in concert. We cannot let pedestrians block the public roadways." Someone shouted, "Why wouldn't you give us a permit to parade?" The police spokesman replied only, "I may not agree with all the laws, but it is my duty to enforce them."

Angry shouts of "No!" broke out over the hill. Someone yelled, "Go get Daley!" Gregory took the microphone again: "Maybe there are some provocateurs in this crowd, maybe provocateurs planted by the police, but whoever they are, they have no place here. Provocation of the police is just stupid. Now make a corridor for our friend from the police and show him that we appreciated his coming here." He left with friendly applause.

Then while Gregory negotiated further with the police and the National Guard we listened to Jean Genet and Pierre Salinger. Like Gene McCarthy, Genet beckoned to the world of exile. Salinger argued in favor of staying with the Democratic Party. After Bob Kennedy's death, he said, he just about decided to quit politics altogether, but the energy and spirit of the young people working for McCarthy and McGovern and protesting in the streets had convinced him it was worth staying in and fighting.

Gregory then reported failure to reach agreement with the police. Some young men shouting "Go! Go! Go!" started pushing down the hill toward the boulevard.

"Wait a minute!" cried Gregory. "I have two questions to ask. Do you want a general for this affair, and do you want me as your general? I don't go in things like this without a general, because too many people can get hurt. Do you want a general?" There was an overwhelming "Yes!" "Do you want me to be your general today?" Again an overwhelming "Yes!" Then pointing to the ones who had been pushing, he said, "So just sit down and listen to the general. We are going to be orderly all the way."

Gregory continued: "They say we can't march south to the convention hall, but they haven't said and they have no right to say that I can't take you all home with me for dinner, and I live south. It's just too nice an afternoon not to walk, and too much has happened this week not to walk. So guess who's coming to dinner? There are a lot of black bugs in the ghetto who would love to see you.

"Legally," he said, "I think you have a right to accept my invitation to walk to my house with me on the sidewalk. Remember the address: 1451 East Fifty-fifth. It's a long way from the convention but at least it's south. We'll stay on the sidewalks and cross streets only when the traffic lights let us, but I can't promise they won't arrest you because they don't quite buy this argument."

Gregory invited the delegates present to lead the march. He wanted dignitaries, officials, older people, and all those with suits and ties to walk up front because he was sure it would have "a marvelous effect on the manners of the police." A clergyman blessed us and called for an end to unjust force in Chicago and Vietnam. Then we stumbled through "The Star-Spangled Banner," did much better with "America the Beautiful," and were on our way.

Once again I was wondering how far I was prepared to go, but Gregory had struck no false note and the songs we were singing— "Onward, Christian Soldiers," "The Battle Hymn of the Republic," and "We Shall Overcome"—were hardly conducive to retreat.

At the very front, next to Gregory, was a Hubert Humphrey delegate from Oklahoma being pushed in a wheelchair. Walking two or three abreast, we passed by a great sign looming overhead: "RICHARD J. DALEY WELCOMES YOU."

At Eighteenth and Michigan we faced a complete military barricade. While Gregory parlayed with officials, a young black man grabbed the microphone. "You are entering black territory," he said. "Black people don't want you white people here, so turn back. And you black people in this march, get out and leave these white people to fight their own battles." Word passed that he was with a group of Panthers, though others said they were Blackstone Rangers. Several of them walked the length of the procession, pointing to the several hundred black participants to get out. The black man next to me just looked at them and didn't move. I saw no black participant leave the line.

In front and alongside of us were armored personnel carriers and jeeps with barbed-wire fencing mounted like snow plows. There seemed to be more police and National Guardsmen than the two thousand marchers. "They won't use clubs or gas tonight, with all you tie people here," a young protester, who had been bruised in earlier encounters, predicted. For a while he was right.

Then the National Guard commander said that if we continued to walk forward we would be "choosing to enter the zone of arrest." The twenty-five convention delegates caucused and after a few minutes announced they would proceed toward Gregory's house, exercising their right to walk peacefully on the public sidewalks in protest against the lawlessness of the night before. Gregory reminded us of his address and stepped into the "zone of arrest," followed by the Humphrey delegate in the wheelchair and fifteen or twenty others. They went single file, at easy intervals, going through the line of guns and climbing into a waiting police wagon.

Trying to think fast, I asked myself: Should I go into the "zone of arrest"? By continuing to walk on the sidewalk we would be constitutionally testing what we had good reason to believe was an unconstitutional police edict (just the kind of testing that Justice Abe Fortas specifically approved in his essay "Concerning Dissent and Civil Disobedience"). It was not even clear that we were violating any order at all. The Guard commander had warned us of a "zone of arrest"—which was a public sidewalk—and given us a choice.

There were responsibilities at home to think about, too, and I tried to guess how my arrest would affect the new college we were starting at Old Westbury. Would it endanger the college's standing or legislative support? Would it be a good example for students or faculty?

Also running through my head was the taunt by my Gandhian friend Rammanohar Lohia, who asked me every time we met, "When are you going to jail?" Like Gandhi, he believed that every man, at least once, should court jail on some important point of principle, and enter prison cheerfully "as a bridegroom enters the bridal chamber." Lohia, as a member of Parliament in India, had visited Mississippi in 1964 and succeeded in going to jail briefly during one of the demonstrations of "Freedom Summer." He could not understand why the occasion had never come my way—and I wondered myself. For twenty years, ever since reading Gandhi's *Autobiography* and Thoreau's *Essay*, I had told myself I was ready for truly *civil* disobedience. At Eighteenth and Michigan, on the evening of August 29, the requisite conditions seemed to obtain.

When I reached the line of troops, the Guard colonel was telling a woman in front of me that he was not going to let any more people go through. She protested that he had promised everyone the choice. "All right, lady, if you insist, you can walk over there and get arrested, but it's your choice," he said. His men lowered their guns and let her pass.

When he repeated the "choice" directly to me, I almost congratulated him for stating the doctrine of civil disobedience so well: every law is a question which the citizen must answer by obeying it, if he deems it constitutional and just, or respectfully disobeying it and accepting the consequences, including possibly prison, if he deems it unconstitutional or unjust. But it was not the time for conversation. My turn had come and I went through the row of guns and climbed into the police wagon. As I entered the van, a reporter asked me to put in three words why I was doing it. I said, "Bob Kennedy, John Kennedy, and Martin Luther King."

After seventy-nine of us with ties and titles had been quietly arrested, the police ordered the dispersal of the remaining marchers. Then, with little if any notice, they threw tear gas and drove the jeeps with barbed-wire grates against the thousand or more people who had overflowed into the avenue. Some were hurt, others were arrested, as they were driven or fled back toward the Conrad Hilton.

Jail is another country, and not an easy one for a man with a tie to get a passport to. Thanks to Mayor Daley, I made it. One old fear had at least been laid to rest: that I would be arrested for violating a just law, like the one against speeding, but never for violating an unjust one. Jaywalkers all, who of us think twice about violating the little laws that are just inconvenient?

"Haven't I seen you before?" asked a young McCarthy worker in the lockup. It turned out he was the vice-president of the student body at the University of Oregon and six weeks before had heard me debate Chancellor Roger Heyns of Berkeley on the question: Should a College or University Be an Agent of Social Change? In arguing the affirmative, I had criticized Northern university presidents who do not believe they or their universities should risk their public or political support by involving themselves directly in matters of injustice or violence nearby (and I had specified "a police department run amuck") but who believe that their counterparts in the South should risk their jobs or institutions by giving leadership on racial integration. "Following the question where it leads, inevitably leads on some occasions into trouble," I had concluded, adding that this was the kind of trouble academia needed more of.

"We wondered whether you meant what you said," commented the Oregon student. "I feel better seeing you here." His skepticism reminded me of the charge by a Peace Corps Volunteer that "if you become a college president you will never say anything, sign anything, or do anything political or controversial."

Soon we were lined up against a wall and frisked. There was a Rockefeller county leader from Kentucky, who looked very Young-Republican and uncomfortable as the jail attendant went up and down his body feeling for concealed weapons. The only combative prisoner in our group was Tom Buckley, the *Times* correspondent recently returned from two years in Vietnam; he was ready to take on anyone, especially a fellow Irishman named Richard J. Daley.

"How would you and your mayor like to have demonstrations and marches like these in New York?" a police officer asked Buckley. "Oh, we love them in New York, they liven up the place," said Buckley. "Mayor Lindsay usually joins them and gives the kids hot dogs. They march all over town and shout anything they want."

"Well, you run your town your way and let us run ours our way, okay?" the policeman said.

With a Southern accent, he could have been a sheriff in Alabama, complaining about the outside troublemakers—the preachers, Yankee politicians, and young people going South for civil rights. There was a difference: the "niggers of the North"—at least in Chicago that week— were the white hippies, student radicals, and youth with long hair. Throughout the week, the class lines around the convention had to do with hair and ties. Hurrying into the Hilton lobby one day, I suddenly found that my younger companions without ties or recent haircuts had been brusquely grabbed by police at the door and shoved into the gutter. The one young man with long hair in the lockup with us (named Steve Smith, "no relation to the Kennedys," he said) became the special target of police hostility, and knew how to goad them in return.

While we were being fingerprinted, Murray Kempton, a New York McCarthy delegate, joined us behind the bars. I recalled Kempton's stirring stories on the Montgomery bus boycott in 1956—and one story in which he bestirred himself too much. He had written about the black men in white uniforms working in the Alabama Capitol building, saying that they might look subservient but that they were really new men—because of the boycott they didn't ride the segregated buses to work but now walked like free men. "You chump, Murray!" the Montgomery *Advertiser* had gloated. It was true that they didn't ride to work on the buses: as prisoners in the state penitentiary they were driven to and from the Capitol in prison vans.

"You chump, Murray," had been my feeling, too, in March 1968, when Kempton wrote a bitter column calling Robert Kennedy a coward for entering the presidential race after McCarthy's victory in New Hampshire. In less than three months, however, Kempton had tried to undo the earlier article in which he had said, "I blame myself, not him, for all the years he fooled me." In his new piece, "RFK—In Sorrow and Shame," Kempton wrote that in "the shadow of death" his previous "language of dismissal" sounded "horrible."

> For I had forgotten, from being bitter about a temporary course of his, how much I liked Senator Kennedy and how much he needed to know he was liked. Now that there is in life no road at whose turning we could meet again, the memory of having forgotten that will always make me sad and indefinitely make me ashamed.

After being photographed with prison numbers hanging around our necks (my mug carried the sign: "CB 257008 29 Aug."), we were crowded into cells equipped with a stinking toilet and two narrow benches. Not quite a "bridal chamber"! But the more ebullient inmates provided some entertainment—the police called it provocation.

"Ladies and Gentlemen of the Convention, come to order!" someone started. "The delegate from Illinois has a candidate to place in nomination."

From another cell a voice boomed: "We nominate that grrreaat American, Richard J. Daley, for King."

"No, Mr. Chairman," called out another. "We nominate Dick Daley for manager of the Animal Farm."

Thanks to a portable radio carried by one of the delegates in the cell with me, we were able to hear snatches of the actual convention going on at the International Amphitheatre. The galleries had apparently been packed with hundreds of city workers who had smuggled in "WE LOVE MAYOR DALEY" signs and were chanting "We want Daley!" Anti-Daley delegates were in an uproar until the lights went down for a memorial film about Robert Kennedy. It ended with the singing of "The Battle Hymn of the Republic," and as the delegates stood and sang chorus after chorus of "Glory, Glory, Halleujah" we picked it up in our cells. The radio anchorman reported that the convention seemed to be rolling all the emotions of the week into one ball, and no gavel could stop that song. Finally there was a film tribute to Martin Luther King and then Hubert Humphrey accepted the nomination. As he waited to begin his address, the band played "Happy Days Are Here Again."

Humphrey began with St. Francis of Assisi: "Where there is hatred, let me sow love. Where there is injury, pardon. Where there is doubt, faith. Where there is despair, hope. Where there is darkness, light." But from where we sat, on the narrow benches in the midst of recurring hot breezes of dispersed tear gas, the speech seemed to go downhill from there. He went through the litany of Franklin Roosevelt, Harry Truman, Adlai Stevenson, and John Kennedy, and then, when he came to Lyndon Johnson, overdid it. When he said, "Thank you—thank you, Mr. President," the hall erupted with applause, boos, cheers, and jeers. About then the battery in our radio ran out.

Around 3 a.m. I was called before a night court magistrate, charged with disorderly conduct for having "failed to obey a lawful order of dispersal," and offered an opportunity to put up a bond to cover the five-hundred-dollar bail. Murray Kempton loaned me the fifty dollars I needed, but I decided not to post it until after breakfast. Having got this far into the strange land called prison, I thought I should at least equal Thoreau's one-night stand in jail. Recalling the adage that a test of a civilization is how it treats its prisoners, I wondered what a regular sleeping cell and a prison breakfast would be like. So I went back to the now empty lockup cell with the two benches and a toilet, and waited.

After a while I went up to the guard and asked when I would be put in a regular cell. He laughed. "You wouldn't get your own cell until noon tomorrow," he said, "but we're not going to give you one. We know people like you are going to put up bail. Do you know how much it would cost the taxpayers of Chicago to process you and install you in a regular cell?" He said the medical exam, delousing, prison clothing, paper work, and other items came to more than four hundred dollars, and rather than go to all that expense they would just wait me out.

Given the size of the prison bureaucracy, I could believe his cost estimates. At each corner of the Cook County jail there seemed to be a new set of policemen or clerks with forms to fill or a line-up to organize. Keeping us in numerical order as we shifted benches from one procedural station to another was the main task of a dozen men hovering around us. It is difficult to get a room at that inn.

Feeling defeated and seeing the last of my colleagues leaving, I signaled that I had bail. The gate was unlocked, the bars closed behind me, and before I knew it, I was back on the Chicago streets. It was nearly 5 a.m. and the sun was beginning to rise. "Hog Butcher for the World . . . City of the Big Shoulders," Carl Sandburg had written of Chicago. It was also the city of Sam Giancana—and the University of Chicago, my alma mater. Having spent a night in its jail, I felt again, as in college days, that it was my town too.

Downtown at the Hilton, at just that hour, the last big police action of the week was taking place. From somewhere in the hotel things had been thrown out of the window on the police and National Guard below. The police alleged that they were pelted by fish, beer cans, ice cubes, and ashtrays, and that the objects came from the fifteenth-floor suites of the McCarthy student workers. After careful checking, Theodore White concluded that there was "no evidence whatsoever that the McCarthy students had themselves been throwing anything" and doubted that anything had been thrown from the fifteenth floor. In their accumulated fury, however, the police charged to the McCarthy rooms, broke open doors, and began striking students with billy clubs and dragging them into the elevators.

By chance, Dick Goodwin arrived to say goodbye to the students while this was going on, and followed the victims to the lobby. Directing the students to sit in a circle until he could get help, Goodwin sent one to find a television crew to record the assault and another to ask McCarthy and Humphrey to come down and help.

Humphrey could not be awakened, but McCarthy came and demanded to know who was the police officer in charge. When no one spoke up, he said, "Just what I thought, nobody's in charge." The police began to disappear, and the students went back to their rooms.

Not knowing about the action at the Hilton, I pondered two choices

444

when I came out of jail: to go to my bed at the Union League or to go to the continuing *Playboy* party for delegates and official visitors, at Hugh Hefner's exotic North Side home. Two evenings before, Bill Mullins had introduced me to the all-night assembly around Hefner's glass-bottom swimming pool off his living room. John Kenneth Galbraith, Max Lerner, Bill Moyers, Warren Beatty, and the bunnies were all there. Beatty was urging Moyers to run for office, and was pursuing questions about the relationship between acting and politics. We had agreed to continue the conversation the last night of the convention. Since the Thursday-night session had lasted so long, I guessed (correctly) that some of them would still be there around the pool. But finally, after the long day and night, prudence prevailed and I went to bed. As the National Guard colonel would say, it was my choice.

Back at Old Westbury, our warmhearted librarian had a private word for me. "May I say something personal?" she asked after I had recounted something of the Chicago story. "Your face looks better, your eyes are warmer, you seem more open since you went to jail." She seemed disappointed when I said, "Are you sure it's not *your* eyes that are warmer? What about the people who look at me with colder, more closed eyes because of Chicago?"

At home, Clare almost proved the point. Reminding me of Nehru's claim that he never saw angrier, less loving looks than those of the troops who beat him when he turned the other cheek, she asked whether I really thought the march and the jail-going had helped the people of Chicago or the country to understand the issues any better. She cited the latest poll, showing that people at large supported Daley's handling of the protesters by a margin of more than two to one.

After our continuing argument of twenty years subsided, our eight-year-old son David asked me to read a chapter from *The World of Pooh*. At home with their families the Chicago police were no doubt as friendly as Piglet, and Richard J. Daley probably had as warm a heart as Winnie-the-Pooh, that faithful Bear of a Positively Startling Lack of Brain. We read of the sad day when everybody in the enchanted forest knew that Christopher Robin was going away.

"What I like doing best is Nothing," said Christopher Robin.

"How do you do Nothing?" asked Pooh.

"This is a nothing sort of thing that we're doing now."

Then suddenly Christopher Robin, who was looking at the world with his chin in his hands, called out, "Pooh!"

"When I'm—when—Pooh! I'm not going to do Nothing any more."

"Never again?"

"Well, not so much. They don't let you."

My sons asked why I had tears and was laughing at the same time. How could they understand that in Chicago, along with the Candidates and Platforms and Protests, the Afternoons and Evenings and Sunrises, there was something more? Marching and going to jail was not much, yet the world doesn't let you do Nothing. Gene McCarthy reading a Poem in the Park was doing something. Hubert Humphrey, trying to satisfy Lyndon Johnson and reach Young People in the Park at the same time was doing something. Stephen Smith with the long hair was doing something. So was the Kennedys' Stephen Smith, promising the return of the Young Man who had gone sailing at Hyannis Port during the convention, but who wouldn't be allowed to do Nothing either.

What did it all mean?

To many, Chicago came to stand for total disillusionment in politics. For them, the confrontation and violence in the streets, the defeat of the peace platform and nomination of Humphrey, and the fresh memory of the assassinations of Martin King and Robert Kennedy together meant more than a temporary defeat.

"The stone was at the bottom of the hill and we were alone," wrote Jack Newfield. In the closing passage of his memoir on Robert Kennedy, the *Village Voice* writer expressed the depression of the spirit felt by millions:

> Now I realized what makes our generation unique, what defines us apart from those who came before the hopeful winter of 1961, and those who came after the murderous spring of 1968. We are the first generation that learned from experience, in our innocent twenties, that things were not really getting better, that we shall *not* overcome. We felt, by the time we reached thirty, that we had already glimpsed the most compassionate leaders our nation could produce, and they had all been assassinated. And from this time forward, things would get worse: our best political leaders were part of memory now, not hope.

At first, I discounted such sweeping rhetoric as the natural despair of a young man grieving at a great loss. Hope would soon spring up again, I predicted, and Newfield and those like him would pick themselves up and start pushing the stone up the hill. But I came to realize that the reaction was deeper, more widespread, and longer-lasting—that 1968 was indeed a turning point.

A perceptive young political scientist, who had been a student leader at Stanford, was amazed when he found me still full of political spirit even after the assassinations and the Chicago debacle. "I guess I can't blame you for not being alienated," he said, "but until you understand the depth of our alienation you will not understand my generation."

With students at Old Westbury, I came face to face with the dark mood setting in. For a brief moment, my jail-going produced a popularity seldom granted an "administrator" in the later sixties, but when students discovered that, despite everything, I intended to campaign for Humphrey, most of them consigned me to one of their unredeemable categories.

"Never trust anyone over thirty," the slogan that had swept out of Berkeley earlier in the decade, had been counteracted by Gene McCarthy and Robert Kennedy in the first half of 1968, but after Chicago that sentiment carried the day on most campuses. "Dump the Hump," "Turn On, Tune In, and Drop Out," and "Paranoia Is True Perception" were among the other slogans and banners raised at Old Westbury and were part of the mind-set of millions of young people.

At Old Westbury it was mainly the black students, whom we had recruited in large numbers, who resisted the withdrawal from public action to personal pursuits. They issued a manifesto declaring that, unlike self-indulgent, middle-class white students, they were not interested in a degree of "GG"—"Grooving in the Grass."

No doubt, at a new college designed to involve students as full partners in the academic enterprise, we experienced (and invited) an extreme form of the counterculture. An experimental college attracts too many experimental students for its—or their—good. With so much leaven, so little lump, the student body was far from representative of American young people. Yet there were many indications that the views expressed so intensely by Old Westbury students were shared in more moderate or subdued forms by a large part of the younger generation.

For a few, 1968 meant a turn to violence. A leader of the Students for a Democratic Society, in a post-Chicago debate on the efficacy of nonviolence, declared, with what sounded like glee, "That whole Gandhi bag is broken, and the good old days of Martin Luther King are gone, and gone forever, and good riddance." After I had argued that the days of King and Kennedy were gone but the memory shimmered the path for us to follow, the SDS fellow called me "the Green Slime." Not long afterwards, he was convicted of practicing what he preached—violence—in Cambridge. In Chicago the next year, the memory of candlelight parades, keeping "Clean with Gene," and flower people chanting "Ooomm" with Allen Ginsberg faded, as the Weathermen, with bombs and other weapons, carried out their "Days of Rage"—and then went into the underground.

It seemed so self-defeating. Robert McNamara in 1968 told an Aspen seminar I was leading that the anti-war march on the Pentagon might have been successful had not some of the protesters turned to violence, in words and deeds. The former Defense Secretary said he watched from a Pentagon window as they approached and said to himself: "If they stick to Gandhi, if they keep their discipline, they can stir the country and paralyze the prosecution of the war." He imagined how he might have trained and led them in effective Gandhian action. Then, when he saw some of the marchers begin to throw bottles and heard obscene epithets shouted, he knew they had lost.

For some, the response was not violence but an odd politics of primarily personal psychic satisfaction. The "blow their minds" approach was first advocated as a form of shock treatment that would result, after the initial anger, in changing the minds of those supposedly jolted out of their dogmatic slumbers. As a sense of hopelessness spread after Chicago, results no longer seemed to matter to many anti-war protesters so much as the pleasure of manifesting opposition in the most exciting and provocative way. In Berkeley the Free Speech movement had degenerated into the Filthy Speech movement, and on many campuses the freedom to shout "Fuck the War" seemed to become more important than effective action to end the war.

A committee of some of the more radical-minded returned Peace Corps Volunteers staged a sit-in occupation of Peace Corps headquarters in Washington, which might have had some persuasive impact if they had not hung Viet Cong flags out the window and convinced most people that they were Communist or crazy. In the name of everyone "doing his thing," protests were multiplied and made louder, but the purpose of persuasion often seemed to be lost.

For far more people, the reaction in 1968 and the years that followed was a turn away from politics of any kind. Cynicism toward all things political and all political leaders amounted to an anti-politics of unusual proportions. Alongside and somehow related to the darkening political development was the youth counterculture—the "Woodstock Nation" and the revolution of Drugs, Sex, and Life Styles. Plato warned that a change in the music of a people could mean a fundamental change in values, and first the songs of Bob Dylan and the Beatles, and then, in different mood, of Jimi Hendrix and Janis Joplin, suggested that something was going on but that not many people over thirty knew what it was. The "me generation" that was soon proclaimed, however, was not an under-thirty phenomenon, but an embodiment of the dominant American mood. Nor was the difference between everyone "doing his thing" and everyone trying to get his thing as great as the prophets of the greening of America had hoped.

The result of all this was the election of Richard Nixon.

A majority of those under thirty who voted apparently voted for the Republican candidate, to the consternation of the self-appointed spokesmen for that generation. More significant was the fact that a majority of the under-thirty population didn't vote at all.

Very late and in lukewarm fashion, Gene McCarthy had finally announced his support of Humphrey, but he had done nothing after the convention to reverse the trend toward withdrawal from politics by the millions of people he had stirred into action earlier that year. Inexplicably, he himself soon withdrew from his seat on the Senate Foreign Relations Committee, deserting the struggle against the war at a critical point, and before long he decided not to run for re-election to the Senate. Poetry in the park and "Grooving in the Grass" turned out to be part of the same process that helped produce the Nixon presidency.

Humphrey, for his part, was caught between Johnson's insistence that peace negotiations were at a delicate, decisive point and thus beyond the pale of public criticism, and the general public's negative reaction to the student counterculture and to the chaos and violence in the streets. He never effectively declared his independence of Johnson or conveyed convincingly a determination to end the war, and thus lost enough of the Kennedy and McCarthy voters to lose the election.

The year, like the decade, had begun well, but ended in as bad a bog as American politics had ever seen.

All this was the last thing Robert Kennedy and Martin King would have wanted their deaths to mean. As a young man, King recognized that "reason was darkened with sin" and toward the end of his life he faced his own Chicago, where he was defeated by massive misunderstanding and outbreaks of violence. Most of all he was tormented by the move toward violence by some blacks, and hated the taunt of a white police officer, about "those nonviolent rocks" protesters had thrown in one demonstration. Yet from the mountaintop in Memphis, in his last sermon, King confirmed that the struggle was worthwhile. However difficult the dialectic of self-government, he affirmed that still it moves, and men and women make it move.

In St. Patrick's Cathedral, when Edward Kennedy gave the eulogy for his brother, he had few words of his own, but turned to what Robert Kennedy had said to the young people of South Africa in 1966 (words drafted in good part by his friend Allard Lowenstein):

There is discrimination in this world and slavery and slaughter and starvation. . . . These are differing evils, but they are the common works of man. They reflect the imperfection of human justice, the inadequacy of human compassion, our lack of sensibility towards the suffering of our fellows. . . .

Some believe there is nothing one man or one woman can do against the enormous array of the world's ills. Yet many of the world's great movements of thought and action have flowed from the work of a single man.

A young monk began the Protestant Revolution. A young general extended an empire from Macedonia to the borders of the earth. A young woman reclaimed the territory of France, and it was a young Italian explorer who discovered the New World, and the thirty-two-year-old Thomas Jefferson who explained that all men are created equal.

These men moved the world, and so can we all. Few will have the greatness to bend history itself, but each of us can work to change a small portion of events, and in the total of all those acts will be written the history of this generation.

Each time a man stands for an ideal, or acts to improve the lot of others, or strikes out against injustice, he sends forth a tiny ripple of hope. And crossing each other from a million different centers of energy and daring, those ripples build a current that can sweep down the mightiest walls of oppression and resistance. . . .

Moral courage is a rarer commodity than bravery in battle or great intelligence. Yet it is the one essential vital quality for those who seek to change a world that yields most painfully to change.

Robert Kennedy saw the depression of the spirit among young people at the end of the decade, and he may have understood the depth of their alienation. In his last campaign, after leaving a tumultuous reception at the University of Kansas, he had said, "You can hear the fabric ripping. If we don't get out of this war, I don't know what these young people are going to do. There's going to be no way to talk to them. It's very dangerous."

He himself had gone deep into despair after his brother's murder in 1963, and in his alienation from President Johnson had let loose some of his own darker impulses of resentment and wrath. But he had pulled himself out of that mood, and set about trying to save the soul of his country—and, in doing so, no doubt, his own, too.

To the mixed messages coming from young people at the end of the sixties, he was reacting as he had to the contradictory and confusing cables coming from Khrushchev during the Cuban missile crisis. Take everything seriously and prepare for the worst, but act on the hopeful possibility: find the opening and go through it.

Out of the widespread negative insights about the war, about the modern bureaucratic system, about politics, politicians, and government of all kinds, Robert Kennedy had started to forge a coalition to end the war, change the system, and demonstrate a new kind of politics. In that same speech in South Africa, he had looked particularly to the young. "Not a time of life but a state of mind, a temper of the will, a quality of imagination, a predominance of courage over timidity, of the appetite for adventure over the love of ease." But he had concluded with a statement of political faith that looked beyond any one generation or decade:

> Like it or not, we live in times of danger and uncertainty. But they are also more open to the creative energy of men than any other time in history. All of us will ultimately be judged and as the years pass, we will surely judge ourselves, on the effort we have contributed to building a new world society and the extent to which our ideals and goals have shaped that event.
>
> Our future may lie beyond our vision, but it is not completely beyond our control. It is the shaping impulse of America that neither faith nor nature nor the irresistible tides of history but the work of our own hands matched to reason and principle will determine our destiny.

No one can be sure that Robert Kennedy would have succeeded. But Robert Kennedy's case for the power of individuals to change history did not depend on optimism. For him, too, the dialectic was deeper and darker than that. He might have pointed to Lee Harvey Oswald and James Earl Ray (and, if he had known, to Sirhan Sirhan) as proof of the power of one person (or a few people) to change the course of history for the worse.

The depression in the spirit of Edward Kennedy in the year or two after his last brother's assassination was another case in point. His temporary course of apparent self-destruction and the tragic culmination at Chappaquiddick is another example of how an individual can do damage to his own destiny and adversely affect the history of his times. Robert Kennedy would have understood that, too, for the compassion people felt in him came, in part, from his knowledge of how far one can fall and rise again.

No one will make sense of the sixties who sees only the bright side, or who cannot see that side at all. No one will begin to understand John and Robert Kennedy and Martin Luther King, their roles and the role of their families in American public life, who does not try to imagine and feel something of what they suffered and learned.

At the Democratic convention of 1976 in New York, Tom Hayden was present as a delegate from California when Mayor Richard Daley was welcomed to the rostrum as a party leader. With Hayden's help, the convention of 1972 had unseated and humiliated the Mayor of Chicago, in retaliation for damage he had done to the party and the country in 1968. I happened to be sitting and talking with Hayden on the convention floor when Daley was introduced at Madison Square Garden, and was interested to find myself—and Hayden—applauding, moderately. When a number of delegates, especially among the Californians, started to hiss and boo, Hayden and I found ourselves rising to stand with the majority who were applauding, moderately.

"Why are you doing this?" a TV man asked Hayden.

"Because on balance I'm glad to see him back," replied the man Daley's police had attacked and prosecuted.

"But didn't you help kick him out in '72?"

"Yes, but we were probably wrong. The politics of exclusion didn't work," said Hayden. Aside to me, he chuckled, "The politics of inclusion may not work either."

"Are you going to go up and shake his hand?" asked the persistent reporter.

"I haven't got that far yet," Tom Hayden said.

Epilogue · Mystic Chords of Memory

*The mystic chords of memory . . . will yet swell the chorus
of the Union when again touched, as surely they will be,
by the better angels of our nature.*

—*Lincoln, First Inaugural*

As Tocqueville noted long ago, Americans are robbed of half their lives
if politics is dead. The anti-politics that spread in late 1968 and became a
wave after Watergate could not last, for our problems remain deeply
political. The widespread complaint of a lack of leadership obviously
arises out of a genuine thirst for leadership, and may indicate a renewed
willingness to let someone lead.

Politics was in everyone's head in the fall of 1979, when many of the
main actors in these stories of the sixties came to Boston for the dedication of the John Fitzgerald Kennedy Library. Coretta King, her son
Martin, and Andy Young were there, saying that they would do everything in their power to see that the millions of blacks now registered in
the South voted for whoever was nominated as the Democratic candidate
in 1980. Alongside Edward Kennedy, sharing the center of the stage in
the outdoor ceremony, was Jimmy Carter, the born-again Baptist whom
Daddy King and Andy Young had helped win the primaries in 1976, and
whose election as the first President since the Civil War from the Deep
South had been assured by an overwhelming proportion of black votes.

Conserving his strength, Martin Luther King, Sr., did not come to
Boston. Although ready to campaign again for his co-religionist and fellow Georgian, Daddy King felt special ties to the Kennedys, including
the same curse of deaths that seemed to afflict their two families. His other
son, Rev. A. D. King, had been found dead in a swimming pool. Mrs.
Martin Luther King, Sr., had been shot and killed by a madman, in the
presence of the congregation, while she was playing a hymn on the church
organ.

At the Kennedy Library dedication, another key character was missing—Rose Kennedy. At eighty-nine, she was recovering from surgery and
gathering her strength to campaign for her last son for President. Not long

453

before, a reporter had found her with Ted, in an Irish pub in Hyannis Port, on the anniversary of her first son Joe's death; she asked the two-man band to play an old ballad about a mother sending her son off to death, to face execution "that old Ireland might be free."

Outside the library, the rest of the Kennedy family trooped onto the sunny platform. Robert Kennedy's eldest son, twenty-seven-year-old Joe, gave a rousing—some thought rabble-rousing—speech against "the concentrations of wealth and power" in America. People looked at each other and smiled—in delight or dismay—at this signal that a new generation of Kennedys was moving onto the political stage and that, whatever fate held in store for Edward Kennedy, he would not be the last of them. After Ted's near-fatal airplane crash in 1964, Robert Kennedy had said, "I guess the only reason we've survived is that there are more of us than there is trouble." (Coming to consciousness in the hospital, Ted, seeing the anxious Robert at his bedside, said: "Are you ruthless?")

In his talk, Edward Kennedy invoked the spirit of his brother's presidency—"its sense of progress and adventure and, above all, the joy of high purpose and great achievement"—and in opposition to the revolution of lowered expectations he said, "Jack believed that America is promises." But it was President Carter who had the trump card of the day. After emphasizing how different the problems of the eighties were from those of the sixties, he recalled a question that had been put to President Kennedy. "Your brother Ted said recently," the reporter began, "that after seeing the cares of office on you, he wasn't sure he would ever be interested in being President." The newsman asked him whether he would work for the presidency again, if he had it to do over, and whether he would recommend it to others. Carter repeated, approvingly, John Kennedy's double-barreled answer: "Yes, I would do it again," and "No, I would not recommend it to others—at least for a while."

Carter's aplomb in the heart of Kennedy country suggested a possible scenario that left many old campaign hands wondering: Would Edward Kennedy turn out to be the brother who is not martyred but beaten? With Chappaquiddick as the lightning rod, he might be the receptacle for years of accumulated resentment and skepticism about the Kennedys. The political air would never be cleared of the Kennedy question until Ted ran, and he seemed programmed by history (and family) to do so—although he seemed also to fear it and draw back from it.

In October 1979, opinion polls showed Kennedy ahead of Carter, two to one, but I saw no easy road for either of them. Only by being tested in a long, hard-fought campaign did Kennedy seem to have a chance of resolving the doubts about his character and judgment. Only if he suc-

454

ceeded in "whipping Ted Kennedy's ass" did Carter seem to have a chance of reviving and reclaiming his faltering Presidency. As the eighties began, it should have come as no surprise to Ted Kennedy, whose brothers' lives and deaths were shaped so much by accident, that wild young revolutionaries in Iran and Soviet tanks in Afghanistan should turn American politics upside down.

Ted Kennedy's immediate fate would depend upon his treatment by the media, for in the eighties more than ever, those who live by the media may perish by the media. Journalists and broadcasters who felt guilty about building up Camelot, or felt they had been unduly charmed by John and Robert Kennedy, were doubtless tempted to take retribution on the more vulnerable one claiming his brothers' legacy. By his actions or inaction after the accident on the bridge, he had brought much of this upon himself. And even without trying to be hard on him, the media were operating in a new era of unlimited probing of our leaders' private lives.

Instead of leaving the electorate more relaxed about matters of personal behavior and family relationships, the so-called sexual revolution seems to have turned the public's natural lust for gossip into an insatiable prurient interest. Though the primary test of Thomas Jefferson in history is what kind of President he was, not whether he had illegitimate children by a slave mistress, the publication of such allegations—or facts—might have kept him from office, as recent disclosures could have been a bar to Franklin Roosevelt (or even, it seems, Eleanor). History shows no clear correlation between the private life of a leader and the ability to lead.

"What will your book say about another Kennedy administration?" I was asked by students at Wakefield High School the day before the dedication of the Kennedy Library. (Former members of the Kennedy administration, and chroniclers such as Art Buchwald and Anthony Lewis, had been asked to spend a day talking to students in the Boston area about "the challenge of public service.") My answer was that if they were going to vote for or against a second Kennedy presidency, they had better try to understand what was wrong and what was right with the first one. To make up their minds about the views and the vision (or lack of it) of those who made the major decisions in the sixties, they should go to the Kennedy Library themselves, I urged, and delve in the records. They should not settle for first impressions and uncomplicated answers, for haste, as Pope John Paul II had said, is "the sickness of this century." It was one of the things wrong in some of the key decisions in civil rights and foreign policy in the early 1960s. So often the urgent was the enemy of the important, and, as Robert Kennedy came to see, energy was no substitute for wisdom.

A larger flaw in the Presidency of John Kennedy was the false pragmatism that put undue weight on the power of guns and dollars, and continued to let the fear of Communism—or the fear of seeming to be soft on Communism—distort if not dominate our world strategy. But that reaction to the cold war was deeply ingrained in American politics before Kennedy, and it outlasted him.

It was under Eisenhower in 1953 that the CIA conspired to reinstate the Shah of Iran, and it was Lyndon Johnson who sent the Marines into the Dominican Republic in 1965. It was Russian expert Zbigniew Brzezinski, a Presidential adviser in 1980, who during the Cuban missile crisis of 1962 telegraphed Arthur Schlesinger: "ANY FURTHER DELAY IN BOMBING MISSILE SITES FAILS TO EXPLOIT SOVIET UNCERTAINTY." It was a top-level 1954 Eisenhower panel that advised against "an implacable enemy" such as Russia: "Hitherto acceptable norms of human conduct do not apply. If the United States is to survive . . . we must learn to subvert, sabotage and destroy our enemies by more clever and more sophisticated and more effective methods than those used against us." And it was Eisenhower's special secret panel of David Bruce and Robert Lovett that warned in 1956 that the CIA's "successes" were "responsible in a great measure for stirring up the turmoil and raising the doubts about us that exist in many countries of the world today." Bruce and Lovett asked: "Should not someone, somewhere in an authoritative position in our government, on a continuing basis, be . . . calculating . . . the long-range wisdom of activities which have entailed our virtual abandonment of the international 'golden rule' . . . ?" If one of the things most wrong in the sixties was the failure to answer it satisfactorily, that question is very much with us still.

One of the things most right about that era, I suggested to the students, was the spirit of public service. Visiting the library, they would sense that spirit in exhibit after exhibit. What a falling off there was from President Kennedy's call upon every citizen to serve the common good and King's dream of the "beloved community" to the slogan of the late sixties, "Do your thing!" Where was the "common thing"—the *res publica*—that is at the heart of the idea of a republic? Yet if a willingness to serve was indeed widespread in the early sixties, it had not sprung full-grown from the mouth of John Kennedy. In the library's exhibit on the Peace Corps, a Volunteer was quoted as saying in 1962, "I'd never done anything political, patriotic or unselfish because nobody ever asked me to. Kennedy asked." His generation proved to be ready when asked. What if someone asked young people today?

The petulance and self-indulgence with which a loud fraction of college students responded to the President's call for registration went beyond pacifism, or just skepticism toward United States overseas policies. Nevertheless, a move toward a military draft was not a fair test of the students' readiness to serve society. The context was too narrow, and the concept of voluntary service, whether in the military or in civilian work, had not really been advanced in any effective way. In one of his last interviews, Robert Kennedy said he thought the Peace Corps idea should become part of the whole of life, not just a passing episode for a relative handful of people. But no such escalation of the idea has yet been tried. The so-called All-Voluntary Armed Forces more accurately should be called mercenary forces, and they amount almost to conscription by poverty.

As a more appropriate course for the 1980s, the first Peace Corps Volunteer to be elected to the Senate, Paul Tsongas of Massachusetts (and Ethiopia 1962–64), and the Senate Democratic leader Alan Cranston, with a bipartisan group of senators, have moved to establish a Presidential Commission on National Service. Before accepting a return to the draft, they want to see whether an effective way cannot be found to ask—but not compel—young people to help meet the military and nonmilitary needs of the nation. So little is asked of the young today, except that they be consumers of goods and services. Who knows how they might respond if asked?

The response of students at the high school where I spoke—and the accounts by others who went to different schools—suggested that young people might be ready to cast off the cynicism of the seventies.* But whether they would rally to a call from any political figure, or to the idea of national service, or to anything else in the political world, was another question. In amazing numbers, the young, and people of all ages and all religions, had been stirred by John Paul II's almost puritan appeal even when they disagreed sharply with some of his prescriptions, but part of his appeal was that he was above politics and above nation, seeking to be a spokesman for the whole tribe of man.

The outpouring for the Pope was no sign of a return to high ideal-

---

* In an unscientific poll, I asked Wakefield High School students whether they would favor the idea of spending a year or more, after leaving school, in some form of full-time voluntary service, either in the armed forces or in non-military programs, at home or abroad, like VISTA and the Peace Corps. A large majority raised hands in support of such a large-scale system for voluntary national service. A smaller number, but still more than half of those present, raised hands indicating their personal interest in volunteering. Their answers were consistent with the results of a nationwide Gallup survey of teenagers in the summer of 1979. See reports of the Committe for the Study of National Service, the Potomac Institute, 1501 18th Street, NW, Washington, D.C. 20036.

ism or easy optimism, and neither at Wakefield High School nor in any other section of the American people is there evidence of a resurgence of conventional liberalism. The curiosity about the Kennedys that I found among the students did not relate primarily to political issues or government programs. What the students mainly asked was: what were John and Robert Kennedy really like?

In the library, visitors could hear the recorded voice of Rose Kennedy telling how she and her husband had brought their children up to render public service and not just loll on the Riviera, and how she and Joe saw to it that their sons and daughters went to church regularly and learned firm moral precepts. I recalled a conversation with her in 1976, a few days after Carter's nomination, when her competitive spirit had been aroused by my account of Lillian Carter at the Democratic convention. In a late television interview just before her son's nomination, "Miz" Lillian had been asked if Jimmy ever lied, and she had said he was a very truthful boy but she wished he didn't tell that white lie about never lying, and the other one about having a perfect marriage. "Rosalynn is a fine wife," Lillian Carter said, "but who ever heard of a perfect marriage?" With barely a smile, Rose Kennedy had quickly responded: "Why, I would never talk like that about one of my sons!" When I said she didn't have to puncture her sons' piety because they didn't pose as pious the way Jimmy did, she remonstrated, "Oh, yes, they have all been very pious!" Then for several minutes I was lectured on their diligence in going to mass every Sunday morning, no matter how late they had stayed up, or how far they had been traveling the night before.

Rose's influence notwithstanding, piety was not her sons' problem. Robert Kennedy was the religious one, but no one can appreciate what he became without remembering what he had been. He followed Emerson's precept, which he underlined in his notebook: *"Do what you are afraid to do."* This took him down paths he had never imagined traveling, on a search that by his death had become, for me and many others, the most interesting as well as the most intense odyssey of our time.

To the inquiring students, I said: Go see the film, shown continuously in the Kennedy Library, of Bob standing in the windy night in Indianapolis, telling black citizens that Martin Luther King had been killed, asking what kind of country we are. Watch him speaking without a note, his voice quavering as he recited from memory: "My favorite poet was Aeschylus. He wrote: 'In our sleep, pain which cannot forget falls drop by drop upon the heart until, in our own despair, against our will, comes wisdom through the awful grace of God.'"

John Kennedy? He was different. They were so different, Robert and John. Politically, John Kennedy wanted to prove, as Alexander Hamil-

458

ton proposed in the First Federalist Paper, that Americans by their conduct and example can demonstrate that they are capable of governing themselves out of reflection and choice and need not be forever governed by accident and force. But he never expected to get all that he wanted, and he learned to live cheerfully—perhaps too cheerfully—with the continuing tension between what we know we are and what we ought to be. He encouraged the country to do the same.

Jacqueline Kennedy gave her own very unpolitical clue to her husband's character in a poem she wrote for him shortly after their marriage in 1953. From the "green land" of his ancestors, there was something he inherited

> *That surged in the depth of his too proud heart*
> *And spiked the punch of New England so tart.*
> *Men would call him thoughtful, sincere,*
> *They would not see through to the Last Cavalier.*

John Kennedy left his own clues. On the silver mug he gave his friend Dave Powers in 1963, he inscribed lines he knew by heart though he didn't remember where he learned them:

> *There are three things which are real:*
> *God, human folly, and laughter.*
> *The first two are beyond our comprehension,*
> *So we must do what we can with the third.*

For the students, and others interested in making sense of the Kennedy era, there is a good prop to the imagination behind the library: the President's boat, the *Victura*, poised gracefully on the grass, as if sailing close to the wind, with the blue harbor on a clear day looming in the background. I think of John Kennedy as a sailor, with a seaman's sins and a skipper's skill. His odyssey was an American one, and it continues.

Appendix · Precursor and Conscience: The Commission on Civil Rights

The first major move in civil rights by the government since 1875 was the Civil Rights Act of 1957 and the creation under that act of the Commission on Civil Rights. Soon after the bus boycott began in Montgomery, President Eisenhower proposed the establishment of a commission to investigate charges "that in some localities Negro citizens are being deprived of their right to vote and are likewise being subjected to unwarranted economic pressures." President Truman's advisory Committee on Civil Rights had recommended such a commission in 1947, but annual efforts by Hubert Humphrey and other members of Congress to enact the necessary legislation had regularly failed. In July 1956 the House passed the measure but it died in the Senate Judiciary Committee, under threat of a Southern filibuster.

In 1957, the bill seemed likely to suffer the same fate. Despite the growing movement for civil rights, the Southern Democratic–conservative Republican coalition continued to control Congress. However, Lyndon Johnson, the Senate Majority Leader, had finally concluded that some congressional action was necessary. He turned all his energies and skills to the task of persuading his Southern colleagues not to filibuster, and his Northern colleagues to accept a compromise the Southerners could swallow: at least a bill establishing a Civil Rights Commission and empowering the Justice Department to sue on behalf of Negroes denied their right to vote.

The junior senator from Massachusetts was one of those who supported Johnson on each key vote. Even at the price of black and liberal criticism, Kennedy voted for the crucial amendment providing a jury trial for anyone charged with criminal contempt in a civil rights case. Without that limitation on judicial action, Kennedy thought there would be no bill, and in any case he considered the limitation constitutionally justified. His position pleased Johnson but antagonized many Negro leaders, who thought Southern white juries would seldom, if ever, agree to a conviction. It became one of the obstacles to Negro support for Kennedy (and one of the reasons for organizing a special Civil Rights Section in his subsequent presidential campaign).

Johnson was weighing political factors, too. His legislative aide, Harry McPherson, with whom I argued and collaborated during this period, believes that Johnson's urge to fix problems would have caused him to take on the race question sooner or later. But he thinks it would have come later if there had not been the 1956 shift of Negro votes to the Republicans. That shift posed a threat to Democrats in future elections, at a time when Johnson needed to reveal himself as a national, not merely a sectional, politician if he were to be seriously considered for President. In setting out to work what political analysts came to call "the miracle of '57," Johnson risked loss of his Southern support, for he knew that in the end he would have to vote for a civil rights bill, which no Texan had done since Reconstruction; yet he also feared that the compromises necessary along the way might win him little Northern or Negro credit.*

During the seven weeks that the bill was before the Senate, I saw Johnson at close range, glorying in his burden and conveying the pain he suffered as part of his appeal for sympathy and support. While lobbying for the bill, I realized the personal power of this big man, who would grab your arm, pull you to him, massage your back, put his face close to you, and tower over you as he made his point, which always finally came down to: "I need your he'p."

Some of my colleagues were sure he was two-faced and not to be trusted. He did talk at least two different lines—one when his arms were around Senator Hubert Humphrey, with whom he discussed the maximum they could get, and the other when he was hand-in-arm with Senator Richard Russell, saying there had to be some kind of "nigra bill." But he wanted to enact the first civil rights law in eighty-two years, and I marveled at the way, through all his political manipulation, he seemed to make reason rule. One way, as Harry McPherson pointed out, was repeatedly to rise on the floor to praise the reasonableness of all sides, which made it difficult for those who wanted to be unreasonable.

When the Senate finally passed the act on August 7, 1957, by a vote of 72 to 18, Johnson's friend Dean Acheson said: "I don't think it an exaggeration to say that the bill is among the greatest achievements since the war, and in the field of civil rights, the greatest since the Thirteenth Amendment." Others considered the relatively weak bill worse than no bill, and predicted that it would defuse the public pressure for further action. I agreed with Johnson's own claim: "It's just a beginning. We've shown that we can do it. We'll do it again, in a couple of years."

To my dismay, however, civil rights spokesmen immediately began to discount the value of the newly created Commission on Civil Rights even before the President nominated its first six members. The Commission was entirely a fact-finding and recommending agency, with no enforcement powers of its own. "Why study the situation any more?" NAACP friends asked. "For nine decades since the Thirteenth Amendment the problem has been studied. We're tired of being studied."

White Southern opponents of the bill did not want to be studied either, but the fury with which they fought the Commission suggested that it might be more potent than others suspected. In a twenty-four-hour speech, Senator Strom Thurmond warned against the Commission's "carte blanche authority to

---

* See Chapter 5, "Sacred Cows and Racial Justice," in *A Political Education*, by Harry McPherson (Boston: Little, Brown, 1972); and Chapter 7, "The Miracle of '57," in *Lyndon B. Johnson: The Exercise of Power*, by Rowland Evans and Robert Novak (New York: New American Library, 1966).

probe and meddle in every phase of the relations between individuals." Those who think the Commission will not be extended at the end of its two-year statutory life "believe in fairies," predicted the minority report in the House Judiciary Committee. Senator Olin Johnston proposed an amendment to provide for "the funeral expenses of the members of the Civil Rights Commission in the unlikely event that the Commission should ever come into being."

Again I found myself in agreement with Lyndon Johnson, who said that the Commission "can sift out the truth from the fancies" and "return with recommendations which will be of assistance to reasonable men." At the request of Stephen Benedict, a friend on the White House staff, I prepared a paper on what the Commission might do to help break the racial impasse; it was sent to the members whom Eisenhower appointed to the Commission.

When those appointments were announced, there was a new wave of skepticism about the Commission. The President's choices seemed to guarantee a stalemate; he was suspected of having deliberately ensured that the Commission would cause no trouble. In conforming to the law's requirement that the Commission be bipartisan, Eisenhower had picked three relatively conservative Southern Democrats, two Northern Republicans, and a priest: John Battle, former governor of Virginia and leader of the Dixiecrat walkout at the 1948 Democratic convention; Doyle Carlton, who was governor of Florida from 1923 to 1933; Robert Storey, dean of the Southern Methodist University Law School in Texas; John Hannah, president of Michigan State University; J. Ernest Wilkins, an Assistant Secretary of Labor; and Rev. Theodore Hesburgh, president of Notre Dame. Negro leaders were particularly displeased that Ernest Wilkins, a stolid Republican attorney with little previous involvement in the civil rights movement, was the only Negro Commissioner. There was no known liberal member to reassure the original proponents of the Commission. This was Father Hesburgh's first major public assignment, and his position was unpredictable.

In January 1958, the Commissioners-designate held their first meeting even though, thanks to Senator Eastland's delays in the Senate Judiciary Committee, they would not be properly confirmed by the Senate until March. After that January meeting I received a telephone call from Father Hesburgh, who asked if I could meet him in Lafayette Park in front of the White House. Though he didn't know anything about me, he had read my October memorandum on the Commission and wanted to talk. I was impressed that a busy executive would initiate a meeting with an unknown author of a memorandum simply because he is interested in the writer's ideas. "Now that you see who the members are, do you still think the Commission can do something important?" Father Hesburgh asked. As we walked around the park on a sunny winter day, I asked whether the North–South division in the Commission could be turned into an asset. Could the divided Commission provide the missing dialogue at the highest level that the racial problem required?

In Father Hesburgh I discovered a man of curiosity, compassion, conviction, and courage. In 1958 he also seemed quite conservative. Open-minded, warm, and direct, he was a promising participant in any dialogue. His approach was obviously to reach and reason with a person, not to manipulate or defeat him. Already he had his sights on the most outspoken segregationist on the Commission, John Battle: if they could work together and find ways forward that they agreed upon, the Commission might make a significant contribution. Hesburgh was not sure it was a good sign that four of the six Commissioners were lawyers; he took his hope from the discovery that all six liked to fish. He himself was also a fisher of men: after several long talks (and checks at my law firm by members of the Notre Dame "Mafia") he asked me to become his legal counsel on the Commission. Each member had the authority to appoint an assistant, who would also be an organizing member of the Commission's staff. The move to the Commission's office on Jackson Place, the other side of Lafayette Square from the law firm of Covington and Burling (where I had been practicing law for nearly four years) seemed right. Still, when I started at the Commission on April Fools' Day, 1958, I wondered whether Father Hesburgh and I were both whistling in the dark.

Eisenhower had emphasized that the problem was one of changing the minds and hearts of people, and said he hoped the Commission would focus on "what can be done in what you might call the educational and even, indeed, the spiritual field." However, our first duty under the act was to investigate and hold hearings on sworn complaints alleging the denial of the right to vote. Moreover, in the matter of voting the law was clear, and action to find the facts and then to bring about enforcement of the law would be the best form of persuasion. "The Law is a teacher," my October 1957 memorandum on the Commission had argued:

> People learn to drive on the right side of the street by driving on that side. The citizens of the thirteen original states came to consider themselves citizens of the United States of America because the Constitution of the United States was ratified, established and enforced. Without the working of the Constitution no amount of talk would have convinced Americans to abandon their parochial loyalties for a higher allegiance.
>
> Today compliance with the Constitution is still the best instruction in our constitutional duties. Negroes voting will do more to change the habits and opinions of those who oppose such voting than any amount of talk. . . .

In other areas of civil rights such as school desegregation and discrimination in housing, there was deep confusion—which Eisenhower had helped compound—and a lot of good talk and thought was necessary. New ways had to be found to disperse hatred, violence, and irrationality, and take the initiative out of the hands of racial demagogues. The larger aim of the Commission should be to discover how to do this.

The Civil Rights Act authorized the Commission to constitute state advisory committees. Such committees, bringing blacks and whites together where almost no communication existed between racial groups, could help communities to know themselves. Through these biracial advisory committees, I had suggested in my October memorandum, the Southern white "might realize that there is a new Negro in his midst, not sent from the North, not

464

primarily stirred up by outside agitators but by the Constitution and the Christian Church. And the Negro might see that there are other wiser Southern voices than the jeers and catcalls of racist mobs and the ranting or slipperiness of political demagogues." While the need for such committees might be greater in the South, it would be important to form them in all regions and thus to recognize that race is not solely a Southern question.

The report produced by a commission proceeding along these lines could, I predicted, serve as a platform for new action by Congress and the President. With luck, we could confound the cynics and take the country by surprise.

At first we in the Commission were the ones surprised. Despite the delaying tactics of Southern legislators who stalled confirmation hearings, budget action, and Senate votes for nearly six months, in late June the Commission had a staff director (Gordon Tiffany, former attorney general of New Hampshire), the nucleus of a professional staff, and an appropriation of $750,000. We were ready for business, but the first business the Commissioners and Congress expected did not come. Though ten months of the Commission's two-year life had passed, not a single sworn complaint alleging a denial of the right to vote had been submitted.

For a while we benefited by the opportunity to read basic literature, collect available information from other sources, and discuss the major issues. The monumental study by Gunnar Myrdal, *The American Dilemma*, published in 1942 following a four-year study funded by the Carnegie Corporation of New York, and the 1947 report of President Truman's Committee on Civil Rights, *To Secure These Rights*, were our initial texts. But after eight monthly Commission meetings, the time for preliminary talk had passed. Everyone was busy, because each Commissioner and his legal assistant had been assigned eight states where they were to organize advisory committees, and three main areas for staff study had been chosen: voting, education, and housing. But since there were no sworn complaints that the right to vote was being denied by reason of race, there was no occasion to invoke the Commissioners' statutory duty to investigate and hold hearings. And, fishermen or not, the members of the Commission were in no mood to go on a fishing expedition for complaints. They had reluctantly accepted the assignment and taken an oath to do their duty, but at least the three Southern members were not inclined to do more.

Without a single affidavit on which to act, the Commission was in danger of falling apart. Quarrels broke out between the Southerners and Ernest Wilkins, and there was suspicion that the staff was too prone toward integration. In addition to my association with King, it became clear that not one of the legal assistants selected by the Southern Commissioners supported segregation. Without sworn complaints, neither the cautious staff director nor the divided Commissioners were going to move. Clearly the only cure was to get some complaints. For several months I had been making just that point to civil rights leaders who were tending to write the Commission off as a lost cause. By not testing the Commission, they were turning their fears into a self-fulfilling prophecy. Why not give us a chance? I asked. What would Congress and the country think if, after all the effort to pass the Civil Rights Act, no one brought a complaint to the Commission?

In talks with Martin King, Roy Wilkins, and others, I found more than skepticism. There was fear that anyone encouraged to file an affidavit would be intimidated, perhaps even killed, and that the Commission would not be able to provide protection. There was also a large factor of inertia: a reluctance to do the difficult, detailed work of finding good cases, persuading people to be complainants, and preparing solid affidavits. "You are willing to lead people into jail," I said to King during this period. "Why can't you get them to file an affidavit?" We agreed that part of the problem was a paradox of non-violent action that Gandhi never solved: 100,000 Indians would follow him to jail, but outside prison he could never get more than a few to persevere with the undramatic constructive program he prescribed for the periods between mass struggles. The lawyers of the NAACP were accustomed to encouraging complainants and to the legal craftsmanship that produces good affidavits, but they were committed to litigation and consumed by school desegregation cases.

When George M. Johnson, the dean of Howard Law School, became chief of the Commission's Office of Laws, Plans, and Research, some of his NAACP colleagues gave us a second, friendlier look. He was a shrewd, wise man. (Johnson had been responsible in 1952 for my going on to finish law school at Yale as well as at Howard; in his practical fashion he wanted to make sure that I knew both worlds.) As head of the Commission's legal staff and as a member of the Commission itself (after Ernest Wilkins' death in January 1959), Johnson played a key role. But for several months his efforts to persuade black leadership to give the Commission a fair test also seemed to be unavailing.

On the assumption that sworn complaints would come someday, a staff of field investigators had been hired, with a former Army colonel in charge. Since the Commissioners would not let them go into the field before a bona fide complaint was in hand, they spent most of the summer in the Library of Congress doing research. They were not scholarly types, and their frustration added to a sense of impending fiasco.

One morning in August, we laughed when an envelope came from a "Professor Bashful." Even when we found that the document inside alleged denials of the right to vote and that it was notarized, we still suspected someone was putting us on. Emmet J. Bashful's affidavit was too good to be true. But when a telephone check found that yes, there was a Professor Bashful, we jumped with delight. Within a week, after assembling all the information we could, we presented Professor Bashful's complaint to the Commission. It was a broad charge, alleging "that through threats of bodily harm and losing of jobs, and other means, Negro residents of Gadsden County, Florida, are being deprived of the right to vote." Some of the Commissioners were understandably troubled that the professor did not claim that he himself was being denied the right to vote. Nevertheless, even though it was not quite the kind of complaint Congress had in mind, the Commission decided by a unanimous vote to conduct an immediate field investigation. News of the Commission's action surprised and encouraged Negro leadership, and soon other complaints, in better order, started coming from Alabama, and then from Louisiana and Mississippi. In each case the Commission unanimously voted to investigate.

At first it was difficult for Commission investigators (almost all of them white) even to locate the Negro complainants. Professor Bashful was neither intimidated nor bashful, but others who had tried to register and been turned down were suspicious of unknown white men, and would often give no information. Investigators had to explain their purpose and prove their identification before doors would open. A smile finally started spreading over the face of an old Alabama Negro woman, who had been rocking silently on her porch while the Commission agent tried to convince her he was there to help. With wide eyes, she finally said, "You mean the Big Government has come? The Big Government has really come all the way down here to help us! The Big Government is finally going to do something to let me vote?" It was the first time in sixty years, she said, that the federal government had shown any interest in the colored people of Alabama.

The impact of the Commission's prompt response—of its investigators appearing on the site, respectfully interviewing complainants, diligently seeking other witnesses, and persistently questioning local registrars and asking for their records—was profound. Negroes often said that the white Southern agents of the FBI in their areas were so closely tied to local officials that they didn't dare go to them with complaints. In instances when the FBI had been asked for help, they contended the FBI invariably accepted the official version and left their names with the local police, who would thereafter taunt and threaten them.

Encouraged by the Commission's action and urged on by Martin King in Montgomery, more and more Negroes in the Black Belt counties of Alabama and other Southern states began submitting detailed sworn allegations that indicated a widespread pattern of restricting registration to whites. In the next months complaints came in from twenty-nine counties in eight states. In fifteen of these counties, including five in Alabama, Negroes constituted a majority of the population but only a relatively small number (or none) were registered.

The greatest number of complaints came from Macon County, Alabama, the location of Tuskegee Institute. In vindication of Booker T. Washington's hopes when he founded the Institute in 1881, the education and economic independence of the Negro community around the Institute provided the base for a voting rights drive throughout that county. Still, whites outnumbered Negroes three to one in registration although there were five times as many Negroes of voting age. As the Commission's investigations spread, it became clear why so few complaints came from the sixteen counties with Negro majorities and not a single Negro registered: they were the areas of the most intimidation—and long-standing hopelessness or apathy among Negroes.

When nineteen sworn complaints arrived from Dallas County, Alabama, I circulated my 1952 law school paper on the state of the Negro there. One of my chief informants, Mrs. Amelia Boynton of Selma, became a key witness for us. She was one of some 150 Negroes registered out of about 18,000 Negroes of voting age in a county where there were two Negroes for every white. In the six years since we had talked she had much personal evidence of unsuccessful efforts to register Negroes in Dallas and in other adjacent counties, where even fewer (if any) Negroes were on the rolls. In Selma, since 1952, she said, more than 800 Negroes had tried to register—some many times—but only two had succeeded. When local Alabama registrars refused to cooperate with investigators, the Commission decided—again unanimously—to use its statutory power to formally request inspection of voting records. Then, on orders of the state's attorney general (soon to become governor), John Patterson, the officials stonewalled, and all six Commissioners voted to hold a hearing at Montgomery, and to subpoena the registrars and their records.

Faced with the first federal civil rights hearing in the Deep South since Reconstruction, several registrars agreed to comply, but an Alabama circuit judge intervened and impounded all registration records. Judge George Wallace, already said to be aiming for the Alabama governorship, told the press: "I will jail any Civil Rights Commission agent who attempts to get the records."

Sixty-six subpoenas to appear at the hearing on December 8 were served to Negro witnesses and pertinent white officials, including officials in Lowndes County, where Negroes constituted 82 percent of the population but none was registered. Montgomery County was dropped from the list when the twenty complaining witnesses and other Negroes received certificates of registration after the hearing was called.

Since integrated accommodations were not possible in Montgomery, the Commissioners arranged to stay at the nearby Maxwell Air Force Base. It took White House intervention to overcome the resistance of the commanding officer, who wanted to maintain good relations with the city. The five white Commissioners were all embarrassed that there was no room at a hotel for their black colleague, an Assistant Secretary of Labor and the chief judicial officer of the Methodist Church.

Television cameras were whirring quietly in the federal building in downtown Montgomery when Vice-Chairman Storey opened the hearing. The former president of the American Bar Association recalled his Southern roots:

> My father was born in Alabama, reared here and educated before he emigrated to Texas. My grandfathers were Confederate soldiers. So, there are many thoughts and memories going through my mind as we meet in Montgomery, the cradle of the Confederacy; but history moves on. We are one nation now. Hence, this bipartisan Commission, composed of two presidents of great universities and four lawyers, has a solemn duty to perform. We are sworn to uphold the Constitution of the United States.

468

All morning Negro witnesses gave their testimony. The Commission was told of the registration board in Macon County that hid its location or the time of its meetings and even went out of operation for many months to avoid black applicants and, when working, would keep Negroes waiting three to nine hours in a back room to fill out the first forms. A twenty-two-year-old woman studying for a master's degree in chemistry never heard from the board after copying Article 2 of the Constitution in eight and a half pages. A veteran of the Korean War said:

> I have dodged bombs and almost got killed, and then come back and denied the vote—I don't like it. I want to vote and I want to take part . . . I have taken part in it when I was in service. I think I should take part in it when I am a civilian.

When local white officials were called to testify, all but two of them refused to respond to the allegations. A registrar of Lowndes County did admit there were no black applicants in a county where Negroes outnumbered whites by four to one, and the county judge in charge of voting records conceded that such a situation "might be unusual, peculiar in some places, yes." State Attorney General and Governor-elect Patterson challenged the Commission's constitutional right to question a judicial officer of Alabama.

Deeply disturbed, Commissioner Battle made a public appeal. Recalling that his Alabama grandfather had been denied a seat in Congress because he had served in the Confederate Army, the former governor said: "I come to the people of Alabama as a friend—returning to the house of my father." None of the white people present, he said, "believe more strongly than I do in the segregation of the races as the right and proper way of life in the South." Battle asked, "As one who is tremendously interested in the Southern cause: Will you kindly reevaluate the situation and see if there is not some way you . . . may cooperate a little bit more fully with this Commission?" An article in the Birmingham *News* said that Commissioner Battle had "raised a sober point as the dark velvet skies gentled down over Montgomery." But a few hours later Attorney General Patterson declared that "the time for retreating has come to an end." He vowed that there would be no cooperation with the Commission's "unlawful invasion."

Most of the nation's press and opinion leaders reacted as Battle had predicted. The Washington *Star* commented that "something is going to fall on Alabama, and this time it will not be stars." *The New York Times* wrote of "the intolerable contempt for law in resistance to this ultra-moderate Presidential Commission." The Atlanta *Constitution* wrote that if Alabama officials will not heed Governor Battle "they will heed no one and the tragedy will have to be played out to the bitter end." Even the usually taciturn President Eisenhower described the action of Alabama officials as "reprehensible."

The Commission itself heard additional Negro witnesses—thirty-three in all, by the close of the hearing—give depressingly repetitive testimony of denials of the right to vote. After one farmer from Bullock County told of being turned down time after time, Father Hesburgh asked, "Are you going to keep trying?" The farmer said, "Oh, yes, I'm determined to register." Departing from the Commission's usual impartial stance, Father Hesburgh said, "God bless you."

Chairman Hannah announced that the record of the hearing would be turned over to the Attorney General of the United States for appropriate action to secure access to the official records the Commission needed. Within a month the government filed suit to require inspection of registration records and federal judge Frank M. Johnson, Jr., ordered local officials to comply, the interposition of circuit judge George Wallace notwithstanding. Wallace said he would burn before giving the records. By turning records over to grand juries, he succeeded in keeping many documents from Commission inspection, but the records that were made available and summarized in a reconvened Commission hearing in Montgomery, January 9, added substantial new evidence of discrimination.

Meanwhile, the Alabama legislature took its own unanimous action: it enacted a bill providing for the destruction of registration records within thirty days after the applications were acted upon. Two months after the Alabama hearing, the Department of Justice filed suit to force the registration of qualified Negroes in Macon County; when the two county registrars both resigned, the suit was dismissed for lack of anyone to sue—and the county lacked a board able to register anyone.

Commission investigation of voting rights complaints continued throughout the seven months left before the report to the President and Congress had to go to press. The statistical picture became very clear: the problem was concentrated in the so-called Black Belt counties, a wide strip of territory crossing eight states, named for its rich black soil, but also known for its predominantly black population. Once the heartland of slave plantations, the Black Belt continued as the bastion of large white farms, whose owners maintained disproportionate power in their state legislatures by disfranchising their Negro tenants. In the states of most concern (and most complaints), the Commission found the following:

ALABAMA—Twelve counties had nonwhite majorities; in 2, no nonwhites were registered; in 7, the number registered was less than 5%. GEORGIA —Twenty-nine counties had nonwhite majorities; in 2, no nonwhite was registered; in 11 others, the number registered was less than 5%. LOUISIANA— Eight parishes had nonwhite majorities; in 4, no nonwhite was registered. MISSISSIPPI—Twenty-six counties had nonwhite majorities; in 6, no nonwhite was registered; in 18, the number registered was less than 5%. Nonwhites were 41% of the state's voting-age population; 4% of total registered voters. SOUTH CAROLINA—Fifteen counties had nonwhite majorities; in one, no nonwhite was registered; in 4, the number registered was less than 5%.

In some places apathy was part of the explanation for the racial disparities in registration. In Atlanta, for example, Negroes could register freely and 29% had done so, in contrast to 44% of the whites. Urban-rural differences were

470

also marked. In Florida as a whole, 40% of voting-age Negroes were registered, 50% in the Miami and Jacksonville areas. But in rural Gadsden County, the locus of the Commission's first complaint, only seven Negroes were registered out of about 11,000 of voting age, and in three nearby farm counties, no Negroes were registered at all.

In all the areas of very low or no Negro registration that the Commission investigated, there was evidence of intimidation or discriminatory use of literacy or other registration procedures. The leader of a registration drive in Gadsden County was fired from his job and left the state altogether after receiving threats of physical violence. Many of the 300 Negro teachers in the county expressed a desire to register but feared they would lose their jobs if they tried.

In Mississippi, with nearly a million Negroes, only 22,000 were reported to be registered, and only 8,000 of these had paid their poll tax and were thus eligible to vote in 1955. In half of the state's 82 counties fewer than 1 percent of voting-age Negroes were registered. Negro applicants told the Commission how they were required to write a "reasonable explanation" of a section of the Mississippi Constitution and then told, "Your replies won't do." One failed to answer adequately the question, "What is class assessment of land?" A minister with two degrees from Columbia University was denied registration. In Terrell County, Georgia, four Negro schoolteachers were turned down because in their reading test they pronounced "equity" as "eequity." In two Louisiana parishes where no Negroes were enrolled, an applicant had to be vouched for by two voters, and no white could be found who would do so. In another parish, Negroes failed to explain adequately the following constitutional provision: "Prescription shall not run against the State in any civil matter."

The Joint Legislative Committee of the Louisiana Legislature launched a statewide campaign in 1958 to reduce Negro registration from 130,000 to 13,000. Advising registrars that "you don't have to discriminate against Negroes" to keep them off registration rolls because "nature has already discriminated against them," the chairman of the Legislative Committee distributed instructions in "Voter Qualification Laws in Louisiana" to officials and white Citizens Councils throughout the state. "We are in a life and death struggle with the Communists and the NAACP to maintain segregation and to preserve the liberties of the people," the foreword to the instructions warned. "The Communists and the NAACP plan to register and vote every colored person of age in the South. While the South has slept, they have made serious progress toward their goal. . . . They plan to divide the people of the South, and to take us over, state by state, and parish by parish."

During May, June, and July of 1959, more than 1,300 of the approximately 1,500 Negro registrants in Washington Parish were stricken from the rolls on the basis of challenges filed by members of the white Citizens Council. The most common basis for the challenges were alleged errors in spelling. The affidavit of one registrar reported that a Negro voter had been disqualified for "Error in Spilling."

While investigating such denials of the right to vote, the Commission also proceeded in the two other areas it had chosen for study: housing and education. Housing had been readily approved as a subject because the problem was centered in metropolitan areas, most of which were outside the South, and all the Commissioners welcomed an opportunity to show that discrimination was nationwide. Some outside critics saw this as a plot by the Southern Commissioners to take the heat off the South. On the contrary, it seemed to us that moral heat outside the South would serve to increase the moral heat everywhere. Discrimination did exist in all parts of the country, and more than half of all Negroes by then were living in the North and West.

Commissioner Wilkins' legal assistant, Eugene Jackson, an able attorney from the National Labor Relations Board, and I were asked to take special responsibility for the housing investigation. The Southern Commissioners no doubt liked the notion of turning the two most obvious integrationists on the staff loose primarily on the North. For basic information we were able to draw on the three-year study of an independent Commission on Race and Housing that had just issued its summary report, *Where Shall We Live?* Headed by Earl B. Schwulst, president of The Bowery Savings Bank, the group had included Clark Kerr, Philip Klutznick, Henry Luce, the Rev. John Cavanaugh (Father Hesburgh's predecessor at Notre Dame), and outstanding black and business leaders. It was supported financially by the Fund for the Republic (an agency described by its president, Robert Hutchins, as a wholly disowned subsidiary of the Ford Foundation). The Schwulst Commission had received much cooperation and data from the Bureau of the Census and various federal housing agencies, and from the National Urban League, the NAACP, interested religious groups, and organizations of builders, mortgage bankers, and real estate brokers. In our one-year study we continued that collaboration between public and private sectors.

By this time advisory committees to the Civil Rights Commission had been organized in almost every state, so we asked each of them to consider the question of discrimination in housing. We received interesting responses. The Indiana committee, for example, reported that there were no Negro residents in thirty of the state's ninety-two counties, and that in some Indiana communities there were signs advising, "Niggers, don't let the sun go down on you." The committee noted: "If one cannot establish residence in one-third of the State, . . . in this way in parts of Indiana the Negro is being deprived of his right to vote by indirection." Nearly every state advisory committee reported varying degrees of racial discrimination in the rental or sale of housing.

During 1959 the Commission held three hearings on housing, to go into greater depth in three different cities: New York, Atlanta, and Chicago. When we speak of housing, Father Hesburgh pointed out in opening the first hearing in New York, we are talking about the face of America now and in the future: "That face must have the beauty and dignity and harmony of the Constitution, not the face of slums and discrimination and chaos." Unhappily, it was the ugly face that we found in much of New York and in the inner city in each of the other places we investigated.

In most Northern cities a "white noose" prevented black access to surrounding suburban areas. Because Atlanta had deliberately broken that noose —in part through a West Side Mutual Development Committee of three whites and three blacks, and in part by aggressive Negro business leadership —Mayor William Hartsfield was able to take the Commission on a tour of impressive modern and well-to-do Negro suburbs. He was embarrassed by the inner-city slum, Buttermilk Bottom, but proud of the West Side. In most Southern cities, partly because of the tradition of servants living on the back lot, neighborhoods were more integrated than in the North. In all the United States between 1935 and 1950 some nine million new homes had been built, but only one hundred thousand were estimated to have been for non-whites. The facts were easy to find; they sprang up from the statistics, they stared out from the tenements, they were described by eloquent witnesses. What to make of the facts—how to remedy the situation—was the problem.

Mortgage lenders and real estate agents defended efforts to exclude Negroes because of the fears of lowered property values. Evidence, however, showed that values often rose after whites fled, and that real estate operators profited from "block busting": bringing in a black purchaser, spreading panic among the whites, buying white homes at low prices and then selling them at high prices to blacks. Builder (later Congressman) James Scheuer explained how profitable it was to turn a residential block into a slum. Witnesses also described successful community efforts to stop the panic and maintain an integrated neighborhood. A PTA leader and housewife said, "It's either this, or taking a rowboat and rowing off Montauk Point, and then who knows . . . you might meet a fish you don't like."

Saul Alinsky, director of the Industrial Areas Foundation, proposed a concerted effort to open neighborhoods and check white flight by agreement on a voluntary quota, setting the number of Negroes to be welcomed in the neighborhood at less than that at which the racial composition would "tip." If the all-white areas of Chicago would work together with Negro groups on those lines, Alinsky predicted, Negroes would have all the opportunities they needed for decent and integrated housing. Some civil rights spokesmen bristled at the thought of "gentlemen's agreements" for integration, but the author of *Reveille for Radicals*, backed by the city's Catholic hierarchy, conveyed his contempt for such liberals. He contended that they eased their consciences by denouncing all forms of discrimination, but were unwilling to make the practical compromises necessary to produce integrated communities.

A sociology professor at the University of Chicago argued that in due course Negroes would follow the path of the once discriminated-against "Polacks, Sheenies, Bohunks and Wops" and other immigrants who had initially congregated together in poor quarters and then moved out to better housing as they made more money. Commissioner George Johnson, a black man who had himself experienced discrimination in housing because of his color, replied that a Negro remains trapped because he can't "lose his high visibility."

Everyone recognized that many Americans prefer to live in neighborhoods with people of their own race, color, religion, or national origin. Roy Wilkins testified that there are "colored people in Harlem who wouldn't move out of Harlem if you gave them a gold-plated apartment." But freedom of choice was the issue, and Negro Americans were far from having that freedom. Baseball star Jackie Robinson, by then vice-president of Chock Full o' Nuts corporation, told of the many evasions and downright refusals he had met in trying to buy a home. Housing is the only commodity in the American market, said banker Earl Schwulst, that is not freely available to nonwhites. In New York, the Commission reviewed the operation of city and state laws against discrimination in housing, the strongest laws of their kind in the nation. By 1959 anti-discrimination statutes had been enacted in thirteen states and thirty-four cities or counties; in many of these areas commissions or agencies were established to enforce open housing. Increasingly middle-class Negroes could find housing in white areas, but there were no signs that the situation was improving for poorer blacks.

Discrimination against the Negro middle and upper class, however, was not the only issue, as our studies kept stressing. According to the Census, nearly 70 percent of nonwhite families lived in dwellings that were dilapidated or had inadequate plumbing. For them, the quality of housing, whether in Negro areas or not, was the main issue. Poverty and the lack of decent low-cost housing were the primary problems. To make matters worse, federally assisted urban renewal slum clearance had all too often turned out to be Negro clearance and slum-spreading. Those uprooted moved into adjacent areas, creating new slums. Public housing projects were placed in the middle of black ghettos where whites would not go, thus further increasing the racial concentration and population pressures.

It was a vicious circle: with limited choice, Negroes would crowd into inner-city apartments, landlords would charge high rents and neglect maintenance, business and city alike would write off the areas as a slum and provide inadequate services, and people in other areas would point to these conditions as reasons to keep blacks out. In the suburbs ringing the city, whites who had fled such conditions would erect zoning barriers to assure pleasant residential neighborhood. Meanwhile, the exodus of middle- and upper-income citizens left the cities with a diminishing tax base, and the circle of deterioration continued.

Justine Wise Polier, for twenty-three years a judge in the Children's Court of New York City, testified about a study of 500 children who had come before her court. Most of them lived in substandard housing. A common denominator of the defendants, she said, was "fear of the real world, an awareness of low family status beyond anything that people who do not meet these little children may realize, little sense of personal worth and terrible discouragement as to their own future." Living in a slum and knowing that Negroes have only a slim chance to live elsewhere "violates a child's sense of justice, certainly his respect for himself," and the young Negro loses his ability "to reach out and function up to his capacity," Judge Polier reported. Yet she was pessimistic about any satisfactory response. "We rarely have enough imagination to understand or to be moved by the suffering of others that we either do not see or know about directly," she said. Disraeli had remarked that there was hardly a woman in England who would not be more disturbed by the smashing of the joint of her small finger in a carriage door than by hearing that a million children had died of famine the preceding week in China. The distance between white suburbs and the black slum, Justine Polier suggested, was as great as that between England and China.

The Commission's study of school desegregation was more cautious and circumscribed. In surveying what already had been done, we went first to the Office of Education in the Department of Health, Education, and Welfare, where we expected to find at least the essential statistical information. We discovered that the Education Office had ceased collecting any information about the racial composition of public schools and claimed to have done so on principle. HEW's response to the Supreme Court's ruling that racial discrimination had no place in public education was that information about continuing racial discrimination had no place in its program.

This was like a police department ceasing to collect information on homicides because murder had been declared illegal. When the Court said the Constitution was color-blind, it did not expect this to mean that the Executive Branch of the government would color-blind itself. While it was difficult to understand the lack of federal leadership, it was easier to sympathize with the predicament of the Southern white. A Northern Negro educator visiting the Commission after a trip South conceded, "I know what a white parent must feel." He had stood on the steps of a new Negro school in a Southern city and "watched those little boys and girls, so many of them in dirty, ragged clothes, carrying their shoes to put on when they went into the new school building. . . . I remembered the shacks and tenements and broken homes they had just come from. I found tears streaming down my face, for them and for the white people, too. For a moment—just a moment—I put myself in the shoes of a white parent."

Before the Commission began, I had toured Negro schools in Alabama's Dallas County and noted the wooden benches and potbellied stoves, the outdoor water pump and privy for 145 students at Sister Springs; the orange crates used for tables at the elementary school in Sardis; and many other manifest results of generations in which so little tax money had gone into the education of the great majority of the community's children. In 1930, $51 had been spent for each white student; $7 for each Negro. By the 1950s, the dollar gap had been closed to about two to one. Pointing to the one new Negro school in Dallas County, a black minister said: "That's what the Supreme Court did." "It's our fault," a white Alabama farmer had admitted to me during my 1952 study. "We neglected the colored all these years. There had to be a war before we realized how little the niggers knew. They didn't even know enough to be able to fight for us. Honestly, though, we just don't have the money to equalize schools all of a sudden." He was sad that Alabama had not long ago heeded the warning of an earlier local educator, minister, and businessman, J. L. M. Currie: "If you do not educate the Negro, he will drag you down to hell."

To demonstrate that there was a better direction, the Commission staff proposed a national conference on cases of school desegregation where constructive action had prevailed. By leaving out the Deep South, where "massive resistance" remained the policy, we got agreement from the Southern Commissioners to a meeting limited to "problems of schools in transition from the educator's viewpoint." For two days in March 1959 school officials convened in Nashville from twelve states and the District of Columbia to share and explain their experiences. They came from rural school districts, small towns, cities of medium size and large cities, from all the border states and Arkansas, North Carolina, Tennessee, and Texas. Nashville was chosen as the site because of its interesting grade-a-year desegregation plan, beginning with the first grade and including a voluntary transfer provision under which a student in a racial minority in his neighborhood school could ask to be transferred to a school where his race was in a majority.

What emerged from the discussions and papers was the fact that with good leadership, advance planning, and, where appropriate, gradual steps, desegregation could take place peacefully, economically, and without lowering academic standards. In areas where there were relatively few Negroes, ending the dual school system saved money, although at first it risked some loss of jobs for Negro teachers and principals. In areas of proportionally large Negro populations, plans for grade-by-grade integration and provisions for voluntary transfer looked promising. The educators at Nashville all thought it possible— and necessary—for desegregation to result in better education. "The way to insure the success of an integrated school is to make that school a great educational institution," the Commission was told. A "superb mathematics teacher" would do more for integration "than a ton and a half of human relations experts."

Was it possible that the acute educational crisis of the long-deprived American Negro could give a lift to all of American education? The young Negro was being urged to jump over the old inadequacies and literally shoot for the moon. The black atomic physicist or engineer of rocketry, the black lawyer, political scientist, or economist trained to meet the new problems of the later twentieth century, would find jobs awaiting him. The old trades were full of vested interests arrayed against Negroes, but the new worlds of automation and atomic energy, of economic development and social revolution, in America and around the world, were waiting for anyone educated for them. If we could discover how to prepare Negroes for these new worlds, it was suggested to the Commission, we would know how to educate all Americans for this fast-moving century.

For anything like that to happen, however, the country would have to listen to what the white Southerner, at his best, was saying, and respond to the reason behind his unreasoning No. The one fact to which he was clinging was the disparity in standards of health, morality, and education between a large proportion of poor blacks and the majority of white children. To be sure, this gap was the legacy of slavery, and of generations of discrimination and separate but unequal schools. White parents did not want to inflict upon their children the price of past sins. But there was another alternative to using the unfortunate results of segregation as an excuse for its perpetuation: the segregationist argument could be turned upside down by accepting the fact of a gap in standards and doing something about it. This would be costly, the Commission was advised, but much less so in the long run than accepting the present demoralization and letting the blackboard jungle spread.

For integration to succeed, the reports at the Nashville conference stressed, a strong network of support was necessary: willing, able, and far-sighted school administrators, cooperative Parent-Teacher Association leadership, newspapers that were not inflammatory, ministers of the Gospel who were not silent on the moral issues involved, state and local officials who helped instead of hindered, a business establishment that accepted the new reality, Negro parents and students who pressed their case but could also compromise, and a wise, patient, and persistent federal court. Even those school officials who had all or most of these factors on their side had faced insults, harassment, and threats.

When the conference adjourned, Nashville's superintendent of schools, who had opposed the Commission's coming, and not even wanted to attend, invited it to come back. "This is the first opportunity that I have had," William Oliver said, "to sit down with a group of fellow men and listen to what they have to say and find out what they think and how they are dealing with this problem." For better or worse, the districts represented were the available models for desegregation, and most of the participants seemed to leave with more of a spirit of pioneering in a vital common venture, and less of a sense of isolation. The response suggested how much could have been done to encourage gradual and peaceful desegregation if President Eisenhower and his administration had worked actively to help.

The Commission's Report to the President and Congress was due on September 9, 1959. Father Hesburgh invited the Commissioners and key staff members to his order's retreat at Land O' Lakes, Wisconsin, to review the draft of the Report and try to agree on findings and recommendations. On July 14, the Commissioners flew to northern Wisconsin from Shreveport, Louisiana, where they had been prevented by court order from holding a hearing on deprivations of the right to vote in that state. Federal district judge Benjamin Dawkins, a segregation-minded Southerner appointed with Senator Eastland's strong concurrence, recognized that he might be overruled by the Supreme Court but said, "It is all part of the game."

Frustrated by the court injunction, the Commissioners spent a long hot night at a federal air base before their flight North. Bombers kept landing and taking off, with searchlights scanning the sky. It seemed like a hell-hole to Father Hesburgh, but he passed part of the late evening, as had become his custom, talking with John Battle. Having discovered the former governor's taste for bourbon, which the president of Notre Dame shared, Father Hesburgh would bring a bottle along whenever the Commissioners met—or leave a message for Battle that it was his turn. They talked of many things together, of family, religion, and politics, as well as of the business before the Commission.

"I'm a tiger on voting," Battle told Hesburgh. The Alabama hearing had gotten to him; something had to be done to secure the Negroes' right to vote, but he couldn't go along on school desegregation. "Don't give me any theological stuff," he said. "I know what the Bible says, I try to be a Christian, but I'm an old dog. My wife says that you're right, but it kills me and I just can't do it."

The next day, sitting on the floor of a military cargo plane that took them to Wisconsin, the Commissioners pondered what to do—what kind of new laws to propose—to end the denial of the right to vote. When they reached the cool Northern lake, Father Hesburgh and his colleagues caught about twenty bass while the staff worked at their final drafts of the Report. There was a full moon over the lake, and an after-dinner glow on the Commissioners when they decided to take up the most controversial recommendations first.

"We must take the bull by the tail," former Governor Carlton said, "and look the ugly facts straight in the face."

In short order, the Commissioners unanimously approved a strong and clear finding that many Americans were being denied the franchise because of race through "legal impediments, administrative obstacles, and positive discouragement engendered by fears of economic reprisal and physical harm." There was "a striking gap"—"a moral gap"—they said, "between our principles and our everyday practices." Concluding that "legislation presently on the books is inadequate to assure that all our qualified citizens shall enjoy the right to vote," they agreed upon a number of specific recommendations dealing with some of the obstacles seen by the Commission.

The most far-reaching recommendation called for Congress to empower the President to appoint temporary federal registrars to register voters for federal elections upon a finding by the Civil Rights Commission that qualified voters were being denied their right to register because of race, religion, or national origin. The temporary federal registrar would be a federal officer already in the area, such as the Postmaster, U.S. Attorney, or Clerk of the Federal District Court.

Such direct registration was designed to cut through the administrative maze of recalcitrant local boards and avoid the lengthy and costly litigation required under existing statutory remedies. Though the proposed law would be limited to federal elections, where congressional power was unquestioned, it was presumed that in most cases local boards would accept such registration for state elections as well rather than risk further litigation.

For a while all six Commissioners were ready to join in this recommendation. Upon reconsideration and with some apology, the "tiger" on voting rights, John Battle, decided he could not go along with the idea of placing "in the hands of the Federal Government a vital part of the election process so jealously guarded and carefully reserved to the States by the founding fathers." He asked Father Hesburgh to forgive him and to try to understand. The two other Southern colleagues stood by the plan, and gave it a five-to-one majority. Battle in no way dissented from the fundamental finding that Negroes were being deprived of their right to vote, but he argued that the discovery of a remedy ought to be left to the Congress.

While supporting federal registrars as a good immediate stopgap, Father Hesburgh, Dean Johnson, and Chairman Hannah pressed an even more sweeping solution: a constitutional amendment to establish universal suffrage. Having concluded that it was impossible to enforce an impartial administration of literacy tests—since where there is a will to discriminate, there is a way—they contended that the quickest and cleanest way to end discrimination would be to eliminate all such tests, as well as poll taxes and other encumbrances on an adult franchise. Noting that literacy tests were still required in only nineteen states, and poll taxes in five, the three Northern Commissioners urged that "the time has come for the United States to take the last of its many steps toward free and universal suffrage." State age and residence requirements would remain but these were objective and readily ascertainable standards. Since the proposed amendment should remove most of the occasions for the kind of continuing federal intervention involved in the federal registrar plan, we hoped that the Southern Commissioners might agree. The two who had gone out on the limb to support federal registrars, however, felt they had gone far enough. Though not a majority "recommendation," the idea was included as a Commission "proposal" supported by half the Commission.

On school desegregation, the Commissioners agreed on a limited set of findings, including two facts that became evident in the Nashville conference: "desegregation by court order has been notably more difficult than desegregation by voluntary action," and school districts "attempting to evolve a desegregation plan have no established and qualified source to which to turn for information and advice." It was important, the Commission thought, to provide affirmative assistance to school districts.

The Commission, therefore, recommended that the Office of Education, in cooperation with the Census Bureau, undertake and publish an annual school census by race in all school districts and in all institutions of higher education. More importantly, it urged that the President propose and Congress enact legislation authorizing a renewed Commission on Civil Rights to serve as a clearinghouse "to collect and make available to states and to local communities information concerning programs and procedures used by school districts to comply with the Supreme Court mandate . . . including data as to the known effects of the programs on the quality of education and the cost thereof."

The Commission also recommended that it be authorized "to establish an advisory and conciliation service to assist local school officials in developing plans designed to meet constitutional requirements and local conditions; and to mediate and conciliate, upon request, disputes as to proposed plans and their implementation." This was an idea that Lyndon Johnson had been advancing for several years. Civil rights leaders tended to look askance at any such approach that implied mediation instead of enforcement, but the Northern Commissioners joined their Southern colleagues in thinking such a service could be constructive.

The Southerners would not join their three Northern colleagues in recommending that federal financial assistance to institutions of higher education be withdrawn from those that refused to admit Negro students. "The reasons for the gradual elimination of racial discrimination in elementary and secondary schools do not obtain in the field of higher education," the proposal of half the Commission contended. Colleges and universities were the principal recipients of more than $2 billion a year of federal funds for education, yet not one federal agency required nondiscrimination as a condition for these grants and loans.

If the Southerners would join in no punitive proposals, they were courageous in agreeing to "two fundamental premises" that became the Commission's concluding statement on education:

> (1) The American system of public education must be preserved without impairment because an educated citizenry is the mainstay of the Republic. . . .
> (2) The constitutional right to be free from compulsory segregation in public education can be and must be realized, for this is a government of law, and the Constitution as interpreted by the Supreme Court is the supreme law of the land.
> The problem, therefore, is how to comply with the Supreme Court decision while preserving and even improving public education. The ultimate choice of each State is between finding reasonable ways of ending compulsory segregation in its schools or abandoning its system of free public education.

On housing, the Commission also agreed upon two basic facts:

> *First*, a considerable number of Americans, by reason of their color or race, are being denied equal opportunity in housing. A large proportion of colored Americans are living in overcrowded slums or blighted areas in restricted sections of our cities, with little or no access to new housing or to suburban areas. . . . The results can be seen in high rates of disease, fire, juvenile delinquency, crime and social demoralization among those forced to live in such conditions. A nation dedicated to respect for the human dignity of every individual should not permit such conditions to continue.
> *Second*, the housing disabilities of colored Americans are part of a national housing crisis involving a general shortage of low-cost housing. Americans of lower income, both colored and white, have few opportunities for decent homes in good neighborhoods.

"Since the home is the heart of a good society," the Commission concluded, "it is essential that this aspect of the promise of equal protection of the laws be fulfilled forthwith." For this, the Commission held, "two things must happen: the housing shortage for all lower income Americans must be relieved, *and* equality of opportunity to good housing must be secured for colored Americans. If racial discrimination is ended but adequate low-cost housing is not available, most colored Americans will remain confined in spreading slums."

The Southern members wanted to emphasize mainly the need for new minority housing and the opportunity for colored neighborhoods to develop outside the inner-city slums, as had happened in Atlanta. The Northern members stressed the need for effective anti-discrimination laws like those in New York City and State. All condemned the situation in Chicago, where the Negroes' primary method of securing better housing was through the mutually unsatisfactory system of blockbusting, with its consequent uprooting of adjacent white neighborhoods and its inevitable racial tension and occasional violence. Unanimously the Commission recommended "that an appropriate biracial committee or commission on housing be established in every city and state with a substantial nonwhite population."

Commissioner Johnson entered a caveat against a policy focused on minority housing, but accepted the moderate approach to biracial housing agencies. To his surprise and to that of his assistant Gene Jackson and me, the Southern members were prepared to go along with our proposed recommendation for a presidential Executive Order against discrimination in federally assisted housing. Following the regional hearings at which federal policies had been repeatedly criticized, the Commission had held a conference with officers of all federal housing agencies. Southern and Northern Commissioners alike were appalled by the official indifference to the ways in which federal funds were being used to reinforce patterns of segregation and discrimination. The proposition of a California court that "when one dips one's hand into the Federal Treasury, a little democracy necessarily clings to whatever is withdrawn" made sense to all the Commissioners.

The Commission agreed upon specific recommendations about each of the major federal housing programs, but its central recommendation was that the President should issue a general Executive Order applying to all federally assisted housing, including housing constructed with the assistance of federal mortgage insurance or loan guarantees, as well as federally aided public housing and urban renewal projects. Without dissent, the Commissioners agreed to recommend:

> That the President issue an Executive Order stating the constitutional objective of equal opportunity in housing, directing all Federal agencies to shape their policies and practices to make the maximum contribution to the achievement of this goal, and requesting the Commission on Civil Rights, if extended, to continue to study and appraise the policies of Federal housing agencies, to prepare and propose plans to bring about the end of discrimination in all Federally-assisted housing, and to make appropriate recommendations.

When the Commission adjourned late that night at Land O' Lakes, Father Hesburgh and I could hardly believe that such a deeply divided group had come together on so many points. His bourbon had helped; so had Dean Johnson's combination of strength and moderation, which had replaced Ernest Wilkins' testiness. Wilkins had been viewed in civil rights circles as an Establishment Republican, perhaps even a professional Uncle Tom; instead, his years of accumulated anger came to a head within the Commission and might have prevented any agreements. His death may in fact have been precipitated by the emotions aroused in him during the Alabama hearings and some of the sharp exchanges within the Commission.

John Hannah's fair and cool chairmanship was certainly instrumental in bringing the Commission together, but with all due respect to the Northern members, much of the Commission's success was due to the three Southerners. They had done their duty, as lawyers and citizens, even when the enterprise had been most painful.

At breakfast the next morning the Southerners were heard to remark among themselves, "We were taken last night!"—"Yes, we agreed to too much."—"But we're gentlemen and we gave our word."

During further meetings they found ways to moderate some of the words in the large 600-page Report and in the 200-page Summary, and they warned us that they would submit "supplementary statements" on education and housing that clarified their views. But they did not go back on their agreement to specific recommendations. In addition to dissenting on the federal registrar plan, John Battle did state his disagreement "with the nature and tenor of the report" which he thought was, "in large part, an argument in advocacy of preconceived ideas in the field of race relations." Still, he expressed his "highest regard" for each of his fellow Commissioners, and said he had "learned a whole lot."

Opposition to sociology had been one of the Southern Commissioners common fronts from the beginning. They had insisted on excluding sociologists from the Nashville conference, and when in somewhat perverse fashion the staff later proposed employing a particular sociologist, the Commission as a whole made it clear it was not going to repeat the mistake of the Supreme Court (which had never heard the end of its citation of Gunnar Myrdal's study and more recent sociological and psychological studies in one superfluous footnote in *Brown v. Board of Education*). One of the last comments at Land O' Lakes was a Southern Commissioner's advice that Myrdal be nowhere mentioned in the final Report, certainly not in a footnote. Prudence doesn't always pay, however, for in one of Senator Eastland's first attacks on the Report he noted triumphantly that Myrdal was not even mentioned, and said: "My conclusion is that the U.S. Supreme Court has more courage than did the Civil Rights Commission."

When the Commissioners presented their Report and summarized their recommendations to President Eisenhower in September 1959, he said he was dumbfounded to find three Southerners and three Northerners agreeing on anything in civil rights. "It's because we're all fishermen," Father Hesburgh said. "Then we need more fishermen," Eisenhower replied.

They told him how they had come, as lawyers and educators, to look the facts straight in the face, and they emphasized the need for presidential leadership. The enterprise had come full circle. In the beginning Eisenhower had urged the Commission to focus on the educational and even spiritual dimensions of the problem. Now the Commission was reminding him that government, as Justice Brandeis once said, "is the potent, the omnipresent teacher" that "teaches the whole people." And Father Hesburgh was making a theological point. "Civil rights were not created, but only recognized and formulated, by our Federal and State Constitutions and charters," he said in a special plea in the last pages of the Commission's Report. "Civil rights are important corollaries of the great proposition, at the heart of Western civilization, that every human person is a *res sacra*, a sacred reality, and as such is entitled to the opportunity of fulfilling those great human potentials with which God has endowed man."

In response to the Commissioners' proposals for action, the President agreed to only one thing: he recommended that the life of the Civil Rights Commission should be extended for another two-year term, and Congress granted the extension in the Civil Rights Act of 1959. On the more controversial points Eisenhower merely indicated that it would take time for such things to be worked out. In the concluding pages of its Report the Commission had addressed itself to that point. Time was, of course, "essential in resolving any great and difficult problem," the Commission said. "However, it is not time alone that helps, but the constructive use of time."

"What is involved here," the Commission said in the closing passage of its Report, "is the ancient warning against the division of society into Two Cities. The Constitution of the United States, which was ordained to establish one society with equal justice under law, stands against such a division."

The Commission's final recommendation was particularly alien to Eisenhower's minimalist view of government. "To eliminate discrimination and demoralization some dramatic and creative intervention by the leaders of our national life is necessary," the Report concluded. "The whole problem will not be solved without high vision, serious purpose, and imaginative leadership. Prohibiting discrimination in voting, education, housing, or other parts of our public life will not suffice. The demoralization of a part of the nonwhite population resulting from generations of discrimination can ultimately be overcome only by positive measures. The law is not merely a command, and government is not just a policeman. Law must be inventive, creative, and educational."

Index